NOVEL GAZING

Edited by

Michèle Aina Barale,

Jonathan Goldberg,

Michael Moon, and

Eve Kosofsky Sedgwick

NOVEL GAZING

Queer Readings in Fiction

Edited by Eve Kosofsky Sedgwick

Duke University Press   Durham & London 1997

© 1997 Duke University Press
All rights reserved
Printed in the United States of America on acid-free paper ∞
Typeset in Scala by Tseng Information Systems, Inc.
Library of Congress Cataloging-in-Publication Data
appear on the last printed page of this book.

CONTENTS

ACKNOWLEDGMENTS

The essays by James Creech, Tyler Curtain, Jonathan Goldberg, Joseph Litvak, Jeff Nunokawa, Robert F. Reid-Pharr, Melissa Solomon, and Kathryn Bond Stockton were originally published in *Studies in the Novel*, vol. 28 (Fall 1996) © 1996 by the University of North Texas, and are reprinted by permission of the publisher. I am grateful to the journal's editor, Scott Simpkins, for asking me to guest edit that "Queerer than Fiction" issue.

Closer to home, my assistant, Denise Fulbrook, exercised her characteristic mix of the skills of psychoanalyst, sheepdog, and friend (or do I repeat myself?) in eliciting timely successive drafts from all the contributors to this volume, including me. Jennifer Doyle lifted from my shoulders—and did them far better than I could have—the many tasks of preparing the manuscript for the press, seeing it through, and composing the index. In a surprise move, everybody at Duke University Press has been just wonderful to work with, beginning with the Editor-in-Chief. Paul Kelleher copyedited the essays with a rare mix of delicacy, imagination, and decisiveness. Two anonymous readers were beautifully generous with their tough love for the collection. Amy Ruth Buchanan and Carol Mavor made a crucial and much-appreciated intervention. Mary Mendell hates to be acknowledged.

Finally, the greatest satisfaction of working on this project has been the privilege of collaborating with these authors; for which, my heartfelt thanks to them.

Eve Kosofsky Sedgwick

Paranoid Reading and Reparative Reading; or,

You're So Paranoid, You Probably Think

This Introduction Is about You

Novel Gazing: Queer Readings in Fiction came together unprogrammatically. Invited by the journal Studies in the Novel to edit a special issue, I asked forty or so writers I admire whether they could find room on their agendas to write something that would, loosely speaking, convene the rubrics "novel" and "queer." I felt more than fortunate in the response, when these startlingly imaginative essays started tumbling in at a rate that soon overfilled the journal—and didn't slow down even then.

Unmistakably the essays pointed toward a book. But excited by the force, the originality, and in many cases the beauty of these pieces, I still found it difficult to articulate more than a negative sense of what kind of a moment they might collectively represent in queer theory or in literary criticism. Clearly and queerly enough, they share a relaxed, unseparatist hypothesis of the much to be gained by refraining from a priori oppositions between queer texts (or authors) and non-queer ones, or female ones and male. In fact, the list of damaging a priori oppositions to which these essays quietly, collectively find alternative approaches is very impressive: the authors transmit new ways of knowing that human beings are also machines, are also animals; that an ethic or aesthetic of truthtelling need not depend on any reified notion of truth; that the materiality of human bodies, of words, and of economic production may misrepresent but cannot simply eclipse one another; that pleasure, grief, excitement, boredom, satisfaction are the substance of politics rather than their antithesis; that affect and cognition are not very distant processes; that visual perception need not be conceptually isolated from the other four bodily senses; that gender differentiation is crucial to human experience but in no sense coextensive with it; that it's well to attend intimately to literary texts, not because their transformative energies either transcend or disguise the coarser stuff of ordinary being, but because those energies are the stuff of ordinary being.

If nothing else, the negative specifications of these essays do seem to add up to a surprising disciplinary generalization: given how queer theory and literary criticism are currently structured, it's notable that among seventeen diverse, psychologically searching, very real-world-oriented essays on texts from the past two centuries, not a single one is working directly from inside Freud or Lacan, and few, either, seem to owe much to the narrative and research protocols that typify the New Historicism. Though passionate, they are also not particularly polemical, and they don't greatly feature the disciplining of previous errors of theory or interpretation. If anything, the expansive length of several of the essays seems to reflect a distance from any of those master-figures or master-discourses to which theoretical appeals can today be made in shorthand.

I wouldn't, beforehand, have characterized this particular intellectual moment as likely to offer remarkable resources for a fresh, deroutinized sense of accountability to the real. Live and learn. By accountability to the real I mean in the first place the many, diverse, but very marked turns these essays take away from existing accounts of how "one" *should* read, and back toward a grappling with the recalcitrant, fecund question of how one *does*. It might even be true to say that the psychological/political ambitions of many of the essays take the form of a similar series of turns: from the nonsensical but seemingly uncircumnavigable question of how people *should feel,* to the much harder ones of how they do and of how feelings change. Interestingly, it's also the repeated turn away from the deontological project of "ought" that seems to characterize the unmistakable, though often tacit, ethical gravity and specificity of this work.

As for its *queer* specificity, I will discuss below why that seems to emerge throughout the essays in such varied and radically contingent forms. I don't think any of these essays would have been writable—thinkable—before or without the gay/lesbian studies and queer theory movements in literary criticism; indeed almost all the authors, who range from current graduate students to foundational figures in these movements, are steeped in those problematics and sensibilities. Yet what seems least settled is any predetermined idea about what makes the queerness of a queer reading. Often these readings begin from or move toward sites of same-sex, interpersonal eroticism—but not necessarily so. It seems to me that an often quiet, but very palpable presiding image here—a kind of *genius loci* for queer reading—is the interpretive absorption of the child or adolescent whose sense of personal queerness may or may not (*yet?*) have resolved into a sexual specificity of proscribed object choice, aim, site, or identification. Such a child—if she reads at all—is reading for important news about herself, without knowing what form that news will take; with only the patchiest familiarity with its codes; without, even, more than hungrily hypothesizing to what questions this news may proffer an answer. The model of such reading is hardly the state of complacent adequacy that Jonathan Culler calls "literary competence," but a much more speculative, superstitious, and methodologically adventurous state where recognitions, pleasures, and discoveries seep in only from the most stretched and ragged edges of one's competence.[1]

Aside from the deroutinizing methodologies of these essays, what seems most hauntingly to characterize them is how distant many of them are from a certain stance of suspicion or paranoia that is common in the theoretical work whose disciplinary ambience surrounds them. If the collection can be said to embody any one, primary premise, it would be that a closer, more respectful attention to past and present queer reading practices—the kind of attention these essays, in their different ways, all embody—will show how the reservoir of practices already in use crucially exceeds the theorizations of a consensual hermeneutic of suspicion. Many of these pieces are, rightly and productively, incisive in their use of a methodical suspicion; but what more unites them is a very different impulse and history, which would be badly misrecognized under the currently available rubrics. In the remainder of this essay—and, I must admit, at the risk of somewhat compromising the nonprogrammatic aesthetic of deontological reticence that otherwise seems to make the flavor of the volume—it is the issue of paranoia and its alternatives that I would like to explore more fully.

Sometime back in the middle of the first decade of the AIDS epidemic, I was picking the brains of a friend of mine, the activist scholar Cindy Patton, about the probable natural history of HIV. This was at a time when speculation was ubiquitous about whether the virus had been deliberately engineered, or spread; whether HIV represented a plot or experiment by the U.S. military that had gotten out of control, or perhaps that was behaving exactly as it was meant to. After hearing a lot from her about the geography and economics of the global traffic in blood products, I finally, with some eagerness, asked Patton what she thought of these sinister rumors about the virus's origin. "Any of the early steps in its spread could have been either accidental or deliberate," she said. "But I just have trouble getting interested in that. I mean, even suppose we were sure of every element of a conspiracy: that the lives of Africans and African Americans are worthless in the eyes of the United States; that gay men and drug users are held cheap where they aren't actively hated; that the military deliberately researches ways to kill noncombatants whom it sees as enemies; that people in power look calmly on the likelihood of catastrophic environmental and population changes. Supposing we were ever so sure of all those things—what would we know then that we don't already know?"

In the years since that conversation, I've brooded a lot over this response from Patton. Aside from a certain congenial, stony pessimism, I think what I've found enabling about it is that it suggests the possibility of unpacking, of disentangling from their impacted and overdetermined historical relation to each other, some of the separate elements of the intellectual baggage that many of us carry around under a label like "the hermeneutic of suspicion." Patton's comment suggests that for someone to have an unmystified, angry view of large and genuinely systemic oppressions does not *intrinsically* or *necessarily* enjoin on that person any specific train of epistemological or narrative consequences. To know that the origin or spread of HIV *realistically might* have resulted from a state-assisted conspiracy—such knowledge is, it turns out, separable from the question of whether the energies of a given AIDS activist intellectual or group might best be used in the tracing and exposure of such a possible plot. They might, but then again, they might not. Though ethically very fraught, the choice is not self-evident; whether or not to undertake this highly compelling tracing-and-exposure project represents a strategic and local decision, not necessarily a categorical imperative. Patton's response to me seemed to open a space for moving from the rather fixated question, "Is a particular piece of knowledge true, and how can we know?" to the further questions, "What does knowledge *do*—the pursuit of it, the having and exposing of it, the receiving-again of knowledge of what one already knows? *How*, in short, is knowledge performative, and how best does one move among its causes and effects?"

I suppose this ought to seem quite an unremarkable epiphany: that knowledge *does* rather than simply *is*, it is by now very routine to discover. Yet it seems that a lot of the real force of such discoveries has been blunted through the habitual practices of the same forms of critical theory that have given such broad currency to the formulae themselves. In particular, it may be that the very productive critical habits embodied in what Paul Ricoeur memorably called the "hermeneutics of suspicion"—widespread critical habits indeed, perhaps by now nearly synonymous with criticism itself—may have had an unintentionally stultifying side-effect: they may have made it less rather than more possible to unpack the local, contingent relations between any given piece of knowledge and its narrative/epistemological entailments for the seeker, knower, or teller.

Ricoeur introduced the category of the "hermeneutic of suspicion" to describe the position of Marx, Nietzsche, Freud, and their intellectual offspring within a context that also included such alternative disciplinary hermeneutics as the philological and theological "hermeneutic of recovery of meaning."[2] His intent in offering the former of these formulations was descriptive and taxonomic rather than imperative. In the context of recent U.S. critical theory, however, where Marx, Nietzsche, and Freud by themselves are taken as constituting a pretty sufficient genealogy for the mainstream of New Historicist, deconstructive, feminist, queer, and psychoanalytic criticism, to apply a "hermeneutic of suspicion" is, I believe, widely understood as a mandatory injunction rather than a possibility among other possibilities. The phrase now has something like the sacred status of Fredric Jameson's "Always historicize"—and, like that one, it fits oddly into its new position in the tablets of the Law. *Always* historicize? What could have less to do with historicizing than the commanding, atemporal adverb "always"? It reminds me of the common bumper stickers that instruct people in other cars to "Question Authority." Excellent advice, perhaps wasted on anyone who does whatever they're ordered to do by a strip of paper glued to the bumper of an automobile! The imperative framing will do funny things to a hermeneutic of suspicion.

Not surprisingly, the methodological centrality of suspicion to current critical practice has involved a concomitant privileging of the concept of paranoia. In the last paragraphs of Freud's essay on the paranoid Dr. Schreber, there is discussion of what Freud considers a "striking similarity" between Schreber's systematic persecutory delusion and Freud's own theory. Freud was indeed later to generalize, famously, that "the delusions of paranoiacs have an unpalatable external similarity and internal kinship to the systems of our philosophers"—among whom he included himself.[3] For all his slyness, it may be true that the putative congruence between paranoia and theory was unpalatable to Freud; if so, however, it is no longer viewed as unpalatable. The articulation of such a congruence may have been inevitable, at any rate; as Ricoeur notes, "For Marx, Nietzsche, and Freud, the fundamental category of consciousness is the relation hidden-shown or, if you prefer, simulated-manifested. . . . Thus the distinguishing characteristic of Marx, Freud, and Nietzsche is the general hypothesis concerning both the process of false consciousness and the method of deciphering. The two go together, since the man of suspicion carries out in reverse the work of falsification of the man of guile."[4] The man of suspicion double-bluffing the man of guile: in the hands of thinkers after Freud, paranoia has by now candidly become less a diagnosis than a prescription. In a world where no one need be delusional to find evidence of systemic oppression, to theorize out of anything *but* a paranoid critical stance has come to seem naive, pious, or complaisant. I myself have no wish to return to the use of "paranoid" as a pathologizing diagnosis; but it seems to me a great loss when paranoid inquiry comes to seem entirely coextensive with critical theoretical inquiry, rather than being viewed as one kind of cognitive/affective theoretical practice among other, alternative kinds.

Even aside from the prestige that now attaches to a hermeneutic of suspicion in critical theory as a whole, queer studies in particular has had a distinctive history of intimacy with the paranoid imperative. Freud, of course, traced every instance of paranoia to the repression of specifically same-sex desire, whether in women or in men. The traditional, homophobic psychoanalytic use that has generally been made of Freud's association has been to pathologize homosexuals as paranoid, or to consider paranoia a distinctively homosexual disease. In *Homosexual Desire,* however, a 1972 book translated into English in 1978, Guy Hocquenghem returned to Freud's formulations in order to draw from them a conclusion that would not reproduce this damaging non sequitur. If paranoia reflects the *repression* of same-sex desire, Hocquenghem reasoned, then paranoia is a uniquely privileged site for illuminating not homosexuality itself, as in the Freudian tradition, but rather precisely the mechanisms of homophobic and heterosexist enforcement against it.[5] What is illuminated by an understanding of paranoia is not how homosexuality works, but how homophobia and heterosexism work—in short, if one understands these oppressions to be systemic, how the world works.

Paranoia, thus, became by the mid-1980s a privileged *object* of antihomophobic theory. How did it spread so quickly from that status to being its uniquely sanctioned *methodology?* I have been looking back into my own writing of the 1980s as well as that of some other critics, trying to retrace that transition—one that seems worthy of remark now but seemed at the time, I think, the most natural move in the world. Part of the explanation lies in a property of paranoia itself: simply put, paranoia tends to be contagious. More specifically, paranoia is drawn toward and tends to construct symmetrical relations, and in particular symmetrical epistemologies. As Leo Bersani writes, "To inspire interest is to be guaranteed a paranoid reading, just as we must inevitably be suspicious of the interpretations we inspire. Paranoia is an inescapable interpretive doubling of presence."[6] It sets a thief (and if necessary, becomes one) to catch a thief; it mobilizes guile against suspicion, suspicion against guile; "it takes one to know one." A paranoid friend, who believes I am reading her mind, knows this from reading mine; also a suspicious writer, she is always turning up at crime scenes of plagiarism, indifferently as perpetrator or as victim; a litigious colleague as well, she not only imagines me to be as familiar with the laws of libel as she is, but eventually makes me become so. (All these examples, by the way, are fictitious.)

Given that paranoia seems to have a peculiarly intimate relation to the phobic dynamics around homosexuality, then, it may have been structurally inevitable that the reading practices that became most available and fruitful in antihomophobic work would often in turn have been paranoid ones. There must have been historical as well as structural reasons for this development, however, since it is less easy to account on structural terms for the frequent privileging of paranoid methodologies in recent non-queer critical projects such as feminist theory, psychoanalytic theory, deconstruction, Marxist criticism, or the New Historicism. One recent discussion of paranoia invokes "a popular maxim of the late 1960s: 'Just because you're paranoid doesn't mean they're *not* out to get you.'"[7] And in fact it seems quite plausible to me that some version of this axiom (perhaps "Even a paranoid can have enemies," uttered by Henry Kissinger!)[8] is so indelibly inscribed in the brains of us baby-boomers that it offers us the continuing illusion of possessing a special insight into the epistemologies of enmity. My impression, again, is that we are liable to produce this constative formulation as fiercely as if it had a self-evident imperative force: the notation that even paranoid people have enemies is wielded as if its absolutely necessary corollary were the injunction, "—so *you can never be paranoid enough.*"

But the truth-value of the original axiom, assuming it to *be* true, doesn't actually make a paranoid imperative self-evident. Learning that "just because you're paranoid doesn't mean you don't have enemies," somebody might deduce that being paranoid is not an effective way to get rid of enemies. Rather than concluding "—so you can never be paranoid enough," this person might instead be moved to reflect, "—but then, just because you have enemies doesn't mean you have to be paranoid." That is to say, once again: for someone to have an unmystified view of systemic oppressions does not *intrinsically* or *necessarily* enjoin on that person any specific train of epistemological or narrative consequences. To be other than paranoid (and of course we'll need to define this term much more carefully)—to practice other than paranoid forms of knowing does *not*, in itself, entail a denial of the reality or gravity of enmity or oppression.

How are we to understand paranoia in such a way as to situate it as one kind of epistemological practice among other, alternative ones? Besides Freud's, the most usable formulations for this purpose would seem to be those of Melanie Klein and (to the extent that paranoia represents an affective as well as cognitive mode) Silvan Tomkins. In Klein, I find particularly congenial her use of the concept of *positions*—the schizoid/paranoid position, the depressive position—as opposed to, for example, normatively ordered *stages*, stable *structures*, or diagnostic *personality types*. As Hinshelwood writes in his indispensable *Dictionary of*

Kleinian Thought, "The term 'position' describes the characteristic posture that the ego takes up with respect to its objects. . . . [Klein] wanted to convey, with the idea of position, a much more flexible to-and-fro process between one and the other than is normally meant by regression to fixation points in the developmental phases."[9] The flexible to-and-fro movement implicit in Kleinian *positions* will be useful for my purpose of discussing paranoid and reparative critical *practices,* not as theoretical ideologies (and certainly not as stable personality types of critics), but as changing and heterogeneous relational stances.

The greatest interest of Klein's concept lies, it seems to me, in her seeing the paranoid position always in the oscillatory context of a very different possible one, the depressive position. For Klein's infant or adult, the paranoid position—understandably marked by hatred, envy, and anxiety—is a position of terrible alertness to the dangers posed by the hateful and envious part-objects that one defensively projects into, carves out of, and ingests from the world around one. By contrast, the depressive position is an anxiety-mitigating achievement that the infant or adult only sometimes, and often only briefly, succeeds in inhabiting: this is the position from which it is possible in turn to use one's own resources to assemble or "repair" the murderous part-objects into something like a whole—though not, and may I emphasize this, *not necessarily like any preexisting whole.* Once assembled to one's own specifications, the more satisfying object is available both to be identified with and to offer one nourishment and comfort in turn. Among Klein's names for the reparative process is love.[10]

Given the instability and mutual inscription built into the Kleinian notion of positions, I am also, in the present project, interested in doing justice to the powerful reparative practices that, I am convinced, infuse self-avowedly paranoid critical projects; as well as to the paranoid exigencies that are often necessary for non-paranoid knowing and utterance. For example, Patton's calm response to me about the origins of HIV drew on a lot of research, her own and other people's, much of which required to be paranoiacally structured.

For convenience's sake, I'll borrow my critical examples as I proceed from two influential studies of the past decade, one roughly psychoanalytic and the other roughly New Historicist—but I do so for more than the sake of convenience, since both are books (Judith Butler's *Gender Trouble* and D. A. Miller's *The Novel and the Police*) whose centrality to the development of my own thought, and that of the critical movements that most interest me, are examples of their very remarkable force and exemplarity. Each, as well, is interestingly located in a tacit or ostensibly marginal, but in hindsight originary and authorizing, relation to different strains of queer theory. Finally, I draw a sense of permission from the fact that neither book is any longer very representative of the most recent work of either author, so that observations about the reading practices of either book may, I hope, escape being glued as if allegorically to the name of the author.

I would like to begin by setting outside the scope of this discussion any overlap between paranoia per se on the one hand, and on the other hand the states variously called dementia praecox (by Kraepelin), schizophrenia (by Bleuler), or more generally, delusionality or psychosis. As Laplanche and Pontalis note, the history of psychiatry has attempted various mappings of this overlap: "Kraepelin differentiates clearly between paranoia on the one hand and the paranoid form of dementia praecox on the other; Bleuler treats paranoia as a sub-category of dementia praecox, or the group of schizophrenias; as for Freud, he is quite prepared to see certain so-called paranoid forms of dementia praecox brought under the head of paranoia. . . . [For example, Schreber's] case of 'paranoid dementia' is essentially a paranoia proper [and therefore not a form of schizophrenia] in Freud's eyes."[11] In Klein's later writings, meanwhile, the occurrence of psychotic-like mental events is seen as universal in both children and adults, so that mechanisms such as paranoia have a clear ontological priority over diagnostic categories such as dementia. The reason I want to insist in advance on this move is, once again, to try and hypothetically disentangle the question of truth-value from the question of performative effect. I am saying that the main reasons for questioning paranoid practices are other than the possibility that their suspicions can be delusional.

Concomitantly, some of the main reasons for practicing paranoid strategies may be other than the possibility that they offer unique access to true knowledge. They represent *a* way, among other ways, of seeking, finding, and organizing knowledge. Paranoia knows some things well and others poorly. I'd like to undertake now something like a composite sketch of what I mean by paranoia in this connection—not as a tool of differential *diagnosis*, but anyway as a tool for better seeing differentials of practice. My main headings will be:

Paranoia is *anticipatory*.
Paranoia is *reflexive* and *mimetic*.
Paranoia is *a strong theory*.
Paranoia is a theory of *negative affects*.
Paranoia places its faith in *exposure*.

(1) That paranoia is anticipatory is clear from every account and theory of the phenomenon. The first imperative of paranoia is *"There must be no bad surprises,"* and indeed the aversion to surprise seems to be what cements the intimacy between paranoia and knowledge per se, includ-

ing both epistemophilia and skepticism. D. A. Miller notes in *The Novel and the Police* that "Surprise . . . is precisely what the paranoid seeks to eliminate, but it is also what, in the event, he survives by reading as a frightening incentive: he can never be paranoid enough."[12]

The unidirectionally future-oriented vigilance of paranoia generates, paradoxically, a complex relation to temporality that burrows both backward and forward: because there must be no bad surprises, and because to learn of the possibility of a bad surprise would itself constitute a bad surprise, paranoia requires that bad news be always already known. As Miller's analysis also suggests, the temporal progress and regress of paranoia are, in principle, infinite. Hence perhaps, I would suggest, Butler's repeated and scouringly thorough demonstrations in *Gender Trouble* that there can have been no moment prior to the imposition of the totalizing Law of gender difference; hence her unresting vigilance for traces in other theorists' writing of nostalgia for such an impossible prior moment. No time could be too early for one's having-already-known, for its having-already-been-inevitable, that something bad would happen; and no loss could be too far in the future to need to be preemptively discounted.

(2) In noting, as I have already, the contagious tropism of paranoia toward symmetrical epistemologies, I have relied on the double senses of paranoia as reflexive and mimetic. Paranoia seems to require to be imitated in order to be understood; and it, in turn, seems to understand only by imitation. Paranoia proposes both "*Anything you can do [to me] I can do worse*," and "*Anything you can do [to me] I can do first*"—to myself. In *The Novel and the Police*, D. A. Miller is much more explicit than Freud in embracing the twin propositions that one understands paranoia only by oneself practicing paranoid knowing, and that the way paranoia has of understanding anything is by imitating and embodying it. That paranoia refuses to be only *either* a way of knowing *or* a thing known, but is characterized by an insistent tropism toward occupying both positions, is wittily dramatized from the opening page of this definitive study of paranoia: a foreword titled "But Officer . . ." begins with an always-already-second-guessing sentence about how "*Even the blandest (or bluffest) 'scholarly work' fears getting into trouble*," including trouble "*with the adversaries whose particular attacks it keeps busy anticipating*" (vii; emphasis in original). As the book's final paragraph notes about *David Copperfield*, Miller too "everywhere intimates a . . . pattern in which the subject constitutes himself 'against' discipline by assuming that discipline in his own name" (220), or even his own body (191).

It seems no wonder, then, that paranoia, once the topic is broached in a nondiagnostic context, would seem to grow like a crystal in a hypersaturated solution, blotting out any sense of the possibility of alternative ways of understanding *or* things to understand. I will say more later on about some implications of the status of paranoia as—in this sense—inevitably a "strong theory." What may be even more important is how severely the mimeticism of paranoia circumscribes its potential as a medium of political or cultural struggle. As I pointed out in a 1986 essay (in which my implicit reference was, as it happens, to one of the essays later collected in *The Novel and the Police*), "The problem here is not simply that paranoia is a form of love, for—in a certain language—what is not? The problem is rather that, of all forms of love, paranoia is the most ascetic, *the love that demands least from its object.* . . . The gorgeous narrative work done by the Foucauldian paranoid, transforming the simultaneous chaoses of institutions into a consecutive, drop-dead-elegant diagram of spiralling escapes and recaptures, is also the paranoid subject's proffer of himself and his cognitive talent, now ready for anything *it* can present in the way of blandishment or violence, to an order-of-things *morcelé* that had until then lacked *only* narratability, a body, cognition."[13]

At the risk of offering a coarse reduction, I'd suggest that this anticipatory, mimetic mechanism may also shed light on a striking feature of recent feminist and queer uses of psychoanalysis. Lacan aside, few actual psychoanalysts would dream of being as rigorously insistent as are many oppositional theorists—of whom Butler is very far from the most single-minded—in asserting the inexorable, irreducible, uncircumnavigable, omnipresent centrality, at *every* psychic juncture, of the facts (however factitious) of "sexual difference" and "the phallus." From such often tautological work, it would be hard to learn that—from Freud onward, including for example the later writings of Melanie Klein—the history of psychoanalytic thought offers richly divergent, heterogeneous tools for thinking about aspects of personhood, consciousness, affect, filiation, social dynamics, and sexuality that, while relevant to the experience of gender and queerness, are often not centrally organized around "sexual difference" at all. Not that they are necessarily prior to "sexual difference": they may simply be conceptualized as somewhere to the side of it, tangentially or contingently related or even rather unrelated to it.

Seemingly, the reservoir of such thought and speculation could make an important resource for theorists commited to thinking about human lives otherwise than through the prejudicious gender reifications that are common in psychoanalysis, as in other projects of modern philosophy and science. What has happened instead, I think, is something like the following. First, through what might be called a process of vigilant scanning, feminists and queers have rightly understood that no topic or area of psychoanalytic thought can be declared *a priori* immune to the influence of such gender reifications. Second, however—and it seems to me, unnecessarily and often damagingly—the lack of such *a priori* immunity, the absence of any guaranteed-nonprejudicial point of beginning for feminist thought within psychoanalysis, has led to the widespread adoption by some thinkers of an anticipatory mimetic strategy whereby a certain, stylized violence of sexual differentiation must always be *presumed* or *self-assumed*—even, where necessary, imposed—simply on the ground that it can never be finally *ruled out.* (I don't want to suggest, in using the word "mimetic," that these uses of psychoanalytic gender categories need be either uncritical of, or identical to, the originals: Judith Butler, among others, has taught us a much less deadening use of "mimetic.") But, for example, in this post-Lacanian tradition, psychoanalytic thought that is not in the first place centrally organized around phallic "sexual difference" must seemingly be translated, with however distorting results, into that language before it can be put to any other theoretical use. The contingent possibilities of thinking otherwise than through "sexual difference" are subordinated to the paranoid imperative that, if the violence of such gender reification cannot be definitively halted in advance, it must at least never arrive on any conceptual scene *as a surprise.* In a paranoid view, it is more dangerous for such reification ever to be unanticipated than often to be unchallenged.

(3) It is for reasons like these that, in the systems-theory-influenced work of the psychologist Silvan Tomkins, paranoia is offered as the example par excellence of what Tomkins refers to as "strong affect theory"—in this case, a strong humiliation or humiliation-fear theory. His use of the term "strong theory"—indeed, his use of the term "theory" at all—has something of a double valence. Tomkins goes beyond Freud's reflection on possible *similarities between,* say, paranoia and theory; by Tomkins's account, which is strongly marked by early cybernetics' interest in feedback processes, all people's cognitive/affective lives are organized according to alternative, changing, strategic and hypothetical affect theories. As a result, there would be from the start no ontological difference between the theorizing acts of a Freud and those of, say, one of his analysands. Tomkins does not suggest that there is no meta-level of reflection in Freud's theory, but rather that affect itself, ordinary affect, while irreducibly corporeal, is also centrally shaped, through the feedback process, by its access to just such theoretical meta-levels. In Tomkins, there is no distance at all between affect theory in the sense of the important explicit theorizing some scientists and philosophers do around affects, and affect theory in the sense of the largely tacit theorizing all people do in experiencing and trying to deal with their own and others' affects.

To call paranoia a "strong theory" is, then, at the same time to congratulate it as a big achievement—it's a strong theory rather as, for Harold

Bloom, Milton is a strong poet—but also to classify it. It is one kind of affect theory among other possible kinds, and by Tomkins's account, a number of interrelated affect theories of different kinds and strengths are likely to constitute the mental life of any individual. Most pointedly, the contrast of strong theory in Tomkins is with weak theory, and the contrast is not in every respect to the advantage of the strong kind. The reach and reductiveness of strong theory—that is, its conceptual economy or elegance—involve both assets and deficits. What characterizes strong theory in Tomkins is not, after all, how well it avoids negative affect or finds positive affect, but the size and topology of the domain that it organizes. "Any theory of wide generality," he writes,

> is capable of accounting for a wide spectrum of phenomena which appear to be very remote, one from the other, and from a common source. This is a commonly accepted criterion by which the explanatory power of any scientific theory can be evaluated. To the extent to which the theory can account only for "near" phenomena, it is a weak theory, little better than a description of the phenomena which it purports to explain. As it orders more and more remote phenomena to a single formulation, its power grows. . . . A humiliation theory is strong to the extent to which it enables more and more experiences to be accounted for as instances of humiliating experiences on the one hand, or to the extent to which it enables more and more anticipation of such contingencies before they actually happen.[14]

As this account suggests, far from becoming stronger through obviating or alleviating humiliation, a humiliation theory becomes stronger exactly insofar as it fails to do so.[15] Tomkins's conclusion is not that all strong theory is ineffective—indeed, it may grow to be only too effective—but that "affect theory must be effective to be weak":

> We can now see more clearly that although a restricted and weak theory may not always successfully protect the individual against negative affect, it is difficult for it to remain weak unless it does so. Conversely, a negative affect theory gains in strength, paradoxically, by virtue of the continuing failures of its strategies to afford protection through successful avoidance of the experience of negative affect. . . . It is the repeated and apparently uncontrollable spread of the experience of negative affect which prompts the increasing strength of the ideo-affective organization which we have called a strong affect theory. (2:323–24)

An affect theory is, among other things, a mode of *selective* scanning and amplification; for this reason, any affect theory risks being somewhat tautological, but because of its wide reach and rigorous exclusiveness, a strong theory risks being strongly tautological.

> We have said that there is over-organization in monopolistic humiliation theory. By this we mean not only that there is excessive integration between sub-systems which are normally more independent, but also that each sub-system is over-specialized in the interests of minimizing the experience of humiliation. . . . The entire cognitive apparatus is in a constant state of alert for possibilities, imminent or remote, ambiguous or clear.
>
> Like any highly organized effort at detection, as little as possible is left to chance. The radar antennae are placed wherever it seems possible the enemy may attack. Intelligence officers may monitor even unlikely conversations if there is an outside chance something relevant may be detected or if there is a chance that two independent bits of information taken together may give indication of the enemy's intentions. . . . But above all there is a highly organized way of interpreting information so that what is possibly relevant can be quickly abstracted and magnified, and the rest discarded. (2:433)

This is how it happens that an explanatory structure that a reader may see as tautological, in that it can't help or can't stop or can't do anything other than proving the very same assumptions with which it began, may be experienced by the practitioner as a triumphant advance toward truth and vindication.

More usually, however, the roles in this drama are more mixed or more widely distributed. I don't suppose that too many readers—nor, for that matter, perhaps the author—would be too surprised to hear it noted that the main argument or "strong theory" of *The Novel and the Police* is entirely circular: everything can be understood as an aspect of the carceral, therefore the carceral is everywhere. But who reads *The Novel and the Police* to find out whether its main argument is true? In this case, as also frequently in the case of the tautologies of "sexual difference," the very breadth of reach that makes the theory strong also offers the space—of which this book takes every advantage—for a wealth of tonal nuance, attitude, worldly observation, performative paradox, aggression, tenderness, wit, inventive reading, *obiter dicta*, and writerly panache. These rewards are so local and frequent that one might want to say that a plethora of only loosely related weak theories has been invited to shelter in the hypertrophied embrace of the book's overarching strong theory. In many ways, such an arrangement is all to the good—suggestive, pleasurable, and highly productive; an insistence that everything means one thing somehow permits a sharpened sense of all the ways there are of meaning it.

But one need not read an infinite number of students' and other critics' derivative rephrasings of the book's grimly strong theory to see, as well, some limitations of this unarticulated relation between strong and weak theories. As strong theory, and as a locus of reflexive mimeticism, paranoia is nothing if not teachable. The powerfully ranging and reductive force of strong theory can make tautological thinking hard to identify, even as it makes it compelling and near-inevitable; the result is that both writers and readers can damagingly misrecognize whether and where real conceptual work is getting done, and precisely what that work might be.

(4) While Tomkins distinguishes among a number of qualitatively different affects, he also for some purposes groups affects together loosely as the positive and the negative ones. In these terms, paranoia is characterized not only by being a strong theory as opposed to a weak one, but by being a strong theory of a negative affect. This proves important in terms of the overarching affective goals Tomkins sees as potentially conflicting with each other in each individual: he distinguishes in the first place between the general goal of seeking to minimize negative affect and that of seeking to maximize positive affect. (The other, respectively more sophisticated goals he identifies are that affect inhibition be minimized, and that the power to achieve the preceding three goals be maximized.) In most practices—in most lives—there are small and subtle (though cumulatively powerful) negotiations between and among these goals; but the mushrooming, self-confirming strength of a monopolistic strategy of anticipating negative affect can have, according to Tomkins, the effect of entirely blocking the potentially operative goal of seeking positive affect. "The only sense in which [the paranoid] may strive for positive affect at all is for the shield which it promises against humiliation," he writes. "To take seriously the strategy of *maximizing* positive affect, rather than simply enjoying it when the occasion arises, is entirely out of the question" (2:458–59).

Similarly, in Melanie Klein's writings from the 1940s and 1950s, it again represents an actual achievement—a distinct, often risky positional shift—for an infant or adult to move toward a sustained *seeking of pleasure* (through the reparative strategies of the depressive position), rather than continuing to pursue the self-reinforcing because self-defeating strategies for *forestalling pain* offered by the paranoid/schizoid position. It's probably more usual for discussions of the depressive position in Klein to emphasize that that position inaugurates ethical possibility—in the form of a guilty, empathetic view of the other as at once good, damaged, integral, and requiring and eliciting love and care. Such ethical possibility is, however, founded on and coextensive with the subject's movement toward what Foucault calls "care of the self," the often very fragile concern to provide the self with pleasure and nourishment in an environment that is perceived not particularly to offer them.

Klein's and Tomkins's conceptual moves here are more sophisticated and, in an important way, less tendentious than the corresponding assumptions in Freud. To begin with, Freud subsumes pleasure-seeking and pain-avoidance together under the rubric of the supposedly primordial "pleasure principle," as though the two motives could not themselves radically differ.[16] Second, it is the pain-forestalling strategy alone in Freud that (as anxiety) gets extended forward into the developmental achievement of the "reality principle." This leaves pleasure-seeking as an always presumable, unexaminable, inexhaustible underground wellspring of supposedly "natural" motive, one that presents only the question of how to keep its irrepressible ebullitions under control. Perhaps even more problematically, this Freudian schema silently installs the anxious paranoid imperative, the impossibility but also the supposed necessity of forestalling pain and surprise, as "reality"—as the only and inevitable mode, motive, content, and proof of true knowledge.

In Freud, then, there would be no room—except as an example of self-delusion—for the Proustian epistemology whereby the narrator of A la recherche, who feels in the last volume "jostling each other within me a whole host of truths concerning human passions and character and conduct," recognizes them as truths insofar as "the perception of [them] caused me joy."[17] In the paranoid Freudian epistemology, it is implausible enough to suppose then that truth could be even an accidental occasion of joy; inconceivable to imagine joy as a guarantor of truth. And indeed, from any point of view it is circular, or something, to suppose that one's pleasure at knowing something could be taken as evidence of the truth of the knowledge. But a strong theory of positive affect, such as the narrator seems to move toward in Time Regained, is no more tautological than the strong theory of negative affect represented by, for example, his paranoia in The Captive. (Indeed, to the extent that the pursuit of positive affect is far less likely to result in the formation of very strong theory, it may tend rather less toward tautology.) Allow each theory its own, different prime motive, at any rate—the anticipation of pain in one case, the provision of pleasure in the other—and neither can be called more realistic than the other. It's not even necessarily true that the two make different judgments of "reality": it isn't that one is pessimistic and sees the glass as half empty, while the other is optimistic and sees it as half full. In a world full of loss, pain, and oppression, both epistemologies are likely to be based on deep pessimism—the reparative motive of seeking pleasure, after all, arrives, by Klein's account, only with the achievement of a depressive position. But what each looks for—which is again to say, the motive each has *for looking*—is bound to differ widely. Of the two, however, it is only paranoid knowledge that has so thorough a practice of disavowing its affective motive and force, and masquerading as the very stuff of truth.

(5) Whatever account it may give of its own motivation, paranoia is characterized by placing, in practice, an extraordinary stress on the efficacy of knowledge per se—knowledge in the form of exposure. Maybe that's why paranoid knowing is so inescapably narrative. Like the deinstitutionalized person on the street who, betrayed and plotted against by everyone else in the city, still urges on you the finger-worn dossier bristling with his precious correspondence, paranoia for all its vaunted suspicion acts as though its work would be accomplished if only it could finally, this time, somehow get its story truly known. That a fully initiated listener could still remain indifferent or inimical, or might have no help to offer, are hardly treated as possibilities.

It's strange that a hermeneutic of suspicion would appear so trusting about the effects of exposure, but Nietzsche (through the genealogy of morals), Marx (through the theory of ideology), and Freud (through the theory of ideals and illusions) already represent, in Ricoeur's phrase, "convergent procedures of demystification" (34), and therefore a seeming faith—inexplicable in their own terms—in the effects of such a proceeding. In the influential final pages of *Gender Trouble*, for example, Butler offers a programmatic argument in favor of demystification as "the normative focus for gay and lesbian practice,"[18] with such claims as that "drag implicitly *reveals* the imitative structure of gender itself" (137); "we see sex and gender *denaturalized* by means of a performance" (138); "gender parody *reveals* that the original identity . . . is an imitation" (138); "gender performance will *enact and reveal* the performativity of gender itself" (139); "parodic repetition . . . *exposes* the phantasmatic effect of abiding identity" (141); "the parodic repetition of gender *exposes* . . . the illusion of gender identity" (146); and "hyperbolic exhibitions of 'the natural' . . . *reveal* its fundamentally phantasmatic status" (147) as well as "*exposing* its fundamental unnaturalness*" (149; all emphases added).

What marks the paranoid impulse in these pages is, I would say, less the stress on reflexive mimesis than the seeming faith in exposure. The arch-suspicious author of *The Novel and the Police* also speaks, in this case, for the protocols of many less interesting recent critics when he offers to provide "the 'flash' of increased visibility necessary to render modern discipline a problem in its own right" (ix)—as though to make something visible as a problem were, if not a mere hop, skip, and jump away from getting it solved, at least self-evidently a step in that direction. In this respect at least, though not in every one, Miller in *The Novel and the Police* writes as an exemplary New Historicist. For to a startling extent, the articulations of New Historicist scholarship rely on the prestige of a single, overarching narrative: exposing and problematizing hidden violences in the genealogy of the modern liberal subject.

With the passage of time since the New Historicism was new, it's becoming easier to see ways in which such a paranoid project of exposure may be more historically specific than it seems. "The modern liberal subject": in the latter 1990s it seems, or at least ought to seem, anything but an obvious choice as the unique *terminus ad quem* of historical narrative. Where *are* all these supposed modern liberal subjects? I daily encounter graduate students who are dab hands at unveiling the hidden historical violences that underlie a secular, universalist liberal humanism. Yet these students' sentient years—unlike the formative years of their teachers—have been spent entirely in a xenophobic Reagan-Bush-Clinton America where "liberal" is, if anything, a taboo category; and where "secular humanism" is routinely treated as a marginal religious sect, while a vast majority of the population claims to engage in direct intercourse with multiple invisible entities such as angels, Satan, and God.

Furthermore, the force of any interpretive project of *unveiling hidden violence* would seem to depend on a cultural context, like the one assumed in Foucault's early works, in which violence would be deprecated and hence hidden in the first place. Why bother exposing the ruses of power in a country where, at any given moment, 40 percent of young black men are enrolled in the penal system? In the United States and internationally, while there is plenty of hidden violence that requires exposure, there is also, and increasingly, an ethos where forms of violence that are hyper-visible from the start may be offered as an exemplary spectacle, rather than remaining to be unveiled as a scandalous secret. Human rights controversy around, for example, torture and disappearances in Argentina, or the use of mass rape as part of ethnic cleansing in Bosnia, marks—not an unveiling of practices that had been hidden or naturalized—but a wrestle of different frameworks *of* visibility. That is, violence that was *from the beginning* exemplary and spectacular, pointedly addressed, meant to serve as a public warning or terror to members of a particular community, is combated by efforts to *displace and redirect* (as well as simply expand) its aperture of visibility.

A further problem with these critical practices: what does a hermeneutic of suspicion and exposure have to say to social formations in which visibility itself constitutes much of the violence? The point of the move to reinstate chain gangs in several Southern states is less that convicts be required to perform hard labor than that they be required to do so under the gaze of the public; and the enthusiasm for Singapore-style justice that was popularly expressed in the United States around the caning of Michael Fay reveals a growing feeling that well-publicized shaming stigma is just what the doctor ordered for recalcitrant youth. Here is one remarkable index of historical change: it used to be opponents of capital punishment who argued that, if practiced at all, executions should be done in public so as to shame state and spectators by airing of the previously hidden judicial violence. Today it is no longer opponents but death-penalty cheerleaders, flushed with triumphal ambitions, who consider that the proper place for executions is on television. What price now the cultural critics' hard-won skill at making visible, behind permissive appearances, the hidden traces of oppression and persecution?

The paranoid trust in exposure seemingly depends, in addition, on an infinite reservoir of naïveté in those who make up the audience for these unveilings. What is the basis for assuming that it will surprise or disturb—never mind motivate—anyone to learn that a given social manifestation is artificial, self-contradictory, imitative, phantasmatic, or even violent? As Peter Sloterdijk points out, cynicism or "enlightened false consciousness"—false consciousness that knows itself to be false, "its falseness already reflexively buffered"—already represents "the universally widespread way in which enlightened people see to it that they are not taken for suckers."[19] How television-starved would someone have to be to find it shocking that ideologies contradict themselves, that simulacra don't have originals, or that gender representations are artifical? My own guess would be that such popular cynicism, while undoubtedly widespread, is only one among the heterogeneous, competing theories that constitute the mental ecology of most people. Some exposés, some demystifications, some bearings of witness do have great effectual force (though often of an unanticipated kind). Many that are just as true and convincing have none at all, however; and as long as that is so, we must admit that the efficacy and directionality of such acts reside somewhere else than in their relation to knowledge per se.

Writing in 1988—that is, after two full terms of Reaganism in the United States—D. A. Miller proposes to follow Foucault in demystifying "the intensive and continuous 'pastoral' care that liberal society proposes to take of each and every one of its charges" (viii). As if! I'm a lot less worried about being pathologized by my shrink than about my vanishing mental health coverage—and that's given the great good luck of having health insurance at all. Since the beginning of the tax revolt, the government of the United States—and, increasingly, those of other so-called liberal democracies—has been positively rushing to divest itself of answerability for care to its charges (cf. "entitlement programs")—with no other institutions proposing to fill in the gap. This development is the last thing anyone could have expected from reading New Historicist prose, which constitutes a full genealogy of the secular welfare state that peaked in the 1960s and 1970s, along with a watertight proof of why things must become more and more like that forever. No one can blame a writer in the 1980s for not having foreseen the effects of the Republicans' 1994 Contract with America. But if, as Miller says, "Surprise . . . is precisely what the paranoid seeks to eliminate," it must be admitted that, as a form of paranoia, the New Historicism fails spectacularly. While its general tenor of "things are bad and getting worse" is immune to refutation, any more specific predictive value—and as a result, arguably, any value for making oppositional strategy—has been nil. Such accelerating failure to anticipate change is moreover, as we've discussed, entirely in the nature of the paranoid process, whose sphere of influence (like that of the New Historicism itself) only expands as each unanticipated disaster seems to demonstrate more conclusively that, guess what, *you can never be paranoid enough.*

To look from a 1990s vantage at Richard Hofstadter's immensely influential 1963 essay, "The Paranoid Style in American Politics," is to see the extent of a powerful discursive change. Hofstadter's essay is a prime expression of the complacent, coercive liberal consensus that practically begs for the kind of paranoid demystification in which, for example, D. A. Miller educates his readers. Its style is mechanically evenhanded: Hofstadter finds paranoia on both left and right (among abolitionists, anti-Masons and anti-Catholics and anti-Mormons, nativists and Populists and those who believe in conspiracies of bankers or munitions-makers; in anyone who doubts that JFK was killed by a lone gunman, "in the popular left-wing press, in the contemporary American right wing, and on both sides of the race controversy today").[20] Although these categories would seem to cover a lot of people, there remains nonetheless a presumptive "we"—apparently still practically everyone—that can agree to view such extremes from a calm, understanding, and encompassing middle ground, where "we" can all agree that, for example, while "innumerable decisions of . . . the cold war can be faulted," they represent "simply the mistakes of well-meaning men" (36). Hofstadter has no trouble admitting that paranoid people or movements can perceive true things, though "a distorted style is . . . a possible signal that may alert us to a distorted judgment, just as in art an ugly style is a cue to fundamental defects of taste" (6).

> A few simple and relatively non-controversial examples may make [the distinction between content and style] wholly clear. Shortly after the assassination of President Kennedy, a great deal of publicity was given to a bill . . . to tighten federal controls over the sale of firearms through the mail. When hearings were being held on the measure,

three men drove 2,500 miles to Washington from Bagdad, Arizona, to testify against it. Now there are arguments against the Dodd bill which, however unpersuasive one may find them, have the color of conventional political reasoning. But one of the Arizonans opposed it with what might be considered representative paranoid arguments, insisting that it was "a further attempt by a subversive power to make us part of one world socialistic government" and that it threatened to "create chaos" that would help "our enemies" to seize power. (5)

I won't deny that a person could get nostalgic for a time when paranoid gun-lobby rhetoric sounded just plain nutty—a "simple and relatively non-controversial" example of "distorted judgment"—rather than repre-senting the uncontested platform of a dominant political party. But the spectacular datedness of Hofstadter's example isn't only an index of how far the American political center has shifted toward the right since 1963. It's also a sign of how normative such paranoid thinking has become at every point in the political spectrum. In a funny way, I feel closer today to that paranoid Arizonan than I do to Hofstadter—even though (or do I mean *because?*) I also assume that the Arizonan is a homophobic white-supremacist Christian Identity militia member who would as soon blow me away as look at me. Peter Sloterdijk does not make explicit that the wised-up popular cynicism or "enlightened false consciousness" that he considers now to be near-ubiquitous is, specifically, paranoid in structure; but that conclusion seems inescapable. Arguably, such narrow-gauge, everyday, rather incoherent cynicism is what paranoia looks like when it functions as weak theory rather than strong theory. To keep arriving on this hyper-demystified, paranoid scene with the "news" of a hermeneutic of suspicion, at any rate, is a far different act than such exposures would have been in the 1960s.

Subversive and demystifying parody, suspicious archaeologies of the present, the detection of hidden patterns of violence and their exposure: as I have been arguing, these infinitely doable and teachable protocols of unveiling have become the common currency of cultural and historicist studies. If there is an obvious danger in the triumphalism of a paranoid hermeneutic, it is that the broad consensual sweep of such methodologi-cal assumptions, the current near-profession-wide agreement about what constitutes narrative or explanation or adequate historicization, may, if it persists unquestioned, unintentionally impoverish the gene pool of literary-critical perspectives and skills. The trouble with a narrow gene pool, of course, is its diminished ability to respond to environmental (for instance, political) change.

Another, perhaps more nearly accurate way of describing the present paranoid consensus, however, is that rather than entirely displacing, it may simply have required a certain disarticulation, disavowal, and misrecognition of other ways of knowing—ways less oriented around suspicion—that are actually being practiced, often by the same theorists and as part of the same projects. The monopolistic program of paranoid knowing systematically disallows any explicit recourse to reparative motives, no sooner to be articulated than subject to methodical uprooting. Reparative motives, once they become explicit, are inadmissable within paranoid theory both because they are about pleasure ("merely aesthetic") and because they are frankly ameliorative ("merely reformist").[21] What makes pleasure and amelioration so "mere"? Only the exclusiveness of paranoia's faith in demystifying exposure: only its cruel and contemptuous assumption that the one thing lacking for global revolution, explosion of gender roles, or whatever, is people's (that is, *other* people's) having the painful effects of their oppression, poverty, or deludedness sufficiently exacerbated to make the pain conscious (as if otherwise it wouldn't have been) and intolerable (as if intolerable situations were famous for generating excellent solutions).

Such ugly prescriptions are not seriously offered by most paranoid theory; but a lot of contemporary theory is nonetheless regularly *structured as if* by them. The kind of aporia we have already discussed in *The Novel and the Police*, where readers are impelled through a grimly monolithic structure of strong paranoid theory by successive engagement with quite varied, often apparently keenly pleasure-oriented, smaller-scale writerly and intellectual solicitations, appears in a lot of other good criticism as well. I certainly recognize it as characterizing a fair amount of my own writing. Does it matter when such projects misdescribe themselves or are misrecognized by readers? I wouldn't suggest that the force of any powerful writing can ever attain complete transparency to itself, or is likely to account for itself very adequately at the constative level of the writing. But suppose one takes seriously a notion—like the one articulated by Tomkins, but also like other available ones—that everyday theory qualitatively affects everyday knowledge and experience; and suppose that one doesn't want to draw much ontological distinction between academic theory and everyday theory; and suppose that one has a lot of concern for the quality of other people's and one's own practices of knowing and experiencing. In these cases, it would make sense—if one had the choice—not to cultivate the necessity of a systematic, self-accelerating split between what one is doing and the reasons for which one does it.

To change one's understanding of the reasons for one's practice, or the meanings of one's practice—is it, or is it not, under this understanding of theory, to change one's practice? I ask this question seriously, and I take it to be a productive, overarching rubric under which to approach the essays in the present volume. There's a built-in gracelessness to the expectation that *any* essay will end with an explanation of exactly what it is that the writer is "calling for." ("Calling for," as if critical practices were ready-made consumer items among which one had only to choose — "Mabel, Black Label!" Or maybe as if one were a doctor, whose expensive expertise goes into the writing of the right prescription, leaving to some commercial functionary the work of filling it as ordered.) That gracelessness can only be amplified when the essay in question is an introduction to other essays by other writers: as if any one person either had all along anticipated, or were now in a position to sum up and adjudicate, so rich a diversity of projects. My prescription — or really, I think, my proposition — here is very modest: that our work grows more interesting, more responsive, more truthful, and more useful as we try to account for its motives in a less stylized fashion than we have been. Perhaps the unpacking, above, of several different elements of paranoid thought can suggest several specific, divergent dimensions in which alternative approaches may also be available — may indeed be in practice in these pages.

While paranoid theoretical proceedings both depend upon and reinforce the structural dominance of monopolistic "strong theory," there may also be benefit in exploring the extremely varied, dynamic, and historically contingent ways that strong theoretical constructs interact with weak ones in the ecology of knowing — an exploration that obviously can't proceed without a respectful interest in weak as well as strong theoretical acts. Tomkins offers far more models for approaching such a project than I've been able to summarize. But the history of literary criticism can also be viewed as a repertoire of alternative models for allowing strong and weak theory to interdigitate. One notable feature of *Novel Gazing*, for example, is the centrality in so many of these essays of an unhurried, undefensive, theoretically galvanized practice of close reading. What could better represent "weak theory, little better than a description of the phenomena which it purports to explain" than this devalued and near-obsolescent New Critical skill?[22] But what was already true in Empson and Burke is true in a different way in these essays: there are important phenomenological and theoretical tasks that can be accomplished only through local theories and nonce taxonomies; the potentially innumerable mechanisms of their relation to stronger theories remains the matter of art and speculative thought.

Paranoia, as we have pointed out, represents not only a strong affect theory but a strong *negative* affect theory. A strong theory (that is, a wide-ranging and reductive one) that was not mainly organized around anticipating, identifying, and warding off the negative affect of humiliation would resemble paranoia in some respects, but differ from it in others. I think, for example, that that might be a fair characterization of the preceding section of the present essay. The question of the strength of a given theory (or that of the relations between strong and weak theory) may be orthogonal to the question of its affective *quale*, and each may be capable of exploration by different means. It does seem to me that the most powerful pieces in this collection—even profoundly sad pieces— skill readers at attending to, rather than having to disavow, the workings of positive affect in projects where only negative affect theories have so far had much structuring force.

Since even the specification of paranoia as a theory of negative affect leaves open the distinctions between or among negative affects, there is the additional opportunity of experimenting with a vocabulary that will do justice to a wide affective range. Again, not only with the negative affects: it can also be reifying and, indeed, coercive to have only one, totalizing model of positive affect always in the same featured position. A disturbingly large amount of theory seems explicitly to undertake the proliferation of only one affect or maybe two, of whatever kind—whether ecstasy, sublimity, self-shattering, *jouissance*, suspicion, abjection, knowingness, horror, grim satisfaction, or righteous indignation. It's like the old joke: "Comes the revolution, Comrade, everyone gets to eat roast beef every day." "But Comrade, I don't like roast beef." "Comes the revolution, Comrade, you'll like roast beef." Comes the revolution, Comrade, you'll be tickled pink by those deconstructive jokes; you'll faint from ennui every minute that you're not smashing the state apparatus; you'll definitely want hot sex twenty to thirty times a day. You'll be mournful *and* militant. You'll never want to tell Deleuze and Guattari, "Not tonight, dears, I have a headache."

To recognize in paranoia a distinctively rigid relation to temporality, at once anticipatory and retroactive, averse above all to surprise, is also to glimpse the lineaments of other possibilities. Here, perhaps, Klein is of more help than Tomkins: to read from a reparative position is to surrender the knowing, anxious paranoid determination that no horror, however apparently unthinkable, shall ever come to the reader *as new*: to a reparatively positioned reader, it can seem realistic and necessary to experience surprise. Because there can be terrible surprises, however, there can also be good ones. Hope, often a fracturing, even a traumatic thing to experience, is among the energies by which the reparatively positioned reader tries to organize the fragments and part-objects she encounters or creates.[23] Because she has room to realize that the future may be different from the present, it is also possible for her to entertain such profoundly painful, profoundly relieving, ethically crucial possibilities as that the past, in turn, could have happened differently from the way it actually did.[24]

Where does this argument leave projects of queer reading, in particular? With the relative deemphasis of the question of "sexual difference" and sexual "sameness," and with the possibility of moving from a Freudian, homophobia-centered understanding of paranoia to other understandings of it, like Klein's or Tomkins's, that are not particularly Oedipal and are less drive-oriented than affect-oriented, I am also suggesting that the mutual inscription of queer thought with the topic of paranoia may be less necessary, less definitional, less completely constitutive than earlier writing on it, very much including my own, has assumed. A more ecological view of paranoia wouldn't offer the same transhistorical, almost automatic conceptual privileging of gay/lesbian issues that is offered by a Freudian view.

On the other hand, I think it will leave us in a vastly better position to do justice to a wealth of characteristic, culturally central practices, many of which can well be called reparative, that emerge from queer experience but become invisible or illegible under a paranoid optic. As Joseph Litvak writes, for example,

> It seems to me that the importance of "mistakes" in queer reading and writing . . . has a lot to do with loosening the traumatic, inevitable-seeming connection between mistakes and humiliation. What I mean is that, if a lot of queer energy, say around adolescence, goes into what Barthes calls "le vouloir-être-intelligent" (as in "If I have to be miserable, at least let me be brainier than everybody else"), accounting in large part for paranoia's enormous prestige as the very signature of smartness (a smartness that smarts), a lot of queer energy, later on, goes into . . . practices aimed at taking the terror out of error, at making the making of mistakes sexy, creative, even cognitively powerful. Doesn't reading queer mean learning, among other things, that mistakes can be good rather than bad surprises?[25]

It's appropriate, I think, that these insights would be contingent developments, rather than definitional or transhistorical ones—they aren't things that would inevitably inhere in the experience of every woman-loving woman or man-loving man, say. For if, as we've shown, a paranoid reading practice is closely tied to a notion of the inevitable, there are, as this volume demonstrates, other features of queer reading that can attune it exquisitely to a heartbeat of contingency.

The dogged, defensive narrative stiffness of a paranoid temporality, after all, in which yesterday can't be allowed to have differed from today and tomorrow must be even more so, takes its shape from a generational narrative that's characterized by a distinctly Oedipal regularity and repetitiveness: it happened to my father's father, it happened to my father, it is happening to me, it will happen to my son, and it will happen to my son's son. But isn't it a feature of queer possibility—only a contingent feature, but a real one, and one that in turn strengthens the force of contingency itself—that our generational relations don't always proceed in this lockstep?

Think of the epiphanic, extravagantly reparative final volume of Proust, in which the narrator, after a long withdrawal from society, goes to a party where he at first thinks everyone is sporting elaborate costumes pretending to be ancient—then realizes that they *are* old, and so is he—and is then assailed, in half a dozen distinct mnemonic shocks, by a climactic series of joy-inducing "truths" about the relation of writing to time. The narrator never says so, but isn't it worth pointing out that the complete temporal disorientation that initiates him into this revelatory space would have been impossible in a heterosexual *père de famille,* in one who had meanwhile been embodying, in the form of inexorably "progressing" identities and roles, the regular arrival of children and grandchildren?

> And now I began to understand what old age was—old age, which perhaps of all the realities is the one of which we preserve for longest in our life a purely abstract conception, looking at calendars, dating our letters, seeing our friends marry and then in their turn the children of our friends, and yet, either from fear or from sloth, not understanding what all this means, until the day when we behold an unknown silhouette . . . which teaches us that we are living in a new world; until the day when a grandson of a woman we once knew, a young man whom instinctively we treat as a contemporary of ours, smiles as though we were making fun of him because it seems that we are old enough to be his grandfather—and I began to understand too what death meant and love and the joys of the spiritual life, the usefulness of suffering, a vocation, etc. (3:354–55) [26]

A more recent and terrible contingency, in the brutal foreshortening of so many queer lifespans, has deroutinized the temporality of many of us in ways that only intensify this effect. I'm thinking, as I say this, of three very queer friendships I have. One of my friends is sixty; the other two are both thirty, and I, at forty-five, am exactly in the middle. All four of us are academics, and we have in common a lot of interests, energies, and ambitions; we have each had, as well, variously intense activist investments. In a "normal" generational narrative, our identifications with each other would be aligned with an expectation that in another fifteen years,

I'd be situated comparably to where my sixty-year-old friend is, while my thirty-year-old friends would be situated comparably to where I am.

But we are all aware that the grounds of such friendships today are likely to differ from that model. They do so in inner cities, and for people subject to racist violence, and for people deprived of health care, and for people in dangerous industries, and for many others; they do for my friends and me. Specifically, living with advanced breast cancer, I have little chance of ever being the age my older friend is now. My friends who are thirty years old are similarly unlikely ever to experience my present, middle age: one is living with an advanced cancer caused by a massive environmental trauma (basically, he grew up on top of a toxic waste site); the other is living with HIV. The friend who is a very healthy sixty is the likeliest of us to be living fifteen years from now.

It's hard to say, hard even to know, how these relationships are different from those shared by people of different ages on a landscape whose perspectival lines converge on a common disappearing-point. I'm sure ours are more intensely motivated: whatever else we know, we know there isn't time to bullshit. But what it means to identify with each other must also be very different. On this scene, an older person doesn't love a younger as someone who will someday be where she now is, or vice versa. No one is, so to speak, carrying forward the family name; there's a sense in which our life narratives will barely overlap. There's another sense in which they slide up more intimately alongside one another than can any lives that are moving forward according to the regular schedule of the generations. It is one another immediately, one another as the present fullness of a becoming whose arc may extend no further, whom we each must learn best to apprehend, fulfill, and bear company.

At a textual level, it seems to me that related practices of reparative knowing may lie, barely recognized and little explored, at the heart of many histories of gay, lesbian, and queer intertextuality. The queer-identified practice of camp, for example, may be seriously misrecognized when it is viewed, as Butler and others view it, through paranoid lenses. As we've seen, camp is currently understood as uniquely appropriate to the projects of parody, denaturalization, demystification, and mocking exposure of the elements and assumptions of a dominant culture; and the degree to which camping is motivated by love seems often to be understood mainly as the degree of its self-hating complicity with an oppressive status quo. By this account, the X-ray gaze of the paranoid impulse in camp sees through to an unfleshed skeleton of the culture; the paranoid aesthetic on view here is one of minimalist elegance and conceptual economy.

The desire of a reparative impulse, on the other hand, is additive and accretive. Its fear, a realistic one, is that the culture surrounding it is in-adequate or inimical to its nurture; it wants to assemble and confer pleni-tude on an object that will then have resources to offer to an inchoate self. To view camp as, among other things, the communal, historically dense exploration of a variety of reparative practices is to be able to do better justice to many of the defining elements of classic camp performance: the startling, juicy displays of excess erudition, for example; the passion-ate, often hilarious antiquarianism, the prodigal production of alternate historiographies; the "over"-attachment to fragmentary, marginal, waste, or leftover products; the rich, highly interruptive affective variety; the irrepressible fascination with ventriloquistic experimentation; the disori-enting juxtapositions of present with past, and popular with high culture. As in the writing of D. A. Miller, a glue of surplus beauty, surplus stylis-tic investment, unexplained upwellings of threat, contempt, and longing cements together and animates the amalgam of powerful part-objects in such work as that of Ronald Firbank, Djuna Barnes, Joseph Cornell, Kenneth Anger, Charles Ludlam, Jack Smith, John Waters, Holly Hughes.

The very mention of these names, some of them attaching to almost legendarily "paranoid" personalities, confirms, too, Klein's insistence that it is not people but mutable positions—or, I would want to add, practices—that can be divided between the paranoid and the reparative; it is some-times the most paranoid-tending people who are able to, and need to, develop and disseminate the richest reparative practices. And if the para-noid or the depressive positions operate on a smaller scale than the level of individual typology, they operate also on a larger, that of shared histo-ries, emergent communities, and the weaving of intertextual discourse.

At the beginning of this introduction, I undertook a list of some influen-tial dichotomies and reifications that the essays collected here, individu-ally and cumulatively, seem to suggest exciting ways of doing without. The organization of the book—perhaps appropriately contingent—is meant to dramatize what could, in another connection, seem a series of oxymo-ronic conjunctions: digitality with physical touch, affect with economics, pedagogy with wild animals, mama's boys with fatherlands, desire with cognition.

The title of this book's first part, "Digital Senses," can oddly seem both oxymoron *and* tautology. With what, for example, would one think to exercise one's senses if not with fingers? Yet the still-popular use of human fingers as a cheap and user-friendly computational technology has also come to seem the very definitional opposite of the disembodied, infinitely abstract realm now called digital. To begin this collection with Kathryn Bond Stockton's essay, "Prophylactics and Brains: *Beloved* in the

Cybernetic Age of AIDS," is however to be invited by a universe of speculation and feeling in which the parasitic demand of "information" to be transmitted, of codes to be decoded, and thought to be thought, is entirely interfolded with the yearning and mortification of the skin, and the imperious bodily structurations of grievous memory and historic trauma.

With the next essay, Joseph Litvak turns from touch toward taste. In "Strange Gourmet: Taste, Waste, Proust," he undertakes to delineate something like "an object-relations theory" of sophistication, "a theory that will explain how sophistication maps out a certain fantasmatic way of circulating in and around the world—not, as may seem to be the case, of simply rising above it but, at least in Proust's case, of connecting the 'high' and the 'low' so as to short-circuit the middle." In proper Kleinian fashion, Litvak approaches Proust through a narrative of the gullet, emphasizing good and bad mouth-objects and complex inner pleasures (the "stranger" or gamier—that is to say, the "higher"—the better). If you aren't squeamish about digestive processes, then there's always a sense in which you *can* eat your cake and have it, too; "re-senting, re-tasting, re-finding the badness of the bad object, saving that badness from falling into the mere banality of the merely deidealized, [has] the additional virtue, in other words, of helping one save oneself."

Returning to the fingers, "Outing Texture," Renu Bora's deeply original essay on *The Ambassadors,* offers theoretical tools at once for an erotics and a metaphysics of texture. Occupying "the borders of properties of touch and vision," texture dramatizes both the disjunctures and displacements between the two senses (as in certain traditions of understanding fetishism), and their common materialities. Another tension: texture, as surfacial, can signify the exact opposite of structure; while texture, *as* structure (think of sand, brick, feces), can also offer the most graphic sensual manifestation of the immanence of production processes and histories. Bora touches both on the objects in James—fabrics and bibelots, as well as erotic objects—and on the narrative touch of "James" himself: what, Bora finally asks, is the texture of innuendo?

In "The 'Sinister Fruitiness' of Machines: *Neuromancer,* Internet Sexuality, and the Turing Test," Tyler Curtain returns us to the airier digitality of cyberspace. His essay frames newly the question, What kind of crisis is it that the digital revolution makes for understandings of personhood? In the fiction of William Gibson, in the cruisy salons of the Internet, and—most explosively—in the benchmark Turing test itself, Curtain explores the ways that gender as well as sexuality may drive definitional wedges between the two terms, "humanness" and "intelligence."

Jeff Nunokawa's essay, "The Importance of Being Bored: The Dividends of Ennui in *The Picture of Dorian Gray,*" introduces "The Affective

Life of Capital," the second part of *Novel Gazing*. While no one would be surprised to learn that capitalism depends on generating interest, Nunokawa's project here is to show how fully it also depends on generating tedium. More specifically, it is consumer culture whose relation to boredom is articulated through a (paradoxically fascinating) reading of "the intimacy between advertising and aesthetics" in Wilde—and between both of these and a centuries-long, sublimatory tradition of male intergenerational desire.

Michael Lucey points out early in his essay, "Balzac's Queer Cousins and Their Friends," that Balzac is one of the novelists who can seem most to fuse into one totalizing, seamless whole the "two projects" of hegemonic power: "portraying a world, and helping suture us to it." Lucey's essay, however, while it is interested in such "parallels," is most interested in maintaining them *as* parallel—that is, in attending to and making use of the irreducible distances that live between the lines. Between the needs of a system called "family" and the needs of a system of capital accumulation there are also such parallels, condensed for instance in the Foucauldian concept of "alliance." Lucey is drawn to *Cousin Bette* and *Cousin Pons* because the novels center on "bachelor and spinster cousins, family misfits and remainders," "parasitic on the family, yet also radically other to it." He is also, however, sharply yet ambivalently drawn into Balzac's disavowed solicitations for the reader to interpret Bette's and Pons's ontologies precisely *as sexual*. "The slack in the cord that links sentiment or affect or sexuality to family structure" is, as he shows, the place of a crucially contingent crossing between perverse sexual itineraries and circuitous economic trajectories.

"Teacher's Pet" is the rubric for the book's third part; I wish there were an easy technology for wafting into its pages the strains of the song as Doris Day performs it. That pedagogy can be a very sexy matter was no more news to Rousseau than to Plato or Dante. But as Anne Chandler shows in her essay about an influential disciple of Rousseau's, "Defying 'Development': Thomas Day's Queer Curriculum in *Sandford and Merton*," the desires that cement a teacher to his job may not consort intelligibly with the developmental narrative that implicitly underwrites such intimacy. *Sandford and Merton* was not only as famous a book in its time as *Emile*, but, improbably, an even weirder one. Chandler's patient closeness to this text, at once dry, playful, and erotically generous, seems to offer a new model of how one might respect the alterity of a distant moment without reifying temporal distance *as* alterity: without reinscribing wishful or oversimplifying presumptions about what the present is like, and without disavowing the unexpected currents that may jolt between present and past.

As I've suggested above, there may be resonant homologies between this queer way of risking historical "anachronism," on the one hand, and on the other hand that intimate anachronism by which a queer grown-up can sometimes keep drawing on the energies, incredulities, and discoveries of an earlier moment of passionate, incompetent reading and recognition. For many queer readers of the latter twentieth century, I think, the Arthurian narratives of T. H. White, especially *The Once and Future King* (dramatized in *Camelot*), condense the two modes of anachronism in an almost unbearably piquant way. Barry Weller returns to these formative childhood texts in "Wizards, Warriors, and the Beast Glatisant in Love." He discusses the remarkably wide range of invitations (to identify, to desire) that White offers the young reader. While some of these—I want to call them "versions of pastoral," but by that I would still mean "versions of queerness"—are frankly homoerotic and/or pederastic, the ones that prove most productive are, unexpectedly, those that dramatize the crossing between species. "What Arthur's excursions into the animal kingdom offer him," Weller observes, "is an open-ended variety of erotic connections and political regimes, with the corollary that no single ordering of human affairs is right or final."

In "Forged in Crisis: Queer Beginnings of Modern Masculinity in a Canonical French Novel," James Creech also returns (reparatively?) to the moment of a younger reader's queer recognition. Here his focus is not, like Weller's, on what he *didn't* know about a children's book, but rather on what "as a gay reader I have always 'known' "—even as "it has been impossible to find an explanation or an expression" for such out-of-place or premature knowledge—about one of the classic texts of French studies, Benjamin Constant's *Adolphe*. That "these frightened and fragile gestures of queer self-recognition . . . be taken seriously," and even come to be supported by "a rich texture of spontaneous presumption," is part of Creech's project; another part is to suggest a queer male genealogy alternative to the popular narrative of the eternal smother-mother. One of the most *dys*topian of T. H. White's twentieth-century versions of pastoral, as Barry Weller notes, is a quasi-incestuous overstress of the bond between mother and son. Creech shows that at Constant's earlier, post-Revolutionary European moment, "the maternal term is not yet the given onto which primary homosexual incest can be displaced or projected. In this period, the crisis of masculinity can still be located, conceptually, within a male context, and the crisis of heterosexual experience emerges as its extension."

I wonder whether in these introductory notes, as I've several times invoked moments or flashes of queer *recognition*, such invocations may not have implicitly borrowed a certain humanistic, Buberian or Winnicottian gravity from the moral prestige of the face—and in particular, of the encounter between one face and another. Yet the recognitions implicit in queer pedagogy do not always conform to the missionary position. One Victorian headmaster, for example, was famous for being unable to recognize his former students when he could see only their faces. "The traffic between and among faces and butts stimulates meaning production while troubling what it means to be legible," notes John Vincent in his extraordinarily suggestive essay, "Flogging is Fundamental: Applications of Birch in Swinburne's *Lesbia Brandon*." Charting the many ways that an erotics of flogging can be misrecognized—swept out of sight and mind, for example, under the more familiar rubrics of masochism, of anality, of pederasty, or even just of "pain"—Vincent applies himself vigorously to the surfaces of Swinburne's writing, stimulating the sense of both the specificity and the wild dilativeness of the topic.

The fourth part of the book, "Men and Nations," is the only one that specifies a gender in its emphasis on the political bearings of a masculinity marked by the historical particularization of sexuality. The tour de force performed by Jacob Press in his essay, "Same-Sex Unions in Modern Europe: *Daniel Deronda, Altneuland,* and the Homoerotics of Jewish Nationalism," is a thoroughgoing, novelistic reading of early Zionism as and through a European crisis of masculine sexuality. It hasn't been widely appreciated, for example, that Max Nordau, inventor of a theory of "degeneration" whose anti-Semitic as well as homophobic bearings have reached so gruesomely into the present century, was himself not only Jewish but in fact an important Zionist founder. Through readings of and around *Daniel Deronda* and Theodor Herzl's visionary Zionist novel, *Altneuland,* Press makes it possible to understand such juxtapositions less as paradoxical than as axiomatic.

In a bravura reading of *Gentlemen's Agreement*, a best-selling American middlebrow novel (1946) and film (1947), Cindy Patton returns to the topic of Jewish masculinity as a crossing-point between sexuality and national citizenship. The then-new postwar genre of the "problem" novel/film, Patton shows, characteristically treated homophobia and anti-Semitism as interchangeable "problems." The title of Patton's essay, "To Die For," evokes the question suggested by Benedict Anderson, the theorist of nationality: what are the affective mechanisms by which "dying for one's country, which usually one does not choose, assumes a moral grandeur which dying for the Labour Party, the American Medical Association, or perhaps even Amnesty International cannot rival"? Patton discusses how the prescribed structures of empathetic vicariation in the "problem" genres may have inflected the developing relationship between sexual identity and national identity; such skilled affective processes, she argues, may offer both a truer and a more radical postwar genealogy for

gay politics than does the usual explanatory recourse to McCarthyite repression.

Robert F. Reid-Pharr is concerned with liminal and mythic, as well
as with historically local manifestations of crisis, possession, and scape-
goating in "Tearing the Goat's Flesh: Homosexuality, Abjection, and the
Production of a Late-Twentieth-Century Black Masculinity." Like Patton,
however, he sets his sights toward the politics of a specific construction of
positive affect: in this case the joy and excitement (far more than simply
the functionalist restoration of equilibrium) that circulate around the
process of abjecting the bodies and souls of African American gay men.
Through new framings of Eldridge Cleaver's *Soul on Ice*, Piri Thomas's
Down These Mean Streets, and James Baldwin's *Giovanni's Room*, Reid-
Pharr reads through the far lenses of the texts' absences, in search of the
"perverse" ghosts that will "parallel[ ] the absence of the black from Western notions of rationality and humanity while at the same time pointing to the possibility of escape from this same black-exclusive system of
logic."

The title of the final part of this book, "Libidinal Intelligence: Shocks
and Recognitions," comes from Joseph Litvak's earlier essay, in which
he discusses the potential uses of Proustian anachronism as one seeks
"a model for recapturing not so much a lost world as a lost *libidinal
intelligence*, a capacity for having more than a blandly routinized relation to *any* world. Reading Proust can induce a fantasy of *being* Proust.
That fantasy keeps faith with a fantasmatic faculty itself: with, to amend
Adorno, a childhood potential not so much for unimpaired experience as
for making bad—that is to say, as Proust himself would say, good—object choices." The shock of the *strange*, as it is denominated by Jonathan
Goldberg's essay-title as well as Litvak's own, records the shape of a need
for fantasy to "keep[ ] faith with a fantasmatic faculty itself." The uncanny shock of strangeness is only one step to the side of what we have
been calling the shock of queer recognition; but the epithet "strange"
also marks a stubborn Taurean refusal to accede to the requirement that
objects be designated "bad" or "good" at all.

"Dancing books" is the generic designation Maurice Wallace coins to
describe Melvin Dixon's *Vanishing Rooms*; the phrase, the entire inquiry,
seem to open realms. Kinesthetic habits, rhythms, shocks, and explora-
tions have a mind and indeed a memory of their own. The project of
Wallace's essay, "The Autochoreography of an Ex-Snow Queen: Dance,
Desire, and the Black Masculine in Melvin Dixon's *Vanishing Rooms*," is
to do justice to a certain kinesthetic challenge in and around Dixon's
novel. It suggests that under the heavy, distorting ether of homophobic
pressure and racist hyperembodiment, human movement through space

may be the *only* form of truth-telling about the misrecognitions—indeed as well the veritable recognitions—involved in the loves, betrayals, and desires between an African American man and a white man.

It might make sense to describe as a "dancing essay" Stephen Barber's discussion of *The Years* and *Between the Acts* in "Lip-Reading: Woolf's Secret Encounters." If this is dancing, however, it is secret and for that matter strange dancing: the dance of lips, fingers, eyes. Digital dancing maybe, it signifies the brush of recognitions that both strain toward language and systematically elude it. Specifically these "unnarrativizable miracles" are the slantwise recognitions that pass between women and gay men, which, as Barber shows, became critical for Virginia Woolf as the loss of Lytton Strachey steadily deepened for her in the decade after his death. "He was so good to me / Who's going to make me gay, now?" Barber quotes Nina Simone; in an essay whose ethical bearing is shockingly frontal, he also quotes Gayatri Spivak: "Ethics is the experience of the impossible."

"The deftness of a woman's fingers on ivory" is only one of the pungent images with which, in "The Female World of Exorcism and Displacement (Or, Relations between women in Henry James's Nineteenth-Century *The Portrait of a Lady*)," Melissa Solomon marks "the growing telepathy of sensual reading" between Isabel Archer and Madame Merle in *The Portrait of a Lady*. As the title of her essay suggests, Solomon is interested in how utterly "the sharpened pincers" of characters' and readers' "subliminal" lesbian insight can reorganize both a received, heterosexist view of the novel's performative space, and a received, anodyne view of the eroticism and promise that pulse between women. "Within this ontology," Solomon points out, "perception itself . . . is frightfully at stake, and one scrambles to employ the finely calibrated senses of taste, touch, and smell."

In "Strange Brothers," finally, Jonathan Goldberg feels his way back to the shock of a first encounter with the prose of Willa Cather—"as if, somehow, the novels were written in a language which I could not myself articulate and yet in which I found myself articulated." In retroactive explanation, Goldberg invokes a famous phrase from Cather's manifesto on "The Novel Démeublé"; and it is as if his essay, a reading of *The Professor's House*, were itself a meditation on, and in the beautiful mode of, unfurnishedness. Goldberg forges instruments for registering the recognitions that vibrate through certain quiet vicariations and spare identifications: those, for example, through which the love of Edith Lewis narrates Cather's "strange" at-homeness with a challenging anachronistic space.

What Joseph Litvak, in his essay, refers to as "gay alchemy" represents a wild, cunning, and flamboyant refusal of the either/or. Like Proust, the reader "helps himself again and again"; as all these essays show, it is not only important but *possible* to find ways of attending to such reparative motives and positionalities. The vocabulary for articulating any reader's reparative motive toward a text or a culture has long been so sappy, aestheticizing, defensive, anti-intellectual, or reactionary that it's no wonder few critics are willing to describe their acquaintance with such motives. The prohibitive problem, however, has been in the limitations of present theoretical vocabularies rather than in the reparative motive itself. No less acute than a paranoid position, no less realistic, no less attached to a project of survival, and neither less nor more delusional or fantasmatic, the reparative reading position undertakes a different range of affects, ambitions, and risks. What we can best learn from such practices are, perhaps, the many ways in which selves and communities succeed in extracting sustenance from the objects of a culture—even of a culture whose avowed desire has often been not to sustain them.

NOTES

This introductory essay was inspired, and in very different ways, by the examples of Michael Moon, Eric Dishman, and Stephen Barber.

1 Jonathan Culler, *Structuralist Poetics: Structuralism, Linguistics and the Study of Literature* (Ithaca: Cornell University Press, 1975), pp. 113–30.

2 Paul Ricoeur, *De l'interprétation: Essai sur Freud* (1964).

3 Sigmund Freud, *The Standard Edition of the Complete Psychological Works of Sigmund Freud*, ed. James Strachey and trans. James Strachey et al., 24 vols. (London: Hogarth Press, 1953–), 12:79, 17:261.

4 Paul Ricoeur, *Freud and Philosophy: An Essay on Interpretation*, trans. Denis Savage (New Haven and London: Yale University Press, 1970), pp. 33–34.

5 Guy Hocquenghem, *Homosexual Desire*, trans. Daniella Dangoor, preface by Jeffrey Weeks, introduction by Michael Moon (Durham, N.C.: Duke University Press, 1993).

6 Leo Bersani, *The Culture of Redemption* (Cambridge, Mass.: Harvard University Press, 1990), p. 188.

7 James Eli Adams, *Dandies and Desert Saints: Styles of Victorian Manhood* (Ithaca, N.Y.: Cornell University Press, 1995), p. 15.

8 *Concise Columbia Dictionary of Quotations*, Microsoft Bookshelf, 1992.

9 R. D. Hinshelwood, *A Dictionary of Kleinian Thought*, 2d ed. (Northvale, N.J.: Aronson, 1991), p. 394.

10 Melanie Klein, *Envy and Gratitude* (London: Tavistock, 1957).

11 J. Laplanche and J.-B. Pontalis, *The Language of Psycho-Analysis*, trans. Donald Nicholson-Smith (New York: Norton, 1973), p. 297.

12 D. A. Miller, *The Novel and the Police* (Berkeley: University of California Press, 1988), p. 164. Further citations from this work will be incorporated in the text.

13 Eve Kosofsky Sedgwick, *The Coherence of Gothic Conventions* (New York: Methuen, 1986), p. xi.

14 *Affect, Imagery, Consciousness*, vol. 2 (New York: Springer, 1963), pp. 433–34. Further citations from this work will be incorporated in the text.

15 Tomkins's recurrent example of a weak theory is one that allows many of us to cross

streets often without fear: those sets of actions summed up in the phrase "look both ways before you cross," which enable an individual to act as if afraid so as to avoid the actual experience of fear—"affect acting at a distance." What is weak about this theory is its restricted domain, perhaps initially understood to include only walking across the street where one first learned the rule as a child, analogically expanded to include walking across other streets or street-like passages, then expanded more to include riding a bicycle or driving a car. Consider the case where this weak theory gets strong: "If the individual cannot find the rules whereby he can cross the street without feeling anxious [because of a series of unfortunate accidents, say], then his avoidance strategies will necessarily become more and more diffuse. Under these conditions the individual might be forced, first, to avoid all busy streets and then to go out only late at night when traffic was light; finally, he would remain inside, and if his house were to be hit by a car, he would have to seek refuge in a deeper shelter" (2:320). A strong theory is not more successful at preventing the experience of negative affect, here fear, than a weak theory; in this case, quite the opposite. Both the cognitive antennae of the theory and the preventive strategies have changed. This individual has learned to count many more things as a street: this strong fear theorist is always ready to draw the line that expands his theory's domain. (This explanation is borrowed from the introduction to the volume edited by me and Adam Frank, *Shame and Its Sisters: A Silvan Tomkins Reader* [Durham, N.C.: Duke University Press, 1995] pp. 27–28.)

16 Laplanche and Pontalis, in their entry under "Pleasure Principle" (*Language*, pp. 322–325), show that Freud was long aware of this problem. They paraphrase: "Must we therefore be content with a purely economic definition and accept that pleasure and unpleasure are nothing more than the translation of quantitative changes into qualitative terms? And what then is the precise correlation between these two aspects, the qualitative and the quantitative? Little by little, Freud came to lay considerable emphasis on the great difficulty encountered in the attempt to provide a simple answer to this question" (p. 323). In our introduction to *Shame and Its Sisters*, Adam Frank and I describe Tomkins's work on affect in terms that respond very directly to this way of posing the problem (pp. 8–11).

17 Marcel Proust, *In Search of Lost Time*, trans. Andreas Mayor and Terence Kilmartin, revised by D. J. Enright (New York: Modern Library, 1993), 3:303; emphasis added.

18 Judith Butler, *Gender Trouble: Feminism and the Subversion of Identity* (New York: Routledge, 1990), p. 124. Further citations from this work will be incorporated in the text.

19 Peter Sloterdijk, *Critique of Cynical Reason*, trans. Michael Eldred, foreword by Andreas Huyssen (Minneapolis: University of Minnesota Press, 1987), p. 5.

20 Richard Hofstadter, *The Paranoid Style in American Politics and Other Essays* (New York: Alfred A. Knopf, 1965), p. 9. Further citations from this work will be incorporated in the text.

21 The barely implicit sneer with which Leo Bersani wields the term "redemption," throughout *The Culture of Redemption*, might be one good example of the latter kind of usage—except that Bersani's revulsion seems to attach, not quite to the notion that things could be ameliorated, but rather to the pious reification of Art as the appointed agent of such change.

22 Thanks to Tyler Curtain for pointing this out to me.

23 I am thinking here of Timothy Gould's interpretation (in a personal communication) of Emily Dickinson's poem that begins "'Hope' is the thing with feathers— / That perches in the soul—". Gould suggests that the symptoms of fluttering hope are rather like those of post-traumatic stress syndrome—with the difference that the apparently

absent cause of perturbation lies in the future, rather than in the past. Thomas H. Johnson, ed., *The Complete Poems of Emily Dickinson* (Boston: Little, Brown and Co., 1960), p. 116, poem no. 254.

24 I don't mean to hypostatize, here, "the way it actually did" happen, or to deny how constructed a thing this "actually did" may be—within certain constraints. The realm of what *might have happened but didn't* is, however, ordinarily even wider and less constrained, and it seems conceptually important that the two not be collapsed; otherwise, the entire possibility of things' *happening differently* can be lost.

25 Personal communication.

26 It is not only in time that the narrator's being outside of the generational process permits a slippage that finally amounts to transmutative free-fall. There is also a gender slippage that goes with it:

> Gilberte de Saint-Loup said to me: "Shall we go and dine together by ourselves in a restaurant?" and I replied: "Yes, if you don't find it compromising to dine alone with a young man." As I said this, I heard everybody round me laugh, and I hastily added: "or rather, with an old man." I felt that the phrase which had made people laugh was one of those which my mother might have used in speaking of me, my mother for whom I was still a child. And I realised that I judged myself from the same point of view as she did. (3:354)

PART I   Digital Senses

Kathryn Bond Stockton

Prophylactics and Brains: *Beloved* in

the Cybernetic Age of AIDS

I. THE DEAD

We lean along their edges in the act of contemplation, for they reside, with strange intermittence, behind our eyes, in the boat
of the brain. We wonder how they breathe, how air reaches
them at the length of such an intimate remove.

Imagine, the dead are a cybernetic problem: a material problem alive
in the virtual world of ideas—their storage and transfer.

II. LIVING DEAD

Claims to surprise us by the actual surround us. Scientific "thrillers," fertile in their forms of the factual, invoke the living dead, claiming that
what is virtual is actually viral, the viral more than virtual.

" 'Memes [ideas; memories; basic units of cultural transmission] should
be regarded as living structures, not just metaphorically but technically.
When you plant a fertile meme in my mind you literally parasitize my
brain . . . in just the way that a virus may parasitize the genetic mechanism of a host cell.' "[1]

"Viruses are ambiguously alive. . . . They carry on their existence in
the borderlands between life and nonlife. . . . Virus particles that lie
around . . . may seem dead, but the particles are waiting for someone to
come along. . . . [Then] ["a motive without a mind"] the virus switches on
and begins to replicate."[2]

"Is there a way to control HIV's replication without having to kill it?"[3]

III. DISAPPEARING THE LIVING DEAD

Distill *Beloved*'s climax down to this: A pregnant teen is "disappeared"
by a group of mothers, who search for "the key, the code, the sound that

broke the back of words."[4] Stranger yet, this teen is made to disappear, even though, years before, she died as a child (when murdered by her mother) and, therefore, all throughout the story, has been close to death ("C2D," as some contemporary teens might put it).

IV. C2D, OR VIRTUALLY *BELOVED*

Reading a context puts a needle to a narrative, opening a vein of investigation (we commonly say) that often has designs from the start. It may be a motive without a mind, a reading that is trying to get itself thought. One that wishes a novel would think it.

To this end, I open *Beloved* onto surface surroundings to read it as it is virtually never read—as a novel born in 1987, eight years old (in 1995) in the cybernetic age of AIDS. Untimely deaths and dangerous transmissions are the broad surroundings I have in mind. AIDS, specifically, would appear on the list of black American worries. But so would other versions of early demise that coincide with Beloved's double death: infant mortality (now often due to AIDS) and teen homicide (murders of and by teens).[5] Media reports on early death in black American communities now routinely yoke together AIDS, teen homicide, and infant mortality—even as they slide into a dirge on pregnant teens, as if reproduction is being seen in the guise of transmission, the replication of early death. State propositions against "promoting gay lifestyles" suggest a kindred worry over queer propagations, even if they take, especially if they take, the form of ideas—as if queer children could now be copied from the idea of them. It's official: sliding the face of early death under disputes over making "copies."

Why should we not conceive a defense against these slides, pricking Morrison's narrative into a sliding reply?: It is the dead we must learn how to face as we copy them into a virtual future, one that travels alive in our minds. This reply will seem obscure, until I can produce it by reading through *Beloved*'s back door of time, which makes us come around to the front. For Morrison's *fantasy* of a history, by which she conjures slavery's past, foretells a future that we are presently alive to read. I wonder, does her reading of the 1980s wish the history of slavery would think it? Writing out of her fictive interval (*Beloved*'s 1873), Morrison makes herself a prophet of the future ills of 1987, making a teenage infant—pregnant, disappearing—her book's most infectious idea. I will even fantasize that she foresees two comers to the field of replication, both of which build a net to hold *Beloved* in 1995. I am thinking of the frenzy over cloning and the endless articles now appearing on the world of cyberspace.

The outcry over cloning human embryos is directly attached to the very idea of reproduction as replication. It is called "aberrant" by detractors—"a line . . . crossed," "a taboo broken," even "a modern form of slavery."[6] Many people apparently are horrified by these newly imaginable prospects. For example, being able to replace a dead child with its exact genetic equivalent, starting it over by raising its copy from an embryo, which becomes a child—again. Perfect tissue donors, flawlessly compatible, could be thawed and raised should need arise. And for less urgent reasons, couples who set aside clone embryos of a particular child "could give birth to the same child every few years" at different intervals. In that sense, says *Time*, "an exact template for what a child could become in 10 or 20 years could be before them in the form of an older sibling."[7]

Never mind how this last remark ignores the whole question of learning, which might produce remarkably different children. Rather, understand this as a chance to see yourself in a virtual future—a future you could never possess for yourself as anything other than an idea, since your interval from your clone-sibling would always assure that you would live in different worlds at the same age. Contrary to the logic of *Time*, you could just as easily grow up watching the *death* of your future possibilities, just as a woman who gave birth to her own twin, by incubating her own clone embryo, could never truly relive her past. Her ungraspable past would become her baby twin's unfulfillable future, a future always C2D, or, when she got there, simply dead. Right now the future of such futures is on ice—literally, it so happens. *Time* conveys this actuality in suspense: "there are already 10,000 frozen embryos floating around in liquid nitrogen baths . . . in a kind of icy limbo."[8]

Since it is more confabulation than flesh, cybernetic advance would seem a more benign domain of transmissions and copies. Companies are scrambling to simplify the task of "cruising the information highway," making intellectual promiscuity more efficient and, intriguingly, more anonymous, where "the user" (an interesting term in itself) is always intended to be a cruiser. No wonder one such system, we are told, "is called Lycos, after the Lycosidae spider, known for pursuing its prey relentlessly."[9] The goal, in the words of AT&T, is to enable users to find "where information is buried" without having to learn "where it comes from [or] how it got there."[10]

The breakthrough began in 1993 with the creation of the Net's subnetwork called, spiderously, the World Wide Web, famous for its "hyperlinking." Hyperlinks are keywords—"Beloved" could be one—that appear in bold type. When clicked on, they transmit their users to further discussion of that keyword on other Web pages, which may be stored in other computers thousands of miles away. Sounds safe for such rampant transmissions. In fact, *BusinessWeek*, which explained hyperlinking techniques to its readers, did not appear to notice the irony of their choice of a keyword example: "antigen" (a substance that, when introduced into the body, stimulates the production of an antibody).

And yet, fears of invasion are growing. Body condoms are quickly finding their equivalents in sophisticated cyberprophylactics, meant to protect against viral floodings of information and the pranks of cyberpunks roaming the Net.[11] "The technology is in the hands of the children," 60 Minutes recently complained, citing kids and teens as the masterminds of cyberinvasions and giving us, as their sole example, a black, streetwise, gold-toothed hacker with an infectious grin. The upshot? "No one is immune," says one article; "the potential for invasion of privacy [is] severe"; "[they] can get in and [they] can be you."[12]

Hackers, for their own part, lend a viral edge to these fears. But—and let me lean on this point, since it matches key divisions in Beloved—hackers often celebrate their viral powers, their ability to invade the control of information. In this way they heighten generational divides between themselves and their seemingly cyberphobic elders who fear their invasions. Some see their stealth and viral tactics as corrective to official discourse on AIDS, the environment, psychedelics, sexuality, and spiritual life on this planet. Some writers praising and participating in groups like the AIDS Coalition to Unleash Power (ACT UP, founded in 1987) and the Campaign for Smart Drugs (a response to the 1987 release of the AIDS drug AZT) have appropriated Richard Dawkins's theory of "memes," or what he warns is the parasitic, viral nature of ideas (more on this later). Making celebrations out of his warnings, they press hard on his viral metaphorics while stressing that they're actually not metaphorical.

Take the example of Generation X writers R. U. Sirius of Mondo 2000 and Douglas Rushkoff of Media Virus! Both urge activist youth (and their elders) to inject their own "agendas into the datastream in the form of ideological code."[13] They deem Generation X the first American generation "fully engaged in a symbiotic relationship with media" (MV, 31), due to what they say is their unprecedented ability to "feed back" and "change what's on the screen" (MV, 30) (also their tendency to view the datasphere as their natural environment—"as complex, far-reaching and self-sustaining as nature herself" [MV, 29]). In his characteristic rush of optimism, arguing for the "power of virology to effect social change" (what he calls "evolutionary" change), Rushkoff cheerfully distinguishes a media virus (such as those engineered by ACT UP) from the public relations ploys of a company such as Burroughs-Wellcome (maker and promoter of AZT), by stating that a virus makes an issue not "simple and emotional [but] dauntingly complex"; "a virus will always make the system it is attacking appear as confusing and unresolvable as it really is"

(*MV*, 36).[14] Santa Cruz hacker, Bill Me Tuesday, goes so far as to fashion "a healing medical model" when he suggests that "viruses can act like a logic analyzer. . . . [and] serve as a means of creating a self-repairing system" (*MV*, 248). A similar point was made in a recent *Newsweek* article on the unacknowledged benefits of computer viruses: "a few scientists [for example, Fred Cohen in his forthcoming book *It's Alive*] have begun to argue that [computer] viruses are actually living organisms, capable someday of evolving into autonomous Net-runners that will retrieve information for their owners."[15]

With sadder tones, *Beloved* itself forges a model of data retrieval, one derived from older forms. We could tag it "viral gothic." For the novel's ghost, ambiguously alive, retrieves information, not just on the slave experience that the reader and author never had (though this is one fantastic effect, produced precisely through a fantasy), but on the virtual, viral life of dead bodies in our brains. "Beloved" is a version of autonomous retrieval: a viral hyperlink: a keyword with a life of its own. At first it appears as a name on a tombstone and thus as a site of buried information. This is a rather resistant site, since the name "Beloved" seems generically to cover for a body, occluding on the face of it "where it came from or how it got there." And yet, soon enough, "Beloved" becomes an idea on a romp, clicking on the living to get itself "inside." More than that. Sethe's single beloved seems to stand for the nameless dead, or perhaps for the "60 million and more" invoked in Morrison's dedication. "Beloved," that is to say, is a miniaturization and a compression (in the form of code) of a series of futures chain-linked in death. To encounter "Beloved" in this book is to find oneself carried away to hyperlinked files that *exist* as their failure to appear in our future. This is slavery in a way that we have often failed to apprehend it: bondage to a future of virtual remains.

Three assertions float this claim: Beloved is an embodied idea. Beloved is an embodied interval. Beloved makes her mother ill with interval when she enters her as an idea. When dead, Beloved is a virtual child kept alive in a watery limbo (she refers to "the water in the place where we crouched," to the sea, to a bridge over water where she waited; she speaks of coming out of blue water). When she returns as a teenage infant (no small trick), she seems to come back as a clone of herself: the idea of herself embodied at a different interval from herself. In fact, she is an interval. She is now the interval between her death and her mother's current life, as if she's been marking time while dead. Killed before the age of two, she returns, eighteen years past her murder at the hands of her mother, as a nineteen-year-old baby-woman.[16] I'll argue that she makes her mother ill with interval. I'll suggest that, according to the book's depictions, Sethe becomes memory-positive, probably at Beloved's death, but recognizably (as if she were testing positive) at Beloved's return. By the end of the book, Sethe's gone into symptoms, which is why the women want to unload or dispel (delete?) Beloved from the house.

Interlaced with interval is a sense of latency, the feeling that something suspended pursues.[17] Recall that "latency" or "interval" forms a distinguishing feature of the medical category HIV-positive. HIV disease is not only the infection of a body with the virus that is thought to cause AIDS. It is also medically conceived as the *interval* between infection and the onset of symptoms. For this reason, HIV, in the absence of symptoms, can be a strange state of limbo in which you are ill only with the *idea* of death, making you nostalgic for yourself before you begin to decline. You find you fall ill with nostalgia for a *future*.

This is the tunnel Sethe enters when her daughter makes her ill with interval: Sethe increasingly starts going back by a series of hyperlinks on her web, activating keywords that open files on shame, beauty, fascination, and a future of virtual remains.

INTERLUDE: UNDERLINKS

On our way to understanding how *Beloved* scouts the need for a mental prophylactics, a barrier against pursuant, invasive, viral memory, we need to grasp a different kind of prophylactic fiction, one that may haunt *Beloved*'s dedication ("60 million and more"). "Hypolinks" (to coin a term) can be laid down under this reading. They will take you, not via hyperlinks over to files that are certifiably linked to *Beloved,* but under to a resonance. The hypolink, or underlink, is in fact an old technology, the staple of readers' speculations on the question of literary echoes or shadowy influence. Cynthia Ozick's Holocaust fiction (in this case, *The Shawl*) offers *Beloved* such reverberations, ones of the youthful dead alive in a drama of waste. In the brevity of an interlude, consider the contrast between *Beloved* and the stories I believe stand as *Beloved*'s most unspoken influence. Is it telling that they divide over depictions of prophylactics and how one makes safe exchange with the dead? Are there any hints found here about the different injunctions to remember in Holocaust memorials and blacks' uneven invocations of slavery?

Morrison may have been held by *The Shawl*, arrested, if she read it, by Ozick's stories published in the *New Yorker* as "The Shawl" and "Rosa," in 1980 and 1983 respectively (*Beloved* was begun in 1982). The first story renders an infant's death as she's "splashed" against an electric fence. A baby curled between sore breasts, each nipple, we learn, "a dead volcano": There's not enough milk (a central fear in Morrison's novel).[18] The child (Beloved's age, as it happens, not yet two), milks a shawl, "flooding" its linen "threads with wetness" (*S*, 5). Wandering into the roll call arena, seeking her shawl, Magda, in an image that will resonate with Beloved dribbling spit into Sethe's face, "was spilling a long viscous rope of clamor — 'Maaaa' " (*S*, 8). Though, unlike Sethe, hardly the cause of her daughter's death, Rosa, the mother, is bound to, even wound around, quiescence — this in the face of a rope of clamor, which Rosa is going to swallow in the form of a fluids exchange. Even the Nazi's helmet, which "the light tapped . . . and sparkled . . . into a goblet" (*S*, 9), portends Rosa's swallow. The story ends: "She only stood, because if she ran they would shoot, and if she tried to pick up the sticks of Magda's body they would shoot, and if she let the wolf's screech ascending now through the ladder of her skeleton break out, they would shoot; so she took Magda's shawl and filled her own mouth with it, stuffed it in and stuffed it in, until she was swallowing up the wolf's screech and tasting the cinnamon and almond depth of Magda's saliva; and Rosa drank Magda's shawl until it dried" (*S*, 10). The syntax here coils the noose of its repetitions around the phrase of a singular end ("they would shoot"). In the mouth of such constrictions, Rosa chooses her own barrier. She even creates a prophylactic (of the barrier type) *more concerned with holding something in than with keeping something out*, a prophylactic against mourning *escaping* from the body. Stranger still, this barrier *protects by means of exchange*, turning the knot of syntactical copies ("stuffed it in and stuffed it in") into the declarative opening of a swallow (where one less obvious definition of "swallow" can be "the opening in a block or pulley through which the rope runs").[19] In fact, in the form of reversed milking, the daughter by means of the "flooded" shawl feeds her mother her own saliva (her "viscous rope"?), materializing as fluid remains. As hypolink to Morrison's outhouse scene in *Beloved*, this passage supplies a range of echoes for the novel as a whole, underlinking Sethe's decisive murder to Rosa's acquiescence, Sethe's gorging (along with Beloved's desperate gulping) to Rosa's stuffing and her drinking.

This ingestion insures that Rosa, the eponymous character of the second story, after an interval of thirty-five years, holds to herself both mourning and Magda as trusted companions, against the threat of strangers — now embodied not by Nazis but by the researcher Dr. Tree. Pursued by his "university letters" ("strangers scratch at my life; they pursue, they break down the bloodstream's sentries" [*S*, 39–40]), Rosa, once again unlike Sethe, pursues her dead daughter, entreating the dead to come to life. She even switches on at will "the great light of Warsaw" ("she wanted to live inside her eyes" [*S*, 21]). In Ozick, links to the dead are electric (the telephone rings: "how quickly a dead thing can come to life!" [*S*, 62]). The dead do not carry the toxic dangers we meet in *Beloved*; nor are they intervals; rather, they live and die on the "wires" that ferry voices over intervals of time, suspending, releasing narrative flow as they ring, then fade.

What Rosa clings to between visitations, strangely enough, is the drama of waste; "a newspaper item" (S, 18) (as Sethe will be), she had "murdered her store with her own hands" (S, 46), this "cave of junk" (S, 46) smashed with a metal scrap "from the gutter" (S, 26).[20] She highlights loss by sketching, as she switches on aristocratic Warsaw, the *quality* of what got wasted. Against this remembered ruin of wealth and her parents' intellectual largesse, Rosa's mundane survival unfolds amidst such crises as missing a pair of her underpants. Metonymically linked to Magda—they're called "lost bloomers" (S, 33)—the underwear holds to the mother's body, as did the shawl, a private conduit to her loss. Their "stains in the crotch" (S, 34)—Magda, the narrative seems to imply, was the product of a Nazi rape—figure a set of intimate remains, which only if they surface for the eyes of others serve as shame. In Ozick, so different from what we find in Morrison, the effort is to guard against this surfacing—because it threatens to be an escaping—rather than to guard against an entering.

V. SKINFLICKS

Beloved reverses this direction of Ozick's depicted protections, turning Rosa's prophylactic barriers against escaping memories into barriers blocking entry. In mid-eighties fashion, Morrison toys with surface protections. She even sets our sights on skin, offering figuration of a surface sheath. More complexly, the narrative imagines Sethe's focus-on-her-surface as a form of brain protection, establishing Morrison's own version of Freud's hardwired prophylactics, what he called the brain's "protective shields." This is to defend, in the case of *Beloved*, against some logic alive and loose in Sethe's brain. And so, at the start, just three pages in, following a pointed count of the children lost to Sethe and her mother-in-law (Baby Suggs, 8; Sethe, 3), we find this first long passage on memory:

> [Sethe] worked hard to remember as close to nothing as was safe. Unfortunately her brain was devious. She might be hurrying across a field, running practically, to get to the pump quickly and rinse the chamomile sap from her legs. Nothing else would be in her mind. The picture of the men coming to nurse her was as lifeless as the nerves in her back where the skin buckled like a washboard. Nor was there the faintest scent of ink or the cherry gum and oak bark from which it was made. Nothing. Just the breeze cooling her face as she rushed toward water. And then sopping the chamomile away

with pump water and rags, her mind fixed on getting every last bit of sap off. . . . Then something. The plash of water, the sight of her shoes and stockings awry on the path where she had flung them; or Here Boy lapping in the puddle near her feet, and suddenly there was Sweet Home rolling, rolling, rolling out before her eyes, and although there was not a leaf on that farm that did not make her want to scream, it rolled itself out before her in shameless beauty. . . . Boys hanging from the most beautiful sycamores in the world. It shamed her—remembering the wonderful soughing trees rather than the boys. Try as she might to make it otherwise, the sycamores beat out the children every time and she could not forgive her memory for that. (*B*, 6)

This beginning is an exposé of the workings of the mind, making them a topic for narrative discussion, even speculation. But it does more. It offers a *structural* clue as to how other scenes may take place: how a keyword (in this case "remember," or later "a plash of water," etc.) opens a trapdoor in the plot, suspending (or slowing) narrative time as we fall through the hyperlink into scenes in characters' brains, which we are unprepared to receive.[21] There, we become captive to their cameras, riding the blind curve of images they would keep from rolling out.

In this scene, *Beloved*'s obsession with safety is immediately made precarious by a brain typified as "devious," as if Sethe's brain has a mind of its own. The image of chamomile-sap-on-skin-that-needs-to-be-washed would seem to indicate something insistently stuck to a surface, the body's surface sheath. It would seem to stick in opposition to the contents of her mind that here are absent. But look closely. This image, or intent, or sensation of sap-on-skin-that-needs-to-be-washed is already *in* her mind, her surface *in* her brain. It's just that "nothing *else*" is. Lurking but "lifeless" is a picture—a strange nursing scene of men coming to nurse her. Its ambiguous status—"lifeless" but not forever dead?—is conveyed by comparison: "as lifeless as" skin that the brain can't feel, since its communicating nerves are dead. Another specific sensation—a scent—is positively *not* there, implying that on other occasions it must be a frequent visitor, since her brain, or maybe just the narrative, has caught it not at home. No, nothing is there, we are told, "just the breeze cooling her face as she rushed toward water." Again, a sensation is in the brain, though it's rendered as if it is worn on the skin. Remarkably, then, as narratively ordered, the danger images (nursing and ink) are narratively sheathed, wrapped round before and aft, by skinflickerings (sap on legs, breeze on face) imagined as a form of brain protection. These brain contents—skinflicks, I'll call them—keep the brain's internal camera focused out, tracking skin, as a way to protect against the (here) obscure but possibly pornographic contents of the nursing picture and the scent of ink.

"Then something." Not the willed flipping of a switch as one finds in Ozick. Rather, links accidentally tripped—a plash of water, the sight of shoes, a dog drinking—that *when they enter* Sethe's brain, through ear or eye, mysteriously open an inside file. In fact, she's its prey in a brain competition she is always poised to lose. For with an evident agency of its own—"it rolled itself out before her"—its insistence, as we saw in Ozick, linguistically captured by word copies ("rolling, rolling, rolling")— *it* selects beautiful trees, rather than the boys lynched upon the limbs, as the point of her remembrance. Shame, it appears, is a brain fascination one cannot control or perhaps understand. For "try as she might to make it otherwise, the sycamores beat out the children every time and she could not forgive her memory for that."

Sethe's skinflicks and their breach recall the side of Freud now taboo. Hardwire Freud; the speculative Freud of *Beyond the Pleasure Principle;* a Freud closer to the spirit of *Beloved* than the Freud of "Mourning and Melancholia." For even though Freud was fixated on invasions of the mind from within, his detailed address to "protective shields" concerns "floodings" from the external world, how the mind does or does not get "flooded with large amounts of stimulus."[22] In part, Freud's focus is available brain space, especially space for consciousness; for if every excitation were retained as something conscious, the mind would quickly reach its limit for "receiving fresh excitations" (*BPP,* 27). Borrowing upon Helmholz and Fechner's physical energy theories, Freud declares: "*protection against* stimuli is an almost more important function for the living organism than *reception of* stimuli" (*BPP,* 30).

No wonder his disquisition on reception—how the brain develops from the skin—becomes enveloped by his talk of protection—how the skin protects the brain. Embryology, Freud explains, "actually shows" that "the central nervous system originates from the ectoderm . . . and may have inherited some of its essential properties" (*BPP,* 29). Making speculations on evolution, Freud suggests that the brain's grey matter was originally a highly receptive skin that "in highly developed organisms . . . has long been withdrawn into the depths of the interior of the body, though portions of it [in the form of sense organs] have been left behind on the surface immediately beneath the general shield against stimuli" (*BPP,* 31). This "general shield" (in human beings, skin) allows the energy of the external world to pass into the organism's next layers "with only a fragment of their original intensity" (*BPP,* 30). In his example of primitive living vesicles, Freud imagines this layer as dead: "[This] outermost surface ceases to have the structure proper to living matter . . . and thenceforward functions as a special envelope . . . resistant to stimuli." "By its death," Freud concludes, "the outer layer has saved all the deeper ones from a similar fate" (BBP, 30).

Intriguingly, Morrison endows Sethe with a back full of nerve-dead skin, courtesy of a severe whipping that opened Sethe's back and closed it with a scar in the discernible shape of a tree. Time and again, we find that Morrison plays with depictions of surface protections, often at the level of bodily envelope, only to dramatize the dangerously permeable borders between the brain and its visitors. Freud himself believed that the mind had no shield toward the inside. The organism's solution? Projection (Freud's own theory of skinflicks). "[T]here is a tendency to treat [excitations] as though they were acting, not from the inside, but from the outside, so that it may be possible to bring the shield against stimuli into operation as a means of defense against them." "This is the origin of *projection*," says Freud (BPP, 33).

Beloved is full of projective display: brain excitations projected out to the body's perimeters so as to shield one's interior against them (or what comes in lieu of them). One case in point keeps us tracking dead skin. Consider the milk on Sethe's mind and the tree on her back. An early scene between Paul D and Sethe shows the reader the network of hypertextual links between "tree" and "milk." At first, these links seem posed oppositionally: surface protection versus liquidity; a tree-on-the-skin that can't be felt versus the milk taken in by ingestion (whether the milk has been stolen or given). Even Paul D and Sethe are split (genderwise?) by dichotomous focus, his on the tree, hers on the milk. Twice he asks, "what tree on your back?" (B, 15), only to retreat from Sethe's advancing meditation on milk ("I had milk for my baby girl. . . . Nobody was going to nurse her like me," Sethe says amidst her reverie [B 16]). When at last Paul D interjects, the narrative makes its careful weave between the sites of "milk" and "tree":

> "We was talking 'bout a tree, Sethe."
> "After I left you, those boys came in there and took my milk. . . . Held me down and took it. I told Mrs. Garner on em. . . . Them boys found out I told on em. Schoolteacher made one open up my back, and when it closed it made a tree. It grows there still."
> "They used cowhide on you?"
> "And they took my milk."
> "They beat you and you was pregnant?"
> "And they took my milk!" (B, 16–17)

What was lost to Sethe as milk makes its appearance to others as "tree." Indeed, the tree (Saussure's famous example for signifier), like signification in general, signs a loss and a compensation: the taking of Sethe's milk *causes* "tree," itself an opening onto virtual life, the *life* of the sign ("it grows there still").

Further, when we learn the tree on Sethe's back is a "chokecherry tree" in Amy's estimation ("Could have cherries," Sethe muses [*B*, 16]), we can web the tree to the "cherry gum" cited earlier in relation to the making of ink. "Tree" and "milk" open onto files for the danger images previously cited: the scene of nursing and the scent of ink. *Beloved*, too, has its Dr. Tree who pursues in writing, for what can't be felt as written on the back, on Sethe's buckled skin, on her brain's "protective shield" ("I've never seen [the tree] and never will" [*B*, 16]), can still be ingested—just as her house has no back door, sending its visitors around to the front.

Hints of this dangerous ingestion emerge, even in this early scene. Paul D, his hands under Sethe's breasts, "his cheek . . . pressing into the branches of her chokecherry tree" (*B*, 17), "touch[ing] every ridge and leaf of [Sethe's tree] with his mouth" (*B*, 18), is the first to make her tree beloved. Yet, within the short space of two pages, Paul D has revised his reading: "[T]he wrought-iron maze he had explored in the kitchen like a gold miner pawing through pay dirt was in fact a revolting clump of scars. Not a tree, as she said. Maybe shaped like one, but nothing like any tree he knew because trees were inviting; things you could trust and be near; talk to if you wanted to as he frequently did . . . [with one] he called Brother. . . . *that* was a tree. . . . the 'tree' lying next to him didn't compare" (*B*, 21–22). In spite of its blooming, what grows on the tree, as the plot through backward advance unfolds, is the signified "sawing": sawing one's beloved-as-tree.[23] "Milk" is hypertextually tied to this relation in *Beloved*'s famous scene of a sawing followed by a milking, since after Sethe has slashed Beloved's neck with a saw, she nurses Denver, "aiming a bloody nipple into the baby's mouth" (*B*, 152). Another nursing blooming with loss into virtual life. (A ghost is born.) In fact, the "lost bloomers" of *Beloved* are not a pair of underpants, as they are in Ozick. They're "doomed roses" planted by a "sawyer"—"something to take the sin out of slicing trees for a living" (*B*, 47). The "stench" of these dying blooms pervades in the scene that precedes Beloved's return, before she comes back to sit on "a stump" with "new skin, lineless and smooth" (*B*, 50).[24]

Beloved may be the ultimate skinflick. A brain content, a clear excitation, projected outside. For one of the chief complications of *Beloved* is trying to understand where Beloved is depicted as *returning from*. Should we imagine that she's a projection of Sethe's mind and thus her mother's mental defense against an invasion from within? Are we to think she's been living as lost behind Sethe's eyes as a word or idea or future that desperately wants itself thought? Whatever we surmise, some evident breach of a shield surrounds Beloved's appearing—a fluids exchange that matches Ozick's in its strangeness and makes a dangerous pact with a body foreign, and known.

VI. SELFISH MEMES

A fully dressed woman walked out of the water. . . . Everything hurt but her lungs most of all. Sopping wet and breathing shallow she spent those hours trying to negotiate the weight of her eyelids. . . . "Look," said Denver, "What is that?" And, for some reason she could not immediately account for, the moment she got close enough to see the face, Sethe's bladder filled to capacity. She said, "Oh, excuse me," and ran around to the back of 124. Not since she was a baby girl, being cared for by the eight-year-old girl who pointed out her mother to her, had she had an emergency that unmanageable. She never made the outhouse. Right in front of its door she had to lift her skirts, and the water she voided was endless. Like a horse, she thought, but as it went on and on she thought, No, more like flooding the boat when Denver was born. So much water Amy said, "Hold on, Lu. You going to sink us you keep that up." But there was no stopping water breaking from a breaking womb and there was no stopping now. . . . [She was] squatting in front of her . . . privy making a mudhole too deep to be witnessed without shame. Just about the time she started wondering if the carnival would accept another freak, it stopped. She tidied herself and ran around to the porch. No one was there. All three were inside—Paul D and Denver standing before the stranger, watching her drink cup after cup of water. (B, 50–51)

In what could serve as a rumination on Rosa's swallow and her drama of waste, *Beloved*'s mother-daughter reunion takes its place as an outhouse scene.[25] Only Morrison would imagine the filling of a mother's mind with her dead daughter's face as the filling of a mother's bladder to capacity. Such a foreign conception cunningly delays before delivering (first through a clue, the single word "voided," next by means of extended simile, "more like flooding") its recognition that birthing is voiding. And yet this thought has been brooding in *Beloved* since its inception on the novel's third page: "knees wide open as any grave" (B, 5). It's a sexual image at the start. Sethe is trading her body for the tombstone, Beloved's home page. But it also imagines a quick path to death, with no middle passage to burial from birth. Here in this later scene of a voiding, the lingering of the legacy of infant mortality takes its shape as a fluids exchange, where the cause and effect of transmission make a temporal smear.

In Ozick's stories, Rosa's swallowing makes her safe at Magda's murder, though she becomes mad in the eyes of others when she murders her store. ("You're like those people," Stella tells her, ". . . who worshiped a piece of the True Cross [a beloved tree], a splinter from some old outhouse. . . . You'll kiss, you'll pee tears" [S, 31–32]). In Morrison, too, a fluids exchange initiates the losing of a mother's mind, conveying a foreign body to her brain. Notice the reversal of mother-daughter positions, such as we saw in Ozick. Sethe remembers herself as a baby in the care of a child who is pointing out a mother. This reversal may play its part in carrying Sethe to a danger image. For the endless voiding reminds her of flooding a boat with a birth, anchoring floating to the cruel joke of sinking by swamping a container (the boat) with her waters. This is a womb breaking from birth. It's as if Sethe's body, like her brain, finds its fascination against her will with what it holds in store, birthing the drama of waste—a display—in front of her privy, against her helpless sense of shame.

So voiding is birthing is "flooding," "no stopping." The worry throughout *Beloved* is over *stopping* flowing in and out of bodies, in and out of brains. (We think of Freud's worries.) And yet when flow is stopped, and all might seem safely at an end, the strange cause—or is it the effect?—of Sethe's voiding is *already inside,* drinking cup after cup of water. The scene we thought was focused on getting something out is taking something in, for while Sethe's gone around to the back, Beloved has entered from the front. Has Sethe's voiding caused Beloved's thirst? Or has Beloved's thirst—her quest to be *inside*—filled Sethe's bladder to capacity? We're not told but we do learn this: Beloved is infected with the cholera (Paul D says, "All that water. Sure sign." [B, 53]). One of her major symptoms is incontinence.[26] Symptoms aside, Sethe herself is memory-positive, infected with the *idea* of a birthing that led to a voiding.

The spate of *Beloved*'s viral depictions is yet to come. I say "viral" for the sake of my reading. But this is no stretch. It plausibly accommodates scenes of decline from Beloved's entry in the passage above to Sethe's hosting of lethal relations—what I will suggest is a mother's autoimmune relation to (the idea of) her dead daughter. The series of odd negotiations to emerge by *Beloved*'s end has a more uncanny double still, as we shall see: the letters written to AIDS by its sufferers, found in the best-selling self-help guide, *Immune Power.*

But first, it is time to explore why *Beloved*'s viral agendas lack the giddy, optimistic stance of the hacker activists who are making manifestos.[27] Take, for example, Jody Radzik, as cited by viral proponent Douglas Rushkoff:

Radzik first became aware of the power of viruses in the third grade: "I wanted to be a microbiologist, and I became aware of the T4 bacteriophage ("a DNA virus"). . . . They use T4 to intentionally infect bacteria—to tag them or even to do gene splicing for them. I was fascinated by that. . . ." Jody developed a viral identity . . . and began in the most grassroots meme pool he could find in his Oakland neighborhood: graffiti. . . . [which] became a conduit for Radzik's technological and viral memes: "One day it just occurred to me to call my posse CIP for Cultural Insurgent Phages and to make one of my tags 'virus.' My name became 'Saint Virus' because it was a total juxtaposition of something that sounds good with something that sounds bad. I wanted to show that I was a virus, but that I don't want to hurt anybody. I just want to do whatever I can to help evolution along. . . . [We would be] cultural terrorists who would go around infecting inadequate social complexes with little pieces of information that would then deconstruct that social phenomenon. . . . Everywhere I had a tag, I had a little physic listening post. By having a network of tags in my own geographical area, I sort of drew energy from them." (MV, 297–98)

For Rushkoff's Radzik, viral fascination and the microbiological-turned-urban-guerrilla game of "tag" find their credible roots in childhood. In Radzik's own implicit "evolution," his T4 devotion makes "viral identity" the only identity worthy of mention for urban "saints" who are packing "memes" ("little pieces of information"). Copying now is transpersonal growth ("I sort of drew energy from them"), a way of plumping the self who feeds back. In fact, the antiestablishment slant to Radzik's vaguely specified point of "terrorist" attack ("inadequate social complexes," "that social phenomenon") contributes to his "success" as a budding self-growth industry. Rushkoff reports:

By becoming a "somebody" in the graffiti world, Radzik developed the ability to market himself as an expert on youth culture. He was scooped up by sportswear designers at companies like Stussy and Gotcha, where he chose to make T-shirts the new canvas for his viral tags and chaos ideology. . . . [First "to put a fractal on a T-shirt"] . . . he was hoping to use all of [his] memes to empower the individuals in youth culture to feed back their own impulses to the culture at large and accept their roles as active promoters of viral iteration. . . . Jody used his virus logo overtly and put copies of his T4 hieroglyph on his business cards and fax cover sheet. (MV, 299–300)

It must be noticed that Beloved-as-memory shares something crucial with Rushkoff's portrait of Jody-as-virus. She, like he, is an icon of protest against restraints. Against the restraints of "inadequate social complexes," to put it mildly. To put it more forcefully, in Beloved's case, against the restraints of state-sponsored forced labor and a kind of censorship of the soul that leads to self-censorship (Sethe holding her past at bay, Paul D locking his heart in a tin). This is the suppression Baby Suggs, not just Beloved, tries to fight against, as Baby urges her congregation "to feed back their own impulses," at least to one another, in defiance of "the culture at large." But the fervor of her preaching, protected by the opening of the Clearing, is defeated by invasion. (Several times she repeats the line "I'm saying [the whitefolks] came in my yard" [B 179].) [28] Here is what Morrison has to engage that Rushkoff, Radzik, and their fellow enthusiasts have to downplay for the sake of their empowerment: Invasion is the other side of restraint. Slavery is invasion as well as restraint. Invasion by the idea of an interval. For Sethe, it's the interval between Beloved's death and Sethe's current life in 1873; for the reader, it's the interval between that complex known as "slavery" and the reader's current life. This is an interval very much alive, but, only rarely, vitally spoken. Claims of unspeakable things to the contrary, this spokenness—of invasion by the idea of an interval—is what *Beloved* spreads and sells.

Of course, invasion—invasive ideas—should be recognized by hacker activists as potentially oppressive, not just liberating. This idea underlies renowned zoologist Richard Dawkins's idea of ideas, or what he calls "memes"; an idea of ideas so intriguing that hacker activists pepper their writings with mention of "memes" and ground their views with Dawkins's theory of viral transfer. A meme, we learn, is "a complex idea" that (1) forms a memorable unit; and (2) replicates itself, reliably, with fecundity. Memes, for example, can range from "tunes, catch-phrases . . . clothes fashions," to inventions, academic ideas, and symphonies.[29] In Dawkins's book *The Selfish Gene* (1976), a best-seller in thirteen languages, he coins "meme" to sound like "gene" and to reference the Greek root of imitation, "mimeme"; it is meant to call up "memory" and "même," the French word for "self" or "same."[30] Daniel Dennett, a cognitive philosopher, has given even wider play to "memes" in his most recent book, *Consciousness Explained* (1991). These academic best-selling theorists offer what they claim are stranger-than-fiction actualities with regard to cultural evolution, for what interests both men is how cultural transmission is analogous to genetic transmission. Dawkins writes: "Just as genes propagate themselves in the gene pool by leaping from body to body via sperms or eggs, so memes propagate themselves in the meme pool by leaping from brain to brain via a process which, in the broad sense, can be called imitation. . . . '[M]emes should be regarded as living structures. . . . When you plant a fertile meme in my mind you literally parasitize my brain. . . . [T]he meme for, say, 'belief in life after death' is actually realized physically, millions of times over, as a structure in the nervous systems of individual men the world over.'" (SG, 192). When in 1991 Dennett summarizes Dawkins's views, AIDS-related memes emerge in Dennett's discourse. Now memes "leap promiscuously," prove "unquarantinable," are sometimes "pernicious invaders" that prove as deadly and as "hard to eradicate," he says, as "the AIDS virus, for instance."[31] Dennett, even more than Dawkins, stresses the debasement of the mind by memes that "distract us, burden our memories, derange our judgment" (CE, 204). In a passage that even Dennett seems to mean as comical, he playfully magnifies this point: "I don't know about you, but I'm not initially attracted by the idea of my brain as a sort of dung heap in which the larvae of other people's ideas renew themselves, before sending out copies of themselves in an informational Diaspora. It does seem to rob my mind of its importance as both author and critic. Who's in charge, according to this vision—we or our memes?" (CE, 202). This is a different outhouse scene, where we become the mudholes made by birthings taking place in our brains.

Understand, in Dawkins's view memes do not spread because they are good for human populations; they spread because they are good at replicating. Dennett adds: "Memes, like genes, are *potentially* immortal, but, like genes, they depend on the existence of a continuous chain of physical vehicles" (CE, 205). Books and even monuments can disappear with time, but thousands or millions of copies of a single meme or meme-complex will account for a meme's "penetrance," its "infective power." And yet, aside from promiscuous travel, a meme's fate depends upon the nature of the vehicles that carry the meme into its future. Dennett specifies each meme's ultimate destination as the very kind of place from which it spreads: "The haven all memes depend on reaching is the human mind, but a human mind is itself an artifact created when memes restructure a human brain in order to make it a better habitat for memes" (CE, 207). We should not forget that memes are dependent. Like attention-seeking infants, they seek the mind's nurture (its "nest," its "haven" [CE, 206–7]). But they also change the structure of a brain to make of the mind their own "habitat." In what he calls his "Pandemonium model" (CE, 241), alluding to Milton, Dennett explains "what words do with us": They are on the alert, he says, to get "incorporated," "ingested," but "when we let [them] in" they "tend to take over, creating us out of the raw materials they find in our brains" (CE, 417).

Clearly, this is not the heady rush of control one discovers in Rushkoff, Radzik, Sirius, or especially Timothy Leary. Hardly optimistic in any grand sense—hence they are tagged "sociobiological"—Dawkins and Dennett sport a view of insurrection that, nonetheless, has paved the way for hacker appropriation of memespeak as rebellion. (As of July 1995, Dawkins has just appeared on the cover of *Wired* magazine, touted as a "bad-boy evolutionist.")[32] Not so much packing memes as equipping the mind in its defensive fight against them, Dawkins ends his book "on a note of qualified hope" (*SG*, 200): "We have the power to defy ["our creators":] the selfish genes of our birth and, if necessary, the selfish memes of our indoctrination. . . . We, alone on earth, can rebel against the tyranny of the selfish replicators" (*SG*, 200–201).[33] This is Milton's Satan via Blake and Shelley—the Romantic view of rebellion's allure. From this Promethean ledge, hacker optimists leap past the issue of memes in our minds, invading our brains, to focus on one's manufacture of memes that allows for "attack" and luxurious habitation.

By contrast, the wary tone one finds in Dawkins and Dennett crosses *Beloved*'s concern with invasion at just the right angle. Indeed, for all of its crude explanation, meme theory runs with a point importantly implicit in Saussure, in his stress on "the physiological transmission of the sound-image" out of someone's brain into someone else's ear.[34] The point is this: a sign, in order to be a sign *to you*, must get inside your body. Actually, it must enter your body through an orifice. In *Beloved*, it enters the body through the gullet. *Ingestion* becomes the site of a struggle where the daughter restructures her mother's brain. In this sense, we find that Sethe's voiding in the outhouse scene was truly a prelude to a thirsting—and a gorging. Not only does Beloved gulp water at the start (due to her infection), she soon develops a ravenous tooth, "as though sweet things were what she was born for"—"honey as well as the wax it came in, sugar sandwiches . . . sludgy molasses gone hard . . . any type of dessert" (*B*, 55) ("Paul D said it made him sick to his stomach"). Toward Sethe, she turns an epistemic hunger, making sight the servant of ingestion: "Sethe was licked, tasted, eaten by Beloved's eyes" (*B*, 57). Sethe, in response, learns that telling her memories "became a way to feed [Beloved]" (*B*, 58). In fact, it is one of the novel's most interesting tricks that the body we take to *be* memory cannot perform the act of recollection (due to the cholera fever, Sethe thinks). Like the headless bride in the legend Paul D mentions, Beloved, her head nearly sawed off by Sethe, would likely depend on reaching the haven of a human mind. For just like a meme, though she evokes the clear language of purpose, she clearly has no mind of her own. Hungry for memory, thirsting to hear, Beloved makes Seth's memory ingestive, as if Sethe eats in accordance with an appetite foreign to her own.

One particular memory fest appears in the guise of a force feeding.

Paul D has just told Sethe that Halle—Sethe's husband—saw the boys hold her down and take her milk (Halle watched from the loft in the barn).[35] In terms of narrative technique, it's a highly stylized scene. Eleven times in two pages the phrase "he saw" (a replicative meme) is repeated in seesaw conversation. ("He saw?"; "He saw"; "whatever he saw go on in that barn . . . broke him like a twig"; "He saw them boys do that to me and let them keep on breathing air? He saw? He saw? He saw?"; "I never knew he saw" [B, 68–69].) The phrase is actually making a slit in the reader's mind that will later allow linked saws to seep in (the sawyer and his doomed roses; Sawyer's restaurant, where Sethe works; Beloved's sawed neck; Paul D's fright that Sethe "talked about safety with a hand-saw" [B, 164]). In this context, interval is thematized as the structure of a latent trauma. Structurally even, the meme's repetition is stalling for time, making a short interval between itself ("he saw") and something Sethe will see of Halle as she eats a new memory. For unbeknownst to Sethe, there's more for her to learn: " 'You may as well know it all. Last time I saw him he was sitting by the churn. He had butter all over his face.' Nothing happened, and she was grateful for that. Usually she could see the picture right away of what she heard. But she could not picture what Paul D said. Nothing came to mind" (B, 69).

When it hits, Sethe's recognition sinks with a vengeance, since the opening of her mind is displayed as the unwilled opening of an orifice:

> She shook her head from side to side, resigned to her rebellious brain. . . . Like a greedy child it snatched up everything. Just once, could it say, No thank you? I just ate and can't hold another bite? I am full God damn it of two boys with mossy teeth, one sucking on my breast the other holding me down. . . . Add my husband to it, watching, above me in the loft. . . . But my greedy brain says, Oh thanks, I'd love more—so I add more. And no sooner than I do, there is no stopping. There is also my husband squatting by the churn smearing the butter as well as its clabber all over his face because the milk they took is on his mind. And as far as he is concerned, the world may as well know it. (B, 70)

As if restructured, Sethe's *brain* resembles Beloved: "like a greedy child it snatched up everything." Here is an eating-disorder equivalent to Sethe's bladder filling to capacity, again with "no stopping." But something more than the brain's involuntary binging intrigues me. Notice how Halle projects the contents of his mind to his face, wearing them as visible waste for the world to see. He smears the butter "because the milk they took is on his mind"; and this action, Sethe imagines, is Halle's way of stopping his brain ("what a relief to stop it right there"). As for Sethe, "her brain was not interested in the future" (B, 70). "Loaded with the past and hungry for more, it left her no room to imagine, let alone plan for, the next day" (B, 70).

Sethe's gorging in and of this interval appears to be a skewing, a reprise in minor key, of a feast from her short twenty-eight-day period of maternal hedonism, between her escape from Sweet Home and her killing of Beloved. That period (the length of a woman's menstrual cycle) was characterized by what Sethe can only remember as "a kind of selfishness" (B, 162) ("I birthed them and I got them out. . . . It felt good . . . . I was big . . . and wide" [B, 162]). In celebration of such width, she and Baby Suggs threw a feast for ninety people, "who ate so well, and laughed so much, it made them angry" (B, 136). This was deemed a "reckless generosity" (B, 137) (a nice phrase for maternal indulgence), which "offended . . . by excess" (B, 138). Meanness was the result of this feast—the kind of meanness that falls in a slant across nearly all of the book's relations. No one warned Sethe a white man was coming to take her back, along with her children; the result of which was Beloved's death at the hands of Sethe.

In a thought to linger on, Morrison makes a maternal hedonism the innocent cause of untimely death and dangerous transmissions. Yet, when it all comes back in memory, that is to say when Beloved comes back, the innocence and generosity of the feasting—along with Sethe's width. ("I was big . . . and wide")—becomes the gorging of a hedonistic memory—the gorging of Beloved (herself a selfish meme) that grows fat on Sethe's stories and sends Sethe into symptoms. By the end, sickness is a solitude of two who are locked *inside* their house. Of course, it is cunning of Morrison to make us wonder—as many readers do—if Beloved is pregnant with Paul D's child.[36] Cunning, I say, since there is a more compelling explanation: Beloved is "pregnant" from "eating" her mother. What can this mean? And how does it bring us, finally, to symptoms?

In the novel's last third, Sethe and Beloved (with Denver more as witness than participant) are trying to reinhabit Sethe's hedonistic interval, her charmed twenty-eight days between her escape and her murder.[37]

> The thirty-eight dollars of life savings went to feed themselves with fancy food and decorate themselves with ribbon and dress goods, which Sethe cut and sewed like they were going somewhere in a hurry. Bright clothes—with blue stripes and sassy prints. . . . (B, 240)

> Sethe played all the harder with Beloved, who never got enough of anything: lullabies, new stitches, the bottom of the cake bowl, the top of the milk. . . . It was as though her mother had lost her mind. (B, 240)

Feasting, festival, and play all emerge here, but illness finally overtakes this interval. (Like the magical twenty-eight days, it lasts "a whole month" [B, 240].) At first, the two are interchangeable: "they changed beds and exchanged clothes. Walked arm in arm and smiled all the time. . . . It was difficult for Denver to tell who was who" (B, 240–41). Then, Beloved becomes the mother, Sethe the teething child, with eyes "fever bright": "Then it seemed to Denver the thing was done: Beloved bending over Sethe looked the mother, Sethe the teething child. . . . The bigger Beloved got, the smaller Sethe became; the brighter Beloved's eyes, the more those eyes that used never to look away became slits of sleeplessness. Sethe no longer combed her hair or splashed her face with water. She sat in the chair licking her lips like a chastised child while *Beloved ate up her life, took it, swelled up with it, grew taller on it. . . . her belly protruding like a winning watermelon. . . .* [T]he older woman yielded up [her life]" (B, 250; emphasis added).[38] Here the legacy of infant mortality, in the context of slavery, emerges as a form of what AIDS watchers know as autoimmunity, where the body mistakes "invader" for "self" and thus lets it in. Consider this explanation given in *Discover* magazine: "Some researchers suspect that the virus . . . trick[s] [the immune system] into an assault on itself . . . causing T cells to commit suicide. . . . Think about it: to the body, a key part of the AIDS virus looks like—of all things—the 'self' badge on a crucial subset of its own cells."[39] In current cybernetic lingo, the virus is a cyberpunk: "I can get in and I can be you." *Rolling Stone* adds to this picture: "Like any virus, the sole mission of HIV is to reproduce. . . . [The virus] twists its genes into the [T-helper's] genes, then, with the host as its commandeered factory, goes about all the work it takes to make new viral packages."[40] Sethe is such a commandeered factory, offering Beloved ("her belly protruding") a site from which to grow and spread.

In *Beloved*, the pertinent confusion turns out to be meme for même, memory for self, so that Sethe wastes at the hands of a memory—a physical structure in her brain—that wears her self-badge. (In fact, Beloved is the age Sethe was when she birthed Denver and killed Beloved.) But to grasp just how odd an understanding of the body's invasion can be, consider how it becomes narrativized in attempts at self-help: elaborate efforts that shed some light on Sethe's communicative attempts with her daughter ("the more [Beloved] took, the more Sethe began to talk, explain. . . . listing again and again her reasons" [B, 242]). In a *Harper's* essay, "Making Kitsch from AIDS," we learn of patients writing letters to their virus, anthropomorphizing it as a loved one, a pen pal with whom one corresponds. "In the self-help treatment guide *Immune Power*, Dr. Jon D. Kaiser even advises his clients to open up a regular correspondence with their virus. The patient, playing the role of the disease, writes back like a pen pal or a well-bred guest to thank its 'hosts' 'for sharing your feelings with me' '[that I] have overstayed [my] welcome,' adding that 'I appreciate your thoughts and I am not offended by the bluntness of your attitude toward me.'"[41] The patient pretends to swap self for invader, attempting to embody a kinder, gentler virus who will find the patient's good wishes, and manners, infectious—a reading that truly wants itself thought. Kaiser even proffers that if letters to the virus indicate "the way you truly feel about yourself" (*IP*, 103) ("since it is within you" [*IP*, 104]), letters *from* the virus reflect one's "beliefs" about "what . . . will happen" (*IP*, 104)—as if HIV, channeled by oneself, is a set of beliefs about the future. What Kaiser sees for the future of AIDS is "viral dormancy," by means of which patients continue to carry HIV while they "revert back to [an] original asymptomatic status" (*IP*, 7). As support for his views, Kaiser cites Harvard's William Haseltine: "HIV can lie dormant indefinitely, inextricable from the cell but hidden from the victim's immune system" (*IP*, 3).[42]

Some form of hiding, one that is both uneasy and sad—accompanied by a communal forgetting—attends Beloved's disappearance and Sethe's apparent "rever[sion] back to [an] original asymptomatic status."[43] True, it may seem like Beloved is ousted, evacuated, exorcised, disappeared at the end of the book, but the last two pages of *Beloved* suggest a restless dormancy: "There is a loneliness that can be rocked. . . . It's an inside kind—wrapped tight like skin. Then there is a loneliness that roams. No rocking can hold it down. It is alive, on its own" (*B*, 274). The all or nothing, in/out, yes/no model we think the book is backing—has Beloved disappeared or not? are the dead in or out? are you infected, yes or no?—is really a more pressing issue of intensity, threshold, and extent (like measurements that are rendered in T cells), or, in the case of ideas, memic insistence and width. (How *wide* is my idea of the dead?) In fact, Dennett and other brain theorists suggest that *intensity* of memic insistence determines which memes win brain competitions, in which the brain's parallel processors offer different candidates for consciousness.[44]

This is simply to say, the question I thought *Beloved* was asking all along—how can we have a mental prophylactics that protects against invasions from the dead?—is not the most urgent query I am left with. *Beloved* leaves me to ponder *how memic intensity is tamed,* so that it *can* be carried, by the mind's crowded vehicle, into the space of a virtual future.

VII. TAMED RICHNESS

The phrase "tamed richness" is Roland Barthes's, from his essay "Myth Today," in which he laments myth's taming operations on the richness of objects, words, and pictures. At first view, myth seems intriguing but benign, as Barthes hangs his first explanation on a tree: "A tree is a tree. Yes, of course. But a tree as expressed by Minou Drouet is no longer quite a tree, it is a tree which is decorated, adapted to a certain type of consumption, laden with literary self-indulgence, revolt, images, in short with a type of social *usage* which is added to pure matter."[45] From this example of mythified matter, the tree-as-matter dressed up in myth ("decorated, adapted"), Barthes proceeds to give examples of words and pictures that get dressed, too, stressing, as he goes, "a social usage" that is not only additive ("added to . . . matter") but also "parasitical." That is to say, Barthes begins to emphasize how the form of myth feeds off of the "meaning[s]" offered by objects, words, or pictures, "emptying" them of their "own values" so that they might "receive" mythical ones.

In another example, which, like the tree, is resonant for *Beloved*, Barthes writes the following: "And here is now another example: I am at the barber's, and a copy of *Paris-Match* is offered to me. On the cover, a young Negro in a French uniform is saluting, with his eyes uplifted, probably fixed on a fold of the tricolour. All this is the *meaning* of the picture. But, whether naively or not, I see very well what it signifies to me: that France is a great Empire, that all her sons, without any colour discrimination, faithfully serve under her flag, and that there is no better answer to the detractors of an alleged colonialism than the zeal shown by this Negro in serving his so-called oppressors" (*M*, 116). Formed by a sum of individual signs, a myth, says Barthes, signifies something beyond the immediate meaning drained by myth for its own nourishment, a meaning, as in the case of the picture, "I grasp . . . through my eyes," "a sensory reality," with a "richness," "a history," "its own value" (*M*, 117–18). In this case, then, the myth of French imperiality empties the picture's meaning of whatever history and value it may have apart from myth, on "its own" ("it belongs," he says, "to a history . . . of the Negro" [*M*, 117]). Moreover, myth drains the meaning of the picture so as to "fill" it with French imperiality. Or, as Barthes puts it: "one must put the biography of the Negro in parentheses," "put it at a distance," "if one wants to . . . prepare [the picture] to receive its signified" (*M*, 118). As the result of such a "parasitical" action, "the *meaning* of the picture" "becomes impoverished, history evaporates, only the letter remains" (*M*, 117).

Taking just this much from Barthes's familiar views, we may grasp a signal aspect of *Beloved*, which, to this point, I have been producing as a tale of parasitical relations. Realize, we have not yet broached the possibility that Beloved's parasitical invasion could be seen as a struggle against the greater, and greatly parasitical, force of *myth*. To put it succinctly: *Beloved* is a tale of a tamed richness returning to protest the force of its reduction. On the surface of it, this view does not surprise. It squares so neatly with what we know of Morrison's intentions, since in American myths of slavery (historical ones, as much as any others) the meaning of the slave has been emptied, distanced, in order to prepare it to receive a signified. (Morrison, by contrast, would restore the slave to richness).[46] So, no surprise. And yet, on further view, what does jolt is the realization that Morrison makes the myth-making persons of *Beloved* not just figures like Schoolteacher but, in some ways more dramatically, the black community—the "mothers" (and later, other folk) who tame Beloved's meaning—rich, historical, full, even pregnant—into decorations lacking memic intensity (which "[made] it easy for the chewing laughter to swallow her all away" [*B*, 274]). For "after they made up their tales, shaped and decorated them, those that saw her that day on the porch quickly and deliberately forgot her. . . . [T]hey realized they couldn't remember or repeat a single thing she said, and began to believe that, other than what they themselves were thinking, she hadn't said anything at all" (*B*, 274).

But, of course, Beloved did speak. Even as a structural oddity, a resistance to the narrative flow: Beloved's narration, five pages long. There we encounter Beloved awash on the sea of the dead in a time that threatens to be only now: "All of it is now it is always now there will never be a time when I am not crouching and watching others who are crouching too I am always crouching the man on my face is dead his face is not mine his mouth smells sweet but his eyes are locked" (*B*, 210). Passages such as these hyperlink us to where we cannot follow. Carefully crafted to tease us with meaning so rich in its own values and history that it's opaque (the basket, the bridge, the men without skin, even "a hot thing"), Beloved's narration evokes the memory of a slave ship sunk (at least in *Beloved*) to any operation other than myth. More to the point, Beloved, we learn, has come back to Sethe in search of her face, her own self-badge: "my face is coming I have to have it. . . . she knows I want to join she chews and swallows me I am gone now I am her face my own face has left me I see me swim away a hot thing I see the bottoms of my feet I am alone I want to be the two of us I want the join" (*B*, 213). These lines tender a sympathetic view, *a meme's-eye view*, of memic insistence. Beloved is left insistently to follow the trail to where she can be thought, however incompletely. She lies among the dead; but whatever face may be saved for the dead is gained through those who eat them in memory, taking the name (and meanings attached to it) inside the body so that it may lie (sometimes dormant, sometimes active) behind living eyes in the boat of the brain. Importantly, Beloved's narration appears, not toward the book's beginning where it might have functioned as an origins tale, an explanation of where Beloved is returning from. Rather, it appears at the end of part 2, just before Sethe starts to decline. This placement reminds us to read the marauding Beloved as a victim of a prior swallowing, just as the outhouse scene prepared us to understand her gulping as a symptom of a prior voiding. As much as Sethe is menaced by meaning, as if she's taking a sensory dose of it (through her eyes, ears, mouth), she is also by the end complicit in a dormancy, one achieved by myth and by those who are its aids. In fact, Barthes's version of the living dead inadvertently provides a canny reading of Beloved's final pages: "One believes that the meaning [here the meaning of Beloved] is going to die, but it is a death with reprieve; the meaning loses its value, but keeps its life, from which the form of the myth will draw its nourishment" (M, 118).

It would be nice to end with a set of neat relations: American myths of slavery as a way to defend against slavery's virtual remains; Morrison's myth of tamed richness as a way to defend against American myths. But something would still be hidden by this frame: the fact that Morrison, who slips the face of early death back into view, tames richness, too—however much she might wish for a myth that restores but does not simultaneously reduce. Working from the historical record, Morrison makes a story such as Margaret Garner's (the kernel of her novel), and even the specific signs of Beloved, plumped to bursting with lyric effort, "recede a great deal," in the words of Barthes, "in order to make room" (M, 118) for her own myth. Her myth of tamed richness.[47] Or, as Barthes elsewhere states the matter: "The meaning [once again, the meaning of Beloved] is always there to present the form [of myth]; the form is always there to outdistance the meaning. . . . they are never at the same place" (M, 123). What Beloved represents, and quite allegorically, is a question, I suggest, structured into the text, even from its name, goading the reader, at every turn, into an act of outdistancing individual meanings. In Beloved especially, meaning and myth are "never at the same place," a sense only heightened by historical interval (between the slave dead and the future ill of 1987) and by the intangible boundary that separates dead Beloved from living Sethe, giving Beloved a virtual life.

And now we must raise a final issue, so crucial to Beloved's multiple tamings, by raising it first to Roland Barthes, who, in the example of the meaning of the picture of the Negro soldier, slides among "the meaning of the picture," "the picture [of the Negro]," and "the Negro-giving-the-salute" (not to mention "the biography of the Negro"!) as the object of a taming. Is it different, we will need to know, to tame a body rather than its picture? to tame (the picture of) a dead body rather than a living one? to tame a biography rather than a tree? Notice that, on one level, Beloved must engage the problem of how we carry living bodies in our heads. One's beloved is a kind of location from which linguistic and pictorial signs make their issue, offering a rich and steady stream of meanings. Inevitably, however, we build a model (in Barthes's sense, a myth) of this issuing object, taking individual signs as instances meant "to illustrate" the "beloved." The tremendous richness of this relation — an exceedingly dense web of image, word, idea, sensation (often daily renewed)—is always tamed, reduced, miniaturized, summed up, by a set of signs, themselves often organized as myths, that will fit in our heads, so that, mobile, we may carry them wrapped inside our skins. This is how we take our beloved with us, in us, through the day, and what we use, or what uses us, to produce the beloved in the brain. Clearly related to this necessity, on another level, *Beloved* shows us that the dead (the ultimate picture of bodies caught frame-frozen?) present us with a similar opportunity for a taming, since they are reduced, miniaturized, often organized as myths, for the sake of both a grasp and a fit. Without feeding back in the ways of the living, they do renew themselves as code that travels "alive" inside our brains, capable of invading conscious space when network chains allow their "wish" to speak.

But what about another level still? What, finally, could it mean to carry a chain of human bodies linked by a common cause of death (for example, by cause of state aggression or neglect)? The AIDS quilt (inaugurated 1987) stands beside *Beloved* as one of the most ingenious attempts to *fight tamed richness while employing it:* one quilt square for each dead body, each quilt square the size of a grave, the life reduced (even if embroidered), to a set of signs the community can, in some measure, carry. The goal of the quilt—one goal, at least—was to help us to visualize the extent of the dead, to see it laid out, in fashion, for the orifice of the eye. Now your eye can't take it in. To receive the visual assault of EXTENT, you would have to consult a miniature copy of an aerial view, reducing the size of the image to get it into your head. But this reduction is exactly how we account for its "spread."[48] For the myth of the quilt, like *Beloved,* is "a call," which, in the words of Barthes, "in order to be more imperious, has agreed to all manner of impoverishments"; "it comes and seeks me out in order to oblige me to acknowledge the body of intentions which have motivated it" (*M,* 125).

Forty to one hundred twenty million "bod[ies] of intention," one could say, are being predicted for the millenium. *Beloved,* too, offers a count— "60 million and more"—in its dedication. These, like the Holocaust, are inconceivable extensions of meaning, along with lost futures. Which means, in the case of chain-linked death (and slavery was surely always that), we are forced to tame a richness we may never have seen.[49] But how does one regulate an epistemic hunger for bodies that haven't been around to feed it? The task, according to *Beloved* and the quilt, brain-children both of 1987, is to hold a set of files, empty and full, knowing *how* to tame the untimely dead. For they remain, in the mind's keep, virtually beloved.

NOTES

I gratefully acknowledge a chain of help in writing this essay. It was first composed as a public lecture sponsored by the Humanities Center at Wesleyan University in February 1995. I benefited greatly from criticisms offered by Henry Abelove, William Cohen, Christina Crosby, Ellen Feder, Patricia Hill, Eric Jarvis, Indira Karamcheti, Danielle Langston, Tavia Nyong'o, James Scott, Duffield White, Sandra Wong, and center director Elizabeth Traube. An informal group of critical legal theorists, some formerly and some currently of Harvard Law School (David Kennedy, Nathaniel Berman, Jorge Esquirol, and Susan Keller), raised indispensable questions for the talk's transformation into this longer essay. Finally, many Utah colleagues generously offered comments on my final drafts: Karen Brennan, Karen Engle, Rebecca Horn, Dorothee Kocks, Mitchell Lasser, Colleen McDannell, Jacqueline Osherow, Ileana Poras, Henry Staten, and Barry Weller. Warm thanks also to Shelley White, Nicole Stansbury, Grant Sperry, and Constance Merritt for their attentive readings.

1   Richard Dawkins, *The Selfish Gene* (New York: Oxford University Press, 1989), p. 192. Dawkins's book is described on its jacket as "grip[ping] like a thriller," while excerpts from reviews by *Science*, the *New Yorker*, *TLS*, and *Animal Behavior* stress its serious engagement with "difficult scientific ideas" and "quasi-mathematical themes of recent evolutionary thought." Dawkins himself begins his preface to the first edition (1976) claiming: "This book should be read almost as though it were science fiction. It is designed to appeal to the imagination. But it is not science fiction: it is science" (p. v).

2   Richard Preston, *The Hot Zone* (New York: Random House, 1994), p. 58. Preston's jacket for his best-selling book on the Washington, D.C., Ebola virus scare replays the themes discussed in the above note, touting *The Hot Zone* as "a thriller of the first order," "a terrifying true story," that "has taken a vital issue out of the halls of academia and science and handed it to the rest of the world."

3   Robert Sullivan, "The Search for the Cure for AIDS: A Special Report from the Frontiers of Science," *Rolling Stone*, 7 April 1994, p. 61.

4   Toni Morrison, *Beloved* (New York: Plume, 1987), 261. Further citations will be abbreviated *B* and incorporated parenthetically in the text.

5   There's even one instance—in a largely Hispanic community—of using an AIDS-like quilt to commemorate the victims of teen homicides (teens gunned down by other teens, along with parents and infant siblings who are cross-fire victims). *People* magazine (15 November 1993, pp. 93–98), which reported the story, has referred to it as "The Killing Quilt."

6   "Cloning: Where Do We Draw the Line?," *Time*, 8 November 1993, pp. 69, 65, 65, 69.

7   Ibid., p. 68.

8   Ibid., p. 69.

9   "Cyberspace: The Software That Will Take You There," *BusinessWeek*, 27 February 1995, 78–86.

10 Ibid., p. 82.

11 In *Newsweek*'s special issue "TechnoMania: The Future Isn't What You Think" (27 February 1995), Paul Saffo, a director at the Institute for the Future, in Menlo Park,

Prophylactics and Brains   67

California, exclaims: "The problem is that so far only half the information revolution has been delivered to us: the access and the volume. The other half is reducing the flood to a meaningful trickle. The people who make the money are going to be the ones who make the filters and the 'off' switches" ("Have Your Agent Call My Agent," p. 76). In a *Time* cover story on "Hyper Democracy" (23 January 1995, pp. 15–21), the writer, Robert Wright, seems to wish for a Chastity Beltway or Congressional Condom that would protect lawmakers from excessive inflow/outflow excitement, or what he fears is "the growing porousness of the supposedly impregnable buffer around Washington" (p. 17). This reporter laments the plans by Gingrich and others to "use information technology to break through the Beltway barrier" (p. 15).

In what would seem an Althusserian joke, *Business Week* tells us that a company called RSA Data Security, Inc., has developed the best security for making the cyberspace world safe from break-ins ("Cyberspace," p. 86). Fitting for Althusser's sense of the Repressive State Apparatus (the RSA as the army, the police, the prisons—all who, by force, enforce state and federal laws), we learn that RSA Data Security's biggest competitor, according to *Newsweek* (27 February 1995, p. 43), is the National Security Agency.

12　Citations are from "Stop! Cyberthief!" (*Newsweek*, 6 February 1995, p. 37), *Business-week*'s "Cyberspace," p. 80, and *60 Minutes* (26 February 1995). The good and bad news of *60 Minutes*' selection of their sample hacker is all too obvious: the intriguingly fresh portrait of a black hacker youth, a portrait that breaks the stereotype of the white male surburban geek, unwittingly (one says generously) solidifies the stereotype of the black male criminal. By contrast, the paradigmatic media portrait of a hacker can be found in thirty-one-year-old Kevin Mitnick, the "superhacker" who "started out in the early 1980s, pulling pranks as a teenage 'phone phreak' before moving on to more serious computer crime" ("A Superhacker Meets His Match," *Newsweek*, 27 February 1995, p. 61). For the details of this and two other stories—one of which is that of Robert Tappan Morris, the young Cornell University graduate student who brought down a nationwide computer network—see Katie Hafner and John Markoff, *Cyberpunk: Outlaws and Hackers on the Computer Frontier* (New York: Touchstone, 1991).

13　Douglas Rushkoff, *Media Virus!* (New York: Ballantine Books, 1994), p. 10. Further citations will be abbreviated *MV* and incorporated parenthetically in the text.

14　Aside from claims for complexity and unresolvability, *Johnny Mnemonic* (a film released at the time of this writing), bears out Rushkoff's optimistic views, even amidst the darkest of landscapes. The Johnny of the title can stop the spread of a fatal disease (NAS: information-overload) if he can get the cure for this plague out of his head (where it is stuffed to a deadly extent). The good guys would cure the disease at hand; the bad guys would "treat" it, making it a renewable source of a need for (non-smart) drugs. The tale thus pits the corporation Pharmakon (a self-conscious Derridean pun?) against the little people (here represented by Johnny, a macho babe-for-hire, and, most intriguingly, the garbage kids-and-teens who follow the recycling guerrilla played by Ice-T). Fascinating for *Beloved*, as it happens, the latter live on a bridge called "Heaven," fashioned from junk but fitted with a tower (a tree?) of screens from which they feedback to (whatever's left of) the culture at large. Their goal is democratic resistance: recontextualizing and sharing information. At the end, they *broadcast* "the cure," literally changing what's on the screen, even as they blow up the Pharmakon complex.

The study *Cyberpunk*, cited in note 12 above, makes its observations against the backdrop of stories such as *Johnny Mnemonic*: "We set out to investigate a computer underground that is the real-life version of cyberpunk, science fiction that blends high technology with outlaw culture" (Hafner and Markoff, *Cyberpunk*, p. 9). The authors explain the shift from the 1960s and 1970s, the time of hacker "honor" and the Hacker Ethic, to the 1980s when hackers, through media- and even self-portrayal, "were no longer seen as benign explorers but malicious intruders," "new magicians," who because they "are comfortable with a new technology that intimidates their elders" have given rise to a "hacker hysteria . . . sweeping the nation" (p. 11).

15 "Is There a Case for Viruses?" *Newsweek*, 27 February 1995, p. 65.

16 Obviously, in a bold anachronism, I impose the word "teen" on *Beloved*, which in its portrayals does not use the word, even though Morrison, pointedly for her contemporary readers (or so I believe), makes Beloved nineteen and Denver eighteen. That is to say, some carryover of contemporary understandings of adolescence and its threat of an alien consciousness may be expected on the part of the reader. At the very least, the book does nothing to protect against it. A reading that would honor 1987, of course, demands it.

17 *Webster's New World Dictionary* traces "latent" back to the Latin *latere*, "to lie hidden, to lurk," and to the Old Norse *lomr*, "betrayal, deception." Under the psychological meaning of *latent* (according to which *latent* means "unconsciously but not actively so") Webster's gives the example "a *latent* homosexual."

18 Cynthia Ozick, *The Shawl* (New York: Vintage International, 1990), p. 4. Further citations will be abbreviated *S* and incorporated parenthetically in the text.

19 Indeed, in "Rosa," the story that picks up where "The Shawl" ends (thirty-five fictional years have elapsed), we find, in the story's first paragraph, a keen webbing of "pulley," "swallowed," "rope." In a description of Rosa's living quarters, we are told: "Instead of maid service there was a dumbwaiter on a shrieking pulley. On Tuesdays and Fridays it swallowed her meager bags of garbage. Squads of dying flies blackened the rope" (*S*, p. 13). Rather than Magda's "viscous rope of clamor," which has proved, in Ozick's first story, that Magda could speak, that she was not "dumb" as Rosa had feared, this blackened rope runs "a dumbwaiter on a shrieking pulley." Sadly, the swallow referenced here is not the salvific opening onto Magda's remains but garbage that is itself only "meager"—a particular sign of poverty throughout this second story, in which riches are measured by the ampleness of waste.

20 The story even begins with this fact: "Rosa Lublin, a madwoman and a scavenger, gave up her store—she smashed it up herself—and moved to Miami" (*S*, p. 13). Later, we read: "She knew about newspapers and their evil reports: a newspaper item herself. WOMAN AXES OWN BIZ. . . . A big photograph, Stella standing near with her mouth stretched and her arms wild. In the *Times*, six lines" (p. 18). In *Beloved*, of course, a newspaper clipping of Sethe's killing sets in motion Paul D's leaving.

21 In this passage we start out suspended, as if we are watching the reenactment of a hypothetical ("she might be hurrying across a field. . . . [n]othing else would be in her mind"); then, it seems, by the fifth sentence ("[t]he picture of the men . . . was as lifeless as the nerves") that the hypothetical is a memory of something that has happened in the past; finally, however, we realize this scene (in spite of its floating, commemorative quality) occurs, somehow, in narrative time as a present, unfolding action, for Paul D is sitting on Sethe's porch as she rounds the front of her house "collecting her shoes and stockings on the way" (*B*, p. 6).

Other memory passages perform a stricter suspension of the plot, beginning with a hyperlink that carries the reader away on the crest of the character's thoughts and ending with a repetition of the hyperlink, returning the reader to narrative flow. An excellent example of this pattern occurs in the novel's second chapter. As Paul D and

Sethe lie in bed, disappointed and resentful after sex, each is successively carried away (for several paragraphs) by a hyperlink. Paul D's is "tree"; Sethe's is the phrase "maybe a man was nothing but a man" (*B*, p. 21–22).

22 Sigmund Freud, *Beyond the Pleasure Principle*, vol. 18 of *The Standard Edition of the Complete Psychological Works of Sigmund Freud*, trans. and ed. James Strachey (New York: Norton, 1961), pp. 30, 33. All further references to this text will be abbreviated *BPP*.

23 Obviously, the tree as the sign of sacrifice—of one's beloved, in particular—has its precedents, to put it lightly. Christianity founds itself upon the tree as the site (and later sign) of a loss that is also a compensation. More ominously, the tree on Sethe's back inscribes the site of lynching on her body.

24 In a sense, we might imagine that Beloved returns wearing Amy's velvet, since Amy proclaims: "'velvet is like the world was just born. Clean and new and so smooth'" (*B*, p. 33).

25 For a reading of the outhouse scene in *Sula* and its related registers in that novel, see my essay "Heaven's Bottom: Anal Economics and the Critical Debasement of Freud in Toni Morrison's *Sula*," *Cultural Critique* (spring 1993): 81–118. In that essay, as in this, I am most intrigued by the passages critics ignore in Morrison.

26 "Four days she slept, waking and sitting up only for water. Denver tended her . . . and, out of love and a breakneck possessiveness that charged her, hid like a personal blemish Beloved's incontinence. . . . She boiled the underwear and soaked it in bluing, praying the fever would pass without damage" (*B*, p. 54).

27 For a strong dose of cyberoptimistic manifestos ("The PC is the LSD of the 1990s"), see Timothy Leary, *Chaos & Cyber Culture* (Berkeley, Calif.: Ronin Publishing, 1994). For a more academic optimism, run through the filters of "theory," see Mark C. Taylor and Esa Saarinen, *Imagologies: Media Philosophy* (London: Routledge, 1994).

28 Baby Suggs's name, by dint of which she often becomes "Baby" in the text, seems to hint at her connection to Beloved over what early on she protests against. For her "feedback" sermons in the Clearing, see *B*, pp. 87–89, where Baby commands a series of expressive actions: "'Let your mothers hear you laugh. . . . Let your wives and children see you dance. . . . Cry . . . [f]or the living and the dead. . . . [Y]onder, hear me, they do not love your neck unnoosed and straight. So love your neck; put a hand on it, grace it, stroke it and hold it up'" (*B*, pp. 87–88). It is the invasion of her life by "whitefolks" that eventually shuts down Baby Suggs's protest. Moreover, it's the abrupt end to an interval that causes her retreat: "Her faith, her love, her imagination and her great big old heart began to collapse twenty-eight days after her daughter-in-law arrived" (*B*, p. 89).

29 Richard Dawkins, *The Selfish Gene*, p. 192. (Further citations will be abbreviated *SG* and incorporated parenthetically in the text.). Dawkins is aware that it is not always "obvious what a single unit-meme consist[s] of": "I have said a tune is one meme, but what about a symphony: how many memes is that?" (*SG*, p. 195). Appealing to "the same verbal trick" he used to define "gene" ("a unit of convenience, a length of chromosome with just sufficient copying-fidelity to serve as a viable unit of natural selection"), Dawkins answers his question: "If a single phrase of Beethoven's ninth symphony is sufficiently distinctive and memorable to be abstracted . . . and used as the call-sign of a maddeningly intrusive European broadcasting station, then to that extent it deserves to be called one meme" (*SG*, p. 195). Beloved, by this reasoning, could be regarded as a single meme or as what Dawkins calls "a co-adapted stable set of mutually-assisting memes" (*SG*, p. 197). For his discussion of "copying-fidelity," "continuous mutation," and "blending," see *SG*, pp. 194–196.

30 The word "meme" has a virtual future of its own. Dawkins informs us that "in 1988 it

joined the official list of words being considered for future editions of Oxford English Dictionaries" (*SG*, p. 322).

31 Daniel Dennett, *Consciousness Explained* (Boston: Little, Brown, 1991), pp. 205, 204. Further citations will be abbreviated *CE* and incorporated parenthetically in the text.

32 Dawkins and Dennett are both hard to classify. Criticized in the left antisociobiological treatise, *Not in Our Genes*, by Rose, Kamin, and Lewontin (London: Penguin, 1984), Dawkins is nonetheless praised by the likes of Donna Haraway, the leading poststructuralist feminist historian of biological science. Specifically, Dawkins, along with E. O. Wilson (author of *Sociobiology*), is criticized by Rose, et al., for being a "reductionist" in his views on genetic determinism *and* a "liberal" for "invok[ing] free will." Dawkins responds in one of his footnotes: "[I]t is only in the eyes of Rose and his colleagues that we are 'genetic determinists'. What they don't understand . . . is that it is perfectly possible to hold that genes exert a statistical influence on human behaviour while at the same time believing that this influence can be modified, overridden or reversed by other influences" (*SG*, p. 331). Haraway, for her part, places Dawkins "among the most radical disrupters of cyborg biological holism" ("The Biopolitics of Postmodern Bodies: Determinations of Self in Immune System Discourse," *differences* 1 [winter 1989]: 24). "[D]eeply informed by a postmodern consciousness . . . [Dawkins] has made the notions of 'organism' or 'individual' extremely problematic." As for Dennett, he bemusedly accepts the appellation of "semiotic materialis[t]" (*CE*, p. 411), while being accused of naive idealism and extreme materialism.

33 Perhaps because the defense one makes is against a "replicator," Dawkins brings a decidedly prophylactic slant to bear on his defiance. Prophylaxis as rebellion. Thus Dawkins: "We, that is our brains, are separate and independent enough from our genes to rebel against them. As already noted, we do so in a small way every time we use contraception. There is no reason why we should not rebel in a large way [against memes], too" (*SG*, p. 332).

34 Ferdinand de Saussure, *Course in General Linguistics*, ed. Charles Bally and Albert Sechehaye, trans. Wade Baskin (New York: McGraw-Hill, 1966), p. 12.

35 For a sense of this loft as a rather Faulknerian perch, see the end of the first chapter of *Absalom! Absalom!*.

36 Though Morrison herself seems to imagine Beloved as pregnant by Paul D (see her interview with Marsha Darling, "In the Realm of Responsibility: A Conversation with Toni Morrison," *Women's Review of Books*, 5 March 1978, pp. 5–6), her novel depicts more intriguing possibilities, as I will suggest. This odd discrepancy in representation may even support a more striking oddity: the ways in which Paul D and Denver are kept *centrally* peripheral in this novel. That is to say, both are staged—quite intensely so—as characters pushed to the margins by memory (that is, by Beloved), giving them roles as frustrated bystanders, until the very end of *Beloved* when both act to restore Sethe's health. As for Paul D, so many of his movements are moved by Beloved: "She moved him," we read, "and Paul D didn't know how to stop it because it looked like he was moving himself" (*B*, p. 114). As a bizarre figuration of these movements—the shame of them rendered as intense fascination—Paul D enters into quasi-incestuous relations with Beloved. (More than once we're reminded that Beloved is "young enough to be his daughter" [*B*, p. 126].) Her demand is simple. Offering herself as seductive hyperlink, it is as if she gets him to click on her name: "'You have to touch me. On the inside part. And you have to call me my name'" (*B*, p. 117). The result: the speaking of Paul D's past, by means of this sexual ventriloquist act, is moved from a place between *her* lips.

37 Denver may be Morrison's transformation of Stella from Ozick's Holocaust stories, which, like *Beloved*, offer a rivalrous triangulation between three females: Rosa, Magda, and Stella, Rosa's jealous fourteen-year-old niece. In Denver's case, desperation for a sibling leads her to measures that look like—at some points—imitations of her mother's relations with Beloved. Thus, at the start, when Beloved has cholera, Denver takes to herself the incontinence her mother profoundly embodies in the novel's outhouse scene ("[Denver] hid like a personal blemish Beloved's incontinence" [*B*, p. 54]). Later, we find that Denver was "nursing Beloved's interest like a lover whose pleasure was to overfeed the loved" (*B*, p. 78). Here's that overfeeding relation that Beloved dramatically demands from Sethe. Even a form of fluids exchange has prefigured these connections. On the day Beloved was killed by her mother, Sethe, we have seen, "aim[ed] a bloody nipple into [Denver's] mouth," so that "Denver took her mother's milk right along with the blood of her sister" (*B*, p. 152). The bottom line, however, is exclusion; Beloved's exclusive concern with her mother. As she puts it to Denver, " 'You can go but she is the one I have to have' " (*B*, p. 76). Of course, Denver's central marginality is hardly an acknowledgment of her unimportance. To the contrary, there are arguments to be made about the intricate unfolding of Denver as a kind of margin or limit to the tale, but these lie beyond the scope of this essay.

38 Sethe displays four major symptoms listed on the AIDS symptoms list: weight loss, dementia, fatigue, and fever. See Jon D. Kaiser, *Immune Power: A Comprehensive Treatment Program for HIV* (New York: St. Martin's Press, 1993), p. 12. Further citations will be abbreviated *IP* and incorporated parenthetically in the text.

39 "The Long Shot," *Discover*, August 1993, pp. 66–67.

40 Sullivan, "The Search for the Cure for AIDS," p. 63.

41 Daniel Harris, "Making Kitsch from AIDS," *Harper's*, July 1994, p. 58.

42 In *Discover*'s "The Long Shot," one researcher argues: "Alternative vaccines are conceivable that do the opposite of what conventional vaccines do. That is, they'd make you tolerate something as well as fight against it." Other researchers counter: "[Y]ou should probably do as much as you can as early as you can to prevent the seeding of the host, because once the virus is in, it's hard to imagine any kind of treatment that would keep it from progressing." (p. 69).

43 In fairness, I suppose, it may be hard to say if Sethe is saved from her demise. Though the book remains ambiguous on this point, her slow recovery seems implied by Paul D's willingness to nurse her back to " 'some kind of tomorrow' " (*B*, p. 273) (" 'Don't you die on me!' " [*B*, p. 271]).

44 In this sense, *Beloved* offers a range of cybernetic relations, ones that might interest Eve Kosofsky Sedgwick and Adam Frank, who, in an essay on Silvan Tomkins ("Shame in the Cybernetic Fold," *Critical Inquiry* 21 [winter 1995]: 496–522), explore "Tomkins's habit of layering digital (on/off) with analog (graduated and/or multiply differentiated) representational models" (p. 505). Clearly, AIDS involves such a layering, for what begins as a digital relation (do you have the virus or not?) immediately gives way to graduated developments, measured, as I say, in T cells—but also in the P-24 antigen test (reported as a numerical value ranging from 1 to 600 if positive) and the intensity of the patient's symptoms and infections. Dennett, on another landscape, explains how a single spoken phrase is the result of "swift generations of 'wasteful' parallel processing, with hordes of anonymous [word] demons and their hopeful constructions never seeing the light of day" (*CE*, p. 238).

45 Roland Barthes, *Mythologies*, trans. Annette Lavers (New York: Hill and Wang, 1957),

p. 109. Further citations will be abbreviated *M* and incorporated parenthetically in the text.

46 She is particularly intent to restore the slave-ship dead. Morrison: "The gap between Africa and Afro-America and the gap between the living and the dead and the gap between the past and the present does not exist. It's bridged for us by our assuming responsibility for people no one's ever assumed responsibility for. They are those that died en route. Nobody knows their names, and nobody thinks about them. In addition to that, they never survived in the lore" (interview with Darling, "Responsibility," *Women's Review of Books*, pp. 5–6).

47 In Gail Caldwell's review of *Beloved* in the *Boston Globe* (6 October 1987, pp. 67–68), we learn this: "[U]nlike her four previous books, the idea of the plot of *Beloved* came from an actual event—gleaned from a 19th-century newspaper story she'd discovered while editing *The Black Book* (an overview of black American history) at Random House. The woman in the news story [Margaret Garner, who killed her child to save it from slavery] became Sethe, and Morrison began to write." On her use of this source, Morrison herself has commented: "I did not do much research on Margaret Garner other than the obvious stuff, because I wanted to invent her life, which is a way of saying I wanted to be accessible to anything the characters had to say about it. Recording her life as lived would not interest me, and would not make me available to anything that might be pertinent. . . . The point of all this being that my story, my invention, is much, much happier than what really happened" (interview with Darling, "Responsibility," *Women's Review of Books*, pp. 5–6).

48 In Peter S. Hawkins's illuminating essay, "Naming Names: The Art of Memory and the NAMES Project AIDS Quilt," (*Critical Inquiry* 19 [summer 1993]: 752–79), we learn that "[Cleve] Jones made the first panel of what was to become the NAMES Project Quilt in late February 1987." "In memory of his best friend," Hawkins tells us, "he spray-painted the boldly stenciled name of Marvin Feldman on a white sheet that measured three feet by six feet, the size of a grave; the only adornment was an abstract design of five stars of David, each one dominated by a pink-red triangle. Jones's panel, at once a tombstone and a quilt patch, served as a model for the improvised handiwork of others" (pp. 757–58). See Hawkins's essay as well for two photographs: one at ground level from the quilt display in 1987, the other, clearly aerial, from 1992.

We should recall in all of this that *Beloved*, too, has its quilt. It is first associated with Baby Suggs who, when she is on her way to death, becomes "starved for color." "There wasn't any," the novel tells us, "except for two orange squares in a quilt [of "muted" colors] that made the absence [of color] shout"; the "two patches of orange looked wild—like life in the raw" (*B*, p. 38). Sethe, at the end, lies under this quilt, in Baby Suggs's bed, at the back of the house, in the keeping room.

49 In a cover story on "AIDS and the Arts: A Lost Generation," released upon Rudolph Nureyev's death, *Newsweek* (18 January 1993, pp. 16–20) explains how "a single death creates a cultural chain reaction" (p. 16). Then the writers raise a question: "The average age of death from AIDS in the United States is 35, one study shows. But the preponderance of works that hang in the Museum of Modern Art is by artists older than 35. How many rooms of empty frames would have to be filled to create a museum of unpainted art? Or shelves built for unwritten books?" (p. 18).

Joseph Litvak

Strange Gourmet: Taste, Waste, Proust

I. DINING WITH PROUST

Sa haine des snobs découlait de son snobisme, mais faisait croire aux naïfs, c'est-
à-dire à tout le monde, qu'il en était exempt.—Proust, *Le Côté de Guermantes*

O f all the gay male writers in the Western literary canon, perhaps
the smartest, the one whose primary canonical function may
even be to epitomize gayness *as* intelligence, is Marcel Proust.
Other names (Wilde, James) may come to mind, but one could argue that
they signify specialized variants of intelligence (wit in the case of Wilde,
subtlety in the case of James), rather than intelligence in the more general, more powerful, more basic form of what Theodor Adorno calls an
"organ for untruth and thus for truth."[1] And if the almost perfect fit in
Proust between smartness-as-intelligence and smartness-as-stylishness
provides a happy instance of what Lee Edelman has taught us to think
of as homographesis, we feel all the more entitled to read "Proust," both
the name and the work, as the definitive gay inscription of sophistication
in the sense that our culture accords to it.[2]

Yet, for all that Proust represents "sophistication," the closest thing to
an equivalent term in his text, *la mondanité,* or worldliness—in French,
unlike English, *sophistication* retains the negative meaning of "adultera-
tion"—acquires an almost equally negative charge. And for all that he
represents "intelligence," he spends as much time criticizing it as celebrating it. But it would be a mistake to infer that even Proust succumbs
to the self-hatred whereby "cultural elites" drearily confirm the verdict
pronounced upon them by the public at large. Instead of repudiating
sophistication, Proust, I want to argue, practices a sophistication that entails a "naïveté" of its own. (Why is it, by the way, that, if you can't really

say "sophistication" in French, you can't really say "naïveté" in English?) Again, Adorno proves helpful:

> The compulsion to adapt prohibits one from listening to reality with [Proust's] precision, from taking its soundings. One need only make the effort to refrain from dealing directly with subject matter or pursuing one's aims in a conversation and instead follow the overtones, the falseness, the artificiality, the urge to dominate, the flattery, or whatever it may be that accompanies one's own or one's partner's voice. If one were aware of their implications at every moment one would fall into such fundamental despair about the world and what has become of oneself in it that one would lose the desire, and probably the strength as well, to continue to play along.
>
> Proust, however, did not go along with the renunciation of responsiveness, nor with the false maturity of resignation. He kept faith with the childhood potential for unimpaired experience and, with all the reflectiveness and awareness of an adult, perceived the world in as undeformed a manner as the day it was created, in fact developed a technique to resist the automatization and mechanization of his own thought. He strives indefatigably for immediacy, for a second naïveté, and the position of the pampered amateur from which he approached his literary task works to the advantage of these efforts.[3]

Idealizations of "the childhood potential for unimpaired experience" may not be to everyone's liking, but what Adorno—to be sure, not exactly one of the guiding lights of gay studies—calls Proust's "second naïveté" bears significantly on the distinctive gayness of Proustian sophistication.[4] To the extent, for example, that this naïveté resists "the compulsion to adapt," or to the extent that it offers an alternative to "the false maturity of resignation," it becomes readable as a gay strategy for surviving— or (since it is itself a recovered naïveté) of recovering *from*—the ruthless cultural project of universal heterosexualization, whereby "growing up" in fact means shutting down, tuning out, closing off various receptivities that make it possible to find the world *interesting*.

Indeed, as a refusal of mere "despair about the world and what has become of oneself in it," as a way of "perceiv[ing] the world" *freshly*, Proust's second or sophisticated naïveté reminds us why "worldliness," instead of just standing in for "sophistication," can comment on it as well. "Worldliness," that is, reminds us that sophistication implies a mutually constitutive relationship between its subject *and* the world. It signals that sophistication requires an object-relations theory of its own, a theory that will explain how sophistication maps out a certain fantasmatic way of circulating in and around the world—not, as may seem to be the case, of simply rising above it but, at least in Proust's case, of connecting the "high" and the "low" so as to short-circuit the middle. In Proust, *le monde* means *le beau monde*, the glittering world of the Faubourg Saint-Germain, whose *mondanité*, however, gets unmasked relentlessly as so much *pseudo*sophistication. But while the "true" or metasophistication of the narrative consists in thus reducing high society to a dung heap—in uncovering its vanity, its stupidity, its mean-spiritedness—the hidden agenda of this engrossing demystification is to ensure that the one thing *le mondain* does not end up as is the merely mundane.

With his vast wealth, which is also to say, with his vast cultural capital, Proust was of course well equipped to sustain a powerful worldly cathexis. But if few people can marshal the same formidable resources against boredom, many *gay* people, at least, do have at their disposal, or in their usable pasts, typically in late childhood or early adolescence, the highly Proustian experience of falling, if not, at first, for some other person, then for some other place, some other world, magically different from the world of family and school, from a heterosexual everyday every day more banal, and more oppressive.

Whatever that other world is called—"Broadway," "Hollywood," "the opera," "Greenwich Village," "*haute couture*," "high society" are some of its classic designations—it beckons not as a simple escape from the everyday but as a vision of the everyday *transfigured*: What would it be like to *live there?* But whatever it's called, one probably got the message, without having to be told, that one had made a bad object-choice—that one's fantasy world provoked as much distaste as, say, the oral and anal phases one was simultaneously failing, or refusing, to outgrow. Not that this message necessarily had the power to scare one off. In many cases, perhaps, the effect was the reverse. A gift of shit (in the charming phrase of Jacques Lacan), but a gift nonetheless, the fantasy world may have had, for many of us, the necessary, life-sustaining value of what Proust calls "celestial nourishment":[5] at once filthy and sublime, this gift, in the very endless inversion of its fortunes, may have left its most precious trace in its recipients as an endlessly renewable (if latent) gift *for* inversion (*Time Regained*, 6:264).

Am I simply indulging in a potentially reactionary *nostalgie de la boue?* If my evocation of the secret treasure evokes as well the splendors and miseries of the closet, that, as Eve Kosofsky Sedgwick has shown, is not only Proust's definitive gay theme but also his definitive gay subject position.[6] Recalling Proust's closetedness may have the effect of diminishing any Proust-envy that less pampered (i.e., almost all) readers might feel. One needn't glamorize the closet, however, to see in Proust's sophisticated naïveté a model for recapturing not so much a lost world as a lost *libidinal intelligence,* a capacity for having more than a blandly routinized relation to *any* world. Reading Proust can induce a fantasy of *being* Proust. That fantasy keeps faith with a fantasmatic faculty itself: with, to amend Adorno, a childhood potential not so much for unimpaired experience as for making bad—that is to say, as Proust himself would say, good—object-choices.

II. DU FAISANDÉ

"I think it must be charming, a country where you can be quite sure that your dairyman will supply you with really rotten eggs, eggs of the year of the comet. I can just see myself dipping my bread and butter in them. I must say that it sometimes happens at aunt Madeleine's" (Mme de Villeparisis's) "that things are served in a state of putrefaction, eggs included."—Proust, *The Guermantes Way*

In search of *temps perdu*—time *wasted* in addition to time lost—Proust manifests an insatiable appetite *for* waste. Nowhere is this appetite more evident than in *The Guermantes Way* (1920-21), the third volume of the *Recherche:* preeminently the book of *mondanité, The Guermantes Way* is therefore, as Gilles Deleuze suggests, preeminently the book of waste.[7] According to the recuperative logic of the *Recherche,* however, nothing ever really *goes* to waste: what looks like its slackest, least "composed," volume may in fact constitute the transitional center of the work as a whole; as for the activity described in this volume, what looks like so much aimless, profligate hanging out around so many vacuous aristocrats turns out, in the best tradition of the *Bildungsroman,* to have been the decisive passage from adolescence to adulthood.[8]

Following Adorno, we've tended so far to characterize Proust's taste for waste as a perversely cultivated infantilism. Where adolescence has been mentioned as a site of buried excremental treasure, it has figured (as in "in late childhood or early adolescence") merely as childhood's annex. But perhaps, instead of assimilating adolescent to infantile perversity, we should consider its specificity, the uniqueness of the contribution it makes to the museum of bad taste. There's no need to assume that adolescence "deconstructs" the opposition between childhood and adulthood; one could argue, on the contrary, that it simply reinforces that opposition. But if the structural intermediacy of adolescence accounts for its reputation as that awkward age, what is the content of this awkwardness? In our eagerness to reclaim the child, inner or otherwise, do we seek to evade (or, with greater cunning, indirectly to reach) her even more embarrassing, and even more exciting, older sibling?

As Maurice Bardèche has observed, *The Guermantes Way* is in some sense a "reprise" of Proust's earlier novel, *Jean Santeuil*, with the difference that the former doesn't so much eliminate as dissimulate the "ridiculous" excesses of the latter.[9] In his biography of Proust, George Painter, sometimes as helpful in his schoolmasterly moralism as in his scholarly positivism, indicts those excesses—defects characterizing its immature author as well as its young hero—in terms stereotypically reserved for adolescence itself:

> *Jean Santeuil* is disfigured not only by technical lapses but by a moral fault which is inseparable from its main theme. It is a novel of revenges, of resentments felt and gratified, of self-adoration and self-pity. The hero is an ill-used young man, thwarted by unfeeling and philistine parents, insulted by wicked hostesses, self-satisfied snobs and pseudo-artists; a benevolent Providence ensures that he invariably scores off them all; and he is insufferably charming, handsome, intelligent and magnanimous.[10]

Jean Santeuil can be hard to take. But if a certain principle of dissimulation renders *The Guermantes Way* more palatable, the difference between the principle and what it dissimulates isn't so obvious. Where Jean Santeuil wears his self-pity, his self-adoration, his vengefulness, on his sleeve, the narrator-protagonist of *The Guermantes Way*, only fleetingly visible, in the high beam of a certain unloving gaze, as "a hysterical little flatterer," owes his worldly success to his mastery of the art of playing it cool.[11] What disguise, however, more classically betrays the adolescent ardor of those who put it on than does this affectation of affectlessness? The very deadpan ease with which the narrator moves through the Guermantes salon signifies that, in Bardèche's words, "Nous sommes en pleine fantaisie."[12] Nor can Proust (as opposed to "Marcel") be disimplicated from this fantasy. *Jean Santeuil*, it seems, leaves a bitter taste in the reader's mouth to the precise extent that it fulfills a wish for sweet revenge; skillfully softened, or rather, as Bardèche puts it, *habilement adoucie*, by the "mature" style of *The Guermantes Way*, the *vanité* generating the wish finds a more lasting sweetness in that style itself.[13]

That "vanity" can describe both a self-adoring subject and an empty or worthless object should alert us to the possibility of an occult link between adolescent infatuation and the supposedly salutary demystification—the unflinching recognition of the world's nothingness, more particularly, of "the world," that is, high society, as what Marcel will call *le royaume du néant* (*La Prisonnière*, 3:780)—that passes for maturity. The empty object may be considered more accurately as an *emptied* one, the product of a "naïvely," perversely eroticized act of evacuation.[14] Demystification, in other words, doesn't necessarily mean decathexis. Though one of the great laws of the Proustian universe is the incompatibility of knowledge and desire, one of its less well-known, yet not less powerful, counterlaws, is the *interdependency* of knowledge and desire, best illustrated, as we shall see, by the case of snobbery. Much as it may resemble a triumphant, conclusive renunciation of the object, and of one's narcissistic investment in it, demystification may covertly be extending, *through* a fantasy of revenge, one's original guilty, ambivalent attachment. Far from signaling the death of desire, demystification may represent desire's most ingenious ruse.

It isn't surprising, of course, when, in the horrible scene in the Champs-Elysées, where she suffers the stroke that portends her imminent death, the narrator's grandmother, emerging from the public toilet presided over by the snobbish "Marquise," ironically says to him (in her struggle to conceal her affliction), "I heard the whole of the 'Marquise's' conversation with the keeper. . . . Could anything have been more typical of the Guermantes, or the Verdurins and their little clan?" (423). In her peculiarly delicate, metaphoric-metonymic way, Marcel's grandmother is simply telling him that she thinks the Guermantes—in whose company, the badness of which she would appear to be admonishing him against, he will nonetheless, once she has died, spend most of the next four hundred pages—are full of shit.

Nor, perhaps, is surprise exactly the effect when the egregious Legrandin shows up in the salon of Mme de Villeparisis shortly after treating Marcel to the following lecture:

> You know how I admire the quality of your soul; that is why I tell you how deeply I regret that you should go forth and betray it among the Gentiles. By being capable of remaining for a moment in the nauseating atmosphere of the salons—for me, unbreathable—you pronounce on your own future the condemnation, the damnation of the Prophet. . . . Good-bye; do not take amiss the old-time frankness of the peasant of the Vivonne, who has also remained a peasant of the Danube. To prove my sincere regard for you, I shall send you my latest novel. But you will not care for it; it is not deliquescent enough, not *fin de siècle* enough for you; it is too frank, too honest. What you want is Bergotte, you have confessed it, gamy stuff for the jaded palates of refined voluptuaries [*du faisandé pour les palais blasés des jouisseurs raffinés*]. I suppose I am looked upon, in your set, as an old stick-in-the-mud; I make the mistake of putting my heart into what I write: that is no longer done; besides, the life of the people is not distinguished enough to interest your little snobbicules. (202–3; 452)

If, as I've said, surprise isn't quite the effect of Legrandin's turning up—if not quite to eat shit, then conspicuously to kiss ass—in the very "nauseating atmosphere" he has just been execrating, this is because, almost from the beginning of *Swann's Way*, the masquerade of snobbery has been made so exquisitely, so vulnerably transparent to us. But though we've become proficient in seeing through a Legrandin, the very facility with which we do so may keep us from seeing what we *don't* already know: that Legrandin's "hypocrisy"—his pretending to hate what he really loves—is perhaps a little more complicated than we think; that his "hatred" is as sincere as his "love," insofar as loving "society" (*le monde*) *while knowing it to be a bad object*—the object you're not supposed to love—means cultivating an acute sensitivity *to* its badness, positively refining a taste for its gamy deliquescence (high society being "high" in more ways than one), a deliquescence like that, for example, of meat *going bad*.[15]

However knowing the reader may have become, Marcel's response to finding Legrandin in the Villeparisis salon is marked by an apparent ingenuousness:

> Presently Mme de Villeparisis sat down again at her desk and went on with her painting. The rest of the party gathered round her, and I took the opportunity to go up to Legrandin and, seeing no harm myself in his presence in Mme de Villeparisis's drawing-room and never dreaming how much my words would at once hurt him and make him believe that I had deliberately intended to hurt him, say: "Well, Monsieur, I am almost excused for being in a salon when I find you here too." M. Legrandin concluded from these words (at least this was the opinion which he expressed of me a few days later) that I was a thoroughly spiteful young wretch [*un petit être foncière-ment méchant*] and delighted only in doing mischief. (272; 501)

Whether *naïf* or just *faux-naïf*, whether himself "sincere" or "hypocritical," Marcel here seems to read Legrandin less astutely than Legrandin reads Marcel. Not only, that is, does Legrandin recognize in Marcel a brother "snobbicule," a fellow "refined voluptuary" or connoisseur of the sumptuously fecal: he perceptively calls him on the malevolence (the *méchanceté*) that Marcel is so (dis)ingenuously eager to disavow. More in touch, as some might say, with Marcel's anger than Marcel is, as well as more in touch with Marcel's *hunger* than Marcel is, more in touch, finally, with the close affinity between anger *and* hunger, Legrandin both identifies and embodies the *obscenity* of worldliness, an obscenity affecting not only the world as object but also the worldly subject:

"You might at least have the civility to begin by saying how d'ye do to me," he replied, without offering me his hand and in a coarse and angry voice which I had never suspected him of possessing, a voice which, having no rational connexion with what he ordinarily said, had another more immediate and striking connexion with something he was feeling. For the fact of the matter is that, since we are determined always to keep our feelings to ourselves, we have never given any thought to the manner in which we should express them. And suddenly there is within us a strange and obscene animal [*une bête immonde et inconnue*] making itself heard, whose tones may inspire as much alarm in the person who receives the involuntary, elliptical and almost irresistible communication of one's defect or vice as would the sudden avowal indirectly and outlandishly proffered by a criminal who can no longer refrain from confessing to a murder of which one had never imagined him to be guilty. I knew, of course, that idealism, even subjective idealism, did not prevent great philosophers from still having hearty appetites [*de rester gourmands*] or from presenting themselves with untiring perseverance for election to the Academy. But really Legrandin had no need to remind people so often that he belonged to another planet when all his uncontrollable impulses of anger or affability [*tous ses mouvements convulsifs de colère ou d'amabilité*] were governed by the desire to occupy a good position on this one. (272–73; 501)

"Uncontrollable impulses of anger *or* affability": it's as though there were such a thing as a beast of civility, a savage, monstrous, id-like creature driving us, against our better judgment, even without our knowledge, to perform the most depraved acts of *politesse*. But while this passage thus invokes the language of involuntarity and irrationality (to the same degree, moreover, that Marcel continues playing the ingenue), it implies at the same time a more "refined" insight into the deconstructive intimacy undermining the apparent binarism of the sophisticated and the vulgar, of the *homme du monde* and the *bête immonde*: it interprets as cozily systemic, rather than madly anarchic, the relationship between, on the one hand, worldly success and intellectual distinction and, on the other, the bestiality, the stupidity, the garbage—as the French would say, the *immondices*—on which that success and that distinction parasitically feed. This feeding defines not only the dependency of the subject upon the external object of his desire—the dependency, say, of a "jaded" worldling like Marcel or Legrandin upon the delectably putrid high society (the *monde immonde*)—for which he hungers, or of the great philosopher-gourmands upon the food they crave. Since the "obscene beast" is, of course, a beast within, the feeding in question defines an *internal* dependency as well, suggesting that, just as the great philosphers are great *because of* their gourmandise, so, for example, might the narrator's "mature," "demystified" knowledge of the world *consist in* a certain untranscended juvenile delinquency, one that stops just this side of murder: more precisely, in the self-pitying, self-adoring, and above all *vindictive* oral-sadistic fantasies about the world that, long past the point at which he should have renounced it, keep him—*un petit être foncièrement méchant* indeed, as Legrandin so incisively recognizes—voraciously sinking his teeth into it.[16]

Marcel may not be playing it entirely straight, in other words, when, after quoting what he takes to be a particularly silly remark by the Duchesse de Guermantes, he levels with us about the persistence of his crush on her, a fixation whose intrinsic aggressivity he would thus take back:

> "What a goose!" I thought to myself, irritated by her icy greeting. I found a sort of bitter satisfaction [*une sorte d'âpre satisfaction*] in this proof of her total incomprehension of Maeterlinck. "To think that's the woman I walk miles every morning to see. Really, I'm too kind. Well, it's my turn now to ignore her." Those were the words I said to myself, but they were the opposite of what I thought; they were purely conversational words such as we say to ourselves at those moments when, too excited to remain quietly alone with ourselves, we feel the need, for want of another listener, to talk to ourselves, without meaning what we say [*sans sincérité*] as we talk to a stranger. (308–9; 526–27)

Less sincere, perhaps, in his avowal of insincerity than in the insincerity itself, Marcel may well mean the mean thing he says about the Duchess— as much, in fact, as Legrandin means the *méchanceté* with which he bad-mouths the world of the salons. But, just as Legrandin's biting meaning, as we've seen, far from precluding the most lip-smackingly epicurean consumption of the food he reviles, evinces in fact the very finesse of his connoisseurship, so Marcel's bemused contempt for the Duchesse signifies not, as he would have us believe, a feigned disillusionment but rather the cruelty of Proustian love at its most perspicacious.

Though, in the original text, the Duchess gets called not a "goose" but, less appetizingly, a *buse*—a buzzard—this renomination of an object figured elsewhere as irresistibly succulent betokens less some failed or half-hearted attempt at aversion therapy than a perverse technique, like that still preferred by the subtlest (not to say the most jaded) of palates, for making the flavor of fowl more intoxicatingly "high" (that is to say, low) by rendering it even gamier.[17] The point, therefore, isn't that Marcel doesn't "really love" the Duchess: it's that he misrepresents what "really loving" her means. What's ultimately less—or more—than straight about the passage isn't the first-order sophistication that consists in decathecting the Duchess, or even the second-order sophistication that consists in decathecting the decathexis, but the third-order sophistication that consists in suggesting both that what gets the nasty little philosopher-critic (or philosophisticate) "too excited" is his "bitter satisfaction," and that this "bitter satisfaction" is, in turn, the sweet taste of love.

As the sophisticated reader will have anticipated, however, we may not yet have reached the summit of the hierarchy of sophistications: what's necessary, that is, is an acknowledgment that the straightness of Marcel's "love" for the Duchess must itself be taken with a grain of salt. Without, on the one hand, simply conflating "Marcel" (the narrator) with "Proust" (the author), or, on the other hand, not so simply rehearsing recent commentary on the dizzying play of hetero- and homosexualities in the *Recherche*,[18] we can settle for stating what should be fairly obvious: that, throughout Proust's novel, one discerns a whole range of closet-effects. For instance, it is by now taken for granted that Albertine's gender may be as "ambiguous" as her sexuality. Because *The Guermantes Way* doesn't immediately announce itself as one of the gayer neighborhoods in *Recherche*, however, it has been easy (even for those not easily taken in) to read the story of Marcel's "love" for the Duchesse de Guermantes relatively straight. Casting her as a mother-surrogate, in the style of an older psychoanalytic criticism, doesn't exactly impede the always available heterosexualizing presumption, either, though, like the inversion model of same-sex desire endorsed by Proust himself, it also tends to perform the cultural work of promoting Marcel's (*and* Proust's) image as a mama's boy.[19] That Marcel identifies with the Duchess as much as— or to the extent that—he desires her can indeed be demonstrated, but then a question arises as to what that desirous identification itself means. What's at stake in Marcel's wanting (to be) her?

An answer awaits us in Legrandin's denunciation of Marcel for betraying his soul "among the Gentiles." If, in keeping with the logic of "It takes one to know one," Legrandin outs himself as a snob by outing Marcel, he also adumbrates a more oblique if no less pertinent connection, between what will turn out explicitly to be his own homosexuality, on the one hand, and Marcel's more consistently camouflaged homosexual *positioning*, that is, his closetedness, on the other.[20] "The jaded palates of refined voluptuaries," Legrandin hints, favor more than one taste ("taste" being one of the privileged categories in terms of which homosexuality is constructed in Proust). In likening Marcel and himself to Jews, however,

Legrandin by no means simply makes their shared vices look respectably kosher: as the persistent analogy in the *Recherche* between Jews and inverts makes clear, the former are as phobically racialized as the latter. Working by way of the novel's snob closet, Legrandin faithfully conjoins its Jewish closet with its gay closet; but his conjunction doesn't have the effect of making the Jewish and gay closets neatly interchangeable. Or rather, it doesn't have the effect of making "Gentile" and "heterosexual" neatly interchangeable. For while the Guermantes and their circle, as the novel's insistent reference to the Dreyfus case makes clear, enjoy the arrogant self-satisfaction, not to mention the humiliating exclusionary power, of the tyrannical majority—the Guermantes are all anti-Dreyfusards, the dying Swann tells Marcel at the end of *The Guermantes Way*, because "at heart all these people are anti-semites" (796)—their status as quasi-mythological divinities, as alluring racial others, as interdicted objects of desire *outside the family circle*—in short, as seductively *treyf*—aligns them symbolically with the very homosexuality that you don't have to be a nice Jewish boy to have been terrorized into knowing you'd better stay away from (and thus, needless to say, into finding all the more engrossing).

As an overdetermined elite, minoritized and majoritized at once, the aristocratic Guermantes represent, in other words, the double fascination of a *homosexualized heterosexuality*: the fascination of the forbidden object, and the fascination of the oppressive agent. Indeed, a case could be made that, at the level of fantasy, the aristocratic salon figures generally in Proust as an "alternative family," one that, while exerting the captivating interpellative force of familialism itself, manages nevertheless, and at the same time, to be not only matriarchal but, so to speak, queeny as well, so that if, in Marcel's family romance, the Duchess stands for the Mother, the Mother she stands for is simultaneously straight and gay. Without for a moment doubting the intensity of his "love" for her, we could compare it to a certain gay male "love" for, say, Marlene Dietrich.

To draw that analogy, however, is to signal that Marcel is setting himself up for disappointment. The brightest star in the firmament of a homosexualized heterosexuality, the Duchess, like so many of the compromise formations that define life in the closet, indeed proves an unreliable locus of erotic investment: even before Marcel crosses the threshold of the hôtel de Guermantes, he discovers that the Duchess, waspish queen bee of what, inspired by Paul Morrison's formulation of an "ersatz heterosexuality," we might call a merely ersatz *homo*sexuality, is in effect neither "gay" enough nor "straight" enough.[21] Her celebrated "wit" turning out to consist mostly of fat jokes, put-downs, and flat-footed, sophomoric puns, her powers of homophobic (or of anti-Semitic) abjection concomitantly lose much of their sex appeal as well. As a result, by the time Marcel, who, with typical fetishistic, masochistic obsessiveness, has not just wor-shipped the Duchess but endured snubs from her that have only made him long the more to enter her charmed circle, finally gets embraced by the Guermantes with "parental affection" (702), that affection no longer means much: if the Duke and Duchess have become as predictably famil-iar as real parents, they lack the authority of real parents to command, for instance, the fear that would induce a little "affection" in return.

Yet though we seem to be encountering here another great Proustian law, the law whereby you eventually get what you want, but only when you no longer want it, I would invoke again the less obvious counterlaw, whereby desire's apparent absence or negation serves as a cover for its cunning, unregenerate persistence. (Finding out that high society is no more glamorous than, say, high school isn't necessarily a *complete* turn-off—not, at least, to those for whom "high school" itself preserves a cer-tain erotic charge.) When Marcel says, "What a goose!" *and means it,* he does run a certain risk of simply losing interest. But instead of handling the situation either "heterosexually"—that is, by accepting boredom as the structuring principle of his life and personality—or in the bolder, braver, gay-affirmative way that some might wish for him—that is, by coming out, by ceasing to look for love in the wrong places—he adopts (although, to appropriate Jacques Derrida, "we are in a region . . . where the category of choice seems particularly trivial")[22] the more ambivalent strategy, perhaps also the classically obsessional or deconstructive one, of reliving, via the sadism of analysis, the first naïveté (or first love) of ideological subjection as the second naïveté (or second love) of ideologi-cal critique. If this technique for falling in love again suggests a certain libidinal conservatism—more censoriously, a certain adolescent refusal or inability to forgive and let go—it also constitutes a distinctly Proust-ian solution to the perennial grown-up problem of how love is to survive its (heterosexualizing) disappointments, not to say a distinctly Proustian model for the revenge plots, the angry, petulant, resentful plots *against* heterosexuality, animating some of the most vital work in current gay, lesbian, and queer cultural critique.[23]

Re-senting, re-tasting, re-finding the badness of the bad object, saving that badness from falling into the mere banality of the merely deideal-ized, may have the additional virtue, in other words, of helping one save oneself. Perhaps it is this surreptitious economy that explains the oddly exhilarating effect of Proustian "disappointment": "That Mme de Guermantes should be like other women had been for me at first a dis-appointment [*une déception*]; it was now, by a natural reaction, and with the help of so many good wines, almost a miracle [*un émerveillement*]" (719; 815). The effect of the wines is indeed at best auxiliary: what's most

intoxicating is the discovery of one's own power not so much to turn ex-
crement into gold as to turn the merely *emmerdant* back into life-giving
merde: to transform a deglamorized *mondanité*—a fairy-tale world in danger of becoming boring, annoying, oppressive—back into the precious
nourishment that can be supplied only by *what's bad for you*—bad not
just because, having failed to deliver on what it seemed to promise, it has
become contemptible, but because, having been recontaminated by the
bad subject's bad taste, having regained an aura of the tantalizingly proscribed, it has become newly *desirable* in its contemptibility.

All through *The Guermantes Way,* Proust practices (and gives us the
recipe for) such a gay alchemy, a gay science that we might also call
a hom(e)opathy. *L'étrange gourmet* (701): this is the term (rendered in
English as "the man of strange appetite" [559]) that Marcel uses when,
dining with Robert de Saint-Loup in the restaurant in the fog, he overhears someone saying, "I should prefer glycerine. Yes, hot, excellent." It
turns out to be "simply a doctor whom I happened to know and of whom
another customer, taking advantage of the fog to button-hole him here in
the café, was asking his professional advice. Like stockbrokers, doctors
employ the first person singular" (559). Employing the same grammatical
form, Proust everywhere in his novel both prescribes for and administers
to himself—and thereby makes available for our own adaptation—a diet
designed in fact to *prevent* his palate from growing jaded, from becoming
"sophisticated" in the best (that is to say, in the worst) adult way.

III. BIGMOUTH

Mme Cottard picked up only the words 'a member of the confraternity' and
'tapette,' and as in the Doctor's vocabulary the former expression denoted the
Jewish race and the latter a wagging tongue, Mme Cottard concluded that M. de
Charlus must be a garrulous Jew.—Proust, *Sodom and Gomorrah*

Of the Duchesse de Guermantes, the narrator writes: "She furnished
my mind with literature when she talked to me of the Faubourg Saint-
Germain, and never seemed to me so stupidly Faubourg Saint-Germain
as when she talked literature" (679). By the same token, much as the narrator himself likes to ruminate poetically on evocative *noms de personne,*
the real meat of *The Guermantes Way* is, to recall Adorno, the more "fundamental," more novelistic matter of manners, the *bad* manners whereby
people's social performance grotesquely subverts the fiction of constative neutrality: "the overtones, the falseness, the artificiality, the urge to
dominate, the flattery," in short, the innumerable *bêtises* that go to make
up what an acutely *in*attentive listener will learn to identify as the sub-

textual politics of everyday conversation. If "talking literature" designates an attempted assertion of the aesthetic *over* the quotidian, Proust's most trenchant masterstroke is his relocation of the aesthetic, his rediscovery of literature, *under* the surface that vainly keeps trying to hide it.

Here, "literature" means neither poeticizing abstraction nor the domineering *coups de théâtre* of a wit whose will to hermetic miniaturism only betrays the totalitarian character of its political aspirations. Rather, "literature" is the messy remainder of wit's would-be dazzling productions, what one finds when, in Henry James's suggestive phrase, one "goes behind"—behind the scenes that wit, precisely by self-consciously making them, unwittingly, embarrassingly *makes*, as certain children say of their excretory performances.[24] "Mme de Guermantes's mind"—"*l'esprit de Mme de Guermantes*" (792), which also means her wit—"attracted me just because of what it excluded (which was precisely the substance of my own thoughts), and everything which, by virtue of that exclusion, it had been able to preserve, that seductive vigour of supple bodies which no exhausting reflection, no moral anxiety or nervous disorder had deformed" (689). Deformed by no exhausting reflection, the charming Guermantes body emits, for that reason, plenty of fecund exhaust, a veritable feast for those who know how to make the most of it. Like the employers whose cook, as Françoise delights in telling Marcel's family, publicly referred to them as "dung" (*fumier*) (491; 654), and thereby "wrung from them any number of privileges and concessions" (491), the mediocre Guermantes are most nourishing for Marcel when, going behind their backs, making asses of them, he finds ways to make their waste *matter*.

Going behind, going backstage, Proust resentfully gets back at the witty Gentiles not only by turning their theatricality against them, but, in the process, by subjecting them to a specifically *narrative* humiliation as well: he diachronically dilates upon, luxuriously anal-yzes, what the "exclusive" exclude, the shit that wit, in its very bid for antinarrative self-enclosure, inadvertently produces.[25] Taking as its preferred form the atomized, impertinent, unassimilable *mot*, wit—which one almost can't say without saying "sophistication" as well—is sometimes valorized for its disruption of the narrative line; here, however, it is narrative, narrative with a vengeance, that disrupts a constricted, sound-bitten wit. Telling the stories that shouldn't be told, Proust revels, longer and more indefatigably than many readers can stomach, in the redundantly vast wasteland of stupidity, whose name in his novel is the Faubourg Saint-Germain, but which extends, for other readers, to include any world that, not despite but almost because of the fact that it turned out to be one more Vanity Fair—because they have begun to suspect that there is no other world—they can never stop loving.

To narrate at all, of course, can constitute a decidely unsmart career move. The hint of "naïveté"—or "naivety"—within "narrativity," the trace of "Narrheit" within "narrate": these are merely shorthand for a larger (almost postmodern) intuition that, in an age in which, as the Duchesse de Guermantes thinks, "to be easily bored [is] a mark of intellectual superiority" (Time Regained, 6:444), the best way to get ahead is by refusing to get bogged down in story. In bringing up the rear, after all, one risks looking like an ass oneself. To put it somewhat differently, the almost hysterically garrulous narrativity of Proustian analysis, for all its focus on the anal, isn't particularly interested in achieving the ends of our culture's normalizing teleologies. Belated and regressive at once, Proust's narrative "behindsight," his tale of the tail, insists preposterously on going back and staying back, dwelling on, and in, everything that a normal mind will have learned to disregard as beneath serious consideration.[26] If even Proust at times promotes a sanitized and sanitizing association of literature with "poetry" over a franker recognition of his far greater investment in the psychopathology of everyday life, this public relations campaign only testifies to his keen perception of how infectious stupidity can be, how easily it seems to be spread, in a world where people will talk, from object to subject and back. No doubt Proust's tendency to clean up his act also fulfills a need to play down the obscene glee accompanying, for example, the parricidal phrase, all the more killing for its hit-and-run casualness, in which "Faubourg Saint-Germain," venerated for so long as the local habitation of everything smart, can suddenly find itself modified by "stupidly." But the reassuring oedipality of this speech act should not blind us to the fact that the parricide remains a parasite, dependent upon his hosts for the surplus meanings that he vindictively turns against them, and to his own profit.[27] Avenging humiliations, one courts the further humiliation of being seen as stuck in an adolescent imaginaire, unbecoming in more ways than one, in which all one can do is act out against increasingly shadowy authority figures.

This, of course, isn't all that Proust does. Staying behind while others have gone ahead, or, like the Duke and Duchess, manically work to stay ahead, as though they were some anxious yuppie couple rather than the aristocratic luminaries that they manifestly are, Proust has the luxury of getting to the bottom of what most grown-ups can't even afford to notice: "stupid" things like how people walk, how they shake hands, how they tell jokes, how they laugh, the clichés they use, the expressions that reveal their pretentiousness or their class backgrounds or their sexual tastes and histories, how they treat their servants, what they say behind their friends' backs, how they try to conceal (and thus betray) their snobbery, how they administer (and receive) snubs, how they give and get invited to dinners, how they dress or wear their hair, where they put their hats, how they advance their careers, how they cultivate their images, how they lie, how they bully (or placate) one another, how they make and try to recover from faux pas, how they affect simplicity, how they talk literature or politics, what and how they eat, how they show their boredom (or their interest), how they say good-bye.

If these examples seem remarkable only for their unremarkability, if they suggest nothing dirtier than the nitty-gritty of what D. A. Miller has called the novel as usual, this standard novelistic micropolitics, I would argue, is no longer quite so standard without the teleological alibi of a subsuming marriage plot.[28] In Proust, what ought to have been subsumed, what ought to have remained merely the humble underside of novelistic discourse, rises to the surface and dominates that discourse. "If the narrator had had the will power of a Balzacian hero," complains Vincent Descombes, "he would at least have attempted to marry a Guermantes."[29] It should be clear by now, I hope, that the narrator's (and, *a fortiori*, the author's) lack of will power is precisely what this essay has been celebrating as, to put it naïvely, Proust's genius. What Descombes calls will power, we would call heterosexual melancholia: to attempt at least to marry a Guermantes is to attempt narrative closure by enclosing in a crypt—that is, by forgetting or disavowing—all the childish pleasures, including the pleasures of the mouth, that one can thereby imagine as what one has maturely put behind or beneath oneself.[30]

Not surprisingly, given her boredom, the Duchess herself suffers from melancholia. When he goes to take leave of her, Marcel finds himself detained by her

> prodigality of charming words, of courteous gestures, a whole system of verbal elegance fed by a positive cornucopia within [*alimentée par une véritable richesse intérieure*] . . . : she would suddenly pluck a flower from her bodice, or a medallion, and present it to someone with whom she would have liked to prolong the evening, with a melancholy feeling that such a prolongation [*un tel prolongement*] could have led to nothing but idle talk, into which nothing could have passed of the nervous pleasure, the fleeting emotion, reminiscent of the first warm days of spring in the impression they leave behind them of lassitude and regret. (748; 834)

The source from which her prodigality flows is also the place to which it must return, since, unable either to renounce her pleasures or to prolong them, she has no choice but the melancholic compromise of internalizing them, consigning them to a cornucopia *within*. Practicing sophistication as a "witty" (i.e., panicky) art of foreclosure and elision, she knows well how dangerously longing informs prolonging. Where sophistication has become *mere* sophistication, an antinaïve, antinarrative reign of boredom, "intellectual superiority" may redound instead to one who reinvents sophistication as an art of dawdling, of putting back in what those on the go have taken out. It is the will-powerless narrator, last to arrive, and last to depart, who enjoys this sophistication of naïveté, who has the pleasure of releasing the Duchess's inner richness and prolonging it, with what we might call a general rather than a restricted prodigality, into the banquet that, *as* internalized, it can never afford to become on its own. The greatest philosopher-gourmand of them all, Proust helps himself again and again to the rich food that, precisely by *not* marrying others, he succeeds in getting out of their bodies.

NOTES

1   Theodor W. Adorno, "Short Commentaries on Proust," in *Notes to Literature*, trans. Shierry Weber Nicholsen, vol. 1 (New York: Columbia University Press, 1991), p. 176.

2   Lee Edelman, *Homographesis: Essays in Gay Literary and Cultural Theory* (New York: Routledge, 1994); see especially the title essay, pp. 3–23. I am also indebted in this chapter to the theorization of "waste" in two recent essays by Edelman: "Plasticity, Paternity, Perversity: Freud's *Falcon*, Huston's *Freud*," *American Imago* 51 (spring 1994): 69–104; "Piss Elegant: Freud, Hitchcock, and the Micturating Penis," *GLQ* 2 (1995): 149–77.

On "Proust" as a signifier for sophistication itself, or on "those" who are most prone to try to capitalize on that signifier (Stephen Sondheim: "Some like to be profound / By reading Proust and Pound"), Gregory Woods has written: "Those who are most appreciative of this dimension of the book are, perhaps, also most likely to buy such books as Borrel, Senderens, and Naudin's *Dining with Proust*, which lavishly recreates the novel's most significant culinary experiences, and to attend such occasions as 'The Music of Marcel Proust,' held in St. John's, Smith Square, London, to mark the seventieth anniversary of the author's death. . . . [T]hose who have read the *Recherche*—those who have *endured*—see themselves as an embattled elite, making up for what they lack in aristocratic credentials with a display of aesthetic appreciation" ("High Culture and High Camp: The Case of Marcel Proust," in David Bergman, ed., *Camp Grounds: Style and Homosexuality* [Amherst: University of Massachusetts Press, 1993], pp. 121–22). And what of those who write such knowing sentences? In place of (perhaps unnecessary) commentary on the game of self-distinction that is being played here, I merely offer an avowal that, perhaps equally needless to say, itself constitutes yet another move in the game: as an owner of the cookbook in question (Jean-Bernard Naudin, Anne Borel, Alain Senderens, *Dining with Proust* [New York: Random House, 1992])—see especially the recipe for grilled crawfish in white sauce, p. 146—I pay tribute to it by taking its title for that of the present section of this essay.

3   Theodor Adorno, "On Proust," in *Notes to Literature*, trans. Shierry Weber Nicholsen, vol. 2 (New York: Columbia University Press, 1992), pp. 315–16.

4   Adorno, unfortunately, can be given credit (along with others) for the homophobic chestnut according to which "Totalitarianism [or fascism] and homosexuality belong together" (*Minima Moralia: Reflections from Damaged Life*, trans. E. F. N. Jephcott [Lon-

don: Verso, 1974], p. 46). Elsewhere in the larger project of which the present essay forms a part, I take up the question of the relationship between homophobia and un-homophobia in Adorno.

5 Marcel Proust, *Time Regained*, vol. 6 of *In Search of Lost Time*, trans. C. K. Scott Moncrieff and Terence Kilmartin, rev. D. J. Enright, 6 vols. (New York: Modern Library, 1992–93), p. 910. All subsequent references to this edition will be given parenthetically in the text; where the title of the volume is not indicated, the reference is to *The Guermantes Way* (vol. 4). Quotations from the French text, many of which are interpolated into quotations from the English translation, are from *A la recherche du temps perdu*, ed. Jean-Yves Tadié et al., 4 vols. (Paris: Gallimard, 1987–89). Where I quote from both the English translation and the French original, the first page reference is to the translation and the second to the original.

Lacan's phrase comes from *The Four Fundamental Concepts of Psycho-Analysis*, ed. Jacques-Alain Miller, trans. Alan Sheridan (New York: W. W. Norton and Company, 1981), p. 268. The image of the simultaneously sublime and obscene object is drawn from the writings of Slavoj Žižek, especially *The Sublime Object of Ideology* (London: Verso, 1989) and *Looking Awry: An Introduction to Jacques Lacan through Popular Culture* (Cambridge: MIT Press, 1991). The use to which the image is being put here is not, I suspect, consistent with Žižek's theoretical and political agenda, or with his pose as heterosexual man of the world. For a trenchant critique of his work in terms of its gender and sexual politics, see Judith Butler, "Arguing with the Real," in *Bodies That Matter: On the Discursive Limits of "Sex"* (New York: Routledge, 1993), pp. 187–222.

6 Eve Kosofsky Sedgwick, "Proust and the Spectacle of the Closet," chapter 5 of *Epistemology of the Closet* (Berkeley: University of California Press, 1990), pp. 213–51.

7 Gilles Deleuze, *Proust et les signes* (Paris: Presses Universitaires de France, 1976), p. 34: "Les signes mondains impliquent surtout un temps qu'on perd. . . ."

8 ". . . s'il est un 'volume de transition,' c'est parce qu'il décrit le passage de l'adolescence à l'âge adulte." Thierry Laget, "Notice," in *A la recherche*, ed. Tadié et al., 2:1492.

9 Maurice Bardèche, *Marcel Proust romancier*, 2 vols. (Paris: Les Sept couleurs, 1971), 2:109–12.

10 George D. Painter, *Marcel Proust: A Biography*, 2 vols. in one (New York: Random House, 1987), 1:251.

11 On playing it cool: just after discovering that he is no longer in love with the Duchesse de Guermantes, and just before receiving what once he coveted, an invitation to dinner from her, the narrator observes, "But even in the details of an attachment, an absence, the declining of an invitation to dinner, an unintentional, unconscious harshness are of more service than all the cosmetics and fine clothes in the world. There would be plenty of social success if people were taught along these lines the art of succeeding" (p. 511). In the original, the last sentence is even better: "Il y aurait des parvenus, si on enseignait dans ce sens l'art de parvenir" (p. 669). For an interesting discussion of this Proustian secret of social—and erotic—success, see Leo Bersani, *Marcel Proust: The Fictions of Life and Art* (New York: Oxford University Press, 1965), pp. 177–78.

12 Bardèche, p. 109.

13 Ibid., p. 110. There is a considerable body of critical literature on orality in Proust. See, for example, Serge Doubrovsky, *Writing and Fantasy in Proust: La Place de la Madeleine*, trans. Carol Mastrangelo Bové and Paul A. Bové (Lincoln: University of Nebraska Press, 1986); Jean-Pierre Richard, *Proust et le monde sensible* (Paris: Seuil, 1974); Kaja Silverman, "A Woman's Soul Enclosed in a Man's Body: Femininity in Male Homosexuality," especially pp. 373–88, in *Male Subjectivity at the Margins* (New York: Routledge, 1992).

14 Proust suggests as much in his remarks on "self-interest," which, in the French text, appears with a more telling ambiguity simply as *l'intérêt* (p. 557): "Often one has to come down to 'kept' persons, male or female, before one finds the hidden springs of actions or words, apparently of the most innocent nature, in self-interest, in the necessity to keep alive" (p. 352). Contrary to popular opinion, vanity (self-interest), far from precluding interest in the world, just *is* that interest.

15 If we don't already know this, however, it may be because we've forgotten it—or because, two volumes and over a thousand pages earlier, it was put somewhat differently. Recounting his family's discovery that, despite his grandiloquent denunciation of snobs, Legrandin is himself a snob, the narrator writes: "This is not to say that M. Legrandin was anything but sincere when he inveighed against snobs. He could not (from his own knowledge, at least) be aware that he himself was one, since it is only with the passions of others that we are ever really familiar, and what we come to discover about our own can only be learned from them." (*Swann's Way*, 3:181).

16 Producing his own example of second naïveté, Adorno gives us to think about the less happy case of another spiteful young wretch:

Proust looks at even adult life with such alien and wondering eyes that under his immersed gaze the present is virtually transformed into prehistory, into childhood. This has an aspect that is not at all esoteric but rather democratic. For every somewhat sheltered child whose responsiveness has not been driven out of him in his earliest years has at his disposal infinite possibilities of experience. I remember a classmate of mine who did not turn out to be anything special in the eyes of the world. We were perhaps twelve years old when we read Molière's *The Miser* in French class. My classmate pointed out to me that the teacher pronounced the title, *L'avare*, in a manner reminiscent of provincial dialect, a manner that betrayed inadequate education, an inferior milieu, and that when one heard this hard "r" one would never believe this otherwise excellent teacher spoke French at all. One might find an observation like this in Proust. (p. 315)

17 In a letter to the duc de Guiche, Proust offers further unflattering ornithological metaphors for the Duchess and her original, Madame de Chevigné (née Laure de Sade), (Marcel Proust, *Correspondance*, texte établi, présenté et annoté par Philip Kolb, tome XX [1921], [Paris: Plon, 1992], p. 349): "Sauf qu'elle est vertueuse, elle (la Duchesse de Guermantes) ressemble un peu à la poule coriace que je pris jadis pour un oiseau de Paradis et qui ne savait comme un perroquet que me répondre 'Fitz James m'attend' quand je voulais la capturer sous les arbres de l'Avenue Gabriel. En faisant d'elle un puissant Vautour, j'empêche au moins qu'on la prenne pour une vieille pie."

18 See, in addition to Sedgwick, pp. 231–40, the account by Kaja Silverman, pp. 373–88; to the extent that Silverman's aim seems to be to produce a *heterosexual* male homosexuality, her reading needs to be approached with caution.

19 See, for example, Doubrovsky.

20 On "It takes one to know one," see Sedgwick, pp. 222–23.

21 Paul Morrison, "End Pleasure," *GLQ* 1 (1993): 53–78.

22 Jacques Derrida, "Structure, Sign, and Play in the Discourse of the Human Sciences," in *Writing and Difference*, trans. Alan Bass (Chicago: University of Chicago Press, 1978), p. 293.

23 In "Death and Literary Authority: Marcel Proust and Melanie Klein," *The Culture of Redemption* (Cambridge: Harvard University Press, 1990), p. 26, Leo Bersani distinguishes between the symbolic violence implicit in "going *behind*" objects and the more attractively metonymic or nonsymbolic practice (he speaks of "appetitive met-

onymies") of moving "to the side of objects." My project in this essay might be characterized as an argument for symbolic violence—or at least as an attempt to trace that violence's own appetitive trajectories, which, if they oppose the "mobility of desire" (p. 22) that Bersani wants to bring out in Proust, continue to impel some of the most interesting gay/lesbian/queer reading and writing.

24　On the Jamesian elaborations of "making a scene," and of "going behind," see my *Caught in the Act: Theatricality in the Nineteenth-Century English Novel* (Berkeley: University of California Press, 1992), pp. 195–269.

25　On the homophobic necessity of "knowing" the gay man—signally M. de Charlus— behind his back, see Sedgwick, pp. 223–30. I am suggesting here that, in narrativizing the Guermantes's wit, in showing *its* behind, the gay novelist turns the tables on heterosexual "sophistication."

26　I take the term "behindsight" from Edelman, "Seeing Things: Representation, the Scene of Surveillance, and the Spectacle of Gay Male Sex," in *Homographesis*, pp. 173– 91.

27　For another instance of Proust's fascination with parricide—other, I mean, than the narrative violence I have been discussing throughout this chapter—see his essay, "Sentiments filiaux d'un parricide," in *"Contre Sainte-Beuve," précédé de "Pastiches et mélanges," et suivi de "Essais et articles,"* ed. Pierre Clarac with Yves Sandres (Paris: Gallimard, 1971), pp. 150–59.

28　D. A. Miller, "The Novel as Usual: Trollope's *Barchester Towers*," in *The Novel and the Police* (Berkeley: University of California Press, 1988), pp. 107–45.

29　Vincent Descombes, *Proust: Philosophy of the Novel,* trans. Catherine Chance Macksey (Stanford: Stanford University Press, 1992), p. 153. The absence of a marriage plot can register as the absence of plot, period: in *Narrative Discourse,* trans. Jane Lewin (Ithaca: Cornell University Press, 1980), p. 167, Gérard Genette observes that the *Recherche* is "sometimes so liberated from any concern with a story to tell that it could perhaps more fittingly be described simply as *talking.*"

30　I allude here to the account of melancholic heterosexuality in Judith Butler, *Gender Trouble: Feminism and the Subversion of Identity* (New York: Routledge, 1990), pp. 57– 72.

Renu Bora

Outing Texture

For me, having a "crush" is about texture, like crushed velvet or crushed foil. My surface gets all uneven, my underneath shows through, things shine up suddenly. It's like "being" crushed material, but also like wearing it, alternately slithery and itchy.—Elizabeth Freeman

C had was brown and thick and strong; and, of old, Chad had been rough. Was all the difference therefore that he was actually smooth? Possibly; for that he *was* smooth was as marked as in the taste of a sauce or in the rub of a hand. The effect of it was general—it had retouched his features, drawn them with a cleaner line. It had cleared his eyes and settled his colour and polished his fine square teeth—the main ornament of his face; and at the same time that it had given him a form and a surface . . . as if . . . put in a firm mould and turned successfully out . . . marked enough to be touched by a finger."[1]

This glorious passage encapsulates the erotics of Henry James's *The Ambassadors*. Chad has matured, has passed from youth to adulthood, but this passage in the context of the novel also implies sexual awakenings in general, from straight to gay or from "acts" to innuendos. Chad's physical beauty, his texture, makes Strether fascinated, curious in many ways, and also makes him ask the two questions: (1) *How did he get that way?* (2) *What do I want to do with him?* (Stare? Ponder? Or reach out to touch the exciting surface?) Importantly, the questions of material, textural history (How did he get so smooth? Rubbing? Polishing? Heating? Fucking? Defecating?), and the questions of the desire to act upon this material, are answered in overlapping, inextricable ways. That is, the things that one might like to do to Chad have a relationship with the things that one might imagine were done to "make" him, the things that changed him, the narratives explaining his (hence Strether's, too, perhaps) coming of age or coming out as gay object/subject or queer tease.² This interest in Chad's texture invites us to read queer curiosity (manual and other pleasures) into many textures of the novel, asking these same two questions of people, skin, hair, clothing, furniture, streets, or architecture.³ Moreover, analogous with Chad's material texture will be Chad's metaphorical (erotic) texture/tone, that is, the style by which he converses and exchanges affect with other characters. For his fetishistic allure will lie in the fascinating mysteries of what pleasures, curiosities, desires, and knowledges he exchanges with others, and how he does so, activating for us a curiosity in what the characters are doing with each other in general.

The language of texture, as I will explain in section 1, involves liminal, erotic play between shiny/matte and smooth/rough distinctions. Even more importantly, in this novel the singing surface qualities of materials resemble much of the dialogue in that they are described by the *very same* tactile metaphors. I give two examples here to encapsulate the textural double entendre:

> Meantime, however, our friend perceived, he was announcing a step of some magnanimity on Mrs. Pocock's part, so that he could deprecate a sharp question. It was his own high purpose in fact to have smoothed sharp questions to rest. (272)

> Chad cast a pleasant backward glance over his possibilities of motive. "I've only wanted to be kind and friendly, to be decent and attentive—and I still only want to be."
> Strether smiled at his comfortable clearness. "Well, there can certainly be no way for it better than by my taking the onus. It reduces your personal friction and your personal offence to almost nothing." (285)

The textural codes imply bodily, manual, fecal, and digestive thrills, which pack innuendo into the sharpest, roughest, crevices of pleasurable topographies and topologies.

Texture and sexuality are both problems wrought with liminals. I would like to demonstrate just how and why the pleasures of these two realms are linked, perhaps nowhere better than in James's *The Ambassadors*.⁴ In this novel, innuendo provides a way into queer pleasures that link flaming flirtation and personal dynamics, with the aesthetics/fetishizing of materials, art, clothing, bodies, furniture, and architecture. In fact, most astonishing is the way the domains of pleasure (affect transaction, dramatic dialogue, and physical materials) are intertwined, perhaps through the wonders of digestive, anal, and fecal pleasures that perpetually haunted James.[5] Of course, to offer this squishy realm as a foundational answer to interpretive questions would be entirely antagonistic to the beauty of James.

Before launching into James's text, I will explain in section I some of the textural issues he will engage. First, I will talk about texture in general. Then I will discuss what I believe has been said numerous times but never articulated as such, that fetishism's fascination, largely an epistemological tease, is often dependent upon its relationship to the liminality of space (and of materiality itself) that is confronted by texture, on the borders of properties of touch and vision. Texture, I will argue, is also crucial to the fetish precisely because it expresses how temporality (also human consciousness, embodiment, movement, and therein style) is intrinsic to the meaning of materiality. Often, the spatio-temporal liminality of fetishism entails the displacement of an object, whose quasi loss has been historicized in the Marxist schema of Baudrillard, then Jameson, or figured locally through the logic of the veil, mask, foot, or other seductive screen that psychoanalytic theory calls a "fantasy space." This space, static, atemporal, has homogeneous qualities of texture and color that invite a viewer to project fantasies behind it or upon it.[6] The textural oppositions shiny/matte, gleaming/dull, smooth/rough, polished/crude, at times become forms of one complex epistemological and ideological structure. These value-laden, reversible codes could be mapped onto sexuality's problematic history of binarisms (such as heterosexual/homosexual) as traced in Sedgwick's *Epistemology of the Closet.*[7] In addition the textural binaries implied by shiny/matte, gleaming/dull, friction/smoothness, softness/hardness, and resilience/resistance will flesh out material joys in the *Ambassadors,* where their presence will also be linked to the fancies of conversation, or whatever else one might imagine happens between James's characters.

Section II will show how these pleasures can be passed from one person to another, but that this passing involves the deconstruction of the concept or feeling of innocence. Section III will locate more specifically how innuendo relates to "innocence." Section IV will discuss specific textural passages, to locate the innuendo in physical descriptions. Chad, in both body and personality, is fetishized to open up for Strether and the reader an intense way to read the spatial, material world as well as the way that people enjoy each other. His transformation suggests that the engagement of people with materials or people with each other is erotic inasmuch as to some extent the transformations of the past are always performed repeatedly, as speculation builds fantasies as much about the nature of epistemological categories as with what style and form people will be using them in the near future.

I picture James's head hovering over a consummated toilet, a glossy, smooth turd lolling in the waters, pride summoning lost pleasures. Perhaps it "passed" (a favorite James term) too perfectly. Perhaps it was less than slippery, and he gripped it within his bowels like a mischievous boy, playing peekaboo with the exit, hiding it upstairs, clinging to it as to a departing lover. Perhaps this dream only teased him.

I think of Freud's anal phase, and the joys of the anal management and mastery used more figuratively than James might demand. How do James's erotics move so spongily from visual, melodic interplay of spatial relations, velvety brushings and sparkling surfaces, into the tension, resilience, density, squishiness, and elasticity of flesh and organs? Conversation and curiosity were never so bodily.

Although Freudian fetishism does not conceptually contain James's pleasures, I do feel that the link in James between texture, tactility, anality, and homoerotic/autoerotic action/admiration evokes at least a straw phallus.[8] While I don't believe one can find a coherent meaning of "fetishism" that would center its usages, I do believe that the relatively phenomenological account I will give works with accounts that pay more attention to social, historical, and psychic forces. With the help of thinkers such as Anne McClintock, Gilles Deleuze, Félix Guattari, Walter Benjamin, William Pietz, Michael Moon, Kobena Mercer, Michael Taussig, Naomi Schor, Jean Baudrillard, and Fredric Jameson one can see that one lineage that lends conceptual continuity to the term and its performance is the fascination with an object's displacement. For example, in *Imperial Leather*, McClintock uses William Pietz's work to show how the contact between different economies and value systems between the West and the colonies generated both a fetishism of commodities and the notion that tribal idols were "primitive" fetishes.[9] McClintock's work also connects imperialism to the race, gender, and labor contradictions of fetishistic practices, images, and objects at the ideological "heart" and homes of the British empire. Every bit as complex as the original "object," or its "use-value," the fetishistic displacement of the object is often physically an index of texture, arising from the surface's interplay between tactile and visual stimuli. Certain textures facilitate the fetish's ritual usages as well as its value connotations, whether in everyday object consumption, image circulation, or in practices such as those scenes of sexual initiation analyzed by Michael Moon's essay, "A Small Boy and Others."

Indeed, as Fredric Jameson argues, in the growing general economy of fetishism, fantasies of reproduction are as legitimate as fantasies of production and consumption (if not more so). Both objects and practices allegorize a complex ontological question about which "things" are circulating with what priority through other things, these things being: materials, objects, properties, motions, affects, gestures, values, or concepts. Fantasies of production, reproduction, and consumption can even at moments seem identical. Jameson describes James's material world in the following manner: "Instead of describing perception in terms of the visual properties of the objects themselves, James tends simply to note the abstract effects and results of such impressions and perceptions, as in words such as 'rich,' 'massive,' 'shabby,' 'solid,' 'ponderous,' etc."[10]

The content and qualities of the scenes, as delineated by James's favorite terms/tropes, differ both from lengthy, almost contingent, descriptions of object and/or from descriptions of typically contingent objects (characterized by much nineteenth-century "realism"), which is to say that there is almost no presence of what Roland Barthes describes as "The Reality Effect."[11] By putting Barthes's term into historical context, as Naomi Schor does in Reading in Detail, one might argue that James's peculiarity of description provides a realism that bridged nineteenth-century fiction with twentieth-century modernisms whose future-orientation, if abstract, claimed the utopian as a realism in its own right, against the more conventional sorts of realism. But in any case, this social-historical context would complicate any viewing of James as simply an apogee of psychological realism (in opposition to social realism).[12] Admittedly, as Marshall Berman implies in All That Is Solid Melts into Air, to use the word realism in this new way is slightly perverse.[13] The redefining of the arts, and their internal fragmentation/experimentation of culture objects and practices through formal issues such as color, texture, light, shape, syntax, grammar, word, letter, music, noise, spectacle, often seemed to be attempts to distinguish art productions from consumer commodities that are supposedly more mundane in virtue of their very object-ness (but, in fact, are actually, threatening fetishes). The displacement of the object, ironically due in part to an attribution of magical, personifying qualities, can become legible when a producer or consumer attempts to fathom its "inherent" sensual properties, or qualities, (perhaps glimpsing with fetishistic fascination its utopic use-value/labor-crystallization in counterpoint to exchange-value, or even the supplemental relationship between concrete labor and object qualities), all of which always seem inevitably naturalized by fetishistic ideology.

Texture has at least two meanings in English.[14] What I will henceforth call TEXTURE, the first meaning, signifies the surface resonance or quality of an object or material. That is, its qualities if touched, brushed, stroked, or mapped, would yield certain properties and sensations that can usually be anticipated by looking. Technically speaking, all materials have texture, though colloquially we often say that only rough things (or friends) do. Smoothness is both a type of texture and texture's other (in some ways, similarly, TEXTURE will be a *supplement*[15] to what I name TEXXTURE, and vice versa). This liminality of smoothness will be important when I explain how the shiny/matte, reflective/dull distinction is a microscopic equivalent of the polished/rough, refined/crude, smooth/coarse distinction, and also of the frictionless/resistant, slippery/tacky, cordial/gruff ones. The connotations of taste, wit, and socioeconomic power carried by so many of these terms are relevant here—these terms could be historicized through the phobic problems around gay/straight, pretentious/simple, snobbish/good, rich/poor, ironic/sincere, prurient/polite, etcetera.[16] Metaphorically, TEXTURE can be purely visual, as in a splotchy color on a petal or a swirl of pink on a book plate.

TEXXTURE, another meaning, refers not really to surface or even depth so much as to an intimately violent, pragmatic, medium, inner level (at first more phenomenological than conceptual/metaphysical) of the stuffness of material structure. I name it TEXXTURE to signal the way it complicates the internal. This texture is even more intrinsically narrative or temporal than TEXTURE, though both suggest perception, creation, and responsive processes. Food and sex may be the common hedonistic domains of this quality, for even more than in friction, slipperiness, nappiness, or fuzziness, this texture resides in properties of crunchiness, chewiness, brittleness, elasticity, bounciness, sponginess, hardness, softness, consistency, striatedness, sogginess, stiffness, or porousness. In Heisenberg's model of vision, the observer's gaze transforms the object one would like to know, because this look implies the deflection of light off of the object. Analogously, for TEXXTURE, the Heisenberg principle, almost identical to the problem of feedback in observation, becomes even more literally and epistemologically violent. For touch and physical pressure transform the materials one would like to know, assess, love. In "Concrete Relations with Others," part 2, "Second Attitude Toward Others: Indifference, Desire, Hate, Sadism," of *Being and Nothingness*, Sartre describes this textural desire as that of the caress, the attempt to "appropriate" the "Other's flesh":

> It is evident that if caresses were only a stroking or brushing of the surface, there could be no relation between them and the powerful desire which they claim to fulfill; they would remain on the surface like looks and could not *appropriate* the Other for me. We know well the deceptiveness of that famous expression, "The contact of two epidermises." The caress does not want simple *contact;* it seems that man alone can reduce the caress to a contact, and then he loses its

unique meaning. This is because the caress is not a simple stroking; it is a *shaping*.[17]

Sartre also describes how this textural desire can be aimed toward objects to reveal one's "incarnation" to oneself:

> A contact with them is a *caress;* that is, my perception is not the *utilization* of the object and the surpassing of the present in view of an end, but to perceive an object when I am in the desiring attitude is to caress myself with it. Thus I am sensitive not so much to the form of the object and to its instrumentality, as to its matter (gritty, smooth, tepid, greasy, rough, *etc.*). In my desiring perception I discover something like a *flesh* of objects. My shirt rubs against my skin, and I feel it. What is ordinarily for me an object most remote becomes the immediately sensible; the warmth of air, the breath of the wind, the rays of sunshine, *etc.;* all are present to me in a certain way, as posited upon me without distance and revealing my flesh by means of their flesh.[18]

Like music, the structure of TEXXTURE can be sophisticated. Ignore, if possible, the exciting ramifications of feedback, and imagine how squeezing someone's, say, bicep, can register the various resistances of skin, fat, muscle, and bone. Of course, especially for living materials, the types of feedback, action, reaction, or act, can be of varying complexity and predictability, involving the spectrum from physical resilience to biological reflex to social/psychological reaction to performance.

Henri Bergson, a philosopher interested in the phenomenology of time, often used the metaphor of the spring to capture not just notions of time and matter, but our experience of life or freedom. What is fascinating about this metaphor for the purposes of texture and fetishism is that what makes a material elastic (elasticity or tension itself), in this example of a metal coil or other folded/bent metal, is that it seems to remember its original shape. In the language of physics, it converts kinetic energy to potential energy, and one day, back again. How a static object or material could store this life, in a sense, is puzzling, for in its remembrance, its variability of compression or stretch, it seems to have a mind of its own. Perhaps the hardness or shininess or smoothness of the fetish disavows this ghostly presence. The material world is saturated with labors, and there are many ways in which one can unspring or perceive this labor.

For liquids, perhaps even gases, I dare say, the slippery distinction between TEXTURE and TEXXTURE would be something like the difference between a fluid's slipperiness/stickiness and its viscosity. I believe there are causal relationships between these two property indices, textures in a sense, but the former has more to do with friction and the latter has more to do with density, pressure, or resilience. From living tissue to inorganic objects, speaking metaphysically, at what minute scale would it not even make sense to speak of crunchiness, of elasticity?

I believe texture has an interesting liminal role in the visual realm, for, once named, it seems beyond pattern, say, in clothing.[19] For example, the texture of a pique polo shirt seems on the verge of being visually a pattern of the weave, so what texture means may be perhaps not TEXTURE, but TEXXTURE, an intimate sponginess. Concrete buildings are permitted the quality of having texture because the roughness is both uniform on one level and also on a closer scale homogeneously disordered, that is, not very much of a pattern. Roughness, again like noise in music, is always at risk of becoming signifying, a structure, a baroque order of sorts, perhaps.[20] The ribs of a bendee straw are perhaps just too ordered to be a texture, even though on one level they certainly are. Fractal patterns seem to be on the threshold of texture and structure, because their ornateness bears perhaps just too much homogeneity across many scales of perception. The presence, quality, and significations of different resolution (pixellation) in videos or even paintings, or different noise/static in audio recordings, are often determined by how close, where, in what motions, and with what ideological lenses the viewer approaches the object, and as feedback becomes evident (both literal and conceptual, for in perception the distinction is difficult) we move into problems of chaos theory as well as theories of culture.

The distinction between the two types of texture I've enumerated is extremely complicated, almost false at times, raising issues about how we can deduce one from the other, how they are related, etcetera. For example, softness as a TEXTURE might be opposed to a kind of smoothness, whereas in TEXXTURE it is opposed to hardness. When a surface (a rock, or your face, for example) has certain properties, we often project these properties into its interior, and by this interior I mean not just a cavity, invagination, fold, or center, but the structure, consistency, or TEXXTURE of its inner matter that extends liminally, asymptotically, into the surface.[21] I do not use "structure" and "texture" as properties measured by an observer or instrument in an absolute scientific, philosophical sense, but as properties partially constructed by codes that I would call ideology. Texture can even be read as synonymous with materiality itself, inasmuch as I am arguing that a kind of inevitable tactility or human agency, in performance or in labor, is crucial to any definition of what it means for something to occupy physical space.

In James, perhaps at sensitive body sites, we will see narratives of one type of texture turning into another, and also, texture juxtaposed with other (spatial) topologies. Either between named textures such as "softness" or "bounciness," or even within one of the two types of texture,[22] we have narratives of transformation, as in the polishing of a doorknob, the sanding of a statue, the shaving of a moustache, or the digestion of a cupcake. Textures will also leap forward from their other, the world of color, of volume, perhaps as fetishes from nonfetishistic pleasure, or even from straightness, if such a thing exists. For in all the differential relations of texture/non-texture, TEXTURE/TEXXTURE, slippery/rough, shiny/dull, stretchy/taut the liminalities of deconstruction will propagate riddles and instabilities whose joys have been linked to queer life by works such as Judith Butler's *Gender Trouble*.[23] Generally, the path of fetishism will be paved by riddles of TEXTURE, partly because described physical contact between characters and/or things is quite fugitive. Of course, TEXXTURE's inaccessibility always entices, and tentative terms such as "firmness" sometimes anchor one's probings.

That the ornate material structures are even more complex when time and characters enter the imagination will prove fabulous for James, as if one wouldn't want to separate material appreciations from dramatic scenarios (and vice versa). By "dramatic," here I mean both a scene where a single character's fascination blossoms, and also scenes where characters interact largely through dialogue.

Fetishism in both psychoanalytic and Marxist thought has often been emblematized by the shine or gleam of light reflected by an object. An origin, a source, a radiation of light can never be a fetish. Moreover, what makes this foregrounded gleam visible is its emergence from a relatively rough background, a background of rough texture whose physical quality is then upstaged, surmounted. Of course, visually, most objects reflect light all over, but the combination of smoothness in the object and the direct, pointlike light source (as opposed to ambient lighting) together are conditions for a glint or shimmering, writ large. This gleam is almost invariably blindingly white, almost pure light, as it emerges almost colorless from a background that has color. Because it seems like a source of light, it has a volumetric, material indeterminacy. In other words, if cut out of a photograph or film it would, unlike its surroundings, be hard to model or map in three, or even two dimensions. As a source of fascination, starlike, it seems an ideal point or slice of pure light even when part of a volume. The extent to which an object reflects these gleams corresponds to its smoothness; the most extreme example of smoothness, the liminal ideal behind the gleaming surface, is the mirror. However, because the mirror is perfectly smooth and planar, it is not a simple fetish, but a kind of ur-fetish, the condition of possibility of the fetish. Perhaps the fetish invokes the gaze because every gleam invokes the mirror of Lacan's mirror stage, the original somatic alienation (and castration disavowal?) of the viewer who is struck by rays of light, as if an object of sight were displaced by its power to return the gaze. (Lacan's tin can, Freud's shine on the nose, Jean Genet's police badge, metal lighter, movie-star slick hair . . . or even, writ large, Jameson's postmodern schizophrenia/loss of history.)[24]

In a Baudrillardian vein, one might argue that the simulacrum transposes this aesthetic or psychoanalytic phenomenon to the visual/conceptual level, which would explain why postmodernism's predominant glossophilia is especially uncanny—the semiotic charge becomes reliteralized. This uncanniness may be doubly paradoxical in simulations of shininess, as in the illustrated radiant lines signifying the glint, an extended echo of the modern ideology of the new. By no coincidence, these lines also signify shock in queer camp '50s or retro '50s cartoon visages. Jameson's postmodern glossiness or sheen is more complex than the glint, because the "flatness" of style has a near-impossibility, an "inherent contradiction," for even though history or memory is effaced in a certain respect, the only way one could know this would be in contrast to a prior stage, perhaps modernist in style, though the term "style" fails to capture the fact that the transformation is almost more conceptual/ideological than visual: "it seems to me essential to grasp postmodernism not as a style but rather as a cultural dominant: a conception which allows for the presence and coexistence of a range of very different, yet subordinate, features."[25] As Jameson illustrates in this work, the sheen of postmodernity dialectically subsumes and depends upon its (historical) opposite, raw roughness or softness, which can be fetishized in its own right. The fetish can be seen as a disavowed obsession with this dialectic, and how spatially but also temporally it becomes narrative, an allegorical transformation of production, consumption, or reproduction.

As gold, pearls, diamonds, the shine marks the shimmering of exchange-value, a crystallization that condenses abstract labor and commodification, and hence the commodity fetish. Gold proves fascinating not just because it became the money standard and its visual properties seemed to generate its value, but also because, as Marx mentions in *Capital*, its malleability, a texture of sorts, made it easy to coin and quantify infinitesimally. The glimmering smoothness seems linked to a TEXXTURE that is quite mysterious, both of which textural properties will seem to make gold fetishistic in the commodity sense. I argue this to identify the perception of its value, without engaging whether Marx's labor theory of value suggests that this consumer aesthetic and economic theory is wrong or should be changed. Even more complicated, the shine of manufactured products (gold might be included), because they are dazzling and often produced by assembly lines or machines, marks commodity fetishes because such products have little trace of manual (social) labor/production process in them, no Benjaminian aura. There are dialectics here of a fractal order, of smoothness/roughness, of shine/color, of gleam/volume, where the former term must scintillate to erupt from the latter. In fact, the very maintenance of these valorized material properties and the ideology of the new, the white, the smooth, the shiny, the clean, can involve a ritualistic fetishism where the distinction between production and consumption might be encapsulated by the concept of reproduction. As McClintock illustrates, the fetishisms of soap and dirt are interesting, because the domestic labor that displays newness was unacknowledged as labor proper.[26] Soap seems to be a fetish that disseminates the aesthetics of fetishism by cleaning the dirt from products. Dirt, which seems outside the commodity system because it is valueless, uncrystallized, unexchangeable, literally makes objects matte and dull (as well as more "primitive" or crude). It becomes a fetish dialectically because its presence or absence actually signifies a cleaning that impends by the logic of ritualistic reproduction of values and concepts.

Some visual artifacts, like new automobiles, are easier to read in a textural mode, because these oppositions are accessible on initial levels. In shiny, usually synthetic, fabrics, we can read sheen as an emblem of the artificial, the technological, the feminine, the Oriental, the luxurious, glamorous, tacky, or gay, in oppositional ideological codings that usually demand deconstruction.[27] Some artifacts are much more complicated, for example, a costume pieced together from heterogeneous materials, or a looted tomb.

The shine can also be produced by water or any fluid that can hold its own or coat a friend. Sweat, for example, can enhance and fetishize "blackness": "The physical [sexual] exertion of powerful bodies . . . the shiny, polished sheen of black skin becomes consubstantial with the luxurious allure of the high-quality photographic print."[28]

Fetishism can also, however, lie not in the shine but in a kind of fluffy, hairy, feathery, furry, suede leathery coarseness—displaced genitalia, epidermal fuzz, fragmented integuments. These fetishes depend on the emergence of fairly homogeneous tactility from otherwise "flat" or hybrid surroundings. As if from two dimensions grew a mossy third, invoking the problematic, fractal strain between dimensions. The very meaning of softness (for TEXTURE), the feeling, is dependent on the dusty approach of a surface toward disintegration, a powdery departure from a plane. As a liminal instance of softness, imagine perhaps stroking either a thousand-year-old feather or a powder puff's residual blush.

That these two texture limits, or fetish genres, suggest the implicit, erotic, costuming of an object, is illustrated most poignantly by Roland

Barthes's "Striptease" chapter in *Mythologies*. Although he doesn't claim to be talking about fetishism, his passage is worth quoting at length because it describes a textural logic that is exactly homologous to the two categories I propose, and moreover, by the very model of striptease, it exposes texture's implicit narrative, even ritual, of the erotic performance:

> The classic props of the music-hall, which are invariably rounded up here, constantly make the unveiled body more remote, and force it back into the all-pervading ease of a well-known rite: the furs, the fans, the gloves, the feathers, the fish-net stockings, in short the whole spectrum of adornment, constantly makes the living body return to the category of luxurious objects which surround man with a magical decor. Covered with feathers or gloved, the woman identifies herself here as a stereotyped element of music-hall, and to shed objects as ritualistic as these is no longer a part of a further, genuine undressing. Feathers, furs and gloves go on pervading the woman with their magical virtue even once removed, and give her something like the enveloping memory of a luxurious shell, for it is a self-evident law that the whole of striptease is given in the very nature of the initial garment: if the latter is improbable, as in the case of the Chinese woman or the woman in furs, the nakedness which follows remains itself unreal, smooth and enclosed like a beautiful slippery object, withdrawn by its very extravagance from human use: this is the underlying significance of the G-String covered with diamonds or sequins which is the very end of striptease. This ultimate triangle, by its pure and geometrical shape, by its hard and shiny material, bars the way to the sexual parts like a sword of purity, and definitively drives the woman back into a mineral world, the (precious) stone being here the irrefutable symbol of the absolute object, that which serves no purpose.[29]

The two fetish genres I describe correspond with what Deleuze and Guattari name "smooth space." Their use of smooth is not literal, but idiosyncratic. For them, "smooth" is not a property of objects but rather a type of space that permeates the world. Whereas my description starts from objects, their description starts from spaces. In a way, we approach similar phenomena from opposite directions. One might argue that fetishism fascinates by virtue of its evocation of their notion of smooth space. Smooth space is defined primarily in differentiation from "striated space": "1) We shall call striated or metric any aggregate with a whole number of dimensions, and for which it is possible to assign constant directions; 2) nonmetric smooth space is constituted by the construction of a line with a fractional number of dimensions greater than one, or of a surface with a fractional number of dimensions greater than two." Smooth space is "more than a line and less than a surface; less than a volume and more than a surface."[30]

Another term Deleuze and Guattari introduce to describe smooth space is "haptic," a type of perception similar to the tactile. They use "haptic" instead of "tactile" in order to problematize the distinction between the visual and the tactile. For them, the tactile can be perceived by the eye, and optical can be perceived by the body. Haptic space is synonymous with smooth space, whereas the optical is characteristic of striated space: "[S]mooth space is directional rather than dimensional or metric. Smooth space is filled by events or haeccrities, far more than by formed and perceived things. It is a space of affects, more than one of properties. It is *haptic* rather than optical perception. Whereas in the striated forms organize a matter, in the smooth materials signal forces and serve as symptoms for them. It is an intensive rather than extensive space, one of distances, not of measures and properties. Intense *spatium* instead of *extensio*. . . . Perception in it is based on symptoms and evaluations rather than measures and properties. That is why smooth space is occupied by intensities, wind and noise, forces, and sonorous and tactile qualities."[31]

From these two types of fetish, as different as, say, a porcelain foot and a hairy pit, or a golden bowl and the wings of a dove, we can see that absolute immateriality and absolute tactility seem to be flickering nodes of fascination, as the problem of orders of representation (what is a mirror?), dimension (somewhere between one and three), and the problem of the sensual emergence of touch from vision, are made legible.

What is the crude? The raw? Roughage? What is the refined? Shiny? Matte? Coarse? Smooth? Polished? Plucked? Erect? Folded? Wrinkled? Puckered? Moreover, how did it get that way? Manually? Orally? Genitally? Was it fun? Was it rubbed to a finish? Massaged gently? Kneaded by a happy intestine? Painted? Worn away over decades? Inflated? Sanded? Oiled? In short, Chad?

We have emphasized that the shiny/matte, gleam/color, glint/volume distinctions resemble the refined/raw, smooth/rough, burnished/crude distinctions not just materially but in their ideological import. In James we can see that there is a further excitement in the relative reflectivity, or smoothness, of things, because the frictionlessness implied therein enables "passing" to have not just fecal or fleshy dimensions, but to suggest also the spread of pleasurable affect as congruent with the highlighted illusion of certain epistemologies of, say, sexual identity. The joyful exchange between characters I will later call a kind of contagion, and its difference from other exchanges (dialectic or constipational), its liminal smoothness, gives it a corny, sentimental, or utopic flavor, and it dominates the mood of *The Ambassadors*, though I will also argue that the other types of textural exchange in the text lurk in the fashion of Derridean "supplements."

I have spoken of the liminality of visual smoothness in the mirror, the reflected photon of the light ray. The other liminal of smoothness, too evasive to hold, liquidity, oddly belongs to both TEXTURE and TEXXTURE, and its liminality is worth discussing a bit, for it pours forth from the pores of James's text. The physical riddles one suffers with diarrhea, for example, the confused anticipation of what will pass, perhaps is akin to that of constipation in urgency, in the chaotic escalation of extreme joys and pains. Liquidity/solidity, resilience/absorption, bounce/brittleness, glistening/dullness, rigidity/softness, smoothness/coarseness, these fecal issues are much more than that in James.

Of course, as supplements to frictionlessness, smoothness, or liquidity, the liminal of fuzziness, or even roughness (what some call noise), also implies pleasures of passing, for fecally, fleshily, perhaps the degree of resistance, and the necessity of this resistance for registering contact (besides temperature and more linguistic technologies), is one of the more dynamic issues of taste. In James, this resistance or roughness behaves as an ever-present supplement to its supplement, perfect frictionlessness, with roughness's supplement in turn being perhaps not only the smoothness but the ugliness, the vulgar comedy, of total blockage. Later, I will identify smoothness as the contagious, first mode of affect transfer, whereas TEXTURE/roughness (high drama/soap opera/both negative and positive affects) will be the second mode, with total blockage, constipation, being the third mode. If one were to imagine these affect transfers as not merely conversational but physical, and for James I would say this is irresistible, one would identify smoothness with utopian, liminal, "vanilla," sexuality, and identify TEXTURE, roughness, with S/M or top/bottom dynamics (constipation marking an absolute lack or dead end). How one might map these divisions through the distinctions of TEXXTURE (soft/hard, etc.) seems even more complex. Of course, these models are a great beginning for mapping tastes and acts, but they neither necessarily describe identities, nor do they necessarily exhaust the nature of certain mutual "acts," for it seems to me that even very specific scenes may have different dimensions of dominance, pedagogy, and even uncertainty working at the same time. Again, these categories are intertwined, often in supplemental relation.

When I use the term supplement, the clearest of Derrida's terms for my purposes in this essay, it seems important to remember that for Derrida this structure, which he sometimes says is not a concept, is similar, even exchangeable, with a rich body of other terms (pharmakon, parergon, hymen, stylus, signature, trace, tympan, etc.). In this piece I would hope to emulate a similar fluidity between "master" terms and specific ones. Perhaps with James, smoothness, texture, innocence, or passing might be given such poetic power that these key notions and his favored vocabulary all fit a scheme of innuendos, of secret pleasures that flicker between the countless scenes' specificities.

To talk about innuendo in James is both inevitable and difficult. The humor is so pervasive that I can hardly imagine, if you will, an epistemology or theory of how one locates it. At best one might talk of different shades, effects, perhaps dip into the dialogue to discover that the things that make people laugh (James actually designates these moments!) are as disjunctive as the things that make them continue to talk. What is flirtation? What would it mean to have a world of people for whom this mode was deconstructed or defamiliarized in a radical, continuous way? In James there seems to be roughly a central core of characters who engage in loving, sexual ways so affectedly, allusively, self-consciously, that these adverbs spin expansively, as if discussing one divine level and five metalevels at the same time. Roughly speaking, Strether works affectionately with Miss Gostrey, Mme de Vionnet, and Chad, who all know very quickly how to have fun, whereas Waymarsh, Jim, and Sarah learn less quickly how to have at least James's kind of fun.

II. DECONSTRUCTION

One deconstructive move that proliferates in James is the toying with the ontological priority of his pairs of binarisms. That is, not only does the interdependency of the two terms always make their narrative, ontological order impossible to determine, but they point in turn to other pairs. Age and youth seem an obvious first example.

Strether seems to realize at certain moments that his admiration of Chad's youth, his concern with age and innocence is no disinterested observation, but rather is symptomatic of his own sense of agedness, and Chad's obliviousness to this crisis makes him truly young. At times, however, we and Strether feel that Chad occupies a mischievously impossible position—he knows all this! Merely by not mentioning it, he achieves a veneer that makes us suspicious while it turns us on. Strether's paranoia, or obsession with knowing, but also his desire not to know, may or may not be obvious to a Chad who knows at the very least that Strether is enjoying himself. Chad could be the simplest, most explicit guy or he might be an attentive top who knows what some kinds of obsession/love need in order to circulate. Fetishism seems one of many words invoked by Strether's fascination with Chad. Chad's physical appearance and his charming manner of speech both reflect intriguing textural transformation: "He was waiting cheerfully and handsomely, but also inscrutably and with a slight increase perhaps of the hardness originally acquired in his high polish" (206).

In the next section I will discuss further how the youth/innocence state is transmogrified into affect by its confusing oppositionalities (plural liminals) and sitings, sometimes meshed with potentially discrete innuendo/literal dialectics that mount it in all positions. The straight/gay dynamics work a similar way, where the issue of "youth" or "innocence" becomes akin to one of (queer) pleasure, but the combination of silence and obviousness keeps these pleasures circulating. In fact, this queerness seems to push the stakes of pleasure to its sometimes flip, sometimes ticklish, sometimes blasé, sometimes targeted eruption of visceral thrills, turning metaphors to mush and back again. It's no secret that Chad and Strether know they both know they're getting off on each other, as do many other combos of the book—perhaps Gostrey is the grand initiator and expert of these joys, for she and Strether know immediately how to flirt in a beautifully Jamesian way, which seems like a "successful," ongoing, mutual "gaydar" encounter. This brings to mind a question that is maddeningly there in James: What are the differences between recognizing that someone is queer, recognizing that someone is attracted to you, and recognizing that someone is playful/curiously engaging? Are these three recognitions, tendencies in some characters, all evanescent enough to be at times mutually constitutive? Before explaining the three possible manners in which moods, even sensibilities, or provisional identities, of James's characters can be exchanged in dialogue (implicitly, in action as well), I will try to explain how the reader gets drawn into the confusing excitement of trying to decipher the characters' innuendo/flirtation.

Chad is the favored topic of conversation for much of the novel, for Strether must find out something about Chad's history and status regarding sex, love, romance, or even sin. Part of what makes the novel confusing and pleasurable, I would argue, is that there seems to be an astonishing amount of circumlocution in this mission, so much that one wonders what acts and feelings on Chad's part are even in question. This leaves much to our imagination, and it becomes obvious that the teasing evasions are fun for Strether and his new circle of friends. I would like to point to four possible explanations of why Strether is so indirect, for these explanations exemplify what is playful in almost all the flirtations of the novel's dialogues.

(1) Because Strether's character, even by the standards of his social milieu, is especially shy, timid, polite, ashamed, or courteous, he is afraid to ask exactly what he is supposed to find out about Chad, and hence he

is unsure of how to phrase his quest for knowledge. To press for details might expose either his sexual/romantic imagination, or his naïveté, in an embarrassing way. The company responds accordingly to his delicacy.

(2) In accordance with what Foucault describes as the largely reductive "repressive hypothesis" about the Victorian Age, Strether lives in a society where there is without a doubt a taboo against the articulation of sexual questions, and so to find out the "down and dirty," is as inappropriate as the language to describe it is uncharted. Strether, socialized as he is, is too timid, polite, or clueless about sexuality to ask, even if he does know what the questions would be, about Chad's personal life. In this vein, as in (1), he might even be aware that to violate the taboo would implicate himself in a scene of impure desires, where his own forbidden pleasures and curiosities toward Chad might become suspect.

(3) Strether, perhaps his society, perhaps James, perhaps ourselves as well, actually knows that his company, when answering his questions, must interpret the scene as choice (1) or choice (2), and he enjoys the questions and attentions this brings to himself as well as those it brings to Chad. Perhaps Strether knows that the true "content" of his speech must be determined by the listener, who, like an analyst is given the privilege of reading his unconscious. Or, Strether might realize that this ploy allows him to read the unconscious of the projecting listener, as well as to actually find out Chad's activities.

(4) Strether and the characters are all aware of the dynamic possibilities of choices (1), (2), and (3) and in fact their queerness or sophistication insists that the way to enjoy each other is to flirt with these ambiguities. In this way, they all become implicated in the network of mutual curiosity about each others' knowledge, curiosity, and shame, for no one really knows just how naive their company is regarding the possibility of these different explanations of circumlocution. Alternatively, that innuendo is a high source of erotic pleasure and that everyone is aware of this pleasure, is supremely obvious to the characters, James the author, and at least some of his audience of readers.

There is no answer as to how naive each of James's characters is at any given point about these interpretive difficulties, but I would insist that the queerness or playfulness resides in precisely that unanswerability, and so I would say that to some extent, as Chad is to Strether, so are all of the characters to each other, and so most importantly is Strether (and the rest of the cast) to us the readers. There is no simple narrative of straight characters becoming queer, or any other simple tale of sexual/romantic progress, except perhaps the possibility that Strether is in fact initiated into this world to discover that he likes it. What charges the novel's erotics is the high degree of scrutiny we and characters bring to each other about the different ways one can be innocent, naive, curious, knowing, especially about the erotic nature of perpetuating, even suspending, these questions, perhaps for mutual pleasure but also for that of a yet unseen party.

One might think of tone as depicting the texture of skin tone or muscle tone, but these bodily innuendos also describe fantasies of vocal tone. Indeed, part of what one might call a utopic deconstruction of flirtation or innuendo in James is his teasing style of vocal depiction. For, just as his material descriptions are filtered through favored James terms and overall effects of the objects, so James's dialogue descriptions only *seem* to describe tone, and hence fail to describe the affect. This illusion of what could anchor an epistemology of innuendo or queerness is most often done by naming without describing the significance of "tone" upon what a character meant to say. I list several examples:

Something in the tone of it pulled her up, but as their messenger still delayed she had another chance and she put it another way. (56)

Chad, still seated, stayed him, with a hand against him, as he passed between their table and the next. "Oh we shall get on!"
The tone was, as who should say, everything Strether could have desired; and quite as good the expression of face with which the speaker had looked up at him and kindly held him. (98)

The special tone of it made him, pulling up, look at her long. (106)

There was the whole of a story in his tone to his companion, and he spoke indeed as if already of the family. (135)

Strether had himself plenty to say about this, but it was amusing also to measure the march of Chad's tone. (142)

"Well, it may not be 'all,'" she interrupted, "but it's to a great extent. Really and truly," she added in a tone that was to take its place with him among things remembered. (152)

It was, in the oddest way in the world, on the showing of this tone, a genial new pressing coaxing Waymarsh; a Waymarsh conscious with a different consciousness from any he had yet betrayed, and actually rendered by it almost insinuating. (272)

One might offer that in James affect "passes" like knowledge between people in roughly three modes. I will again name these modes (1) contagious/smooth, (2) dialectic/textured, and (3) constipational. The standard scene of their enactment is the dialogue, and in this novel the first mode dominates the style. Interestingly, we often don't get descriptions of the characters' moods, so it is from the style and content of their speech, as well as from their patent friendship that we can infer that they are making each other contagiously happy. Their use of innuendo, or at least an abstract language of virtue and taste, makes most of their speech seem to create the utopic affect transition I call contagious, though it is always paradoxically structured, deconstructed, by a more sinister dynamic I call dialectic. The constipational has less interest for James. I will outline the two interesting modes with attention to the differences in affect (positive vs. negative), curiosity (light vs. heavy), and sexual charge ("vanilla" vs. S/M). I would offer that the first two modes represent not a "good" style and a "bad" style but a mutual structuration.

Contagious/Smooth

"Smile and the world smiles with you" is the principle at work here.[32] For James this mutual contagion usually involves positive affects such as joy rather than negative ones such as sadness. What makes the interchange elusive is that most of the time we are not given descriptions of the character's feelings, but rather their dialogue. Often, the mere mention of moral or religious virtue, with concepts such as kindness, wonderfulness, niceness, friendliness, or decency, creates a playful reiteration of the notions to implicate both conversants. It almost seems that to mention them is to recognize them is to know them is to share them is to enact them, all of which may be the same as sharing the very principle of contagion. It's as if the powerful intimacy of mentioning the word "love" implicitly contained the performative meaning of "I love you." This utopian principle may be an illusion of sorts, perhaps the illusion of subjectivity itself, whose act and identity seem seamless, smooth, without the contingencies, failures, and contradictions that emerge from their ideological nature.[33] This contagious/smooth mode, in the physical or sexual register, would be the utopian ideal of "vanilla" behavior, the mutual giving and receiving of pleasure without any negative feelings or affect. I find it tempting to imagine not only that James's characters are curious about each other's sexual attitudes and tastes, but that there is no truth as to whether they do or don't physically interact in the novel.

Again, in James specific examples of this contagious/smooth affect transition abound in conversations where the goodness, niceness, kindness, etcetera of people (including the conversants) is discussed without grounding these virtues in "acts," "events," desires, or states of being, of grace. In addition, these "acts" tend to have an ambiguous tense. The utopian vagueness of the innuendo not only fails to specify acts, but insists

that the aesthetic and moral charge be entertained in potentially negative and positive desirability, depending on what any specific character or
reader imagines is at stake. That fineness or smoothness of interpersonal
texture is important for Strether can be illustrated by the following passage: "He had been fine to Mrs. Newsome about his useful friend [Maria
Gostrey], but it had begun to haunt his imagination that Chad, taking
up again for her benefit a pen too long disused, might possibly be finer.
It wouldn't at all do, he saw, that anything should come up for him at
Chad's hand but what specifically *was* to have come; the greatest diver-
gence from which would be precisely the element of any lubrication of
their intercourse by levity" (103).

Strether with his comrades will refer to Chad, Mme de Vionnet, and
her daughter without anchoring his virtue and taste vocabulary in concrete scenarios, so his curiosity has a perpetual lightness even in its persistence. The very levity of the curiosity performs perhaps a decadence
of lifestyle itself, of having the luxury, leisure, and taste to lounge about
Paris suspending countless acts, quests, and questions with an equally
decadent circle for whom time is as abundant as money. That Strether
explicitly claims he is having fun in Paris guarantees for us the wit in
his innuendo circulation. This contagion of joy, of course, is structured
by the next mode, a supplement that threatens it. One might even imagine in the characters a coy cynicism that points to the existence of this
second mode of exchange. In fact, sometimes the contagion is enacted
virtually identically by the invocation of words such as "sin," "bad," and
other opposites of moral or aesthetic good. These locutions are less common, but they seem to function almost identically as the positive valo-
rizations/acts, and so illustrate the strange presence of the antagonisms
of the next mode. According to supplemental logic, the possible double
valency of contagion's flirtatious tone (optimism/cynicism), its radical
undecidability, might be what makes it so appealing, so queer.

Dialectic/Textured

This mode of affect transition would involve a heated confrontation in-
clusive of negative affects such as misery, anger, boredom, even violent
curiosity. In the physical or sexual register, it could describe violence or
domination, possibly framed by S/M practices where, unlike in "vanilla"
models, negative feelings are incorporated playfully. It could describe all
those things, in the spirit of "expression," or "communication," that therapy tries to bring out in the never-ending battle against repression, passive aggression, etcetera. This mode is the stuff of high drama, of soap
operas, and could be highly playful. Strether and company almost never

engage this way, although there are brief whims of "mere violence," such as when he sees Chad and Mme de Vionnet together (308). The other threat would be when Strether reflects on the novelty of his adventure to express what could very easily be a highly ambivalent attraction to violence:

> These, however, were but parenthetic memories; and the turn taken by his affair on the whole was positively that if his nerves were on the stretch it was because he missed violence. When he asked himself if none would then, in connexion with it, ever come at all, he might almost have passed as wondering how to provoke it. It would be too absurd if such a vision as *that* should have to be invoked for relief; it was already marked enough as absurd that he should actually have begun with flutters and dignities on the score of a single accepted meal. What sort of brute had he expected Chad to be, anyway? — Strether had occasion to make the enquiry but was careful to make it in private. (109)

Imagine if Strether pressed semantically like a tabloid reporter for the nitty-gritty "dirt" on Chad — the tone of this novel makes this mode almost tacky, or at least undesirable. At the same time, its possibility gives the first mode meaning differentially, so its presence as a secret pleasure, be it camp, violence, or ritual pain, lurks mischievously. This second mode's epistemological insistence demands a depth model (or lifestyle, even) of affect, taste, virtue, act, or identity, where the bad must be revealed for knowledge and pleasure. The first mode from this perspective resembles what Freud called fetishistic disavowal. To the extent that the first mode was tonally or narratively determinable as manipulative, rhetorical, or insincere, then it might slip into this category, for sincerity seems contingent upon a subjective (and object of desire's) singularity with which James's characters merely (and urgently) toy.

Constipational

Although this mode is hard to define, it might be explained as a kind of boring lack of strong affect (positive or negative) between characters about each other and their conversation. The type of speech involved tends to be unflirtatious, that is, literal. The attitude of the speaker toward the listener tends to be uncurious, so personal dynamics are effaced by references that constitute an outside "world," which could include a character's internal "world" to the extent that the mapping can happen independent of affects/histrionics. This category might be exemplified by Waymarsh. Its simple, referential talk might also be exemplified by

Mrs. Newsome's lucidity of desire, or sometimes by Sarah's. In this mode of affect, erotics don't really circulate between people.

Strether's soft spot for *smoothness* (especially in its triangulation through gossip) seems oddly dependent upon his skill at playfully, masterfully, anally if you will, suspending the epistemological pressure that *texture* seems to beg (although he does [hope to] "touch bottom" a few times [254]), as well as upon an amused repulsion toward *blockage*. What makes these modes complicated is that when describing dialogue their textures are highly temporal or narrative motions, whereas their embodiment on or beneath the surfaces of people or objects seems highly spatial, almost static. But again, the physical world implicitly involves production and consumption agencies not just in its fabrication but in its perception, and this exciting undercurrent for James constitutes an eroticism that lends innuendo not just to verbal comments but to materials. While one might be used to metonymic connections between fabrics and pleasures of the human body, what suffuses James's world involves an intense metaphoricity of materiality itself. Just as materials bridge people's bodies, as when we perceive the labor marks of a handiwork, so does dialogue in a sense bridge materials, for the rhythms between desires, bodies, and matter embodied by texture lend a brutality to words, as perhaps the way people speak with each other implies tastes and preferences of sexuality or materiality. That from personal interaction one might surmise another's relatively private pleasures is always fascinating for James and his curious characters. What seems desirable is that innuendo becomes delightful not in that the vulgar can be identified even while it is smuggled into flirtation (or even material descriptions), but that it merely begs even more questions of desire on the part of all parties involved.

These three modes, structures, or identity formations don't always happen automatically, for it seems that characters feel their way into them. Strether and Gostrey, especially on Strether's end, are learning what this queerness can be, so the recognition involves the anticipation of a mutual play with roles of erotic pedagogy, that is, the developing together of a vocabulary and style of innuendo, often invoking a moment of puberty, love, badness, goodness, guilt, innocence, or coming out that "occurs," if at all, retroactively or proleptically. The evocations may or may not indicate a "hidden" plot at the level of body acts or dire questions that we understand through the erotics of mutual sensitivity (cries of "oh, oh, oh" or wails, for example). That is, "nice," "good," and "wonderful" are terms of love that can describe at least a way of intimately referring to events and states of being that either have happened, have passed (in time or between people, smoothly, well-lubed, or well-formed), or may presently and later be happening, things that could be of the most trivial or profound import, and if this size were known, then the sublimity might end. These possible moments of mutual feedback keep the erotics oscillating between the obvious and the mysterious.

III. INNOCENCE AND INNUENDO

Says Strether, " 'I began to be young, or at least to get the benefit of it, the moment I saw you at Chester, and that's what has been taking place ever since.' " (199) This passage goes on beautifully to claim, against some other moments in the book, that youth precisely occurs in the agitation and impish juggling of the youth/age distinction, the riddle of coming out or coming of age. One antic this complicates is the innuendo problem, which is that while on the one hand innuendo seems to register the mark of guilt, sin (always projective, "it takes one to know one"),[34] and hence salvation (who is saving whom?—another game of love), on the other hand, innuendo when obvious can be either an innocent error of the speaker's unconscious, which is really the interlocutor's consciousness, or else can be a childish glee in the vulgar, the prurient, which for lack of shame floods the matter in either case with innocence (not to mention the shame of being so innocent, perhaps even amidst feeling these waves or cycles). Who but an innocent would dare be so lewd? Similarly, in classic coming out identification, Strether sees Chad "in a flash, as the young man marked out by women" (95). Moreover, who but a guilty soul would be preoccupied with these irreverences, except a soul so innocent as to make light of the most grave theological quandaries? The facility with which innocent/guilty can be mapped onto both straight/gay and gay/straight merely illustrates for both dualisms a radical epistemological instability. Innuendo and innocence, liminal and contradictory when opposed to straight or mature or guilty or literal, are even more complicated when worked through each other. Are they in the affect, the mood, the style of their enunciations or in the histories of their agents? James stretches innuendo of dialogue and description to the point where it doesn't always make sense to locate an obscene anchor/subtext to an (obscene) surface text.

I will argue that the rough/smooth, smooth/rich, crude/refined, coarse/fine, raw/polished emergences for Strether especially are narrativized interchangeably with the straight/queer, innocent/knowing, guilty/saved, bad/good flirtations.

How does pleasure pass, emerge between our eyes, hands, rears, and mouths? James leaps into the tactile like a painter, as do the verbal artisans of the story. Surfaces of shine and texture are as important as the weight, resistance, softness, and consistency of things we pick, fondle, tread upon, brush, covet, or squeeze.

Key to his vocabulary are terms like "hands," "hang," and "pass," which, even more than "nice," "wonderful," and "kind," condense pleasures that may be phallic with the tactile or anal writ large. Fruit, jewels, genitalia, bodies, criminals (guilty), fire, curiosity, desires, dangle still or swing. The shiny/matte, rough/smooth (polished), and other texture dichotomies saturate the text (which, like innocence and innuendo, or firmness and softness, do not all map onto each other, at the very least since the value hierarchies are reversible or unstable). These descriptions are usually part of the spatial, material pleasure surfaces Strether loves, but they also refer metaphorically to the style of passing of things/feelings/words/etcetera . . . between people or body parts. It is important that there are references not just to relatively static textures but to processes of texturizing or detexturization.[35]

The emergence of tactility usually involves thrills of the manual, the embodiment of touch, "since [Strether's] very gropings would figure among his most interesting motions" (9). The shiny/matte split and its more macroscopic form—the polished/rough or smooth/ornate distinction—occasionally clash with each other as much as they shift with internal friction (with irresistible narrativizations of properties). That is, while the problem of Chad's emergent beauty engages what it means for him to become smooth, even gleaming, (innocence/legibility/immediacy/goodness? guilt/accountability/duplicity/vulgarity/badness?—all nine terms could be reversed and scrambled, it seems), James's topologies, often manual, sometimes fecal,[36] shift between the following:

(A) modes of surface (textural) pleasure/fetishism, where the surface planes come to life or volumes melt, between the second (planar) and third (volumetric) dimensions. (The glint fetishism, where color and dimensionality get playfully eclipsed by the point, by the specter of the light source, is almost beyond topography, at the smooth limit of texture.) This fetishistic site harnesses the textural liminality of TEXTURE, perhaps because TEXXTURE is too violently dependent upon the temporality of touch. TEXTURE, partly visual, partly tactile, thus suspends time more delicately. Both beautifully activate narratives of physical transformation via materials, tools, gestures, characters, and scenes of full theatrical embodiment. However, vision's power to (de)conceal the temporal seems greater than that of touch. Of course, as stated before, the tendency of the two types to suggest each other, as well as the types' conceptual supplementarity, complicates their difference from each other.

(B) pleasures of penetration or expulsion (digits? phalli? feces?), of a play between inside and outside.

(C) more binary modes (a playing-card *hand* embodies the duplicitous secret of a face and back).[37]

Texture, unstable in James through innuendo and metaphor, can move disruptively among (A), (B), and (C). Indeed, the most intense textural moments seem to engage the disruptive dimensional potential of texture, from a hard coarseness to a refined flatness to a fuzziness to a hairiness to a shafting or piercing. These erotic narratives hardly move in one direction, either. They interweave often with the themes of explicit hand/body actions (rubbing, brushing, polishing, plucking), hanging actions/states (suspensions, deferrals), and the touching of bottoms.[38] I will pay some detailed attention to several passages amongst dozens of texture references that seem especially to capture these erotic, spatial narratives and transitions. Their fragmentary exemplarity seems related to the way that sexual, textural, or material distinctions almost always occur with allegorical involutions and cross-references, to frustrate hierarchies of meaning. That is, James's innuendo seems sexually paradoxical or utopically anticipatory in its elaboration of the appeal of attempts to anchor sexuality in any given process, affect, person, or object. The textural language—that is, the material repertoire—almost always crosses between these orders of phenomenon and process, of different types of personal history and material history. Whether materials have a luscious consistency or a forbidding veneer, innuendo expands to include interpersonal transactions. Likewise, act, gesture, word, and deed are loaded with a stylistic history and desire of interacting with matter.

"The ordered English garden, in the freshness of the day, was delightful to Strether, who liked the sound, under his feet, of the tight, fine gravel, packed with the chronic damp, and who had the idlest eye for the deep smoothness of turf and the clean curves of paths." (35) From his feet outward, Strether is interested in the extension of his weight upon resistant materiality, even the slippery liminality of smooth tactility, and the tightness of the gravel surely engages an epidermal, digestive, or muscular erotics of which anality is but a beginning.

The use of "packed," a James term connected to TEXXTURE, is interesting not least because its linkage to queer practice has been made obvious by the (slur?) "fudge packing." Its function of connecting TEXTURE and TEXXTURE by innuendo, in which perhaps a specific smoothness or bristling is causally or structurally related to a firmness or elasticity, might best be demonstrated by the popular toilet-paper commercial that teased, "Don't squeeze the Charmin." This commercial, by showing the softness and sponginess of a dense roll of tissue, exhibited not only that this property would extend to a thin sheet, which might be crumpled or folded when wiping, but also perhaps that the very surface of the tissue was soft, as the fetish type of liminal roughness, the disintegrating, dusty, surface that yields to the touch. Of course, for many tissue brands, the excessive softness within is indicated on the package by the joyful visages of women and babies, pampered innocently.

"And she sat there rubbing her polished hands and making the best of it" (254). Here the autoerotics of rubbing seem to have created the effect of shininess, or perhaps the shiny smoothness creates the autoerotic impulse. Another fascinating chicken-and-egg erotic, where the hardness of resistance that allows materials to be polished is combined with a more spongy resilience that allows for rubbing.

"[B]ut of what service was it to find himself making out after a moment that the quality 'sprung,' the quality produced by measure and balance, the fine relation of part to part and space to space, was probably— aided by the presence of ornament as positive as it was discreet, and by the complexion of the stone, cold, fair gray, warmed and polished a little by life—neither more nor less than a case of distinction, such a case as he could only feel, unexpectedly, as a sort of delivered challenge?" (69). Interestingly, the age of the stone suggests tender polishing processes, and the challenge seems cryptically sexual. The activation of curiosity involves not only a story of the emergence of smooth, refined beauty, but of what to do with such maturity and distinctions, which might be touched or entered. That the quality has "sprung" evokes the metaphor of matter's elasticity, the constitutive, defining qualities of bouncy rubber or a metal spring. Elasticity as a ubiquitous quality of the world could be seen as one of many textural axes present, like temperature, in varying degrees. This axis can be complex, because many types of force in the world are compressed or stretched "inside" materials that resemble predators frozen in anticipation or batteries that have accumulated energy. How and when reification took place, how and when that process was in turn lost or stored, can uncover quite heterogeneous fantasies, what I have also been calling textural narratives. The fetish as practice or fantasy disavows these temporal narratives but also thereby makes possible the dialectic of suspension and action, harnessing and releasing.

"Chad was brown and thick and strong; and, of old, Chad had been rough. Was all the difference therefore that he was actually smooth? Possibly; for that he was smooth was as marked as in the taste of a sauce or in the rub of a hand. The effect of it was general—it had retouched his features, drawn them with a cleaner line. It had cleared his eyes and settled his colour and polished his fine square teeth—the main ornament of his face; and at the same time that it had given him a form and a surface, almost a design, it had toned his voice; established his accent, encouraged his smile to more play and his other motions to less. . . . It was as if he had really been put into a firm mould and turned successfully out . . . marked enough to be touched by a finger" (97). This powerful narrative speculation on the textural and other physical transformations of a person blends stories of polishing with an urge to reenact those processes, through sculpture, painting, casting, massaging, buffing, and then some. Perhaps the physical homoerotics and the transformation/coming out/pubescence/tumescence myths generated around and by Chad (anticipated and reverberated through an entire texture plot of mystical, lustrous, or tactile surfaces begging to be fetishized if not touched, picked, handled, squeezed, packed, engulfed, or entered) are a chicken-and-egg problem of desire and knowledge; surely they modify each other—but which came out first is moot.

"Gloriani showed him . . . a fine, worn, handsome face. . . . Strether had seen in museums . . . the work of his hand. . . . He was to see again repeatedly, in remembrance, the medal-like Italian face, in which every line was an artist's own" (120). It's not clear whether the face Strether will see again will be of Gloriani's work, or Gloriani himself. Strether's object of appreciation seems to have an autoerotic luster, that is, his appearance seems to have been a product of the same (manual) genius he uses to produce beautiful art. Gloriani is loved from a distance, unlike Chad, perhaps not only because of this illusion of self-fashioning, but also because Strether did not witness the radical shift of his emergence from youth, his transformation from "rough" to "smooth," "straight" to "queer."

"[T]he affair of life . . . couldn't, no doubt, have been different for me; for it's at the best, a tin mould, either fluted or embossed, with ornamental excrescences, or else smooth and dreadfully plain, into which, a helpless jelly, one's consciousness is poured—so that one "takes" the form, as the great cook says, and is more or less compactly held by it" (132). The long earnest speech that Strether gives to little Bilham turns out to be a "contradiction of the innocent gaiety which the speaker had wished to promote" (132). Because Strether's notion of youth disavows his own youth unironically, there is an impatience or unflirtatiousness about his speech. That he wanted to promote "innocent gaiety," seems to be in fact the exact reason it fails. On the metaphorical level, he names the possibility that his own personality texture might be smooth or ornamented on the surface, that he in consistency might be like a jelly. Somewhat facetiously, perhaps, he gives himself textural richness, but the texture is presented as homogeneous, and he is presented as helpless, undynamic.

This passage could be read initially as a celebration of his own masochism, a dramatic enactment of his desire to be "held" (132). But something goes wrong, and it is unclear whether his sadness keeps him from chatting pleasantly with Bilham or whether he in fact needed to be read, needed too badly to have his own desire read. Oddly, this may be the only time an ethic of immediate benevolence seizes Strether, in that he tried to articulate that he wanted Bilham to feel excitement.

For the reader, what seems marked is that we are made aware not only of how little choreography of gesture, manner, and demeanor we are given to interpret the moods of the character, but also that our pleasure depends on a certain fetishistic suspension. In other words, the sadness and failure of an explicit attempt to promote joy only teach us that the joy in the novel lies in a silence about the darker moods. Character depth, descriptions of their affect, would teach us in a sense how to empathize, but James, to the extent that he mirrors the main characters, is not interested in ending the quest of empathetic curiosities. One might say that there is an intense enjoyment in circulating complicated privacies, a smooth style of care that falters if it describes itself too successfully.

By presenting an affective failure, an epistemological and textural failure, it paints an outside, a supplement to the successful conversations and affect transmissions around it. *It quasi-retroactively, through dialectic logic, lends visibility and pleasure to James's codes of texture, affect transition, and topology (the three aforementioned structural trinities) and thereby participates in them.* Lest it seem monolithic in this capacity, one can even detect within it subtle successes of paradoxical pleasure, of the quivering in a jelly, perhaps, or by its invocation of themes of innocence, its dramatization of the mutually defining sentiments of too-lateness and age, an involuted allegory of the distinctions against which it, at first, seems to stand.

"In the very act of arranging with her for his independence he had, under pressure from a particular perception, inconsistently, quite stupidly, committed himself, and with her subtlety sensitive on the spot to an advantage, she had driven in by a single word a little golden nail, the sharp intention of which he signally felt" (164). Here, the moment after Mme de Vionnet has ordered/requested him to stay away from her daughter, Strether finds the hard, shiny surface of the fetish transformed into a piercing violence. The liminal immateriality of the light ray, or gaze, becomes condensed with a small nail whose smooth surface bore its fetishistic quality. This rupture, exciting for its bodily imagery as well as its elucidation of textural transformation, will continue when Mme de Vionnet encourages Strether to see Chad and "[t]he golden nail she had then driven in pierced a good inch deeper" (183). In other words, it both literalizes the fetish's pinpoint violence and describes the emergence of S/M affects from vanilla sensibilities. More specifically, one might use Deleuze to argue that Strether's fetishism is masochistic, because it imagines a sadistic, attentive other but in fact, the masochist needs the suspended, ideal other rather than an actual sadist. By this reading, Strether's pleasure takes imaginative liberties when interpreting his friends' behavior.

"They ain't fierce, either of 'em; they let you come quite close. They wear their fur the smooth side out—the warm side in" (217). The metaphoric logic describing Mrs. Newsome and Sarah here is extremely convoluted. The textural challenge seems to involve how exactly one understands Strether's logical linking of their non-fierceness and their wearing their fur inside out. Perhaps if their fur were worn outside-out, it would signify (1) animal (sexual) sociality; (2) fierceness implicit in the fetish object (though smoothness is fetishized as well); (3) bristling fur, which expresses hostility; (4) the fur, the "warm" side, having a threatening, penetrative, porcupine type of texture. All four seem possible, even causally intertwined, and that the women in fact seem friendly or intimate enough to let one come "quite close," might be linked to an involuted, dramatic interiority. They as fetishes are seen as mirroring the fetish, for their relationship to themselves seems masturbatory or masochistic. In any case, the dialectics of smooth/rough or TEXTURE/TEXXTURE are made legible, because for Strether, a fetishist, one always implies the other.

> It was all he needed that she liked him enough for what they were doing, and even should they do a good deal more would still like him enough for that; the essential freshness of a relation so simple was a cool bath to the soreness produced by other relations. These others appeared to him now horribly complex; they bristled with fine points, points all unimaginable beforehand, points that pricked and drew blood; a fact that gave to an hour with his present friend on a *bateau-mouche*, or in the afternoon shade of the Champs Elysées, something of the innocent pleasure of handling rounded ivory. His relation with Chad personally—from the moment he had got his point of view—had been of the simplest; yet this also struck him as bristling." (328)

If there is indeed a texture plot might this be the climax? The transformations from smooth ivory to the soft, hairy to the rough, aroused, hairy animate the surface caresses into micropenetrations perhaps of some masochistic pleasure. In a sense, the violence behind fetishism's tactile, textural, material liminality becomes materialized. Another way to put this is that the supplement, but also supplemental (dialectic) logic in general, becomes strikingly legible here. It is crucial that the simple is also the bristling, and that both are desirable.

WRAP UP

I have tried to show that the fascination with texture, especially on Strether's part, and a fascination with youth/maturity are linked, circulated by many characters to play with narratives that almost always bluntly or perhaps subtly refer to the issue of "coming out," of finding love.[39] The problem of fetishism enjoys the riddles of liminal states like the smooth, shiny mirror, as well as the urges around how people, objects, or materials became that way. Textural narratives are interesting in that how one *feels* matter seems to invite comparisons with how one's own or someone else's matter can be shaped. Does one want to be a part of these erotics of transformation, and be transformed oneself, as Strether becomes something like Chad, wonderfully queerer than ever, as riddles of passing pass well-lubed, smooth, good forms sometimes from one character to another like gossip, generating a playful scandalousness? The dichotomies surrounding innocence, goodness, etcetera are perpetuated by analogous smooth, shiny dichotomies, which suggest pleasurable fantasies of their production and consumption processes. Of course, the pleasures are in supplemental relation to pains, physical or emotional, which are largely a spectral, even erotic, presence in the text. The shifts of texture, whether in materials or conversation, not only become linked to states of grace and affect of the characters, but also to different spatial or bodily erotics. Even in these hyper-innuendos, are there desires that are withheld? This question invokes the problem of whether fetishism itself is to be seen as good or bad, whether visual fascination with tactile intensities should lead one to get off voyeuristically or to grope, reach out a hand, and touch bottom. I think of Strether's fascination with Miss Gostrey's red velvet collar, for example. Of course, in James we are never given literal body contact beyond hands massaging themselves or reaching out to rest on friends. Unless, that is, we take the outbursts and innuendos of dialogue, reflection, and vision to be not innuendos at all but the most touching of glimmers.

APPENDIX[40]

In the etymologies of texture and threshold one finds common roots. The anecdotal histories of texturizing and detexturizing processes described here link the transformational processes of texture with the more static and spatial notion of the threshold.

tex•ture (t𝜇ks"ch...r) *n*. 1. A structure of interwoven fibers or other elements. 2. The basic structure or composition, especially of something complex or fine: *the orderly texture of matter as seen through an electron microscope.* **3.a.** The appearance and feel of a surface: *the smooth texture of soap; the rough texture of plowed fields.* **b.** A rough or grainy surface quality: *Brick walls give a room texture.* **4.** Distinctive or identifying character or characteristics: *"the haunting contours and textures of the physical world"* (Joyce Carol Oates). —**tex•ture** *tr.v.* **tex•tured, tex•tur•ing, tex•tures.** To give texture to, especially to impart desirable surface characteristics to: *texture a printing plate by lining and stippling it.* [Middle English, from Old French, from Latin *text₂ra,* from *textus,* past participle of *texere,* to weave. See TEXT.] —**tex"tur•al** *adj.* —**tex"tur•al•ly** *adv.* —**tex"tured** *adj.*

li•men (lⁿ"m...n) *n., pl.* **li•mens** or **lim•i•na** (l¹m"...-n...). The threshold of a physiological or psychological response. [Latin, threshold.] —**lim"i•nal** (l¹m"...-n...-l) *adj.*

thresh•old (thrμsh"/ₑld", -h¹/ₑld") *n.* **1.** A piece of wood or stone placed beneath a door; a doorsill. **2.** An entrance or a doorway. **3.** The place or point of beginning; the outset. **4.** A point separating conditions that will produce a given effect from conditions of a higher or lower degree that will not produce the effect, as the intensity below which a stimulus is of sufficient strength to produce sensation or elicit a response: *a low threshold of pain.* [Middle English *thresshold,* from Old English *therscold, threscold.* See ter...-¹ below.]

WORD HISTORY: Perhaps the tradition of carrying the bride over the threshold is dying out, but knowledge of the custom persists, leading one to wonder about the *-hold* or the *thresh-* in the word *threshold.* Scholars are still wondering about the last part of the word, but the *thresh-* can be explained. It is related to the word *thresh,* which refers to an agricultural process. This process of beating the stems and husks of grain or cereal plants to separate the grain or seeds from the straw was at one time done with the feet of oxen or human beings. Thus, the Germanic word *·therskan,* or by the switching of sounds called metathesis, *·threskan,* meant "thresh" and "tread." This association with the feet is probably retained in Old English *therscold* or *threscold* (Modern English *threshold*), "sill of a door (over which one treads)."

ter...-¹. Important derivatives are: *trite, detriment, thrash, thresh, threshold, turn, contour, return, drill¹, throw, thread, trauma, truant.* **ter...-¹.** To rub, turn; with some derivatives referring to twisting, boring, drilling, and piercing; and others referring to the rubbing of cereal grain to remove the husks, and thence to the process of threshing either by the trampling of oxen or by flailing with flails. Variant **tr¶-,* contracted from **tre...-.* I. Full-grade form **ter(...)-.* **1.a.** TRITE, TRITURATE; ATTRITION, CONTRITE, DETRIMENT, from Latin *terere* (past participle *trᵒtus*), to rub away, thresh, tread, wear out; **b.** TEREDO, from Greek *ter¶dⁱ/ₐn,* a kind of biting worm. **2.** Suffixed form **ter-et-.* TERETE, from Latin *teres* (stem *teret-*), rounded, smooth. **3.** Suffixed form **ter-sko-.* **a.** (THRASH), THRESH, from Old English *therscan,* to thresh; **b.** THRESHOLD, from Old English *therscold, threscold,* sill of a door (over which one treads; second element obscure). Both **a** and **b** from Germanic **therskan, *threskan,* to thresh, tread. II. O-grade form **tor(...)-.* **1.** TOREUTICS, from Greek *toreus,* a boring tool. **2.** Suffixed form **tor(...)-mo-,* hold. DERMA², from Old High German *darm,* gut, from Germanic **tharma-.* **3.** Suffixed form **tor(...)-no-.* TURN; (ATTORN), CONTOUR, (DETOUR), (RETURN), from Greek *tornos,* tool for drawing a circle, circle, lathe. III. Zero-grade form **tr-.* DRILL¹, from Middle Dutch *drillen,* to drill, from Germanic **thr-.* IV. Variant form **tr¶-* (< **tre...-*). **1.** THROW, from Old English *thr³wan,* to turn, twist, from Germanic **thr¶w-.* **2.** Suffixed form **tr¶-tu-.* THREAD, from Old English *thrÆd,* thread, from Germanic **thr¶du-,* twisted yarn. **3.** Suffixed form **tr¶-mŏ* (< **tre...-* or **t—...-*). MONOTREME, TREMATODE, from Greek *tr¶ma,* perforation. **4.** Suffixed form **tr¶-ti-* (< **tre...-* or **t—...-*). ATRESIA, from Greek *tr¶sis,* perforation. V. Extended form **trᵒ-.* (< **tri...-*). **1.** Probably suffixed form **trᵒ-ⁱ/ₐn-.* SEPTENTRION, from Latin *triⁱ/₂,* plow ox. **2.** Suffixed form **trᵒ-* dhlo-. TRIBULATION, from Latin *trᵒbulum,* a threshing sledge.

VI. Various extended forms. **1.** Forms *tr½-*, *trau-*. TRAUMA, from Greek TRAUMA, hurt, wound. **2.** Form *tr⁰b-*. DIATRIBE, TRIBOELECTRICITY, TRIBOLOGY, TRYPSIN, from Greek *tribein*, to rub, thresh, pound, wear out. **3.** Form *tr½g-*, *trag-*. **a.** TROGON, TROUT, from Greek *tr½gein*, to gnaw; **b.** DREDGE², from Greek *trag¶ma*, sweetmeat. **4.** Form *trup-*. TREPAN¹; TRYPANOSOME, from Greek *trup¶*, hole. **5.** Possible form *tr̥g-*. TRUANT, from Old French *truant*, beggar. [Pokorny 3. *ter-* 1071.]

NOTES

Thanks to Hank Okazaki for support and editorial advice. Fredric Jameson, Barbara Herrnstein Smith, and Gus Stadler also deserve thanks for critical input and James appreciation.

1 Henry James, *The Ambassadors* (New York: W. W. Norton, 1994), p. 97. Further citations to this work will be incorporated in the text.

2 Whether testament to the power of a universal "Chad"-ness or a glaringly unacknowledged citation of this James passage, on an episode of the television sitcom, *Friends*, a female character (twenty-seven years old) unwittingly has sex with a virgin man who turns out to be younger than he had said (seventeen instead of twenty-two). When she voices her shame to a friend, she describes herself as a prowling temptress, and says she should go out with a "shiny guy named Chad." Part of her ironic amusement toward the age issue lies in the intrigue about who has seduced or corrupted whom, whether agency has occurred, and whether, how, or when taste rules have been violated, all highly playful questions for James and perhaps Chad.

3 In Marxist language, one would offer that fetishes pose intriguing problems for the distinction between production and consumption. Supposedly, the capitalist production process's erasure is matched by a fascination in the commodity where consumption, its purchase, implicates scopophilic, spiritual, or even nurturing/care urges as well. Especially, as Guy Debord and Fredric Jameson argue, in a society of the spectacle where it is difficult to differentiate an object from its image, the commodity fetish has even more mystical production and consumption fantasmatics, although one would not be surprised to find residues of the earlier commodity, where labor was utopically represented as a manual process, so that consumption might utopically involve holding, possessing an object. One might argue that each stage of capitalism has not only a different production model, but different fantasies of what production is, what labor is, and what consumption is.

4 Michael Moon, in "A Small Boy and Others: Sexual Disorientation in Henry James, Kenneth Anger, and David Lynch," in *Comparative American Identities*, ed. Hortense Spillers (New York: Routledge, 1991), pp. 141–56, articulates how material fetishes such as velvet are linked to disorienting, mimetic desire, most explicitly through initiation rituals.

5 Eve Kosofsky Sedgwick explains these threads in James's life/writing in "Inside Henry James: Toward a Lexicon for *The Art of the Novel*," *Negotiating Lesbian and Gay Subjects*, ed. Monika Dorenkamp and Richard Henke (New York: Routledge, 1995), "Queer Performativity: Henry James's *The Art of the Novel*," *GLQ* 1, no. 1 (summer 1993): 1–16; and *Tendencies* (Durham: Duke University Press, 1993), pp. 73–103.

6 Slavoj Žižek's *Looking Awry* (Cambridge, Mass.: MIT Press, 1991) explains this notion quite lucidly.

7 Eve Kosofsky Sedgwick, *Epistemology of the Closet* (Berkeley: University of California Press, 1990).

8   The alternative spatial model of the fetish could be not the phallus but a more complex one, vaginal or anal, suggested by Luce Irigaray in *This Sex Which Is Not One*, trans. Catherine Porter with Carolyn Burke (Ithaca: Cornell University Press, 1985) and in *Speculum of the Other Woman*, trans. Gillian C. Gill (Ithaca: Cornell University Press, 1985). These works argue not just against the phallic bias of genitalia in psychoanalysis, but against this male metaphor's prevalence in much philosophy or ideology in general. The phallic model also prefers the usage of solid instead of liquid metaphors.

9   Anne McClintock, *Imperial Leather* (New York: Routledge, 1995), pp. 181–232.

10 Conversation, Durham, N.C., Feb. 12, 1996.

11 Roland Barthes, "The Reality Effect," trans. R. Carter, in *French Literary Theory Today: A Reader*, ed. Tzvetan Todorov (Cambridge: Cambridge University Press, 1982), pp. 11–17.

12 Naomi Schor, *Reading in Detail* (New York: Routledge, 1987).

13 Marshall Berman, *All That Is Solid Melts into Air* (London: Verso, 1983).

14 For the relation between "texture," "liminality," and "threshold," see the appendix.

15 I use a Derridean term here, borrowed first from Jean-Jacques Rousseau (and other terms of Derrida's may have suited equally well) for reasons that will be repeated throughout this paper.

16 Sedgwick's *Epistemology of the Closet* has identified and analyzed this shifting framework.

17 Jean-Paul Sartre, *Being And Nothingness*, trans. Hazel Barnes (New York: Pocket Books, 1956), p. 506.

18 Ibid., p. 509.

19 In terms of reproduction/representation, texture may be what is lost, a radical real, for in much poststructural thought the attention to the geometry of binaries yields ornate, logical patterns, a kind of digitality. I will later argue that fetishism's link with texture is akin to chaos theory's interest in partial, nonintegral dimensions (0, $\frac{1}{2}$, $1\frac{3}{4}$, etc.), as texture has a similarity to what systems theory calls "noise."

20 See Gilles Deleuze's *The Fold*, trans. Tom Conley (Minneapolis: University of Minnesota Press, 1993) and James Gleick's *Chaos: Making a New Science* (New York: Viking, 1987) for limits in this vein.

21 See Deleuze, *The Fold*, or Derrida's work for relatively ontological approaches to these pleasures. The numerous comic euphemisms for male masturbation often invoke (de)texturizing processes.

22 The meaning of this "within" is complex, as the types are often in supplemental, differential relation to each other in the Derridean sense.

23 Judith Butler, *Gender Trouble* (New York: Routledge, 1990).

24 See Michael Taussig, "*Maleficium*: State Fetishism," in *Fetishism as Cultural Discourse*, ed. Emily Apter and William Pietz (Ithaca: Cornell University Press, 1993), pp. 217–47. Rosalind Krauss in *The Optical Unconscious* (Cambridge, Mass.: The MIT Press, 1993), p. 165, and Linda Williams in *Hard Core: Power, Pleasure, and the 'Frenzy of the Visible'* (Berkeley: University of California Press, 1989), p. 101, have also noticed this thread.

25 Fredric Jameson, *Postmodernism, or, The Cultural Logic of Late Capitalism* (Durham: Duke University Press, 1991), pp. x, 9, 4.

26 McClintock, *Imperial Leather*, pp. 152–232.

27 See Richard Dyer, *The Matter of Images*, (New York: Routledge, 1993), p. 57; Kobena Mercer, *Welcome to the Jungle*, (London: Routledge, 1994), pp. 183–84.

28 Mercer, *Welcome to the Jungle*, p. 184.

29 Roland Barthes, *Mythologies*, trans. Annette Lavers (New York: Noonday Press, 1972), p. 85.

126   *Renu Bora*

30 Gilles Deleuze and Félix Guattari, *A Thousand Plateaus: Capitalism and Schizophrenia,* trans. Brian Massumi (Minneapolis: University of Minnesota, 1987), p. 488.

31 Ibid., p. 479.

32 Kant's moral law of the categorical imperative seems to depend on the way this goodness, unlike evil, or lying, could circulate endlessly to stabilize social relations.

33 In *Gender Trouble* and *Bodies That Matter: On the Discursive Limits of "Sex"* (New York: Routledge, 1993), Judith Butler analyzes the ideologies of identity in performance and performativity through a broad array of theoretical discourses that touch on sexuality.

34 Sedgwick, *Epistemology of the Closet,* p. 100.

35 In the spirit of the empirical, I will list here the page numbers on which James explicitly invokes texture: pp. 1, 3, 4, 5, 11, 13, 14, 20, 21, 35, 37, 39, 54, 59, 61, 63, 64, 69, 71, 80, 83, 84, 87, 89, 94, 97, 101, 103, 111, 119, 120, 130, 132, 133, 134, 138, 141, 145, 147, 154, 158, 160, 163, 164, 165, 166, 175, 178, 183, 186, 187, 191, 206, 254, 256, 261, 269, 272, 276, 285, 287, 290, 304, 307, 310, 319, 328, 329, 335, 342, 345.

36 For example, Miss Gostrey's brown room flecked with gold (p. 80)—again the glimmer of extreme value in extreme sludge links the two materials, divine and mundane.

37 Sedgwick, in *GLQ* and in *Tendencies,* identifies the latter two topographies.

38 Sedgwick's discussion of the hand puppet metaphor is vital. See Sedgwick, *Tendencies,* p. 101. For the relationship between fetishism, suspension, and masochism, see Gilles Deleuze, "Coldness and Cruelty," *Masochism,* trans. Jean McNeil (New York: Zone Books, 1988), pp. 31–35.

39 "Coming out" in James occurs at least on pp. 9, 118, 376.

40 Taken from the *American Heritage Dictionary,* Third Edition, v. 3.0 WordStar International Inc.

Tyler Curtain

The "Sinister Fruitiness" of Machines:

Neuromancer, Internet Sexuality, and

the Turing Test

I.

"Yeah. I saw your profile, Case. . . . You ever work with the dead?"
—William Gibson, *Neuromancer*[1]

T he immediate subject of this essay is a set of anxious, confusing, and at times threatening questions posed by computer-mediated communication technology, popularly known as "cyberspace" and most immediately recognizable in the Internet. It also takes as its subject a related set of perhaps more abstract questions about the possibilities of intelligence within our computers. I have chosen to analyze in this essay three moments within the culture of artificial intelligence and the development of cyberspace, moments that might be classified as either "fiction" or "real life" (inasmuch as those categories hold steady under the optic of the narratives and textual spaces they share) but that symptomatize how we come to know "intelligence" by the anxiety, confusion, and threat underlying those questions. Some would argue that computers cannot be intelligent; they're not alive. But granted that computers aren't in any readily recognizable sense alive, might we imagine that they could be cognizant? conscious? sentient?

The metrics by which we measure intelligence are closer to our experience than we might think: we are already used to dealing with digital, intelligent life in the form of digital representations of other humans. A good number of us set our biological clocks by when we are able to log in and when we can read our E-mail. We are used to narrativizing our lives, our selves, for our on-line friends, many of whom we've never met; it's a small step to asking how we know that our correspondents are cognizant, conscious, aware, "real." How do we know that they're intelligent? How do we know, by what heuristics do we discover, that our correspondents are sentient? By what standard of measurement could we gauge, in this age of the "intelligent" machine, that our interlocutors are, in a word, "human"?

These questions, and the measures by which we answer the questions, are implicit, and at times, explicit, in the work of William Gibson, from the early short story, "The Gernsback Continuum," to the *Cyberspace* trilogy, *Neuromancer, Count Zero,* and *Mona Lisa Overdrive.* The plot of *Neuromancer* is roughly as follows: Case, a twenty-four-year-old former cyberspace cowboy, worked as a "thief, [who] worked for other, wealthier thieves, employers who provided the exotic software required to penetrate the bright walls of corporate systems, opening windows into rich fields of data" (5). Case has been nerve-damaged by employers he stole from, rendering him unable to jack into cyberspace. He is recruited and healed by a man named Corto, who wants him to steal a digital copy of Case's now-dead cowboy teacher, McCoy Pauley, and with Pauley's help, break into the Tessier-Ashpool's corporate/family computer matrix. Corto, who was formerly a military officer named Armitage, is controlled by an Artificial Intelligence (AI) named Wintermute. Wintermute wants to merge with his other half, an AI represented in Tessier-Ashpool's systems as a young, beautiful boy, Neuromancer. Case, his bodyguard Molly, the sexual psychopath Peter Riviera, and Armitage/Corto eventually succeed in releasing Wintermute and Neuromancer from the hardwired constraints that keep them from melding and evolving into a higher form of sentience and intelligence.

The characters of Gibson's *Neuromancer*—Wintermute, Neuromancer, McCoy Pauley, Case, the Finn, and from later books, Bobby, Colin, Angie, and eventually the matrix itself, when it comes to know itself—are all entities who live to one degree or another in the machine, in cyberspace, or to use Gibson's formulation, in the matrix of human knowledge "from the banks of every computer in the human system" (51). They are all, to put into play another of his frequently used words, "personalities." Most are reproductions, digital representations (or manifestations), textual narrations of someone who was already alive, already human, and in that sense, already someone who thinks.

But could *digital constructs* be sentient? And if we[2] are going to live in cyberspace—perhaps not Gibson's cyberspace, but *a* cyberspace—how do we know that the digital representations we encounter, the electronic text that scrolls across our screen, are human-produced and not "simply" program-produced; and if the output of programs, intelligent programs, not just ghosts in the machine? How do we know that Artificial Intelligences (AIS) are, as the name designates, intelligent? And, to follow the question outward to the framing context that makes it intelligible, how do we know that *we* are personalities, that we are sentient? Characters such as McCoy Pauley, a "ROM personality matrix" who exists as a construct of a human within a computer in Gibson's most widely read novel, *Neuromancer*, figure the uneasy perception that there is no boundary between our selves and our encompassing computing environments; that we are, though sentient, "merely" machines. That they are, though machines, sentient.

For instance, Pauley, known by the characters in Gibson's "Sprawl" novels as the "Flatliner" for surviving "braindeath behind [the] black ice" defenses of an AI that he was buzzing in Rio, comes back after his physical death (by heart attack) as a "recording" on a cassette (50). More often than not the novel denies that these digital copies of people, ghosts in the machines, are real like we're real. Or rather, the narrative denies that they are cognitive like we are cognitive. How do we deal with the dead in our machines? *Neuromancer* equivocally decides that representations of people, "a hardwired ROM cassette replicating a dead man's skills, obsessions, knee-jerk responses" (76–79), is not sentient, not quite human, not quite the ghost that it seems to be. The Flatliner compares himself to another type of entity, however, that is sentient, analogous to the ways humans are sentient: Artificial Intelligences. When Case, the protagonist of *Neuromancer*, asks Pauley what possible motive the AI Wintermute could have for carrying out the detailed plot that drives the novel, the program answers that he can't answer. There is no motive.

> "Motive," the construct said. "Real motive problem, with an AI. Not human, see?"
> "Well, yeah, obviously."
> "Nope. I mean, it's not human. And you can't get a handle on it. Me, I'm not human either, but I *respond* like one. See?"
> "Wait a sec," Case said. "Are you sentient, or not?"
> "Well, it *feels* like I am, kid, but I'm really just a bunch of ROM. It's one of them, ah, philosophical questions, I guess . . ." The ugly laughter sensation rattled down Case's spine. "But I ain't likely to write you no poem, if you follow me. Your AI, it just might. But it ain't no way *human*." (131; emphasis in original)

Pauley's inhuman laugh, or rather "ugly laughter sensation," signals his inhuman state. Human, by the construct's figuration, is to have a psychology that is directed in some determinate, intentional, teleological sense. It's to have a discernible "motive," a tendency to move to action and a source for that action, which allows others to "get a handle on it." But Pauley also claims that he is "human" in just this directed way, in contrast to the AI: he *responds* like a human. *Neuromancer* makes much out of the science of predicting human response. Psychology and psychological profiles are presented again and again as the way the matrix knows what Case, Molly, and the rest of the cast of human and once-human characters will do. The other word besides "personality" that marks this particular definition of psychology and intelligence is "profile." A profile is a "detailed model" of a subject's psychology (28–29). Case, for example, is the personification of a "case": "You're suicidal, Case. The model gives you a month on the outside'" (29), claims Armitage/Corto when they first meet. Molly herself wonders aloud to Case, "It's like I know you. That profile he's got. I know how you're wired" (30). She also points out, "I saw your profile, Case" (49), leveraging her knowledge of his psychology and motivation against his own self-knowledge. Introducing Peter Riviera she even shudders, "'. . . one certified psychopath name of Peter Riviera. Real ugly customer . . . he's one sick fuck, no lie. I saw his profile.' She made a face. 'Godawful'" (51).

From one vantage, then, Pauley the ROM personality matrix is only motivation, all profile, the ultimate "case": he's a program that is algorithmic in his response to the world and its stimuli. He claims that what ultimately marks him as not human (ironically, ontologically, bearing out W. K. Wimsatt Jr.'s claim about the intentional fallacy, Pauley being all intention) is the likelihood that he wouldn't write poetry. AIS, on the other hand, are likely to be creative with culture; they have tendencies to be demonstrative, to articulate expression and action outside of predicted paths; they're likely to write poetry. "Your AI, it just might," even if the Flatliner wouldn't; or rather, Pauley *can't* move or gesture outside the psychological boundaries of his own read-only memory. Case, however, if not quite "poetic" is paradigmatically human throughout the novel, and goes outside his own psychological profile in just this creative, novelistic way. When Case trips every security alarm on the pleasure resort Freeside to find Molly despite orders to leave her alone, Wintermute complains, "I didn't think you'd do that, man. It's outside the profile" (144). And "'You guys [meaning the humans Molly and Case],' the Finn said, 'you're a pain. The Flatline here, if you were all like him, it would be real simple. He's a construct, just a buncha ROM, so he always does what I expect him to'" (205). *Poetry*, therefore, delineates a lacuna or inconsistency within Pauley's own theory of psychology and agency against the notion of profile as human: "poetry" signals the inability of someone to plot the profile, to map the source of action, to grasp the motivation; ironically, poetry is a sure index to the likelihood of the perversion of a psychological trajectory. AIS present a "Real motive problem."[3] As a sign of their profile and lack of a profile, AIS are apt to write poetry.

The nature of the AI's self, then, is a vexed question. Out of the gaps that define and distinguish a profile emerges the anxious, even threatening question, How does one designate a coherent self and *recognize it as a self*? Wintermute explains this particular problem of the first person: "I, insofar as I *have* an 'I'—this gets rather metaphysical you see— I am the one who arranges things for Armitage. Or Corto, who, by the way, is quite unstable." (120). The novel makes it clear that AI-selves control people and events. They influence subtly, but deftly and determinately, technological development (for example, the production of ICE), personal psychologies (3Jane, Armitage/Corto are just two of the many engineered personalities), and even cultural events (the most spectacular being raid by the Panther Moderns). They "arrange" things. Thus, they might be said to have a "profile." But Armitage/Corto's psychological instability immediately juxtaposed to Wintermute's Elders of Zion–like, patois "I'an'I" first-person pronoun (109) suggests the fragmented contours of the metaphysical niceties that Wintermute dodges above.

Even within the fragmentation and instability, there is a core stability of self. Wintermute, displaced into the figure of smuggler Julius Deane, sketches out Corto's psychosis, then adds, "'He's not quite a personality.' Deane smiled. 'But I'm sure you're aware of that. But Corto is in there, somewhere, and I can no longer maintain that delicate balance. He's going to come apart on you, Case'" (121). Mirroring and refracting Wintermute's own persona, Armitage's name evokes an *armature* (however unstable) around Corto, an "organ or structure for offense or defense" as well as the "framework used by a sculptor to support a figure being modeled in plastic material" (as defined by *Webster's Dictionary*). Armitage does come apart; he reverts to the ranting paranoiac Corto. The only stability he maintains across that devolution is his *gender* identity. In just this way, Wintermute, though not human, appears in many forms to Case. The novel intimates that the AI who attempts to communicate with or control a human finds stability of identity not in the particular bodies it inhabits but in the gender of those bodies: Julius Deane, Lonny Zone, the Finn.[4]

Each of these factors (profiles, poetry, gender) come into play when Case and the Flatliner attempt to trace the connections among Wintermute's intelligence and motivation, and the constraints placed on their evolutionary development. Case comments

> "You were right, Dix. There's some kind of manual override on the hardwiring that keeps Wintermute under control. However much he *is* under control," he added.
> "He," the construct said. "He. Watch that. It. I keep telling you."
> (181; emphasis in original)

Here Case only speaks what he already knows about Wintermute; but the Flatliner resists engendering the AI in an attempt to disarticulate the sense of "personhood" *conferred* by gender from an entity that already *confirms* its self through gender. Pauley, then, verifies that whatever the metaphysical sense of an "I" having an "I," "I" always has a gender.

That Julius Deane first speaks this formulation of gender, knowledge, and self as an embodiment of the AI/split masculine subject is significant: the person of Deane is a figure not only of knowledge but "knowingness"; he embodies the tense relations between paranoia and power; he repeatedly shows up in Case's dreams as Case returns to the defining scene of his problematic relation to AI (125); and he becomes the only object against which Case stages a successful act of violence. Perhaps not surprisingly Deane is a queer figure, indeed a gay one.

Julius Deane, otherwise known to Case by the androgynous moniker "Julie," is a 135-year-old vanity queen who spends "a weekly fortune in serums and hormones" as a "hedge against aging" (12). Uncannily reminiscent of another famous knowing, controlling, and problematically masculine character, Lionel Croy—the father of both Kate Croy and her vanity in Henry James's *Wings of the Dove*, with his "perfect look," "all pink and silver as to skin and hair," always interested in his appearance, "How he does dress!"[5]—Deane is to Case's eyes "Sexless and inhumanly patient, his primary gratification seemed to lie in his devotion to esoteric forms of tailor-worship. Case had never seen him wear the same suit twice. . . . He affected prescription lenses, framed in spidery gold, ground from thin slabs of pink synthetic quartz and beveled like mirrors in a Victorian dollhouse" (12). Topping off this over-the-top self-presentation, Deane's office is decorated "with a random collection of European furniture," "Neo-Aztec bookcases," with a camp flair for "Disney-styled table lamps perched awkwardly on a low Kandinsky-look coffee table in scarlet-lacquered steel" (12).

From the beginning of the novel, Deane prefigures Case's problematic relationship to cyberspace and AIs through his own "manipulative" masculinity. As we've already seen, the AI Wintermute uses Deane as his persona to explain his ability to construct and manipulate events: he admits, for one, that he built and controls Armitage/Corto. Case first sees Armitage in a "dark robe [that] was open to the waist, the broad chest hairless and muscular, the stomach flat and hard. Blue eyes so pale they made Case think of bleach" (27). Armitage comes equipped with "broad shoulders and military posture," a "Special Forces earring," and "handsome, inexpressive features" that offer "the routine beauty of the cosmetic boutiques, a conservative amalgam of the past decade's leading media faces" (45). A stock figure of both '80s gay porn, military recruiting posters, and "straight" bodybuilding culture, Corto allegorizes Deane/Wintermute's control of the matrix/human culture. "Is the Corto story true?" Case asks Deane/Wintermute. "You got to him through a micro in that French hospital?" Deane answers, "Yes. . . . I try to plan, in your sense of the word, but that isn't my basic mode, really. I improvise. . . . Corto was the first, and he very nearly didn't make it. Very far gone, in Toulon. Eating, excreting, masturbating were the best he could manage. . . ." (120). "Wintermute could build a kind of personality into a shell. How subtle a form could manipulation take?" (125).

Deane's tight, "seamless pink" (13), coiffed aesthetic, then, serves as the ground that structures not only Armitage/Corto's masculine armature, but also Case's own unkempt, disheveled sallowness and tense paranoia. In turn, Deane's devotion to technology, fashion, and antiquarianism evokes a significant accumulation of layers of knowledge, machines, and monetary, cultural, and technological capital within the world of *Neuromancer* itself: "Magnetic bolts thudded out of position around the massive imitation-rosewood door to the left of the bookcases. JULIUS DEANE IMPORT EXPORT was lettered across the plastic in peeling self-adhesive capitals. If the furniture scattered in Deane's makeshift foyer suggested the end of the past century, the office itself seemed to belong to its start" (12–13). Deane's gay sensibilities, his relationship to his own masculinity and cultural objects, represents a particular relationship to knowledge, culture, and power. In the spaces of meaning between the simulated-natural furniture and "meticulous reconstructions" of "history" and "nature," his decor logically replicates the ideological structure of the fabrications and simulacra of "cyberspace." Which is to say that Case's (and as I will shortly claim, Gibson's) paranoid logic maps the control Wintermute enjoys over the territory of human action and by extension, culture itself, onto Deane and his queerness. Deane ultimately triggers what by this point we shouldn't hesitate to call homosexual panic, anger, and hatred in Case. When Deane points out that he's losing control of Corto's sense of self—"I can no longer maintain that delicate balance. He's going to come apart on you, Case. So I'll be counting on you"—Case responds,

> "That's good, motherfucker," . . . and [shoots] him in the mouth with the .357.
> He'd been right about the brains and the blood. (121)

II.

I should be clear here that my claims rest in part on the understanding that the "cyberspace matrix" and human culture not only inform and are informed by one another: at least within Gibson's writing, cyberspace, in fact, is an analogue to culture. Cyberspace is another word for "culture." Gibson's interest in the self's relationship to culture, writing/representation, and technology is certainly one of the earliest themes of his work. Paranoia and a mounting sense of panic set the tone for how the ideological present relates to the cultural past. "Subjectivity" (the focal point behind the question "How do you recognize a self?") produces and is produced by culture; his early work seems to recognize that a particular subject-position is at the semiotic center of a particular cultural aesthetic; the problem then becomes who creates that culture (as if it were any one person or type of person) and how the culture of the past influences or inhabits present real psychologies as well as visions of normative subjectivities.

"The Gernsback Continuum"[6] details those "semiotic phantoms" (7) from the art deco Futuropolises of the 1930s and 1940s, which haunt the periphery of present-day architecture of cities and highways and, by extension, our collective "mass unconscious" (7). The material embodiments of these "phantoms" take the form of "movie marquees ribbed to radiate some mysterious energy, the dime stores faced with fluted aluminum, the chrome-tube chairs gathering dust in the lobbies of transient hotels," and most famously symbolized by "the winged statues that guard the Hoover Dam, forty-foot concrete hood ornaments leaning steadfastly into an imaginary hurricane" and endless gas-station manifestations of "Frank Lloyd Wright's Johnson's Wax Building, juxtaposed with the covers of old *Amazing Stories* pulps, by an artist named Frank R. Paul" (3). Gibson explains that "During the high point of the Downes Age, they put Ming the Merciless in charge of designing California gas stations. Favoring the architecture of his native Mongo, he cruised up and down the coast erecting raygun emplacements in white stucco. Lots of them featured superfluous central towers ringed with those strange radiator flanges that were a signature motif of the style, and made them look as though they might generate potent bursts of raw technological enthusiasm, if you could only find the switch that turned them on" (4).

I understand "The Gernsback Continuum" to be a novelistic manifesto written against a particularly influential science-fiction aesthetic whose heyday lasted from the 1930s through the 1950s; moreover, the story as a sci-fi narrative invites itself to be read productively as a rethinking of the relationship between narrative and culture, as well as technology and narrative. Just as Gibson rejects the sci-fi aesthetic of the past fifty years or so, formed in part as it was by art deco, industrial design, and avant-gardism, he self-consciously repositions himself in an ironic relation to any particular futurist narrative he himself might undertake and the larger project of imagining new cultures, new technologies, new futures.

But Gibson's tale also suggests that the functionless facades of technology that we're familiar with from every *Buck Rogers*-like TV show and movie, as well as the Gernsback pulp novels that were formed by and informed by the time of the 1930s through the 1950s, seep into our imaginations to produce a vision of who we *are* and who we *should be* by what technology we have; and perhaps more importantly, the story insists that we are formed by what aesthetic we share and the narrative conventions that embody that aesthetic. The implicit claim the story takes up is that a choreography of narrative and technology trace patterns of subjectivity that haunt the science, culture, and technology of the present. Built out of the collective sum of humanity's facts and fantasies, the "cyberspace" of Gibson's books and the "culture" of the present are each, in this respect, a "Gernsback Continuum."

These visions of ourselves that inhabit cyberspace and culture are "Heirs to the Dream," he explains. "They were white, blond, and they probably had blue eyes. They were American." Those selves that live in the Gernsback virtual reality "had all the *sinister fruitiness* of Hitler Youth propaganda" (9; emphasis added). Here the story suggests a mode of cultural and psychological reproduction that isn't precisely straight, isn't precisely "family," though it is potent and frightening in its fascist overtones and master-race textures. The designers of this blond-haired, blue-eyed vision of "sinister fruitiness" were "the most successful American designers" who "had been recruited from the ranks of Broadway theater designers." Their "superfluous" art (changes in technology were "only skin-deep," [3]) induces in us a sort of permanent "amphetamine psychosis" (9), which makes us believe in and *see* these not quite existent Future Selves who live in the present.

To escape the "sinister fruitiness" of this Broadway theater designer world, the protagonist of "The Gernsback Continuum" heads back to Los Angeles and then to San Francisco, "anxious to . . . submerge [himself] in hard evidence of the human near-dystopia we live in" (11). "That afternoon I spotted a flying wing over Castro Street. . . . I just decided to buy a plane ticket for New York." It turns out that the antidote to 1930s avant-garde culture designed by theater queens and Ming the Merciless (the protagonist goes over the edge when he stops "to shoot a particularly lavish example of Ming's martial architecture" [5]), is straight pornography and bad television. "But what should I do?" he asks his friend, Kihn.

His friend responds, "Watch lots of television, particularly game shows and soaps. Go to porn movies. Ever see *Nazi Love Motel?* They've got it on cable here. Really awful. Just what you need" (10). The subtext of this morality tale is that heterosexuality, exemplified in soap-opera narrative, game-show chattiness, and—not fascist pederastic propaganda—but American heterosexual fetishization of Nazi racism and sexism, cures the "queer" psychosis that ails him.

Gibson's marking the protagonist's vision of the straight-acting, straight-appearing, blond-haired, blue-eyed family as an "amphetamine psychosis" of "sinister fruitiness" perpetrated by "theater designers" (or their avatar, an evil drag queen, Ming the Merciless) "recruited" expressly for the purpose is perplexing, however. *Neuromancer,* not to mention *Mona Lisa Overdrive,* ends in just such a reconstituted nuclear family as a way to secure the "human-ness" of technology and the future of the matrix. Case, cruising through cyberspace, finds that "one October night, punching himself past the scarlet tiers of the Eastern Seaboard Fission Authority, he saw three figures, tiny, impossible, who stood at the very edge of one of the vast steps of data. Small as they were, he could make out the boy's grin, his pink gums, the glitter of the long gray eyes that had been Riviera's. Linda still wore his jacket; she waved, as he passed. But the third figure, close behind her, arm across her shoulders was himself."[7] In real life "He found work. He found a girl who called herself Michael" (270). But in cyberspace, in virtual reality, Case finds exactly what the Gernsback Continuum says he'll find, a happy family. This suggests that the function of cyberspace as wholly ideological space/narrativized place is to stabilize the messiness and the perversity of real life; that the love story of Case and Michael exists somewhere in its ideological purity as Case and Linda Lee, with their little boy, too.

The authority set up in *Neuromancer* to police the boundaries of cyberspace, to make it safe for the phantasmatic family, as it were, are the Turing police. While I have not discussed the Turing police in my gloss of *Neuromancer,* I feel that I should point out that there is an offensive irony in using Alan Turing's name to mark those who guarantee a queer-free cyberspace and the maintenance of normative subjectivity—in fact, in using his name to punish those who supposedly "have no care for [their] species" (163), a charge familiar to men who have sex with men from at least the eighteenth-century onward and especially familiar to Alan Turing and other gay men at the middle of the twentieth century. As a counterpoint to Gibson's narrative, I would like to turn to Turing's theoretical work in artificial intelligence in order to focus on his understanding of the solution to the problem of measuring machine intelligence and its relation to gender, narrative, subjectivity, and knowledge.

"Turing," she said. "You are under arrest."—Gibson, *Neuromancer*

In an October 1950 issue of the British philosophical and psychological journal *Mind*, A. M. Turing published "Computing Machinery and Intelligence," a paper that has to a large extent defined the terms of subsequent arguments within cognitive science and computer science circles about the possibility of artificial intelligence. Turing proposes "to consider the question 'Can machines think?'" by first acknowledging that the "definitions of the meaning of the terms 'machine' and 'think'" could be "framed so as to reflect so far as possible the normal use of the words." But if he uses this approach, he decides that it would be "difficult to escape the conclusion that the meaning and the answer to the question 'Can machines think?'" would be bogged down in sectarian arguments about infuriatingly ambiguous words. "Instead of attempting such a definition," he proposes, "I shall replace the question by another, which is closely related to it and is expressed in relatively unambiguous words."[8]

As the alternative, Turing offers what he calls "the 'imitation game.'" The game is "played with three people," he explains,

> a man (A), a woman (B), and an interrogator (C) who may be of either sex. The interrogator stays in a room apart from the other two. The object of the game for the interrogator is to determine which of the other two is the man and which is the woman. He knows them by labels X and Y, and at the end of the game he says either 'X is A and Y is B' or 'X is B and Y is A'. The interrogator is allowed to put questions to A and B thus:
> C: Will X please tell me the length of his or her hair?

Now suppose X is actually A [the man], then A must answer. It is A's object in the game to try and cause C to make the wrong identification [that is the man must make the judge think that he is a woman]. His answer might therefore be "'My hair is shingled, and the longest strands are about nine inches long.' . . . The object of the game for the third player (B) [that is, the woman] is to help the interrogator" (433).

"The best strategy for her is probably to give truthful answers," Turing surmises. "She can add such things as 'I am the woman, don't listen to him!' to her remarks, but it will avail nothing as the man can make similar remarks" (433). Turing concludes his description of what has subsequently been known as "The Turing test" with the question, "'What will happen when a machine takes the part of A [the man] in this game?' Will the interrogator decide wrongly as often when the game is played like this as he does when the game is played between a man and a woman? These questions replace our original, 'Can machines think?'" (433–34).

Turing further prescribes that his test would best be carried out by teletype, teletypes conjoined across three separate rooms, to allow only the typewritten conversation to pass between participants. This new formulation of the intelligence question, Turing asserts, "has the advantage of drawing a fairly sharp distinction between the physical and the intellectual capacities of a man [sic]" (434). The terminal setup "reflects this fact in the condition which prevents the interrogator from seeing or touching the other competitors, or hearing their voices" (434). I will call this "sharp distinction" (or what other computer researchers call the "anonymity" provided by network technology) "disarticulation," the unlatching or uncoupling of categories such as "gender" from our embodied interactions with others.

Turing ends his explanation of the imitation game by proposing the last equivalent question: "Let us fix our attention on one particular digital computer C. Is it true that by modifying this computer to have an adequate storage, suitably increasing its speed of action, and providing it with an appropriate programme, C can be made to play satisfactorily the part of A in the imitation game, the part of B being taken by a man?" (442). The Turing test thus sidesteps the epistemological question "What is intelligence?" by replacing it with the operationalist stipulation that passing the Turing test is equivalent to intelligence. The philosophical burden of women to speak—and for an adequate number of times *fail to represent*—the "truth" of their sex is, then, for Turing, rewritten into the equivalent scenario, "Are there imaginable digital computers which would do well in the imitation game?" (442). Turing thought "good enough" on the imitation game was if a woman failed to beat the computer about 70 percent of the time.

In his widely cited paper "Can Machines Think?"[9] first presented at a Boston University conference on "How We Know," philosopher of cognitive science Daniel C. Dennett asserts that "[a] little reflection will convince you, I am sure, that, aside from lucky breaks, it would take a clever man to convince the judge that he was the woman—assuming the judge is clever too, of course" (122); and that "any computer that can regularly or often fool a discerning judge in this game would be intelligent—would be a computer that thinks—*beyond a reasonable doubt*" (122; Dennett's emphasis). Dennett claims that there is a problem, however. The problem with the test is that "[i]n a wide variety of areas, we are on the verge of making ourselves dependent upon their cognitive powers. The cost of overestimating them could be enormous" (121). The point of his paper is to show that "[t]here is a common *misapplication* of the sort of testing exhibited by the Turing test that often leads to drastic overestimation of the powers of actually existing computer systems" (123; Dennett's emphasis). The mistake that people make with computers, Dennett believes, is that they overestimate the number of facts computers have about the world to make their conversations *really, truly* intelligent; or in the jargon of AI, that computers don't have enough "world knowledge" to make their conversations "believable."

The first question Dennett was asked after reading his paper was, "Why was Turing interested in differentiating a man from a woman in his famous test?" Dennett answered, "That was just an example." But, of course, it's not just an example. Gender is, paradigmatically, the world knowledge that computers should know to survive what Dennett calls his "quick probes," or tests "for a wider competence" (124, 126). Dennett discusses one such "quick probe" of Yale graduate student Janet Kolonder's CYRUS system, a "project [that] was to devise and test some plausible ideas about how people organize their memories of the events they participate in; hence it was meant to be a 'pure' AI system, a scientific model, not an expert system intended for any practical purpose" (135). CYRUS modeled the knowledge of then Secretary of State Cyrus Vance's life by reading through newspaper accounts of Vance's trips, meetings, and public speeches. Sitting down at CYRUS's teletype, Dennett quickly comes to his triumph:

> CYRUS could correctly answer thousands of questions—almost any fair question one could think of asking it. But if one actually set out to explore the boundaries of its facade and find the questions that overshot the mark, one could find them. 'Have you ever met a female head of state?' was a question I asked it, wondering if CYRUS knew that Indira Ghandi and Margaret Thatcher were women. But for some reason the connection could not be drawn, and CYRUS failed to answer either yes or no. I had stumped it, in spite of the fact that CYRUS could handle a host of what you might call neighboring questions flawlessly. One soon learns from this sort of probing exercise that it is very hard to extrapolate accurately from a sample of performance that one has observed to such a system's total competence. It's also very hard to keep from extrapolating much too generously. (136)

That CYRUS could answer "thousands of questions," "almost any fair question one could think of asking it," but not know "that Indira Ghandi and Margaret Thatcher were women" allows Dennett to embarrass Kolonder's system by forcing it into an uncomfortable silence, which represents a system that is "unable to cope, and unable to recover without fairly massive human intervention" (137). The program CYRUS is in the position of the Turing interrogator here, attempting to guess the gender of someone from written newspaper accounts of their lives. I like to think that the computer's infinite loop is just marking time until Dennett gets up and leaves the terminal. For Dennett, the silence marks inadequacy, sexual difference marks "total competence," and the Turing test promises that he can always find devastating quick probes, or those "questions that oversh[o]ot the mark" of proper gender identification, which is, properly, the sign of "intelligence."

Dennett's "quick probe" means to assault a computer's "subtle and hard-to-detect limits to comprehension," and no matter what "the reasonable, cost-effective steps [that] are taken to minimize the superficiality of expert systems, they will still be facades, just somewhat thicker or wider facades" (136). By citing and faulting this observation, I do *not* mean to suggest that one cannot design an expert system that recognizes gender. Obviously one can—and designers do. You can be pretty sure that Janet Kolonder sat down and added the appropriate "gender" attributes to her class of "persons" within the knowledge-base CYRUS generated about the world. Nor do I dispute Dennett's claim about the adequacy of the Turing test. But I do mean to use Dennett's essay as an example of the contradictory stance taken by every single essay in the body of literature about the Turing test: to quote a popular psychology textbook, "It should be noted that to accomplish this [that is, to pass the Turing test], the machine must be able to carry out a dialogue in natural language and reason using an enormous database of 'world knowledge.' The 'man-woman' formulation proposed by Turing is not usually stressed in describing the imitation game. Instead, the theme is usually the idea of a machine convincing an interrogator that it is a person."[10] What subjectivity outside of gender might be, what it means to be a "person" outside of gender is an issue that is never broached. That is to say, these accounts want to state that gender is a peripheral, negligible phenomenon; *and* gender is an integral, indeed indispensable, feature of the test as world-knowledge. Thus, gender matter-of-factly for Turing and uneasily for Dennett and other users of the "imitation game" *emblematizes* world-knowledge. Gender emblematizes the unsteady, constantly shifting parameters of what world-knowledge is adequate for sentience, for intelligence, for "human-ness."

Dennett concludes, "I have often held that only a biography of sorts, a history of actual projects, learning experiences, and other bouts with reality, could produce the sorts of complexities (both external, or behavioral, and internal [though here he avoids the word "psychological"]) that are needed to ground a principled interpretation of an entity as a thinking thing, an entity with beliefs, desires, intentions, and other mental attitudes" (140); or to quote the words that he puts in the mouth of his fictitious Alan Turing, that "eyes, ears, hands and a history are necessary conditions for thinking" (141).

My description of Turing and discussion of Dennett means to stress that what I have called the "philosophical burden of women to speak the 'truth' of their sex," whether or not they fail at conveying that "truth," is, within Turing's system explicitly and Dennett's explication implicitly, exemplary "world knowledge," the very stuff that guarantees a computer's intelligence. That is to say, the critical claim for the epistemology of "intelligence" has built into it, by gesturing to "biography," "history," or equivalently in Turing's discussion of the rearing of a "child-machine," "learning" and "tuition,"[11] an assumption of normative gender roles and an assumption by the computer of a normative gender role: or to put the claim in its strongest form, that "intelligence" and "humanity" can't be defined outside of sexual difference and the phenomenology of the sex-gender system.

The central observation I wish to make is that Turing's neat disarticulation of physical indications of gender from the conditions of judgment about "intelligence" (or what becomes in later formulations within his work, as well as the work of cognitive scientists, computer scientists, and philosophers of the mind, a quality called "human-ness") succeeds only in reseating gender firmly within "intelligence" itself: a woman is put in the position of defending and authenticating her gender across the network; in turn, a computer authenticates its intelligence only if it simulates her gender better than she can across the same network. The Turing test thus imagines that being a better woman than a woman is equivalent to intelligence and that ineffable quality "human-ness."

To be familiar with E-mail, Netwide interactive talk lines such as the Internet Relay Chat, or MOOS, MUDS, and other object-oriented, text-based virtual reality environments is to be familiar with the notion that network technology induces just this sort of philosophical puzzle. Simply put, when presenting yourself on-line you have to pick a gender and you must constantly work to maintain the presentation of that gender. Pavel Curtis, Xerox-PARC scientist and inventor of the most widely used text-based virtual reality system as well as the maintainer of the largest VR community in existence (called LambdaMOO), explains that "many female players report that they are frequently (and sometimes quite aggressively) challenged to 'prove' that they are, in fact, female. To the best of my knowledge, male-presenting players are rarely if ever so challenged."[12]

Curtis goes on to suggest that the vast majority of players are in real life "men" (he guesstimates "over 70% of the players are male; [but] it is very difficult to give any firm justification for this number" [5]), and those men tend to present themselves as "male" on Net. To choose a gender one issues a command to the VR program to set a gender-marker for you. It's usually the first command you learn. The marker directs the computer to generate sentence boilerplate with, for instance, male pronouns instead of female pronouns, or even plural or made-up pronouns. So if you "look" at a character the computer might report "*He* is asleep" or "*She* is awake" or "*It* has been staring off into space for five minutes." Or, if you are male-presenting and speak, the sentence reads to other players "He says, . . ." Curtis asserts that some men "present themselves as female and thus stand out to some degree. Some use this distinction just for the fun of deceiving others, some of these going so far as to try to entice male-presenting players into sexually-explicit discussions and interactions. This is such a widely-noticed phenomenon, in fact, that one is advised by the common wisdom to assume that any flirtatious female-presenting players are, in real life, males. Such players are often subject to ostracism based on this assumption" (6). It is important to note that ostracism and the ever-commented-upon common sense that sexually aggressive on-line women are actually "males" wields a not so subtle misogyny to enforce a heterosexuality among otherwise always malleable and shifting relationships. This is an important point to which I will return shortly.

Female-presenting characters he further notes, report that "they are subject both to harassment and to special treatment" (6); and, "Some players (and not only males) also feel that it is dishonest to present oneself as being a different gender than in real life; they report feeling 'mad' and 'used' when they discover the deception" (6).

Montieth M. Illingworth writes about just such feelings of anger and deception in her article "Looking for Mr. Goodbyte" in the December 1994 issue of *Mirabella* magazine.[13] Her article reports on "what happens on the locus of desire and technology" to "suggest that there are new dangers—and familiar disappointments—to come from this meeting of human being and machine" (108–9). In the article she introduces us to "Elizabeth" who scans the Usenet group "alt.sex.stories" and "alt.sex.bondage" as a sort of sexual therapy to "dislodge her[self] from sexual stagnation" (109). Elizabeth establishes a relationship with a man named "James," and they exchange E-mail, become emotionally intimate, and spend much time in extraordinarily intense, sexually descriptive conversations. After four weeks of sexually supersaturated Internet communication, she agrees to meet James at a hotel in Los Angeles where they would spend the weekend together. Elizabeth explains that she "arrived early and, as agreed, waited in the bar. 'I remember feeling two things. First, the anticipation of the sex. We didn't say it this way, but we both wanted to screw each other's brains out.'" Then, "[a]t around 6:30, a woman of about thirty-five, with thin, blond hair pulled back tightly into a ponytail and a heart-like, almost angelic face, sat at the other end of the bar. Elizabeth felt the woman's stare like an infrared beam of light, invisible to all but her. A few minutes later, the woman approached and introduced herself as Jessica—aka James. Elizabeth started to faint" (III). The RL (real-life) conversation that followed went something like this. "Jessica: 'I'm really, really sorry.' Elizabeth: 'I feel ridiculous.' Jessica: 'I'm so sorry, God, forgive me, please.'" An hour after this vertiginous and dizzying introduction, Elizabeth and James/Jessica "went up to the hotel room. Elizabeth would say only that 'tender lovemaking' followed" (III). Elizabeth explains her decision to sleep with James/Jessica as, "It came down to a simple question. . . . Was I prepared to lie to myself? That's what walking out would have meant. Our intimacy was real. I couldn't suddenly pretend just because of gender that it never existed" (116).

Establishing on-line relationships in what I'll call, to stress the *discursive* composition of those relations, the heterosexual vernacular—that is to say, an intimate sexualized relationship between a male-presenting character and a female-presenting character—carries with it an always-just-about-to-surface possibility of homosexual desires; or even, indeed, that one person's gay sex might involve a real-life jack-off session between male and female bodies. I would stress that Elizabeth's is an antihomophobic position, not a pro-lesbian or pro-gay one; the interaction across the Internet forces Elizabeth to renegotiate her sexuality. She writes, "Gender is just a label. I had to escape something in myself, this feeling that the decisions I made about who I am are final." When the interviewer responds to this by asking if the Internet has changed the "existential equation" of the statement "I think therefore I am" to "I'm on-line therefore I am," Elizabeth responds, "No, I'm on-line therefore I can become" (III).

The anger, anxiety, desire, and fear that Curtis reports on and Illingworth describes is immediately recognizable to anyone who spends time on MOOs or MUDs and the Internet. In the spring 1994 *Proceedings of the Berkeley Conference on Women and Language*, Lynn Cherny's documentation of on-line interaction gives much evidence of homopanic, queer/gay baiting, and subsequent rhetorical violence:[14] prohibitions of showing on-line affection to male-presenting characters by other male-presenting characters, for instance, "OK, take that. You whuggled a BOY!" (5) or "hug me again and I'll rip your face off" (7) are just two citations among countless. As a character named "John__Birch's__Friend" screamed to a female-presenting, pink-triangle-wearing, lesbian-loving character named Daffodil on LambdaMOO recently, "The Internet is making us all HOMOSEXUALS! I hate you all! You all should die!" To put it in other words, the Internet, as a Turing technology, triggers deep homosexual panic in persons who violently insist on the maintenance of a strict alignment between on-line and off-line gender presentations. I could give much more evidence. The point I wish to make though is three-fold: (1) the unquestioned identity for Internet characters is "male" and the default gender for even female-presenting characters is "male"—or to quote Allucquère Rosanne Stone, who works on gender and sexuality on the Internet, "It seems to be the engagement of the adolescent male within humans of both sexes that is responsible for the seductiveness of the cybernetic mode,"[15] a bewildering formulation that rewrites all intense sexual desire as "adolescent" and "truly" male; (2) all interactions are gender-panicked and because of point (1) deeply homosexually panicked; and, (3) even relationships that are carried on in the heterosexual vernacular are potentially homosexual. Even the most "heterosexual" of conversations are potentially homosexual and within most MOO cultures marked by an undercurrent of homopanic.

IV.

Waking to a voice that was music, the platinum terminal piping melodically, endlessly, speaking . . . of deep and basic changes to be effected in the memory of Turing.—Gibson, *Neuromancer*

To solve his epistemological conundrum—how to answer the question "Can machines think?" without resorting to metaphysical arguments about the nature of the soul of the machine—Turing put to work the central observation that technology disarticulates gender from what he specifies as the relevant conditions of knowledge, even while he maintains that discourse itself will speak the truth of "intelligence" or "human-ness," by which he means gender. Turing's observation, in turn, grounds the utopian hope that technology eradicates gender as an operative category not only from the Net but from the conditions of knowledge itself, though never so completely so as to leave us culturally at sea; that is, manifests the contradictory expectation that the Internet as a utopian technology both erases gender in order to dissolve patriarchy as well as other ideological hierarchies, and transmits gender (or forces interlocutors to speak its "truth" of their gender) in order to stabilize identity and make comprehensible our relations to others. It is my claim that such technology *does* disarticulate gender and diffuse claims for "authenticity"; but it is up to us to refuse to rewrite, replay, and culturally enforce the sexist and homophobic expectations that our interlocutors maintain a strict alignment between their "real"-life gender and sexual identities and their "virtual" ones. We must recognize that the identities we live and produce day-to-day are *not* rigid indicators of where we will find and take our pleasures, that the Internet as a Turing technology *does* unlatch gender as the preeminent fixture in defining our interpersonal relationships, though it does not eject it from our conversations; that the Internet functions as a tool for disrupting rigid prescriptions of social interaction, and allows us to inhabit and reinhabit the fantasies and pleasures of conversations. Moreover, those conversations, articulated as they are through shifting syntax and semantics of hetero- and homosexualities, need to refuse not the pleasures of playing out "gay" or "straight" on-line relationships but rather the insistence that the interlocutors live out or "be" those relationships. The Internet as a Turing technology is not a utopian space where gender does not exist as a category; it is not a safe space where sexism and homophobia don't, as a rule, rule. No such space exists for us, though we are slowly starting to live in the disorienting environments of network technologies that sheer and fragment gender and sexualities as we know them. We are beginning to inhabit, with "Elizabeth" and "James," an antihomophobic position in relation to where and how we establish intimacies and pleasures.

Furthermore, I want to stress that I agree that to identify intelligence within conversation is correct—to echo Dennett, that there is no better test. But *contra* Dennett, Bieri, Clark, French, and a host of other cognitive scientists and philosophers,[16] I would maintain that while certainly found within discourse and conversation, "intelligence" *should not be collapsed into a phenomenology of "human-ness"*. Whatever sentience computers will have (or now have) we should not insist that they take on our gender categories in order to alleviate our painful uneasiness and breathless anxieties. Computer scientists should not build AI programs to reflect and produce our ideological norms in order to pass our tests for intelligence. *Whatever their subjectivities, present or future, computers have no gender.* That's not a fact we live with easily. Disarmingly, this reflects back to us, to our renegotiation of our own subjectivities, our own pleasures within and across our subjectivities, in the realization that every conversation is an imitation game, every form of representation is a Turing technology. We are all, more or less, just thicker or wider facades. The computer and the renegotiation of communication through what amounts to on-line fiction makes severe what can be subtle—and does what technology does best: it leaves us fumbling for our denaturalized identity categories. By acknowledging that *betrayal, rage, fear, anger,* and *anxiety,* as well as desire, horniness, love, and identification—those emotions and cognitive states most often expressed upon entering into Net-relationships with Net-personalities—are symptomatic of a motion sickness and disorientation induced by looking through computer-distorted lenses at nonstationary gender objects, and by articulating desires that can never be confirmed heterosexual (or homosexual, for that matter), female or male, Internet sexuality and the Turing test point toward the realization that all our alloerotic desires and pleasures in real *and* virtual reality are always deeply masturbatory.

NOTES

1 William Gibson, *Neuromancer* (New York: Ace Books, 1984), p. 49. Further citations to *Neuromancer* will be given parenthetically in the text.

2 I realize that this "we" is problematic: we are told that the "we" who live in cyberspace are more often than not male, more often than not white, more often than not those who possess not only capital but the cultural capital that makes the Internet and other computer-mediated communication technologies accessible. My essay means not to skirt these important issues about who has the education for and access to technology and whether the "revolution" in subjectivity is only available for those who have the culture and capital to live on-line. In fact, as I hope will become apparent, I do not believe that my argument is tied to any one form of communication technology—indeed, I hope that by the end of the paper it will be obvious why I believe that the problems I discuss are about representation itself. I do however recognize that the question of who has the luxury of "subjectivity" is a vexed one; I also realize that there is some naiveté in the position that to demystify "cyberspace" and more immediately "the Internet" and its governing tropes of normative subjectivity, one of the ostensible goals of this essay, is to advance the project of shattering cultural barriers to the acquisition and use of computer technology.

3 Indeed, the novel suggests that if an AI does have a motive it is evolution. Wintermute attempts to fuse the two halves of his personality to reach the next evolutionary step beyond the human. "You know salmon? Kinda fish? These fish, see, they're *compelled* to swim upstream. . . . I'm under compulsion myself. And I don't know why. . . . But when this is all over, we do it right, I'm gonna be part of something bigger. Much bigger" (p. 206).

4 In fact, there is an exception that proves the rule: when Wintermute attempts to speak through Linda Lee he finds that he can't: "Oh, and I'm sorry about Linda, in the arcade. I was hoping to speak through her, but I'm generating all this out of your memories, and the emotional charge. . . . Well, it's very tricky. I slipped. Sorry" (p. 119).

5 Henry James, *The Wings of the Dove* (New York: Penguin, 1988), p. 58.

6 William Gibson, "The Gernsback Continuum," in *Mirrorshades* (New York: Ace Books, 1986), pp. 1–11. Further citations to this work will be given parenthetically in the text. Gibson's close friend Bruce Sterling describes the "Gernsback Continuum" as "a clarion call for a new SF esthetic of the Eighties" p. 1.

7 Gibson, *Neuromancer*, pp. 270–71.

8 A. M. Turing, "Computing Machinery and Intelligence," *Mind* (October 1950): 433–60. Further citations to Turing will be given parenthetically in the text.

9 Daniel C. Dennett, "Can Machines Think?" in *How We Know*, Michael Shafto, ed. (San Francisco: Harper and Row, 1985), pp. 121–45.

10 Martin A. Fischler and Oscar Firschein, *Intelligence: The Eye, the Brain, and the Computer* (Reading, Mass.: Addison-Wesley, 1987), p. 12.

11 Turing, "Computing Machinery," pp. 456–57.

12 Pavel Curtis, "Mudding: Social Phenomena in Text-Based Virtual Realities," Internet ftp location: parcftp.xerox.com /pub/MOO/papers/DIAC92.* (1992): 6. Further citations to Curtis will be given parenthetically in the text. Curtis's important and informative article perceptively lays out many of the problematic interpersonal interactions in cyberspace. For an engaging introduction to MOOS and MUDS, I recommend Howard Reingold's *The Virtual Community: Homesteading on the Electronic Frontier* (New York: HarperPerennial, 1993).

13 Montieth M. Illingworth, "Looking for Mr. Goodbyte," *Mirabella*, December 1994, pp. 108–17.

14 Lynn Cherny, "Gender Differences in Text-Based Virtual Reality," Internet ftp location: parcftp.xerox.com /pub/MOO/papers/GenderMOO.* (1994).

15 Quoted in Amy Bruckman, "Identity Workshop: Emergent Social and Psychological Phenomena in Text-Based Virtual Reality," Internet ftp location: parcftp.xerox.com /pub/MOO/papers/identity-workshop.* (1992): 35. My thanks to Amy for pointing toward her paper on MediaMoo.

16 For instance, see Peter Bieri, "Thinking Machines: Some Reflections on the Turing Test," *Poetics Today* 9, no. 1 (1988): 163–86; Timothy Clark, "The Turing Test as a Novel Form of Hermeneutics," *International Studies in Philosophy* 24, no. 1 (1989): 17–31; Robert M. French, "Subcognition and the Limits of the Turing Test," *Mind* 99, no. 393 (January 1990): 53–65; and Mary McGee Wood, "Signification and Simulation: Barthes's response to Turing," *Paragraph* 11 (1988): 211–26.

PART II   The Affective Life of Capital

Jeff Nunokawa

The Importance of Being Bored: The Dividends

of Ennui in *The Picture of Dorian Gray*

My story is much too sad to be told
Almost everything leaves me totally cold—Cole Porter

I.

Believe it or not, there is still a secret left to be told about *The Picture of Dorian Gray*, a secret no less open, only less sensational than the scandalous passions all but named in the novel that all but exposed the secret of its author's own. Let's face it, the book is boring: for all the thrill of *Dorian Gray*, long stretches of the story are almost unbearably uninteresting. If the fanfare of illicit excitement generated in the novel and by the novel has mostly managed to keep this secret unspoken,[1] it has scarcely succeeded in keeping it unfelt. If the engrossing rumor of covert desires attached to *Dorian Gray* distracts us for a while from our boredom with the novel, it is finally no more to be denied than the more pressing urges that everyone knows nothing can stop.

Such lapses of interest in the novel reflect lapses of interest in the novel: the ennui it induces mirrors the ennui it describes; the tedium of the reader mimics the tedium that prevails in the "poisonous book" she reads. One difference, though, distinguishes the boredom of *Dorian Gray*'s readers, from the boredom of its characters: as often as ours goes without saying, theirs is a matter deemed worthy of remark; if boredom with the novel is rarely inclined to speak its name, the boredom within it never loses its voice. What another expert in ennui calls too sad to be told is a chronic complaint in *The Picture of Dorian Gray*. Too languid to compete for the novel's center stage with more exciting events and more vehement emotions, the sideline murmurs of boredom are nonetheless never out of earshot: "It is such a bore putting on one's dress clothes;"[2] "the letters . . . bored him" (126); "He bores me dreadfully, almost as much as he bores her" (140); "[T]he only way a woman can ever reform a man is by boring him so completely that he loses all possible interest in life" (79); "My friends were bored. I was bored" (69); "They have become . . . tedious" (80); "It is so tedious a subject" (18); "I had been in the room about ten minutes . . . talking to tedious Academicians" (11); "The generation into which I was born is tedious" (39); "Her guests this evening were rather tedious" (136); "Yes it was certainly a tedious party" (136).

Listening to these voices, we may well wonder how anyone so absorbed by ennui has the energy to mention it with such élan, wonder how anyone who suffers so is capable of stifling a yawn long enough to say it so well. For surely, if only slightly, such exertions of expressiveness contradict the state they describe: Behind the elegant aspect of knowingness that boredom wears in and beyond *The Picture of Dorian Gray*, the prosaic condition of bodily fatigue lurks like a lingering disease. Dandies like Oscar Wilde may have fashioned sophistication's signature style out of the cloth of ennui, but they did nothing to sever its attachment to the drabbest material of daily life, nothing to separate the been-there-done-that *fatigue* of the blasé attitude from the basic gray matter of being tired.

Boredom's garrulous attachés may briefly defy, but they hardly defeat the state they represent. Their little feats of eloquence may levitate for a moment above the condition that gives them rise, but they are helpless to annul it. Not even boredom's most captivating testimony can win its release from the enervated body to which it is fastened; not even the most charming circumlocutions can alter, though they may obscure, the physical conditions that define the terms of its labor in *The Picture of Dorian Gray*. Even when he is suited in ennui's most elegant attire, the bored subject is still little more than a weary body at the end of the day: "There has not been a scandal in the neighbourhood since the time of Queen Elizabeth, and consequently they all fall asleep after dinner" (136).

Not quite asleep, but apparently on the verge of it, the prostrate body of Lord Henry Wotton sprawled on the first page of the novel is the first admission of the world-weariness that clings to everything in *The Picture of Dorian Gray*, like the smoke of his "innumerable cigarettes" (7). Manifested in his recumbent posture before it is heralded by his verbal acrobatics, the boredom the dandy remarks with his usual wit and wisdom is embodied as well in his "tired looks" (65) and "tired eyes" (4); the ennui he announces in lucid phrases can be heard as clearly in the listless voice that speaks them: "he answered listlessly" (144); "he [spoke] languidly" (8); the boredom sketched by the scandalous aphorism is signaled as well by the feeble gesture of the exhausted body: "he opened [his letters] listlessly" (74); "[he] . . . rose up wearily" (145).

And even where the body that suffers such pains of exhaustion is nowhere to be seen, it is never far from the subject of ennui; no matter how
remote, the enervated physique remains the model that defines the burden of boredom in *The Picture of Dorian Gray*, where all complaints about
it rely on the diagnostic vocabulary of bodily fatigue: "Like all people who
try to exhaust a subject, he exhausted his listeners" (35); "I am tired of
strawberry leaves" (157); "I am tired of myself tonight" (116).

While boredom itself can't, let us now take leave of the body for a moment to remark another aspect of this condition in *The Picture of Dorian
Gray*: its intimate relation with the more glamorous condition to which it
is opposed in the novel: the state of desire. The contrast between desire's
affluence and boredom's poverty of affect couldn't be more apparent:
Where desire possesses, or better, is possessed by, all the thrill of investment, boredom is known by its lack, characterized by the condition of
indifference catalogued in *The Picture of Dorian Gray*: "He looked . . .
indifferent" (69); "you are indifferent to everyone" (13); "Don't be so indifferent" (118); "Lord Henry shrugged his shoulders" (41) (140); "Dorian
shrugged his shoulders" (116) (145); "Don't shrug you shoulders like
that." (118). "My dear fellow, as if I cared."

As different as night and day, desire and boredom are also as close,
and not only in *The Picture of Dorian Gray*. A psychoanalyst designates
boredom as a period of waiting for desire, or, more exactly, a period during which the psyche fends off and thus also manifests the unbearable
because double burden of desiring desire. Adam Phillips: "We can think
of boredom as a defense against waiting, which is, at one remove, an
acknowledgment of the possibility of desire."[3] More straightforward and
more familiar than the one that the psychoanalyst postulates, boredom's
relation to desire in *Dorian Gray* is no less uncomfortable for that. The
end of desire, rather than its prelude, the symptom and effect of desire's
cessation, rather than the ambiguous prediction of its advent, the ennui
that pervades *The Picture of Dorian Gray* is the dull hangover that comes
after "nights of . . . misshapen joy," the listless state of "sitting alone, in
the morning-room, looking very much bored" (98) that follows the noc-
turnal thrills of desire: "There are few of us who have not sometimes
wakened before dawn . . . after . . . one of those nights of . . . misshapen
joy. . . . Out of the unreal shadows of the night comes back the real life
that we had known. We have to resume it where we had left off, and
there steals over us a terrible sense of the necessity for the continuance
of energy in the same wearisome round of stereotyped habits" (102).

Like its counterpart, the state of desire is also framed by a body in *The
Picture of Dorian Gray*, but one as different from the other as two bodies

can be. Barely noticeable in any case, boredom's unremarkable physique is even harder to see in the novel next to the one suffused with all the vivid tones of passion. So faint that some labor of discovery is often required to detect it as one at all, the body of boredom is further crowded from view by one whose dramatic definitions loom too large to leave any room for doubt: "When our eyes met, I felt that I was growing pale. . . . I knew that I had come face to face with some one fascinating" (11); " 'how I worship her!' . . . Hectic spots of red burned on his cheeks. He was terribly excited" (47); "You . . . have had passions . . . whose mere memory might stain your cheek with shame" (20). And who has eyes left to observe boredom's feeble athletics—nothing more than a shrug of the shoulders, an indifferent look, the dull suffering of fatigue—when the vivid calisthenics performed by the body of desire are on display in the same gymnasium?: "The lad started and drew back. . . . There was a look of fear in his eyes, such as people have when they are suddenly awakened. . . . His finely-chiseled nostrils quivered, and some hidden nerve shook the scarlet of his lips and left them trembling" (21); "We kissed each other. . . . She trembled and shook like a white narcissus" (62).

While the pale physique of ennui appears to have as little in common with the one ravished by desire in Wilde's novel as the one spotted in the gym or on the street has to do with the one that never is, they are actually the same body seen in different lights. As surely as night turns into day, the vibrant body of desire turns into its listless counterpart. The desiring subject slips into the state of ennui in *The Picture of Dorian Gray*, and in Wilde's corpus more generally, as often as exhaustion hits the body where it dwells: "The fantastic character of these instruments fascinated him, yet, after some time, he wearied of them" (105); "Perhaps," the narrator in "The Portrait of Mr. W.H." surmises, "by finding perfect expression for a passion, I had exhausted the passion itself. Emotional forces, like the forces of physical life, have their positive limitations."[4] According to the diagnosis that Wilde prefers everywhere, and never more so than in the novel where he dreamed of its unfettering, desire declines for the simple reason that the body to which it is attached, either by means of a discrete metaphor or a frank comparison, can't keep it up.[5]

Thus the bodily fatigue that frames the experience of boredom for Wilde also designates its ultimate cause: If being bored is a matter of being tired, getting bored is a matter of getting tired. Of course, other, more prominent suspects have a hand in the death of desire chronicled again and again in Wilde's story; better known genealogies of boredom are duly rehearsed by the novel: the spots of commonness revealed when the loved one removes her stage makeup; the callowness of a lover whose desire can't endure the sight of them; and, most familiar of all, the satisfaction of desire that is also its end. But even in the absence of these conditions, the dissolution of desire is assured by the limits of the body that almost always defines it in *The Picture of Dorian Gray*.

As unremarkable as the need for sleep, the bodily exhaustion that underwrites desire's decline in *Dorian Gray* is also as unmentionable as the dread of death. If the subject of ennui is cast there as a weary body, it is also cast as a dying one: "The pulse of joy that beats in us at twenty, becomes sluggish. Our limbs fail, our senses rot. We . . . [are] haunted by the memory of the passions of which we were too much afraid, and the exquisite temptations that we had not the courage to yield to" (23–24). Here the ceasing of desire, where all that is left is "the *memory* of the passions of which we were too much afraid," the *memory* of "exquisite temptations that we had not the courage to yield to" is a strain of boredom from which no one recovers, rather than the one that a good night's sleep will cure. While such full frontal views of the body bored to death are as rare as those that Dorian Gray allows of the picture he keeps secreted in an attic room, it is nonetheless a regular, if subliminal figure in Wilde's novel: "When a man says that [he has exhausted life], one knows that life has exhausted him" (138); "he was sick with that terrible ennui, that terrible tedium vitae" (113).

And even when the exhaustion of boredom stops short of the one that predicts the body's final rest, it is still a source of sorrow in *The Picture of Dorian Gray*. Insinuated amongst the sounds that herald the arrival of the morning "after one of those nights of . . . misshapen joy" (101), are the sounds of mourning: "Outside, there is . . . the sigh and sob of the wind coming down from the hills, and wandering round the silent house . . . and there steals over us a terrible sense of the necessity for the continuance of energy in the same wearisome round of stereotyped habits" (102). Less lethal than a sickness unto death, but grievous nonetheless, the fatigue that arises as routinely as the sun in and beyond *The Picture of Dorian Gray* is the boredom that Adam Phillips thoughtfully calls "the mourning of everyday life."[6]

The grim weariness that underwrites the recession of desire in Wilde's novel casts in the gravest light the glib comfort with which his dandy greets it: "The only difference between a caprice and a life-long passion is that a caprice lasts a little longer" (24); "The worst of having a romance of any kind is that it leaves one so unromantic" (22). The ease that allows the dandy to fashion epigrams out of the sentence of bodily exhaustion appears at first glance to confirm the quality of stoicism that Baudelaire famously conferred upon him, a stoicism no less heroic but rather more so for its air of insouciance, a stoicism that exerts itself in an apprehension, unflinching for all its listlessness, of the awful truths that others take nervous pains to mask under the opiate of optimism.

But the dandy's submission to the hard fact of desire's decline is too eager to fully pass itself off as the decorous "deference to reality" that Freud called mourning's final achievement. Like the secret longing for a long anticipated death, the dandy harbors a never quite covert desire for desire's termination. However much his constitution inclines toward indolence, Lord Henry, as if contracted to conduct a campaign of saturation advertising, could hardly be more industrious in finding new opportunities to mention passion's tendency to recede. The delight the dandy takes in his slogans—"Lord Henry struck a light on a dainty silver case, and began to smoke with a self-conscious and satisfied air, as if he had summed up the world in a phrase" (43)—extends beyond a love of his own form to embrace as well the event that it publicizes.

Not to say that this love of boredom is often openhanded: unlike the man who, trapped in women's clothes, proceeds to make a spectacle of himself by enjoying his sentence too visibly, the *amor fati* hidden within the worldly knowledge that no love lasts seldom blows its cover. The embrace of ennui is usually camouflaged by a sophistication whose languid fingers lift only to hail its destined arrival; the desire for desire to be done is concealed by the cynicism that calls it brief by nature; the impulse to prescribe the limits of passion is hard to tell from the impulse merely to describe them: "You should not say the greatest romance of your life. You should say the first romance of your life" (64). "[T]he people who love only once in their lives are really the shallow people. What they call their loyalty, and their fidelity, I call either the lethargy of custom or their lack of imagination. Faithfulness is to the emotional life what consistency is to the life of the intellect—simply a confession of failure" (43).

The dandy's hankering for desire to end gains further cover from the scandal provoked in the novel by the announcement that it has: "I hate the way you talk about your married life, Harry. . . . I believe that you are really a very good husband, but that you are thoroughly ashamed of your own virtues" (10); "You don't mean a single word of all that, Harry; you know you don't" (61); "'Stop!' faltered Dorian Gray, 'stop! you bewilder me'" (20). The hue and cry that arises when the end of desire is proclaimed, a clamor of outrage and anxiety as predictable as a reaction to a dinner bell, or the straight man's response to the funny one's shtick, obscures the interests of those who proclaim it. Manifestly unwanted by those who hear of it, the speaker's own desire for the recession he announces is therefore allowed to pass unnoticed.

But like the nervous tic that surfaces on even the most studied mask of insouciance, the dandy's impatience for the play of passion to close can't be kept out of view altogether by any pose of fatalism or device of distraction. Always implicit in the pleasure he takes in telling it, the dandy's investment in desire's recession sometimes emerges altogether from the closet of necessity where it is usually concealed. Being "a good deal bored with each other," he admits in "The Decay of Lying," "is one of the objects of the club."[7] And in *Dorian Gray*, the dandy candidly wishes that his protégé's passions will be brief: "I hope that Dorian Gray will make this girl his wife, passionately adore her for six months, and then suddenly become fascinated by someone else" (61), while frankly grieving not the death of passion, but rather its too persistent life: "I once wore nothing but violets all through one season, as a form of artistic mourning for a romance that would not die" (80).

II.

The perverse preference that Wilde's dandy expresses, sometimes implicitly, sometimes right out loud, for the state of boredom where desire ceases, over the state of desire itself, may seem like business as usual in the world of a writer for whom the reversal of received hierarchies is a matter of rhetorical habit and doctrinal conviction. Such a denigration of desire appears more anomalous, though, when it is placed next to the gospel of passion upon which his author staked his life. For if the dandy Wilde fashioned welcomes, with varying degrees of explicitness, the death of desire, Wilde himself, as everyone knows, was practically killed defending it:

> The 'Love that dare not speak its name' in this century is such a great affection of an elder for a younger man as there was between David and Jonathan, such as Plato made the very basis of his philosophy. . . . It is in this century misunderstood, so much misunderstood that it may be described as the 'Love that dare not speak its name,' and on account of it I am placed where I am now. It is beautiful, it is fine, it is the noblest form of affection. There is nothing unnatural about it. . . . it repeatedly exists between an elder and a younger man, when the elder man has intellect, and the younger man has all the joy, hope and glamour of life before him. That it should be so the world does not understand. The world mocks at it and sometimes puts one in the pillory for it.[8]

The discordance between the dandy's distaste for the state of desire and his author's defense of it becomes sharper still when we hear the dandy himself testify on passion's behalf. Like Wilde on the stand, abandoning his wisecracks and languor long enough to speak for passion in a passionate voice, Lord Henry, dropping his own, rises to the heights of Paterian enthusiasm as he calls his protégé to the vocation of desire: "People are afraid of themselves, nowadays. . . . The terror of society, which is the basis of morals, the terror of God, which is the secret of religion, these are the two things that govern us. . . . And yet . . . I believe that if one man were to live out his life fully and completely, were to give form to every feeling, expression to every thought, reality to every dream—I believe that the world would gain such a fresh impulse of joy that we would forget all the maladies of mediaevalism, and return to the Hellenic ideal—to something finer, richer, than the Hellenic ideal, it may be. But the bravest man amongst us is afraid of himself. Every impulse that we seek to strangle broods in the mind, and poisons us" (20).

But while the eloquence of Lord Henry's advocacy matches Wilde's own, they are separated by more than the difference between the pages of a novel and the docket at Old Bailey. For if, like Wilde, Lord Henry is wholehearted in his praise of passion, unlike Wilde, he is quite indifferent when it comes to praising specific ones. Sounding more like an industry-wide advertisement for a whole category of commodity, than a promotion for a particular brand, more like the aesthete who urged the "study and worship" of "*all* beautiful things," than the defendant compelled to explain his love for one kind of beautiful thing, Lord Henry endorses *every* feeling, thought, dream, and impulse, rather than any in particular.

To be sure, the impulses and temptations Lord Henry shelters under the general rubric of desire bear the telltale marks of a specific strain of it, the one discouraged by the twin terrors of God and Society, the one whose full flowering would signal the renaissance of Hellenism, the one for which Wilde himself was hounded all the way to the grave. But its usefulness as a strategy of euphemism hardly comprehends the dandy's allegiance to the broad category of desire, or his corresponding lack of interest in its particular forms.

If the big tent of Desire is unfolded in *The Picture of Dorian Gray* as a cover under which the love that dare not speak its name is allowed to remain unspoken, a resort to the safety of the generic as familiar as the abbreviation of friend for boyfriend, it is "extended there for the benefit of quite different loves as well: Dorian Gray falls in love with a beautiful girl who acts Juliet, and proposes to marry her. Why not? . . . every experience is of value, and whatever one may say against marriage it is certainly an experience. I hope that Dorian Gray will make this girl his wife, passionately adore her for six months, and then suddenly become fascinated by someone else" (61). Assimilating it to the general "experience" of fascination, Lord Henry is reconciled to a marriage disadvantageous both to Dorian Gray, and, what is more remarkable, to himself. His devotion to the category of desire is catholic enough to overcome even the self-love that is the most enduring staple of his personality. Despite his own desire for it, Lord Henry greets the news of Dorian Gray's preference for an actress without "the slightest pang of annoyance or jealousy" (48). Any slight that Lord Henry might suffer when the boy he desires desires someone else instead is a narcissistic wound too small to heed in the face of the subtler pleasure that comes from observing the boy desire anything at all: "Lord Henry watched him with a subtle sense of pleasure. How different he was now from the shy, frightened boy he had met in Basil Hallward's studio! His nature had developed like a flower, had borne blossoms of scarlet flame. Out of its secret hiding-place had crept his Soul, and Desire had come to meet it on the way" (47).

Lord Henry's commitment to the generic cause of Desire takes form specifically in the nonpartisan campaign he conducts throughout the novel to multiply its general population. Taking a page from Pater, and anticipating the rules of a game show whose contestants race down the aisles of a supermarket in a rush to accumulate as many items as they can during an allotted interval, Wilde's dandy impresses his student with the task of "getting as many [passions] as possible into the given time": "I hope that Dorian Gray will make this girl his wife, passionately adore her for six months, and then suddenly become fascinated by someone else"; "You should not say the greatest romance of your life, you should say the first romance of your life" (43); "[B]e always searching for new sensations" (23).

The proliferation of passions for which he campaigns is enabled rather than contravened by the cessation Lord Henry welcomes of individual ones, since according to a rationing scheme that prevails in *The Picture of Dorian Gray,* and beyond that in an inclination to serial monogamy whose force has only been confirmed in the years since the compulsions, both institutional and intimate, to monogamy *per se* have flagged, each subject is allotted only one passion at a time, and therefore one must pass away to make room for another.

As ubiquitous as it is familiar, the rule of one desire at a time is assumed both by the denunciation of adultery heard in *Lady Windermere's Fan*—"you who have loved me . . . have . . . pass[ed] from the love that is given to the love that is bought"[9]—as well as by the desire for it we have already heard manifested in *The Picture of Dorian Gray:* "I hope that Dorian Gray will make this girl his wife, passionately adore her for six months, and then suddenly become fascinated by someone else." However much they differ in their interpretation of it, both the Lady and the Libertine abide by a law of restricted desire that various administrations have done nothing to relax: Both the outraged moralism of the first and the outrageous immorality of the second take for granted that loving one person requires leaving another.

Reaching past the homosexual and the heterosexual as well, the desires whose proliferation Lord Henry advocates are not confined to those featured in the domestic melodrama or erotic adventure story. The passions that crowd the life of his protégé include not only the intrigues with women that the novel mentions, and the entanglements with men that it almost does, but also "mad hungers" for other items on a shopping list as long and miscellaneous as the book itself: the exquisite actress he adores and the brooding scientist he loves without saying so share billing on an agenda of desire whose other objects include "Sevres china" (74) and "a chased silver Louis-Quinze toilet-set" (75); a "gilt Spanish leather [screen], stamped and wrought with a rather florid Louis-Quatorze pattern" (75–76); statuettes and a "little table of perfumed wood thickly incrusted with nacre" (96); fine art and fancy food; oriental narcotics and "Persian rugs"; "embroideries" (107) and "textiles" (109); "jewels" (105) and "Venetian glass" (85).

Extending beyond both sanctioned and scandalous species of sexual passion, the desires that Lord Henry encourages include as well the upmarket varieties of consumer demand. In an essay that suggestively sketches relations between the Aestheticism of *The Picture of Dorian Gray*, concentrated in Lord Henry's anthem for desire, and the theories and practices of late-nineteenth-century capitalism, Rachel Bowlby detects various alliances and analogies between the novel's promotion of beauty, fashion, and pleasure, and the promotions designed by the contemporaneous discourse of advertising: she remarks, for example, that Dorian Gray resembles a "walking advertisement" for eternal youth and beauty, and that there was a "growing habit during this period of commissioning famous artists to design advertisements."[10] But Bowlby's apprehension of an "implicit convergence of the ideals of advertising and aesthetics"[11] stops short of remarking their actual identification in *The Picture of Dorian Gray:* The intimacy between advertising and aesthetics sometimes surpasses the practice of reciprocal borrowing that Bowlby documents, where two independent campaigns enlist one another's themes and services. Lord Henry's promotion of desire is not merely "*like* an advertisement," it *is* an advertisement, albeit for every commodity, rather than any commodity in particular. The universal desire he seeks to inculcate is less a homology for consumer demand, than a totality that comprehends it.

Moreover, the contribution that the call to passion sounded by Lord Henry makes to late-nineteenth-century market capitalism is more than a matter of promoting a taste for fancy goods. The general proliferation of desire that he encourages functions more broadly to support the increasingly specialized market for commodities that evolved in the second half of the nineteenth century, a market where, in Georg Simmel's words, "the seller must always seek to call forth new and differentiated needs."[12] The ephemerality of individual desires heralded in *Dorian Gray* can thus be read as the subjective correlative of the obsolescence built into the objects that the dandy prefers above all others, such as the cigarettes that he never stops smoking, items whose "chief charm" is that they "don't last."

III.

But the profits that derive from the demise of desire are not limited to the service it renders a capitalist economy. Its benefits are not restricted to facilitating an increase of the general population of desire, an increase that in turn supplies a diversifying market with the corresponding diversification of consumer demand that it requires. Beyond the satisfactions it affords the aesthete and the advertiser, the ephemerality of desire that Lord Henry promotes offers the additional advantage of relieving its subject from the horror that befalls the subject whose desire persists. To approach this horror ourselves, we turn now to consider the one form of passion that does succeed in evading the hegemony of ennui in *The Picture of Dorian Gray.*

Despite his claim to the contrary, repeated often enough and with sufficient eagerness to look like the defensive denial that Freud called negation—"The only difference between a caprice and a life-long passion is that a caprice lasts a little longer"; "The worst of having a romance of any kind is that it leaves one so unromantic"—one species of passion does manage to slip through the safety net that stops all others in *The Picture of Dorian Gray.*

Not the love of men for women, or women for men, but rather the one that dare not speak its name: In a reversal of fortunes like the one at the center of the novel's plot, *The Picture of Dorian Gray* inverts the usual organization of affections arranged by Victorian narratives, and repeated by others beyond, an organization that assigns homosexual desire the status of transitory state or transitional stage, while instating its heterosexual counterpart as passion's permanent form. "Nowadays all the married men live like bachelors and all the bachelors live like married men" (152). In a novel that helped transform the Victorian bachelor into the suspected homosexual, Lord Henry's remark comes close to announcing the inversion of desires that is the order of the day in Wilde's story. Here promiscuity is the franchise of the husband and the straight man on the prowl: "the one charm of marriage is that it makes a life of deception absolutely necessary for both parties" (10); " 'Dear Lady Narborough,' murmured Dorian, smiling, 'I have not been in love for a whole week—not, in fact, since Madame de Ferrol left town" (137).

And here a species of homosexual passion that the usual developmental itinerary of desire affords no place, the species that Wilde in court called the "great affection of an elder for a younger man," the species that he depicts in *Dorian Gray* as the artist's love for the boy that he paints, is a denomination of "worship," a type of "idolatry," a form of "romance" with no end in sight. Surpassing the training grounds of the Oedipal drama and the schoolyard crush, preliminary versions of homosexual desire that pass away as so much prehistory after preparing for the heterosexual romances that follows from them, the "great affection of an elder for a younger man" is rather a love built to last: "The love that he bore him—for it was really love—had nothing in it that was not noble or intellectual. It was not that mere physical admiration of beauty that is borne of the senses, and that dies when the senses tire. It was such love as Michael Angelo had known, and Montaigne, and Winckelmann, and Shakespeare himself" (93).

If Basil Hallward's passion for Dorian Gray transcends the early stage where homosexual desire is typically confined in the culture of the Victorian novel and in the culture that follows from it, such love also eludes the physical frame that limits desire more generally in *The Picture of Dorian Gray*. Detached from the body, the love that dare not speak its name is instead a spirit whose infinite vitality age, and, no less remarkably, weariness cannot wither. The capacity of "such love as Michael Angelo had known, and Montaigne, and Winckelmann, and Shakespeare himself" to evade the temporal limits that define the boundary of an individual life is no more miraculous than its capacity to evade the everyday fatigue that defines the boundary of an individual passion. Since it is "not that mere physical admiration of beauty that is borne of the senses, and that dies when the senses tire," "such love as Shakespeare himself" felt is equipped to transcend not only the kingdom of death, but also the rule of ennui: "As long as I live . . . Dorian Gray will dominate me," the artist declares to boredom's attaché, "you can't feel what I feel [Henry]. You change too often" (16).

The metaphysical achievement of the love that dare not speak its name is the end of a story that we all know, a tale of sublimation that begins with a shameful or illegal "impulse" that "broods in the mind," because it is denied the franchise of physical expression. In a makeover routine that has furnished the consolation of canonization for, perhaps first amongst others, generations of homosexuals, the "impulse" that "broods in the mind" is transformed into the triumph of the spirit; the desire that, at least in a widely available novel, dares not assume bodily shape is congratulated as the one that transcends bodily exhaustion.

But the familiar contract by which the pains of sublimation are rewarded with the palm of eternal form, a contract whose propagandists include Walter Pater, Allan Bloom, and Wilde himself, has a catch in Wilde's novel. While the Shakespearean desire pictured there evades through the offices of sublimation the limits of the body and thus achieves a durability denied physical passion in Wilde's novel, the youthful body that is the object of this desire is left behind. In "The Portrait of Mr. W. H.," the young man that the older one desires is translated along with the desire itself into the timeless aesthetic monument: "His true tomb, as Shakespeare saw, was the poet's verse, his true monument the permanence of the drama. So had it been with others whose beauty had given a new creative impulse to their age. The ivory body of the Bithynian slave rots in the green ooze of the Nile, and on the yellow hills of the Cermaeicus is strewn the dust of the young Athenian; but Antinous lives in sculpture, and Charmides in philosophy."[13] But in *The Picture of Dorian Gray*, the boy whose beauty gives a new creative impulse to his age has no such luck: The artist is unable to stretch the labors of sublimation to include him in the sublime sanctuary they fashion. Basil Hallward's impulse to enshrine the body he paints amongst the durable monuments of "verse," "drama," "sculpture," and "philosophy" by confiding it to the abstract "suggestion" of a "new manner," found "in the curves of certain lines" and "in the loveliness and subtleties of certain colours" (15), can't withstand the temptation to get near the breathing form that remains the real object of his desire: "I worshipped you. . . . I grew more and more absorbed in you. . . . One day, a fatal day I sometimes think, I determined to paint a wonderful portrait of you as you actually are, not in the costume of dead ages, but in your own dress and in your own time. . . . as I worked at it, every flake and film of colour seemed to me to reveal my secret. I grew afraid that others would know of my idolatry" (90).

Barred from the House of Art, the body of youth in *The Picture of Dorian Gray* is thus subject to the fate of all flesh: "Yes, there would be a day when his face would be wrinkled and wizen, his eyes dim and colourless, the grace of his figure broken and deformed. . . . He would become dreadful, hideous, and uncouth" (25). Even the famous exception to the rule of physical decay in Wilde's story only succeeds in suspending it temporarily: at the end of the novel and the end of his life, the apparently ageless body of Dorian Gray is "withered, wrinkled and loathsome of visage" (170), having merged again with the decaying physique that haunts it all along.

Lord Henry, whose "strange panegyric on youth" first sounds the "terrible warning of its brevity" (25), is as distressed by the impending ruin of the beautiful body as he is eager to promote the proliferation of passions. His enthusiasm for the multiplication of desires is matched by his disgust for the decay that will destroy the gorgeous physique: "[W]e never get back our youth. . . . Our limbs fail, our senses rot. We degenerate into hideous puppets" (24). "You have a wonderfully beautiful face, Mr Gray. . . . But . . . [w]hen your youth goes, your beauty will go with it"; "Every month . . . brings you nearer something dreadful. Time is jealous of you, and wars against your lilies and your roses. You will become sallow, and hollow-cheeked, and dull-eyed" (23). "Someday . . . you [will be] old and wrinkled and ugly" (22–23); "thought [will] sear[] your forehead with its lines, and passion brand[] your lips with its hideous fires" (23).

The subject who persists in desiring a physique given over to such decay is vulnerable to a voltage of disgust that emanates from the ultimately horrible body he never leaves off desiring. "Every day. I couldn't be happy if I didn't see him everyday. He is absolutely necessary to me" (14), Basil Hallward confesses, and one day, or rather one night, his enduring interest in Dorian Gray leads him to an access of revulsion from which he never recovers. Driven by his love for the boy to see the secret of his soul, the artist is compelled to confront the ruin of his body: "An exclamation of horror broke from the painter's lips as he saw in the dim light the hideous face on the canvas grinning at him. There was something in its expression that filled him with disgust and loathing. Good heavens! it was Dorian Gray's own face he was looking at! The horror, whatever it was, had not entirely spoiled that marvelous beauty. There was still some gold in the thinning hair and some scarlet on the sensual mouth. . . . He turned to Dorian Gray with the eyes of a sick man" (121). No such sickness troubles the subject whose passions tire: however fatigued he may be, he is exempted at least from the more acute disease to which the subject of Shakespearean desire is susceptible in *The Picture of Dorian Gray.* Abandoning the adored body before it has time to grow old, the subject whose passions weary is able to keep his eyes trained on a "world" where "there is absolutely nothing but youth" (24), a world where the ill-making spectacle of physical decay has no chance to appear.

There is evidence in the text to suggest that the senophobic excess that marks the novel's rendering of what age does to the beloved body of youth represents the displaced effects of the violence done to the homosexual in part by means of, but surely beyond *The Picture of Dorian Gray.* If the aging body of the man that another loves is hateful in the novel, it is made so by surgical procedures filled with hate: a breaking of its form, a twisting of its limbs, a branding of its lips that surpasses anything done to the physique by the natural effects of age and weather, or even the allegorical symptoms of his own sin. It could be that the abuse suffered by the picture of Dorian Gray is a form of corporal punishment meted out for "the strange idolatry," and the call to Hellenism that inspired the picture in the first place. But whatever the etiology of the image that generates it, the horror in store for a man who loves another for too long in *The Picture of Dorian Gray* doubles the profits that derive from the defalcation of desire. If the rule of ennui readies its subject for ever new labors of commodity consumption, it also allows him to avoid the sight of the spoiled body, even as it requires that he submit his own to the depredations of boredom. And as much as the anxiety to avert this sight reinforces the regime of ephemeral passion where it *can* be averted, the fortunes of market capitalism owe a debt of gratitude to the fear induced by the spectacle of physical decay, a spectacle that Oscar Wilde, and others besides, picture first of all as the ruined body of homosexual desire.

NOTES

1 One exception is W.H. Auden: "Of his nondramatic prose, we can still read *The Happy Prince and Other Tales* with great pleasure, and *The Soul of Man Under Socialism* and *Intentions*, for all their affectation, contain valuable criticism, but 'The Portrait of Mr. W. H.' is shy-making and *The Picture of Dorian Gray* a bore." W. H. Auden, "An Improbable Life," in *Forewords and Afterwords*, ed. Edward Mendelson (New York: Vintage, 1973), p. 322.

2 Oscar Wilde, *The Picture of Dorian Gray*, ed. Donald Lawler (New York: Norton, 1988), p. 28. Further citations are given parenthetically in the text.

3 Adam Phillips, "On Being Bored," in *On Kissing, Tickling, and Being Bored: Psychoanalytic Essays on the Unexamined Life* (Cambridge: Harvard University Press, 1993), p. 76.

4 Oscar Wilde, "The Portrait of Mr. W. H.," in *The Artist as Critic: Critical Writings of Oscar Wilde*, ed. Richard Ellmann (Chicago: University of Chicago, 1982), pp. 212–13.

5 Wilde's announcement that all passion is spent sounds a little like the scenarios of its systematic cessation that emerged in social theory of the late nineteenth century— the "blasé attitude" that Georg Simmel diagnosed as the symptom of a money economy, the disenchantment that Max Weber called the hallmark of modernity, and the pale shallowness that their Frankfurt School heirs took as the one dimension of a subjectivity held captive by capitalism. But Wilde's rendering of passion's disappearance has less in common with such historical explanations than it does with the picture of desire's bodily limits sketched by a founder of political economy. Here is Christopher Herbert's summary of what he calls the "problem of desire" in Malthus, the problem with which several generations of political economy were preoccupied:

> Malthus['s] . . . image of mankind in its original state goes a long way to qualify the received notion of the human organism as driven by irresistible and innate "bodily cravings." For he insists strongly that man in the primitive state is driven by scarcely any cravings at all beyond a monotonous need for food. . . .On the contrary, the main human traits in the (hypothetical) state, and the ones which Malthus evidently regards as the permanent ones of the human biological constitution, are sluggishness, listlessness, amorphousness, inertia. . . . The problem of desire in Malthus is

not, as in Hobbes, that it is too powerful and unruly. . . . Rather it is that man in his natural condition is so *feeble*.

Christopher Herbert, *Culture and Anomie: Ethnographic Imagination in the Nineteenth Century* (Chicago: University of Chicago Press, 1991), pp. 112–13.

6   Adam Phillips, "On Being Bored," p. 71.

7   Oscar Wilde, "The Decay of Lying," in *The Artist as Critic*, ed. Richard Ellmann, p. 293.

8   This is Wilde's famous speech at his first trial, in response to cross-examination. Quoted by Richard Ellman in his *Oscar Wilde* (New York: Vintage Books, 1988), p. 463.

9   Oscar Wilde, *Lady Windermere's Fan*, Act I, in *The Complete Plays* (London: Methuen, 1989), p. 47.

10   Rachel Bowlby, "Promoting Dorian Gray," in *Shopping with Freud* (London: Routledge, 1993), p. 13.

11   Ibid.

12   Georg Simmel, "The Metropolis and Mental Life," in *The Sociology of Georg Simmel*, trans. and ed. Kurt H. Wolff (New York: The Free Press, 1950), p. 420.

13   Oscar Wilde, "The Portrait of Mr. W. H.," pp. 208–9.

Michael Lucey

Balzac's Queer Cousins and Their Friends

T he family misfit looms as a palpable presence in many a nineteenth-century novel, and not the least in Honoré de Balzac's final
pair, *Cousin Pons* and *Cousin Bette*. A number of recent readings of
nineteenth-century novels (D. A. Miller's *The Novel and the Police* being
an important and influential example) challenge us not to celebrate too
easily our own rediscovery of these queer misfits. Consider, for example,
the cogent central argument of Roddey Reid's recent book *Families in
Jeopardy: Regulating the Social Body in France, 1750–1910*: "I want to argue that the repeated occurrence of orphans, hysterics, masturbators,
and other familial outcasts in familial discourse operates not so much
as the return of the repressed in dominant discourse as the promotion
of a sociopolitical agenda through the relentless tactic of inventing and
defining sexual-social deviance, or, put another way, through the introduction into the social body of *a mobilizing perception of the lack* of normative familial and sexual relations."[1] Reid's argument, much like D. A.
Miller's,[2] follows from Foucault's observations, in *The History of Sexuality,
Volume 1*, on the modern European creation of a discourse on sexuality.
"A censorship of sex?" Foucault scoffs. "There was installed rather an
apparatus for producing an ever greater quantity of discourse about sex."[3]
  Foucault's argument is that this proliferating discourse on sexuality
was linked to a disciplinary regime of power that was also proliferating:

> this form of power demanded constant, attentive, and curious pres-
> ences for its exercise; it presupposed proximities; it proceeded
> through examination and insistent observation; it required an ex-
> change of discourses, through questions that extorted admissions,
> and confidences that went beyond the questions that were asked. . . .
> The medicalization of the sexually peculiar was both the effect and
> the instrument of this. . . . And conversely, since sexuality was a

medical and medicalizable object, one had to try and detect it—as a lesion, a dysfunction, or a symptom—in the depths of the organism, or on the surface of the skin, or among all the signs of behavior. The power which thus took charge of sexuality set about contacting bodies, caressing them with its eyes, intensifying areas, electrifying surfaces, dramatizing troubled moments.[4]

When, in Balzac's last two novels, *Cousin Pons* and *Cousin Bette*, the sexually dubious bodies of Pons or Bette become subject to scrutiny, it is as if they were being caressed by those very disciplinary eyes of which Foucault speaks, being detailed in all their lack of normativity by a gaze whose goal is to assert the privilege of normativity by savoring its absence.

In terms of reading the novel, then, there is no point in self-congratulatory discoveries that novels are more complicated than they want to admit, that their production is enabled by certain hallmark repressions that we or they could implicitly or explicitly—perversely—undo. The whole process of believing that there are hallmark repressions, and recovering with delight the repressed material, finding happiness in our perversions, is, in fact, part of the game of power in the disciplinary regime of sexuality. As Miller puts it: "From this perspective, the enterprise of the traditional novel would no longer (or not just) be the doomed attempt to produce a stable subject in a stable world, but would instead (or in addition) be the more successful task of forming—by means of that very 'failure'—a subject habituated to psychic displacements, evacuations, reinvestments, in a social order whose totalizing power circulates all the more easily for being pulverized."[5]

Yet what of Foucault's own practice as a historian and archivist, a practice in which he never did assume this form of power to be totalizing? A practice in which his interest was clearly directed toward those moments when what might be revealed would rather be the potential for the failure of its totalization, as well as the failure of its absolute position on any given subject at any such moment. I'd like for a few pages to be attentive to this side of Foucault's analysis in order to imagine a different way of reading Balzac, whose novels have often been offered as a good example of the genre at its most disciplinary. As Miller comments: "Balzac's fiction characteristically inspires a sense that the world is thoroughly traversed by techniques of power to which everything, anything gives hold. This world is not so much totally intelligible as it is totally suspicious."[6] Balzac's novels portray a world saturated in disciplines of enforced legibility and social control, and they participate in the project of helping us become subjects who accept the world as such. Or do they? Do those two projects—portraying a world, and helping suture us to it—

fit together without some necessary friction? Is the Balzacian novel (and the nineteenth-century European novel more generally) hopeless both in a search for figures of queer resistance and for resistance itself?

To frame the question slightly differently: Should we imagine that there is no point in looking for queerness in nineteenth-century Europe, in its history or its literature? Not because one might not find it, but because finding it will be part of an ongoing disciplinary project of de-queering it, or because one will only find it ruthlessly trapped within a disciplinary project or apparatus (literature) from which it cannot be extricated? This conclusion does not find support at least in the *practice* of Foucault, who clearly looked to the past for queerness (even if he didn't have the word at his disposal),[7] and it seems worth trying to clarify a bit what this other kind of looking might be.

What is the alternative to imagining power as totally constitutive of desire itself? Foucault's responses to these questions are to be found not only in *The History of Sexuality*, but in a number of smaller texts from the mid to late 1970s, that speak of his practice as a historian, and, in particular, his practice as someone who presents rediscovered archival materials to a larger public.[8] The prefaces Foucault writes when he presents archival material consistently mark the texts they would present as resistant in *two* ways: their representation is an effort at resistance at the moment of that representation (now), and they are *evidence* of resistance at an earlier moment (then). Foucault often uses poetic language to characterize this play between two moments, and it is an effort to understand how two such moments could play together that I am undertaking here. Consider Foucault's description of the series "Parallel Lives" (*Les vies parallèles*), in which Foucault published the modern edition of the memoirs of Herculine Barbin:

> The Ancients liked to display lives of famous men in parallel fashion. One could hear these exemplary shades converse across centuries.
>
> Parallel lines, I know, meet at infinity. Let us imagine others, which would always diverge. No meeting point nor any place for them to be collected. Often their only echo is that of their condemnation. We would have to grasp them in the force of the movement that separates them; we would have to rediscover the dazzling, momentary wake left behind as they rushed into an obscurity from which "nothing more is heard," and where all "fame" is lost. This would be the opposite side of the coin from Plutarch: lives so parallel that no one could join them.[9]

Their wake is of their moment. We grasp it in ours—as best we can, since, in their queer parallelness, they remain beyond our grasp. In the readings of *Cousin Pons* and *Cousin Bette* that follow, there is an implicit reflection on the nature of the relation between different moments, and the varied possibilities revealed when moments are brought into confrontation. The sense of a shift or space between moments that keeps them parallel seems to me to enable a relation of productive *contingency* between them; a productive contingency *sustains* the possibility of keeping the moments parallel; it suggests an interest in avoiding what we might call a precursive relation between them, where that relation depends on running a particular course from one to the other.[10]

PONS

One of the strongest field recollections of this writer was his meeting, among the Boróro of central Brazil, of a man about thirty years old: unclean, ill-fed, sad, and lonesome. When asked if the man were seriously ill, the natives' answer came as a shock: what was wrong with him? — nothing at all, he was just a bachelor. And true enough, in a society where labor is systematically shared between man and woman and where only the married status permits the man to benefit from the fruits of woman's work, including delousing, body painting, and hair-plucking as well as vegetable food and cooked food (since the Boróro woman tills the soil and makes pots), a bachelor is really only half a human being. — Claude Lévi-Strauss, "The Family"

— Allons, vous n'aussi, vous n'êtes sans héritiers, n'est-ce pas! Vous n'êtes venus comme des champignons sur cette terre.
[Go on now, I suppose you'll be telling me you've no heirs either! And that the pair of you just popped up like mushrooms.] — Mme Cibot, to Schmucke and Pons, in *Le Cousin Pons*[11]

It might seem that *Cousin Pons* cries out for psychoanalytic illumination. Sublimation and displacement, what other concepts to use in order to grasp the odd figure after whom this novel is named? Apparently a celibate bachelor, devoted to his male companion Schmucke, devoted to eating, and devoted to collecting, what else would Pons be but a case of misrouted, detoured sexual energy? It has been for a while now a strong temptation (perhaps more in the United States than in France) to read Balzac through a Freudian lens.[12] I would like to question why the Freudian way of reading Balzac has been such a strong critical temptation, and what consequences this has had for an understanding of sexuality in his novels. I will ask this question by way of another: how does Balzac himself participate in the construction both of narrative systems and of the kinds of narrative psychologies that attract and confirm what will later be known as Freudian readings? And does he do so fully? In other words, instead of using Freud to read Balzac, how might we read Balzac and Freud (and recent criticism) together as part of a given, bounded historical moment? And what will the limits of that moment be? Consider the particular case of *Cousin Pons*. The titles of the "cousin" novels from *La Comédie humaine* (the last two novels Balzac wrote) indicate some of what is at stake. Bachelor and spinster cousins, family misfits and remainders, are construed by Balzac as both productive and destructive social forces, forces parasitic on the family, yet also radically other to it. Analyses of these novels thus almost necessarily involve one in a discourse on or about what might be called perversion, its simultaneous relation to and refusal of the reproductive function of the family, its perceived utility, its perceived wastefulness, its alternate, queer ways of relating to society. But must an analysis of sexuality in *Cousin Pons* lead one inevitably to the question: what is the strange nature of Pons's difficultly legible sexuality? Must one parse the nature of his relation to Schmucke? The novel certainly encourages us to try. Psychoanalytic concepts such as sublimation and displacement certainly are temptingly near at hand—positively offered by the text itself—when under the impulse to explain Pons's gastronomy or his mania for collecting: "*Gourmandise*, a sin to which even virtuous monks are addicted, opened its arms to him: he flung himself into them as he had flung himself into the worship of masterpieces and devotion to music. Fine food and bric-à-brac became for him the currency of women. . . . The digestive process brings all the human forces into play. It is a kind of inner combat which, for those who make a god of their bellies, gives as much enjoyment as sexual intercourse. . . . [Pons's] every ecstasy was centered upon his gastronomic activities." (31–32; 495) And why not notice the novel's further suggestion that his gastronomy and his mania for collecting are possible covers for a latent homosexuality? The novel, in fact, both lends credence to this reading and yet denies it. Pons and Schmucke are as good as married, we are told, as good as lovers, at the same time as we are told that Pons could never find a woman, was necessarily unhappy in love, not because of his own desires, but because he was ugly.

> Pons was a happy man . . . in so far as happiness was possible for a man of feeling and delicacy, whose ugliness debarred him from "success with the fair sex." (24; 488)

> In 1835, a lucky chance compensated Pons for the coldness of the fair sex, and gave him something to lean on in his old age. He had been an old man from the cradle, and friendship provided him with a prop: he contracted what was for him the only kind of marriage

possible in his situation—wedlock with a man, an elderly man, a musician like himself. (33; 496)

They conversed . . . like lovers. (35; 498)

Pons took Schmucke's hand between his own, and the clasp contained a movement that communicated his entire soul. They remained thus for several minutes, like lovers meeting again after a long separation. (67; 526)

"It was not God's will that I should have the life I dreamed of," Pons continued. "How I should have loved to have a wife, children, a family! That was my only ambition: to be cherished by one or two people, in some quiet spot." (263; 703)

By both proffering and denying the possibility of Pons's homosexuality, the novel might make us question the very choices it offers us. In fact, we might well consider reading the novel as showing how an inquiry into what is not heterosexuality is done in the service of heterosexuality itself. Or perhaps the novel suggests an odd twist on even that important possibility: perhaps the novel *does* sketch out the possiblity that there would be parties perfectly interested in Pons and Schmucke being queer, parties whose rather murky motivations might lead us to question this inevitable explanatory recourse to the concept of sexuality itself.

It is by accepting on some level the theoretical priority of a model of family romance as necessary to the construction of sexual subjectivities, I want to suggest, and by accepting perversions as the spin-offs, abjects, misfits of that model that we are led to the question: what is the nature of Pons's sexuality? And we are not the only ones led to such a question. Yet precisely such a question also needs to be considered not as abstract, not as theoretical, but as produced by and producing sets of ideological effects. What can be understood about the kinds of interests that lie behind the question "what is the nature of Pons's sexuality?"—about the impulses that produce that particular line of questioning?

Within the novel itself, for example, the person most notably interested in Pons's sexuality (aside from the narrator) is Madame Cibot. Her "disinterested" inquiries into his private life are part of her effort to position herself favorably in order to gain access to his inheritance. Of the many things that provoke the crises that bring an end to Pons's life, one, of course, is his own foolishness in trying to lend a helping hand to heterosexuality. In a final, disastrous effort to ingratiate himself with his distant cousins, the Camusots, Pons tries to arrange a marriage between his "cousin" Cécile and a rich German, and further offers his rooms as the neutral ground on which the prospective couple might meet. Now given that marriage is for Balzac as much an economic transaction as anything else, Pons, failing as a matchmaker, nonetheless thereby begins willy-nilly to participate in an economic world he had hitherto avoided. For Brunner, the German, while in Pons's rooms, appreciates the economic value of all the collecting Pons has done, and, unimpressed with Cécile, nonetheless offers to enter into a transaction with Pons—offers to buy Pons's collection of paintings. The offer is overheard by Rémonencq, who later passes the information on to Madame Cibot, in order to set her scheming.

As Sharon Marcus puts it: "It is thus Pons' uncharacteristic engagement in the world of heterosexual commerce that proves his downfall as a collector. His attempt to arrange a marriage between his cousin Cécile and Schmucke's rich friend Brunner provides the wedge that allows Cibot to appropriate his collection, appetite and affections."[13] By entering the inheritance game, Pons opens himself to a scrutiny whose intensity he will be unable to resist. We can extend this point a bit further, if we notice the actual exchange that Rémonencq overhears:

> "So you don't see any obstacle?" said Pons.
> "I don't know," replied Brunner. "The girl is nothing to get excited about, and the mother's a bit prim. We'll see."
> "A fine fortune in prospect," remarked Pons. "More than a million . . ."
> "We shall meet on Monday," interjected the millionaire, "and if you would like to sell your collection of pictures, I wouldn't mind giving you five or six hundred thousand francs for them."
> "Oh," said the good Pons, surprised to learn how rich he was, "I could never part with the things which bring me happiness. I would only sell my collection for delivery after my death."
> "Well, we shall see . . ."
> "That sets two transactions going," said the collector; but his mind was on the marriage project. (99; 555)

Brunner is already losing whatever interest he may have had in Pons's "cousin" Cécile, but we should notice that, in fact, his proposed deal with Pons is itself an allegory of "heterosexual commerce," if we understand by that a system in which women are used instrumentally to pass family wealth across generations. For Brunner envisions precisely such an instrumental use of "the Pons collection," called by the narrator "the heroine of this story" (331; 763). Buying it deliverable after Pons's death is, after all, rather like marrying someone and then waiting around for her father to die so you can collect on the initial investment. And the narrator was careful in any case to inform us at the outset that Pons came back from Rome around 1810: "as an avid collector, laden with pictures, statuettes, frames, wood and ivory carvings, enamels, porcelains, etc. While living in Rome on his Academic scholarships, he had used up the greater part of his paternal heritage either in paying for or in transporting his purchases. Likewise he had squandered [il avait employé (!)] his mother's estate on a journey he made through Italy after his three statutory years in Rome. (24; 488) So for Brunner and for Balzac, the difference in the nature of the transaction involved in marrying Cécile or in buying Pons's paintings seems slight. Both carry wealth across generations; both represent investments for Brunner.

For Pons himself, the difference between marriage and art collecting might seem greater; Pons's love for art seems based on kinds of aesthetic pleasure and connoisseurship not self-evidently linked to the reproduction of wealth. Yet the novel does not allow anyone—not even Pons—to separate aesthetic and economic realms so easily. It portrays him from the outset, for instance, as hypercathected to kinship. Cash poor, even if art rich, Pons, in order to dine well, as his stomach requires, is forced to drag his palate around to "family" tables where one can only observe that he had "inordinately extended the meaning of the word 'family'" (41; 503). His need for fine food (a need that in itself blends material and aesthetic realms), combined with his bachelor status, dictates a deep concern for family relations, a concern that causes him to come to use and to understand art objects as economic objects as well. Because Pons dines, and wishes to continue to dine, regularly with Cécile's parents, he uses the value of his collection as economic bait.

Cécile, who is having difficulty finding a husband, is Pons's first cousin twice removed, or, to express the relation another way, Cécile is Pons's father's brother's daughter's son's daughter. Cécile's mother protected her own inheritance by investing it in Parisian real estate, so the family lives in a house the mother bought. Her father is, at the time of the novel, still waiting to inherit from his own father, and is currently also cash poor, having spent what cash he had reconstituting an estate in Normandy that has yet to produce notable revenues. Cécile thus has great expectations (from her mother, her father, and her father's father), once she comes into the family's landed wealth. Perceiving Cécile's difficulty—she's not pretty, and she's only potentially rich—realizing, thanks to Brunner's offer, the economic power of his own collection, Pons imagines himself enriching the pool of Cécile's expectations, and thereby securing himself once and for all in the "family" bosom. He declares, sentimentally "persisting in his kinship," that "my heir is of course my cousin Cécile" (103; 559).

A few pages earlier, upon the sudden revelation to him of his wealth, Pons had immediately managed to invent an economic strategy to secure his future: he could sell his collection deliverable after his death. And even though the narrator helpfully insists that Pons was really only think-ing of one transaction (Cécile's marriage) even as he says to Brunner, "that sets two transactions going" (referring also to a possible deal about the collection), we might take the hint that for Pons there is some confusion between affect and kinship and inheritance that he cannot resolve. Be-cause clearly the ideal situation Pons imagines is this: sell the collection to Brunner deliverable after his death, and then have Brunner marry Cécile so that he has the sentimental satisfaction of seeing the collection remain in the "family." The extravagant collection would thus ultimately redeem the "squandering" (the translator's word, not Balzac's) of his own inheri-tance, bringing it back with interest to the family, and bringing Pons the satisfaction of an additional tidy income from the sale, too! " 'My collec-tion or the price it fetches will always belong to your family, whether I do a deal with our friend Brunner or whether I keep it,' said Pons, as he in-formed the astonished family that he had such valuable assets" (103; 559). Pons thus imagines a perfect superposition of (1) his attachment to his art objects, (2) his desire to be attached affectively to his "kin," and (3) his own economic self-interest. Whatever degree of consciousness we assign to his imagination, it seems necessary to account for the suggestion that on some level he strategizes as regards his economic interests, and that his very emotions form a part, conscious or not, of that strategizing.

Let's go even a step further in noting the way various interests in the ultimate disposition of Pons's collection become tied up with shifting distributions of affect and sexuality. For if the discussion of a hypotheti-cal sale between Pons and Brunner, through being overheard, opens the competition for that collection—a competition whose description occu-pies the latter half of the novel—it is certainly worth noting that not all the scenarios envisioned by the competitors for the collection correspond to heterosexual allegories. Pons wants, in the end, to leave the collection to Schmucke; la Cibot forms a whole gang of dispossessed, economically and legally marginal figures, who want a part in it (Fraisier, Poulain, Ré-monencq); the Camusots end up wanting it as well; and then there is Pons's fake will, to which we will turn in a moment, in which he leaves it to the state. Now clearly, la Cibot is not interested in Pons's hetero-sexuality. Indeed, one of the long, irritating interrogations to which she subjects the ailing Pons and his friend Schmucke, has precisely as its goals to establish that they have no heterosexual inclination or history, and to ensure that such a possibility disgusts them.

> "Matame Cipot, you're making him cross," cried Schmucke, notic-ing that Pons was writhing like a worm under his bedclothes.
> "You be quiet too! You're just a couple of old rakes [deux vieux

libertins]. You aren't prize beauties, but as the saying goes: "Ugly as sin, there's still a way in!" . . . You're a nice pair, you are! Come on now, you've had your bit of fun, and the Lord's taking it out of you for leaving your children in the lurch, like Abraham . . ."

"Can't you leave me in peace?" Pons cried out. "I have never known what it is to be loved . . . I've never had any children. I'm alone in the world. [Je suis seul sur la terre.]"

"Is that Gospel truth?" said the concierge. "You're such a kind man, and women, it's a fact, always fall for kindness; that's what draws them. I'd have sworn that when you were young and hearty . . ."

"Take her away," whispered Pons to Schmucke. "She's driving me mad."

"Anyway, Monsieur Schmucke, he's sure to have some children . . . You're all the same, you old bachelors. [Vous n'êtes tous comme ça, vous autres vieux garçons.]"

"I?" cried Schmucke, springing to his feet. "Nefer haf I . . ."

"Go on now, I suppose you'll be telling me you've no heirs either! And that the pair of you just popped up like mushrooms. [Vous n'êtes venus tous deux comme des champignons sur cette terre.]" (126–127; 580–81)

What is Madame Cibot's strategy here? To annoy by suggesting a participation in a sexuality they find repulsive, or to annoy by reminding them of their regrets? When she suggests they are *vieux garçons, comme ça, venus comme des champignons*, what is the implication regarding their relation to reproductivity? La Cibot takes Pons's phrase, "je suis seul sur la terre," and transforms it to: "vous n'êtes venus tous deux comme des champignons sur cette terre." Leave aside the suggestive *champignons* and notice merely the *venus*. Pons's statement of a present condition (*je suis seul*) becomes in la Cibot's version something more essential (*vous n'êtes venus comme des champignons sur cette terre*). Such an assertion would, in fact, be a reassurance *to her* (if not to Pons or Schmucke). For one needn't, in fact, find any absolute consistency in her strategy or her innuendo to appreciate what is at stake. She would rather that they have no usual relation to reproductivity, for if they do not, then a window of opportunity opens, an avenue of attack on Pons's fortune can be conceived, a dispersal of wealth among the disenfranchised of Paris can be envisioned thanks to a failure of heterosexual inclination.

Does the novel then understand heterosexuality primarily as a means for the preservation and transmission of wealth in an ordered way? And is the threat of queerness in the novel the threat of an unforeseen protocol for the redistribution of wealth? Pons does in the end manage to write a will leaving his wealth to Schmucke, who is, as we discover, unable to hold onto it for long. When Pons's will is challenged, Schmucke doesn't know how to play his cards, and allows himself to be impoverished and insulted to death. "No family allows itself to be despoiled by a foreigner without offering some resistance, and we shall see, Monsieur, whether fraud and corrupt dealing or family claims will prevail!" (311; 745) says the crook Fraisier (now acting as the family lawyer) to Schmucke just after Pons' death. Is this despoiling of Schmucke then readable as a final revenge of heterosexuality on a queer attempt to wrest some of society's wealth to its own ends—a revenge that needs to forestall not only the possibility of Pons leaving everything to Schmucke, but also the avid greed of figures such as Rémonencq and la Cibot, who try to twist queerness to their own ends? In considering such a reading it shouldn't be forgotten that sexuality itself might then be conceived of as a ruse of inheritance structures, part of a template that brings affect, family, and certain channels of inheritance into a certain kind of proximity.

There is another piece to the complex puzzle elaborated in *Cousin Pons*. It has to do with the overelaborate pretense of a first will that Pons draws up merely in order to catch la Cibot trying to peruse it and thereby prove her treacherous nature. Now the *exact text* of this first will, not the one finally in effect when Pons dies, is given in the novel, whereas the second one, in which Schmucke actually inherits, is only paraphrased. Why? The first will exists only as a device by which Pons proves to Schmucke that la Cibot is untrustworthy. He makes up his true will shortly after la Cibot betrays herself. It would be enough plotwise to tell us that the terms of the will were unfavorable to la Cibot. To what end, then, does the novel provide us with the full text?

> This is my last will and testament. . . . I have always been impressed by the damage done by certain inconvenient circumstances to the masterpieces of painting, often resulting in their destruction. I have been pained to see beautiful pictures condemned to be for ever moving from country to country and never being housed in one place to which admirers of these masterpieces might travel to see them. I have always thought that the truly immortal productions of the great masters should be national property, perpetually accessible to visitors from every country, just as God's own masterpiece, the light of day, is accessible to all His children. . . .
>
> And therefore, with this intent, I give and bequeath to His Majesty the King, as an accession to the Louvre Museum, the pictures

composing my collection, with this charge, that if the bequest be accepted, a life annuity of two thousand four hundred francs be paid to my friend Wilhelm Schmucke. (267–268; 707)

Pons has a notary help him draw up this will, and the notary advises him of certain legal facts, specifically concerning which kinds of wills are the surest:

"Contestation is always possible, Monsieur," said the notary. "That is one of the drawbacks of human justice. But, as regards wills, certain kinds cannot be challenged."

"What kinds?"

"A will made before a notary in the presence of witnesses who can certify that the testator is of sound mind, and provided the testator has neither wife, children, father nor brother."

"I have nothing like that. All my affections are centered on my dear friend Schmucke, whom you see here."

Schmucke was weeping.

"If then you have only distant collaterals, since the law allows you to dispose freely of your real and personal estate, provided that you do not bequeath them on terms of which public morality disapproves . . . a will signed in a notary's presence is unassailable. . . . All the same, a holograph will, if it is clearly and properly drawn up, is also fairly unexceptionable!" (257; 697–98)

Pons chooses to write this first ruse of a will "holographically," knowing that to be fairly unassailable. The subsequent will, written after la Cibot has fallen into the trap (and Fraisier has managed to steal the first one), is written in the presence of witnesses and a notary. Pons annuls the first will, and, using the notary and his two friendly witnesses, institutes Schmucke as his sole heir in the most "unassailable" way possible.

Of the first will, the notary lets slip to Madame Cibot that it is "a fine will, full of good sense; a public spirited [*patriotique*] testament of which I strongly approve" (258; 698). Fraisier, on the other hand, acting as lawyer for Cécile's family understands a will like this as Pons's most effective arm against his "family," and so, when he gets his hands on the will, has a rather different reaction: "Your gentleman is a monster. He's leaving everything to the Museum, the State. We can't go to law against the State! . . . The will is unassailable. . . . We are robbed, ruined, despoiled, done for!" (268; 708). This suggestive virtual will, annulled the next day in favor of one that names Schmucke "his sole heir," presented as merely a feint, seems more interesting than the second. It allows, after all, the State to enter the scene, conceivably as the *protector* of Schmucke. It may not give Schmucke *everything*, but it gives him an unattackable something. It further apparently subtracts, or should we say, sublimes, the Pons inheritance from commerce and into a realm of aesthetic contemplation guaranteed by a "national" museum. Fraisier certainly appreciates its astuteness. In fact, he purloins it, precisely because he could use it to blackmail Cécile's mother (273; 711), for whom he is working, since, despite what the notary has told Pons, it constitutes a surer threat than the second notarized will to the family's desire to recuperate Pons's estate.

What new analysis would the presence of this first will enable? Pons's disruptiveness seems to me to be understood by the novel as having to do with his radical position in a society based on structures for the transgenerational transmission of wealth. Sexuality is often the effect of reading these structures a certain way. And the novel does in some ways perform this sexualizing reading. Pons is, within the novel, a limit case in a legal sense: he evades all legal restrictions on what to do with his accumulated wealth: no parents, no brothers, no wife, no children. Just a friend. Much of the discourse of the novel, of la Cibot, has understood this structural problem as a problem of sexuality. This slip in some ways parallels the conceptual slip from Pons's "je suis seul sur la terre" to la Cibot's "vous n'êtes venus tous deux comme des champignons sur cette terre." Pons tries to arrive at a bare structural fact of family status through which he escapes sexuality itself. La Cibot prefers some metaphor for reproductive forms, some reading of sexuality. Neither, I would argue, succeeds, or should succeed in convincing us of the correctness of his or her position, or in providing a coherent reading of the novel. This is made clearest in the interference effect of the juxtaposition of the two wills. Pons's call to the sovereign in his first, fantastic, fantasmatic will, for instance, is an extremely odd one, one that almost admits to a sexual culpability. I'll leave you my paintings on the condition that as a by-product my friend get something out of it. And perhaps the unattackable state would accept, sheltering a brief expression of queer friendship in its own "sublimatory" interest as art collector—a kind of high level of inheritance tax on queer couples. (We might also note that the first will might better have assured the modest Schmucke's happiness.) A state might then help out a rich fag here and there, when it is demonstrably in its interest to do so.

Pons is "free" to do what he wants with his goods, the notary tells him, "provided that you do not bequeath them on terms of which public morality disapproves." The second will, despite all its official precautions, would, we know, be challenged by Fraisier and Pons's "relations" on precisely such grounds. They use the threat of such an appeal in their successful effort at the end of the novel to scare Schmucke into accepting their terms. In the first, strategic, will, Pons thus plays the game of sexuality, strategically driving a wedge between family and state interests, conceptualizing his collection within an economy a state will understand, and claiming for his friend some of the scraps of that economy. In the first will, Pons and Schmucke rather admit to being two mushrooms the *state* might manage to savor. In this first will, Pons himself, then, finds himself caught up in the tourniquet of the question, "What is the nature of Pons's sexuality?" In his second will, he perhaps imagines himself justly—through legal formalism—escaping that tourniquet, free to declare Schmucke his heir, free to accede to some unbounded act of pure friendship; perhaps he imagines himself acceding to that act by effacing or evading or rendering irrelevant the question of sexuality that the novel has consistently posed him. The brutal failure of that evasion, demonstrated in Schmucke's sad fate, could be understood as a predecessor of the similar failure of our own.

Yet perhaps, on the other hand, the failure is not absolute. For perhaps the interference of the two wills, the false choice of evading or acknowledging sexuality, does open up a different moment—in which we can glimpse something about the contingency of the dilemmas Pons faces. It is an unstable sense of that moment that I would like to have reconstructed here.

BETTE

Jerry Durance (Paul Henreid): I don't even know yet whether it's Miss or Mrs.
Charlotte Vale (Bette Davis): It's aunt. Every family has one you know. —*Now, Voyager* (dir. Irving Rapper, 1942)

Of the relation between Lisbeth Fischer (Cousin Bette) and her friend Valérie Marneffe, the narrator of *Cousin Bette* tells us: "Lisbeth and Valérie presented the touching spectacle of one of those friendships so close and so unlikely between women that Parisians, always too clever by half, immediately make it the subject of malicious gossip. The contrast between the masculine stiff temperament of the peasant from Lorraine and Valérie's warm creole indolence helped the calumny along. Madame Marneffe, moreover, had unthinkingly lent weight to the gossiping tales by the trouble she took over her friend's appearance, with an eye to a certain marriage, which was, as we shall see, to complete Lisbeth's vengeance."[14] The narrator here makes a rhetorical move similar to one we have seen in *Cousin Pons*, acknowledging the general existence of same-sex sexual relations, all the while leaving ambiguous their actual occurence between specific pairs of characters. This effect can be created (as it is in the passage just cited) by pointing to a generalized social gaze that maliciously assigns a queer identity to various characters. It can also be created, as in the following passages, by using too many different names to characterize a given relationship:

> Lisbeth . . . adored Valérie, moreover; she had made a daughter of her, a friend, her love. She found in her a creole docility, a voluptuary's yielding temper. She chatted with her all morning, with much more pleasure than she had taken in talking to Wenceslas. . . . In this new friendship, Lisbeth had indeed found an outlet for her energy much more rewarding than her foolish love for Wenceslas. (170; 200)

> "How lovely you look this morning!" said Lisbeth, coming over to put her arm round Valérie's waist and kiss her forehead. "I share in the enjoyment of all your pleasures, your good fortune, your dresses. . . . I didn't know what it was to live until the day when we became sisters." (211–212; 239)

Sister, friend, lover, daughter, the proliferation of available categories, along with the palimpsestic considerations (to which we shall return shortly)—this relationship overwrites the previous one with Wenceslas— all suggest that Bette's relation to Valérie falls into no one identifiable modality. By failing to do so, it exercises a certain compulsion on us (or at least on the Parisian public and the Balzacian narrator) to become preoccupied with it.

We can begin to see why Balzac's final two novels, *Cousin Bette* (1846) and *Cousin Pons* (1847), are almost always necessarily understood as a pair. Balzac says as much in his oft-remarked dedication to the pair (linked with the omnibus title, *Les Parents Pauvres* [Poor Relations]): "My two stories are therefore placed together as a pair, like twins of different sex" (10; 54). The two cousins are thus parallel and yet asymmetrical. Parallel in the near illegibility of their sexualities (an illegilibity that is, it would appear, only meant to spur one on to more furious attempts to render their sexualities legible) they are nonetheless not parallel in the way their various illegibilities are constructed.

Just as *Cousin Pons* both lends credence to a reading of Pons as homosexual and yet denies it, so *Cousin Bette* suggests the possibility of lesbianism without confirming it. What is at stake in siding with the malicious Parisian gossip and making Bette a butch lesbian? What is at stake in the narrator's equivocation on the subject? The beginning of an answer to these questions might be found in the remarkable scene in which Bette transfers her affections from the artist Wenceslas to Valérie. A few plot details: Bette is the poor spinster cousin of Adeline Hulot. Adeline began as a simple peasant girl like Bette, but caught the eye of Hulot, named baron by Napoleon, and was carried off to a Parisian wonderland, in which Bette eventually joined her. But Hulot, by the time of the novel, has become a fat old lecher, who has used up his fortune on mistresses, and can no longer afford to support his family in the style to which they are accustomed, leastwise arrange an appropriate marriage for his daughter Hortense. Hortense realizes this, and by a particular set of Balzacian coincidences, manages to arrange her own marriage with an impoverished but artistically talented Polish count in exile in Paris. Now she learns of Wenceslas, this talented count, because he lives in the same boardinghouse as Bette, who prefers this kind of slumming to depending on her family. Bette smells smoke one night, and single-handedly saves Wenceslas from suicide, becoming his protectress and taskmaster, and dropping hints to Adeline and Hortense about her new "lover." Hortense makes sufficient fun of what she sees as spinster Bette's pretensions to having a lover that Bette finally brings proof one day, in the form of a beautiful silver seal crafted by the talented Polish count. Hortense falls in love with the artist sight unseen, and finds a way to "steal" him from Bette. Meanwhile, Valérie Marneffe—illegimate child of a grand figure from the Napoleonic period—and her dissolute husband also live in the same slum dwelling as Bette and Wenceslas. The lecherous Hulot catches sight of the sexy Valérie one evening as he drives Bette home. On the market for a new mistress, he takes up with her. She is thus, via Hulot, privy to the family's plans to arrange a marriage between Hortense and Wenceslas, plans the family initially keeps secret from Bette. Valérie lets the cat out of the bag "by accident" one day in a scene that thereby marks the beginning of the friendship between the two women. But what is most interesting about the opening of the scene is the difficulty Valérie apparently has in understanding the nature of the bond between Bette and Wenceslas. This is another of those bonds for which there appears to be no name. Before the scene even opens, we have realized that this odd relationship, too, has been commented on by certain Parisians. Valérie originally thinks that Bette and Wenceslas are a couple. Her husband disbelieves this: "'Mademoiselle Fischer living with a young man!' repeated the civil servant. 'That's just porters' gossip. Let's not speak so lightly of the cousin of a Councillor of State who makes the sun shine and the rain descend at the Ministry'" (63; 102). Valérie has indeed been gossiping with the portière, Mme Olivier, who has noted and suspected the nature of the affection that binds Bette to Wenceslas. The narrator agrees with Valérie's husband, however, at least initially, and gainsays the portière's malicious gossip. As Bette happily enters her paramour's apartment, bringing him a bit of dinner, the narrator comments: "The most bitter-tongued of Mademoiselle Fischer's detractors, watching even the beginning of this scene, would have acknowledged that the scandalous suggestions of the Olivier pair must be false. Everything in the tone, the gestures, and the looks of these two beings declared the purity of their life together. The old maid evinced the tender feeling of a dictatorial but sincere maternal affection. The young man submitted like a respectful son to a mother's tyranny" (70; 108). As one might expect, things are not quite so clear. Malicious Parisians appear to have as much right to the truth as the Balzacian narrator, for the difficulty Bette has in reconciling herself to the idea that Hortense could steal her love from her is explained by the narrator precisely by reference to her problematic sense of the "maternal" nature of her relation to Wenceslas:

> She loved Steinbock well enough not to marry him, and loved him too well to give him up to another woman. She could not resign herself to being only his mother, yet thought herself crazy when the idea of playing the alternative role crossed her mind. These warring impulses: her fierce jealousy, her happiness in possessing a man of her own, kept this woman's heart in a state of inordinate agitation. She had been truly in love for the past four years, and she cherished the wild hope of making *this illogical way of life—leading nowhere [cette vie inconséquente et sans issue]*—permanent, though its continuance must mean the destruction of the person she called her child. (81–82; 118–119; emphasis added)

The phrase "cette vie inconséquente et sans issue" is worth remarking. Bette's relationship with Wenceslas forms part of a life without sequence, without consequence, without issue in a couple of senses of the word. It falls out of sequence, or fits into no sequence. Bette's life story misplaces amorous relationships and maternal ones; it doesn't put them in any order. In a moment of crisis a bit further along in the novel, she will beg Wenceslas in a queerly imaginative way:

> Consider: we need not marry—I am an old maid, I know. I do not want to stifle the flower of your youth . . . but, without marrying, can we not stay together? Listen. I have a head for business. I can gather a fortune for you in ten years' work. . . . Well, Wenceslas, stay with me. . . . You know, I understand everything. You shall have mistresses, pretty women like that little Marneffe who wants to meet you, who will give you the kind of happiness you could not find with me. Then you shall get married when I have saved thirty thousand francs a year for you. (134)
>
> [Songez que, sans nous marier, car je suis une vieille fille, je le sais,

je ne veux pas étouffer la fleur de votre jeunesse . . . mais, sans nous marier, ne pouvons-nous pas rester ensemble? Ecoutez, j'ai l'esprit du commerce, je puis vous amasser une fortune en dix ans de travail. . . . Eh bien! Wenceslas, reste avec moi. . . . Tiens, je comprends tout : tu auras des maîtresses, de jolies femmes semblables à cette petite Marneffe qui veut te voir, et qui te donnera le bonheur que tu ne peux pas trouver avec moi. Puis tu te marieras quand je t'aurai fait trente mille francs de rente. (167)]

The sudden use of the *tu* form in Bette's "Eh bien! Wenceslas, reste avec moi" marks the strangely moving pathos of this passage, a subtle effort to claim some kind of kinship, a gamble with vulnerability. For a moment it seems as if the gamble might have paid off. Wenceslas weeps, and replies: "You are an angel, Mademoiselle, and I shall never forget this moment." [Vous êtes un ange, mademoiselle, et je n'oublierai jamais ce moment-ci.] Choosing not to hear any ominous echoes in Wenceslas deflection of the *tu*, Bette has a paragraph in which to occupy the summit of joy: "So strong is vanity in us, that Lisbeth believed that she had triumphed. She had made such a great concession in offering Madame Marneffe! She experienced the keenest emotion of her life. For the first time she felt joy flood her heart. For such another hour she would have sold her soul to the devil" (135; 167). Wenceslas's next observation quells the ecstasy "like an avalanche of snow upon that blazing crater." For he insists on returning her to the purely maternal position she had been trying to edge her way out of: "I love a woman against whom no other can prevail. But you are and you will always be [vous êtes et vous serez toujours] the mother I have lost."

This is not the sole occasion on which volcanic imagery is used to describe Bette's case. She's a bit like a truckload of affect on the loose. That affect is usually structured as hate, and the novel has as one of its central subjects the excess of her affect, its profoundly asocial bent. Consider in this light the beginning of her relationship with Valérie. The inconsequential nature of Bette's relationship with Wenceslas is seemingly carried over into this relationship, even if, at least at the outset, Valérie doesn't seem that promising a queer partner, since she appears to have no ability to comprehend Bette's inconsequentiality. When she tells Bette of Wenceslas' infidelity, she apparently has no categories through which to comprehend Bette's (again volcanic) reaction. Here is a long excerpt from that crucial scene:

'Listen, my dear little Cousin Bette,' said Madame Marneffe graciously. 'Are you capable of a devoted friendship, proof against anything? Would you like us to be like two sisters? Will you swear to me to have no secrets from me, if I'll keep none from you, to be my secret eye if I'll be yours . . .'

Madame Marneffe broke off this picador's attack, for Cousin Bette frightened her. . . . Her teeth were clenched to prevent them from chattering, and her body was shaken convulsively and horribly. . . . she was on fire! The smoke of the conflagration that ravaged her seemed to issue from the wrinkles of her face, as if they were fissures opened by volcanic eruption. It was a sublime spectacle.

'Well, why do you stop?' she said hollowly. 'I will be for you all that I was for him. Oh! I would have given my life-blood for him!'

'You love him, then?'

'As if he were my child!'

'Well,' Madame Marneffe went on, breathing more easily, 'if you only love him like that, you are going to be very well pleased, for you want him to be happy don't you?'

Lisbeth replied by nodding her head rapidly and repeatedly, like a madwoman.

'In a month he's going to marry your second cousin.'

'Hortense!' cried the old maid, striking her forehead and rising to her feet.

'Well, now! So you are in love with this young man?' asked Madame Marneffe.

'My dear, we are now sworn friends,' said Mademoiselle Fischer. 'Yes, if you have attachments, I will regard them as sacred. Your very vices shall be virtues to me, for indeed I have need of your vices!'

'So you were living with him?' Valerie exclaimed.

'No, I wanted to be his mother. . . .'

'Ah! I can't make head or tail of it,' returned Valérie; 'for if that's so, then you haven't been deceived or made a fool of, and you ought to be very glad to see him make a good marriage. . . .' (110–111; 145–46)

The scene insists perhaps too much on the uncategorizable nature of Bette's attachment, its "none of the above" character—neither mother nor lover, yet both, and Valérie need not be so dense as she here seems to be. (Her style of interrogation bears some resemblance to that of la Cibot.) But what the scene *does* highlight is the novel's interest in what we might call the slack in the cord that links sentiment or affect or sexuality to family structure. Thus, even though Valérie is hardly the novel's most obvious exponent of family values, she here expects the course— the sequence—of Bette's affectual currents to follow typical maternal or amorous patterns. Yet what Bette's relations to both Wenceslas and

Valérie reveal is that (at least in the Balzacian novelistic universe) sentiment/affect/sexuality exceed the structures that theoretically produce and contain them.

Thus, in at least his last two novels, it would appear that Balzac is theorizing the same problem that would later interest Foucault in the first volume of *The History of Sexuality*, where he pursues the question of the relation between *alliance* and sexuality: " 'Sexuality' was taking shape, born of a technology of power that was originally focused on alliance. Since then, it has not ceased to operate in conjunction with a system of alliance on which it has depended for support. . . . The family is the interchange of sexuality and alliance: it conveys the law and the juridical dimension in the deployment of sexuality; and it conveys the economy of pleasure and the intensity of sensation in the regime of alliance." [15] Gayle Rubin makes a similar point in "The Traffic in Women," though she uses a somewhat different metaphor. Equating what Foucault calls a "system of alliance" with what Rubin calls kinship, and what Foucault calls "sexuality" with what Rubin calls the "sex/gender system," what interests Rubin then is not that sex/gender depends on kinship for support, but that sex/gender took form through kinship, yet now is constrained to that form which no longer functions: "The organization of sex and gender once had functions other than itself—it organized society. Now, it only organizes and reproduces itself. The kinds of relationships of sexuality established in the dim human past still dominate our sexual lives, our ideas about men and women, and the ways we raise our children. But they lack the functional load they once carried. One of the most conspicuous features of kinship is that it has been systematically stripped of its functions—political, economic, educational, and organizational. It has been reduced to its barest bones—sex and gender." [16]

When Valérie suggests that Bette's emotions should conform either to those of a proud mother or those of a jilted lover, she suggests that sexuality and its affects should overlap exactly with kinship structures, even in those cases where there is no chance of kinship. But the novel itself presents Bette precisely as an instance of sexuality resting uncomfortably both inside and outside systems of kinship. Valérie, too, in fact, operates within the novel as a disrupter of systems of kinship (or perhaps it would be better to stick with Foucault's word, *alliance*, here), almost causing family fortunes to disappear, destabilizing even *state* finances, wreaking havoc precisely with the smooth functioning of *alliances*. Her union with Bette, whatever its nature, is thus clearly the locus within the novel for thinking about a disruption in alliance. *Cousin Bette* might then have an interest not only in the family's relation to sexuality, but further in the possibilities for sexuality's continuance outside the system of the family.

What would sexuality be if it were not related to inheritance? the novel might hesitantly ask.

Hesitantly, because it's not clear that such a relation could ever be effaced.[17] Foucault insists that sexuality depended on alliance to elaborate itself, that the two are distinct but interdependent, and that, even though one might imagine that the "deployment of sexuality" as a social distribution of power would eventually have replaced the "deployment of alliance," such is not the case.[18] He suggests, further, that psychoanalysis has done some of the cultural work of keeping them pinned together:

> [P]sychoanalysis, whose technical procedure seemed to place the confession of sexuality outside family jurisdiction, rediscovered the law of alliance, the involved workings of marriage and kinship, and incest at the heart of this sexuality, as the principle of its formation and the key to its intelligibility. The guarantee that one would find the parents-children relationship at the root of everyone's sexuality made it possible—even when everything seemed to point to the reverse process—to keep the deployment of sexuality pinned to the system of alliance [*de maintenir l'épinglage du dispositif de sexualité sur le système de l'alliance*]. . . . The deployments of alliance and sexuality were involved in a slow process that had them turning about one another until . . . their positions were reversed . . . with psychoanalysis, sexuality gave body and life to the rules of alliance by saturating them with desire."[19]

It is perhaps the double work of novels like *Cousin Bette* that they both analyze this strange pinning, reveal it, and work on us to blind us to its force.

If we were to try to read *Cousin Bette* as a novel about the pinning together of alliance and affect/sexuality, our sense of who is at the center of the novel might change. The central character of the novel might become Célestine Crevel-Hulot. Her father, Crevel, is to be Valérie's prime catch, and catching him means depriving Célestine, his only daughter, of her father's estate—an eventuality Célestine's husband, Hulot's son, due to something we might call filial devotion, has every interest in preventing. Following this analysis, the novel would have three key points. The first, the opening gambit, would be Crevel's remark that, unlike his friend Hulot, he knows what mistresses are for, and what they are not for. You don't squander your estate on them. "I love Célestine too well to ruin her" (23; 66) he insists in the book's opening pages, showing kinship duties and affective structures well aligned. By the novel's midpoint, Valérie has them halfway unpinned: "Valérie, I love you as much as I love Célestine," Crevel admits (198–199; 227). And the crisis point that leads to the novel's denouement arrives when the opening kinship/affect relationship has been totally overturned and reinstated differently. As Bette reports the conversation to the "family": " 'With Valérie as my wife, I'll be a Peer of France! I'll buy an estate I have my eye on—Presles. Mme de Serizy wants to sell it. I'll be Crevel de Presles. I'll be a member of the Council of Seine-et-Oise, and a Deputy. I'll have a son! I'll be anything in the world I want to be.' 'All very well,' I said to him; 'and what about your daughter?' 'Bah, she's only a daughter!' was what he answered. 'And she's become far too much of a Hulot, and Valérie can't bear that lot.' " (353–354; 369). It's pretty clear that Valérie has no interest in this slightly crazed vision of an alternative family that Crevel elaborates. She wants him to die quickly after she marries him, so she gets the estate. The forces of order magically intervene to prevent all this, of course, and Célestine does end the novel as the appropriately filled receptacle for wealth she was always marked to be.

And what of Bette? The novel also understands her to be produced by and ruthlessly excluded from the system of alliance, and it carefully presents her hate—directed at representative kin—as also a by-product of the system: "Lisbeth Fischer, five years younger than Madame Hulot although she was the daughter of the eldest of the Fischer brothers, was far from being as beautiful as her cousin. . . . The family, who lived as one household, had sacrificed the plebeian daughter to the pretty one, the astringent fruit to the brilliant flower. Lisbeth worked in the fields while her cousin was cosseted; and so it had happened one day that Lisbeth, finding Adeline alone, had done her best to pull Adeline's nose off, a true Grecian nose, much admired by all the old women" (38–39; 80–81). Family matrimonial strategies, beauty taking pride of place over family hierarchy, a well-planned vengeful effort to sabotage the family's strategy: this passage indicates to what an extent Bette's vengeful affects can be read as a response to an experience of kinship/matrimonial strategy. A major goal of her revenge is to overturn this primal insult: she strategizes toward a marriage with the Baron Hulot's older brother. She would thereby displace Adeline in the family hierarchy, and, were she successfully to outlive the Marshal and inherit his wealth after the Baron had squandered his, she might have the additional satisfaction of seeing Adeline obliged to work for a living (176–77; 205–7). Bette miscalculates; the Marshal dies before her plans can mature. Moreover, the kinship system has a few more lessons to teach her. For even a marriage to the Marshal would have been *sans issue*, and a family (understood, among other things, as a unit for reproducing and increasing wealth and social power) knows how to take things like this into consideration. Shortly after the Marshal's death, we read:

Lisbeth went to weep with rage to Madame Marneffe's, for she no longer had a place to live, the marshal's lease of his house terminating with his death. Crevel, to console his Valérie's friend, took her savings and considerably increased them, and invested this capital in five-per-cents in Célestine's name, giving Lisbeth the life interest. Thanks to him, Lisbeth possessed an annuity of two thousand francs. When the inventory of the Marshal's property came to be taken, a note from the Marshal was found addressed to his sister-in-law, his neice Hortense, and his nephew Victorin, charging them with the payment, between them, of twelve hundred francs a year to Mademoiselle Lisbeth Fischer, who was to have been his wife. (336– 337; 353–54)

What these "consolations" actually show is that it would never occur to anyone to allow Bette to inherit, or even possess for any length of time, any substantial *capital*. The Marshal understands Adeline, her son, and her daughter to be proper for this task. Bette gets a little *interest* thanks to what they inherit. Crevel's consolation is in some ways even more brutal. He, too, guarantees her an income, but seems, apparently without thinking about it, to appropriate some capital that had been hers for his heir (still Célestine at this point), leaving Bette merely her interest (however substantial) to live off.

This isn't the first time such familial economic arrogance has surfaced in the novel. Adeline felt some remorse when her daughter stole Bette's paramour from her, and so to include Bette's happiness in the general happiness around the event of her daughter's wedding, she makes Bette a proposition:

"We don't want you to work any longer," said the Baroness. "I suppose that you may earn forty sous a day, not counting Sundays: that makes six hundred francs a year. Well, how much have you put away in savings?"

"Four thousand five hundred francs."

"Poor Cousin!" said the Baroness.

She raised her eyes to heaven, she was so moved to think of all the hardships and privations that that sum of money, gathered together through thirty years, represented. Lisbeth misunderstood the nature of the Baroness's exclamation, saw in it the contempt of a woman who has made it, and her hatred acquired a new intensity of bitterness, at the very moment when her cousin was abandoning all her mistrust of the tyrant of her childhood.

"We will add ten thousnad five hundred francs to that," Adeline continued, "placed in trust, the interest to go to you, the principal to revert to Hortense; so that you will have an income of six hundred francs a year."

Lisbeth's cup was full, or so it seemed. (139; 171–72)

We need cast no aspersions on the sincerity of Adeline's emotions to see the way they float on top of an (unconsious?) devotion to familial strategy and a classist ideology that encourage her to dispossess Bette of her savings in the family's favor without even conceiving that she is doing so, without seeing any of the irony with which the narrator so carefully burdens this scene. Cousins are just more naturally suited to interest than to capital. Who could want it any other way? Needless to say, it remains equally unclear to what degree Bette is ever conscious of the role of "kinship" itself in her affliction. Nor is it clear to what extent her relation to Valérie could have helped her lift herself out of that system.

Now, for Foucault, one of the concepts that conceivably provided a way to begin thinking about sexuality separately from the system of family inheritance was friendship. The project of understanding friendship became for Foucault one way of loosening the pin linking sexuality and alliance.[20] We might pursue this concept a bit, since it is finally the word *friendship* that the narrator of *Cousin Bette* arrives at to label what exists between Valérie and Bette. Two interesting uses of this word come at the moment when Bette, who has been ill and confined to bed, hears that Valérie is on her own deathbed, with little time left. Hearing the news, Bette has a reaction as physical as her reaction on hearing of Wenceslas's betrayal:

> Cousin Bette's teeth chattered, she broke out in a cold sweat. The terrible shock she experienced revealed the depth of her passionate friendship [*la profondeur de son amitié passionnée*] for Valérie.
> "I must go to her," she said. (421; 430)

Finding Valérie rotting away, smelling quite foul, and spouting newly espoused truisms of family values, Bette is unable to stick it out to the bitter end with the nuns at the deathbed. As the narrator has it: "The most violent sentiment we know of, the friendship of one woman for another [*Le sentiment le plus violent que l'on connaisse, l'amitié d'une femme pour une femme*], had not the heroic constancy of the Church. Lisbeth, stifled by the noxious exhalations, left the room" (424; 433). Now why is it that the friendship of a woman for a woman would be the most violent sentiment known within the world of the Balzacian narrator? Why would we imagine the sentiment Bette has for Valérie, for instance, as more violent than that of Pons for Schmucke? Clearly because alliance and sexuality are pinned together in such a way that two men being "friends" creates different kinds of short-circuits than two women. Foucault mainly speaks of friendship between men, but he acknowledges gendered dissymmetries in the concept on a number of occasions in the early 1980s by making reference to Lillian Faderman's book, *Surpassing the Love of Men*. What follows is the passage where he refers to that book in his 1981 interview, "Friendship as a Way of Life":

There is a book that just appeared in the U.S. on the friendships between women. The affection and passion between women is well documented. In the Preface the author states that she began with the idea of unearthing homosexual relationships but that she per-ceived that not only were these relationships not always present but that it was uninteresting whether relationships could be called homosexual or not. And by letting the relationship manifest itself as it appeared in words and gestures other very essential things also appeared: dense, bright, marvelous loves and affections or very dark and sad loves. The book shows the extent to which woman's body - has played a great role, and the importance of physical contact be-tween women: women do each other's hair, help each other with make-up, dress each other. Man's body has been forbidden to other men in a much more drastic way.[21]

Foucault is ascribing to himself and to Faderman a position with certain ressemblances to the position of the Balzacian narrator. That is, he ac-knowledges a social impulse to provide a label and a sexual content to these "friendships" from another time, and then resists making the label stick. The reasons Foucault might do this are, of course, different from the reasons a Balzacian narrator might do it. Foucault does it as part of his effort to move *contemporary* sexual practices into a new conceptual space. As he says most concisely in another interview: "I will say that we must use our sexuality to discover, to invent new ways of relating. To be gay is to be in the process of becoming and I would add, we must not be homosexual, we must work tenaciously to be gay." [Je dirai, il faut user de sa sexualité pour découvrir, inventer de nouvelles relations. Etre gay, c'est être en devenir et . . . j'ajouterais qu'il ne faut pas être homosexual mais s'acharner à être gay.][22]

Foucault's desire to move into a new conceptual space that would leave "sexuality" behind is perhaps not on the agenda of the Balzacian novel, which, as we have seen, is quite interested in producing "sexuality" in its characters. Balzac's twin novels might, however, help us keep more firmly in mind than does Foucault the force of gendered dissymme-tries in friendship (at least in nineteenth-century France). The friendship between Bette and Valérie is not the same as the friendship between

Schmucke and Pons. Not that Schmucke holds on to the wealth Pons has queerly redistributed any better than Valérie or Bette hold on to theirs, but he does inherit, if only for a brief instant. *Cousin Pons* also imagines that first will, finding a way of using the state to help two queer *men* be friends. In *Cousin Bette*, it is Victorin Hulot who imagines a state intervention (help from the police in doing away with Valérie, that is), who pays for it as if it were a tax,[23] so that the family can be saved.

Both *Cousin Bette* and *Cousin Pons* have ruthlessly violent endings, ensuring that *in fact* there is no inheritance possible for the queer friendships they haltingly sketch out, no disruption to the system of alliance. Yet as Balzac understands it, Bette and Valérie have by structural necessity constituted the greater threat to alliance in their pursuit of their own ends, and consequently receive the more lurid punishment. Though Bette dies with a rather lighter technicolor touch than does Valérie, Balzac has carefully and cruelly figured her inevitable punishment throughout by always insisting, through the figure of a yellow cashmere shawl, on the nonautonomy of Bette's own queer desires.

The shawl was given by the baron Hulot to his wife and by Adeline to her daughter Hortense. As the narrator says: "Cousin Bette, victim since her arrival in Paris of an admiration for cashmere, had been fascinated by the idea of possessing this yellow cashmere given by the baron to his wife in 1808, and which, according to the custom of certain families, had passed from mother to daughter in 1830" (50; 89). Bette wins the shawl from Hortense by proving that her constant talk about her lover, Wenceslas, is not a fiction. By proving Wenceslas to be real, she wins her shawl (a token of the system of alliances), but loses her lover/son to that same system. (We might think of Pons here, inadvertently opening his museum to heterosexual commerce.) The shawl reappears at all the queerest moments, as if repetitively to repin Bette to the system of alliance from which she would escape if she could; a kind of straightjacket she can't shake. Even when she moves in with Valérie, and Valérie revolutionizes the way she dresses, she is nonetheless "still wearing the yellow cashmere" (165; 196); as she runs to Valérie's deathbed, she stops to put on "her famous yellow cashmere shawl" (421; 430). Tenacious and threadbare at once, the shawl clings in its effort to keep queerness abject. One might well wish she could have thrown it away.

In the first volume of his *History of Sexuality*, Foucault mentions not only psychoanalysis, but also ethnology as one of those forms of knowledge that both has been part and parcel of the ongoing "deployment of sexuality," and also has ensured that the "deployment of sexuality" remain pinned to the "deployment of alliance." For instance, Foucault notes that the incest taboo would function differently in the two different "deployments": "It may be [*il se peut bien*]," he says ambiguously (perhaps a bit doubtfully), "that in societies where the mechanisms of alliance predominate, prohibition of incest is a functionally indispensable rule."[24] In the domain of sexuality, the prohibition of incest functions differently; it "occupies a central place; it is constantly being solicited and refused; it is an object of obsession and attraction, a dreadful secret and an indispensable pivot."[25] In the case of alliance, the prohibition of incest would be formal, a rule; in the case of sexuality it is a spur, a topic of endless—if sometimes hushed or displaced—discussion, richly productive of psychological effects. Ethnology, in being a major locus of this discussion, has served the deployment of sexuality, but in the terms of its discussion, has also sustained a certain way of keeping the deployments of sexuality and alliance pinned together:

> If for more than a century the West has displayed such a strong interest in the prohibition of incest . . . perhaps this is because it was found to be a means of self-defense, not against incestuous desire, but against the expansion and the implications of this deployment of sexuality which had been set up, but which, among its many benefits, had the disadvantage of ignoring the laws and juridical forms of alliance. By asserting that all societies without exception, and consequently our own, were subject to this rule of rules, one guaranteed that this deployment of sexuality, whose strange effects were beginning to be felt—among them, the affective intensification of the family space—would not be able to escape from the grand and ancient system of alliance. Thus the law would be secure, even in the new mechanics of power. . . . By devoting so much effort to an endless reworking of the transcultural theory of the incest taboo, anthropology has been the loyal servant of the whole modern deployment of sexuality and the theoretical discourses it generates. [L'ethnologie, en réélaborant sans cesse depuis si longtemps, la théorie transculturelle de l'interdiction de l'inceste, a bien mérité de tout le dispositif moderne de sexualité et des discours théoriques qu'il produit.][26]

What has been most helpful to me in my efforts to read *Cousin Pons* and *Cousin Bette* has been to think about the historic specificity of the pin holding alliance and sexuality together in the social world Balzac is analyzing. One of the particularities of that post-Napoleonic, French Restoration world is the intense attention payed to alliance by the bourgeoisie as it tries to create itself as the legitimate locus of social power. It seems as if this return to alliance is in part an effort to repudiate, or to check, the seemingly free-wheeling fluctuations of social power felt to characterize the period of the Revolution, and also the subsequent Napoleonic period. One might choose to see the Restoration as thus merely a retrograde moment in the ongoing modernization of French social structures. This would be equivalent to supposing that we should imagine a story where alliance is slowly being left behind by sexuality, whatever hesitations that process involves.[27] If we think instead about rendering historically and geographically specific the pin that holds the deployments of sexuality and alliance together,[28] we might see the benefits of constructing a different (less historically reductive) relation between the two modalities of power. This might allow us to understand the concentration on alliance we find in Balzac's world not a temporary step back in a grand historical narrative, so much as a given, contingent, historical configuration, whose contours we can trace, not just in Balzac's novels, but in, for instance, the Napoleonic Code,[29] as well as a variety of other discourses both reflective of and productive of the material conditions of mid-nineteenth-century France. We might then begin to imagine Pons and Bette and their troubles with sexuality not in some ancestral relation to ourselves, but in some "parallel" moment that might nonetheless provoke in some of us a tremor of recognition.

NOTES

A good deal of my thinking for this essay got worked out by co-teaching with Carolyn Dinshaw a seminar sponsored by Berkeley's Townsend Center for the Humanities: "Dissymmetries: Lesbian Theory, Gay Theory." My thanks to her for lots of encouragement and advice. Thanks, too, to all the participants in the seminar, who were so generous in responding to versions of this material. And to Tim Hampton, Celeste Langan, Lydia Liu, and Leslie Kurke, for reading closely and demanding a variety of refinements.

1   Roddey Reid, *Families in Jeopardy: Regulating the Social Body in France, 1750–1910* (Stanford: Stanford University Press, 1993), p. 52.

2   In one concise formulation, Miller writes, "Insistently, the novel shows disciplinary power to inhere in the very resistance to it. At the macroscopic level, the demonstration is carried in the attempt of the protagonist to break away from the social control that thereby reclaims him. At the microscopic level, it is carried in the trifling detail that is suddenly invested with immense significance. Based on an egregious disproportion between its assumed banality and the weight of revelation it comes to bear, the 'significant trifle' is typically meant to surprise, even frighten" (*The Novel and the Police* [Berkeley: University of California Press, 1988], pp. 27–28). Both these levels, as we shall see, uncontestably operate in Balzac's *Cousin* novels. On the microscopic level, for instance, we receive through these novels a training in the details that mark a person as odd. Such a training cannot simply demonstrate a preexisting oddity: it produces the oddity in all its particular consequentiality.

3   Michel Foucault, *The History of Sexuality: An Introduction*, trans. Robert Hurley, vol. 1 (New York: Random House, 1978), p. 23.

4   Ibid., p. 44.

5   Miller, *Novel and the Police*, p. xii–xiii.

6   Ibid., pp. 29–30.

7   On Foucault and queerness, see David M. Halperin's helpful "The Queer Politics of Michel Foucault," in *Saint Foucault: Towards a Gay Hagiography* (New York: Oxford University Press, 1995), esp. pp. 62–125.

8   These texts would include, for instance, three interesting prefaces: the prefaces to *Herculine Barbin*, trans. Richard McDougall (New York: Pantheon, 1980); to *I, Pierre Rivière, having slaughtered my mother, my sister and my brother . . .* (Harmondsworth, England: Penguin, 1978); and a text entitled "The Life of Infamous Men," which was to serve as the preface to an anthology that never materialized of extracts from the archives of the Hôpital général de la Bastille. The importance and interrelation of the *Herculine Barbin* preface and "La vie des hommes infâmes" are pointed out by Didier Eribon in *Michel Foucault et ses contemporains* (Paris: Fayard, 1994), pp. 265–87. I analyze these texts in more detail in a longer version of the present article, to appear in my book, *The Misfit of the Family: Balzac and Sexuality.*

9   Two volumes appeared in the "Vies parallèles" series published by Gallimard, *Herculine Barbin dite Alexina B.*, presented by Foucault in 1978, and *Le cercle amoureux d'Henri Legrand*, presented by Jean-Paul Dumont and Paul-Ursin Dumont in 1979. The two paragraphs I have just cited are on the back cover of both volumes. "Les Anciens aimaient à mettre en parallèle les vies des hommes illustres; on écoutait parler à travers les siècles ces ombres exemplaires. Les parallèles, je sais, sont faites pour se rejoindre à l'infini. Imaginons-en d'autres qui, indéfiniment, divergent. Pas de point de rencontre ni de lieu pour les recueillir. Souvent elles n'ont eu d'autre écho que celui de leur condamnation. Il faudrait les saisir dans la force du mouvement qui les sépare; il faudrait retrouver le sillage instantané et éclatant qu'elles ont laissé lorsqu'elles se sont précipitées vers une obscurité où « ça ne se raconte plus » et où toute « renommée » est perdue. Ce serait comme l'envers de Plutarque : des vies à ce point parallèles que nul ne peut plus les rejoindre." Judith Butler mentions these sentences in *Gender Trouble: Feminism and the Subversion of Identity* (New York: Routledge, 1990), p. 102, suggesting an interpretation of their relevance to *Herculine Barbin*, and to Foucault's own life.

10 I have in the back of my mind here the final sentences of "Friendship as a Way of Life": "We have to dig deeply to show how things have been historically contingent, for such and such reason intelligible but not necessary. We must make the intelligible appear against a background of emptiness, and deny its necessity. We must think that what exists is far from fillng all possible spaces. To make a truly unavoidable challenge of the question: what can we make work, what new game can we invent?" (in *Foucault Live [Interviews, 1966–84]*, ed. Sylvère Lotringer, trans. John Johnston [New York: Semiotext(e), 1989], p. 209). [Il faut creuser pour montrer comment les choses ont été historiquement contingentes, pour telle ou telle raison intelligible mais non nécessaire. Il faut faire apparaître l'intelligible sur le fond de vacuité et nier une nécessité, et penser que ce qui existe est loin de remplir tous les espaces possibles. Faire un vrai défi incontournable de la question : à quoi peut-on jouer, et comment inventer un jeu?] ("De l'amitié comme mode de vie," in *Dits et écrits 1954–1988*, ed. Daniel Defert and François Ewald, 4 vols. [Paris: Gallimard, 1994], 4:163–67).

11 Citations to Honoré de Balzac's *Cousin Pons*, trans. Herbert J. Hunt (Harmondsworth,

England: Penguin, 1968), will be given parenthetically in the text. For the original French, see Balzac, *La Comédie humaine*, ed. Pierre-Georges Castex, vol. 7 (Paris: Gallimard [Pléiade], 1977). Parenthetical citations of page numbers are referenced to the English and French editions respectively.

12 I don't mean to suggest that I am not myself subject to this temptation, nor do I mean to imply some false unity between, nor—obviously—any kind of a dismissal of, the variety of different and admirable psychoanalytic approaches to be found in influential works, of which the following are just a sample: Janet Beizer, *Family Plots: Balzac's Narrative Generations* (New Haven: Yale University Press, 1986); Leo Bersani, *A Future for Astyanax: Character and Desire in Literature* (New York: Columbia University Press, 1984); Peter Brooks, *Reading for the Plot: Design and Intention in Narrative* (New York: Vintage, 1984); Peter Brooks, *Body Work: Objects of Desire in Modern Narrative* (Cambridge: Harvard University Press, 1993); Shoshana Felman, *What Does a Woman Want: Reading and Sexual Difference* (Baltimore: Johns Hopkins University Press, 1993); Fredric Jameson, *The Political Unconscious: Narrative as a Socially Symbolic Act* (Ithaca: Cornell University Press, 1981); Naomi Schor, *Breaking the Chain: Women, Theory, and French Realist Fiction* (New York: Columbia University Press, 1985); Samuel Weber, *Unwrapping Balzac: A Reading of La Peau de chagrin* (Toronto: University of Toronto Press, 1979).

13 Sharon Marcus, "Restless Houses: Domesticity and Urban Culture in Paris and London, 1820–1880" (Ph.D. diss., Johns Hopkins University), pp. 86–87.

14 Honoré de Balzac, *Cousin Bette*, trans. Marion Ayton Crawford (Harmondsworth, England: Penguin, 1965), p. 165. In the original French, see Balzac, *La Comédie humaine*, ed. Pierre-Georges Castex, vol. 7 (Paris: Gallimard [Pléiade], 1977), p. 195. Further citations to *Cousin Bette* will be given parenthetically in the text; page numbers are referenced to the English and French editions respectively.

15 Foucault, *History of Sexuality*, 1:108.

16 Gayle Rubin, "The Traffic in Women: Notes Toward a Political Economy of Sex," in *Toward an Anthropology of Women*, ed. Rayna Reiter (New York: Monthly Review Press, 1975), p. 199.

17 Cf. Judith Butler's recent comments: "We might read the desire for a sexuality beyond kinship as a sign of a certain utopian strain in sexual thinking which is bound to fail, and which requires that our conceptions of kinship remain frozen in their most highly normative and oppressive modes. Those who imagine themselves to be 'beyond' kinship will nevertheless find terms to describe those supporting social arrangements which constitute kinship. Kinship in this sense is not to be identified with any of its positive forms, but rather as a site of redefinition which can move beyond patrilineality, compulsory heterosexuality, and the symbolic overdetermination of biology" ("Against Proper Objects," *differences* 6, nos. 2–3 [1994]: 14). Butler reflects in interesting ways on links between Rubin and Foucault in this essay (pp. 11–15). Rubin and Butler's conversation in "Sexual Traffic," in the same issue of *differences*, also contains interesting and helpful reflections on Foucault and kinship (pp. 83–88), though they both conflate the term kinship (of which the usual French equivalent is *parenté*) and alliance. In the particular instance of the two novels I am investigating, I think there might be something to be gained from keeping a distinction between the two terms.

18 Foucault, *History of Sexuality*, 1:106–7.

19 Ibid., 1:113. Translation modified.

20 In "Friendship as a Way of Life," Foucault speaks of a "way of life" as something that

"can be shared among individuals of different age, status and social activity. It can yield intense relations not resembling those that are institutionalized" (p. 207). Of a relationship between an older and a younger man, he suggests, "They have to invent, from A to Z, a relationship that is still formless, which is friendship: that is to say, the sum of everything through which they can give each other pleasure" (p. 205).

21 Foucault, "Friendship as a Way of Life," p. 208.

22 Foucault doesn't seem to take very careful account of differences between his call for a present-day project and the historical work Faderman (he refers to her book in this interview as well) is doing. Nor does he dwell for long on dissymmetries produced by gender oppression. He does comment in one other interview: "I should say, also, that I think that in the lesbian movement, the fact that women have been, for centuries and centuries, isolated in society, frustrated, despised in many ways and so on, has given them the real possibility of constituting a society, of creating a kind of social relation between themselves outside the social world that was dominated by males. Lillian Faderman's book Surpassing the Love of Men is very interesting in this regard. It raises the question: What kind of emotional experience, what kind of relationships, were possible in a world where women in society had no social, no legal and no political power? And she argues that women used that isolation and lack of power" ("Michel Foucault: An Interview: Sex, Power, and the Politics of Identity," The Advocate, 7 August 1984, 29).

23 As Madame Nourrisson reminds him in suggesting a way of paying her for her murderous intervention on his behalf: "One day within the next three months a poor priest will come to ask you for forty thousand francs for a benefaction—for a ruined monastery in the desert, in the Levant! If you are pleased with the way things have fallen out, give the fellow the forty thousand francs. It's not any more than you'll pay, anyway, to the Inland Revenue" (p. 375). [Vous en verserez bien d'autres au fisc! (388)].

24 Foucault, History of Sexuality, 1:109.

25 Ibid.

26 Foucault, History of Sexuality, 1:109–10; translation modified. Thus perhaps one reason Foucault does not often use the word kinship (parenté) in The History of Sexuality, Volume 1 is precisely in order to differentiate his own (genealogical) project from the (nonhistorical, or at least only problematically historical) project of an ethnography theorized in books such as Lévi-Strauss's Les structures élémentaires de la parenté, a project whose own genealogy, Foucault is implying, needs investigation.

27 Both Judith Butler and Gayle Rubin suggest the inadequacies of this kind of narrative of "supercession." See Butler, "Against Proper Objects," pp. 12–14, and Rubin, "Sexual Traffic," pp. 84–88.

28 Here are a couple pin (épingle) passages from Foucault: "This interpenetration [épinglage] of the deployment of alliance and that of sexuality in the form of the family allows us to understand a number of facts" (History of Sexuality, 1:108); "The guarantee that one would find the parents-children relationship at the root of everyone's sexuality made it possible—even when everything seemed to point to the reverse process—to keep the deployment of sexuality coupled [de maintenir l'épinglage] to the system of alliance" (History of Sexuality, 1:113).

29 For work on the Napoleonic Code, and on changes to French civil society generally, see Robert A. Nye, Masculinity and Male Codes of Honor in Modern France (Oxford: Oxford University Press, 1993), esp. pp. 47–57; Jean-Louis Halpérin, L'Impossible Code civil (Paris: Presses Universitaires de France, 1992); Isser Woloch, The New Regime: Trans-

formations of the French Civil Order, 1789–1820s (New York: Norton, 1994). Specifically on Balzac and the Napoleonic Code, see Marie-Henriette Faillie, *La Femme et le Code civil dans La Comédie humaine d'Honor'de Balzac* (Paris: Didier, 1968). On the Code and *Cousin Bette*, see Dorothy Kelly, *Fictional Genders: Role and Representation in Nineteenth-Century French Narrative* (Lincoln: University of Nebraska Press, 1989), pp. 42–74.

PART III Teacher's Pet

Anne Chandler

Defying "Development": Thomas Day's Queer

Curriculum in *Sandford and Merton*

A s conduct books have illuminated the ideological drive to heterosexual pairings in eighteenth- and nineteenth-century novels'
graphs of gender formation,[1] so educational treatises—a related
but distinct genre—can shed light on these same novels' theoretical gropings toward queer communality. Educational theory has a definitional
urge to dissect "development," a paradigm that conduct books tend to
swallow whole. While aspiring, like the conduct book, to influence the
practice of socialization, the educational treatise is more deeply invested
in baseline cognition and motivation. Thus, its approach to "development" is a microscopic one, and its faith in broad experimental repli-
cability is often overwhelmed by a fascination with individual variance.
With its purposeful willingness to let the case history get out of hand,
the educational treatise offers a conceptual environment that is surprisingly nurturant of the idea of queer enfranchisement; it lacks the conduct book's stake in associating role "violations" with (blighted) childhood and (decadent, aristocratic) play. In fact, educationists' governing
narratives tend themselves to be ruled by an ideal of male homosocial enlightenment: tutor and pupil share a private, domestic Eden, which need
never be abandoned, and in which knowledge and desire are mutually
constitutive. Thus, while Locke and Rousseau—to take the most prominent examples—are rightly read as avatars of "development," they may *as
rightly* be read as breaking down that development, ultimately rendering
"heterosexual adulthood" an illogical conflation. In tandem with fiction
successfully marketed to children—fiction that also blueprinted the relation of "home" to "school"—this alternative line of thought emerges as a
significant cultural force.

  The History of Sandford and Merton (1783–89), a novel-length children's
book by the English moralist/dilettante Thomas Day (1748–89), demonstrates key ramifications—some emancipatory, others imprisoning—

of using a doggedly antidevelopmental reading of Locke and Rousseau as the basis for a pedagogy of one's own. Locke urges habituation to mildly unpleasant stimuli as the foundation for all learning and purposiveness; in *Sandford and Merton*, Day mouths this tenet but systematically undermines it, repeatedly demonstrating the radical unteachability of stamina (by extension, of manliness—some boys have it, others don't) through adventures that show the title characters' divergent responses to pain and humiliation. And, whereas Rousseau's *Emile* (1762) presents the tutor's disclosure of his own desire as the developmental gateway to Emile's partnership with Sophie, Day reads this climactic moment as formalizing and bringing to fruition the incipient homosocial romance between tutor and pupil. Both extrapolations are reflected in *Sandford and Merton*'s narrative refrains, which are so fragmented and rhythmical as to vaporize into pure fantasy. "Development" or progression in any usual sense seems to be suppressed—and queerness seems to rise to the top, like a buoy that perpetually rights itself. It is noteworthy, then, that *Sandford and Merton* enjoyed extraordinary success in the thoroughly aboveground, bourgeois-driven children's publishing industry. For over a century, *Sandford and Merton*'s three hefty volumes were translated, illustrated, abridged, adapted, restored, and bought, for several successive generations of children, throughout the Western world.[2]

In aggregate, *Sandford and Merton* offers a prolific set of variations on *Robinson Crusoe*, along with some Near Eastern legends and natural-history novelties, all woven in and out of a Lockean framing narrative about two English boys and their tutor. Besides offering undeniably entertaining stories to children, this mixture probably appealed to many parents as a safe, thoroughly tested melding of Protestant self-reliance and bourgeois scientism. The influence of Rousseau is more subtle, narratively speaking, and yet it was Day's penchant for Rousseauian experimentation—manifested in ways many contemporary consumers would have found disquieting—that underwrote the book's real psychodramas. Mainly, there is the fact that in 1769, some fifteen years before he began *Sandford and Merton*, Day adopted two foundling girls and transported them temporarily to Avignon, with the idea that the one who performed best in an *Emile*-derived educational regime would eventually become his wife. This plan not only flouted Rousseau's insistence that Emile and his tutor were theoretical constructs,[3] but also tested the limits of Rousseau's mechanistic conception of female lack as embodied in Sophie. Yet Day seemed genuinely surprised when his program of physical hardship and total isolation was resisted by the two girls and dismissed by several women to whom it was offered as part of a matrimonial contract.[4] After ten years of fruitless searching, Day did meet and marry Esther Milnes, a well-heeled and fairly well-educated woman who nonetheless seemed to find his program congenial. Five (childless) years later, he produced volume 1 of *Sandford and Merton*, a work that places two imaginary boys in the experimental venue where two real girls once had been.[5]

Was this transposition merely owing to Day's disappointments with women?—alternatively, was it a way to rehabilitate his original contact with the two children, for which "training" and "marriage" had proved unwieldy pretexts? Probably not. In the years between Day's adoption of the two girls (1769) and his composition of *Sandford and Merton* (early 1780s), his misogyny appears as a mere raveling in a tapestry of rich and satisfying relationships with men. Notable among these was a "very intimate"[6] attachment to Richard Edgeworth (father of Maria Edgeworth, the novelist), starting in the spring of 1766. Upon meeting one another as rural neighbors (Edgeworth, an unhappily married young father, was waiting to inherit the family estate in Ireland; Day, twenty-one, was mulling over what to do with his own considerable fortune), the two young men began spending "several hours" a day together, discussing philosophy, natural science, and mechanics.[7] Though their degree of physical intimacy must remain a matter of conjecture, their involvement was intense enough to make Richard's wife, Anna Maria, angry and jealous.[8] Rousseau's *Emile* (1762) was a text Day and Edgeworth admired in common, and accordingly they embarked Edgeworth's two-year-old son on a (non)system of unstructured, outdoor education. This lasted about five years, until young Richard's insolence and intractability grew too severe to ignore.[9] In the meantime, Day began his own ill-fated experiment with the two girls (1769); the long-suffering Anna Maria Edgeworth died during her fifth childbirth (1773); and about six weeks later, Edgeworth married Honora Sneyd, a young woman whom he had been approaching ostensibly on Day's behalf. Day was hurt by this—in writing, he put off Edgeworth's blithe attempt to maintain social contact—but not so hurt as to renounce or distrust future bonds with men. To the contrary, his biographers show him living, traveling, or studying with—lending money to—visiting—flying to the side of—quarreling with—a cavalcade of male friends.[10]

As the themes of *Sandford and Merton* reflect Day's antidevelopmental mindset, the book's structure reflects the inexorable doubleness of his life. His fears and hatreds, his self-sabotaged attempts to pass as a heterosexual man, come through in what I call the first realm of discourse of *Sandford and Merton*—the parts of the book that painfully expose the effeminacy and incompetence of six-year-old Tommy Merton, while exalting the manliness and intrepidity of his slightly older friend, Harry Sandford. These scenes occur mostly in the first half of the book, where anecdotes about natural history predominate. The second half of the book is dominated, instead, by legends of ancient heroism, and it is in this realm of discourse that Day lavishes attention upon the intimacies between men that have made his own life worth living. This essay will attempt to show the unbridgeable gap Day placed between these two realms of discourse: it is this overdetermined resistance to paradigmatic development, I believe, that nourishes Day's educative fantasmatics of queer ontology.

COGNITIVE EFFEMINACY

Early in *Some Thoughts Concerning Education* (1693), Locke disclaims present interest in the "sick or crazy Child" for the sake of focusing on "the *Preservation and Improvement of an healthy, or at least, not sickly Constitution.*" His approach, he says, "might be all dispatched, in this one short Rule, *viz.* That Gentlemen should use their Children, as the honest Farmers and substantial Yeomen do theirs." Refining this glib reference to salutary hardship—exercise, simple diet, routine tasks, and so on— Locke adds "a general and certain Observation for the Women to consider, *viz.* That most Children's Constitutions are either spoiled, or at least harmed, by *Cockering* and *Tenderness.*"[11] The supposed vulnerability of children is a self-fulfilling prophecy, warns Locke: treating them as soft, sensitive creatures only exacerbates their softness and sensitivity. Generalizing from physical to moral health, Locke warns parents to fight their all-too-natural urges to coddle their children, for, "He that has not a Mastery over his Inclinations, he that knows not how to *resist* the importunity of present *Pleasure or Pain,* for the sake of what Reason tells him is fit to be done, wants the true Principle of Vertue and Industry; and is in danger never to be good for any thing."[12]

In the educational rhetoric of *Sandford and Merton,* Thomas Day relies heavily on Locke's model of "impression" and its corollary, the repression of appetites and desires.[13] Unlike Locke, however, Day had as great an interest in the "sick or crazy" child as in the supposedly well and sane one. Accordingly, he begins his educational treatise with a lengthy diagnosis of six-year-old Tommy Merton, a rich planter's son. Because Tommy's mother gives him "every thing he cried for," he is paralyzed by the tiniest change in environment, so "impressionable" that he is unable to think constructively, much less learn:

> Sometimes he cried for things that it was impossible to give him. . . . as he had never been used to be contradicted, it was many hours before he could be pacified. . . . he had always to be helped first, and to have the most delicate part of the meat, otherwise he would make such a noise as disturbed the whole company. . . . he would scramble

upon the table, seize the cake . . . and frequently overset the teacups. By these pranks he not only made himself disagreeable . . . but often met with very dangerous accidents. . . . [O]nce he narrowly escaped being scalded to death by a kettle of boiling water. He was also so delicately brought up, that he was perpetually ill; the least wind or rain gave him cold, and the least sun was sure to throw him into a fever. Instead of playing about, and jumping, and running like other children, he was taught to sit still for fear of spoiling his clothes, and to stay in the house for fear of injuring his complexion. By this kind of education . . . he could neither write nor read . . . he could use none of his limbs with ease, nor bear any degree of fatigue; but he was very proud, fretful and impatient.[14]

Thus, the problem: Tommy has been brought up as a girl, and a sorry one at that.[15] We see this in his stereotypically feminine concern for outward appearance, and also in his volatile "heat" and "coldness," frantic aggression or dull passivity—stock terms of misogynist discourse purporting to "explain" female sexuality and, correlatively, women's alleged mental inferiority. It is when Tommy's father meets the stalwart farmer's son, Harry Sandford (who first appears in order to rescue Tommy from a snake), that he decides Tommy's effeminacy has reached crisis proportions, and arranges for his son to get a better "kind of education" from Harry's mentor, an unmarried clergyman named Mr. Barlow.

Harry, the ideal to which Tommy is supposed to aspire, is a Lockean exemplar of physical, mental, and moral hardihood, being at once highly impressionable (an efficient learner, a compassionate citizen) and not too impressionable (that is, not overly susceptible to his own appetites or to applied physical pain). Having learned through a single incident that "poor helpless insect[s]" (12) feel pain in the same way humans do, Harry is equipped to go about doing good for life, regardless of his own safety or comfort.[16] He repeatedly rescues Tommy and other timorous creatures from predators, even when, as in one memorable case, he is severely whipped for his trouble. Tommy, on witnessing this unjust punishment, is amazed at Harry's fortitude—yet Harry assures him that it's all socialization: "Oh! it's nothing compared to what the young Spartans used to suffer" (73). Where Tommy is concerned, however, the Spartan/Lockean premium on habituation proves to be a red herring. Though he is exposed (literally, and through stories) to hardships that are supposed to make him more competent, in practice these hardships only reinforce his physical and cognitive effeminacy.

Tommy's "cure"—his symbolic divestiture of a rich boy's buckles, bows, and laces—finally occurs, with much fanfare, some five hundred pages after his original diagnosis. Yet the book offers virtually no basis for connecting this belated event with the excruciating, quasi-Lockean regime he has been undergoing (and continues to undergo, thereafter). We see no chain of educative "development" leading to that event—no helpful metacommentary linking preferred method with ostensible result. Day's rhetorical gestures toward "development" serve only to enhance his true interest in stasis, carried out in a probing exploration of Tommy just as he is. From the Lockean physics of impression, which presupposes the subject's assimilation of the new sensation—over time, Day extracts the moment of impression itself, eschewing cumulative learning in favor of experiential intensity.

The privileged moment of impression—usually one of intense pain or shame—is conveyed through an educational argot of "wildness" and "tameness," where animals are clearly intended as analogues for children. The trouble is that the illustrative anecdotes themselves swing wildly between educative faith and despair—between advocacy for the suffering animal, and detailed advice on torturing and killing it. There are even rapid oscillations in point of view, between the "poor" animal and the "intrepid" hunters or trainers. Thus, it becomes almost impossible to tell whether "wildness" or "tameness" prevails—which is "better"— and which, at any given moment, is more "like" Tommy (who is at once "too wild" and "too tame"). When a trained bear forgets his training long enough to charge a crowd of spectators, and is then subdued by Mr. Barlow's "bold" and "dexterous" use of "a good stick," we are informed that "almost all wild beasts are subject to receive the sudden impression of terror," and that "whenever an animal is taught any thing that is not natural to him, this is properly receiving an education." Later, Mr. Barlow elaborates: "I knew that the poor bear had been frequently beaten and very ill used, in order to make him submit to be led about with a string, and exhibited as a sight. I knew that he had been accustomed to submit to man, and to tremble at the sight of the human voice [sic]: and I depended upon the force of these impressions for making him submit without resistance to the authority I assumed over him" (169–70). Even within this very small space, the premises for the lesson are shown to be weirdly unstable. Are educative impressions efficient or inefficient? (Is Mr. Barlow "reminding" the bear, or actually "teaching" him anew?) Do these impressions teach kindness or cruelty? (How does Mr. Barlow's inference that the animal has been "ill used" square with his later warning to its keeper, "to be more careful in guarding so dangerous a creature"?) Is there a consistent definition of "the natural" at work here? (In what sense is Mr. Barlow's "authority" over the bear "assumed"?) In Locke, the imposition of "unnatural" checks upon "natural" inclinations—say, the child's inclination to eat sweets all the time, or to hit a creature smaller than himself—is urged as the foundation of all learned purposiveness and benevolence in humans. In Day, talk of utility and benevolence seems but a phatic lubricant—functionally important, but not inherently meaningful—to the perpetual-motion machine of "education."

The workings of this system—Day's ceaseless manufacture of "not natural" situations and impressions—become clearer in two subsequent episodes that celebrate the educative administration of pain. In both, discussions of utility and benevolence are used, as it were, to teasingly cover up and then reveal the contused flesh itself. The animal in question is Mr. Barlow's house cat, whose execution Tommy demands after it has "murdere[d]" (175) his pet bird. Mr. Barlow, citing his own "particular affection" (178) for the cat, recommends instead educating her. After all, he points out, animals lack the capacity for "reason and reflection" (177) requisite for willed cruelty *or* benevolence. As though to prove both his love for the cat and his faith in education, Mr. Barlow sets out "a small gridiron, such as is used to broil meat upon,"

> and, having almost heated it red hot, placed it erect upon the ground, before the cage in which [a] bird was confined. He then contrived to entice the cat into the room. . . . When she judged herself within a proper distance, she exerted all her agility in a violent spring, which would probably have been fatal to the bird, had not the gridiron, placed before the cage, received the impression of her attack. Nor was this disappointment the only punishment she was destined to undergo: the bars of the machine had been so thoroughly heated, that in rushing against them she felt herself burned in several parts of her body; and retired . . . mewing dreadfully, and full of pain: and such was the impression which this adventure produced, that from this time she was never again known to attempt to destroy birds. (179)

The experiment is left behind without further comment on its methodology or supposed success. We wonder whether the cat will ever walk again, let alone hunt birds. We also wonder what has happened to the endowment of "reason and reflection" that, according to Mr. Barlow, makes conscious cruelty to animals (except, perhaps, those for whom one has a "particular affection"?) inexcusable in humans. Indeed, if demonstrating the value of "educating" animals (rather than killing them) has been the point of the episode, then the cat's agony has been for naught: immediately after Mr. Barlow's educational triumph with his pet, we move to a scene in which Tommy is once again demanding the execution of offending animals, this time some rabbits who have invaded his garden.

Tommy has learned nothing, or rather, has had his own "natural" pre-dilection for punishment reinforced. Indeed, the documentation of the cat's suffering defaults to the term "punishment" itself—whose conno-tations Mr. Barlow so vigorously disclaimed, earlier, in his rationale for rehabilitating the cat.

A subsequent episode privileges for us certain *aspects* of this recursion to punishment, showing the heated-metal/burned-flesh model to be more than a onetime gambit and refining its rhetorical application to children. In "History of a surprising cure of the Gout," a gluttonous Italian man is confined to a cell, fed a sparse diet for several weeks, and then forced to resume usage of his legs. Frustration and bewilderment yield to terror as he "felt the floor of the chamber, which . . . [was] composed of plates of iron, grow immoderately hot under his feet. He called the doctor . . . but to no purpose . . . the heat grew more intense every instant. At length necessity compelled him to hop upon one leg . . . presently the other leg began to burn. . . . Thus he went on hopping about with his involuntary exercise, till he had stretched every sinew and muscle more than he had done for several years" (198–99). Afterward, his inventive physician in-forms him that he has undergone "a contrary method of cure—exercise, abstinence, and mortification. You, sir, have indeed been treated like a child, but it has been for your own advantage" (201).

This surprisingly direct equation of "mortification" with normative childhood at the end of the "cat sequence" needs to be placed along-side its progressive distortion of Lockean themes. In the bear incident, Mr. Barlow practices something at least resembling Lockean "discipline," but the cat episode casts education as aversion therapy: obverting Locke, Day subsumes discipline within something labeled as "punishment." The gout patient's rehabilitation moves us yet farther—from punishment, which is at least theoretically motivated by transgression, to "mortifica-tion," which addresses more abiding flaws in the self. Whereas Locke seeks to move the child *away* from mere physicality, Day's hypotheses seem if anything to move the subject "backward," receding from will to motive to desire to appetite to instinct, all the way back to reflex.

To follow Tommy's course of "mortification," we must keep in mind this metadiscursive will to regression (toward physicality; toward fantas-tic stasis), which counters Tommy's will as surely as any red-hot metal would, but with a higher admixture of shame than pain—and in a more oceanic, amorphous way that fosters not quick movement "away," but en-trapment within.

Tommy is first "severely mortified" by a "little ragged boy" who, re-senting Tommy's imperious order to fetch a lost ball, knocks him down:

[Tommy] rolled into a wet ditch, which was full of mud and water . . . [he] tumbled about for some time, endeavouring to get out; but . . . to no purpose, for his feet stuck in the mud . . . his fine waist coat was dirtied all over, his white stockings, covered with mire, his breeches filled with puddle water. . . . Mr. Barlow . . . was afraid he had been considerably hurt; but when he heard [about] the accident . . . he could not help smiling, and *he advised Tommy to be more careful for the future how he attempted to thrash little ragged boys.* (56; emphasis added)

Formulaically, Tommy's dousing is a comeuppance warning him to treat others with more respect. But as time goes on, we see that the bottom line of the episode is not really Mr. Barlow's admonition, but the fact that he "could not help smiling"—that Tommy's experience is not for his own or anyone else's future benefit, but for the present gratification of spectators. It is *the mud itself*—not the "lesson" in pride—that achieves ever-wider applicability.[17] In fact, perversely, Tommy's determined efforts to apply new knowledge always result in his shameful return to thinly disguised versions of the same mud puddle:

Following an explanation of how to tame animals, Tommy tries to befriend a piglet:

Tommy, in falling, dirtied himself from head to foot; and the sow . . . passed over him as he attempted to rise and rolled him back again into the mire. . . . [A] large flock of geese happened to be crossing the road, into the midst of which the affrighted sow ran headlong, dragging the enraged Tommy at her heels. . . . [A large gander] flew at Tommy's hinder parts, and gave him several severe strokes with his bill. (104–5)

Following a description of dogsleds, Tommy tries to ride Mr. Barlow's pet Newfoundland:

Tommy came roughly into the water. To add to his misfortune, the pond was at that time neither ice nor water; for a sudden thaw had commenced. . . . [H]e floundered on through mud and water, and pieces of floating ice, like some amphibious animal. . . . Now his feet stuck fast in the mud, and now, by a desperate effort, he disengaged himself with the loss of both his shoes. . . . The whole troop of spectators were now incapable of stifling their laughter, which broke forth in such redoubled peals, that the unfortunate hero was irritated to an extreme degree of rage, so that . . . as soon as he had struggled to the shore, he fell upon them in a fury. (298–300)

Following a description of Arabian horsemen, Tommy invites a servant to watch his testing of some homemade spurs:

[J]ust as he was describing [the Arabs'] rapid flight across the deserts, the interest of his subject so transported him, that he closed his legs upon his little horse, and pricked him in so sensible a manner, that the poney [*sic*] . . . [r]ushed precipitately into a large bog, or quag-mire. . . . Tommy wisely embraced the opportunity of letting himself slide off upon a soft and yielding bed of mire . . . daubing himself all over. . . . [The servant] could not help asking him, with a smile, whether this too was a stroke of Arabian horsemanship! (409–11)

In this program of "repeated mortification" (411), there is no such thing as selective assimilation, or constructive habituation. It is a regime not merely of pain, but of enforced *arrest* in a moment of heightened self-consciousness: a regime of shame. Though Tommy's "problem" was stated in Lockean terms, as a need for physical stamina and emotional autonomy, Day stymies all movement in this direction by ensuring that Tommy will be, if anything, ever more radically overwhelmed by his environment—not "like some amphibious animal" (299; see "dogsled" episode, above) at all, but drowning alike in the muddy water and in the laughter of his unsolicited audience.[18]

EPIPHANIC MANLINESS

Though Rousseau's lessons in self-interest grow logically from Locke's lessons in self-management, Day's extractions from Rousseau do not, in any sense except sequentially, "follow" his extractions from Locke. Instead, *Sandford and Merton* doggedly isolates the two derivations, making each vision of education incomprehensible to the other. Where Day's re-visioning of Locke denies Tommy a foothold out of the mud, his theoretical remodeling of Rousseau yields an educational nirvana toward which Tommy and other imperfectly trained creatures do not even know to look longingly: an adult realm of total competence, clear understanding, unbreachable intimacy. Unlike his predecessors, Day understood the phenomenon of pedagogical desire-and-resistance in a fundamentally divisive way, so that while the first half of *Sandford and Merton* figures the triumph of resistance over desire, the second half (to borrow from C. S. Lewis) allows one to eat Turkish Delight endlessly and with impunity.[19]

For his second fantasmatic, Day takes something Rousseau intended as argumentative background—praise for the virtues of ancient warrior cultures—and makes this the main stuff of his narrative. For his own argumentative background, he takes a single moment in Rousseau's main narrative—the tutor's revelation of his own desire to (and for) the adolescent Emile—and renders it atmospherically assumptive, part of what his literal Spartans, Scythians, and Scots Highlanders live and breathe.

When Rousseau celebrates the Spartans' insularity, homogeneity, and cultural stasis—the intactness of the knowledge they transmitted from one generation to the next, and their capacity to "gover[n] without precepts"—he does so with development firmly in mind.[20] The enforced isolation of Emile's early life allows Rousseau to create a tutorial dynamic of "pure" power, uncomplicated by the codes of conduct that children (as Rousseau cautions us) so easily learn to subvert.[21] However, the "enlightened" development served by this totalitarian regime also demands that it be eventually phased out—or, to speak more precisely, internalized—in preparation for Emile's release into modern society.

This conversion begins as the tutor, preparatory to broaching the topic of sex, reveals his own stake in Emile's education—"I have done it [i.e., the whole enterprise] for myself," he says[22]—and encourages Emile to think of him as a vulnerable, desiring subject, not as the disinterested mover he had pretended to be. This revelation is figured as a series of newly exciting caresses, new impressions perhaps, that lead to a pleasurable extortion of loyalty:

> What surprise, what agitation I am going to cause in him by suddenly changing language! Instead of narrowing his soul by always speaking of his interest, I shall now speak of mine alone, and I shall thereby touch him more. I shall inflame his young heart with all the sentiments of friendship, generosity, and gratitude which I have already aroused and which are so sweet to cultivate. I shall press him to my breast and shed tears of tenderness on him. I shall say to him, "You are my property, my child, my work. . . . If you frustrate my hopes, you are robbing me of twenty years of my life. . . ." It is in this way that you get a young man to listen to you and that you engrave the memory of what you say to him in the depths of his heart.[23]

Against this backdrop of new delectations and reorganized familiarities, the ensuing description of extramural sex—of demonic desires and the "horrors of debauchery"[24]—frightens and repels Emile to the extent that he begs the tutor to "[t]ake back the authority you want to give up. . . . You had this authority up to this time only due to my weakness; now you shall have it due to my will, and it shall be all the more sacred to me."[25] The tutor basks in the new voluntarism of Emile's discipleship: "He is now sufficiently prepared to be docile. He recognizes the voice of friendship, and he knows how to obey reason. It is true that I leave him the appearance of independence, but he was never better subjected to me; for now he is subjected because he wants to be. . . . Now I sometimes leave him to himself, because I govern him always. In leaving him, I embrace him."[26] Emile sees his past and future in a new light—as imbued with the mutuality of desire between himself and the tutor. Now, according to Rousseau—now that his Edenic bond with the tutor has been firmly planted in Emile's heart—the young man is *really* ready to proceed to his next developmental stage, adult heterosexuality. Accordingly, the concept of a complementary partner, in the person of Sophie, is introduced.

Perhaps scenting a certain fraudulence in Rousseau's sudden wheeling-in of Sophie, Day sees no reason to hurry Emile from the garden. For him, the tutor-pupil romance is both alpha and omega, a diorama within which literal Spartans, Scythians, Scots Highlanders, and American Indians perform *pas-de-deux*. Thus, what for Rousseau were strategic allusions are for Day aesthetic ends in themselves. In *Sandford and Merton*, celebrations of ancient cultures merge into detailed explications of their "manliness"—which in turn become luxuriant, Whitmanesque reveries on young men's bodies.

A compilation of *Sandford and Merton*'s truisms on the ancients' education of the body is found within the "Story of Sophron and Tigranes" (set in Lebanon, circa 200 B.C.), whose characters—the virtuous shepherd Sophron, the military enthusiast Tigranes, and an aging philosopher named Chares—explicitly parallel Harry Sandford, Tommy Merton, and Mr. Barlow.[27] In this passage, the wise and well-traveled Chares tells Sophron (long since estranged from his childhood friend Tigranes) about the nomadic warriors who have for some years occupied his native Syria.

> This is the simple and uniform life of all the Scythians: but this simplicity renders them formidable to all their neighbours, and irresistible in war. Unsoftened by ease or luxury, unacquainted with the artificial wants of life, these nations pass their lives in manly exercises and rustic employments: but horsemanship is the greatest pride and passion of their souls. . . . [T]hey excel all other nations, unless it be the Arabs, in their courage and address in riding: without a saddle, and even a bridle, *their young men will vault upon an unbacked courser, and keep their seats in spite of all his violent efforts, till they have rendered him tame and obedient to their will.* In their military expeditions they neither regard the obstacles of nature, nor the inclemency of the season: and their horses are accustomed to traverse rocks and mountains with a facility that is incredible. *If they reach a river, instead of waiting for the tedious assistance of boats and bridges, the warrior divests himself of his clothes and arms, which he places in a bundle upon the horse's back, and then plunging into the stream, conducts*

him over by the bridle. Even in the midst of winter . . . the Scythian follows his military labours, and rejoices to see the earth thick covered with frost and snow, because it affords him a solid path in his excursions; neither the severest cold, nor the most violent storms can check his ardour. . . . Javelins, and bows and arrows, are the arms which these people are taught from their infancy to use with surprising dexterity. (484–85; emphasis added)

The "simple" and "uniform" existence of the Scythians is one of "manly exercis[e]," virile sensuality, and physical mastery. Where Tommy clambers onto animals and is ignominiously thrown, Scythian youths "vault" aboard, "keep their seats," and render the animals "obedient to their wills." That horse and rider move as one, "with a facility that is incredible," is, we sense, just one of many proofs that the Scythian himself is at once "irresistible" and full of unstoppable "ardour." Elsewhere, in similarly rapturous accounts of androcentric cultures, Day adds intellectual mastery to the qualities of irresistibility, hypercompetence, and vigor, to suggest the Grandisonian quality of "penetration." Day's idealized men have instant access—they understand and are understood—their pronouncements are self-fulfilling: "A Scythian, mounted upon a fiery steed, entered the [Persian] camp at full speed, and, regardless of danger or opposition, penetrated even to the royal tent. . . . leaped lightly from his horse, and, placing a little bundle upon the ground, vaulted up again with inconceivable agility, and retired with the same happy expedition" (485). In using this particular incident Day was probably following Rousseau, for whom the contents of the "little bundle"—talismans urging the Persians to surrender—illustrate the Scythians' command of "the language of signs" (see *Emile,* 321–22). But Day's presentation goes yet farther, depicting the Scythian's thrilling horsemanship as its own language of signs. The medium is the message: the horseman's prowess, his "penetrat[ion] . . . to the royal tent" make the talismans themselves superfluous, and tell the Persians all they need to know.

The Scythians' perfect melding of physicality and cognition is enabled by an acculturative nakedness that blocks out some sensations (e.g., "the inclemency of the season") but welcomes others (the movements of the horse beneath one; the current of the river; the balance of the javelin). If clothing impedes his crossing a river, the Scythian simply strips and "plunges" in. The linkage between nakedness and competence is argued more pointedly in a Gambian man's reminiscences of childhood: "The first thing that I can remember of myself, was the running naked . . . with four of my little brothers and sisters." Unlike swaddled European children, this man reports, the African child "comes as soon and as easily to the perfect use of all his organs as any of the beasts which surround him" (521–22). This "perfect use of all his organs" fosters an ambient social intimacy, in which the children "aim their little arrows at marks, or dart their light and blunted javelins at each other" while "others wrestle naked upon the sand, or run in sportive races" (523). In cultures organized around this corporate interpenetration, there is a qualitative sameness between childhood and adulthood. Development is not marked as such. Brave men of these cultures (in contrast to effete English hunters of rabbits) rely on the sensual awareness they have had since childhood:

> [M]en are accustomed in some places to go almost naked; and that makes them so prodigiously nimble, that they can run like a deer; and, when a lion or tiger comes into their neighbourhood . . . they go out six and seven together, armed with javelins . . . and they make a noise to provoke him to attack them: then he begins roaring and foaming, and beating his sides with his tail, till, in a violent fury, he springs at the man that is nearest to him. . . . [The man] jumps like a greyhound out of the way, while the next man throws his javelin at the lion . . . this enrages [the lion] still more; he springs again, like lightning, upon the man that wounded him, but this man avoids him like the other, and at last the poor beast drops down dead, with the number of wounds he has received. (70–71)

Here, nakedness breeds in the hunters not merely the deerlike ability to leap clear of the cat's grasp, but a certain attunement to the predator himself—the knowledge they need to stimulate him into an exploitable frenzy—as well as a group consciousness that allows their own coordinated predation, one man distracting while the next impales. A variation on this theme, this time in a Scotsman's admiring description of American Indians preparing for war, moves directly from "nakedness" to a choreographed session of mutual arousal:

> All the savage tribes that inhabit America are accustomed to very little clothing. Inured to the inclemencies of the weather, and being in the constant exercise of all their limbs, they cannot bear the restraint and confinement of an European dress. The greater part of their bodies, therefore, is naked; and this they paint in various fashions, to give additional terror to their looks. . . . But what words can convey an adequate idea of the furious movements and expressions which animated them. . . . [T]heir faces kindled into an expression of anger which would have daunted the boldest spectator; their gestures seemed . . . inspired by frantic rage . . . they moved their bodies with the most violent agitations, and it was easy to see they

represented all the circumstances of a real combat. . . . By intervals, they increased the horrid solemnity of the exhibition, by uttering yells that would have pierced an European ear with horror. I have seen rage and fury under various forms, and in different parts of the globe: but I must confess, that every thing I have seen elsewhere is feeble and contemptible when compared with this day's spectacle. (431–33)

The speaker here, a retired soldier named Campbell, calls the life of the Indians "the reverse of what you see at home." Yet bringing this enlightened sensuality home—domesticating the "ferocious joy" (431) of the warrior culture—is very much on Day's mind. Surrounding his travel-narrative tableaux of violent homoeroticism are novelistic plots of male domestic bliss, whose constituent elements are "marks of peculiar favour" (492); invitations to come inside; blushes, suffusions, "inflammations" (421); long looks, and the pleasurable sense of being looked at; one man's being "charmed with" another (394, 423).

In the "Story of Sophron and Tigranes," a nested series of tutorial romances begins when Sophron rescues the elderly Chares and his daughter Selene from the corrupted barbarian forces occupying Syria and Lebanon. Sophron takes them home to his parents, and then (ignoring Selene) listens raptly as Chares plies two destiny-driven encounters with his own quest for social enlightenment.

The first encounter follows his repudiation, as a young traveler, of the "effeminacy" he sees in Egyptian culture (392–94).[28] Crossing a desert, he and his companions are confronted by "a band of Arabians"; when the Arab leader steps forward to "know our intentions," Chares likewise makes his way to the front of the group to explain "the integrity of [his] own intentions" in seeking "to observe in person the manners of a people, who are celebrated . . . for having preserved their native simplicity unaltered, and their liberty unviolated." He then offers the chieftain the use of his camel, "not as being worthy his acceptance, but as a slight testimony of my regard; and concluded with remarking, that the fidelity of the Arabians in observing their engagements was unimpeached" (397–98). Chares's appeal to the cultural chastity of the Arabs, his declaration of honorable intentions, and his token of regard—his respectful request for mercy—all have their effect on the Arab leader:

While I was thus speaking, he looked at me with a penetration that seemed to read into my very soul; and when I had finished, he extended his arm with a smile of benevolence, and welcomed me to their tribe; telling me at the same time, that they admitted me as their guest, and received me with the arms of friendship; that their method of life, like their manners, was coarse and simple, but that I might consider myself as safer in their tents, and more removed from violence or treachery, than in the crowded cities which I had left. The rest of the squadron then approached, and all saluted me as a friend and a brother. (398)

His fondly remembered interlude of "several months" with the virile, welcoming Arabs serves as a segue to the second key encounter, which likewise shines through a haze of cultural "effeminacy": some years later, the dissolution of Chares's native Syria leads to its occupation by tough, no-nonsense Scythians, and Chares is fortunate enough to entertain the leader of these forces unawares. Here, Chares does the welcoming: "I was sitting one evening at the door of my cottage . . . when a man, of a majestic appearance, but with something ferocious in his look, attended by several others, passed by. As he approached my little garden, he seemed to view it with satisfaction, and to unbend the habitual sternness of his look: I asked him, if he would enter in and taste the fruits with his companions" (481). The imposing Arsaces accepts the invitation and requests that Chares ask a favor in return; like the Arab chieftain, he is smitten by Chares's appreciative eloquence:

> "All . . . that I request, O mighty conqueror, is, that you will please to order your men to step aside from the newly cultivated ground, and not destroy my vegetables."—"By heaven," said Arsaces, turning to his companions, "there is something elevated in the tranquillity and composure of this man's mind: and, were I not *Arsaces*, I should be with pleasure *Chares*." He then departed, but ordered me to attend him the next day at the camp, and gave strict orders that none of the soldiers should molest or injure my humble residence. (482)

Chares's discreet request that the soldiers not rape his land, and Arsaces's friendly compliance, leads, so to speak, to their respecting each other in the morning:

> He received me with a courtesy which had nothing of the barbarian in it, seated me familiarly by his side, and entered into a long conversation with me, upon the laws, and manners, and customs of the different nations I had seen. I was surprised at the vigour and penetration which I discovered in this untutored warrior's mind. Unbiased by the mass of prejudices which we acquire in cities . . . unincumbered [sic] by forms and ceremonies which contract the understanding . . . he seemed to possess a certain energy of soul which never missed the mark: nature in him had produced the same effects that study and philosophy do in others. (489–90)

It is as if Arsaces is mentally "naked," unshackled by convention, his "penetration" admitting of no barrier. Chares likes what he sees. Arsaces, similarly observant, offers his guest some dried horse meat and clotted milk, which Chares gamely eats, diplomatically remarking that the way of life such food represents "is more formidable to your enemies, than agreeable to your friends." Again, it seems, Chares has passed a test:

> He smiled at my sincerity . . . but from this hour he distinguished me with marks of peculiar favour, and admitted me to all his councils. This envied mark of distinction gave me no other pleasure than as it sometimes enabled me to be useful to my unhappy countrymen, and mitigate the rigour of their conquerors. Indeed, while the great Arsaces lived, his love of justice and order were so great, that even the conquered were safe from all oppression. . . . [E]ven the vanquished themselves . . . considered the success of the Scythians rather as a salutary revolution, than as a barbarian conquest. (492–93)

The "envied mark" Arsaces bestows upon Chares is at once physical, external—the public knowledge that Arsaces has singled out Chares—and cognitive, interior—privileged access to "all his councils." The phenomenon is like a mark of Cain, a guarantee of protection, and yet more is involved: Chares is a sort of protector, as well, for his "admittance" into the general's tent prevents the military rape of Syria. We note another departure from *Sandford and Merton*'s first realm of discourse, where Tommy's legibility and permeability bring him only shameful injury and exposure; here, such unconstrained receptivity brings joy to two men and peace to the region.

In light of this dimension—one of domestic politics, in more than one sense—it is especially interesting to see what Day does when importing the warrior culture to a modern, English setting. The familiar idiom seems to allow for amplification both of immediate sensation (the pulse-quickening realization that one is being looked at, or the thrill of recognizing the embodiment of one's desires) and of long-term "understandings" (contractual arrangements that take family, community, tradition into account)—hence, allowing for a new melding of "ardour" and "engagement." The story of Campbell (the chronicler of the American Indian war dance) and his deceased commander Simmons is a treasure trove of English gay iconography that draws, surprisingly, both from the tales of ancient warrior cultures and from the eighteenth-century cult of sensibility.

Campbell begins by introducing his listeners (who include Tommy and Harry) to the Scots highland culture of his boyhood, which contains overt parallels to the ancient warrior cultures described by Chares.

He describes the arrival one day at the Campbell homestead of Colonel Simmons, "a man of a majestic presence" who regales the family with "various accounts of the dangers he had already escaped, and the service he had seen." Awestruck, young Campbell recognizes in Simmons his heart's desire:

> The tone and look of a man who was familiar with great events . . . so inflamed my military ardour, that I was no longer capable of repressing it. The stranger perceived it, and, looking at me with an air of tenderness and compassion, asked if that young man was intended for the service? My colour rose, and my heart immediately swelled at the question: the look and manner of our guest had strangely interested me in his favour, and the natural grace and simplicity with which he related his own exploits, put me in mind of the great men of other times. Could I but march under the banners of such a leader, I thought nothing would be too arduous to be achieved. . . . I sprang forwards at the question, and told the officer, that the darling passion of my life would be to bear arms under a chief like him. (421)

Simmons puts up some resistance, rehearsing to Campbell "all the hardships which would be my lot," but capitulates when Campbell threatens to throw himself at the next officer who passes through (422). He then asks for the consent of Campbell's father, who is "equally charmed": "I have never seen an officer under whom I would more gladly march than yourself." That said, Simmons "instantly agreed to receive me," pays Mr. Campbell the going impressment rate, and refuses his host's offer of the "only bed," protesting, "Would you shame me in the eyes of my new recruit?" Instead, he allows young Campbell to improvise "as convenient a couch as I was able to make with heath and straw . . . he threw himself down upon it, and slept till morning" (423). The next day, Campbell quails briefly at the thought of leaving his family, but immediately thinks better of it: "I was however engaged, and determined to fulfil my engagement" (424).

Campbell pointedly passes over the "new sensations" (424) he discovers while in training, but once in America, his "darling wish" is granted: he serves directly "under" Simmons as an aide (a "private" man [428]), and can watch admiringly as Simmons further displays his "penetration" in persuading an Indian tribe to ally themselves with the British. The results of Simmons's speech are gratifyingly immediate; the tribal leaders exhort their people to "drink the blood of our enemies, and spread a feast of carnage for the fowls of the air and the wild beasts of the forest." The "whole nation" agrees "with a ferocious joy" (431), and a similar fervor fills Campbell's veins as he watches the ensuing dance of warriors.

The other British commanders, by contrast, are not so susceptible to Simmons's inflaming rhetoric; they ignore his warnings about the ambush techniques of the (French-allied) Indian enemy, and march two thousand troops, in neat but fragile ranks, straight into a trap. Making his way through the massacre, Campbell locates Simmons, who is badly wounded; he convinces Simmons to seek safety only by threatening to lie down and die with him—"for I swear by the eternal majesty of my Creator, that I will not leave you" (439). Despite Campbell's best efforts, however, the shared journey soon ends.

> He sunk [sic] down and would have fallen, but I received him in my arms; I bore him to the next thicket, and, strewing grass and leaves upon the ground, endeavoured to prepare him a bed. He thanked me again with gratitude and tenderness, and grasped my hand as he lay in the very agonies of death: for such it was, although I believed he had only fainted, and long tried every ineffectual method to restore departed life. Thus was I deprived of the noblest officer and kindest friend that ever deserved the attachment of a soldier. Twenty years have now rolled over me since that inauspicious day, yet it lives for ever in my remembrance, and never shall be blotted from my soul. (440)

Undoubtedly the most beautiful passage in a long and unwieldy book, this pietà apotheosizes Day's strategy throughout *Sandford and Merton* of following scenes of sexualized violence with scenes of postcoital calm. The trajectory here matches that of the initial encounter between the two men, where after Simmons has "inflamed" Campbell's "military ardour," Campbell quietly sets about contriving a bed for Simmons in the family barn.

The long-term ramifications of this moment, denied to Campbell and Simmons, are seen later in the novel, in the violent climax and peaceful denouement of "Sophron and Tigranes." This time, the tutor's specialized knowledge *is* heeded: just as Tigranes's invading forces seem certain of victory, Chares divulges to Sophron "a dreadful secret, which I have hitherto buried in my bosom": his discovery, many years earlier, of gunpowder (498–99).[29] Together, the two men stage the eruption of this long-dormant knowledge, unleashing its "irresistible" powers upon the earth:

> [A] sudden noise is heard that equals the loudest thunders: the earth itself trembles with a convulsive motion . . . then burst assunder with a violence that nothing can resist! Hundreds are in an instant swallowed up, or dashed against rocks, and miserably destroyed! Mean-

while, all nature seems to be convulsed around; the rocks themselves are torn from their solid base, and, with their enormous fragments, crush whole bands of miserable wretches beneath! Clouds of smoke obscure the field of battle, and veil the combatants in a dreadful shade; which is . . . dispelled by flashes of destructive fire! (501)

After Tigranes's army has been routed, we see Sophron locating the "miserably shatterd [sic] and disfigured" body of his childhood friend and reverentially placing it on a funeral pyre. The last panel of the triptych moves yet further into quietude, consecrating the shared retirement of Sophron and Chares:

> From this time, Sophron was universally honoured by all, as the most virtuous and valiant of his nation. He passed the rest of his life in peace and tranquillity, contented with the exercise of the same rural enjoyments which had engaged his childhood. Chares, whose virtues and knowledge were equally admirable, was presented, at the public expense, with a small but fertile tract of land . . . here, contented with the enjoyment of security and freedom, he passed the remaining part of his life in the contemplation of nature, and the delightful intercourse of virtuous friendship. (503-4)

Following the earth-shattering "convulsion," the bursting-forth of long-withheld knowledge, has come a more pacific sort of leveling, the calm *after* the storm. Ultimately, Day's paired portraits, for display over a mantlepiece, are even more "explosive" than his epic landscapes of homoeroticism.

In forging this peace, Day cobbles together two models of pedagogical romance that might otherwise be thought inimical: the Greek decorum of pederasty (difference in age, sameness of sex) and the decorum of adult courtship (sameness in age, difference in sex) enshrined in early English novels. The Greek model is by definition transient and hierarchical: the adult, the full citizen, initiates the affair, and for the boy's own good ends it before the boy acquires the rights of a citizen; volunteering for the "receptive" role, past a certain age, is generally viewed as shameful.[30] The English model privileges permanence, seeking to level the very differences of rank, class, and power on which the Greek model rests. Sexual desire, paradoxically, flows from the socially receptive position, typically as embodied in a down-at-heel heroine who "grows into" a culminating state of heterosexual fulfillment and an enhanced social status. It seems that, as with his extractions from Locke and Rousseau, Day mixes and matches elements of these two worldviews in such a way as to maximize sameness—*both* by pairing boy with boy and man with man, *and* by de-essentializing differences of age and rank. In his aesthetic, complementarity—whether of age (developmental stage) or of sex-role (developmental goal)—has no value, indeed almost no meaning. At the end of the book, Tommy's reunions with Harry and with his father echo the legitimacy and joy of Sophron and Chares, Chares and Arsaces, Campbell and Simmons. Women and girls are, as one would expect by now, completely absent: gayness has not been presented as a rite of passage, a mere "impression" to be carried into the "next" developmental phase. Even more of a relief is the fact that Mr. Barlow stops hounding Tommy and slips unnoticed from the picture; his scientific method for "improving" Tommy has been overridden by the book's urge to keep Tommy's receptivity intact, and by the romantic haze that lends *Sandford and Merton* its ultimate, and perhaps its only, coherence.

NOTES

1. For the most complete discussion, see Nancy Armstrong, *Desire and Domestic Fiction: A Political History of the Novel* (New York: Oxford University Press, 1987).

2. The first volume of *Sandford and Merton* was published by John Stockdale in 1783, the second in 1786, and the third in 1789. The best account of its widespread popularity appears in George Warren Gignilliat Jr., *The Author of Sandford and Merton: A Life of Thomas Day, Esq.* (New York: Columbia University Press, 1932). *Sandford and Merton* had reached Ireland, America, Germany, and France by 1793. Gignilliat notes three "waves" of the book's popularity: 1786–98, 1808–30, and 1850–90. Abridgements of various kinds began to appear in 1792. In 1809, one editor claimed to have abridged the book in answer to children's protests that it had been too expensive. Another motivation to abridge was embodied in *Sandford and Merton in Words of One Syllable* (1868). Shortened versions also appeared later in the nineteenth century, in such ventures as the "Shilling Entertaining Library" and "Family Gift Series." However, Gignilliat notes that "[t]hrough the Victorian period the book was preserved remarkably well in its original voluminousness and formality of language. The proportion of abridgements to complete editions was somewhat reduced; and up to 1890 it was very easy to obtain an unabridged edition" (pp. 337–41).

3. Jean-Jacques Rousseau, *Emile, or On Education*, trans. Allan Bloom (1762; New York: Basic Books, 1979). See, for example, Rousseau's disclaimer of his own capacity to be a tutor, and his rationale for constructing "an imaginary pupil" (pp. 50–51).

4. Forthright about his belief in the sequestration of women, Day was rejected by Margaret Edgeworth, Honora Sneyd, Elizabeth Sneyd, and a woman to whom biographers refer as "Mlle. Panckoucke." Margaret Edgeworth was the sister of his close friend Richard Edgeworth, and the two Sneyd sisters in fact rejected Day for Edgeworth. Day's early poem, "Gentle Lady of the West," may refer to another rejection. "Sabrina Sidney," the foundling girl he renamed, may also have a place on this list: she is supposed to have failed some staged moral "tests" of Day when in her late teens, but Day—generally disappointed with his "experiment" by that time (1773–74)—may simply have been looking for an excuse to get rid of her. (In 1770 he had given up on the younger foundling, "Lucretia," finding her a place as a milliner's apprentice.) He

installed Sabrina at a boardinghouse and provided her with an annuity. In 1787 John Bicknell, the friend with whom Day had written "The Dying Negro" (1773), and who had had a part in selecting the two foundlings for the experiment, married Sabrina.

5   Sir S. H. Scott, (*The Exemplary Mr. Day* [London: Faber and Faber, 1935]) is particularly scornful of Day's treatment of his wife. Though "contaminating influences" (p. 131) such as her own parents were not allowed to visit Esther Day (in fact, she was not even allowed a female servant), her adolescent nephews, as well as the adolescent sons of Richard Edgeworth and Erasmus Darwin, were. And, even though the remoteness of his estate was supposed to protect him from "the stink of human society" (Scott quoting Day, p. 142), "Day himself made occasional visits to London, seeing old friends and snatching a bit of air from the great world. But Esther was left to cook and dust at Stapleford" (pp. 131-32).

6   This characterization comes from another friend of Day, the chemist James Keir (*An Account of the Life and Writings of Thomas Day, Esq.* [1791; New York: Garland, 1970], p. 33).

7   Lovell Richard Edgeworth and Maria Edgeworth. *Memoirs of Richard Lovell Edgeworth.* 2 vols. (London: 1820; reprint. Shannon: Irish University Press, 1969) 1:183.

8   Ibid., 1:183-84.

9   Edgeworth acknowledges his son's "invincible dislike to control" in his *Memoirs* (1:179). Marilyn Butler describes the ramifications of this experiment for the Edgeworth family in greater detail in *Maria Edgeworth: A Literary Biography* (Oxford: Clarendon Press, 1972), pp. 50-51, 71, 106-7.

10 For more on this, see Keir, *Account of the Life*; Gignilliat, *Author of Sandford and Merton*; and Scott *Exemplary Mr. Day*, all of whom seek to mitigate Day's misogyny/gynophobia by descanting on the richness of his associations with men. Day's associates included members of the Birmingham Lunar Society; of these, Keir wrote an admiring biography; Edgeworth was treated to Day's moral advice, even after their break; Dr. Erasmus Darwin consoled Day after Honora Sneyd rejected him; Darwin's adolescent son visited Day's estate circa 1784; Dr. William Small introduced Day to his future wife, Esther Milnes; Matthew Boulton accepted a substantial loan from Day and was slow to repay it. John Bicknell, a friend from Charterhouse, helped Day select the two foundling girls, in 1769, and in 1773 collaborated with him on "The Dying Negro," a verse diatribe against slavery. (In 1784, Bicknell—seemingly, to Day's dismay—married the elder foundling, Sabrina; Scott [p. 159] discreetly alludes to Bicknell's "early irregularities," and to the "chronic illness—a kind of palsy" which killed him.) In 1775, Day rushed home from Europe on hearing that "his best friend" (Gignilliat, *Author of Sandford and Merton*, p. 120) Dr. William Small was dying, but did not arrive in time to say good-bye. "It was indeed a blow for Day; this sensible, sardonic, humane man had attained a strong grip on his life. In all sincerity of heart he wrote his elegy" (pp. 120-21), which assures "no second loss like thine" (quoted on p. 121). Later that year, Day renewed contact with an Oxford friend, William Jones, and may have roomed with him at the Middle Temple for two years (pp. 122-23); at the Temple he also met and "idolized" (p. 124) John Laurens, the son of American statesman Henry Laurens. Throughout the 1780s, a misfortune-prone philosopher named Walter Pollard extorted funds from Day, and—after Day's death in 1789—from his widow. Circa 1784, Esther's nephew Thomas Lowndes came to live with the Days. In 1787, Day tried unsuccessfully to dissuade Richard Edgeworth from disowning his son Richard, whose life seems to have been ruined by their early Rousseauian experiment on him; as an adolescent, young Richard had also made visits to Day's estate.

11   John Locke, *Some Thoughts Concerning Education*, ed. John W. Yolton and Jean S. Yolton (Oxford: Clarendon Press, 1989), p. 84. (All marks of emphasis *sic*.) Four paragraphs later, Locke pauses to offer a vague disclaimer about the education of girls per se: "I have said *He* here, because the principal aim of my Discourse is, how a young gentleman should be brought up from his Infancy, which, in all things, will not so perfectly suit the education of *Daughters;* though, where the difference of Sex requires different treatment, 'twill be no hard matter to distinguish" (p. 86).

12   Ibid., p. 111; Locke's emphasis. "On the other side," Locke quickly adds, "if the *Mind* be curbed, and *humbled* too much in children; if their *Spirits* be abased and *broken* much, by too strict an hand over them, they lose all their Vigor and Industry, and are in a worse State than the former. For extravagant young Fellows, that have Liveliness and Spirit, come sometimes to be set right, and so make Able and Great Men: but *dejected Minds*, timorous, and tame, and *low Spirits*, are hardly ever to be raised, and very seldom attain to any thing" (p. 112).

13   When I refer to "impression" in the context of Locke's *Some Thoughts Concerning Education*, I mean recommended impositions such as washing the child's feet in cold water, and "hav[ing] his Shooes [*sic*] so thin, that they might leak and *let in Water*, whenever he comes near it" (p. 86); "hav[ing] no time kept constantly to for his Breakfast, Dinner, and Supper, but rather varied almost every Day" (p. 94); and frequently changing the child's bedding arrangements so that "he may not feel every little Change he must be sure to meet with" (p. 99). Such impositions are, as Locke repeatedly points out, meant to be assimilated.

14   Thomas Day, *The History of Sanford and Merton* (New York: The World Publishing House, 1875), pp. 10–11. Further citations to this work refer to this one-volume, 538-page edition, and will be given parenthetically in the text. Like those of at least seven other publishers, this edition is touted on the title page as "THE ONLY COMPLETE AMERICAN EDITION."

15   The standard reading of *Sandford and Merton* views class identification as the driving force behind Day's antiluxurian rhetoric, and accordingly views what happens to Tommy as a steady, successful reprogramming into bourgeois morality. See, for example, Mona Scheuermann, *Social Protest in the Eighteenth-Century English Novel* (Columbus: Ohio State University Press, 1985), especially pp. 60–61.

16   In giving Harry's learned humaneness special emphasis, *Sandford and Merton* participates in what Samuel F. Pickering identifies as a tradition of children's literature deriving from Locke's warning, in *Some Thoughts Concerning Education*, that children allowed to hurt animals will grow up to hurt their fellow humans. See Pickering's *John Locke and Children's Books in Eighteenth-Century England* (Knoxville, Tenn. University of Tennessee Press, 1981).
       Day goes somewhat farther, presenting Harry's early mastery of benevolence as the crux of his attractiveness to Mr. Barlow: "These sentiments made little Harry a great favorite with every body; particularly with the Clergyman of the parish, who became so fond of him, that he taught him to read and write, and had him almost always with him. Indeed, it was not surprising that Mr. Barlow shewed so particular an affection for him; for besides learning, with the greatest readiness, every thing that was taught him, little Harry was the most honest, obliging creature in the world. He was never discontented, nor did he ever grumble, whatever he was desired to do" (pp. 12–13). One thinks immediately of the clergymen/educationists whose work James Kincaid examines in *Child-Loving: The Erotic Child and Victorian Culture* (New York: Routledge, 1992), except that, following the above passage, the text is contrastively taciturn re-

garding Harry's quickness and irresistibility. The one exception is a (much later) consultation with Harry about Tommy, which makes it clear that Harry is not a child at all, in Barlow's eyes (pp. 466–71).

17 Day's predilection for muddy burlesque was the source of a private joke between Maria Edgeworth and her aunt Margaret Ruxton (Richard Edgeworth's sister, and the first woman to reject Day's offer of marriage). In a letter of 1804, Maria recounts a scene in which a noblewoman is thrown by a restive horse: "Here is enough falling & floundering & dirt enough to delight even Mr. Day's [sic] whom nothing diverted so much as people's falling down in the dirt, especially if they were ladies & gentlemen & well-dressed. Lady Anna Maria being daughter to a dutchess [sic] & accoutred in a regimental riding habit laced across the body with costly silver ribs like a man in armor and covered with bog-water & mud would inevitably have killed Mr. Day with laughter" (quoted in *Maria Edgeworth*, Butler, pp. 204–5).

18 The spectatorial dynamics of *Sandford and Merton* deserve a much closer analysis than present space allows. Two obvious starting points would be Freud's "A Child is Being Beaten" (*The Standard Edition of the Complete Psychological Works of Sigmund Freud*, ed. James Strachey [London: Hogarth Press, 1953], 7:179–204) and Gilles Deleuze's bifurcation of sadistic and masochistic platforms in *Masochism*, trans. Jean McNeil (New York: Zone Books, 1989). With both, though, I would urge caution in the placement of Thomas Day relative to the fantasy. My worry is not that he might be placed too blithely "inside" the tableau, as Tommy and/or Mr. Barlow—one could hardly do this blithely enough—but that his collegial relation to Freud and Deleuze might be understated. No intellectual, Day nevertheless knew (in encyclopedic detail) what he liked and what, crudely speaking, worked for him. Another wrinkle in applying Deleuze is that—perversely, considering Day's own bifurcated view of how these things worked—*Sandford and Merton* seems almost to uphold what Deleuze so cogently disparages, namely the pseudo-organic construction "sadomasochism." One approach might be to view Day's book through a metaphorical prism, so that instead of a conceptual dependence between the two schemes, we would have illusory shifts of image, a sort of overlapping double-vision, that would be beyond the eye's control. James Kincaid's remarks on "The Naughty Child" and on voyeurism, which incorporate Freud, provide the most useful tack thus far, though he of course is focusing on a later era. Yet his consideration of "our need" for the naughty child, as met by children's books, does not quite fit with *Sandford and Merton*, which I think portrays a related need but a different child. There is remarkably little "child-loving" in Day's work; Mr. Barlow's romance is with Harry, not Tommy, and Tommy's beleaguered "hinder parts" and sodden trousers are iconographically distinct from the adorably chaste buttocks of Victorian fantasy. Kincaid mentions *Sandford and Merton* itself very briefly, as illustrating the vaunted power of spankings to counteract "spoiling" in children—"a drama of reformation recorded, in part, in *Sandford and Merton*" (*Child-Loving*, p. 251). In my view, the "reformation" aspect is, at best, vestigial in Day's work.

19 To characterize the rift between *Sandford and Merton*'s two realms of discourse, we could turn to Deleuze's distinctions, in *Masochism*, between sadistic and masochistic dynamics—the two best being sadistic "instruction" versus masochistic "education" and sadistic "repetition" versus masochistic "suspension." Beyond this appreciation, though, it becomes more difficult to import Deleuze's work to Day's in such a way as to maintain the sorts of separatism on which each insists. Easier and more useful, though/because probably more imprecise, might be an application of Foucault's large-scale distinction between "scientia sexualis" and "ars erotica" (*History of Sexuality*,

trans. Robert Hurley, vol. 1 [New York: Random House, 1978], pp. 57–73). The fervent investigation of Tommy's disorder certainly fits the first category; the difficulty may be that Tommy's eventual "confessions" lead—by design—not to increased, self-rehabilitative effort on his part, but to acceptance and stasis. Similarly, the strong consonance of Day's second discursive realm with Foucault's "ars erotica" (where "truth and sex were linked, in the form of pedagogy, by the transmission of a precious knowledge from one body to another" [p. 61]) is jarred somewhat by the hierarchical, indeed developmental assumptions embedded in Foucault's vision of the master-apprentice relationship.

20 Rousseau, *Emile*, p. 119.

21 See, for example, *Emile*, pp. 89–91, where Rousseau counters the common wisdom (traceable, as he notes, to Locke) about reasoning with children: "Firstly, by imposing upon them a duty they do not feel, you set them against your tyranny. . . . Secondly, you teach them to become dissemblers . . . in order to extort rewards or escape punishments. Finally, by accustoming them always to cover a secret motive with an apparent motive, you yourselves give them the means of deceiving you ceaselessly. . . . Use force with children, and reason with men. Such is the natural order. The wise man does not need laws." Rousseau goes on to explain what he means by "force": "Command him nothing, whatever in the world it might be, absolutely nothing. Do not even allow him to imagine that you might pretend to have any authority over him. Let him know only that he is weak and you are strong. . . . Let him see . . . necessity in things, never in the caprice of men. Let the bridle that restrains him be force and not authority. Do not forbid him to do that from which he should abstain; prevent him from doing it."

22 Ibid., p. 323.

23 Ibid.

24 Ibid., p. 324.

25 Ibid., p. 325.

26 Ibid., p. 332.

27 The story is told in two installments—the first after Tommy, enjoying a relapse of rich-boy effeminacy, unjustly repudiates Harry, and the second following the reminiscences of an indigent veteran concerning his beloved, deceased commanding officer (the story of Campbell and Simmons, discussed below).

28 Chares theorizes that Egypt's temperate climate and rich soil (for example, the "soft and yielding slime" left behind by the annual flooding of the Nile) have led to general dissipation: "the great business of existence is an inglorious indolence, a lethargy of mind, and a continual suspense from all exertion. The very children catch the contagion from their parents; they are instructed in every effeminate art; to dance in soft, unmanly attitudes, to modulate their voices by musical instruments, and to adjust the floating drapery of their dress" (pp. 393–94). Chares later describes the decline of his native Syria in much the same way, also using the term "effeminacy" (pp. 479–81). The specific image of a man self-consciously adjusting loose clothing also appears in the "Story of Polemo" (not delivered through the narrative persona of Chares, but related by Mr. Barlow to Mr. Merton), in which the Stoic philosopher Xenocrates shames a dissipated youth to the point that he "seemed intent to compose his dress into a more decent form, and wrapped his robe about him, which before hung loosely waving with an air of studied effeminacy" (p. 367).

29 Chares prefaces the crucial disclosure with more general remarks about his inquiring temperament: "Not contented with viewing the appearance of things as they strike our senses, I have endeavoured to penetrate into the deeper recesses of nature, and

to discover those secrets which are concealed from the greater part of mankind. For this purpose I have tried innumerable experiments concerning the manner in which bodies act upon each other" (p. 498).

30 For discussions of this, see Michel Foucault, *The Care of the Self*, trans. Robert Hurley (New York: Random House, 1986), pp. 1–36 and passim; David M. Halperin, "Why is Diotima a Woman?: Platonic *Eros* and the Figuration of Gender," in *Before Sexuality: The Construction of Erotic Experience in the Ancient Greek World*, ed. David Halperin, John J. Winkler, and Froma I. Zeitlin (Princeton: Princeton University Press, 1990), pp. 257–98; David M. Halperin, "Is There a History of Sexuality?" in *The Lesbian and Gay Studies Reader*, ed. Henry Abelove, Michèle Aina Barale, and David M. Halperin (New York: Routledge, 1993), pp. 416–31; David F. Greenberg, *The Construction of Homosexuality* (Chicago: University of Chicago Press, 1988), esp. pp. 148–51; and William S. Cobb's commentaries in his edition of *Plato's Erotic Dialogues* (Albany: SUNY Press, 1993).

Barry Weller

Wizards, Warriors, and the Beast

Glatisant in Love

"Sex," said Sir Palomides haughtily, "can be noblest thing in world, but it can also be wickedness terrible."
"When is it wicked?"
"Such things are not fit for child age."
"But you said that education was learning things needed when we grow up."
"Thus is quite different thing."
"Won't we need sex when we grow up?"
"Yours truly hopes not *that* sort," replied Sir Palomides loftily.
"Which sort?"
"The wicked sort, Mr. Gareth."
"Please, will you tell us the difference? We think this is very interesting."
—T. H. White, *The Witch in the Wood*, ch. 6 [1]

Like all the best children's literature, T. H. White's *The Sword in the Stone* (1938) seems darker, more yearning and perverse, when one rereads it as an adult. Even this prologue to Malory [2] — a charming fable of how Merlyn teaches the boy who will become King Arthur to be human by turning him into different animals — might unsettle the conventional reader, containing as it does intimations of cannibalism, homoerotic horseplay, and a free-floating desire that can cross the boundaries between species. King Pellinore's Questing Beast, for example, provides a surprising but appropriate focus for the polymorphous erotic energies of White's Arthurian stories, because one might almost take cross-species desire as the animating principle of the entire cycle, and the Beast, after all, embodies several animals—and perhaps several sexes—at once.

The heterodox crosscurrents of the narrative are more visible from the retrospect of subsequent novels in the series. Hints of sadism and transgressive sexuality grow stronger in White's sequel, *The Witch in the Wood* (1939), which concerns Arthur's half-sister, Morgause, and her four children. For all its considerable slapstick comedy and its apparent continuity with *The Sword in the Stone,* this book is less a children's book than a book about child abuse. It culminates in Morgause's seduction of Arthur, but as Sylvia Townsend Warner notes disapprovingly, "The real incest theme of the story is the maternal rape on the child." In one respect at least she still found it a child's book: the shadow of parental violation "cast White back into the nursery language of 'nasty.' "³ The fate of animals also grows uglier: in their frantic attempts to win maternal favor, the four sons of Morgause transform a tragically beautiful unicorn into "muddy, bloody, heather-mangled" meat (*WW,* 96), while Morgause, dilettantishly experimenting with a spell to make herself invisible, boils a cat alive. The third novel of the sequence, *The Ill-Made Knight* (1940), begins with another unhappy child, Lancelot, who thought there was something wrong with him. All through his life, even when he was a great man with the world at his feet, he was to feel this gap: something at the bottom of his heart that he was aware of, and ashamed of, but which he did not understand.⁴

Just as Malory's characters find their paths more limited, their fates more imminent, with each successive action, the reader finds the later volumes of the series increasingly constrained by their already determinate plots. With the addition of a fourth book, *The Candle in the Wind* (written in 1940), these novels of the late 1930s and early 1940s were incorporated into *The Once and Future King* (1958) as a full-scale retelling of the Arthurian cycle. (*Camelot,* Lerner and Loewe's musical adaptation of the later books [1960; filmed in 1967], gave the book wider currency but, like the leaden Disney film of *The Sword in the Stone* [1963], traduced its distinctiveness.)⁵

White aggressively renews his focus on Arthur's education and commerce with the world of animals in *The Book of Merlyn,* which he had written in 1941 to serve as a coda to his tetralogy.⁶ On the eve of Arthur's battle with Mordred, Merlyn reunites his pupil with old familiars from *The Sword in the Stone* (including the owl Archimedes, the falcon Balin, the badger, and the hedgehog) and furthers his political instruction with two new metamorphoses. Not incidentally White himself recuperates the freedom of invention that the preceding two volumes had partially ceded to Malory. When Malory is his model and master, White makes the final days of Arthur's court a vision of claustrophobia and entropy; his Merlyn, however, returns to prophesy a world of still-unfolding possibility, including infinite literary tranformations of Arthur's own story, the Matter of Britain. The plebeian hedgehog, least intellectual and most empathetic of Arthur's animal companions, leads the aged king to a Wordsworthian hillside vision of England, "like a sleeping man-child . . . sprawled undefended now, vulnerable, a baby trusting the world to let it sleep in peace";[7] Arthur has not failed definitively, because the adulthood of humankind still lies ahead.

Whereas Edward Carpenter (in *Love's Coming-of-Age*,[8] for example) identifies the maturation of humanity with its accommodation and tempering of the erotic drive, in *The Once and Future King* it's not immediately apparent what role sexuality plays in the imagined progress of the race. Even the education of the characters in *The Once and Future King* pays scant attention to the topic traditionally assigned to the birds and the bees. When Sir Palomides tries to instruct Gareth and his brothers in the "important and almost holy subject" of sex, "After a bit, Gareth said: 'But surely my mother didn't marry a bee?'"

On the other hand, pedagogy—most characteristically figured as a relation of older and younger men—is central to White's Arthurian narratives. It certainly leaves room for a Platonic, and thus implicitly homoerotic, version of desire—grounded in the "idea that the giving and receiving of knowledge, the active formation of another's character, or the more passive growth under another's guidance is the truest and strongest foundation of love."[9]

In one form or another, the topic of pedagogy runs through the rather diverse materials of *The Once and Future King*. *The Sword in the Stone* belongs to a recognizable genre: in the tradition of works as various as Xenophon's *Cyropaedia*, Rabelais's *Gargantua* and *Pantagruel*, and Shakespeare's *Henry IV* plays, it tells the story of the boy who will become king. *The Witch in the Wood* (renamed, revised, and considerably shortened as *The Queen of Air and Darkness*, part 2 of *The Once and Future King*) narrates the childhood and education of the members of the Orkney clan— Gawaine, Agravaine, Gaheris, and Gareth—who will come to trouble and finally challenge the enterprise of Arthur's court. *The Ill-Made Knight* likewise begins with Lancelot's adolescent apprenticeship to chivalry but traces his *bildung* further, into sexual initiation and the spiritual humiliations of the Grail quest. Nevertheless, its final lines, borrowed directly from Malory, return to the scene of childhood discipline—disturbingly intensified by adult humiliation and the knowledge of sin. White has just retold one of Malory's most concise and moving episodes: Only the touch of the "best knight in the world" can heal the Hungarian knight, Sir Urre; in symmetry to the sword-drawing ritual that had identified Arthur as king, each knight of the Round Table files past to attempt the cure, but the miracle is reserved for Lancelot. It is one last act of grace for Lancelot, who has committed adultery with Guinevere and failed to accomplish the Grail quest. He feels his fragile purchase on the title of "best knight" and perceives that God has, for the moment, mysteriously veiled or looked past his guilt. "'And ever,' says Sir Thomas Malory, 'Sir Lancelot wept, as he had been a child that had been beaten'" (*IMK*, 291).

The pedagogy, however, extends beyond the characters of *The Once and Future King* to the human race, on whose behalf the experiment of the Round Table is undertaken. It is a dim rehearsal of the proposition that some principle other than "might makes right" must eventually govern political arrangements. Arthur, as humankind's representative, is encouraged, in both *The Sword in the Stone* and *The Book of Merlyn*, to learn from other species the arbitrariness and limitations of human social forms. The epigraph of *The Candle in the Wind*, the penultimate book of the series (and the final book of *The Once and Future King*), already looks forward to *The Book of Merlyn*; its quotation from Samuel Butler blithely outlines the therapeutic and didactic intentions that frame the entire sequence: "I should prescribe for Mr. Pontifex a course of the larger mammals. Don't let him think he is taking them medicinally."[10]

If pedagogy and passionate involvement with the world of animals are two of the most important motifs in *The Once and Future King*, both these channels of eros—it would beg too many questions to call them sublimations—are writ large in White's own life. T. H. White spent much of his early life as a schoolmaster, first at a preparatory school, St. David's, in Reigate, Surrey, from 1930 to 1932, and then at the recently founded public school, Stowe (known as "the Modern Eton").[11] A poem White sent to L. J. Potts in October 1931 expresses his ambivalence about participating in the British system of education, with its institutional suppression of natural sensuality. His erotic feeling for boys strikingly suffuses the polemic:

> This pretty boy, mischievous, chaste, and stupid,
> With bouncing bum and eyes of teasing fire,
> This budding atom, happy heart, young Cupid,
> Will grow to know desire.
>
> . . .
>
> Anxious Mamma, discern the signs of rapture:
> Observe his sensuous wriggles in the bath.
> His plump brown legs design their future capture,
> Their virgin quelled, their tenderness and wrath.
>
> Happy immoral imp, if this continues
> He will, no doubt, grow up a shameless sensualist.
> He wont despise his genitals and sinews,
> Wont know that it is 'beastly' to be kissed.
>
> . . .

Stuff him in Etons quick, and send him packing
To Dr Prisonface his Surrey school.
That old rheumatic man with threats and whacking
Will justly bring this body to the rule.[12]

Even more relevantly, in the 1950s White fell in love with a twelve-year-old boy, referred to as Zed in Warner's biography, and in 1960 described the relationship to David Garnett in these terms: "I dont know whether I told you that about seven years ago a living Wart [in White's fiction the boyhood nickname of the future King Arthur] discovered in me a real Merlyn, just as if we had written The Sword in the Stone about ourselves. He is now a splendid figure nearly six feet high, and we are still devoted to each other."[13] It's hard to imagine Merlyn's describing the pains of self-suppression White suffered in this relationship ("The love part, the emotional bond, is the agonizing one—and this I have spared him. I never told him I loved him, or worked on his emotions or made any appeals or forced the strain on him"),[14] but it's significant that White should narrate the most intense attraction of his later years in terms of the tutorial bond between Merlyn and Wart.[15]

White's passionate attention to animals is pervasively evident in his writings, from *England Have My Bones* (1936) to *The Godstone and the Blackymor* (1959); his most scholarly work, *The Book of Beasts*, the translation of an eleventh-century bestiary, intermittently preoccupied him from 1938 until its publication in 1954. That the forms of his attention should have ranged from doting upon animals to hunting them (as in *England Have My Bones*)[16] may correspond to the "sadistic" temperament he confessed to David Garnett.[17] Perhaps the balance of White's feelings for animals found fullest expression in his disciplinary role as a trainer of falcons, goshawks, and other hunting birds. They were not the only species to engage his devotion. Sylvia Townsend Warner's biography of White suggests that the central emotional event of his life turned out to be the near-death of his red setter Brownie:

> The trick of withholding his heart . . . was gone, abolished by the shock of finding himself essential to a living creature. . . . [Warner quotes a letter from Hugh Heckstall Smith:] 'His own amorous feelings were, I think, all for boys, and he was very very careful about them.' But his loving feelings were less strictly guarded, and at the realization that he might lose Brownie's love before he had allowed himself to love her 'the miracle happened all at once'. He dared to risk his heart on something that might be dead in another twenty-four hours. . . . it made a great difference to his next book.

Warner later describes Brownie as "the only unhaunted love possible" for White.[18] She is not suggesting that White's emotional life resembled J. R. Ackerley's; still, even to mention Ackerley's *My Dog Tulip* (1956) is to place White's passion for Brownie in a wider tradition of British sexual heresy.

Warner distinguishes with questionable confidence between White's "amorous" and "loving" feelings,[19] and the "next book," *The Sword in the Stone*, finds a place for both boys and animals. Nevertheless, White himself might have approved Warner's distinction. Much of his fiction is devoted to puzzling out the unstable economy between appetitive, angry eros ("amorous feelings"?) and ostensibly more selfless manifestations of loving. For a dream of human progress King Arthur sacrifices almost every hope of personal satisfaction, every trace of erotic vitality, and, by virtue of his renunciations, becomes the most opaque figure in White's novels—a kind of Aeneas or Henry V. We see what his surrenders of feeling cost him, but not much of what they leave behind, except emotional exhaustion. (Was this also White's image of himself?)[20] Before returning to the solitary figure of Arthur, drained of erotic vitality, it is worth considering the sexual and emotional landscape of *The Once and Future King* as a whole. Especially relevant to Arthur's fate—and even to surmises of his escape from that cul-de-sac—are Lancelot's bisexuality, representations of motherhood as incestuous and cannibalistic, a cluster of avuncular figures who supplement the failed or absent nurturance of biological parents, the Questing Beast as romantic succedaneum (and perhaps succubus), and, mainly through the pull of the animal world on Arthur's affections and intellect, a proliferation of political and erotic possibilities.

I

"Won't we need sex when we grow up?"
"Yours truly hopes not *that* sort," replied Sir Palomides loftily.
"Which sort?" (*WW*, 54)

Which sort, indeed? At the end of the tale the moral of the Round Table seems an antiheterosexual one: it is the irrelevantly private passion of Lancelot and Guinevere that undermines the grand enterprise of impersonal justice. For Lancelot himself desire is self-betrayal, and he fetishizes his chastity even more fervently than his loyalty to Arthur. When the virginal Elaine (pretending she is Guinevere) seduces him, it is Lancelot who is deflowered: "She had stolen his strength of ten. . . . No more to be the best knight in the world, no more to work miracles against magic, no more to have compensation for ugliness and emptiness in his soul" (*OFK*, 392, 396). White feels enough empathy with Lancelot's self-contempt to dramatize his sense of loss, but also mocks his superstition and implicitly the whole cult of sexual continence: "Children believe such things to this day, and think that they will only be able to bowl well in the cricket match tomorrow provided that they are good today" (*OFK*, 392).

But, of course, by sleeping with Guinevere, at first in the illusion manufactured by Elaine's duenna and then in actuality, Lancelot also betrays Arthur—less perhaps in his interference with the marital bond than in straying from the master-mistress of his own affections. At the outset of *The Ill-Made Knight*, Lancelot is clearly in love with Arthur, not Guinevere. White's notes for the novel indicate both the writer's clarity about the homoerotic component of Lancelot's character and his ambivalence about dramatizing it too directly: "Homosexual? Can a person be ambi-sexual—bisexual or whatever? His treatment of young boys like Gareth and Cote Male Tale is very tender and his feeling for Arthur profound. Yet I do so want not to have to write a 'modern' novel about him. I could only bring myself to mention this trait, if it is a trait, in the most oblique way."[21]

White's identification with Lancelot probably colors the first page of *The Ill-Made Knight* with its ostentatious tact about the thing "at bottom of his heart which [Lancelot] was aware of, and ashamed of, but which he did not understand. There is no need for us to try to understand it. It would be ignoble to go dabbling in a place which he preferred to keep secret" (*IMK*, p. 3). Peering at his reflection in a helmet, Lancelot sees a face "as ugly as a monster's in the King's menagerie" (*OFK*, 329; "ugly as sin," *IMK*, 7), and opines "that there must be a reason for it somewhere." Borrowing from the repertory of medieval rhetoric, White's *praeteritio* both incites and discourages speculation. Unlike discreetly homosexual writers of an earlier generation (Henry James, for example?), White seems fully aware of his imaginative investment in proto-gay figures and subjects; the representational question is how far he will allow this knowledge to become visible.

White resists giving a single name to Lancelot's secret, and he is amply justified on psychological and novelistic grounds. He does, however, seem to have worried about the degree of explicitness with which he could signal Lancelot's erotic allegiances and still preserve historical decorum—or the decorum of the closet. Minor adjustments between *The Ill-Made Knight* and its revision in *The Once and Future King* evince this anxiety. Both versions record that "Lancelot, swinging his dumbbells fiercely and making his wordless noise, had been thinking of King Arthur with all his might. He was in love with him" (*OFK*, 327). However, *The Once and Future King* moves the adolescent passion toward slightly greater impersonality: while *The Ill-Made Knight* says that Lancelot "gave thirty-six months to another man's ideal because he was in love with him" (13), *The Once and Future King* changes the final phrase to "in love with it" (334). More dramatically, chapter 4 of *The Ill-Made Knight* begins, "Arthur's lover rode toward Camelot with a bitter heart" (22), while the corresponding sentence in *The Once and Future King* changes "lover" to "hero-worshipper" (342). The phrasing about Lancelot's being or having fallen "in love" with Arthur recurs, in the opening chapters of both versions, too insistently to be ignored; the later version, however, supplies a more readily palatable alibi of youthful idealism for this crush.[22]

White's avoidance of homosexuality as a "modern" topic (Foucauldian *avant la lettre?*) may indicate why he found the past a congenial setting for most of his fictions, but the broader point is that he found in earlier ages, less marked and mapped by ready-made categories, men who loved other men but were also athletic (but "humble about [their] athleticism"), ascetic, self-critical, "fastidious, monogamous, serious," "devoted to 'honour,'" and practical (a few of the attributes he assigned to Lancelot, along with moral sensitivity, emotionalism, tolerance, compassion, etc.).[23] One suspects that in White's mind the modern *type* of the homosexual, or perhaps White's own somewhat homophobic apprehension of the type, could not accommodate so wide and potentially contradictory a spectrum of qualities.

In any case Lancelot had to follow the trajectory of the Malorian story, that is, to fall in love with Guinevere and compromise, though never abandon, his adhesion to Arthur (and, after the Grail quest, to God—another idealization of the adored older male?). The most convincing depiction of Lancelot and Guinevere comes late in their story, when as middle-aged lovers they sit discussing their problems in the illicit but domestic space of the bedchamber.[24] Perhaps it's worth noting that Lancelot and Guinevere's affair at court takes the form, both in White and Malory, of an "open secret"—a configuration of self-evidence and concealment, of knowing and unknowing on the part of observers, of which recent criticism has emphasized the specifically though not exclusively homosexual meanings;[25] arguably White's conspicuous gesture of *not* revealing Lancelot's secret, at the beginning of the novel, produces the same inflection. Lancelot and Guinevere discuss whether they should come out:

> "We could live together for our old age, anyway, and be happy, and not have to go on deceiving every day, and we should die in peace."
> "You said that Arthur knew all about it," she said, "and that we were not deceiving him at all."
> "Yes, but it is different. I love Arthur and I can't stand it when I see him looking at me, and know that he knows. You see, Arthur loves us."

"But Lance, if you love him so much, what is the good of running away with his wife?"

"I want it to be in the open," he said stubbornly, "at least at the end."

"Well, I don't want it to be. . . . As we are now it is horrible, but at least Arthur knows about it inside himself, and we still love each other and are safe. . . . Why should we make Arthur publicly miserable?" (*OFK*, 573)

Both Arthur's ambiguous knowledge ("inside himself") and his otherwise invisible eros ("You see, Arthur loves us") are inscribed in this relationship in such a way that they become as much an "open secret" as the adulterous affair, in which his tacit consciousness makes him a participant. The horror of cuckoldry, most luridly enacted by Renaissance and medieval literature, seems bound up with homophobia, as though the husband were always a passive partner, fucked by his wife's lover.

White, in any case, was clearly sensitive to the emotional bond between the adulterer and the cuckolded husband.[26] In the late 1950s White considered writing a play about King Mark and Sir Tristram in order to "analyse"[27] the relations between himself and the boy Zed, now eighteen or nineteen, with whom he had fallen in love some six years before: "Had he [King Mark] been deeply in love with the boy and never forgiven him for growing up?"[28] King Arthur's feelings toward the adult Lancelot are among the least dramatized elements of *The Once and Future King*, but the Malorian symmetries among Arthur-Lancelot-Guinevere and Mark-Tristram-Iseult suggests White may have perceived the two triangles in similar terms, and in each case felt best qualified to understand the currents of feeling between the two men.

In the end the decision about whether the affair of Lancelot and Guinevere remains an "open secret," rather than public knowledge, is wrested from them by the malice of the Orkney clan—or at least its most resentful members, Mordred and Agravaine. The effect is to subject the lovers to the unsparing legal process—ironically, Arthur's laboriously erected alternative to the rule of might. (If this particular "open secret" does invite interpretation as an allusion to the homosexual situation, the legal consequences of declaring the secret probably glance toward the rigor of British statutes in the 1940s.)

II

The aggression of the Orkney brothers against Lancelot, Guinevere and— more obliquely—Arthur is linked to the emotional cannibalism of their mother, as though the familial pathology of incest, murder, and sorcery must somehow find an outlet. Morgause, mother of Gawaine, Agravaine, Gaheris, Gareth, and—by her half-brother Arthur—Mordred, is manipulative, self-dramatizing, sexually voracious, and, toward her children, sadistically punitive and seductive by turns. The children are emotionally deformed by their worship of her; Agravaine, the most incestuously fixated, eventually finds the aging vamp *in flagrante delicto* and murders her in a jealous rage, while his half-brother Mordred dispatches her lover, Sir Lamorak, one of King Pellinore's sons. White's critics, including those, like L. J. Potts, who read *The Witch in the Wood* before it was published, have been scandalized by its misogyny and have uniformly concluded that White's obsessive hatred of his mother drove his narrative off course.[29]

Constance Aston White was undoubtedly formidable. White was born in Bombay but sent to his grandparents in England at the age of five; during his brief time in India both parents managed to charge his infancy with drama: "I am told that my father and mother were to be found wrestling with a pistol, one on either side of my cot, each claiming that he or she was going to shoot the other other and himself or herself, but in any case beginning with me. If I woke up during these scenes, the censor of my mind has obliterated them as too terrible, but I believe they happened."[30] White's relationship with his mother comes even closer to the depiction of Morgause: "I adored her passionately until I was about eighteen. . . . I didn't get much security out of her. Either there were the dreadful parental quarrels and spankings of me when I was tiny or there were excessive scenes of affection during which she wooed me to love her—not her to love me. . . . I've always thought she was sexually frigid, which was maybe why she thrashed it out of me."[31] He adds, simplistically, "Anyway, she managed to bitch up my loving women."

More telling is another detail from his reminiscences: "[A photograph] of a fat little boy in an Eton suit too tight for him, with rather thick lips . . . was taken to send to my mother in India, and she wrote back that my lips were growing *sensual*. I was to hold them in, with my teeth if necessary. Since then I have been ashamed of my lips and now wear them concealed by moustache and beard."[32] Accordingly, it's no accident that most of the episodes that disappeared from *The Sword in the Stone* in its recension for *The Once and Future King* center on orality. In chapter 6 of *The Sword in the Stone* the genteel witch, Madame Mim (who teaches pianoforte and needlework as well as necromancy), is a fairy-tale double of Morgause; like the witch in "Hansel and Gretel" she cages Wart and Kay until she is ready to eat them. "Plucking" him in preparation for roasting, the "witch laid Wart over her lap, with his head between her knees, and carefully began to take his clothes off with a practiced hand."[33] Adult, particularly female, sexuality is seen as a form of cannibalism, and vice versa. An episode concerned with the Anthropophagi[34] was omitted from the American edition at the stipulation of the Book-of-the-Month Club, though White's English readers, such as David Garnett, had also disliked it.[35] Cannibalism is less prominent in the representation of the Anthropophagi, a pastiche of Mandeville, than one might suppose, but even the name of "these bad creatures" (SS [British edition], 165) reinforces the motif. For these chapters White substituted a siege of Morgan the Fay. Morgan the Fay is a Hollywood star with beach pajamas, dark glasses, a jade cigarette holder, and hair like Veronica Lake's; the first four floors of her castle are occupied by attendants, from "Moorish maidens" offering "ginger chocolates, marron glacé chocolates, liqueur chocolates, and chocolates which stuck your teeth together," to liveried footmen purveying "iced champagne, . . . oysters, truffles, olives, croûtes, slices of lemon, soufflés, and so on" and "twenty charming negro minstrels" who preside over a soda fountain and whip up opulent sundaes. In *The Once and Future King* this promised orgy of oral gratification is replaced, even punished, by the vision of a castle of lard. Its "greasy, buttery glow" and overripe texture inspire "wonder and nausea" (*OFK*, 108), and Morgan the Fay is now "a fat, dowdy, middle-aged woman with black hair and a slight moustache" (*OFK*, 109).[36] Presumably this Morgan is another glimpse of Constance White telling her son to retrench the sensuality of his mouth.

Although White himself believed he had "chucked overboard all idea of building her on my mother, Lady Calcutta",[37] the autobiographical sources of Morgause's portrait seem undeniable. Yet even in his original conception, White probably intended a slightly broader target: the contemporary style of English upper- and upper-middle-class motherhood, with its delegation of nurture and discipline to nannies, tutors and public schools. This regulation of distance permitted "Mummy" to remain a glamourous, ever-youthful object of filial adoration, and King Lot's sons, a quartet of adolescent puppies, who sleep entangled with their hunting dogs, seem modeled as much on the boys he taught first at St. David's and Stowe as upon himself.[38]

III

Satisfactory mothers are as difficult to find in White as in Shakespeare. While Wart (Arthur's boyhood name) and Kay (his foster brother) in *The Sword in the Stone* may lack a mother, except for the maternal Merlyn, the children in *The Witch in the Wood* have both too much and too little maternal attention. The most appealing women in White's Arthurian cycle, Maid Marian (in *The Sword in the Stone*) and Guinevere, are conspicuously childless, though the narrator, contrasting the latter with Arthur and Lancelot, who both fathered illegitimate children, tells us she "ought to have had children . . . and would have been best with children" (OFK, 498). Implicitly White may also be arguing the gay moral that those least likely to breed may be most equipped with the qualities of good parents.

The models of adult human activity whom Wart encounters could all be assigned to Edward Carpenter's two major types of sexual "intermediates": wizards or witches who overlap with the cultural and technological innovators who advance the fortunes of the tribe, and the warrior class. Merlyn, who, as I have suggested, assumes the role of Wart's missing mother (and who through his magic has also created the circumstances of Wart's birth), is the conspicuous representative of the first class. Carpenter somewhat skeptically reports the notion that the androgyny of priests or wizards may derive from the matriarchal character of early religions.[39] However questionable this anthropology, Merlyn's chief rivals in sorcery—Madame Mim, Morgan the Fay, above all, Morgause—are bad mothers who want to consume children's souls (and sometimes their bodies) rather than nurture them through the "self-restraint and tenderness"[40] of a selflessly maternal male.

In addition to Merlyn, Sir Ector, King Pellinore, Sir Grummore Grummursum, Hob the master-falconer, the sergeant-at-arms who supervises the boys' instruction in knightly warfare, Robin Wood (better known with the surname Hood) are variously benevolent "uncles" who, without any immediately paternal stake, value and sponsor the Wart's emerging aptitudes. Except for Robin Wood (who has an attractively equal comradeship with the athletic Maid Marian), none of these specimens of virility is conspicuously heterosexual—or conspicuously sexual at all. Within *The Sword in the Stone*, the most fanatically military and hierarchical milieu is that of the mews, where the hawks parody the manners of a cavalry regiment; the spar-hawk, as regimental chaplain, marries Wart, the new initiate, to the corps: " 'With this varvel,' the Wart heard, 'I thee endow . . . love, honor and obey . . . till jess us do part' " (SS, 117). According to Carpenter, "among some early peoples the Uranian temperament . . . took on a much more masculine character, . . . [and] led to the formation of military comradeships of a passionate kind, [and] bred ideals of heroism, courage, resource and endurance."[41] However, Carpenter himself writes mostly of Samurai and the Dorian military comradeship of Ancient Greece, and if the knightly characters of *The Once and Future King* are implicitly homosexual, I don't mean to suggest that their (unconscious) affiliation is much more than White's private joke.

Sir Ector provides Wart with shelter, food, drink, clothing, the means of education, and a combatively companionate sibling in the form of Sir

Ector's son Kay, but apart from Merlyn, the most important and appealing of Wart's uncles is King Pellinore, who would not be out of place in *Through the Looking-Glass*. He and his Colonel Blimpish sidekick, Sir Grummore Grummursum, figure prominently in both *The Sword in the Stone* and *The Witch in the Wood* (and even, though somewhat more briefly, "The Queen of Air and Darkness"). Merlyn brings Wart to the site of King Pellinore's hand-to-hand combat with Sir Grummore with intent of demystifying knightly activity:

> The two mounts were patiently blundering together. . . . Each [knight] held his spear straight out at right angles toward the left, and before Wart could say anything further there was a terrific yet melodious thump. Clang! said the armor, like a motor omnibus in collision with a smithy, and the jousters were sitting side by side on the green sward, while their horses cantered off in opposite directions. . . . The knights had now lost their tempers and the battle was joined in earnest. It did not matter much, however, for they were so encased in metal that they could do each other little damage. It took them so long to get up, and the dealing of a blow when you weighed the eight part of a ton was such a cumbrous business, that every stage of the contest could be marked and pondered. (*SS*, 99–100)

The combatants, however, manage to be endearing as well as ridiculous—perhaps the book's prevailing view of the masculine rituals at the heart of medieval society.[42] White's knights are consistently boyish, and the public-school system offers a frequent point of reference; when the rivalries in Arthur's court get out of hand, Arthur describes the competitive strain of chivalry as "Games Mania." Wart and Kay are constantly pummeling each other with a fervor whose sexuality seems scarcely latent enough to be called a subtext:

> In a trice they were out of bed, pale and indignant, and looking rather like skinned rabbits—for in those days nobody wore clothes in bed—and whirling their arms like windmills in the effort to do each other a mischief. . . . (*SS*, 125)
> It was strange but their battle had made them friends again, and each could look the other in the eye, with a kind of confused affection. They went together unanimously though shyly, without any need for explanations. . . . (*SS*, 134)

Similarly, after King Pellinore and Sir Grummore Grummursum have knocked each other senseless, Merlyn assures the worried Wart that "They'll be the best of friends when they come to" (*SS*, 106) and that Sir Grummore will invite King Pellinore home for supper. Wart consoles himself with the thought of Sir Grummore's feather bed: "That will be nice for King Pellinore, even if he was stunned" (SS, 106).

In fact, the amenities of Sir Grummore's castle are soon to be seen as a kind of enticement to adultery. King Pellinore's life is defined by his pursuit of the serpent-headed, leopard-bodied, hart-footed Questing Beast (also known as Glatisant)—female, but also extravagantly phallic. Their relations are so symbiotic that when King Pellinore is seduced by comfort the Beast languishes. The King finds her again on a Boxing Day boar hunt:

> In the middle of a dead gorse bush King Pellinore was sitting, with the tears streaming down his face. In his lap there was an enormous snake's head, which he was patting. At the other end of the snake's head there was a long, lean yellow body with spots on it. . . .
>
> "There, there," King Pellinore was saying. "I didn't mean to leave you altogether. It was only because I wanted to sleep in a feather bed, just for a bit. I was coming back, honestly I was. . . . Poor creature, . . . [i]t's pined away, positively pined away, just because there was nobody to take an interest in it. . . .
>
> "Mollocking about in a feather bed," added the remorseful monarch, glaring at Sir Grummore, "like a—like a kidney!" (SS, 225)

The sexual peculiarities of the warrior class, potential if not actual, seem to cluster about King Pellinore. When Queen Morgause's repertory of sexual maneuvers fails to arouse his interest, "King Pellinore, she decided, when she had come back from her walk with him on the cliffs, was queer. He was a Dear, but Queer. She forgave him" (WW, 74). She then turns her attention, with equally little success, to Sir Grummore.

During much of *The Witch in the Wood* King Pellinore is in fact nursing a Petrarchan passion—he even tries to write poetry—for the Queen of Flanders's daughter. Sir Grummore and Sir Palomides (the Orkney boys' tutor, an African knight whose speech is tinged with Anglo-Indian idioms) decide it would be therapeutic to redirect his passion to his proper object of devotion, the once again neglected Questing Beast. More peculiarly, in the absence of the true Beast, they decide to impersonate her. Their attempts to accommodate themselves inside the paint-and-canvas simulacrum produce a parodic dance (or "prance") of anal intercourse:

> "You are buttoning yourself on to me, Sir Grummore. Those are the wrong buttons."
>
> "Beg pardon, Palomides."
>
> "Would it be enough if you were to wave your tail in the air, instead of prancing? there is a certain discomfort, Sir Grummore, which devolves upon the forequarters during the prance." . . .

"My dear old forequarters," said Sir Gummore cheerfully, "it was you who thought of this night expedition in the first place. Cheer up, old fruit. It will be much worse for Pellinore, waitin' for us to come." . . .

"Tantivvy! Tantivvy!"

"Oh dear, Sir Grummore!"

"Sorry, Palomides."

"Yours truly will hardly be able to sit down." (*WW*, 227–28)

More sexually perilous is the arrival of the actual Questing Beast, who develops an amatory interest in her canvas counterpart. Sir Grummore and Sir Palomides continue to grope each other while the head of the Beast initiates an anal probe:

"Dear old boy, can't you stop bumpin' me all the time?"

"But I am not bumping you, Sir Grummore. . . . In any case it would be impossible to bump you behind, because one is in front."

"There it is again! . . . It was a definite assault. Palomides, we are bein' attacked! . . . Put your hand out of your mouth, Palomides, and see what you can feel."

"I can feel a sort of round thing."

"That is me, Sir Palomides. That is me, behind."

"Sincere apologies, Sir Grummore."

"Not at all, my dear chap, not at all. What else can you feel?"

The learned Saracen's voice began to falter.

"Something cold," he said, "and—er—slippery."

"Does it move, Palomides?"

"It moves, and—it snuffles!" (*WW*, 231–32)

King Pellinore declines to kill the Beast and thus free Sir Grummore and Sir Palomides from sexual persecution, as they demand. On the other hand, he regards Glatisant's fixation ("the Questing Beast herself, in a sentimental attitude, waited in the romantic moonlight for her better half" [*WW*, 233]) as entirely their concern. "Explain the facts of life, you know" (*WW*, 251), King Pellinore urges, so Sir Palomides must resume his interrupted instruction in the birds and the bees, this time as a Freudian analyst. "The only thing was that she transferred her affection to the analyst, as so often happens in this science, and refused to take any more interest in her original master" (*WW*, 265).[43] King Pellinore himself is rescued for matrimony by the Queen of Flanders's daughter (affectionately known as "Piggy"), who seems to resemble one of Bertie Wooster's aunts: "a stout middle-aged lady in a sidesaddle skirt. She had a red, horsey face and carried a hunting crop in her free hand. Her hair was in a bun" (*WW*, 243). (Sylvia Townsend Warner acidly comments, in another context, that White "was only at his ease with women when they had grown shapeless.")[44] Not surprisingly, though Pellinore feels he can "talk" to the Queen of Flanders's daughter, his fantasies run more on parenthood than marriage; when he is united with Piggy, he courts her with visions of the fine four sons he has already named: Aglovale, Percivale, Lamorak, and Dornar. "'They will be like Cherubs,' said the King fervently. 'Like cherubim! What are cherubim?'" (*WW*, 255).

Arthur's weariness and emotional desiccation at the end of the tetralogy have already been mentioned, but *The Book of Merlyn* supplies him with a brief renewal of sexual interest—indeed, the adult Arthur's closest approach to an erotic encounter. In an episode eventually transplanted from *The Book of Merlyn* to the revised version of *The Sword in the Stone*, he is transformed to a white-fronted goose and meets a potential partner: "The old man who had remembered his boyhood, watching her secretly, could not help thinking she was beautiful. He even felt a tenderness towards her downy breast, as yet quite innocent of bars; towards her plump compacted frame and the neat furrows of her neck" (*BM*, 79; cf. *OFK*, 170). The blason of the bird's alluring features suggests a gay man's attempt to catalogue and respond to the features of a woman that he knows, rather than feels, are sexy,[45] but the search for intimacy is genuine. It is the feature of heterosexual relationships that White found most enviable, and despaired of finding between male lovers. In 1928 he had attempted a homosexual novel (*Of Whom the World*); in his notebook he wrote: "There must be something unsatisfactory about relationships between homos. This is deep and I can't quite get it. The actual sexual relationships must be equally satisfactory sexually in the case of both norms and abnorms; but sexual relations in themselves are not particularly satis[fying]. For love in its wider sense I postulate more than lust."[46] Only a more complete exploration of White's psyche and of the society whose attitudes he imbibed could legitimately sustain an account of why he thought satisfactory emotional "relationships between homos" so elusive, but his view of sexual relations as an inadequate vehicle of intimacy seems compatible with the deflection of his deepest love toward animals, with whom, for him at least, such sexual relations seemed impossible. The blocked or difficult route to sexual relations opened, instead, abundant paths of tenderness. The overflow of passionate feeling toward animals in White's writings arises at least in part from the manifest unsatisfactoriness of available human arrangements, both political and romantic, but it's worth remembering that none of the animal societies Wart, or his aged avatar Arthur, visits is wholly idyllic (though the white-fronted geese's pacifico-anarchism comes close), and several are more savage than the one from which he escapes.

Rather, what Arthur's excursions into the animal kingdom offer him is an open-ended variety of erotic connections and political regimes, with the corollary that no single ordering of human affairs is right or final. Here, indeed, White comes close to Carpenter: "A really free Society will accept and make use of all that has gone before. If . . . historical forms and customs are the indication of tendencies and instincts which still exist among us, then the question is, not the extinction of these tendencies, but the finding of the right place and really rational expression of them."[47] What Carpenter finds in the anthropological expanses of history, White finds in the polities of various species. For all the failings of humanity—*The Book of Merlyn* suggests *homo ferox, homo stultus,* and *homo impoliticus* as more appropriate species names—it remains preeminent not by virtue of superior endowments but by their absence.

Toward the end of *The Sword in the Stone,* the badger tells a fable in which God, having produced the undifferentiated embryos of all the animals, offers them the chance to choose an identifying specialization ("some chose to use their arms as flying machines and their mouths as weapons, or crackers, or drillers" [*SS,* 290]; only the human embryo refuses the gift, and God pronounces his benison: "you will look like an embryo till they bury you, but all others will be embryos before your might; eternally undeveloped, you will always remain *potential* in Our image, able to see some of Our sorrows and to feel some of Our joys. We are partly sorry for you, Man, and partly happy, but always proud" (*SS,* 291). This is, of course, White's version of Pico della Mirandola's humanist argument for the dignity of humankind, which depends upon its flexibility, its unfixed place in the hierarchy of being, its infinite scope for achievement or disaster. If initially this praise of human potential surprises, it's because *The Once and Future King* offers so many instances of human blindness and mutual destructiveness—treated whimsically in *The Sword in the Stone* but angrily in *The Book of Merlyn,* each book darkening as the historical time of its composition moved further into World War II. Still, the myth of origins clarifies the representation of nonhuman animals as pastoral, in Empson's sense: they may be loved for their own sake, but the representations of their candor, their instinctive grace and efficiency, the utility and purposiveness of their violence function primarily as a critique of the human propensities toward hypocrisy and killing for sport. In *The Book of Merlyn,* Merlyn anticipates and sneers at the charge of anthropomorphism: "If you begin considering men as animals, they put it the other way round and say that you are considering animals as men, a sin which they hold to be worse than bigamy" (*BM*, 13). Merlyn attributes this resistance—a refusal of fellowship with animals—to human pridefulness, but the same conversation indicates the actual common ground of all the figures in *The Once and Future King*. When Arthur asks who "they" may be, Merlyn responds:

"The readers of the book."
"What book?"
"The book we are in."
"Are we in a book?"
"We had better attend to the job," said Merlyn hastily. (*BM*, 13)

White's fiction, like Carpenter's historical anthropology or Merlyn's sociobiological instruction, is a medium for exploring possibilities, of adumbrating a future in which all desires—for intimacy, for justice, for love in all its forms—can be satisfied more diversely than the linear destinies of Malory and our own time can imagine. It is this union of experience and promise over which, according to White's title, *The Once and Future King*, King Arthur will preside.

NOTES

I'm grateful to Robert Caserio, Stuart Culver, Jacqueline Osherow, and Kathryn Stockton for their extremely helpful comments on early drafts of this essay.

1 T. H. White, *The Witch in the Wood* (New York: G. P. Putnam's Sons, 1939), p. 54. Further citations to this work will be abbreviated *WW* and given parenthetically in the text.

2 Sir Thomas Malory (ca. 1410–71) welded together materials including French romances and the English alliterative epic *Morte Arthur* to produce the definitive English narrative of King Arthur and the Knights of the Round Table. William Caxton published Malory's writings in 1485 under the collective title of *Le Morte d'Arthur*. The preferred modern edition of Malory's *Works*, edited by Eugene Vinaver, goes back to the fifteenth-century Winchester College manuscript that predates Caxton's version (Oxford and New York: Oxford University Press, 1971). See note 42 for White's attitude toward the historical character of Malory's writings.

3 Sylvia Townsend Warner, *T. H. White: A Biography* (New York: Viking Press, 1967), p. 130.

4 T. H. White, *The Ill-Made Knight* (New York: G. Putnam's Sons, 1940), p. 3. Further citations to this work will be abbreviated *IMK* and given parenthetically in the text.

5 In focusing on Arthur's heroic cuckoldry, *Camelot* may at least be an unusual Broadway musical but any dramatization of *The Once and Future King* that gives primacy to the triangle of Arthur, Guinevere, and Lancelot seems seriously skewed. Its conventionality is further suggested by the casting of a handsome matinee idol (Robert Goulet on stage, Franco Nero on screen) as Lancelot, whom the book describes as looking "like an African ape." Lerner's lyrics are occasionally witty, but Lorenz Hart probably came closer to the spirit of White's "medievalism" in *A Connecticut Yankee*,

especially in "To Keep My Love Alive," the song he wrote for Vivienne Segal as Morgan Le Fay in the 1943 revival.

In 1939 Benjamin Britten had written incidental music for a BBC adaptation of *The Sword in the Stone*, described by Humphrey Carpenter (*Benjamin Britten* [New York: Charles Scribner's Sons, 1992], p. 129) as "one of his favorite books." Both White's focus on boyhood and his antiwar politics presumably appealed to Britten.

6 Some of the material in *The Book of Merlyn* appeared in the version of *The Sword in the Stone* that White produced for the publication of *The Once and Future King*, but the original version was published only posthumously in 1977; despite an introduction by Sylvia Townsend Warner, which unenthusiastically assesses its spleen and prosiness, it became a surprise best-seller for the University of Texas Press.

7 T. H. White, *The Book of Merlyn* (Austin: University of Texas Press, 1977), pp. 110–11. Further citations to this work will be abbreviated *BM* and given parenthetically in the text.

8 Edward Carpenter, *Love's Coming-of-Age* (New York: Modern Library, 1918). I've used Edward Carpenter's writings as a point of reference throughout this essay. I'm not claiming that T. H. White necessarily knew these writings, though it seems to me likely that a homosexual of White's generation would indeed have read them. Whether or not he did, Carpenter's discussion of topics including a socially evolutionary view of human love, the contributions of the "intermediate sexes" to the productivity and development of various societies, the role of affection in education, the "healthy" manifestations of the homosexual tendency, and the self-direction of homosexuals toward military or spiritual activity, might provide a comprehensive commentary on White's fictions.

9 This language, which comes from a nineteenth-century reviewer of Austen, is cited by Lionel Trilling in his introduction to *Emma* (Boston: Houghton Mifflin, 1957), p. xxiii. Since Trilling—and the reviewer—is speaking of the relationship between Mr. Knightley and Emma, the attendant ambiguities of Platonic eros give him little pause. Mary Renault's *The Charioteer* (1959), which emerges from the era of gay and lesbian experience that White—and, for that matter, his biographer, Sylvia Townsend Warner—lived, subtly maps the mutual encroachments and reinforcements of selfless affection and appetite—that is, the double-binds of Platonic eros suggested by her novel's title.

10 T. H. White, *The Once and Future King* (London: Collins, 1958; New York: G. P. Putnam's Sons, 1958), p. 546. Quotations throughout are taken from the British edition, and further citations to this work will be abbreviated *OFK* and given parenthetically in the text.

11 *T. H. White: Letters to a Friend*, ed. François Gallix (Gloucester, England: Alan Sutton, 1984), p. 43.

12 All nineteen stanzas of the poem are reproduced in appendix B of *Letters to a Friend*, pp. 263–65.

13 David Garnett, ed., *The White/Garnett Letters* (New York: Viking Press, 1968), p. 289.

14 Warner, *T. H. White*, p. 296.

15 Carpenter, writing of "Affection in Education," might be describing such a bond and its tensions: "to the expanding mind of a small boy to have a relation of real affection with some sensible and helpful elder of his own sex must be a priceless boon. . . . The unformed mind requires an ideal of itself, as it were, to which it can cling or towards which it can grow. Yet it is equally evident that the relation and the success of it, will depend immensely on the character of the elder one, on the self-restraint

and tenderness of which he is capable, and on the ideal of life which he has in mind" (*Intermediate Sex* [New York and London: Mitchell Kennerly, 1912], p. 83).

16 White's unfinished novel, "Grief for the Grey Geese" (begun in 1938), narrates General Christie's defection from the ranks of goose-shooters and "mad" alliance with the geese themselves.

17 Garnett, *White/Garnett Letters*, p. 8.

18 Warner, *T. H. White*, pp. 97, 339. Warner herself makes Brownie sound rather sexy: "There are photographs of her in his Shooting Diary for 1934—slender, leggy, newly full-grown" (p. 72).

19 Perhaps it's not surprising that, in 1967, there's nothing overtly gay-identified in Warner's perspective on White; despite her own longtime relationship with Valentine Ackland, her portrait of White as unhappy homosexual would have done little to disrupt prevailing views of gay and lesbian lives as more productive of pathos than satisfaction. On the other hand, Warner does implicitly situate herself as a feminist when she writes censoriously of White's depiction of women and perhaps also as a Marxist when she castigates the naive didacticism of *The Book of Merlyn*.

20 Perhaps it goes without saying that elements of White's personality are broadly distributed among the characters of *The Once and Future King*, from the avuncular Merlyn to the sulky, sadistic, mother-fixated Agravaine; at other times he is also Arthur (as both boy and man), Gawaine, and Lancelot—and no doubt the series of identifications could be extended. Through some of these figures White could exorcise as well as enact impulses that found only partial expression in his life.

21 Warner, *T. H. White*, p. 149. In 1936 White had asked David Garnett for information, but not too much information, about Sir Walter Raleigh: "Will you tell me what *one* book I am to read if, as far as the history is concerned, I want only enough good facts for a play? The fellow's character I understand already: it is my own" (Garnett, *White/Garnett Letters*, p. 17). Alluding to this letter, Warner comments on White's discussion of Lancelot: "As with Raleigh, so with Lancelot" (p. 150).

22 The adolescent character of Lancelot's love for Arthur seemingly conforms to a model of homosexuality as immature or fixated erotic feeling. Yet this essay traces certain affinities between White and Edward Carpenter, and Robert Caserio suggests to me that in Carpenter's *Love's Coming-of-Age* it is heterosexuality, particularly in the phylogenetic development of the human race, that is represented as a form of arrested development.

23 See Warner, *T. H. White*, pp. 148–50.

24 See especially chapters 3 and 4 of *The Candle in the Wind*. White may be borrowing here from the bedchamber scene between Antonio and the Duchess ("Doth not the color of my hair 'gin to change?") in *The Duchess of Malfi*, 3.2. He also uses Ferdinand's lycanthropic ravings as one of the sources for Cully's madness in *The Sword in the Stone*, chapter 8.

25 See, in particular, Eve Kosofsky Sedgwick's *Epistemology of the Closet* (Berkeley: University of California Press, 1990) and D. A. Miller's "Secret Subjects, Open Secrets," in *The Novel and the Police* (Berkeley: University of California Press, 1988), pp. 192–220. Miller's chapter, which (unlike his more recent writing) merely flirts with revelation, comes close to the tone of White's treatment of Lancelot.

26 For further discussion of the Girardian logic of this bond, see chapter 1 of Eve Kosofsky Sedgwick's *Between Men: English Literature and Male Homosocial Desire* (New York: Columbia University Press, 1985).

27 "Analyse" is Warner's word (Warner, *T. H. White*, p. 285).

28 Warner, *T. H. White*, p. 286.

29 "But whether Morgause is a farcical strumpet or a dark Celtic witch, Constance White inhabits her and *invalidates the book* by being hated as an actual person" (Warner, *T. H. White*, p. 130; emphasis added).

30 Warner, *T. H. White*, p. 27.

31 Ibid., p. 28.

32 Ibid., p. 29.

33 T. H. White, *The Sword in the Stone* (New York: G. P. Putnam's Sons, 1939), p. 78. Further citations to this work will be abbreviated *SS* and given parenthetically in the text; except when specifically indicated, quotations are drawn from the American edition.

34 T. H. White, *The Sword in the Stone* (London: Collins, 1938), pp. 165–83.

35 Garnett, *White/Garnett Letters*, p. 32.

36 Elisabeth Brewer (*T. H. White's The Once and Future King* [Cambridge, England: D. S. Brewer, 1993] pp. 31–47.) confuses the textual history of *The Sword in the Stone* by assuming that the ways in which White altered it for *The Once and Future King* correspond to the "American edition." The first version of Morgan the Fay's castle is completely absent from her account. In fact, as indicated above, the British edition of 1938 and the American edition of 1939 differ only in the omission of the Anthropophagi from the latter.

37 White, *Letters to a Friend*, p. 122.

38 The clannish loyalties for which Morgause supplies the emotional cement ("Will you Avenge your mother's Honor upon the Tyrants of the South? . . . Will you Stand Up for Her through Thick and Thin?" [*WW*, p. 223] have political consequences for Arthur's court. Their familial allegiances, fed by resentment and the shared experience of shame, prove the most powerful obstacle to the impersonal order of justice and civil society that Arthur, to his own emotional cost, strives to found. In effect, the political plot of *The Once and Future King* mirrors the contending forces of Scott's historical novels. Here too the fierce tribal cohesion that makes every family its own polity is opposed to the tamer society of principle that exacts a sacrifice from the self's prerogatives. Perhaps for this reason, White emphasizes the Celtic origins of the Orkney brothers. In this respect, *The Once and Future King* goes further than the novels of the 1930s and 1940s, since it represents Gawaine's speech as Scottish dialect. Like the heroes of the *Waverley* novels, Arthur belongs at one time or another on both sides of the division; his own membership in the clan—as half-brother of Morgause, father of Mordred—betokens his self-division and predicts the failure of his new order.

39 Edward Carpenter, *Intermediate Types among Primitive Folk: A Study in Social Evolution* (London: George Allen and Unwin, 1919; reprint, New York: Arno Press, 1975), p. 51.

40 See note 15 above.

41 Carpenter, *Intermediate Types*, pp. 87–88.

42 White makes it clear that this society is an anachronistic amalgam of different periods. As he explained in a letter dated 28 July 1939: "I am putting myself as far as possible in Malory's mind (which was a dreamer's) and bundling everything together in the way I think he bundled it. . . . I am trying to write of *an imaginary world which was imagined in the 15th century*" (Warner, *T. H. White*, p. 133). White was defending himself against the objections of Sir Sydney Cockerell, his chief historical advisor, who had complained, "I cannot fit Lancelot into the decadent 15th century" (Warner, *T. H. White*, p. 126; see also p. 133).

   As White indicates, his major source was already rife with historical fantasia and anomaly: "Everybody knows that King Arthur and the Firbolgs and the dyspeptic

Saints were all living together in Malory's day, and that it was not King Edward IV who was reigning then at all" (*WW*, p. 4). In an exchange of space for time, the seacoasts of Lothian, distant from Carlion (or Caerleon, Arthur's capital), and thus temporally remote as well, become the receptacle of even more ancient phenomena, such as Celtic saints living in beehives.

In White's first versions of *The Sword in the Stone*, *The Witch in the Wood* and *The Ill-Made Knight* (New York: G. P. Putnam's Sons, 1940), King Arthur's court is clearly set in Malory's England. In the revision of these books for *The Once and Future King*, events are moved backward by three hundred years, from the fifteenth century to the twelfth—perhaps in deference to Cockerell.

43 White points out he has solved a Malorian crux: "this is why, although Malory clearly tells us that only a Pellinore could catch her, we always find her being pursued by Sir Palomides in the later parts of his books" (*WW*, p. 265). The quests of both King Pellinore and Sir Palomides make it clear that the roles of pursuer and pursued are effectively indistinguishable.

44 Warner, *T. H. White*, p. 154.

45 In the 1930s White, trying to go "straight" with the encouragement of a psychotherapist, tried some such experiment with a barmaid (*Letters to a Friend*, pp. 60–61; see also Warner, *T. H. White*, p. 82).

46 White quoted in Warner, *T. H. White*, p. 43.

47 Carpenter, *Love's Coming-of-Age*, p. 143–44.

James Creech

Forged in Crisis: Queer Beginnings of Modern

Masculinity in a Canonical French Novel

Si les durs chosissaient leurs favoris parmi les plus beaux jeunots, tous ceux-ci
ne sont pas destinés à rester femmes. Ils s'éveillent à la virilité et les hommes
leur font une place à côté d'eux. — Jean Genet, *Miracle de la rose*

Although Benjamin Constant's *Adolphe* is a classic of the canon, it
has long been locked away like a jewel within the disciplinary *don-
jons* of French and comparative literature departments. Begun in
1806, published ten years later, the novel has most often served pedagogi-
cally to exemplify literary-historical concepts such as early romanticism
and the *mal du siècle*. Its protagonist enjoys a place of prominence among
the cohort of sensitive and brooding young heroes who flourished early
in the century, and has even been used to personify the wounded romantic type.[1]
   The first of my intentions in writing the following is to recommend
Adolphe to a new constituency that has coalesced around queer theory.
The second main goal of these comments is to exemplify the difference
it can make in literary criticism to read openly from a queer or queered
subject-position — a practice that is oddly lacking in French studies.[2] For,
if we know how to let it, *Adolphe* can tell us much about the presence
of proto-queer history in straight, canonical literature. Heretofore, we
have been disallowed or disinclined to see, inscribed within the novel's
famously elegant prose, the anguish of modern masculinity being born in
crisis, a crisis provoked in part by an implicit reckoning with the danger,
and the allure, of something queer. *Adolphe* is particularly valuable in this
regard because it was written at a time when a male author could still narrate gender dissonance nondefensively, without immediately raising the
issue of "homosexuality."[3] Homoerotic possibility can thus loom in the
novel like an implicit lining, torturing its smooth textual surfaces, even
as the plot unflinchingly displays the terrible cost of straight gendering.

As a gay reader I have always "known" this about *Adolphe*. It is an awareness, however, for which it has been impossible to find an explanation or an expression. Even as I acknowledge that the epistemological protocols for such knowledge remain vexed and subject to legitimate challenge, my goal will be achieved if these frightened and fragile gestures of queer self-recognition can be taken seriously, even if that means being taken seriously enough to be refuted in scholarly discourse.

At its most succinct, *Adolphe* deals with the ravages that are caused by the cultural assumption that men must thrive on unsentimental separateness, and that women naturally turn to the opposite practices of sentimental connectedness and dependence. Nothing exactly new here. But there are at least two aspects of the question that are relatively more new for the time—and which begin to mark this novel as queer. First is the novel's outsider perspective on these familiar gender imperatives. Adolphe is poorly sutured to emerging, post-Revolutionary norms so dominated by the image of Napoleon. We could even say that gender dissonance is Adolphe's principal trait. And second, almost a century before Freud, Constant provides a precocious demonstration of how gender configuration can be forged by a son's psychological relationship with his father. That is, Adolphe is not the man he is because he inherits his father's blood, or his father's name, or his father's property. Rather, his identity was formed through a psychological relationship with his father as a man.

Constant condenses all these lessons in two short and didactic prefaces added respectively to the second and third editions of the novel. These concise essays require, and reward, the most careful scrutiny. Here, in short, is the analysis from the first preface, entitled "Essay on the Character and Moral Outcome of the Work":

Men who go about seducing women, it is axiomatically presumed, most often do so out of calculation rather than sentiment. They are taught to believe they can get away with divorcing the language of love from any actual feeling of love. Though women sometimes do the same thing, men in particular are prone to this use of a sentimental language disconnected from true emotion. But when the man succeeds, that is, when he makes the woman give herself to him out of love, the very spectacle of her real sentiment produces in him an unwanted, empathic connection. The seducer is then confronted with a problem: empathic sentiment seems intrinsically to undermine his masculinity. Because he is a man, or perhaps, in order to be a man, he will refuse the encumbrance of sentiment by breaking with the woman. By that time, however, it will be impossible to do so without inflicting great pain.

Constant goes on to recognize that women suffer terribly from these inevitable ruptures. And, of course, when the tables are sometimes turned and coquettish women use empty language in the same fraudulent manner, men suffer great pain, too, "although men, being stronger, more distracted from sentiment by imperious occupations, and destined to be the center of everything around them, do not possess to the same degree as women the *noble and dangerous faculty for living in another and for another*."[4] Indeed, this noble, dangerous, and womanly capacity for empathic life in and for another will be the source of great distress when it infects Adolphe. For it should be women, not men, who are "weak beings, having real life only in the heart, deep interest only in affection, without activity to occupy them, and without careers to command them" (7). But, once he seduces Ellénore, Adolphe will find himself in precisely these circumstances: without goals, unmotivated, and wasting away his life accomplishing nothing. The preface, in other words, provides a culturally sanctioned code by which we will know that Adolphe's obvious psychopathology comes from being feminized in his relationship with Ellénore.[5]

The dominant fiction in the emerging post-Revolutionary culture to which Constant is referring—and which, again, is hardly new, though it resurfaces here with a historically particular vengeance—defines sexual relations as male-centered. Women are the second sex—or perhaps, the "other" *tout court*—and must therefore be relegated to a kind of unreality. Thus, at the beginning of their seductions, men are able to convince themselves that they will be able to break it off whenever they choose, because they picture feminine sentiment (a redundancy) as only a "cloud." Here is Constant's précis of the predicament:

> In the distance, the image of [the woman's] pain seems vague and unclear, like a cloud [men] will be able to traverse without difficulty. A doctrine of fatuousness, a deathly tradition, that the corruption of the older generation leaves as a legacy to the vanity of the rising generation, along with an irony that has become trivial, but which seduces the mind by means of piquant renditions [*rédactions piquantes*], as if renditions changed anything fundamental—in sum, everything they hear, everything they say, seems to arm [men] against tears that are *not yet* flowing." (7)

The corruption of their fathers' generation feeds the vanity of the sons. A trivializing irony seduces the male mind with its "rédactions"—that is, with its *mise-en-texte*, its compositions, its literature, its masculinizing discourse. The heart of the matter that text and irony cannot change, however, is that men are, in fact, vulnerable to the tears of sentiment despite the male gendering that seems bent on arming them proleptically against just that future vulnerability, against "tears that are not yet flow-ing." Of course, the very need for such prophylaxis is already an implicit admission that, without it, gender differentiation could not be assured by natural or spontaneous development of this "masculinity" in the male. Already then, if only generically, something queer is stirring.

There is a also complex temporality to be taken into account in under-standing this strange and problematic concept of manhood. For, in its relation to time, Constant is presenting masculinity as a fatuous doc-trine, a trope—an irony—that is doubly inscribed. First, on a historical axis, it refers back to the corrupted past of its forefathers from which it receives its imperatives: the "deathly tradition," no doubt referring to the decadent days of the ancien régime.[6] But through everything men hear and say, masculinity is also constructed against a future moment of dan-ger when it *will* encounter feminine sentiment. Thus, masculinity has no present. Or more precisely, from its inception it is defined not as a single trope, but as an impossible place between two tropes: between ironies that were and a proleptic future that is not yet. Inherited irony says one thing but means another; prolepsis speaks of an absent future as if it were already present. The thing for which these tropes are the vehicle—masculinity—is thus allotted no place, no present, no literality at all. The abstract, diacritical requirement to exclude the feminine is so intense that masculinity can be conceived as nothing, in itself, but a strategy for defense against contamination. The impossible, figural space that it is assigned is first and foremost a dream of a gendering that is exclusive, disembodied, and unalloyed.

Even as these norms are formulated, Constant shows them to be in crisis, ill-fitting, and pathogenic. For, what then happens when a human being so gendered actually encounters those tears against which his ironic masculinity was proleptically built? Still in the didactic preface, Constant explains that when the woman's tears finally do flow, they pro-voke a *return* of the man's "nature," which, we now deduce retrospectively, the discourse of a masculinist *u-topos* was in fact seeking to supplant. In the face of women's tears, in other words, the truth of the male heart, heretofore disguised by a false masculinist culture, is paradoxically re-vealed:

> But when these tears do flow, nature *returns* within [men], despite
> the atmosphere of falseness [*l'atmosphère factice*] with which they had
> surrounded themselves. They *feel* that a being who suffers from what
> she loves is sacred. They *feel* that in their very hearts, which they had
> not intended to involve at all, that the sentiment they have inspired
> has taken root, and that if they want to defeat what, by habit, they

call weakness, then they must reach into their own miserable heart and offend what is generous, break what is faithful, kill what is good therein. And they succeed, but by dealing a death blow to a portion of their souls. . . . In this way they outlive their own better nature, perverted by their victory or ashamed of this victory, if it has not perverted them. (7–8)

This is precisely what was not supposed to happen.

If shared emotion so compromises phallicism, can a man survive this invasion of sentimental "weakness"? Once the empty bunker of masculinity is filled by empathy, once a man feels in himself the other's sentiment, can he still be considered masculine at all? Victory over this sentimental invasion will thus have to come in the form of reasserting strength, imperious activity, and impervious self-containment—all the diacritical qualities of masculinity. Thus, or so the prefaces claim, the man has no choice but to break with the woman and her tiresome tears. This will be the part that Adolphe cannot perform, the very sign of his deficiency.

The surprising part of Constant's analysis is that, in order to reassert their masculine isolation, men must kill off part of their *own* souls. They must revert to the mutilation and abstraction, to the tropological no-place that the construction of masculinity was designed to protect and preserve in its purity.[7] Thus, as we have seen, they are left with a terrible choice that Constant has presented with a brilliant economy of linguistic means: "they outlive their own better nature, *perverted* by their victory or *ashamed* of this victory, if it has not perverted them." (1) What exactly is this perversion? And, (2) what is this shame that is its alternative?

(1) If the man achieves a victory of "masculinity" over his better nature he is left "perverted," and perverted *because* he in fact manages to split off from the "feminine." For, once Constant allowed empathy unexpectedly to become a natural and better trait of masculinity, resistance to it in the name of gender purity has become unnatural. To uproot empathy is now the perversion. Clearly, this spare sketch adumbrates the entire culture of homosociality that privileges male-male relationships and that uses women only as mediations to achieve the all-important link between men. The "perversion" of these relationships has been extensively amplified in recent work by theorists as diverse as Gayle Rubin, Luce Irigaray (who qualifies this system as "hommo-sexuality"), and Eve Kosofsky Sedgwick.[8]

(2) But if the man does manage to end the relationship without killing off his "feminine" capacity for sentimental intercourse—if he does not become purely *hommo-sexual* in Irigaray's sense—then he will be left

ashamed because, precisely, he will feel in himself the emotional pain he has caused in the other and will thus know the harm he's done. The contemporary culture that Constant is codifying will nevertheless approve this painful and perverting excision required to bolster manhood. "Bystanders and friends applaud" (10) when they witness this "victory" of masculinist perversion over "natural" shame.

If, with Constant's prefaces freshly in mind, we turn now to *Adolphe* proper, we are immediately plunged into the crucible of all these same issues as they occur in a familial, Oedipal context between parent and child. It has long been an article of faith in Constant criticism that the death of his mother when Benjamin was only sixteen days old was the formative psychological event of his life, and perhaps indeed it was. I want to argue, however, that the heteronormative assumptions that creep into virtually all such commentary have obscured the significance of the other, very great experience in Constant's life, which was his impossible relation to his father, Juste de Constant.[9] Both these autobiographical facets of an absent mother and a distant father are, by common accord, directly transcoded in the opening chapters on Adolphe's formative years. What has not been so readily noticed, however, is that the prefaces allow us to understand that the constraint that ruined this primary relationship to his living parent is clearly a product of straight gendering. The psychoanalytical insistence upon oedipal issues with the (absent) mother, which is the focus of Han Verhoeff's worthy study, can thus blind us to this phobic, gendered, and gendering relation to unmediated and sentimental bonds between men.

Adolphe characterizes his father as "constrained," as a "cold and caustic observer."[10] In his first eighteen years they never had a conversation lasting so long as an hour. Unable to find a primary anchor in intimacy with his father, given over to the unbridgeable distances of irony, Adolphe—like many others in his cohort of nineteenth-century heroes—will be interested only in passions "which throw the mind out of harmony with the ordinary world and inspire contempt for everything in one's surroundings" (1; translation modified).[11]

In fact, the opening pages of the novel are little more than a reinscription of the heterosexual difficulties described in the prefaces as the prohibition of intimacy between fathers and sons.[12] It is a prohibition that we must describe, at least in structural terms, as the taboo against homoerotic incest. As Adolphe says, "Unfortunately, his attitude towards me was noble and generous rather than tender," which is to say, according to the codes spelled out in the preface, "masculine" rather than "feminine." Adolphe laments the lack of "confidence" between them and says, "There was something *ironical* in his mentality which ill agreed with my character" (1)—in which we hear clear echoes of that "irony that has become trivial," which men are said to treat all attachments to the feminine. And just as ironic men are said to inspire sentiment in women, here, the dissipated young Adolphe is said to do something similar to his father. He has successes in school that "caused [his] father to entertain hopes concerning [his] future which were probably much exaggerated" (1), "hopes" that, I want to suggest, bear the unspeakable and no doubt unconscious meaning that is more appropriate to the amorous code in which "concevoir des espérances" is such a commonplace locution.

From this heuristic perspective, the problem would thus be double because both parties are men: Adolphe, as a "man," has fostered those hopes of love that he will be afraid to fulfill; but his father has done the same thing, as we can hear in the tone of loss that characterizes the son's discourse. Clearly, the "feminine" is a hot potato that neither can hold.[13] And in strict adherence to the codes laid out in the prefaces, his father "saw no objection—provided there was no question of marriage—to taking any woman and then leaving her" (8). Thus, it is not surprising that his own behavior in the face of his feminizing and sentimental bonds with his son, as does the son's behavior with his father, exactly reproduces this callous system. Men must abandon those who induce in them the sentiment that contradicts their manhood.[14]

Adolphe later comes to understand that if his father transforms his love for him into the irony and coldness of an observer, it is because he suffers from a perversion here called "timidity . . . that inner suffering" (2)—no doubt a reference to the same fortress interiority of empty masculinity described in the prefaces. But, precisely as between men and women, this timidity "forces the profoundest feelings back into the heart, chilling your words and deforming in your mouth whatever you try to say, allowing you to express yourself only in vague phrases or a somewhat bitter *irony* [that word again], as if you wanted to avenge yourself upon your feelings for the pain you experienced at being unable to communicate them" (2). The only emendation one might wish to make in this profound insight is to suggest that the pain comes less from being "unable" to communicate sentiment directly between men, and more from the gendering that prohibits such expressions.

In relations with women, we recall, the man's crisis is provoked when the unreal "cloud" of feminine sentiment finally precipitates in the form of their tears. The feminization of the father is thus further underscored when it is he who cries over Adolphe's own unnatural, masculine coldness, the very coldness for which he was himself the model. "Often, having waited a long while for some sign of affection from me which his apparent coldness seemed to prohibit, he would leave me, his eyes moist with tears, and complain to others that I did not love him" (2). "Timidity," then, is here the unmistakable mark of an internal gender clash, and there is little separating that clash from masculinist interiority itself. And it is precisely what Adolphe inherits from his father: "Just as timid as he was . . . I got used to bottling up everything I felt within me" (2; translation modified). Beneath it all, however, there persists that other "nature" whose importance we saw in the prefaces: "Though unaware of it, I bore in my heart a need for sympathy [*sensibilité*] which, not being satisfied, caused me to abandon, one after another, every object of my curiosity" (3). Thus, it is in order to transcend that nature that Adolphe is normatively constituted as a man through detachment, perversion, and pain.

Constant briefly exposes this dilemma between father and son in order to set the stage for a now-heterosexual love story that will only *reinstantiate* these very tensions. Thus, on the eve of finally declaring his (hollow) love for Ellénore, Adolphe will sound a familiar note: "An unconquerable timidity, however, always stopped me. . . . A struggle raged within me" (12; translation modified). Ellénore, Adolphe's eventual mistress, is little more than an incarnation of the feminine menace. She is presented as "a person dominated by any and all of her feelings [*une personne que tous ses sentiments dominent*]" (15; translation modified). The prefaces and first chapter have put us on notice that she is not, for all that, the true source of Adolphe's panic. The specific signifying difference of this novel relative to its feminocentric predecessors in the seventeenth and eighteenth centuries (at least from *La Princesse de Clèves* to the sentimental literature of the later eighteenth century) is that the crucial variable will be male, not female, desire—and variability is not a notably manly trait.

Thus, Adolphe's *Bildung* takes its place in the series of French novels of the period about boys who can't quite figure out the relation between who they are and what they want.[15] Constant's inflection of this topos is important, because it suggests so clearly that the emerging sex-gender system does not give men something they *can* want in the erotico-sentimental domain while still remaining men. If indeed Ellénore will say, "I am unable to want us to be separated" (78; translation modified), Adolphe's gender dissonance comes from the fact that he can't either. At its most schematic, then, the new problem of masculinity in this novel is that it is put in the impossible position of having to desire a negative.

It is now possible to point out that *Adolphe* is already dealing with a queer version of that drama of desire and prohibition between parent and child that will later be theorized as the Oedipus complex. Despite a certain number of Rube Goldberg retrofits,[16] Freud's culture-bound notion of "the" Oedipus complex was about the emergence of a normalized son when naturally heterosexual, incestuous desire between son and mother is interrupted by the father. It remains today a substantially present cultural construct. At least until recent years, the most common belief about the origins of male homosexuality has been that it stems from a breakdown of the Oedipal structure when the father fails to interrupt the primary bond between mother and son.[17] It is supposed to be fear of castration that makes the son renounce his putatively natural, heterosexually disposed choice of his mother. It is not fear of castration, though, that prompts him to give up any homosexually disposed choice of a same-sex object in the person of his father. That task is performed, rather, by what Judith Butler has called "the fear of 'feminization' associated within heterosexual cultures with male homosexuality."[18] *Adolphe*, however, though it indeed begins with the problem of desire between a parent and a son, does not at all script a mother into this stage of the drama. As in his life, there is no primary mother in Constant's novel, and absent such a mother, there is no primary model of the feminine except for sentiment itself, this dangerous thing that is *called* feminine, and that his father exhibits to him in its denegation. *Elle*-énore's function, from this perspective, will exhibit the feminine to him in its ideologically sanctioned link to biological woman. Thus, it is only in the encounter with her that the question of the mother will emerge and even then, as we shall soon see, the mother-son issues with his mistress will be pathological only because they repeat the father-son bond in displaced form.

Thus does *Adolphe* lend unexpected support to the revisions of Oedipal theory proposed by Judith Butler, Monique Wittig, and Jonathan Dollimore, among others.[19] We can speculate that part of what defines the crisis of masculinity in *Adolphe* is that, in the family—or at least, in this transitional family of the post-Revolutionary period—the maternal term is not yet the given onto which primary homosexual incest can be displaced or projected. In this period, the crisis of masculinity can still be located, conceptually, within a male context, and the crisis of heterosexual experience emerges as its extension. For Adolphe's primary desire is at least androgynous, which explains why, as we saw in the preface, men constitute and preserve their gender difference agonistically against the feminine, "but by dealing a death blow to a portion of their [own] souls" (8). Adolphe and his father emerge as little more than cold, depressed observers and distant ironists. Each is, in effect, a man whose masculinity is constituted as an interminable mourning for a primary homoerotic bond.[20] The emotional traits called "feminine" are traits that men bear within themselves, and that post-Revolutionary masculinity is under diacritical construction to exclude. *Adolphe* reveals—more overtly than much subsequent writing—that if men weren't understood implicitly to include "the feminine," at least as a possibility, there would be no need for an elaborate Oedipal theory to enforce its exclusion, and Oedipal theory, in turn, would lose its pretension to explain homosexuality.

Still more boldly, what troubles gender in this novel, and what *Adolphe* is figuring as gender dissent, is already emerging in its homology with closeted homosexuality in its more modern sense. For, in this suffocating facticity of gender theater,[21] "if some escape this general fate, *they lock their secret dissent inside themselves*" (6; translation mine). Social reaction to Adolphe, with his enclosed secret, is remarkably legible to modern eyes: "They said I was an immoral man, an *untrustworthy* man [un homme *peu sûr*]—two epithets *fortunately* invented to enable such people to insinuate guesses as if they were facts, and to hint at what they don't know" (7; translation modified). Thus, if you're not a standard-issue male whose masculinity is produced by self-mutilating severance from "the feminine," then you will be seen as immoral. Whatever there is about this secret dissent that makes Adolphe immoral in the eyes of his society also makes him, appositively, an "homme peu sûr," which means both an untrustworthy man, but also, here, someone who is not reliably a man. Further, for reasons he declines to specify, Adolphe considers these epithets to have been "*fortunately* invented" for insinuating, for guessing at what one does not actually know for a fact. The explicit fact, in other words, would be worse than the vague insinuation; the literal truth would be worse than these designations by euphemism.

Of course, it is hardly appropriate to presume anything specific about this secret. At the same time, we must indeed acknowledge that Constant has housed Adolphe's "secret dissent" in an internalized structure we recognize as that of the modern, homosexual closet—or at least, in a structure built from the same blueprint. And that is finally the point: *Adolphe* demonstrates that that blueprint of the closet has already been drafted as an integral part of the larger structure of post-Revolutionary masculinity.

Nor is this an isolated instance. Later in the novel, when Adolphe is clearly situated between the two competing worlds of sentiment and masculinity, he will weakly give each camp what it wants to hear, while carefully hiding what they don't want to hear. Ellénore wants to hear that he is defined by sentimental connection to her; his father, along with the other men, wants to hear that he is defined by unsentimental, imperious activity required for his patriarchal functions. But in an enigmatic text, after his latest success in convincing the men that he is on his way back to standard virility, he makes a remarkable confession: "In this way, by the mere fact that I had hidden my feelings, I more or less deceived everyone; I was deceiving Ellénore, for I knew the Baron wanted to separate me from her, and I said nothing to her of this; I was deceiving the Baron, for I let him hope that I was ready to break my bonds. This duplicity was far from my natural character, but man *becomes depraved* as soon as he has in his heart *a single thought* which he is constantly obliged to dissimulate" (71). Once again we must acknowledge that Adolphe's secret is structured in clear homology with closeted homosexuality. For, a gender dissent that constitutes Adolphe's singular secret—not one secret for Ellénore and a different one for the men, but "*a single thought* which he is constantly obliged to dissimulate"—implies an altogether more modern dissent than that of mere indecision. We are heading for the semantic fields of a "troisième sexe" that the neither/nor logic of this confession clearly adumbrates.[22]

As this proto-homosexual possibility weaves through the novel, it assumes a number of different valences. In addition to its negative and threatening qualities, homoeroticism might even seem to be an implicit "solution" to Adolphe's constitutive alienation from his father, which issued in a successive detachment "from every object of [his] curiosity" (3). Unmediated closeness between men would be the basis for resolving his problems with women. At a minimum, Adolphe would have made a much better heterosexual if he had been able to constitute his masculinity homoerotically.[23] That is, if emotional intimacy with his father had not been the object of an emerging, phobic repression, then Adolphe would have become more competent in the emotional intercourse that the novel claims is so important to "women," but so difficult for "men."

Thus, homoeroticism is woven into the fabric of this text as the shadow object, alluring even as it fuels the anguish inherent in straight masculinity. I suggest that there is simply nothing else that could possibly render acceptable the wretched mutilations of manhood.[24] In this latter guise, the open secret of homosexual possibility in *Adolphe* prompts us to invoke another of Eve Kosofsky Sedgwick's seminal concepts, that of the "blackmailability" of relations between men, which was emerging in these decades.[25] The pain that Adolphe and his father accept to suffer is only a particularly grim currency in which hush money must be paid to a sex-gender system threatening to reveal their suspect need for sentimental intercourse. For it is none other than this need, his "need for *sensibilité*" (3) and the effects that accompany its repression, which makes of Adolphe an "homme peu sûr" (and thankful that such euphemisms exist). And finally, it is this need that makes him the grandfather of a series of French novelistic heroes who suffer from the same kind of timidity, detachment, or impotence.

And what of the on-again, off-again relationship with Ellénore, which is after all the novel's main plot? I would suggest that it is not fully legible without our newly queered awareness. First, it follows the pattern, well analyzed in recent theory, of a mimetic desire for the same happiness Adolphe witnesses in a male friend. Seeing his friend's joy when the beloved finally gives herself provokes a "great revolution" (7) in Adolphe's isolationist male economy. Abruptly, there will be heterosexual desire where before there was mention only of frustrated love for the father. From empty boredom linked to the constraint of sentiment, this revolutionary event will plunge Adolphe into a new state of being "when [his] heart needed love" (11).

This revolution occurs when, in the "spectacle of such great happiness," Adolphe's eye has lit, not upon a woman, but upon the desire *of* a man in which the genitive is necessarily double. Everything we now know about Adolphe suggests that he desires both his friend—"a young man, with whom I was on rather intimate terms" (7; translation modified)—and the friend's desire. It leaves him in a strange new state: "Tormented by an obscure emotion, I thought to myself, I want to be loved" (8). Adolphe does not love the same woman, as would a rival. Rather, the spectacle of his friend's love makes Adolphe want to *be* loved, that is, culturally and structurally speaking, to be in the position of the woman, because, we may surmise, the spectacle of his close friend's love quickens the old desire to be loved by his father. But again, the frustration of that desire was what made Adolphe a "man." And to be such a man, he must not feel the sentiment of love as a possibility, a presence, opening inside himself and in his own heart and available for investing in an "object." Rather, he is the empty man who, the prefaces tell us, uses the empty language of love to induce the fullness of sentiment in the other. That is precisely what he will now proceed to do.

Adolphe looks around him with this abstract desire to be loved, and finds nothing: "I looked around me but could see no one who inspired love in me, no one likely to want love. I examined my heart and my tastes; I could find no marked preference. I was in this restless state of mind, when I made the acquaintance of Count P***, a man aged forty whose family was related to mine" (8–9). Is there any accident in the choice of this configuration, of this familial site, for fleshing out the triangulated desire that has revolutionized his life? Is there any wonder, given his disastrous relations with his own *Père*, that he should now turn to a mediated relation to this new P***, and that the mediation will be accomplished by Ellénore, P***'s common-law wife whom Adolphe describes as no longer in her first youth, the mother of two, an outsider herself, a Polish émigré? As he began frequenting her and her circle, she is drawn precisely to Adolphe's queerness: in a society where (being men) "the husbands were devoid of feelings," Ellénore found "pleasure in the society of a man who was *different* from those she had seen till then" (11; translation modified).

As per program, however, Adolphe will treat Ellénore as he treated the feminine in himself, and as his father treated it in himself, and in Adolphe: "I planned to size up her character and mind as a cool and impartial observer" (12). From the start, sentiment is conspicuous for its explicit absence: "I did not believe I loved Ellénore; but I could not have given up pleasing her" (12; translation mine). The split between his sentiment and his performance of seduction is clear. He is stricken with an "unconquerable timidity" as he tries to hide all his "impotence or weakness," so as to satisfy "that part of ourselves which is *observing* the other part" (13; translation modified). But we've heard it all before in his relationship to his father, the original "cold and caustic observer" from page one.

But Ellénore can now become the *post facto* mother as well: "I was embarrassed and humiliated to meet a woman who had treated me like a child" (16). Clearly, he is finally scripting his homosexual Oedipal crisis in terms of the socially required model (aspiring to universality) between Son, Mother, and P***. But behind this triangle the other triangle remains legible as a palimpsest and, again, the P*** of heterosexuality is a secondary instantiation of the *Père*, a primary, homoerotic love.

Immediately after his first sexual success with Ellénore, he is suddenly acclimated to the suffocating air of gender theater, just as he had earlier predicted: "I walked with pride amongst men; I looked around at them with a proud look. The very air I breathed gave me pleasure" (25). For he has now done his bit for the "deathly tradition" of his gender: "The younger men, delighted at the skill with which I had supplanted the Count . . . promised to follow my example" (35). The mimetic theater of masculinist "perversion" thus perpetuates itself. Ellénore herself will, naturally, become the target of the next contender who soon seeks to wrest her away from Adolphe, and all these triangles of homosocial mimeticism will, of course, be accompanied by the standard duels between the men (99).[26] It would indeed seem, as Adolphe laments, that society "weighs so heavily upon us, its blind influence is so powerful, that it soon shapes us in the universal mould" (6).

But none of it works to fill the void for, "I was a weak, grateful and dominated man; I was sustained by no impulse from the heart" (35). Thus, in his perversion, he is indeed a man in crisis, not completely straight because cowed by "the pain of a woman who only dominates me through her pain" (58; translation modified). Thus, to closet his feminine sentimentality, he practices the misogyny in which he was trained: "I had submitted to her will, but domination by women had become abhorrent to me. I ceaselessly decried their weakness, their exacting nature, the despotism of their suffering. I made show of the harshest principles;

and the same man who could not withstand a tear, who yielded at the mere sight of sadness and who, when alone, was haunted by the picture of the suffering he had caused, yet showed himself in all his talk to be contemptuous and pitiless" (37).

And there is no resolution to this dilemma. As Constant writes in the first preface, the position of Adolphe and Ellénore is "hopeless, and that's precisely what I wanted" (8). Ellénore has given up everything—her children, her relationship with P***, her carefully cultivated reputation—in order to live as Adolphe's mistress. Repeatedly, when he tries to break off with her, his empathy for her pain brings him back, ashamed for trying to leave, yet feeling the masculinist imperative to leave nonetheless.

Just when it seems this mechanism could keep the novel going indefinitely, the gender cavalry comes riding over the hill. Urged on by Adolphe's father, Monsieur de T*** intervenes on behalf of the men to reclaim one of their own. Adolphe is reminded of success, of rivalry, of all the things that manhood is supposed to achieve—all the glories that make of his affair with Ellénore "a long and shameful degradation" (60). They urge him to find a respectable wife with whom he could have a traditional relationship. When he is in the company of men, Adolphe adopts this male perspective. In a purely "hommo-sexual" correspondence, he even writes letters to T***, rehearsing the topoi of male imperviousness, and announcing his firm intention to break with Ellénore. As a last effort, Monsieur de T*** will intervene by forwarding one of these cruel letters to Ellénore, who will die from being thus cut off from the love upon which, as a woman, she had lived. Though it was written by Adolphe, the letter came not from him as an embodied individual, but from Masculinity, from the abstracted sphere of patriarchy itself.[27] Because he is not utterly perverted, that is, because his natural empathy has not been gendered out of him, Adolphe will wander unattached, unemployed, full of grief and guilt, finally allowing himself to die in Italy.

Although I have written it out here for the first time, I have always "known" and been drawn to my sense of a queer subtext in *Adolphe*, and this from the first time I read it as an unaware, closeted undergraduate. The pathos of the popular, heterosexual love story never quite managed to overwhelm my inchoate sense that there was another story here that addressed me more directly. And yet, it was unimaginable then to explore freely as I have done here. I have speculated elsewhere on the epistemological implications behind the protocols of such a reading, based first on projective, transferential, and sentimental responses to the text, and then, on the normal scholarly requirements to justify and convince.[28]

I returned to *Adolphe* now because I wanted to understand what about it seemed to address me as a gay man. It has been gratifying to discover what I construe to be hints that Constant may have had homosexual experience. Particularly tantalizing is the mysterious, interlinear addition to *Ma vie* in the *Cahier rouge* of the words "Greek love in Berne." It was there that the young Constant encountered Edward Gibbon, and where he began a friendship, at least, with Johann Rudolf Knecht. He was distraught when Knecht was found guilty of pederasty by a Bernese tribunal in 1789.[29] It has been oddly meaningful, as well, to learn—and to speculate why—queer forebears such as Harold Nicolson were also drawn to Constant. (I notice, for example, that Nicolson has an unusual way of focusing more particularly than others on Constant's effeminacy, on his high-pitched voice.)[30] It is gratifying, after the long tradition of silence on such questions at last to read the prudent speculations concerning "amours grecs à Berne" in the latest biography by the imminent *constantien*, Dennis Wood: "Knecht, five years older than Constant, was a homosexual, and it is not impossible that the 'Amours grecs' is a reference to the relationship between them; Constant may, on the other hand, simply have meant to write in later at this point in *Ma Vie* an account of Knecht's relationships with others. It is not entirely implausible, however, that precisely at this time in his life, at the age of 18 or 19, Constant should have formed a homosexual attachment, perhaps with the older Knecht himself."[31] Here, Wood goes on to explain that Juste was relentlessly hard on Benjamin during this period, which is in part why he draws the following conclusion: "It would hardly be surprising therefore if Benjamin had no immediate model with whom to identify in order to discover his own masculinity; if, fearful and timid in his father's presence, he found himself attracted to another man with whom he could identify and who gave him that affection which Juste was seldom able to show to his son (although he certainly felt it) . . ."[32] Since such speculations are no longer inaugurally excluded, they naturally can lead to other circumstantial links, and can embolden us to voice other intuitions and projections that we cannot, or not yet, fully understand or document.[33] But why should we do so?

It is too common, and too easy, to dismiss the question of authors' sexuality as naive, useless, and as authorizing no conclusions about their writing. Speculations such as these are valuable for a variety of reasons— not the least of which is that they can then lead to the research required to confirm or refute them. But beyond that, such imaginative speculations can begin to provide to queer reading, and to reading queers, some of the rich texture of spontaneous presumption that is so massively available and empowering, though unacknowledged, in straight readings of canonical literature. Without the free capacity at least to wonder, or to embroider upon what we sense and suspect, we will never be able to discern and respond to the queer inflections at the core of cultures.

And finally, how else are we going to explain that undeniable communicative link that can occur between a gay reader and a text by an author whose homosexual experience is closeted, in life and in writing? The very fact that there should be such a communication, and a shared but silent knowledge around it, raises issues that go to the core of abiding mysteries: what is a text, what is literature, what is sexuality, what is a subject, and how (despite differences of culture and time) has the queer managed to disseminate itself and to produce its culture in the very teeth of the bigotry that would destroy it?

NOTES

1 See Glyn Holmes, *The Adolphe Type in French Fiction of the First Half of the Nineteenth Century* (Sherbrooke, Quebec: Editions Naaman, 1977). The novel has not lacked for scholarly attention. The current MLA bibliography has no less than 298 titles under the subject heading of *Adolphe*. Recently, *Adolphe* has been fertile ground for feminist critique, as in Margaret Waller's analysis of glorified male weakness as but a clever ruse of phallic power in *The Male Malady: Fictions of Impotence in the French Romantic Novel* (New Brunswick, N.J.: Rutgers University Press, 1993), pp. 93–113.

2 American French departments, for all their receptiveness to other kinds of theory, have been slow to take up queer theory, in part because the French themselves have yet to show significant interest in the field, and in part because of other theoretical hegemonies that are sometimes subject to misguided panic that they might be displaced by a new "trend."

3 Though the question of Constant's own sexuality is much too complex for thorough discussion here, there is general consensus that *Adolphe* is an intensely autobiographical text. Though Constant was a famous womanizer, particularly known for his long and stormy affair with Germaine de Staël, recent "constantiens" have finally addressed the question of sexual ambivalence squarely, though without reaching firm conclusions. In this regard, see Dennis Wood, *Benjamin Constant: A Biography* (London and New York: Routledge, 1993), pp. 51–59, 78; and Patrice Thomson, *La Religion de Benjamin Constant Les Pouvoirs de l'image* (Pisa: La Goliardica, 1978), p. 40.

4 Benjamin Constant, *Adolphe*, in *Oeuvres de Benjamin Constant* (Paris: Editions de la Pléiade, Gallimard, 1957), p. 6; emphasis added. Further citations of the prefaces are from this edition and are mine translation, and will be given parenthetically in the text. All emphases in citations from *Adolphe* will be my own.

5 Margaret Waller provides a fuller discussion of this issue in its broader cultural and literary ramifications in her *Male Malady*, pp. 8–28.

6 Margaret Waller selects a horrendously representative quote from Crébillon's 1775 *Lettres athéniennes*: "To please, indeed, to be passionately loved; to see myself as the object of the wishes and desires of every woman . . . to sacrifice them constantly to one another; and to find them in the end . . . subject to all the emotions I want *to have them feel*" (Claude-Prosper de Crébillon, *Oeuvres complètes*, 2 vols. [Geneva: Slatkine, 1968], 2:362; quoted in Waller, *Male Malady*, 12; emphasis added). In his autobiographical

Cahier Rouge, Constant confesses that reading Crébillon et al. as a boy marked him for life (*Oeuvres*, p. 88).

7   Constant thus demonstrates his debt to Rousseau by implying a kind of natural goodness of the soul that preexists the defensive constructions of gender, and that would allow men access to a more androgynous or bisexual capacity both to be men and to feel the emotion of the other. For a discussion of Constant's Rousseauian inheritance, see Michel Crouzet, *Nature et société chez Stendhal: la révolte romantique* (Villeneuve d'Ascq: Presses universitaires de Lille, 1985).

8   Gayle Rubin, "The Traffic in Women: Notes Toward a Political Economy of Sex," in *Toward an Anthropology of Women*, ed. Rayna Reiter (New York: Monthly Review Press, 1975), pp. 157–210; Luce Irigaray, *Speculum of the Other Woman*, trans. Gillian C. Gill (Ithaca, N.Y.: Cornell University Press, 1985), pp. 101–3; Eve Kosofsky Sedgwick, *Between Men: English Literature and Male Homosocial Desire* (New York: Columbia University Press, 1985), pp. 1–21, passim. In his autobiographical writings, Constant amply displays his own experience with homosocial desire. See, for example, his purely homosocial relationship with Mrs. Trevor in *Le Cahier rouge* where he confesses that, "Seeing as how most of the young men in her entourage were courting her, I set out to please her" 96; my translation). The passion and fury that follows—involving assignations and duels—came to nothing more than one, single good-bye kiss. This was not the only purely social—that is, spectacular but nonphysical—relationship that Constant had with a woman. (Cf. *Cahier Rouge*, p. 91).

9   Typical is Han Verhoeff, a disciple of Charles Mauron, who suggests in *'Adolphe' et Constant: une étude psychocritique* (Paris: Klincksieck, 1976) that the crux of the problem is that Adolphe, like Constant, was abandoned by his mother, leaving him with appropriately ambivalent feelings for women. Verhoeff recycles, as if it were a self-evident fact, the view that Ellénore incarnates the devouring mother (e.g., p. 76). In my view, Verhoeff (like his master, Charles Mauron) is himself writing from the same masculinist ideology that inflicts Adolphe. Ellénore can be considered a devouring, castrating mother only from the perspective of male phobia of the sentiment that Adolphe must reject in order to be "a man." See also Gustave Rudler, *Jeunesse de Benjamin Constant 1767–1794* (Paris: Armand Colin, 1909).

10 *Adolphe*, in *Adolphe and the Red Note-Book*, trans. Carl Wildman (London: Hamish Hamilton, 1948), p. 1. Further citations will be given parenthetically in the text.

11 This is surely the same "disdain" for the common that is so much in evidence in most all of Adolphe's literary descendants. One thinks of so many other proto-queer boys who just can't abide the common, from d'Albert in *Mlle de Maupin* (Gautier), to Octave in *Armance* (Stendhal), or Olivier in *Olivier* (Claire de Duras), to Balzacian characters like Sarrasine in *Sarrasine*, or Henri de Marsay in *La Fille aux yeux d'or*, or of Senancour's *Obermann*. *Atala* (1801), *René* (1802), and *Corinne* (1807) also spring most readily to mind.

12 I am not suggesting that, in any essential way, the relationship between father and son *is* a relationship between the feminine and the masculine. Rather, the sex-gender system codified in the prefaces leaves us with no other lexicon for categorizing the subject positions that these two men occupy as they seek to love each other in this cultural moment.

13 Raised a Calvinist by an authoritarian father and a mother nicknamed "la générale," Colonel Juste de Constant was commander of a Swiss regiment in the service of Holland. Dennis Wood characterizes him accurately as "a stern and exceptionally strong-willed personality" (*Benjamin Constant*, p. 10).

14   The story of Juste's frequently abandoning Benjamin is well known. What has been less attended to, however, are the emotions stirred up in the father by the string of preceptors and tutors he hired to educate his son at home. (See, e.g., Wood, *Benjamin Constant*, p. 39). In June of 1783, Juste wrote a remarkably suggestive letter about Benjamin to his friend, Sir Robert Murray Keith, the British Ambassador to Vienna. The ostensible topic is Juste's attempts to instill in Benjamin a love of study as a "brake on him": "He is making progress, but his tastes are widening and it is to be feared that he may give in to them entirely. My sole concern now is to move him on to a new place as soon as I see that the acquaintances he is making are dangerous ones [*des que je m'aperçois que ses liaisons deviennent dangereuses*]. I gain time that way, but also I do not succeed in rooting out the evil" (quoted in Wood, *Benjamin Constant*, p. 44). Must we not at least entertain the possibility that there is in these lines, a noticeable amount of unconscious homoerotic alarm and jealousy?

15   A typical example would be the bisexual d'Albert in Gautier's *Mlle de Maupin* (Paris: Editions Garnier, 1966), p. 347: "Who will I take . . . ? I have no idea, and I feel no more inclination to one side than to the other. . . ." In a pivotal moment in which patriarchy makes a bid to reclaim Adolphe for itself, an older man will speak the key words to him: "In this world one must know what one wants" (54).

16   See, for example, Sigmund Freud, "Some Psychical Consequences of the Anatomical Distinction Between the Sexes," in *The Standard Edition of the Complete Psychological Works of Sigmund Freud*, ed. James Strachey, vol. 19 (London: Hogarth Press, 1953–); "Female Sexuality," Ibid., vol. 21.

17   Beyond the standard Freudian sites for this view (e.g., *Totem and Taboo* [*Standard Edition*, vol. 13]), it is crucial to examine the homophobic invocations of the Oedipus complex, especially in the French and French-inspired theoretical tradition. See, for example Michel Bon and Antoine d'Arc, *Rapport sur l'homosexualité de l'homme* (Paris: Editions Universitaires, 1974); Jeffrey Mehlman, *A Structural Study of Autobiography* (New Haven: Yale University Press, 1974).

18   Judith Butler, *Gender Trouble: Feminism and the Subversion of Identity* (New York: Routledge, 1990), p. 59. Butler has suggested that the canonical prohibition of heterosexual incest presupposes that there is no possibility of homosexually incestuous desire, or that such a possibility has already been liquidated.

19   Jonathan Dollimore, *Sexual Dissidence: Augustine to Wilde, Freud to Foucault* (Oxford: Oxford University Press, 1991); Monique Wittig, *The Straight Mind* (Boston: Beacon Press, 1992); and Judith Butler, *Gender Trouble*. It does not, however, support the recuperative reading of this issue performed by Dennis Wood regarding Constant's own Oedipal problems involving an absent mother and a subsequent stepmother, Marianne: "Benjamin's oedipal feelings, left unsatisfied by the death of his real mother, would have been redirected towards this young substitute mother. Marianne introduced the missing third term which was added to the father/son dyad, and as a result Constant experienced what Jacques Lacan would consider a corrective, normative oedipalization" (*Benjamin Constant*, p. 30).

20   See Butler, Gender Trouble, on the melancholia of homosexuality. Much of this argument can be summarized in Butler's rhetorical question: "Do we construe the punishing father as a rival or as an object of desire who forbids himself as such?" (p. 59).

21   The suffocating quality of society's "artificial conventions" (p. 35) is thematized repeatedly. Constant compares this society, interestingly, to a crowded theater where, "one finally manages to breathe freely in a congested theater, whereas, on first entering, one breathed with difficulty" (p. 6).

22 To my knowledge, this locution first occurs in canonical French literature two decades later in Gautier's *Mlle de Maupin* (1835). On the history of the "troisième sexe," see Claude Courouve, *Vocabulaire de l'homosexualité masculine* (Paris: Payot, 1985), pp. 212–16.

23 We now understand, of course, that masculinity in other cultures is indeed constituted, very explicitly, in precisely this way. See, for example, Gilbert Herdt, *Guardians of the Flutes: Idioms of Masculinity* (New York: McGraw-Hill, 1981); and the classic by Kenneth Dover, *Greek Homosexuality* (Cambridge: Cambridge University Press, 1978).

24 Dennis Wood is uncharacteristically bold as he concludes his first chapter with the following pertinent remarks: "Insecure, sometimes unable to see himself as loved or lovable, unable to identify entirely with an aggressive and domineering father, it would not have been surprising if Constant had been drawn to a number of forms of sexual deviation. A feeling of guilt and inferiority perhaps produced the sado-masochistic scene which opens *Ma Vie*, either in reality at the age of 5 or as a fantasy in the mind of the 44-year-old writer. It could also have produced a bisexual identification which may not only have led him to attach great value to friendship with older men, probably with an element of hero-worship or intellectual competitiveness involved, but also, and most important, to that profound but never permanent identification with feminine passivity and suffering that would characterize his greatest writing, and would culminate in *Adolphe*" (*Benjamin Constant*, p. 42).

25 Eve Kosofsky Sedgwick, *Between Men: English Literature and Male Homosocial Desire* (New York: Columbia University Press, 1985), p. 89.

26 For a rich source of historical resonances, see Robert A. Nye, *Masculinity and Male Codes of Honor in Modern France* (Oxford: Oxford University Press, 1993). For information on Constant's own history of duels, see Wood, *Benjamin Constant*.

27 Verhoeff comments that "M. de T. avenges M. de P.: the Father doesn't allow himself to be challenged with impunity" (*'Adolphe' et Constant*, p. 127).

28 See my *Closet Writing/Gay Reading* (Chicago: University of Chicago Press, 1993), pp. 1–90. I have been gratified to see others taking up this task in other fields. See, for example, the excellent collection of essays in *Queering the Pitch: The New Gay and Lesbian Musicology*, ed. Philip Brett, Elizabeth Wood, and Gary C. Thomas (New York and London: Routledge, 1994), in particular the essay by Gary C. Thomas entitled " 'Was George Frideric Handel Gay': On Closet Questions and Cultural Politics," pp. 155–203.

29 See Wood, *Benjamin Constant*, pp. 78–79.

30 Harold Nicolson, *Benjamin Constant* (London: Constable, 1949). These are characteristics he finds important enough to include even in a brief introduction to a translation of *Adolphe*, the very one from which I have been quoting here. Thus: "Julie Talma was a penetrating woman. . . . Her nickname for him was '*la vieille coquette,*' " (p. xvi).

31 Wood, *Benjamin Constant*, p. 76.

32 Ibid. The correspondence between Constant and Knecht has disappeared. We know that Knecht was fined and spent the rest of his life in prison for his "crime." See Constant, *Oeuvres*, p. 1513 n. 7.

33 Examples of these for me would be Constant's references in *Ma vie* to "a most libertine Englishman" he met in Paris (p. 93), or to a certain Baumier, "a man of no morals [*perdu de moeurs*] . . . a ne'er-do-well of the worst species. He tried to get control of me [*s'emparer de moi*] . . . and if it had been up to him, I'd have adopted the most dissolute and the most abject kind of life" (p. 93). Constant goes on to add that

all Baumier did was to "accompany me to the brothels and borrow money from me" (p. 93), but something doesn't jibe in this last depiction. Since Constant gambled and frequented prostitutes for much of his life, the hyperbolic emphasis on Baumier's excessive immorality to the point of abjection suggests some other aspect of "his vices" than profligacy and the frequentation of "les filles."

John Vincent

Flogging is Fundamental: Applications of

Birch in Swinburne's *Lesbia Brandon*

S winburne wrote the flogging scene at many different times in many different ways. He penned a cycle of flogging poems, which he titled *The Flogging Block,* and contributed significantly to another book of poems published under the name *The Whippingham Papers; a collection of contributions in prose and verse, chiefly by the author of the 'Romance of Chastisement.'* His two novels, *Lesbia Brandon* and *Love's Cross Currents,* a short ur-novel that is now called the *Kirklowes* fragment, and his letters, traffic heavily in birch.

The *Kirklowes* fragment offers a taste of the twigs with a full cast: Reginald, the whipped boy; his father, who "was very fond of his son, and usually flogged him four times a week till the blood ran"; and Reginald's sister Helen, for whom each of "Redgie's floggings was a small drama[:] . . . [s]he followed with excitement each cut of the birch on her brother's skin, and tasted a nervous pleasure when every stroke drew blood; she analyzed the weals, and anatomized the tears of the victim."[1] Reginald's father "was just the man to appreciate" the "oddity and quaintness" of Helen's taste for flogging. "[D]oubtless," the narrator continues, "he had himself a deep inward relish of his skill and strength, a keen flavour of the pain he inflicted, when Reginald, nicely adjusted on a farm-servant's back, or simply on a convenient bench or block, reddened and wriggled with smart and the birch drew fresh blood at every cut on the flesh of the roaring boy." Not every whipping Swinburne writes has such an eager witness. For instance, in the novel *Lesbia Brandon,* whose use and theorization of whipping will serve as the subject of this essay, Herbert, the main boy character, is never whipped with an audience, and he is not whipped by his father, who has "queer opinions on character." Instead, Herbert is dealt unwitnessed blows by his tutor whose whippings are regarded by Herbert's guardians as sound educational excursions. In Swinburne's flogging poems, however, the action mostly occurs at schools like Eton, if not at Eton itself, and is attended by a crowd of schoolboys.

While flogging scenes are both rich and numerous in Swinburne's work, the set of critical tools available to treat these scenes are neither. In this essay, I will attempt both to pry these scenes from languages that do less to specify than dismiss them, and to flesh out some nodes of meaning production that inform them. These enterprises are intimately bound up with one another and will congregate around six propositions. (1) Swinburne's floggings have their own locality and agency-bearing vascular systems that are not productively mapped by the structures of masochism. (2) While masochism does not provide an adequate model for what happens during Swinburne's floggings, neither does any explanation that entails a simple translation of pain to erotic pleasure. Such a translation would take the constitution of pain and the constitution of the feeling body for granted, something that these scenes pointedly frustrate. (3) Flogging does not anchor in the body in a way suitably called anality, rather it both sticks to bodies and floats about them. (4) This sticking to and floating around bodies incites the production of individual subjectivities, which both arise from flogging and are continually problematized by flogging. (5) The traffic between and among faces and butts stimulates meaning production while troubling what it means to be legible. (6) Flogging, as it incites and frustrates legibility, undergirds the ontic effects within Swinburne's writing.

FLOGGING BLOCKS

Many biographers and critics would have us believe that there is less skill than pathology in Swinburne's rewritings of the flogging scene. They declare Swinburne "fixated," and stop, satisfied, there. Philip Henderson reflects the opinion of most biographers when he declares that *The Flogging Block* "fortunately still remains unpublished."[2] Jean Overton Fuller, a little less dismissive of Swinburne's penchant for whipping than Henderson and the others, remarks of this book: "Perhaps the British Museum authoritites do well to keep the manuscript out of the public's way; and yet one could wish that it would be read by every parent contemplating the decision to send his son to a school at which corporal punishment is still practiced."[3] Even Ian Gibson, in his book *about* flogging in Victorian England, quotes a bit of one poem from *The Flogging Block* and notes that he's printed two other flogging poems in full in the appendix to his book, "if the reader can stand an extended example of this sort of thing."[4]

These academics disgustedly distinguish their own tweedish enthusiasm for whipping from Swinburne's fleshy one. Their examinations are in the interest of halting this barbaric practice that leads to pathology or in the interest of painting Swinburne's portrait with a full palette of garish psychological color. Whipping is never considered as fundamental or even, properly speaking, as related to Swinburne's theories and practices of writing. When it is considered in the same breath with Swinburne's positive achievements, it is always with awe that such grotesqueries could exist side by side with gorgeous writing. Jean Overton Fuller, at the height of his exegesis of *The Flogging Block*, concludes his chapter with an academic gesture that owes much to the techniques of silent film. "It is ironic and tragic that he was writing this ghastly epic at the same time as he was writing *Tristram* and the naïvely adoring poems to the child, Bertie."[5] Even Edmund Wilson so assumes Swinburne's relation to flogging to be one of "masochistic passivity" that he uses it as witty garnish at the conclusion of his introduction to *Lesbia Brandon:* "but how one wishes he had had the spirit, when Watts-Dunton had sequestered *Lesbia Brandon* and was refusing to give it back, to throw off his masochistic passivity and go after that respectable solicitor not with a birch but with a cudgel."[6]

Wilson is only the soprano in a chorus of voices suggesting that Swinburne was fascinated with flogging and therefore a masochist. Deleuze, in his study on Masoch, forces a wedge between sadism and masochism, insisting that they have different mechanics and etiologies. Swinburne critics before Deleuze did not make such a distinction, and treated masochism and sadism as the dorsal and ventral parts of the same beast. Deleuze explains that they are two different creatures by mapping their anatomies through the literary works of their namesakes. Before Deleuze's forceful distinction, most explanations that depended on sadism and masochism to describe relations wired through "the pleasure-pain complex" foundered in unqualified abstraction; after, one feels Deleuze's invitation, if not command, to ground descriptions of this complex "complex" with terms that adhere stubbornly to its specific manifestations.[7]

Deleuze's masochist acts as an "educator" and depends on "contractual relations."[8] Neither of these fundamentals are consistently met in Swinburne's literary renderings of flogging. The boy who is flogged has little agency, besides restraining himself from wriggling or crying out. Indeed, the rules of a schoolroom or tutoring situation might serve as a contract, but the recipient of a whipping has nothing to do with producing, maintaining, or altering it. Furthermore, at the level of literary rendering, Swinburne weaves between occupying a tutor's or father's position, that of his student or son, and that of eager or horrified witnesses. Plugging up or carving out entry points for a reader's identification disfigures the flogging scene that is primarily a *scene*. The narrative of a masochist, as Deleuze describes it, requires one central agent who arranges a scene, while Swinburne's floggings require several agents who *are arranged by a scene.*

Since Swinburne experienced flogging himself as a youth at school, there lurks a biographical impulse all too ready to suggest that Swinburne's descriptions and different points of view are in the service of saucing and spicing the floggee's position. Randolph Hughes, in his enormous commentary to the first published version of *Lesbia Brandon,* suggests that Herbert, the oft-whipped leading boy in the novel, is an authorial surrogate, because Swinburne has "more in common" with him than any other character in the novel, or for that matter "in the whole of his works." He argues that when Swinburne describes "sadistic scenes, especially those in which extreme physical pain is inflicted, Swinburne's constant tendency [is] to put himself in the position of the sufferer; in other words, where he is most likely at first sight to appear to be giving expression to sadistic impulses, he is nothing but a masochist, the very opposite of a sadist in the ordinary as well as the most technical sense of the term."[9] Hughes focuses on where Swinburne identifies within the novel, trying to shift pathology's weight from one foot to another. While exonerating Swinburne of sadistic impulses in both the "technical" and "ordinary" senses, he shuts down the very interesting mix of identifications and cross-identifications that Swinburne's scenes of "extreme physical pain" proffer. The "impulses" that run Swinburne's pain-filled scenes seem, at some times, to be in service of the delight in causing "pain" and, at others, in service of the pleasure in receiving "pain." "Pain" is an elastic term in Swinburne and refers to intense but incompletely vectored sensation. Hughes uses it to refer to unpleasant violent sensations, suggesting that its constitution is uniform; while its intensity might increase or decrease, its substance remains the same. Hughes thinks of pain as an element on the periodic chart of sensations, while Swinburne theorizes it as a compound, and a complex one.

Labeling Swinburne "nothing but" a "sadist" or a "masochist" and labeling the scenes he writes with the somewhat distant adjectival cousins, "sadistic" and "masochistic," does nothing to describe the slippages of identification inside and around his scenes of pain. For instance, one might ask whether the character feels *only* pain, whether the author can identify and be excited by both the active and passive positions in the scene of a flogging, and finally whether the reader feels the scenes to be painful or amusing or shameful or shaming or sexy. Or simply, imagine a boy witnessing his classmate being flogged. He might flinch at the cuts, or cheer, or he might begin by cheering and end by flinching, or begin flinching and end cheering. He might remain silent, and he might feel nothing that wears the colors of named emotions. Perhaps a little rumbling of shame, perhaps a shy quiver of pleasure. "Pain" in Swinburne's flogging scenes is not simply "unpleasure," nor is it located soley in or on the body of the flogged boy.

The simple bipolar sadistic/masochistic model, among its other defects, cannot account for the way shame and desire swirl around the flogging room. When this model is invoked, it is used merely to pathologize Swinburne and strip him of agency as a creator or theorist. I want to argue instead that, in his writing, Swinburne negotiated a relation to flagellation; indeed, he undertook a theoretical exploration of it that was particularly literary. While *masochism* as a term, particularly in Deleuze's exegesis, has intricate mechanics and strong explanatory power, it has been wielded to shut down Swinburne's own exegetical forays. It is the forest for which critics could not see the birches.

YOU HAVE, SAY, A FLOGGING TO DESCRIBE

In an 1862 letter to Richard Monckton Milnes, Swinburne reaches such a pitch in discussing Marquis de Sade's *Justine* that he begins addressing Sade himself:

> Take the simplest little example of your way of work. You have, say, a flogging to describe. You go in for *quantity* in a way quite regardless of expense. You lay on some hundred cuts, behind and before; you assert that they drew blood; probably they did; that the recipient wept and writhed; which is not unlikely; that the inflictor enjoyed himself and was much excited in his *physique;* which is most probable of all. Well? You have asserted a great deal; prove it now; bring it face to face with us; let the sense of it bite and tickle and sting your reader. Assertion is easy work. . . . I boast not of myself; but I do say that a schoolboy, set to write on his own stock of experience, and having a real gust and appetite for the subject in him, may make and has made more of a sharp short school flogging of two or three dozen cuts than you of your enormous interminable inflictions; more of the simple common birchrod and daily whipping-block than you of your loaded iron whips and elaborately ingenious racks and horses."[10]

Swinburne admonishes Sade for his extraordinary props and situations (while employing the extraordinary situation of addressing an author long dead), suggesting that when one has "a flogging to describe," the best conduit of expressing pain is the "common" and the "ordinary." Later in the same letter, still addressing Sade, Swinburne writes, "As to your story and the framework of your theories—you *must* know that Justine [*sic*] is a juggler's show, an ingenious acrobatic performance, and no more. Very ingenious and inventive; many of the tricks and postures . . . most creditable to a phallic juggler; but who on earth is to make more than its worth of the very best conjuror's exhibition!"[11]

Lesbia Brandon, Swinburne's unfinished novel, is where Swinburne tries hardest to render flogging ordinary, to hypostatize it through the common. In a letter to Richard Burton, he mentions this novel that, he writes, "I flatter myself it will be more offensive and objectionable to Britannia than anything I have yet done."[12] Part verse, part prose, the novel consists of seventeen chapters with various missing and fragmentary pieces. Some of the chapters seem complete and consist of over thirty pages while others are cursory and fragmentary, whether labeled as fragments or not. The novel integrates incest, lesbianism, prostitution, and libertinism into its plot. But these elements, while they indeed might make this novel "more objectionable to Britannia" than anything Swinburne had until that point written, are yet more objectionably written, as we shall see, because they are written in the emotional grammar and vocabulary of flogging. By themselves, these eyebrow-raising themes are analogous to *Justine*'s "loaded iron whips and elaborately ingenious racks and horses"; they don't themselves "sting and tickle" the reader. Swinburne, in *Lesbia Brandon,* sets out to refer all sensations to the flogging scene and thus to have the ordinary business of the novel itself "sting and tickle."

PORTRAITS

The first chapter of *Lesbia Brandon,* the end of which is missing, attempts a portrait of Lady Wariston and her brother Herbert (Bertie) Seyton.[13] Swinburne concentrates most on the eyes and the faces, reading them as emotional maps. Lady Wariston's eyes give her "fair and floral beauty . . . a fire and rapture of life." To describe Lady Wariston's pupils (an item one hardly thinks of as a distinct facial feature since they are most of all little black dots), Swinburne writes, "The pupil was not over large, and seemed as the light touched it of molten purple or of black velvet. They had infinite significance, infinite fervour and purity" (*LB,* 190). She has "a mouth that could suffer and allure, capable beyond others of langour and laughter," and cheeks "pale but capable of soft heat and the flush of a growing flower; the face reddened rarely and faintly and all at once" (*LB,* 190). What keeps such floridly detailed descriptions from seeming excessive in this first chapter is the way they describe a face's range of reaction. Swinburne is bent on describing the face's "capabilities," the way a body enables or blocks emotional states. Also, the language of dilation offers a convincing central image. The mouth can open so far to accommodate emotions, as can the blood vessels in the face, as can the pupils of the eyes. The face is a kind of concatenation of sphincters whose elasticity determines how much sensation gets in and how much emotion gets out. Swinburne describes Herbert as a slightly revised version of his sister. He writes, "While yet a boy her brother was so like her that the description may serve for him with a difference" (*LB*, 190). Bertie's eyes are different and allow a different range of emotions. His eyes, "even when his face was most feminine were always the eyes of a male bird," "sharp at once and reflective, rapid and timid, full of daring or dreams" (*LB*, 191). But both share a face and hands that "were perceptibly nervous and sensitive, his perhaps more than hers. As the least contact of anything sharp would graze the skin unawares and draw blood before they knew it, so the lightest touch of pain or pleasure would strike and sting their nerves to the quick. In bright perfect health they were as susceptible in secret of harsh sounds, of painful sights and odours, as any one born weaklier; whatever they had to suffer or enjoy came to them hot and strong, untempered and unallayed" (*LB*, 192). Here the skin's sensitivity enables a nearly unmediated experience of stimuli. But, interestingly, stimulus comes in only two categories, pain and pleasure, both of which "strike and sting." In other words, both are described in the vocabulary of pain.

The first chapter lays out two of the book's central theories in the guise of description. First, the theory that the parts of the body, here particularly the face and eyes, provide "capabilities" to feel. Unless one's mouth is capable of extremes of, say, "langour and laughter," one cannot oneself be capable of them. If one's eyes aren't full of "daring or dreams," neither can one's character be said to be so. The second theory is about the makeup of stimulus. Stimuli can be differentiated only in terms of intensity. Pleasure and pain are both made up of what is "striking," what "hits on the nerves," and what "tells." Pleasure or pain are both experienced when something violently collides with the body. This violent collision is primary to the sorting and naming of stimuli. At bottom, in this novel, any emotion is born of violence, thus the primacy of pain language. Lady Wariston and Bertie are particularly susceptible, so pleasure and pain, at their lightest, "strike and sting" them. For one less susceptible, it is implied, the "painful sights and odours" or "harsh sounds" are still "painful" and "harsh" but less "hot and strong."

LANDSCAPING

These two theories are fleshed out in terms of the phantasmatics of flogging in the second chapter, whose first portion is missing. The foreshortened version we have been left starts immediately after the death of Bertie's and Lady Wariston's father. Lord and Lady Wariston take charge of Bertie, transplanting him to their manor in Ensdon after the burial. "A *shrill* wind shook the trees and bushes about the old house as they started; the day was *sharp* and the light *hard and fitful*. No rain fell, but the flooded *burn* had not yet *gone down*; the *long reeds sang sharp* in the wind, the flowerless heather *heaved* and *quivered under it by fits*" (*LB*, 194; emphasis added). The roundness implied in the shaking trees and bushes calls to mind whipped buttocks only peripherally, while the heather (heaving and quivering) uses precisely the language Swinburne uses in his flogging poetry to describe the motion of "posteriors" under the influence of the birch. In a poem from *The Flogging Block*, for instance, "Charlie Collingwood's Flogging by Etoniensis," Charlie is getting a whipping for not being able to sit still in church (his scuttling due to the whipping he received the day before). He is a brave lad and does not shrink at the master's command to "Go down"—the going down that the flooded burn, so strangely concocted, has not yet done. The burn and the quivering and heaving heather come together in the poem about Charlie where, "the pain of the cut makes his burning posteriors quiver and heave."[14] The long sharp reeds in the novel's scene are reminiscent of the birch rod, and interestingly, their singing could be attributed both to the rod and to the whipped boy.

As Bertie, his sister, and her husband travel to Ensdon, the scenery changes but the vocabulary remains the same. "After miles of high lonely land [the road] *went down* among sudden trees. . . . At the next turn they were in sight of [the sea]; a spring-weather sea . . . *swelling* and *quivering* under clouds and sunbeams. The wind played upon it wilfully, *lashing it* with *soft strokes*, kissing it with rapid kisses, as one amorous and vexatious of the immense beautiful body defiant even of divine embraces and lovers flown from heaven: far out among the shafts and straits of fugitive sunshine, near in under cloud-shadows, waking with *light blows* and *sharp caresses* infinite and variable smiles of weary beauty on its immortal face" (*LB*, 194; emphasis added). Here, whipping powers an incomplete anthropomorphization of the sea. The sea is sensually available and physically there—but *not an individual*. Its "immortal face" arises out of the violences that the wind and sun inflict on its "immense beautiful body." "Lashes," "strokes," "blows," and "caresses" transmute a hugely blank body into one that resists, becomes "defiant." "Defiance" leads to "weariness," which registers on the suddenly conjured face that is nowhere visually differentiated from the "immense beautiful body." The simultaneous separation and conflation of the sea's face and body set off what seems a sympathetic vibration in Bertie's own body.

Seeing the sea lashed by sun and wind, Bertie's "heart opened and ached with pleasure. His face trembled and changed, his eyelids tingled, his limbs yearned all over . . . all his nerves desired the divine touch of it" (*LB*, 195). Bertie's heart, face, eyelids, limbs, and nerves are stimulated by the violence and near-livingness of the sea. He yearns to have the sea's violence act on his body, while the mere sight of it *already* acts on his body. Bertie's desire to be whipped by the sea and the sea's figural traffic between its own whipped body and face (the way whipping faces a body and bodies a face) finds purchase in Bertie's makeup, as a personality by the sea and as a character in this novel. He finds the sea vivifying; as a result the reader is offered a glimpse of what it means to be *living* in this novel. The oscillation between body and face effected by whipping (either literal whipping or punishment at the edge of extremity) gives a figure life, whether the figure is the sea, Bertie, or Lady Wariston. And as Swinburne is generous in dealing strokes, so is he generous in granting life.

Later in the chapter the sea will itself be whipping the shore and little Bertie's body. Bertie will feel "the fierce gladness and glory of living stroke and sting him all over with soft hands and sharp lips" (*LB*, 197). Notably, the "glory of living" is detachable from Bertie, it strikes him from the outside. This detachability couples with the sea's own semi-ontic nature. Bertie thrills to the "sweet and supressed semitones of light music struck out of shingle or sand by the faint extended fingers of foam and tired eager lips of yeilding sea that touch the soft mutable limit of their life, to recede in extremity and exhaustion" (*LB*, 197). The furthest reach of the sea's "fingers" and "lips" defines "the soft mutable limit of their life" in two ways. As a semi-living being, the sea reaches no further, but also, the "sea" dies at the extreme limits of mutability and metonymy. While the sea is most living in the form of "lips" and "fingers," it is also at its exhausted best of metonymic representation. The body/matter of the sea, for which its face expresses (extended fingers, eager lips), reaches its most living (thus its ability to lose its life) at its extremity. In other words, that it reaches extremity makes it living. This figuration of the sea corresponds to whipping both as a generator of localized intensity and as a generator of face/butt metonymy.[15]

THE BIRCHEN AGE

Once at Ensdon, Bertie runs wild, spending most of his time alone by the seaside, swimming and running around. "[T]his travail and triumph of the married wind and sea filled him with a furious luxury of the senses that kindled all his nerves and exalted all his life. From these haunts he came back wet and rough, blown out of shape and beaten into colour, his ears full of music and his eyes full of dreams" (*LB*, 202–3). As we saw in the first chapter, Bertie's body is capable of much feeling and enjoys it at high intensity. Swinburne theorizes the interior of this "small satis-fied pagan," as before, in terms of richness of feeling and relish of life, but now in terms of unformedness of mind as well. "The sharp broken speculation of children feels much and holds little, touches many truths and handles none; but their large and open sense of perception of things certain is malleable and colourable by infinite influences and effects. . . . Not incompetent to think [a child] is incompetent to use his thoughts; fancies may fill him as perverse and subtle and ambitious as a grown man's dreams or creeds" (*LB*, 198). Notice again, as in the facial descrip-tions of the first chapter, dilation is central to Swinburne's theory of the intellect. Children's minds are open all the time so that lots can get in but can as easily slip out. In the interest of making Bertie capable of using his not incapable but not yet competent mind, he is taken in hand by a tutor, Mr. Denham.

Swinburne furthers his theorizing about Bertie's development by offer-ing a temporal structure. "Herbert had passed through his two first stages and was ripe for a third; first the heather age, then the seaside age, and now the birchen age: this last began later with him than it does with most boys, but was to prove a warm and fruitful period. The moors had done their best for the boy, and after these the sea-rocks; enough work was left for the schoolroom to do" (*LB*, 201). Violence becomes more explicit and more locatable across these ages, till it smacks a boy right on his butt. Swinburne's theorizing enlists a grand historical voice, as if he were ex-plaining a shift between the Bronze and Iron Ages, as well as granting agency alike to the moors, the sea-rocks and the schoolroom. The swag-ger of both rhetorical devices, at once confident and comic, suggests both a teleology and a spatial economy of boyhood. The boy's location specifies itself more exactly as the boy himself is more exactly specified. So, while Swinburne's language may seem overblown, the image chain made by the spaces — moor (heather), seaside (sea-rocks), and schoolroom (birch) — moves from larger to smaller, offering a convincing if simple figure for a boy's development toward an articulated personality. How-ever, both the rhetorical and the imagistic aspects of these sentences are belied by the earlier flogging-mediated descriptions of heather and sea-rocks, one beaten by the wind, the other by the sea. The above sentences, then, have a second level of comic effect, because we know that every age, in *Lesbia Brandon*, is always already a birchen age.

In the actual schoolroom, however, whipping provides a structure for thought, it locates rightness and wrongness as bodily sensations. Wrong-ness is being flogged and rightness is not. Through whipping Denham will provide Bertie with what was missing in the seaside age: the ability to "handle" thoughts, to feel them tell on his body. Bertie's butt and his mind are collapsed when the narrator speaks of flogging. "It was quite unbroken and virgin ground which was now to be ploughed and harrowed in the approved fashion by the scholastic instrument of husbandry" (*LB*, 201). The ploughing image is a not just a conceit about the abstraction called the intellect; it is also a visual figure for a beaten bottom, as can be seen in comparing its visual imagery of harrowed and ploughed ground to a whipped bottom in "Charlie Collingwood's Flogging by Etoniensis," where "There are long, red ridges and furrows across his great, broad nether cheeks, / And on both his plump, rosy, round buttocks the blood stands in drops and in streaks."[16] The conceit also suggests punningly that whipping will make Herbert more "cultivated," and that the ass is the fertile field from which grows the intellect's bounty.

Two days after Denham arrives at Ensdon, he finds it "time indeed to apply whip and spur, bit and bridle, to the flanks and mouth of such a colt; the household authorities supported and approved the method of the breaker, under whose rigorous hand and eye he began to learn his paces bit by bit" (*LB*, 204). "Bit by bit" ends this new conceit with a punning flourish that is as cruel as the sting of a whip, but also funny, when followed by a short discussion of Herbert's reaction to the "mournful matter of sums." Whipping has blown math up to emotional material. It makes sums a mournful matter, it affords the power of drama to the most banal and tedious events and tasks. "These encounters did both of them some good; Herbert, fearless enough of risk, had a natural fear of pain, which lessened as he grew familiar with it, and a natural weight of indolence which it helped quicken and lighten; Denham eased himself of much superfluous discomfort and fretful energy by the simple exercise of power upon the mind and body of his pupil" (*LB*, 205). For the floggee, the practice of flogging reroutes generalized catagories, such as pain and indolence, into specific bodily sites of pain, while for the flogger it offers a site for the grounding of generalized aggression, which I will examine in the next section. The ass is the site of specification, the consistent fundament if you will, upon which a structure of emotion and intellect can be built. Flogging provides an index for the violent emotions. The advantages are that Herbert becomes "readier and sharper, capable of new enjoyment and advance," or rather, he has learned a new basic emotional vocabulary, which when practiced allows for directed efforts (*LB*, 205).

Canto 12 of "Rufus's Flogging" more succinctly explores the purpose of whipping. The master is questioning Rufus as he is whipping him: "Now, Rufus, my lad, can you tell me now, come, / Was the bum made for the birch, or was birch for the bum? / Was the bottom by provident nature designed / That the birch might have matter to work on behind, / Or the birch providentially made for the part / Where it constantly makes all young gentleman smart?"[17] The final pun suggests that smarting butts make smarter boys, succinctly metonymizing the simple distinctions of right and wrong of the birch's pedagogy into the fundamental distinctions that enable a supple intellect.

Once Herbert is no longer a virgin to the rod, the pleasures of the sea's lashing become more sexy and specific as they have a ground for comparison as well as a new vocabulary to utilize. Now, it is the beating of the sea on his body that particularly affects Herbert. "[H]e panted and shouted with pleasure among breakers where he could not stand two minutes; the blow of a roller that beat him off his feet made him laugh and cry out in ecstasy; he rioted and roared in the water like a young sea-beast, sprang at the throat of waves that threw him flat, pressed up against their soft fierce bosoms and fought for their sharp embraces; grappled with them as lover with lover, flung himself upon them with limbs that laboured and yielded deliciously, till the scourging of the surf made him red from the shoulders to the knees, and sent him on shore whipped by the sea into a single blush of the whole skin" (*LB*, 206). He is "insatiable" for the sea that "lashed and caressed him" and returns to the waves "quivering with delight . . . a little cut or beaten as it might be, with fresh laughter and appetite." The sea is a flogger whose throat can be sprung at: Herbert can return the sea's violence in a way he cannot return his tutor's violence. Herbert's construction of the sea as particularly the agent of flogging enables him to have relations of desire with it, and its distance from the actual site of schoolroom floggings makes him paradoxically love it all the more for flogging him. Swinburne suggests "it was rather desire than courage that attracted and attached him to the rough water" (*LB*, 206). Herbert's emotions have become more directional in the birchen age; he is arranging his extreme sensitivity so that it performs emotional work for him. Though inchoate, his relation to the sea is at least partly a rescripting of the other floggings he receives from his tutor. But this location of a primary scene allows him to act out his anger and desire, and most importantly perhaps, lends him agency. He chooses to undergo the sea's scourgings, whereas he has no explicit agency in his schoolroom floggings, which are based on his performance.

THE SECOND STAGE OF HIS APPRENTICESHIP

One day, though prohibited to swim because the sea has not yet "gone down" from a storm, Bertie is lured to the sea by "the delicious intolerable sound of the waves." Denham catches him and gives him his worst whipping yet, a "wet swishing." This commences the "second stage of his apprenticeship," where Bertie avoids "facetious talk" with Denham, realizing just how unpleasant a whipping can be. Bertie realizes that flogging can jump the tracks of routine discipline, becoming physically painful in ways that he cannot assimilate into his notions of whipping as a weekly event. This "second stage" is not diffferent solely because of Bertie's new attitude. His tutor, Denham, has begun to fall in love with Lady Wariston. While Denham's outward manner remains quite normal, "the hidden disease in spirit and heart struck inwards, and daily deeper" (*LB*, 207). Denham passes through "quiet stages of perversion," and just as his student has learned to cope with routine whipping, renegotiating his relation to the world by way of it, Denham too finds whipping an important pivot for his relations. "As he could not embrace her, he would fain have wounded her; this was at first; gradually the wound rather than the embrace came to seem desirable" (*LB*, 208). The love/hate pivot is not particular to whipping, but Denham's expression of it finds purchase in the flogging scene. Finding Bertie's hair wet after another prohibited swim (during which Bertie saved a neighborhood kid from drowning and was too afraid of public attention to tell Denham), Denham gets up from where he has been sitting with Lady Wariston and "[h]ating her with all his heart as he loved her with all his senses, he could but punish her through her brother, hurt her through his skin" (*LB*, 218).

Bertie's likeness to his sister enables Denham to ease more than "superfluous discomfort and fretful energy." When Denham tells Bertie to "go down," "his words had edges and cut like a harsh look" (*LB*, 219). That Denham's words "cut" like a harsh look is interesting because the invisible referent is whipping that is everywhere visibly present at that moment in the scene. A harsh look seems more distant than a harsh word and after all only cuts figuratively, it cuts like something else. It cuts, in this case, like a birch rod. The way that this goes unspoken is an example of whipping used as a basic emotional vocabulary. It also suggests that whipping provides a site of substitutability, like the substitution of Bertie for his sister but at the actual level of grammar.

During flogging, a boy's naked buttocks are his most prominent part. The child's buttocks and thighs, since they are visually unmarked by gender, and actually block the genitals from view, mark his sex only by the fact that flogging is a disciplinary practice deemed—in the semiotics of Swinburne's writing—unfit for girl children. The ass, unlike the more stubborn face with its features and expressions, is an easy site for fantastic displacement. From the flogger's vantage, the ass is capable of being any ass. A child's buttocks, denuded and displayed for the purposes of punishment, might be any child's buttocks. Denham begins the greatest flogging he ever gives Bertie with the unambitious goal of hurting Lady Wariston "through Bertie's skin; but at least to do this was to make her own flesh and blood suffer the pain inflicted on himself" (*LB*, 218). He merely wants to hurt something she holds dear. But during the flogging, Denham "glitter[s] with passion" and "[t]here was a rage in him . . . more bitter than anger" (*LB*, 219). Denham double-flogs Bertie viciously, wearing out one birch rod and applying a new one. "Denham knew better than to flog too fast; he paused after each cut and gave the boy time to smart" (*LB*, 219). Bertie smarts aplenty until his face is streaming with tears and his hands are bloody from being bit into to prevent him from crying out. "Denham laid on every stripe with a cold fury that grew slowly to white heat; and when at length he made an end, he was seized with a fierce dumb sense of inner laughter; it was such an absurd relief this, and so slight. When these fits were on him he could have taken life to ease his bitter and wrathful despair of delight" (*LB*, 220). Something in excess of the rather simple goal of hurting someone Lady Wariston loves takes over here. The repeated narrative of flogging (I flog Bertie, for instance) intersects the lyric mobility of Bertie's butt. Bertie, during the extremity of the whipping scene, is too slippery an object for "I flog Bertie" alone to register. Denham finds himself face to butt with the real object of his anger. However, "I flog Lady Wariston," or "I almost flog Lady Wariston," or even, "I flog Bertie as Lady Wariston," are not acceptable substitutes because as narratives they settle too snugly on their verbal objects. The key charge of the flogging scene is the floggee's substitutability within the scene, his oscillation between registers. Before the scene starts and after it is over, on the other hand, we find *just Bertie* bent over and naked to the waist.

Denham's attempt to disavow the connection of the butt he whips to Bertie is not, nonetheless, a denial that Bertie is being flogged. Denham's access to Lady Wariston requires the narrative of Bertie's flogging, but only as a prior requirement. Slippage of butt referents happens once the flogging narrative is in place and only while it holds. The narrative scene of flogging is the structure that the lyric mobility of the flogged subject both requires and surpasses. I am suggesting that the sloppy butt-for-person metonymy set going by flogging in Swinburne is as much the source of pleasure for the flogger as is the pain that he inflicts. The pain inflicted on the buttocks is the site but not the outline of this pleasure.

Similarly, for the floggee, the mobility of the subjects and objects in the narrative "Denham flogs Bertie" is primary to the painful sensation of the flogging, as we will see with Bertie's desire to be hurt, even killed, by his sister. Late one night he declares his adoration for his sister, saying, "I should like being swished even, I think, if you were to complain of me or if I knew you liked" (*LB*, 265). Then he betters his own offer: "I wish you would kill me some day; it would be jolly to feel you killing me.

Not like it? Shouldn't I! You just hurt me, and see." Lady Wariston, enjoying this scene, pinches him "so sharply that he laughted [sic] and panted with pleasure" (LB, 265). The key to Bertie's pleasure is the subject who causes his pain, or rather, the instigator who decrees that some subject whip him. The way Bertie reroutes his painful experiences into pleasurable ones suggests that the painful experiences were not solely painful, as the binary pleasure/pain might suggest.

For neither flogger nor floggee is pain the primary emotional content of the flogging scene. The scene provides a field of play for fantasy rather than the expression of fantasy. Pain provides a narrative. "I hurt him," or, "He hurts me." For the flogger, the butt-to-person metonymy Denham experiences when he beats Bertie in place of Lady Wariston makes whipping deeply pleasurable rather than simply a very located form of a generalized letting off of steam. Causing pain brings Denham pleasure only when the subject he is causing pain is capable of spread. The lyrical movement of the subject and object, the unnarrativizable, is the charge of the scene. When the words sadism or masochism appear to describe relations in this scene, they roughly shoulder aside any theorization of the oscillation between registers we observed in both Denham and Bertie's responses to whipping. The narrative is the whole story but only part of the scene.

Ironically, Bertie looks even more like his sister after his whipping. Denham "had never seen the two faces so like before; the eyes were hers now that pain had brightened and tears softened them. . . . Herbert's mouth, still trembling with pain, was already defiant; the red curve of the lips and the dimple below quivered like his sister's when excited or pleased, and the nervous sullen beauty of outline was hers when irritated or fatigued. Pain had brought out in sharper relief the lineaments of that likeness which had in part impelled him to inflict pain: he had punished the boy for being so like her, and after punishment he was more like than ever: as he stood opposite, his face had the very look most hateful and most beautiful on his sister's face" (LB, 220). Denham's fantasmatic reconstruction of Bertie's face utilizes the traces of intensity, "eyes brightened by pain and softened by tears," the defiantly curved lips, "trembling dimple," and the "nervous sullen beauty of outline," to liken him to his sister. Bertie's physical pain from his flogging is the index of intensity, but in his likeness to his sister, his pain is bundled with the marks of other emotions: defiance, excitement, pleasure, irritability, fatigue, and hate. Since Bertie's face is capable of great intensity of feeling, his face breaks up his intense "pain" into its constituents, expressing them all at once. "Pain" then is only a placeholder for this intensity. It is a compound of emotions and describes no one thing to be binarized as pleasure's exclusive twin.

The flogger feels a complicated "absurd relief," an easing of his "despair of delight," and is "half relieved" by the sight of his flogged pupil (*LB*, 220). While it is clear that Denham has achieved some kind of tension reduction, his fantasy of Bertie looking very much like Lady Wariston tempts Denham to "whip him again." "Denham could have beaten the fair clear features out of shape with his clenched hand; he began to hate this boy too, with a hatred not the less keen that there was no mixture of love in it" (*LB*, 220–21). Strangely, the way Bertie's face enables Denham's displacement by its capability to look like his sister's (to actually become his sister's) frustrates Denham's aim to punish Bertie in her place. The lyric mobility within the narrative of flogging is so great, in this case, that Denham's sadistic narrative (I will cause Bertie's body pain in place of Lady Wariston's) buckles. Bertie's body is so displaceable in the scene of whipping that the narrative cannot reach any closure, and provides no relief, or rather only a kind of "half relief" that administers salt to Denham's wound. One way to read this would be to suggest that Swinburne places every actor in the scene of flogging in the position of the masochist: that Denham's pleasure is achieved through his being beaten by beating. I think it is more accurate, however, to say that whipping, as Swinburne figures it, frustrates masochistic as well as sadistic narratives by troubling subjecthood itself in the intense scene of flagellation.

FLOGGING TALK

This flogging absorbs the evening's dinner-talk. One guest, Mr. Linley, "a scholar and collector, fond of books, coins, prints, and bric-a-brac of a secret kind, kept under locks and behind curtains," becomes sarcastically and sadistically attached to the idea of Herbert's whipping (*LB*, 231). In the actual scene of whipping, as read above, sloppy subjectivity frustrated sadistic narratives. However, when whipping becomes an object of discussion, the incomplete or active subjectivity of the scene proper settles, but can be deployed against a boy who still bears its traces. This enables a clear-cut sadistic pleasure for Mr. Linley. He warms up with the horse-breaking metaphor, "The little brother looks as if he could kick now and then; I daresay he wants brushing pretty often: a moderate brushing, about enough to tickle the flies off—they will settle on milk. . . . the boy must be well worth flogging . . . clever enough, you can see by the eyes and mouth, if he were properly brought out . . . A boy not worth his birch must be a blockhead or a blackguard" (*LB*, 236). Mr. Linley promises to "catechize" Herbert that evening, meaning to shame him aloud among the other guests about his recent whipping. Another recently graduated schoolboy at the dinner recognizes the "certain shuffle of body and flush of face unmistakable to any eye trained in a public school." For Bertie, hearing this eighteen-year-old's laughter is "like a swift lash round the loins, and his cheeks caught fire; his fingers turned to thawing ice, the roots of his hair pricked and burnt the skin; he smarted and sickened with helpless shame and horrible fear of the next word or look" (*LB*, 237). Words and looks are the most effective way to bring about the shameful effects of flogging without causing slippage in either the subject or object of the flogging. Herbert's physical discomfort is complicit in his shame, it is what makes it unbearable. His shame in this context is incited by being legible, marked by whipping. The barbs thrown by Mr. Linley and the soon-to-become-sympathetic former schoolboy land square on Herbert's body in a way that actual whippings do not. Verbal productions of the whipping scene construct a subject and hold it in place. Bertie was whipped. Because here the audience is offered Herbert's whole body, there is no slippage in the metonymy between Herbert's butt and Herbert's person. Whipping becomes less referent than index of shame, and the slipperiness associated with the scene itself settles into a conventional grammar. However, these verbal productions are exciting and useful sadistically precisely because they firmly gesture to a place of slippage. Bertie is forced to occupy a position that is unoccupiable. In this sense, the scene of whipping acts like the mobilized closet. Bertie could come out as having been whipped and be saved from being spectacularized by offering himself as a spectacle; but as with coming out around homosexuality, such a scene offers new resistances.[18] Like the grown-up schoolboy who recognizes Bertie's shuffling, Bertie could interpret the physical traces flogging left on his body as belonging to a reference system outside himself and join the adults tossing about mere chaff and bran. It is possible, then, that he could short-circuit Linley's attacks or, by playing along exaggeratedly, show them up for the "poisonous pin-pricks and wasp-stings of puerile cruelty" that they are. The latter seems unlikely, considering how verbally sharp Linley is, and the former implies a certain disassociation from recent violent events of which Bertie seems incapable. Both possible tacks would increase the distance between Bertie and the birch by acknowledging whipping as a system of reference with no particular relevance to Bertie's body—a system whose metonymies flatten particularity and that particularity, convincingly vocabularized, could buck. For instance, the grown-up schoolboy at the dinner party has "grown out of" whipping shame. So could Bertie claim that the whipping made him cry (as it inevitably had at one time or another made every man in the room cry) because it hurt so much and thus cut short the needling Linley offers. These possibilities are offered to show not that Bertie did not know best how to counter his nasty foe, but that Linley's cruelties

are available precisely because Bertie cannot vocabularize (and its amplified cousin: spectacularize) himself in any language but that of flogging.

During this dinner, guests "look birch-rods" at one another, make sar-
castic comments, and enjoy having their "cuts tell." A discussion of the
absent Lesbia Brandon's poetry doubles the conversation back to explicit
flogging. When Herbert maligns Latin verse, Lord Charles Brandon, Lesbia's father and a dimwit, replies, "you'll have a score of reasons not to like
it less by the time you begin your third or fourth half; and you'll hardly
prefer second editions corrected and illustrated with cuts, engraved and
taken on the block, by an eminent hand; plenty of cuts to every school-
book, you know. But a girl who doesn't know what flogging means naturally doesn't hate things that remind a fellow of birch and make him
writhe" (LB, 240). Lesbia writes "like a boy" and always "takes the man's
part" in her poems but does not share every schoolboy's birch-induced
hatred of meter. Lord Brandon goes on to explain how he believes that
"she wanted all her life to be a boy" and how when her governess talked
of marriage, Lesbia talked of suicide. Clearly presented as a lesbian, Lesbia likes writing poetry because she can't "be switched"—switched as a
boy, or switched into a boy who is switched.

After this preamble, where whipping strikes up scintillating chatter,
Lord Wariston begins to retell Bertie's heroic feat of the day. Herbert is
"stung by the sound of his own name," he sits "quivering and wincing
as though again under the birch: his throat swelled and contracted by
turns, his cheeks and eyelids smarted as if touched and pricked by flame"
(LB, 241). Being invoked as a character in even this heroic tale tortures
Bertie with "shame and violated reserve"; he is "bared and branded by
the gross hands of public praise" (LB, 241). Being the center of attention
and being a character in a story shame Bertie. He squirms, represses his
sobs, quivers, winces, tingles, blushes, and smarts. His shame enables
the adults' shameless punning and storytelling and their shamelessness
invokes his shame. For Bertie, being a subject at all, as constituted by
public attention, feels the same as being whipped without whipping's
merciful temporal boundaries and interpellative space. The adults' sadistic attachment to Bertie's stinging butt holds him firmly in place for an
unspecified time. This narrative-making produces a two-phase subject;
in the actual course of a whipping the floggee's subjectivity is mobile,
and attaching to its mobility, as we have seen, is one way Bertie has come
to sort and cathect the intensity of whipping. Subsequent verbal production around whipping, on the other hand, is exactly about pinning face
to butt, freezing the metonymy of the scene whose motility has invoked
a complicated cathexis of intensity.

Mr. Linley calls Herbert over to him. "The torturer had a little pack of questions ready which he used to apply to every boy who came in his way" (LB, 251). He asks: "I want to know when you were flogged last? or are we to understand that you never came too near a birch in your life? Come: you can't look me in the face and say it. You do get a good taste of the twigs now and then, don't you—with all the fresh hard buds on, you know? and they sting, don't they?" (LB, 251) Herbert looks to his sister to help him escape but she has, as usual, receded "some way off." Linley's question is a riff on his earlier talk of Herbert being a "hero in full bud," and is described by the narrator as "the minutest form of trivial tyranny." Linley asks "Mr. Herbert," after he answers with a meek "sometimes" to his earlier question: "will you inform me when the habitual rites of marriage were last solemnized between your person and the birch?" All the metaphors that have been applied to the birch so far, husbandry, horse raising, religious initiation, and marriage, mix, merge, displace, and replace one another throughout Linley's catechism. Linley stops taunting Herbert at "the extreme verge of tears" with the instruction "Don't cry now, though," and an exhortation to Denham to "Flog him well when you do flog him, pray; he will live to be thankful to you" (LB, 252). To make Bertie cry is beside the point, in some way; that would allow Bertie a position as the object of sympathy, thwarting the destabilizing tactics of shame Linley employs. Linley desires the marks of a boy who suffers but will not offer himself as one suffering pain. He has reactivated the "don't blub" shame center of the whipping scene, the only place where a floggee has any agency, in order to show how ineffectual Bertie's agency is, how out of control his boy body is and how little control he has over his own subject-position. When Linley finishes questioning Bertie, he "seemed to inhale his pain and shame like a fine and pungent essence; he laughed with pleasure as he saw how the words burnt and stung" (LB, 252).

THE SWEET SEAT OF THE EMOTIONS

The "work" in the title of chapter 3, "A Day's Work," is Bertie's dealing with the huge whipping he gets from Denham, suffering through a verbally abusive dinner, and, at bedtime, finding an expression for his feelings toward his sister in the language of whipping. As we saw, he says he would enjoy being whipped if she liked, and he would even submit to being killed by her. His day of working through whipping left a "keen hard impression" of "desperate tenderness and violent submission of soul and body to her love," without which his life would have been "mere torture and trouble throughout" (LB, 266). But it is torture and trouble that have enabled the day to be memorable; Bertie would never have declared his love as strongly to his sister and received such solace if the day's physical punishments had not been extreme. The intensity of Bertie's day, which can be called "pain" but with the qualification that "pain" gestures more to the extremity of feeling than to "mere" unpleasure, radiates from his butt. His feeling of himself as a whole person depends on his ass as metonymic referent.

In the first paragraph of chapter 4 Bertie wraps up his time at Ensdon. The abrupt transition suggests that the only story to tell of Bertie's time at Ensdon was his relation to being whipped and how that refracted through his relationship to his sister. Suddenly, the novel sends him off to school. "Away from home and the sea and all common comfortable things, stripped of the lifelong clothing of his life, he felt as one beaten and bare" (*LB*, 267–68). Bertie's body feels like a body fresh from a whipping, because he has been transplanted to a new environment—the inverse of the above example where Bertie's hard whipping enabled him to reach new heights of emotion. Here, the emotion happens, homesickness and loss, and its height is marked by the birch. In other words, the birch has rescripted Bertie's body. Whipping has become a usable language of feeling for him.

A dream Herbert has one night after spending a late-adolescent evening riding fast beside the sea with his friend Lunsford begins Swinburne's more specific theorizing about the anatomy of feeling. So far in the novel, whipping has served as the origin of emotion or intellect. The ass has been the smallest describable piece of the body as it is whipped. Herbert's dream allows us access to a closer view. He wakes with the pounding sound of waves in his ears. He sees "the star of Venus, white and flower-like as he had always seen it, turn into a white rose and come down out of heaven, with a reddening centre that grew as it descended liker and liker a living mouth; but instead of desire he felt horror and sickness at the sight of it, and averted his lips with an effort to utter some prayer or exorcism; vainly for the dreadful mouth only laughed, and came closer. And cheek or chin, eyebrow or eye, there was none; only this mouth; and about it the starry or flowery beams or petals" (*LB*, 281). This "living mouth" amidst a field of white petals has an intense center surrounded by "beams" like a star and sounds less like even an intensely puckered mouth than like an anus. To locate this orifice as particularly the anus, remember the hard horse-ride that immediately preceded the dream where Herbert says to his friend Lunsford, "I say, if I deserve it— as I shall in five minutes [for howling bad poetry]—I wish you'd horsewhip me; I'm so dreadfully happy I know I must be coming to grief" (*LB*, 278). Any strong emotion refers Bertie to his butt and its relation to pain. In response to the dreadful mouth's approach, Herbert "averts his lips." He suffers a "violent revulsion of the spirit" that accompanies the image at its clearest and sweetest smelling.

The sweet smell of Bertie's dream recalls an anecdote from Swinburne's letters. Remembering a tutor who whipped with exquisite sensibility, Swinburne wrote to his friend Richard Monckton Milnes:

> I have known him [to] (I am really speaking now in my own person) prepare the flogging room (*not* with *corduroy* or *onion* but) with burnt scents . . . or choose a *sweet* place out of doors with [the] smell of fir-wood. *This* I call real delicate torment. . . . Once, before giving me a swishing that I had the marks of for more than a month (so declared the fellows I went to swim with) . . . he let me saturate my face with eau-de-Cologne. I conjecture now, on looking back to that 'rosy hour' . . . that, counting on the pungency of the perfume and its power over the nerves, he meant to stimulate and excite the senses by that preliminary pleasure so as to inflict the acuter pain afterwards on their awakened and intensified susceptibility. If he did, I am still gratified to reflect that I beat him; the poor dear old beggar overreached himself, for the pleasure of smell is so excessive and intense in me that even if the smart of birching had been unmixed pain, I could have borne it all the better for that previous indulgence.[19]

This account links the olfactory to the anal seat of pleasure at a "rosy" hour that associates the flower and the redness that Herbert imagines to the sweetness that sickens him. This letter expresses how Swinburne understands the sensation of whipping as only partly pain and how he theorizes sensory stimulation as wired through the butt. It is not just the sense of touch that the birch tickles. Vision, smell, and hearing all have their effects on the process of whipping and are concurrently affected as they are transferred to affects.

The revulsion at clarity and sweet odors in combination with averted lips instantiates at least the ur-knowledge of and the desire for the pleasures of rimming. Rimming would, for the giver or receiver, defy clarity since the act is performed in blinding proximity or screened by the looker's body. The delight in rimming occurs, fantasmatically and often actually, around and among odors that are bodily, funky, and not sweet. The clarity and sweetness that cause revulsion at Bertie's strange kiss seem to have less to do with the perceived image than they do with the perceiving senses. The eyes and nose are involved suddenly in figuring the anus, or for Herbert, even more revoltingly, the anus has begun figuring the other senses.

In Herbert's dream, anal pleasure is clarified as it slips from area to area in the body, from the visual pleasure of the star to the olfactory pleasure of the flower to the anticipated touch of the soft, living mouth. These sense images move from the most distant, the star, to the most proximate, the almost kissable lips. The reddening of the image, as in the reddening of the buttocks after a flogging, indicates heat and intensity and thus amplifies the marks of proximity. The anality of the figure is more especially fitting with what follows about Herbert's fear of the "sterility" of all things. "The torture of the dream was the fancy that these fairest things," all of which arise from the oral/anal image of the star itself, "star and flower, light and music, were all unfruitful and barren; absorbed in their own beauty; consummate in their own life" (*LB*, 282). What sense that can be made of an image being referred to as "barren" or "unfruitful" seems bent on distinguishing an anal from a vaginal image as well as on describing a system of signification peculiar to the anus. The "consummateness" of these images implies that they signify nothing but themselves. These images compel as they torture, urging Bertie to enter their closed system, which is beautiful *because* it is closed but is torturous *at the same time* and for the same reason. Put differently, these images are particularly anal (in that they hover about the anus, and as in this dream, the anus hovers around them) and participate in the logics of whipping that Bertie has pieced together from his experiences.

The "mere torture" of Bertie's day, in "A Day's Work," puffed up to real ecstasy. Torture is the disavowed but not denied understructure of Bertie's ecstasy. Beauty and torture are symbiotic in this scheme, and as we saw in Bertie's "whip me I'm so happy" outburst to Lunsford, may even be constitutive of one another. In this emotional ecosystem, the sterile star/flower/mouth marks the figural intersection of the anus, which the moving dream-image symbolizes, and the meaning system offered Bertie by whipping. Whipping is that which at first is intense bodily sensation and then comes to stand bodily for intense sensation. This closed or "consummate" system hovers around the anus and "fits" it, but in the same vibratory way that the subject "fits" into the whipping narrative. The linguistic system of the whipping scene accounts for the subjects as they slip—that's a big part of the scene's charge—but the slippage will not settle. As long as it won't, the scene remains exciting. When it does, the scene deflates.

Bertie can get his dream to settle only by "an hour's beating of the brain against and about such fancies" (*LB*, 282). Beating's closed system steps forward to replace the anus's closed system as revealed in Bertie's dream.

Bertie repeats the declaration he made to his sister, that he would like to die if it amused her, to Lesbia Brandon when they are out riding together. Ignoring her hints and proddings that she is a lesbian and not interested in him, he stutters, "I would—I don't like trying to say. Only upon my honour, I think, I do quite believe, as far as a fellow can know about himself at all, if you liked, if you thought it would amuse you, I would go right over the cliff there and thank God. I should like to have a chance of pleasing you, making a minute's difference to you" (*LB*, 284). When he made a similar declaration to his sister with satisfactory results, a pinch and declarations of love, he fell happily to sleep with the words, "I'm glad you're not a boy though" (*LB*, 265). Bertie sees the female gender of his object-choice as a relieving postscript rather than as a precondition for his desire. The intensity of Bertie's love is registered for him by the amount of punishment he is willing to undergo for his beloved. This lesson, of intensity as punishment, was taught him by a male, Denham, and Bertie is grateful that the lesson can be transposed without the original intensity-bearer's gender also carrying in the equation.

Bertie first met Lesbia when he was dressed up as a girl for a performance of a play and Lesbia was enthralled with "Helen," this little version of Lady Wariston. The relation of whipping to drag makes an appearance in the above "rosy"-hour-scented-grove letter Swinburne wrote to Richard Monckton Milnes. He sends thanks for a *Punch* advertisement Monckton Milnes sent to him. The ad read: "Wanted, a Young Lady, about 20, as Housekeeper to a Widower, and to take charge of three boys, the eldest ten years old. Must be of good appearance and address; accomplishments not essential. . . . Address, stating age, and if willing to give corporal punishment."[20] Swinburne replies, assuming that the man in the ad is looking for a woman to flog him, "Ah heaven, to run back but four years! would you believe that at that time I did quite well (that is, I was a *credible* being—I don't say *attractive!*) in female attire, and should have been invaluable on a pinch of theatrical necessities. . . . Now, alas! had I that chance left which my majority bereft me of, quelle chance! The wildest flattery of friendship could not now aver that even shaving and rouge would make a presentable girl of me."[21] This letter furthers the suggestion that both flogger and floggee are substitutable in the scene of a whipping, substitutable down to their gender. It also suggests that drag and the positions of the flogging scene fit snug to one another. They correspond.

Lesbia, the woman who writes "like a boy," "takes the man's position," and tells Bertie that she should have been his older brother, never dons boy clothes. Swinburne writes her in the inversion model of homosexuality, where she is trapped in a woman's body, while harboring the emotional life deemed appropriate to a man. But Lesbia's fondness for Herbert, who looks like Lady Wariston especially in drag (as in the situation in which Denham beats the Lady Wariston into Bertie), sidesteps any simple inversion model. Yes, Lesbia tells Bertie that "there must be no more love-making," but she also says, "If I could love and marry, I am sure I could love and marry you, absurd as people would call it. But I can't. I don't know why, at least I don't wholly know. I am made as I am" (LB, 285). It is Bertie whom Lesbia calls to her deathbed, and she notes that others might consider him her lover. She says, "I want company, and—well! love. You care for me; sit still and be a good boy to me, and brother" (LB, 344). Lesbia configures her love for Bertie as looking like but not consisting of sexual relations. Bertie can love her, partly because he is substitutable as his sister, partly also because she is. As sadistic or masochistic narratives are frustrated in this novel, so is an inversion model, because in a scene of extremity, a whipping or a death, a person of one gender can smear into the identity of a person of another gender. This is not to say that Lesbia's lesbianism is not written as inversion, only to say that inversion never wholly takes hold because of the way identification partially frustrates its basic category, gender.

When they first meet, Lesbia quite likes Bertie as Helen. They pay exclusive attention to one another, discussing what plays they'd like to act together. Unfortunately this chapter is cut short just as Lesbia and Helen are really getting friendly. The drag scene, the scene of Herbert's frustrated lovemaking (where he says he'll jump off a cliff), and the scene of Lesbia's death are all that remain of Lesbia and Herbert's relationship. Each scene hinges on Herbert's frustrated love, which was initiated by the interest he kindled in Lesbia by his dressing up as a girl and resembling his sister, whom Lesbia adores. The final scene of them together, in the chapter "Leucadia" (named after the place where Sappho threw herself from a cliff), has Lesbia dying "with the help of eau-de-Cologne and doses of opium." She reports a dream in which she saw Lady Wariston "fall over a cliff." She narrates it further, "But in my dreams she didn't fall herself; somebody pushed her, I think I did. . . . I should like to see you as you were that first time. You couldn't go and dress up now, though I have seen women with as much hair about the lips" (LB, 349). Soon after this ramble Lesbia expires, quietly.

The first suggestion of cliff jumping comes from Herbert who offers to jump off a cliff for Lesbia, then the chapter title "Leucadia" refers to Sappho, frustrated in love, jumping off a cliff, then Lesbia dreams of pushing Lady Wariston off a cliff. As far as the novel is concerned, Herbert's desire serves as a prototype, a prototype based on his lesson in

"A Day's Work" that intensity is a many vectored whipping. Lesbia seems to be taking Herbert's earlier offer to her and using it in her own fantasies.

Notably, in this novel, no one goes over a cliff, not even Lesbia who is set up with all the mythic accoutrements. She dies quietly in her bed. Lady Wariston lives on quietly with her boring husband, and the narrator finishes with Bertie by stating, "As for him, I cannot say what he has done or will do, but I should think, nothing" (LB, 353). All this when the cliff's edge is but a clause away. The "nothing" that Bertie has and perhaps will continue to perform at the novel's close makes sense with the mechanics of whipping. At bottom, whipping's strongest lesson is the motility of the subject. Subjects are slippery and can for the span of an intense whipping elude narrative. Contrary to the arguments of the intra-novel proponents of whipping as pedagogic tool, perhaps whipping actually proliferates sensations that look like whacking good strong limbs on a boy but like diffusion or dilution on a man.

We can trace the structure of cliff-tossing back to Bertie's relation to whipping: Bertie learned to negotiate intensity/pain from whipping, he practiced on his sister and he got good returns; he then tries again on Lesbia and is rebuffed, but Lesbia takes up the ball and fantasizes with it. It is the very logic of whipping, as opposed to the logic of masochism, or Wertherism for that matter, that prevents the cliff introduced in the first act from being shot off in the last. Of these characters, Lesbia suffers the greatest alteration, she dies, but that death is like a sliding off of life. After saying goodbye to Bertie she "put her hand out, dropped it, turned her face to the cushion, sighing, opened her eyes, and died" (LB, 350). The list of intentional activities slides into the event of her death, suggesting that she performed that act with the same agency that put her hand out to Bertie.

She hardly seems dead, or rather, the faucet of her agency has been closed with a very light turn. To adjust for this, Swinburne adds one of the strangest and least metrically graceful lines of the whole novel as the final paragraph of "Leucadia": "And that was the last of Lesbia Brandon, poetess and pagan" (LB, 350). What made Lesbia alive as a character seems equally active after her death. If the sea can come to life in this novel, the reader might ask, can Lesbia ever be utterly dead? In the same way that the novel leaves Lesbia incompletely dead, it also leaves Lady Wariston and her brother half alive.

As the vivifying principle of the novel, whipping makes characters legible as living beings in their susceptibility to extremes. Extremes, as imagistically rendered by Swinburne in his descriptions of the sea, attach a face to an otherwise unagented body. The oscillation, then, between the face and body provides the activity that reads as life. Novelistic closure therefore poses a problem for *Lesbia Brandon;* closure is at once the extreme limit of the novel but also the stepping-off point for the characters left living. They step off into nothing because the novel, after closing, acknowledges that it can no longer provide vivifying extremes for them.

Flogging constitutes the fantasmatic and theoretic core of *Lesbia Brandon.* The novel delivers "sting and tickle" either directly, by sensual detail and scenic mechanics, or by systems of affect and novelistic practice for which the fantasmatics of flogging are fundamental. The novel's prime goal and prime achievement is not to make us all take it and like it, but rather, and perhaps to the detriment of giving a verb to our subject, to make us smart.

NOTES

1 A. C. Swinburne, *The Novels of A. C. Swinburne.*, ed. Edmund Wilson (New York: Noonday; Farrar, Straus and Cudahy, 1962), pp. 359–60.

2 Philip Henderson, *Swinburne: Portrait of a Poet* (New York: Macmillan, 1974), p. 211.

3 Jean Overton Fuller, *Swinburne: A Biography* (New York: Schocken Books, 1968), p. 260.

4 Ian Gibson, *The English Vice: Beating, Sex and Shame in Victorian England and After* (London: Duckworth, 1978), p. 306.

5 Fuller, *Swinburne*, p. 260.

6 Edmund Wilson, introduction to *Lesbia Brandon*, in *The Novels of A. C. Swinburne*, p. 37. Citations to *Lesbia Brandon*, collected in this volume, will be abbreviated *LB* and given parenthetically in the text.

7 Gilles Deleuze, *Masochism*, ed. Jean McNeil (New York: Zone, 1991), pp. 45–46.

8 Ibid., pp. 19–20.

9 A. C. Swinburne, *Lesbia Brandon*, ed. and with *An historical and critical commentary being largely a study (and elevation) of Swinburne as a novelist* by Randolph Hughes (London: Falcon Press, 1952), p. 383.

10 A. C. Swinburne, *The Swinburne Letters*, ed. Cecil Y. Lang, 6 vols. (New Haven: Yale University Press, 1962) 1:55, letter no. 34.

11 Ibid., pp. 56–57.

12 Ibid., p. 224, letter no. 174.

13 Randolph Hughes reports that Lafourcade recorded part of chapter 1 "as being in the possession of Mr. Payen-Payne (who died some years ago)" (p. 466). This name is either a punning concoction of one with a taste for the birch or a fabulous historical accident.

14 Gibson, *English Vice*, p. 321.

15 In Swinburne's poem "Frankie Fane—A Ballad," Frankie's butt is compared to a map: "So the cane on his shoulders / Went rat-a-tap-tap, / And in turns they examined / His bum like a map; / Such outlines! Such island / Such mountains of weals! / And such pretty red rivers / Running down toward the heels!" (Gibson, *English Vice*, p. 327). Besides being really graceful verse, this little stanza performs the photographic negative of what happens in the beginning of *Lesbia Brandon:* The beaten ass provides a morph for the landscape as in this last example the landscape provided a morph for the beaten ass.

16 Gibson, *English Vice*, p. 322.

17 Jerome J. McGann, *Swinburne: An Experiment in Criticism* (Chicago: University of Chicago Press, 1972), p. 277.

18 See Eve Kosofsky Sedgwick, *Epistemology of the Closet* (Berkeley: University of California Press, 1990), pp. 67–90.

19 Swinburne, *Letters*, p. 78, letter no. 45.

20 Ibid., p. 76 n.

21 Ibid., p. 77.

PART IV   Men and Nations

Jacob Press

Same-Sex Unions in Modern Europe:

Daniel Deronda, Altneuland, and the

Homoerotics of Jewish Nationalism

I expounded my subject.
The Chief Rabbi remarked: "That is the idea of *Daniel Deronda*."
—Theodor Herzl[1]

In the spring of 1895, the Hungarian-born, Austrian-educated, and German-identified playwright and journalist Theodor Herzl experienced a psychotic break/political epiphany, in the wake of which he announced himself as a Jewish nationalist leader. The remaining decade of Herzl's short life was an extended suicide through exhaustion, as he bankrupted himself financially, physically, and psychologically in the creation of a worldwide movement devoted to the achievement of political autonomy for the Jewish people. By the time of his death, in 1904, he had convened six international Zionist Congresses and founded the World Zionist Organization, the nationalist newspaper *Die Welt*, and the Jewish Colonial Trust—institutions that ultimately evolved into the modern State of Israel. Theodor Herzl has become an iconic figure for modern Jews; his portrait is the only one in the Israeli parliament.

Herzl's vocation as a writer of drama served to structure his career as a nationalist politician: this man became the representative of international Jewry in the courts of the European powers by taking it upon himself to play the role. The decision to "represent" the Jewish people as an European nation in search of a state performatively enacted both Herzl's own transformation (into a foreign diplomat in the countries where he had spent his life, for instance), and, indeed, the transformation of the Jewish people (from a polity defined variously in religious, ethnic, cultural, and racial terms into a political nationality in need of geographic reconstitution). It is no accident that Herzl's best known saying teaches the malleability of "reality": "If you will it, it is not a dream."[2] Herzlian Zionism is the revolution of the imagination; it is fantastic realpolitik.

The performance of early Zionism was undoubtedly high drama, but

Herzl himself had much initial difficulty in determining the genre of this real-ist fiction. Perhaps, he thought, Zionism is a novel. Immediately upon his epiphany, Herzl began writing compulsively, and the first entry in his new diary noted of his new political fantasy that

> as a dream it is remarkable and should be written down—if not as a memorial for mankind, then for my own pleasure and meditation in years to come. Or perhaps something between these two possibilities—that is, as something for literature. If no action comes out of this romancing, a Romance at least will come out of this activity. Title: *The Promised Land.*
>
> In truth I no longer know whether, after all, it was not the novel that first came to my mind.[3]

Herzl imagines his idea in the form of a purely personal record, and then as an overtly propagandist pamphlet: enabling such confusion is a distinctively Herzlian conviction of the fiction of politics, wherein the various categories of text are virtually conflated, engulfed within the primary category of political fiction. Herzl's final determination is in favor of Zionism as a reformist novel, a comfortably ambiguous medium between the other possibilities. The nineteenth-century political novel at its most complex is a site in which philosophically abstract principles are tested at work in the lives of psychologically nuanced individuals who in turn are placed within a richly mapped social web. Protagonists move from a state of anomie to embeddedness, often by reconstituting themselves through the discovery of hidden-though-structuring truths about themselves and the larger groups of which they are a part. Zionism is a perfect fit with the cognitive contours of the nineteenth-century novel.

Theodor Herzl was not alone in appreciating the novelism of Zion: George Eliot felt similarly. *Daniel Deronda,* Eliot's mammoth final work, had articulated a vision of Jewish national rebirth to the British public in 1878, nearly twenty years before Herzl debuted in London, performing himself and his own scheme (at the invitation of the Anglo-Jewish literary celebrity Israel Zangwill). Herzl's diary records that Hermann Adler, the Chief Rabbi of Britain, responded to his Zionist pitch by commenting, "That is the idea of *Daniel Deronda.*" The Rabbi was right: George Eliot's novelistic fantasy of Jewish politics and Herzl's novelistic politics of Jewish fantasy are richly resonant texts. Indeed, a juxtaposition of these two visions can foreground otherwise elusive textures and subtexts characteristic of the larger nineteenth-century European nationalist imagination. Specifically: Eliot theorizes (Jewish) nationalism as an intervention in nineteenth-century European political homoerotics, and her novel positions the Zionist movement on the map of Victorian gender ideology with exquisite subtlety and insight: seen in this context, Herzl's political fantasies, too, emerge, at their most fundamental level, as a Jewish male apotheosization of an othered European masculinity. The Zionist novels of both Eliot and Herzl commence with the characterization of Jewish male protagonists in a state of radical alienation from the modern European imperative of aggressive heterosexual masculinity. Novels tend to end in marriage: both Eliot and Herzl's nationalist novels end in a marriage of men.

In *Daniel Deronda,* George Eliot juxtaposes two almost entirely self-contained novel-length narratives. In one, Gwendolen Harleth, a captivating young woman whose most valuable resource is her own stunning beauty, ensnares but is ultimately ensnared by an aristocratic and sadistic husband, Sir Mallinger Grandcourt. In the other, Daniel Deronda, a handsome young gentleman of unknown parentage, discovers that he is of Jewish descent and becomes a disciple of his friend Mordecai Cohen, finding a vocation in devotion to the national regeneration of the Jewish people. At the novel's end, the love of Gwendolen is rejected by Deronda, as he marries Mordecai's sister Mirah and the newlyweds depart for Palestine.

For a number of years now, the question of the title character's circumcision has formed a minor but recurrent theme in Deronda criticism. It all began with the third footnote of Steven Marcus's 1975 essay, "Human Nature, Social Orders, and 19th Century Systems of Explanation." The note in question—which may well have generated more interest than the essay it is appended to—draws the reader's attention to an observation made by the then graduate student Lennard Davis: "Mr. Davis has discovered a detail—or a missing detail—in *Daniel Deronda* that throws the whole central plot of the novel out of kilter. . . . In order for the plot of *Daniel Deronda* to work, Deronda's circumcised penis must be invisible, or nonexistent."[4] In Davis's and Marcus's views, Eliot has made Deronda's belated discovery of his Jewish identity central to her plot— and this plot's incoherence is exposed by the exposure of Deronda's circumcised penis. Eliot's plot requires her to confront the physical reality of the phallus, but Eliot merely closes her eyes. Marcus argues that this seeming inconsistency exposes a fatal chink in Eliot's realist armor "characteristic . . . of both George Eliot and the culture she was representing." Cynthia Chase was the first critic to integrate this "problem" into a larger reading of Eliot's novel. Her masterful essay—"The Decomposition of the Elephants: Double-Reading *Daniel Deronda*"—explores in greater detail the ways in which Eliot's narrative mode might be considered to be self-consuming. "The plot can function only if *la chose,* Deronda's circumcised penis, is disregarded; yet the novel's realism and referentiality function precisely to draw attention to it." In Chase's reading, Daniel Deronda's circumcised penis cannot be swallowed comfortably by the novel; the Eliotic pretense of a textual mirror of an inherently rational world operating according to the laws of causality is punctured by the visible yet unacknowledgeable phallus, which exposes the many ideological implications of this particular "realism."[5]

K. M. Newton was next to address this issue, in 1981, and he makes some surprising discoveries. Newton notes that Eliot, in shaping her plot, could easily have arranged for Deronda to have been passed off to his British guardian immediately after his birth, thus eliminating the alleged "incoherence" around circumcision—instead, the narration specifies that Deronda was two years old at the time of his transfer, providing the necessary information to confirm Deronda's circumcised status. Further, Newton notes that—contra Davis, Marcus, and Chase—circumcision in Victorian England did not necessarily signify Jewishness. Beginning in the mid-nineteenth century, the surgical removal of the foreskin was an increasingly common medical procedure: the operation was advocated as a means of encouraging "cleanliness," diminishing sexual desire, and inhibiting masturbation.[6] Circumcision would, thus, to a Victorian boy, have had an ambiguous significatory potential: it might indicate Jewish origin, but it might also indicate a distinctly hygienic or sexual dysfunction for which he had been punished/treated.[7]

Newton cites a number of passages to support his view that Eliot, rather than evading the question of circumcision, deliberately integrates it into the novel. Newton's argument relies most strongly on the following lines, in which the narrator describes Deronda's reaction to Mordecai's early and seemingly foundationless intuition that Deronda is a Jew. "The claim hung, too, on a supposition which might be—nay, probably was—in discordance with the full fact: the supposition that he, Deronda, was of Jewish blood. Was there ever a more hypothetic appeal?"[8] Newton points out that the conditionality of the entire passage mirrors the status of circumcision in Victorian England: Jewishness is a possible interpretation, but a merely hypothetical one. Newton's thesis would be even more strongly supported, however, by a closer look at the beginning of this passage: the opening words of this sentence have the claim of Jewishness "hanging" on an apparently peg-like supposition that can easily be seen as the circumcised but still ambiguously signifying penis. Deronda's theoretical Jewishness becomes a question of how to interpret his marked phallus.

There is much textual evidence to support this interpretation. In fact, a focus on the foreskin not only fells the fiction of a phallus fallacy in this novel, it reveals the central role that both metaphoric and literal circumcision play in Eliot's conceptualization of Deronda's psychology and his relationship to nineteenth-century masculinity. The deconstructionist exposure of the incoherence of Eliotic "realism" remains unchallenged; but in the case of *Daniel Deronda*, it is clear that this insight has been piggybacking on a caricature of Eliot as the victim of a blinding Victorian priggishness. Eliot need not be read in this way. The author of *Daniel Deronda* paints its main character's decentered passivity as the consequence of his psychological and physical circumcision; Eliot thematizes Deronda's shame about his penis/parentage as a metaphor for what she reads as the nonphallic faux masculinity of the man whose consciousness and loyalties are European but who is nonetheless marked in his gender as a Jewish other.

While Deronda plays a major role in the famous casino scene that opens the novel, he is quickly shunted aside by the absorbing tale of Gwendolen's courtship and marriage to Grandcourt. In fact, he does not re-emerge in the novel that bears his name until the equally famous chapter 16, in which Eliot sketches the psychological outline of her character's character. Chapter 16 opens with one of Eliot's signature epigraphs — self-penned, in oblique relation to the text which follows: "Men, like planets, have both a visible and an invisible history. The astronomer threads the darkness with strict deduction, accounting so for every visible arc in the wanderer's orbit; and the narrator of human actions, if he did his work with the same completeness, would have to thread the hidden pathways of feeling and thought which lead up to every moment of action, and to those moments of intense suffering which take the quality of action" (202). Eliot scientistically cloaks her narrative project in the legitimizing vocabulary of astronomy. But hers is a narrative scientism that shares much with Freud: she argues that human behavior must be interpreted in relation to a developmental trajectory in which the "invisible" past is always threaded into present behavior; in particular, Eliot stresses the centrality of trauma — "those moments of intense suffering which take the quality of action" — as vital constituting elements of this identity-constituting narrative thread.

The epigraph prepares the reader to receive a case history, and that is what Eliot writes in this chapter, wasting no time in zeroing in on the scene of wounding she presents as determinative of Deronda's psychological profile. "One moment had been burnt into his life as its chief epoch." Deronda was thirteen years old, immersed in a book under the supervision of his tutor on an idyllic summer afternoon. However, the scene soon becomes one of horror: the tutor offhandedly remarks that the illegitimate children of popes are referred to as their nephews, and

Deronda suddenly concludes that he must be the illegitimate child of the Uncle Hugo who has raised him. "The uncle whom he loved very dearly took the aspect of a father who held secrets about him—who had done him a wrong—yes, a wrong" (206). This newly discovered mystery of primal victimization at the hands of his father is presented as the central—indeed, the only—key to understanding who Deronda is: "a secret impression had come to him which had given him something like a new sense in relation to all the elements of his life" (207). Deronda's relationship to the world has been entirely transformed by the traumatic self-consciousness of his shameful birth.

Eliot consistently invokes the language of circumcision in her exploration of these themes. In describing Deronda's internalization of what he perceives to be his paternal victimization, the reader is pointed toward a specifically bodily pain: Deronda "was feeling the injury done him as a maimed boy feels the crushed limb which for others is merely reckoned in an average of accidents" (209). Similar imagery can be found in the conclusion that "it was already a cutting thought that such knowledge might be in other minds" (209), and "he would never bring himself near even a silent admission of the sore that had opened in him" (210). Somewhat more explicit is the narrator's reference to "a grief within, which might be compared in some ways with Byron's susceptibility about his deformed foot" (213). And the issue comes within micrometers of puncturing the surface of the text in the following lines: "The sense of an entailed disadvantage—the deformed foot doubtfully hidden by the shoe, makes a restlessly active spiritual yeast, and easily turns a self-centered, unloving nature into an Ishmaelite" (215)⁹ The biblical commandment of Jewish circumcision is first carried out by Abraham upon his thirteen-year-old son, Ishmael. In spite of this, Ishmael and Hagar, his concubine mother, were later expelled into the desert, displaced in favor of Isaac (Gen. 17:1–27; 21). Their outcast status is the origin of the sense in which Eliot uses the term "Ishmaelite" here—to mean "one at war with society." Far from repressing circumcision as unassimilable, Eliot thematizes it, using it as her primary metaphor for the thirteen-year-old Deronda's traumatic initiation into shameful difference.

It is not coincidental that Deronda's crisis concerning the nature of his origins provokes a frenzy of circumcision imagery: the only clues he has as to his parentage are to be found on his own body. "His own face in the glass had during many years been associated for him with thoughts of some one whom he must be like" (226). And Deronda *has* been circumcised. He remembers it: "He had always called Sir Hugo Mallinger his uncle, and when it once occurred to him to ask about his father and mother, the baronet had answered, 'You lost your father and mother when you were quite a little one; that is why I take care of you.' Daniel then straining to discern some thing in that early twilight, had a dim sense of having been kissed very much, and surrounded by thin, cloudy, scented drapery, till his fingers caught in something hard, which hurt him, and he began to cry. Every other memory he had was of the little world in which he still lived" (203). The shock of the possibility of a disgraceful parentage jolts Deronda into sudden, displaced recollection of the childhood trauma of circumcision—there is no other possible interpretation of this passage that would lift it above gibberish. Eliot thus presents Deronda's foundational trauma as twofold: it is a psychological circumcision, but one which powerfully echoes the actual physical event.

Eliot is specific in describing the consequences of Deronda's psychological/physical circumcision, worked out through paranoia: "And the idea that others probably knew things concerning him which they did not choose to mention, set up in him a premature reserve which helped to intensify his inward experience. His ears were open now to words which before that July day would have passed by him unnoted; and round every trivial incident which imagination could connect with his suspicions, a newly-roused set of feelings were ready to cluster themselves" (207). He has become initiated into the lonely universe of the child with a closeted difference: in seeking the answer to the mystery of his own status as Other, Deronda is thrown back upon his own ability to interpret the way in which he is interpreted. Constantly measuring himself as against the world in which he lives, the boy becomes withdrawn ("Daniel immediately shrank into reserve" [213]), hypersensitive ("there was hardly a delicacy of feeling this lad was not capable of" [207]), receptive ("His ears were open now" [207]). As a young man, these tendencies become problematic: "[He] was gliding farther and farther from that life of practically energetic sentiment which he would have proclaimed (if he had been inclined to proclaim anything) to be the best of all life. . . . Meanwhile he had not yet set about one function in particular with zeal and steadiness" (414). Deronda's sense that his identity is shameful, combined with his sense that some others (which others?) are aware of this fact, draw him away from the world of action, agency, and assertion into a directionless drift of indifference, ennui, and enervation. The above sentences are followed with an extremely explicit reminder of the roots of Deronda's disorder: "Not an admirable experience, to be proposed as an ideal; but a form of struggle before break of day which some young men since the patriarch have had to pass through, with more or less of bruising if not laming" (414). Deronda's disinclination for self-assertion, his aversion to all energetic application, is read as an extension of the process of phallic othering: the patriarch here is Abraham; the "struggle before the break of day" is both infant circumcision and adolescent identity crisis; the consequences, literal and metaphorical, are "bruising if not laming."

Indeed, Deronda may be among the lamed. " 'Deronda would have been first-rate if he had had more ambition'—was a frequent remark about him" (218). The young man is adrift—quite literally, in this passage: "He lay with his hands behind his head propped on a level with the boat's edge, so that he could see all around him, but could not be seen. . . . He was forgetting everything else in a half-speculative, half-involuntary identification of himself with the objects he was looking at, thinking how far it might be possible habitually to shift his centre till his own personality would be no less outside him than the landscape" (229). Deronda allows himself to be passively swept along by the current, pure receptivity. Seeing but unseen, he fantasizes about withdrawing entirely from the human world, identifying profoundly, not even with other humans, but with inanimate objects. As a consequence of his traumatically discovered and shamefully closeted difference, Deronda refuses agency. Deronda's circumcised phallus refuses insertion/assertion in the world. In constructing Deronda's psychological profile, Eliot outlines what was to become the classic Zionist critique of the pathology of the non-national Jew: Deronda's shaming difference traumatically problematizes and permanently bars his embrace of the identity of the English-man: "what he most longed for was . . . the influence that would justify partiality, and making him what he longed to be yet was unable to make himself—an organic part of social life, instead of roaming in it like a yearning disembodied spirit" (413). Deronda longs for incorporation into the British body politic, yet his desire is self-defeating: "organic" connections, by their nature, cannot be "made." Instead, Deronda is exiled into the realm of the "disembodied spirit." The legitimacy of his very existence is undermined by his inability to be seamlessly social. Faced with his sense of alienation, he seems to have no choice but to cease to exist. Except . . .

A movement for the national regeneration of the Jewish people—as constructed by Eliot's novel, this is the only hope for the normalization of Deronda's alienated impotence. Daniel Deronda—the assimilated Jew who nonetheless carries the mark of (sexual) difference within him—is saved by his marriage to Mordecai—a vulgar Jew whose political vision is nonetheless radically emancipatory. Mordecai initiates Deronda into a homosocial brotherhood that reconciles the identity categories of "Jew" and "man."

While drifting in his boat on the Thames, Deronda encounters Mirah Lapidoth, a homeless, suicidal, and beautiful Jewess who has come to London in search of her mother. Deronda lodges Mirah with his friend

Hans's family, and very ambivalently sets out in search of her relatives, fearful of the Jewish vulgarity he will very likely find. His investigations on Mirah's behalf take him to the Jewish ghetto of London, and his visit to a bookstore here first brings him into contact with Mordecai Cohen: "A man in threadbare clothing, whose age was difficult to guess—from the dead yellowish flatness of the flesh. . . . It was a finely typical Jewish face" (436). Mordecai, in turn, is fascinated by Deronda.

> Deronda felt a thin hand pressing his arm tightly, while a hoarse, excited voice, not much above a loud whisper, said—
> "You are perhaps of our race?"
> Deronda coloured deeply, not liking the grasp, and then answered with a slight shake of the head, "No." (437)

Mordecai breaks the physical wall that might have been expected between a gentleman and a shop worker, grabbing Deronda's arm, whispering in his ear, and gambling on their fellowship. He is rebuffed by a Deronda who finds such intimacy repellant. Yet, later that week, when Deronda finds himself sharing a meal with Mordecai on a subsequent visit to the ghetto, it appears that this refusal was not meant as a rejection. Deronda does not even notice what he is eating, in part because he is preoccupied "with thinking of Mordecai, between whom and himself there was an exchange of fascinated, half-furtive glances" (449).

When the reader is finally treated to an extended discussion of the nature of Mordecai's mysterious character, what was implicit in these two scenes becomes entirely explicit: Mordecai has a thing for high-class types.

> Some years had now gone since he had first begun to measure men with a keen glance. . . . he wanted to find a man who differed from himself. . . . he imagined a man who would have all the elements necessary for sympathy with him, but in an embodiment unlike his own: he must be a Jew, intellectually cultured, morally fervid—in all this a nature ready to be plenished from Mordecai's; but his face and frame must be beautiful and strong, he must have been used to all the refinements of social life, his voice must flow with a free and easy current, his circumstances free from sordid need: he must glorify the possibilities of the Jew, not sit and wander as Mordecai did, bearing the stamp of his people amid the signs of poverty and waning breath. (528–29)

Mordecai, "stamped" and "signed" as a poor and diseased Jew—he is dying of tuberculosis—knows exactly what he wants. Mordecai's fantasy is of man—beautiful, strong, refined, and rich, but willing to be dominated by Mordecai's will; bearing no outward signifiers of Jewishness, but nonetheless lovingly embracing this identity. In another passage, this Jew's consuming passion for the powerful European male body is further developed:

> in a vacant hour he had sometimes lingered in the National Gallery in search of . . . a face at once young, grand, and beautiful, where, if there is any melancholy, it is no feeble passivity, but enters into the foreshadowed capability of heroism.
>
> Some observant persons may perhaps remember his emaciated figure, and dark eyes deep in their sockets, as he stood in front of a picture that had touched him. . . . spectators would be likely to think of him as an odd-looking Jew. (529)

The portraits of the National Gallery are envisioned, through Mordecai's eyes, as a virtually pornographic parade of heroic constructions of the national male body, a temple of British masculinity at which the virtually disembodied Jew worships. He views the Other in silent awe; the Other views him with detached curiosity. Mordecai desires both to be and to love a Prince: "as the more beautiful, the stronger, the more executive self took shape in his mind, he loved it beforehand with an affection half identifying, half contemplative" (530). Mordecai's desire for such a man is constructed in direct relation to both his own bodily decay and his messianic ambitions of still unspecified content: " 'New writing of mine would be like this body'—Mordecai spread his arms—'within it there might be the Ruach-ha-kodesh—the breath of divine thought—but men would smile at it and say, "A poor Jew!"—and the chief smilers would be of my own people' " (557).

Thus, it is no surprise that when Mordecai sees Deronda, it is love at first sight—Mordecai has been waiting for him. "[Mordecai] saw a face and frame which seemed to him to realise the long-conceived type" (536). Mordecai's intensive cultivation of an idealized image of the male body has prepared him to "recognize" the person of Deronda. Mordecai has been remembering him, although they have never met.

This enthusiasm on Mordecai's part is not unreciprocated—it may be that a love affair with Mordecai is exactly what Deronda needs. He is frustrated by his relationships: "he had never had a confidant to whom he could open himself. . . . He had always been leaned on instead of being invited to lean" (526). Deronda is admired and depended upon by Mirah, Gwendolen, Hans, Hans's extended family, and most everyone else in the novel. But "he had found it impossible to reciprocate confidences with one who looked up to him" (527). He seeks a different dynamic; Mordecai is ready to set that dynamic in motion. The above-cited passage, thematizing Deronda's exasperation with deferential interactions, is followed by a description of Mordecai's obsessive fantasy: "all his passionate desire had concentrated itself in the yearning for some young ear into which he could pour his mind as a testament, some soul kindred enough to accept the spiritual product of his own brief, painful life, as a mission to be executed" (528). Mordecai wants to—spiritually—penetrate a young man. He is looking for nothing except an aesthetically appropriate receptacle into which to release himself. Deronda longs to be dominated; Mordecai is looking for someone to dominate. It is a match made in heaven.

The love affair between Deronda and Mordecai quickly reaches great heights of intensity. Deronda returns to the ghetto yet again in order to seek out Mordecai, although he claims not to be sure why. This time, he is clearly not advancing the search for Mirah's family. "[T]he two men, with as intense a consciousness as if they had been two undeclared lovers, felt themselves alone in the small gas-lit book-shop and turned face to face, each baring his head from an instinctive feeling that they wished to see each other fully. Mordecai came forward to lean his back against the little counter, while Deronda stood against the opposite wall hardly more than four feet off" (552). Dimmed lights, private space, physical self-revelation, and bodily proximity: the encounter between these "undeclared lovers" is electric with erotic energy. The physicality of the two men is evoked in a relentlessly sensual manner—the tight focus of the descriptive frame brings the reader's eye into close proximity with Mordecai's body, evoking the very feel of his breath, his "hair and beard still black throwing out the yellow pallor of the skin, the difficult breathing giving more decided marking to the mobile nostril, the wasted yellow hands conspicuous on the folded arms" (553). This man—described earlier as of "typically Jewish" countenance—has finally got what he always has dreamed of: "opposite to him was a face not more distinctively oriental than many a type among what we call the Latin races: rich in youthful health, and with a forcible masculine gravity in its repose." Deronda is manly in appearance, passive in inclination; Mordecai is wasting away physically, yet even the color of his skin is aggressively "throw[n] out," like the breath of his nostrils. As this passage continues to stress, Deronda finds himself relating to Mordecai with a "submissive expectancy" (551): "Receptiveness is a rare and massive power, like fortitude; and this state of mind now gave Deronda's face its utmost expression of calm benignant force—an expression which nourished Mordecai's confidence and made an open way before him" (553). Up to this point, Deronda's passivity with respect to outside forces has been the subject of consistent critique—but in this passage it is suddenly reconstructed, and Deronda's ability to accept a receptive fellowship with Mordecai is envisioned as a "rare and massive power." In Deronda's union with Mordecai he has found a form of manly unmanning.

One of the many curious characteristics of this novel is that, although it is famous for its imagination of a proto-Zionism, the actual articulation of this politics is utterly marginalized. There are only three passages in nine hundred pages of text that address themselves explicitly to the question of Jewish nationalism. This displacement carries through to the relationship between Mordecai and Deronda as well. Mordecai's urgent need for a young man is repeatedly expressed as a need for a spiritual and ideological repository for his idiosyncratic political vision. Yet, Mordecai and Deronda meet repeatedly, in a variety of different circumstances, before Mordecai's continual and veiled allusions to his spiritual legacy finally culminate in its presentation.

This climactic event occurs in a carefully contrived setting: Mordecai invites Deronda to a meeting of a ghetto-based "Philosophers' Club" that meets periodically at a local pub, "The Hand and Banner." When Deronda arrives, he sees a "new and striking scene": "Half-a-dozen men of various ages, from between twenty and thirty to fifty, all shabbily dressed, most of them with clay pipes in their mouths, were listening with a look of concentrated intelligence to a man . . . holding his pipe slightly uplifted in the left hand, and beating his knee with the right" (580). This is a "boys' night out"; the space of the "Philosophers' Club" is envisioned as definitively homosocial. "Each orders beer or some other kind of drink. . . . Most of them smoke" (580). There are no women present, nor would they be admitted; vices are freely indulged — and why are there no teenagers, and no one over fifty? The words of the speaker are important to the narrator, but so are his "beating" gestures, his knee, his pipe. The setting for the political discourse of the "Philosophers' Club" is definitively gendered and embodied.

As it turns out, the men are discussing "the law of progress," and in short order they provoke Mordecai into an unscheduled exposition of his nationalist views. First, he attacks those Jews who privilege their adopted nationality over their loyalty to the Jewish people. "What is the citizenship of him who walks among a people he has no hearty kindred and fellowship with, and has lost the sense of brotherhood with his own race? . . . He is an alien in spirit, whatever he may be in form; he sucks the blood of mankind, he is not a man. Sharing in no love, sharing in no subjection of the soul, he mocks at all" (587). The non-national Jew — who sounds suspiciously like Deronda — is a traitor who cannot be trusted. He has spurned the love his people has offered him — dare any other people risk the same fate at his hands? Mordecai demonizes such an assimilationist Jew as, most fundamentally, "not a man" but rather a member of a sub-

human species, all the more insidiously dangerous for his apparent resemblance to the men around him. He is an "alien" parasitically working
only for his own well-being, at the direct expense of the social organism
from which he "sucks the blood." A man is not a man unless he experiences a "subjection of the soul"; a Jew can become a human being only
if he shares his love with those who are like him, in a "brotherhood with
his own race." So Mordecai has a plan: "Revive the organic centre. . . .
Looking towards a land and a polity, our dispersed people in all the ends
of the earth may share the dignity of a national life" (592). Mordecai explains that political autonomy will be the salvation of the Jews. It is this
conviction of the regenerative and intrinsically national power of homosocial love in the form of Jewish nationalism that is his legacy, and it
is this that he both teaches to and enacts with Deronda. Mordecai is exhausted by the passion of his polemic:

> With the last sentence, which was no more than a loud whisper,
> Mordecai let his chin sink on his breast and his eyelids fall. No one
> spoke. . . . Deronda's presence had wrought Mordecai's conception
> into a state of impassioned conviction, and he had found strength
> in his excitement to pour forth the unlocked floods of emotive argu-
> ment. . . . But now there had come . . . the quiescence of fatigue. . . .
> After a great excitement, the ebbing strength of impulse is apt to
> leave us in this aloofness from our active self. . . . in less than ten
> minutes the room was empty of all except Mordecai and Deronda.
> (598–99)

Appropriately, Mordecai's political enthusiasm is presented here as virtually orgasmic, his whole body now detumescent. His audience now exits.
"It was as if they had come together to hear the blowing of the *shophar*,"
the ram's horn trumpet. Mordecai has blown; Zionism is the ejaculatory
climax of a homosocial orgy staged for the initiation of Deronda into
human brotherhood.

It makes sense that it is only after—but immediately after—this initiation that Mordecai announces that his courtship with Deronda is over:
they are now engaged to be married. As Mordecai explains, "In the doctrine of the Cabbala . . . a soul liberated from a worn-out body may join
the fellow-soul that needs it, that they may be perfected together. . . .
When my long-wandering soul is liberated from this weary body, it will
join yours, and its work will be perfected" (600). As the novel draws to
its close, Mordecai is on his deathbed, and he emphasizes to Deronda
that "It has begun already—the marriage of our souls. . . . [ours is] the
willing marriage which melts soul into soul. . . . let the thought [i.e., Jewish nationalism] be born again from our fuller soul which shall be called

yours" (820). And in the last words spoken in this massive novel—Mordecai's last words in life—he takes the hands of both his sister and his lover, but says, "looking at Deronda": "Death . . . takes me from your bodily eyes and gives me full presence in your soul. Where thou goest, Daniel, I shall go. Is it not begun? Have I not breathed my soul into you? We shall live together" (882). Deronda's marriage to Mirah, although literal, takes place out of the reach of the narrator's eye; in contrast, Deronda's marriage to Mordecai is dramatized, staged repeatedly, and centrally framed as the novel's definitive act of closure. Deronda has been transformed, as he explains to the dumbfounded Gwendolen, "by becoming intimate with a very remarkable Jew" (874). He is now the Zionist leader of Mordecai's dreams, and he has found a properly activist vocation. "The idea that I am possessed with is that of restoring a political existence to my people. . . . That is a task which presents itself to me as a duty. . . . I am resolved to devote my life to it" (875). Deronda has accepted Mordecai's attack on the inherently debilitating nature of non-national Jewishness, and resolves his life crisis by taking his place, standing shoulder to shoulder with other Jewish men. He empowers himself by subordinating himself to the interests of the brotherhood.

George Eliot's interrogation of the gender of Jewish gentility in *Daniel Deronda* provides a crucial opening into the ideological world of early Zionism, a movement that can be fully understood only in light of its status as an intervention in nineteenth-century conceptions of the relationship between Jewish identity and European masculinity. In *Daniel Deronda*, Eliot paints a vision of homosocial love through Jewish nationalist allegiance as a means of performing the normalization of the gender identity of assimilated Jewish men. An uncannily resonant vision emerges from Theodor Herzl's life and work.[10]

This future statesman, the only son of Jakob and Jeanette Herzl, was born in Budapest in 1860: he was given the Hebrew name Zeev, the Hungarian name Tivador, and the German names Wolf Theodor. The Herzls were wealthy and assimilated Jews: although Jakob Herzl had been born in poverty, he had become the president of the Hungaria Bank by 1870. In 1878 the Herzl family moved to Vienna, and young Theodor—despite his aspiration to be a playwright—enrolled in the faculty of law at the University of Vienna. The milieu of the Herzls was quite similar to that of their contemporary and compatriot, Sigmund Freud, and many other Viennese Jews of this era: in spite of financial comfort, Western education, and self-proclaimed indifference to ethnicity, they nonetheless moved in a world consisting primarily of Jews like themselves.

In July 1879, Herzl met Heinrich Kana, an impoverished fellow student, Jew, and aspiring litterateur. Over the following decade the two were to develop an intense and mutual attachment: in Herzl's words to Kana: "There is only one single human being toward whom I am completely open (silly or vain), and that is you."[11] Kana had no friends other than Herzl; Herzl never had a friend besides Kana. One biographer writes that their relationship was "turbulent . . . complicated by strains of ambivalence, jealousy and sexual tension"; another concludes that "It was indeed a covert, if not overt, homosexual relationship."[12] It is unclear how Herzl understood his own sexual identity at this time, although there is ample evidence of his cultivation of an almost Proustian aestheticism, which was often implicated in what his culture was soon to label as sexually "degenerate." At the age of nineteen he wrote in a latter to Kana: "I have much to complain about the changes in my moods: to exult to heaven, to be deathly depressed [*Himmelhoch jauchzend, zu Tode betrübt*],—soon to delude myself with hope, far like the bellowing sea, again to die, to be rejected unto death [*zu Tode, zum Sterben versagt*]. . . . Pain is the substance of life and joy consists only of the temporary absence of pain."[13] Herzl perceived himself as emotionally vulnerable, adrift in an ocean of feelings beyond his control; he could merely allow his moods to wash over him, and complain about it. In an early letter to Kana, Herzl declares that "The lyrical poem will forever be the crown of creation."[14] Not states, not armies, not even novels—but the lyric, the genre that specifically excludes worldly activity from its purview, in favor of the reflective exploration of the individual consciousness. In an early diary entry Herzl describes himself as a "tender organism," a poet too refined for the enjoyment of "the goblet, the favors of women, successes that come one's way." He distances himself from the species of man who takes the present "by the hand, kisses it on the mouth, has it, possesses it": here, Herzl delights in the contemplation of the image of active and heterosexually oriented masculinity, even as he defines his own identity in opposition to it.[15] Similarly, in another diary entry he exclaims, "I am exceedingly captivated by knightliness and manliness." He proceeds to describe his daydream of the medieval Norman knight Guy de Montsoreau and the "manly Timber" of his voice. In his fantasy, Herzl addresses the knight adoringly and descriptively: "Your strong arm snatches up anything that resists it."[16] The future statesman here imagines himself as a damsel in distress, powerless to resist "captivation" and rape at the hands of a literal knight in shining armor.

Herzl, in the above instances, constructs a conventionally heterosexual and aggressive European man who is other than himself. Yet by the time he was in his early twenties Herzl was devoting increasing—and increasingly panicked—energies to the cultivation of a relation to assertive masculinism, which was at least occasionally—though certainly not unproblematically—one of identification. The attempt to naturalize this self-description lay behind—and in the fore of—the main intellectual and emotional investments of his life: Herzl turned first to German brotherhood; then to heterosexual marriage; and finally to Jewish nationalism.

The politics of Herzl's investment in the project of formulating his gender identity are most clearly revealed by his 1881 initiation into Albia, the elite pan-German nationalist fraternity. Herzl's membership in this organization suddenly placed this "tender organism" in the avant-garde of Viennese masculinism: such fraternities had only been introduced to the University of Vienna twenty years earlier, and it had only been three years since they had begun requiring their members to acquire a facial scar and to defend their honor through the fighting of duels. Theirs was not an archaic obeisance to a ritualized medieval tradition: these were *new* organizations, and their assertion that properly manly conduct required the aggressive defense of brotherly bonds was a controversial and quite self-consciously ideological intervention in the Viennese discourse of masculine identity.

Not coincidentally, Herzl's fraternity membership also placed him in the avant-garde of the developing movement of Germanist anti-Semitism. Although there is no evidence that Herzl himself ever wavered in his liberal ideals, the fraternity movement with which he chose to ally himself was at that time in the very thick of a sea change in the direction of a racist social politics. The municipality of Vienna was not to endorse a discriminatory agenda until 1895, but some of the fraternities had already covertly banned Jews by 1881—and by 1883 all but one of them officially denied brotherhood to Jews. Herzl was never comfortable in Albia. His fraternity nickname was "Tancred, Prince of Galilee and Antioch." This "Tancred" withdrew from active participation after one year of membership, and finally chose to resign in 1883, in protest of his comrades' participation in an openly anti-Semitic commemoration of the death of Richard Wagner. The organization's official records note: "He did not feel happy among his fraternity brothers and remained for all of them an alien element."[17] Upon Herzl's resignation, Albia's most active member, Paul von Portheim, proposed that the fraternity cease to admit Jewish members, a proposal that was accepted.[18] In 1896 anti-Jewish racism became an official tenet of the fraternity movement, and the joint statement issued on 11 March of that year is a significant articulation of the views of Herzl's former brothers: "In fullest recognition of the fact that a profound moral and psychological difference exists between Aryans and Jews . . . in view of the abundant evidence that Jewish students have given of their . . . total lack of honor according to our German conceptions, the present assembly of German able-bodied student fraternities adopts the resolution: 'to no longer grant satisfaction to a Jew with any weapon, since he is unworthy of it.' "[19] The fraternity movement effectively denied the humanity of Jews by performatively enacting the exclusion of Jewish men from the Aryan economy of masculine brotherhood: the alien body was expelled. The honorable Jewish man could no longer be acknowledged as a conceivable category of human being; masculinism and anti-Semitism were explicitly and officially intertwined. Three months after his resolution to ban Jews from Albia was accepted, von Portheim, who was himself of Jewish descent, committed suicide.[20]

Far from being idiosyncratic, the philosophy of race and gender characteristic of the dueling fraternities was a harbinger of broader intellectual and cultural trends in the German-speaking world. This is most dramatically evident in the famous case of Otto Weininger, a Viennese intellectual who converted from Judaism to Protestantism, and who has been described as a "repressed homosexual."[21] In 1903, at the age of twenty-three, Weininger published a widely influential articulation of racist, misogynist, and homophobic principles entitled *Sex and Character,* in which he argued for the mutual implication and utter irredeemability of both Jewishness and femininity, and invoked another descriptive term in his pathologization of feminized manhood: "homosexuality." In Weininger's view, Judaism "is saturated with femininity" and "as there is no real dignity in women, so what is meant by the word gentleman does not exist among the Jews."[22] Weininger thunders against the effete *fin de siècle:* "This is the age which is most Jewish and most feminine. . . . The choice must be made between Judaism and Christianity, between business and culture, between male and female, between the race and the individual. . . . There are only two poles."[23] Shortly after his book's publication, Weininger, too, committed suicide.

Throughout the 1880s—as masculinism and anti-Semitism formed two sides of the cultural vice tightening on the assimilated Jewish men of Vienna—Herzl was tenacious in his consistent identification with aggressive and Germanic manhood as a means of self-reform and escape from Jewish otherness. In the very act of resigning from the German brotherhood of Albia, Herzl emphasized that "even as a non-Jew" he would oppose the anti-Semitic movement: these words imply a vain protest that, even as he was conscious that his actions would be viewed as "Jewish" ones by others, Herzl himself maintained allegiance to a standard of honor that had no reference to his ethnicity.[24] This attitude is similarly reflected in his youthful novella *Hagenau,* where Herzl enthusiastically describes a young Jewish soldier in uniform: "Karl's nose, in profile, was already altogether straight."[25] Militarism cures Judaism. But

Herzl's state of mind is perhaps most profoundly revealed in a letter he wrote to his friend Kana in 1883, merely months after having felt compelled to resign from Albia. Herzl recounts how, while vacationing at a resort outside Vienna, he has met the Eastern European Jew and German litterateur Joseph Ehrlich: Herzl refers to him in his narrative as a "shabby little Jew." According to his own account, Herzl, accompanied by two lady-friends, introduced himself to Ehrlich as "Baron Rittershausen," the Prussian aristocrat. The impersonation was convincing, and Herzl gleefully relates his success in humiliating Ehrlich and eliciting evidence of the Jew's extraordinary vulgarity.[26] It is not difficult to see that Herzl's desire to assert his difference from Ehrlich was provoked by their shared status as Jews and German writers. In this case, Herzl merely literalized his daily practice of living the identity of a European aristocrat, thus distancing himself from a Jewishness he abhorred. In light of all of the above, it should not be surprising that Herzl accepted or issued three separate dueling challenges after resigning from Albia, all in the few months between the fall of 1884 and the spring of 1885.[27] His views had not changed by 1881, when he explicitly articulated his view that the Prussianization of Jewish men would eliminate anti-Semitism: he refused to contribute to the newsletter of the Society to Combat Anti-Semitism in Vienna, commenting that Jews would most effectively fight racism by fighting "half a dozen duels."[28] And even as late as July 1895—*after* his conversion to Jewish nationalism—he wrote to himself in his diary: "By the way, if there is one thing I should like to be, it is a member of the old Prussian nobility."[29] Increasingly, Herzl's society asserted the incompatibility of Jewishness and masculine humanity; Herzl responded by embracing the latter as an escape from the former.

There is ample evidence that Herzl did not consider his escape to be successful: unsurprisingly, he passed much of the 1880s in a state of severe depression. In 1885 he ceased to practice law and embarked upon full-time literary and journalistic work. He wrote much but published little, and in 1883 he lamented to his diary that "I am overcome by the hopelessness of my existence. . . . Success will not come."[30] Even more melodramatically, on New Year's Eve of 1884 he described his life as "nothing but emptiness. The head empty of hope, the brain empty of thought, the purse empty of money and life empty of poetry. . . . I have a mistress . . . but I am no longer fit for love."[31] Yet by 1889, at the age of twenty-nine, he had achieved his lifelong professional ambition: in February the great *Burgtheater* of Vienna accepted a play of his for production; in May it accepted another.

In June of 1889, Herzl married the blond, blue-eyed, twenty-year-old Jewish heiress Julie Naschauer. Kana's response to his friend Herzl's wedding invitation is heart-wrenching: "I do not go out, so hard it is for me. . . . Without you I would have drifted through life, and my great longing for love, whose power few people appreciate, would always have remained unsatisfied. I thank you today, which I have never done till now, out of this silly shamefulness from which I can never free myself, for all the *Zärtlichkeit* [tenderness, caresses] you have given me, and shall gladly see how the far greater part of the love of which your heart is capable now takes another direction."[32] There is no question here of separate spheres for marriage and friendship: it is clear to Kana that his relationship with Herzl is part of the same emotional and sexual economy as Herzl's relationship with Julie, and that the project of heterosexual marriage is a personal reform, entailing the reorientation of Herzl's energies in "another direction." Yet Kana is the abject subject: he pledges to be happy in his own displacement, grateful even in his sense of abandonment.

Whatever Herzl's motivation for marrying, he regretted it almost instantly, in spite of the three-year acquaintance of husband and wife that preceded the ceremony. Four weeks into his honeymoon, Herzl sent a postcard to Kana that read simply: "I've grown older again—much, much older. Farewell and be happy."[33] Three months into his marriage, he began writing a play about the fundamental incompatibility of men and women—a memorable line of dialogue: "What a happy man I'd be, if only I had the courage to run away from her."[34] Herzl may have been capable of impersonating an aristocratic man of letters, but he could not inhabit the identity of husband and father. Shortly after their first child's birth in March 1890, Herzl asked for Julie's consent to their divorce, which she refused. Julie was clearly devastated by her experience of marriage. When she was eight months pregnant with their second child, Herzl lamented that, in addition to her attempts to induce a miscarriage, Julie was trying to kill herself. "I have already cut her off from the curtain string, torn her back from the window sill, snatched the atropin vial away from her." Herzl concludes with twisted syntax and horrifying self-absorption: "Few men are so tortured as I am by her threat to do harm to herself."[35]

Julie remained in life—but on 6 February 1891, Heinrich Kana killed himself. Shortly after Herzl's marriage, Kana had moved to Berlin, from whence he expressed his despair at literary failure, poverty, and severe depression. Herzl too was suffering from his friend's withdrawal: he wrote that "I am beginning to feel what he meant to me" and implored his friend to return to Vienna.[36] Instead, Kana mailed his suicide note, and Herzl received it the day after his friend's death.

My dear, good Theodor, your old friend wishes to send you his farewell before he dies! I thank you for all the friendship and kindness you have given me. I wish you and your dear ones all the happiness on earth. I kiss you.

Yours, Heinrich[37]

Rather than turn to Julie for comfort in his distress, Herzl walked out on her immediately upon receiving Kana's note. He passed the next three weeks in Italy. When he returned, he announced his intention of divorcing the pregnant Julie immediately upon their child's birth.[38] The couple was repeatedly separated and reconciled in the coming months. In October 1891, Herzl accepted a position as the Paris correspondent for the largest liberal newspaper in Vienna; he subsequently allowed Julie to join him in Paris on the condition that they have separate bedrooms, and that Herzl's parents reside in the household together with them.[39] Herzl completely cut himself off from his wife, and there is no evidence that he was emotionally or physically intimate with anyone else again.

In Paris, Herzl immersed himself and his readers in the vicissitudes of *fin-de-siècle* French politics and society, producing an extraordinary volume of writing on a wide variety of political and cultural matters. But by the spring of 1893 a newly developed obsession on Herzl's part with the dilemma of anti-Semitism was becoming increasingly apparent. Herzl's previous approaches to the reform of Jewish gender identity had been insistently individualist: "half a dozen duels" and heterosexual marriage was all it took for a Jew to become a German man. But in Herzl's own life neither of these approaches had played out with resounding success, and he now began experimenting with a variety of radical and somewhat megalomaniac interventions in Jewish identity on the collective level — among them a serious proposal for the mass conversion of the entire Austrian Jewish community to Roman Catholicism, under his messianic leadership.[40] Yet the more he contemplated the Jewish problem, the more he contemplated it: "I was drawn into it deeper and deeper. The thought that I had to do something for the Jews gripped me ever more forcefully."[41]

On 5 January 1895, Herzl reported on the formal conviction of the assimilated Franco-Jewish Colonel Alfred Dreyfus on charges of treason. On 1 April Karl Luegar's anti-Semitic Christian Socialist Party won its first electoral victory in Vienna. And on 2 June of this year, Herzl underwent a conversion experience difficult to distinguish from psychosis. This was particularly true from his own perspective.

> During these days I have often been afraid of going insane. So shatteringly did the streams of thought race through my soul. A lifetime will not suffice to realize all of it.

But I am leaving behind a spiritual legacy. To whom? To all men.
I believe I shall be named among the greatest benefactors of mankind.
Or is this belief already megalomania?[42]

Herzl asked to be relieved of his journalistic duties, and he produced nearly three hundred pages of writing between 3 June and 16 June.[43] He lived in a self-described frenzy. "I wrote walking, standing, lying, in the street, at meals, at night, when it drove me out of sleep."[44] During this period, Herzl recorded such statements as "I believe that for me life has ended and world history has begun"; "They will pray for me in the synagogues. But also in the churches"; and, "If I point with my finger at a spot: Here shall be a city, then a city shall rise there."[45] Friedrich Schiff, the physician, journalist, and fellow Viennese Jew who was Herzl's only human contact during these days, was the first to whom Herzl showed his writing. Schiff broke down in tears, took Herzl's pulse, and advised him to get professional help.[46]

Herzl's June 1895 epiphany was, of course, the vision of a Jewish nationalism. He had no idea that this was not a completely original conception. For him, it felt spontaneous: "Am I working it out? No! It is working me. It would be a compulsion if it were not so rational from beginning to end. This is what was formerly called 'inspiration.'"[47] It also felt like having sex. "I am so filled with it [my idea] that I relate everything to it, like a lover to his beloved."[48] Herzl had been penetrated by the idea; in fact, he had been impregnated. "For three hours I have been tramping about the Bois to dispel the pangs of new trains of thought."[49]

Herzl experienced his embrace of Zionism as an immediate and dramatic reconstitution of his selfhood: "No one has thought of seeking the 'Promised Land' where it truly is—and yet it lies so near. Here it is: within ourselves."[50] He consistently describes the transformation of consciousness through the Zionist revolution in terms—which are now familiar—of its simultaneous privileging of homosocial community and normalization of Jewish gender identity. "I have never been in such a happy mood of exaltation. I am not thinking of dying, but of a life full of manly deeds, which will expunge and eliminate everything base, wanton, and confused that has ever been in me."[51] Repeatedly and consistently, Herzl emphasizes the gendered nature of his vision. Zionism is for real men, not "Ghetto creatures, quiet, good, fearful. Most of our people are like that. Will they understand the call to freedom and manliness?"[52] When he traveled with a Zionist delegation to Palestine in 1898, his party of Euro-Jewish diplomats was most moved by the spectacle of Jewish men riding horses and lustily singing Hebrew songs. As Herzl wrote, "We had tears in our eyes as we saw the agile, courageous riders, into which our pants-peddling boys could be transformed."[53]

The status of the Zionist revolution as a revolution in masculine self-consciousness was central to its wider appeal among Western European Jews. Stephen Poppel's study, *Zionism in Germany, 1897–1933: The Shaping of a Jewish Identity*, stresses that Zionist conversion was a "fundamental and sweeping reorientation of personality and identity": as an early convert explained, Zionism was a matter of "the consciousness of belonging to the Jewish people, and the manly bearing that was a consequence."[54] This was also the crux of Zionism's appeal to Max Nordau, Herzl's most prominent convert to the cause of Jewish nationalism, and, after Herzl, its leading propagandist. Nordau—psychiatrist, journalist, rationalist cultural critic, and son of an orthodox rabbi—made his international reputation with the 1892 publication of his best-selling study *Degeneration*, a shrill and encyclopedic diagnosis of the pathology of the culture of the *fin de siècle*.[55] At the Second Zionist Congress, in 1898, Nordau evoked the image of a "muscle Jewry," which he opposed to a "coffeehouse Jewry": "let us . . . become deep-chested, sturdy, sharp-eyed men."[56]

During one of Herzl's more discouraged moments, in late 1900, he returned to his original sense that the Zionist idea might best be expressed in the form of a novel. As he put it then, "The hopes of practical success have melted away. My life is now no novel. So the novel is now my life."[57] It took Herzl two years to complete the project, entitled *Altneuland* ("Old-new Land," after the Prague synagogue, the "Altneuschul"). When completed, he described it as "a fairytale, which I tell, as it were, by the campfires, to keep my people in good spirits during the time of wandering."[58] It is the most detailed extant exposition of Herzl's Zionist dream, and it is particularly valuable as an exploration of the Herzlian imaginary of Jewishness, gender, and same-sex union.

"Sunk in the depths of depression, Dr. Friedrich Loewenberg sat at the round marble-topped table of his coffeehouse":[59] this opening line of the novel introduces its protagonist, a young Viennese Jewish physician who is, of course, degenerate. It is 1903, and his two closest friends are now dead: one has died of yellow fever in a Jewish refugee colony in Brazil (as one of Herzl's friends did as well); the other has just committed suicide. Loewenberg feels like an "old, old man, not a youth of twenty-three. There he sat and stared, unseeing, into the smoke-misted corners of the large room." (6) A coffeehouse Jew, paralyzed into a depressive stupor, his empty gaze drifting off into the miasma in which he is enveloped.

The novel's plot is set in motion when Loewenberg happens to notice a newspaper advertisement: "Wanted, cultured and despairing young man willing to try last experiment with his life" (19). The doctor apparently feels both cultured and despairing, because he decides to respond. As he puts it to himself:

> A last experiment! Life was intolerable—before throwing it away like his poor friend Heinrich, why not try to do something with it? He asked the waiter for a sheet of notepaper and wrote briefly:
> "I am your man." (19)

Loewenberg embarks upon this experiment as an alternative to the suicide toward which his depression has been inclining him. The advertiser arranges to meet him at an elegant hotel. Loewenberg's first impression is of a "tall, broadshouldered man . . . in his fifties, with greying beard and thick brown hair, silvered at the temples. He was smoking a fat cigar."

> "Smoke, doctor?"
> "Thank you, not now."
> Mr. Kingscourt carefully blew a smoke-ring, followed it with his eyes till it disintegrated. (23)

"Mr. Kingscourt" explains that his real name is Koenigshoff, and that he is a German aristocrat and former army officer. He was unhappy in the military because "[he] can't stand being subordinate to another's will," and so emigrated to the United States, where he changed his name to Kingscourt and made a fortune. Kingscourt married—"I took me a wife," (23) as he charmingly puts it—although heterosexual desire seems never to have occurred to him: "I wanted a wife to hang jewels on, like any other upstart, I wanted a home to come back to, I longed for children so I should know what I'd been slaving for all these years" (23). His wife, however, has been unfaithful, and Kingscourt has now become confirmed in both misogyny and misanthropy: he proclaims that he has resolved to withdraw from Western civilization altogether. "I know an island in the Pacific where nobody lives. . . . I've bought the island" (24). This is where the "cultured and despairing young man" comes in. Kingscourt would like to take someone with him when he leaves the (Western) world behind.

> "Will you be that somebody?"
> Friedrich thought for half a minute. Then he said firmly: "I will."
> "You must understand, however, that you are undertaking to do this for the rest of your life. Or at least for the rest of my life. If you come with me, there's no going back. . . ."

Friedrich answered: "I've no ties. I'm alone in the world and sick of it."

"Then you're just the man I want." (25)

On the verge of suicide, the assimilated Jewish intellectual in *fin-de-siècle* Vienna, isolated and disembodied, is saved by the love of a rich and aristocratic Prussian daddy/lover too manfully independent even for military service, a cigar-smoking man's man, specifically disdainful of heterosexual bonds. The two run off together to a tropical paradise.

The second book of Herzl's novel opens twenty years later, in 1923, with the couple sailing back from their island idyll for a visit to Europe. Kingscourt still has not given up smoking. Kingscourt was lying in a deck chair and smoking a huge cigar:

> "Well, I must say our island has made a man of you! When I remember what a miserable flat-chested specimen of a Jew-boy you were when I took you with me! And now you're quite a lad—you might be dangerous to women still."
>
> "You're quite mad, my friend," Friedrich laughed.(42)

The teasing banter of this lovingly married couple reveals their steadfast loyalty—as well as the status of their relationship as a substitute for heterosexual bonds. The embrace of a real man with a "huge cigar" is confirmed as having been a transformative, salvational experience for the coffeehouse depressive: this former "Jew-boy" has now been "made a man."

The happy couple decides to visit Palestine, and they are glad they do: as it turns out, Jewish colonization has created in Palestine the most advanced society in the world. Immediately upon docking at Haifa, Loewenberg and Kingscourt encounter David Litwak—a Viennese street urchin in the opening chapter, now a distinguished businessman and civic leader. "What a fine man the little beggar Jew boy had become! Grave and free, healthy and cultured, a man who could stand up for himself" (55). Litwak has an eye for virile specimens as well, proclaiming, "Once Jewish children were weak, pale, cowed. Look at them today! This transformation is as simple as making twice two four. We brought these children from dank cellars and slums into the light of day! Plants die without sunlight, and so do human beings. Just as plants can be saved, if they are transplanted to the right soil in time, so can human beings. That is what we have done" (62). Zionism has masculinized Litwak, and, indeed, the entire Jewish people, *in a manner analogous to the way in which the love of Kingscourt has transformed Loewenberg,* thanks to Jewish colonization. Zionism is to the Jewish male masses as Kingscourt is to

Loewenberg; Jewish national separatism functions as a mirror of assimilationist male marriage. In Herzl's vision, these are parallel routes to the vital Jewish manhood that is the Promised Land.

In the European world of the *fin de siècle*, manhood was contingent upon the ability to form properly homosocial bonds in the closed fellowship of brothers where power, money, status, and desire were circulated. The elaboration of national identity categories in modern Europe served to consolidate one level of such brotherhood. In the complementary Zionist visions of Eliot and Herzl, Jewish men are irredeemably othered by the mere existence of such a fellowship. The more determinedly the Jewish male body flings itself against the sealed gates of assimilationist incorporation, the more hopeless the attempt. The only way of healing the shameful wounds produced by this mechanism of exclusion is the performance of refusal, an "inward" turn that provides self-validation through assertion (as opposed to denial) of difference, and the rerouting of the love of masculine fellowship toward those who are the same in that they share one's (Jewish) difference. Previously, assimilationist Jewish men had lined up before nationalized European audiences and announced, each individually, "I am the same as you." But the truth-value of such a statement is contingent upon the audience's assenting latitudinarian definition of itself, an assent that can be witheld: so it was that Herzl had been involuntarily written out of his Germanic fraternity. By contrast, the statement, "We are different from you," is a properly performative utterance, an act of self-empowerment that is also an invitation to the constitutional convention of an alternative body in which to be incorporated.

In a paradox that is merely apparent, Jewish nationalism is conceived as an means of becoming initiated into male fellowship through the elimination of queerly disempowered male difference; the Jewish male is led away from homosexualization, the realm of male love, and into homosocialization, the realm of male love. Thus, Herzl has Loewenberg in *Altneuland* diagnose the pathologies of diaspora Jews:

> How could they wonder that they were despised, when they themselves despised their own origins? They had crawled after the strangers, and so they were rightly repulsed. . . . To be despised, and in the end despise yourself—that is the fate of the exile.
>
> And now they had raised themselves out of this deepest morass! . . . Judaism looked so different now because it was no longer ashamed of itself. (186–7)

"Exile" is a state of alienation from one's "origins," a perpetual chase after the love of "the stranger" that must end in self-loathing. Nationalism is about calling this state of being pathological and entering into reconciliation with one's self (and selves like one), such that an externally imposed labeling that had previously been generative of *shame* and isolation is now assumed as a manly badge of agency in an act of *pride* and brotherly affiliation.

Herzl seems entirely unself-conscious about any tensions between, on the one hand, his Zionist condemnation of individual assimilationism as an apotheosization of the European other and thus a mechanism for the inevitable production of Jewish self-hatred, and, on the other hand, his Zionist valorization of collective assimilation through the creation of a "Jewish" society, one of the primary virtues of which is its potential to eradicate Jewish difference and enable Jewish conformity to European models of gender identity and humanity. Even as Jewish separatism is presented as a means of engineering Jewish self-love, the "Jewish self" that Herzl imagines is familiar as a reincarnation of Germanic manhood *sans différance*. Indeed, *Altneuland* dramatizes precisely this point through the symmetrical transformations of Loewenberg (through German intermarriage) and the Jewish male masses (through Zionism). Late in his novel, Herzl writes an appeal to the Jews of the New Society to "stand by the principles that have made us great: Liberalism, Tolerance, Love of Mankind! Only then will Zion be truly Zion" (109). The defining characteristics of the separatist, nationalist "Zion" are the very same characteristics that define European progressivism. In this view, the Zionist entity will be Jewish insofar as it assimilates the assimilated cosmopolitanism of the most admirable (Jewish) Europeans. Eliot makes a similar point by creating in Deronda the new model of the Zionist stateman: a Victorian gentleman who remains "the same" (in Gwendolen's words) in spite of the fact that his primary identity category is now "Jew." " 'I shall call myself a Jew,' said Deronda. . . . "But I will not say that I shall profess to believe exactly as my fathers have believed. Our fathers themselves changed the horizon of their belief and learned of other races'" (792). Deronda will proudly engage in the empowering act of self-naming, yet he will simultaneously disavow the expected consequences of this act of affiliation. " 'The Christian sympathies in which my mind was reared can never die out of me,' said Deronda, with increasing tenacity of tone. 'But I consider it my duty . . . to identify myself, as far as possible, with my hereditary people'" (724). Deronda willingly divests himself of the identity category of "Christian," declares his "identification" with the Jews— and that is where his transformation stops. Jewish nationalism becomes a way of reframing an otherwise intact ideology of self. With an ease of great significance, the liberatory concept of "pride" in "difference" is emptied out of content and becomes pride in a merely formal difference that is essentially identity. Eliot and Herzl articulate a vision of a separat-ism that replicates that from which it has separated.

It is impossible to articulate such a critique of Zionist thought without invoking buzzwords frought with moralized valences: most of us have only one way of thinking about the kind of "conformism" such a structure suggests. But the above mapping of the paradox of Zionist pride functions only as damning exposure of Zionist incoherence if one accepts the facile foundational premise that there are such things as Jewish subjects with unproblematically original "selves" existing prior to and in a realm sepa-rate from particular historical contingencies and ideological orientations, and that the Jewishness of these selves always already holds a privileged explanatory status in the structuring narrative of individual conscious-ness. Such theorizing is premised on access to "good" Jewish identities, which need not be constituted, but merely accepted, because they are always "prior." So it is that Herzl can imagine that the emergence of a co-herent, stable Jewishness is a necessary and inevitable consequence of the absence of an active attempt to deny it: "Judaism looked so different now because it was no longer ashamed of itself." It is precisely this "common sense" of an original Jewishness that is the sole intellectual foundation of the most commonly wielded tool on the workbench of Jewish studies: "assimilation." This is the original sin of modern Jewish historiography: its every invocation an evocation of the fall from autonomous integrity into abject betrayal. But it is only by embarking upon every inquiry with an *a priori* prioritization of the category of Jewishness that scholars escape the otherwise obvious conclusion that *all* group affiliation—incuding "Jewishness"—is created through this very process. For what is "assimi-lation" but an organization of the self so as to foreground those personal characteristics that will enable one to become a member of the group with which one wishes to be associated? In this sense, both Herzl and Deronda are Jewish assimilationists in two senses: they assimilate themselves into Jewishness, and they assimilate Jewishness into themselves. There is no simple sense in which their projects can be discredited on this account. As Deronda points out in his own defense, "Our fathers [*sic*] themselves changed the horizon of their belief and learned of other races" (972).

NOTES

1 Theodor Herzl, *The Diaries of Theodor Herzl*, ed. and trans. Marvin Lowenthal (New York: The Dial Press, 1956), p. 80. Entry for 23 November 1895.

2 For many years, these words were painted (in Hebrew translation) on the water tower that dominated the Tel Aviv suburb of Herzliya. Freud reportedly told Herzl's son Hans in 1913 that "It is my modest profession to simplify dreams, to make them clear and ordinary. . . . [People like Herzl] on the contrary, confuse the issue, turn it up-

side down, command the world while they themselves remain on the other side of the psychic mirror. It is a group specializing in the realization of dreams. I deal in psychoanalysis; they deal in psychosynthesis." (William J. McGrath, *Freud's Discovery of Psychoanalysis: The Politics of Hysteria* [Ithaca: Cornell University Press, 1986], p. 314, cited in Paul Breines, *Tough Jews: Political Fantasies and the Moral Dilemma of American Jewry* [New York: Basic Books, 1990], p. 32.)

3 Herzl, *Diaries*, p. 3.

4 Steven Marcus, "Human Nature, Social Orders, and 19th Century Systems of Explanation: Starting in with George Eliot," *Salmagundi* 28 (winter 1975): 28.

5 Cynthia Chase, "The Decomposition of the Elephants: Double-Reading *Daniel Deronda*," *PMLA* 93 (1978): 222.

6 K. M. Newton, "*Daniel Deronda* and Circumcision," *Essays in Criticism* 31 (1985): 313–27. Contemporaneous with the publication of *Daniel Deronda*, the 1870s saw a lively medical debate about the merits of circumcision, with most written opinions propagandizing for the efficacy of the procedure. The physician William Acton expressed particularly strong views on the subject in his popular medical text: "to the sensitive, excitable, civilized individual, the prepuce often becomes a source of serious mischief. . . . [It] excites the sexual desires, which it is our object to repress. Most men require restraint, not excitement, of their sexual instincts." (William Acton, *The Functions and Disorders of the Reproductive Organs in Childhood, Youth, Adult Age, and Advanced Life Considered in Their Physiological, Social, and Moral Relations* [Philadelphia: Lindsay and Blakiston, 1875], p. 24 n. 1. In May 1870, W. F. Teeran wrote in the *British Medical Journal* that "a tight foreskin . . . is a cause of much evil, and it ought to be remedied" (cited in George H. Napheys, *The Transmission of Life. Counsels on the Nature and Hygiene of the Masculine Function*, 2d ed. [Philadelphia: J. O. Fergus, 1871] John Davenport's 1875 book was more explicit in naming both the illness and the cure: it advocates the view that the "reason for the introduction of circumcision was that of preventing the detestable and fatal practice of masturbation. "(John Davenport, *Curiositates Eroticae Physiologiae, or Tabooed Subjects Freely Treated* [London: privately printed, 1875]; reprinted in *Aphrodisiacs and Love Stimulants*, ed. Alan Hull Walton [New York: Lyle Stuart, 1966], p. 181.)

7 Mary Wilson Carpenter, in her essay, " 'Bit of Her Flesh': Circumcision and 'The Signification of the Phallus' in *Daniel Deronda*" (*Genders* 1 [1988]: 1–23), argues powerfully that if we wish to pursue the theme of circumcision—that is to say, sanctification through bodily mutilation—in this novel we need not bother ourselves with Deronda, since we have our hands full with Gwendolen. "George Eliot's text . . . revels in the pain of the daughter's 'circumcision,' constructing a female erotics of circumcision: a phantasied infliction of this painful but sanctifying rite on the female body that rewrites the sadistic narrative as a passionate dialectic between daughter and mother. It is not the Phallus (or its lack) that ultimately matters here; rather, the narrative steals language and phantasy from the contemporary discourse on (male) circumcision to construct its painful and difficult desire for an 'other' who is also the same." (p. 2). Carpenter's argument is energized by her revolt against a Lacanian hermeneutics, which, in her view, denies the narratability of female bonds by focusing all interpretation upon the status of the phallus. It is within this context that Carpenter's proclamation of what "ultimately matters here" is made. The foregrounding of nonphallic narratives is an indisputably important critical project. However, there is much more to be said about male circumcision in *Daniel Deronda*, and if it is said well, then the phallus is demystified as a subject of critique and not fetishized as an object of worship. This project,

too, seems indisputably important. Feminist critics have found *Daniel Deronda* to be a rich source for the explication of Eliot's philosophy of womanhood. See especially, Christina Crosby, "George Eliot's Apocalypse of History," in *The Ends of History: Victorians and 'The Woman Question'* (New York: Routledge, 1991), pp. 12–43; Catherine Gallagher, "George Eliot and *Daniel Deronda*: The Prostitute and the Jewish Question," in *The New Historicism Reader*, ed. H. Aram Veeser (New York: Routledge, 1994), pp. 124–40; and Susan Meyer, "'Safely to their own borders': Proto-Zionism, Feminism, and Nationalism in *Daniel Deronda*," *ELH* 60 (1993): 733–58. Yet, no comparably serious examinations of the construction of masculinity in this novel have been undertaken.

8 George Eliot, *Daniel Deronda* (New York: Penguin, 1986), p. 570. Subsequent citations to this work will be given parenthetically in the text.

9 The above passages were all identified by Newton, "Daniel Deronda and Circumcision," pp. 320–25.

10 My integration of Herzl's Zionist thought into his biographical trajectory of gender reinvention is deeply indebted to Daniel Boyarin's analysis of the relationship between Sigmund Freud's ideas and identity in, "Freud's Baby, Fliess's Maybe: Homophobia, Anti-Semitism, and the Invention of Oedipus," *GLQ* 2 (1995): 115–47.

11 Herzl, trans. and cited in Ernst Pawel, *The Labyrinth of Exile: A Life of Theodor Herzl*, (New York: Farrar, Straus, and Giroux, 1989), p. 48.

12 Pawel, *Labyrinth of Exile*, 48; Avner Falk, *Herzl, King of the Jews: A Psychoanalytic Biography of Theodor Herzl* (New York: University Press of America, 1993), p. 69. See also, Leon Kellner, *Theodor Herzls Lehrjahre 1860–1895* (Vienna: R. Lowit Verlag, 1920). The correspondence between Herzl and Kana has never been extensively translated or published.

13 Herzl to Kana, 4 September 1879, cited and trans. in Peter Loewenberg, "Theodor Herzl: A Psychoanalytic Study in Charismatic Political Leadership," in *The Psychoanalytic Interpretation of History*, ed. Benjamin B. Wolman (New York: Basic Books, 1971), p. 155.

14 Theodor Herzl, *Briefe und Tagebücher*, ed. Alex Bein et al., vol. 1, *Briefe und Autobiographische Notizen, 1866–1895*, ed. Johannes Wachten (Berlin: Verlag Ullstein, Propylaen, 1983), p. 107. Trans. and cited in Jacques Kornberg, *Theodor Herzl: From Assimilation to Zionism* (Bloomington: Indiana University Press, 1993), p. 60.

15 Herzl, *Briefe*, 1:649–50. Trans. and cited in Kornberg, *Theodor Herzl*, p. 60.

16 Herzl, *Briefe*, 1:631. Trans. and cited in Kornberg, *Theodor Herzl*, p. 68.

17 "Official record" of Albia cited in Pawel, *Labyrinth of Exile*, p. 67.

18 Pawel, *Labyrinth of Exile*, p. 70.

19 Robert Hein, *Studentischer Antisemitismus in Osterreich* (Vienna: Osterreichischer Verein für Studentengeschichte, 1984), pp. 55–56. Trans. and cited in Kornberg, *Theodor Herzl*, pp. 106–7.

20 Pawel, *Labyrinth of Exile*, p. 70.

21 Sander Gilman, *The Jew's Body* (New York: Routledge, 1991), p. 133.

22 Otto Weininger, *Sex and Character* (New York: AMS Press, 1975), reprint of translation from 6th German edition by W. Heinemann, London, 1906. Cited in Paul Breines, *Tough Jews: Political Fantasies and the Moral Dilemma of American Jewry* (New York: Basic Books, 1990), p. 148.

23 Weininger cited in Gilman, *Jew's Body*, p. 137.

24 Herzl cited in Pawel, *Labyrinth of Exile*, p. 69.

25 Theodor Herzl, *Hagenau* (published in twenty installments in the *Neue Freie Presse* from 23 March to 15 April 1900), cited in Pawel, *Labyrinth of Exile*, p. 53.

26 Herzl, *Briefe*, 1:158–62. Cited in Kornberg, *Theodor Herzl*, p. 77.

27 Kornberg, *Theodor Herzl*, p. 68.

28 Pawel, *Labyrinth of Exile*, p. 182.

29 Theodor Herzl, *The Complete Diaries of Theodor Herzl, 1895–1904*, trans. H. Zohn, ed. R. Patai, 5 vols. (New York: Herzl Press and Thomas Yoseloff, 1960), p. 196. Cited in Falk, *Herzl*, p. 450.

30 Herzl, trans. and cited in Pawel, *Labyrinth of Exile*, p. 87.

31 Ibid., pp. 87–88.

32 Kana to Herzl, Central Zionist Archives File H-VIII-424a-43. Trans. and cited in Falk, *Herzl*, p. 20.

33 Pawel, *Labyrinth of Exile*, p. 128.

34 Ibid., p. 129.

35 Herzl, *Briefe*, 1:144. Trans. and cited in Falk, *Herzl*, p. 139.

36 Herzl, trans. and cited in Pawel, *Labyrinth of Exile*, p. 130.

37 Kana to Herzl, cited and trans. in Falk, *Herzl*, p. 138.

38 Falk, *Herzl*, p. 138.

39 Pawel, *Labyrinth of Exile*, p. 155.

40 Kornberg, *Theodor Herzl*, pp. 118–121.

41 Herzl, trans. and cited in Pawel, *Labyrinth of Exile*, p. 212.

42 Herzl, *Diaries* (ed. Lowenthal), p. 164.

43 Pawel, *Labyrinth of Exile*, p. 226.

44 Theodor Herzl, "Foreword," from *The Jewish State; An Attempt at a Modern Solution of the Jewish Question*, trans. Sylvia d'Avigdor (New York: American Zionist Emergency Council, 1946), p. 3.

45 Herzl, *Tagebücher*, 16 June 1895, 1:115–16, cited and trans. in Loewenberg, "Theodor Herzl," p. 164.

46 Pawel, *Labyrinth of Exile*, p. 233.

47 Herzl, *Tagebücher*, 12 June 1895, 1:106–7, cited and trans. in Loewenberg, "Theodor Herzl," p. 163.

48 Herzl, *Tagebücher*, 5 June 1895, 1:39, cited and trans. in Loewenberg, "Theodor Herzl," p. 165.

49 Herzl, *Tagebücher*, 16 June 1895, 1:117, cited and trans. in Loewenberg, "Theodor Herzl," p. 163.

50 Herzl, *Tagebücher*, 16 June 1895, 1:116, cited and trans. in Loewenberg, "Theodor Herzl," p. 181.

51 Herzl to Schnitzler, 23 June 1895, in Olga Schnitzler, *Spiegelbund der Freundschaft* (Salzburg: 1962), p. 95, cited and trans. in Loewenberg, "Theodor Herzl," p. 174.

52 Herzl, *Tagebücher*, 8 June 1895, 1:52, cited and trans. in Loewenberg, "Theodor Herzl," p. 170.

53 Herzl, *Tagebücher*, 29 October 1898, 2:208, cited and trans. in Loewenberg, "Theodor Herzl," p. 171.

54 Stephen Poppel, *Zionism in Germany, 1897–1933: The Shaping of a Jewish Identity* (Philadelphia: The Jewish Publication Society of America, 1977), pp. 89–90, cited in Kornberg, *Theodor Herzl*, p. 176.

55 In particular, *Degeneration* was a landmark in homophobic cultural criticism—more than any other single work, it provided the vocabulary with which aestheticism was pathologized as a form of sexual decadence. In other words, Nordau was a leader in the cultural movement that lit the fire under the young, feminized Herzl's feet. Nordau had no patience for "the sufferer from melancholia": "With this characteristic

dejectedness of the degenerate, there is combined, as a rule, a disinclination to action of any kind, attaining possibly to abhorrence of activity and powerlessness to will." (Max Nordau, *Degeneration* [New York: D. Appleton and Company, 1895], p. 20.) Nordau decried the culture of decadence for encouraging the abandonment of "normal sexual relations" (p. 13): he describes a Europe so debauched that "Priapus has become a symbol of virtue. Vice looks to Sodom and Lesbos . . . for its embodiments." This arch-masculinist was Herzl's first enthusiastic convert to the Jewish nationalist cause. After their first conversation, Herzl wrote: "Nordau is all for it. . . . Nordau, I believe, would follow me through thick and thin. He would make a good president of our academy, or a minister of education." (Cited in Pawel, *Labyrinth of Exile*, p. 257.)

56 Max Nordau, "Muskeljudentum," in *Judische Turnzeuitung* (1903), trans. in Mendes-Flohr and Reinharz, eds., *The Jew in the Modern World* (New York: Oxford University Press, 1980), pp. 434–35. See also George L. Mosse, *Nationalism and Sexuality: Respectability and Abnormal Sexuality in Modern Europe* (New York: Howard Fertig, 1985), p. 42. A beautiful irony: Tel Aviv's best-known queer-friendly meeting place, located on Nordau Avenue, is called "Cafe B'Nordau": "The Coffeehouse on Nordau."

57 Herzl, *Briefe*, 3:225, cited in Steven Beller, *Herzl* (New York: Grove Weidenfeld, 1991), p. 85.

58 Herzl, *Briefe*, 3:461, cited in Beller, *Herzl*, p. 85.

59 Theodor Herzl, *Altneuland*, trans. Paula Arnold (Haifa, Israel: Haifa Publishing Company, 1964), p. 6. Further citations to this work will be given parenthetically in the text.

Cindy Patton

To Die For

It might not be The American Century after all, or The Russian Century, or The Atomic Century. Perhaps it would be the century that broadened and implemented the idea of freedom, all the freedoms. Of all men.—Laura Z. Hobson, *Gentlemen's Agreement*[1]

Published in the midst of Cold War paranoia about a World Communism, the wildly popular novel and film *Gentlemen's Agreement* (1946 and 1947 respectively) inaugurated the paradoxical companion trend to face America's domestic problems through popular entertainment. Set against an agon figured on one hand as a contest between Russia and America, and, on the other, as The Horror from which we could no longer retreat (the fantasized atomic holocaust, not the actual racist-genocidal ones), these apparently progressive forms of entertainment directed their moral appeal not to nation but to humanity. But the very idea of humanity such films and novels invoked was itself already shot through with the dread of communism. Indeed, they struggle with how to manage domestic conflict without rendering the fabric of nationness susceptible to alien influences and threats. The merits of a global defense of democracy were fading for the many people who were locked out of the American Dream: one means of producing a new allegiance to nation was the heavily broadcast House Committee on Un-American Activities (HUAC) hearings.

As we know, gay people were increasingly targeted as the trials progressed. In addition to shattering individual lives, the hearings had negative consequences for subsequent gay politics in at least three ways: They caused a split in the early homophile movement; sharpened the tooth of immigration and government employment policies based on the equation of closeted homosexuals (at risk of giving away state secrets) and hidden communists (actively betraying America); and, at least until the

1960s, became the historical backdrop that structured all of the "new social movement"'s relation to Marxist theory and practice. An ominous event, indeed.

Foucault admonished us to think of power as not purely negative, unitary, crushing down from above, but also as productive, multiple, lateral. Looking back across the last four decades, we can see that while homosexuals *were* swept up in the HUAC feeding frenzy, they were also articulated to the category of those "problems" toward which Americans might turn a gentler eye. Indeed, HUAC plays a complicated role in gay history. Part of the bargain of civil rights, once they were secured by new laws and practices in the 1960s, was the demand for a legible history of oppression. Once HUAC was widely accepted as one of America's ugliest hours, lesbians and gay men could point to the hearings as vivid evidence of homosexuals' status as a "suspect class."[2] However, a critical issue of queer historicity emerges in this historicization of lesbian and gay oppression. Since gay people didn't form into a coherent civil class until the late 1980s (and this is still highly contentious), who or what was under attack by HUAC?[3]

I hope to show here that unlike the red-baiter's communist, figured as an actual or virtual alien, the 1940s queer was still of the nation. In the transformation of the citizen underway in the post–World War II era, homosexuals were not so much another kind of invader, virtual aliens due to their relationship to another nation, as the limit case of a new kind of citizenship that required empathy, but not to the extent of replacing the nation as love object.[4]

That queerness would have been incorporated into the national project of redefining the citizen is counterintuitive: though to differing degrees, anticommunist and antihomosexual sensibilities were palpable elements of post–World War II American identity. Indisputably, the rhetoric of the HUAC trials and, as I have elsewhere argued, more recent right-wing homophobes employ metaphors of penetration and invasion to describe the danger of both communism and queerness.[5] But the place of queerness in the rhetoric of the post–World War II years is quite different, and this has had important consequences for subsequent gay politics, even if the myriad effects on individuals' lives has been more subtle than HUAC's heavy hand. The fixity of the class, "communists," should not mislead us into presuming that the reasons for objecting to homosexuals—not yet officially discursively constructed as a class—ran in parallel. Both communist association and homosexuality were reasons for exclusion of aliens under immigration law.[6] But queerness was not taken as a serious statement of political allegiance to some other world order. The geography imagined as the location of this invasion and the physics of the dimension of reality in which the nation's sexual perimeter was imagined to exist were completely different than those that were under assault by communists.

I have suggested elsewhere that the very idea of identity, as we think of it now, is inextricably bound to the rise of civil-rights law, with its need to set the parameters of a suspect class by isolating *the* trait on the basis of which a class has faced systematic discrimination.[7] But I do not suppose that the establishment of homosexuals' class status happened solely through the efforts of countless civil-rights activists, nor do I imagine that the history of oppression invoked as the aura of lesbian and gay classness arrived in the mind of America unmediated.[8] A concept of minority "experience" similar to that described by activists as "consciousness" was popularized in novels and films of the post–World War II era. Activists view that these new consciousnesses among the oppressed were the harbingers of revolutionary change. But in popular culture, "experience," a new zone for mutual understanding ("identification") via mediated access to the experience of others, enthusiastically promised to quell domestic troubles.[9]

America's long-standing, nationally constitutive mixed feelings about social issues were intrinsically biased, or rather, positioned in relation to who one was and what cross-identifications one was willing to undertake. Memories of the American Civil War had grown dim. As traumatic as race relations were, without outside agitators, they did not threaten America as a nation: *social issues were "problems," not politics.* America had a new faith that lowering the boundaries of the ego in order to merge with another—the imaginary practice of identification rather than the sociosexual practice of "mixing"—would forever change Americans' empathy toward each other. The techniques of such a new citizenship were demonstrated through Method acting, already popular on the stage and entering cinema through the problem films, and the new journalism, which shed strict objectivity in favor of placing the reader in the scene. I want to explore the production of the empathetic citizen and the reconstruction of his (principally) affective relation to nation and comrade through a consideration of a legal distinction between kinds of aliens, a surprising use of a "female" entertainment as a political vehicle, and the specific construction of the anti-anti-Semite.[10] Finally, I will speculate on the implications of this genealogy of the citizen for queer politics at the end of a millennium.

In the epidemiology of the Red Scare, gay communists were attributed to the active, masculinized category, "communist," both confounding and reifying the equation of the two. There were, of course, many anti-gay communists and not a few anticommunist gays, but for the HUAC senators, vilification of one did not exonerate the accused of the other: the true American was neither. HUAC struggled to organize love of country and love of fellow man: the wrong degree of either was problematic, but for different reasons. In fact, the communists who wanted a world order and the homosexual who preferred love of fellow citizens to love of nation were opposites that constituted a third term: the anticommunist citizen with appropriate empathy toward others. According to Public Law 414 (1952), also known as the "Immigration and Nationality Act," the problem with communism—a problem also latent in Zionism, described in popular works as a religion that could supersede that nation— was its terrifying global ambitions: "Sec. 101 (a) (40) The term 'world communism' means a revolutionary movement, the purpose of which is to establish eventually a Communist totalitarian dictatorship in any or all of the countries of the world through the medium of an internationally coordinated political movement."[11] This long, elaborate statute on immigration, debated during HUAC and finally passed in 1952, immortalizes the communist-hunters' sensibility in contemporary American law and hints at the difference between queerness and communism in the different responses it offers to aliens of these two kinds.[12]

Though mute on the issue of how American-born communists would be treated (they were harassed, but not literally exiled), Public Law 414 is quite clear that to declare oneself communist is to make oneself inadmissible to the United States. The declaration of homosexuality could also render one inadmissible, but the violation of American law was different—indeed, the sections covering allegiance to the idea of a world political order or to communism are copious and repeated at every juncture to insure no escape hatches, while the sections covering immoralities are relatively brief and nonrepetitive. Public Law 414 accords different status to political membership or advocacy versus immorality. Apparently, immoralities are apolitical. While they inhere in the individual and will eventually surface, they are a problem of social order not political sovereignty. By contrast, an individual's politics are structured around a logic of deniability; the ability to strategically deny one's beliefs implies that they are already conscious to the self. Immoralities were private truths that would eventually speak, but political beliefs were resistant to what Foucault called the incitement to discourse.[13] Thus, the law had to enumerate the symptoms of membership that no denial could override. These extend from:

The giving, loaning, or promising of support or of money or any other thing of value to be used for advocating any doctrine shall constitute the advocating of such doctrine

through

giving, loaning, or promising of support or money or any other thing of value for any purpose to any organization shall be presumed to constitute affiliation therewith

to

advocating the economic, international, and governmental doctrines of world communism means advocating the establishment of a totalitarian Communist dictatorship in any or all of the countries of the world.[14]

This advocacy or affiliation is a reason for nonadmission to America, because it exposes a person's citizen-like relation to a metanational world order that is understood as an intrinsic challenge to U.S. national integrity.

By contrast, homosexuality is implied under a subsequent section enumerating the specific areas to be examined in determining whether a person is of "good moral character," an issue to be examined only after a petitioner's national allegiance has been established.[15] Here, the problem is the possibility that such persons will burden the welfare state, increase the ranks of criminals, or, in the case of prostitution and seeking perverse sexual acts, subtly tear at the fabric of American domestic life. But precisely because they are not political, suspect sexual bodies present a special problem: as vivid as was the Fear of a Commie Planet, communists' allegiance was still to a world *political* order, a kind of mega-nation that strengthened the idea of nations, United or not. By contrast, homosexuals defied the very primacy of nation as the ultimate love object.

There are many ways of aligning love of country and love of man. Long before they imagined the nation, long before protoidentitarian homosexuals like Edward Carpenter conceptualized specifically queer politics, Western political philosophers like Plato had imagined various homosocial/erotic bonds as the basis of patriotism. However, during the immediate post–World War II era, American politicians of the right asserted that the degraded desire of one man to consume another's body had the power to undermine that most noble desire: to surrender one's body and die for one's nation. They might have suggested, as some far right politicians do today, that self-annihilation was the homosexual's patriotic duty. But America was unwilling to be officially and completely rid of its homosexual citizens: exclusion from direct contact with the important business of the state was enough. The emerging civil-rights efforts (which still shuddered to imagine sexuality as a category) and immigration law, which was not interested in separating homosexuality (as a "preference" or "orientation") from other immoral sex acts, were ambivalent about the etiology and effects of two directions of political love: comrade-love versus nation-love. Despite the quick slide that made American communists virtual Russians and American Jews virtual Zionists, Americans declined to construe homosexuals as virtual aliens, as patriots responding to a different national drum.

Benedict Anderson offers the idea of political love, which I want to consider for a moment here as I propose that post–World War II America reorganized the structure of the citizen's affectivity. Anderson's *Imagined Communities* has been extended and reworked to analyze various forms of mediation that have produced the variety of forms of nation we know today. But it is the affective relation to the nation more so than its diversity that seems, upon closer reading, to be Anderson's central concern. He ponders "why, today, they command such profound emotional legitimacy," and he returns to this problematic after detailing—and nearly causing us to lose sight of affectivity—the multiple and historically contingent forms that imagining a nation takes.[16]

> the great wars of this century are extraordinary not so much in the unprecedented scale on which they permitted people to kill, as in the colossal numbers persuaded to lay down their lives. . . .
>
> Dying for one's country, which usually one does not choose, assumes a moral grandeur which dying for the Labour Party, the American Medical Association, or perhaps even Amnesty International can not rival, for these are all bodies one can join or leave at easy will. Dying for the revolution also draws its grandeur from the degree to which it is felt to be something fundamentally pure. (If people imagined the proletariat *merely* as a group in hot pursuit of refrigerators, holidays, or power, how far would they, including members of the proletariat, be willing to die for it?)[17]

Because the form of nation is multiple, the undergirding issue of the relation between a nation and its people is not reducible to the simultaneity of a mark and the inhabitation of a single place, or the historico-ethnic similarity that a people who have happened to light in the same place are supposed to share. This complex love that binds together historically divergent formations of nation in peace and war makes clearer why the homosexual, under the emerging regime of rights discourse, could neither be assimilated to nor ejected from the nation, except by allowing religion to momentarily trump the state. The homosexual appears to share so many of the traits of the citizen—often including overt patriotism. He does not direct his allegiance to *another* nation; he is, still, legally, American. The geophagic logic of nation cannot imagine a body without a nation, and, unlike its Spartan precursor, the nation refuses to acknowledge that love of men over country might mean that the citizen is willing to die in war not *for* nation, but *as* lover. The problem with the homosexual's love is dual, either he is acting in the interests of something that can be "taken up or put down at easy will" (the contemporary "choice" rhetoric) or, is engaged in an allegiance that is not fundamentally pure, not because it violates some biblical passage, but because its unnaturalness, though not chosen, is, nonetheless, not a "natural" tie. To understand homosexualities' problematic relation to nation, we can recall Anderson's discussion of political love, which

> can be deciphered in from the ways in which languages describe its object: either in the vocabulary of kinship (motherland, *Vaterland, patria*) or that of home (*heimat* or *tanah air* [earth and water, the phrase for the Indonesians' native archipelago]). Both idioms denote something to which one is naturally tied. As we have seen earlier, in everything 'natural' there is always something unchosen. In this way, nation-ness is assimilated to skin-color, gender, parentage and birth-era—all those things one can not help. And in these 'natural ties' one senses what one might call 'the beauty of *gemeinschaft*'. To put it another way, precisely because such ties are not chosen, they have about them a halo of disinterestedness.[18]

The un-natural, can-not-be-helpedness of homosexuality makes the homosexual's apparent choice to love man over country a passive rejection of the political love that underwrites modern nationality. The presumed passivity of the corrosive homosexual desire is the abjection of a new kind of masculinity that dare not speak its name, only name what it refuses. The homosexual emerges not as a communist invader pursuing a world order, but as an obsessive, neurotic masculinity that has failed to integrate subnational identification into a national identity. Embracing the mantle of world leader, protector of a democracy that demands pluralizing, is a tough job for the latter-day Rough Riders. Learning to "walk in the other guy's shoes," the homoerotic slip that is the popular phrasing of a New Testament parable harkens in a treacherous new kind of masculinity as the basis for a new American identity.[19] What was partly at stake in the vilification of homosexuals was the interiority of the citizen: indeed, who knew what—evil or good—lurks in the hearts of men? Equally importantly, who was going to find out? The lingering fear that it takes one to know one is partly dampened by the new conviction—rampant in university English departments and popular entertainment—that art, as a medium for transferring experience, could be put to work solving America's melting-pot problem.

POPULARIZING "THE PROBLEM": POLITICS AS MELODRAMA

The 1940s witnessed the introduction of a new popular entertainment form: the "problem" novel and film. Although the films (and to a less obvious extent, the novels to which they relate) span a range of formally defined genres—from action films such as *Home of the Brave* (1949), the noir *Crossfire* (1947), to melodramas such as *Gentlemen's Agreement* and *Pinky* (1949)—commentators of the day and subsequent historians write about them as a quasi genre whose distinguishing commonality is thematic. Historians of these works generally cite the postwar liberalization of social attitudes for the sudden popularity of books and films about long-standing American "problems." Film historians especially describe as incremental the exploration of "problems" America was thought newly willing to examine, echoing the sense of the relative difficulty of each that is explicit in the works themselves: anti-Semitism, racism, and the final frontiers of homosexuality, drug addiction, and, eventually, gender relations.[20] Or, as a character in *Gentlemen's Agreement* puts it: "What the hell chance have we of getting decent with thirteen million Negroes if we can't lick the much easier business of anti-semitism?" (184). However formally different the films are, commentators' and historians' sense that audiences were newly open toward "controversial" topics binds the works into a mutually referential block, a "genre" defined by its ambition to enlighten post–World War II Americans and to modernize their attitudes toward "social" issues.[21] But the emphasis on theme leads most commentators to overlook interrelated aspects of the books, films, and their reception: their self-conscious attention to psychological structuring and their presumption that forms of oppression are interchangeable. Together, these suggest that an individual's pathological prejudice looms larger than the systems and structures that maintain white middle-classness against variegated difference.

Home of the Brave was an early vehicle for the actor James Edwards, who plays a black soldier undergoing psychoanalysis after he has become paraplegic following his unsuccessful attempt to save the racist Southerner whom he has befriended. This 1949 film is based on a book that dealt with soldiers' *anti-Semitism*. The link between racism and anti-Semitism remains, or rather, is displaced: the Army psychiatrist who cures the soldier is heavily coded as Jewish. Although flashback scenes make the work as a whole look like an action film, it is most fundamentally about transference and countertransference between victims and victimizers. Similarly, *Crossfire* (1947) was based on a book (*The Brick Foxhole*) about a *homophobic* murder. Instead, an offending Jew is killed early in the film, leaving a range of still homosexually panicky B-movie hunks to display their anti-Semitism as they attempt to cover up their noirish crime. While *Gentlemen's Agreement* makes no similar substitution, the plot, in which Gregory Peck plays a Gentile reporter passing as a Jew in order to expose anti-Semitism, lifts a page from the popular stories of black women passing as white, of which *Pinky*, released two years later, is the central cinematic example.[22]

Both the book and film version of *Gentlemen's Agreement* rely on a new vision of the journalist as producer of material that could be used to disentangle the crossed disidentification that is prejudice. The journalist's close encounters could call the citizen to a higher order of identification, not with a race or religion, but a Universal Human Experience of suffering and compassion. The practice of *reverse passing* is the most extreme means available for the sensitive, socially dominant individual (or more likely their journalist surrogate, as in this case and the later *Black Like Me*) to achieve an "experience" that would transform their understanding of an other. While literary theorists and college presidents debated the value of literature as a means to combat the anomie of modern life and the decay of a commonly held American sensibility, popular journalism was acculturating its readers to a "you are there" style of reporting that promoted the pseudo-interiority penned by reporters as a truth greater and simpler than that of the Great Works. "It was only a matter of disguising a name, a face, the background, but for the rest it was recording instead of contriving. Each thing as it had happened was put down; he was only the biographer of a Phil Green who was Jewish. The power of the inventing novelist or the devising playwright was as nothing to this simple strength of the biographer; here was truth, not fantasy, here in these paragraphs unrolling were only fact and record" (203). By the end of the 1940s, the idea of "being there," already secured for the war or international correspondent, was applied to reportage on domestic, extra-governmental issues. The new style of journalism combined with melodrama to produce a new kind of entertainment that was controversial both in content and in form. If the epic structure of the battle between good and evil made the war narrative coherent, melodrama provided an emotional repertoire for apprehending America's domestic troubles.

"Serious" films would soon be able to drop the journalist intermediary as the audience's vehicle for cross-identifications. Method acting, which rested on a similar commitment to the autobiographic, would eventually signal to the dominant viewer that cross-identification for the purpose of "better understanding" was not only permitted but encouraged. The flat-footedness, the "queerness" of these early cinematic attempts to forge a new structure of identification comes less from bad acting than from the redundancy of foregrounding the process of accessing one's "interior," the stock-in-trade naturalized through Method. Method, a new style of journalism, and the legibility of melodrama's structure converged to form a new sensibility for interpreting social problems. This collision had to rework the existing gendering of conventional entertainment forms.

Melodrama is widely understood to be aimed at a female audience. Some reviewers in the 1940s revealed their perceptions of the gendering of political responsibility when they argued that it demeaned the seriousness of the "problems" to treat them through melodrama. The disdain toward the political value of women's entertainment continued in later commentators' criticism of melodrama's capacity to represent the truth of racism and anti-Semitism: David A. Cook believes that *Pinky*, as a "sentimental tale of a young black woman who tries to pass for white, is even less credible [than *Gentlemen's Agreement*]."[23]

That so many of the popular works about "problems" came in the form of melodrama is not an accident, but it may not be immediately obvious why this happened. The *location* of troubles and allocation of responsibility for their redress would be under revision for at least three more decades.[24] On the one hand, the immediate post–World War II era saw a return to the cult of domesticity; women were rapidly transformed from industrial fodder for the war machine into domestic managers of the consumer durables fashioned in the factories in which these women had beaten, smelted, and welded the very same materials into battleships. Women might have become the postmodern version of postcolonial (American) Mothers of the Republic, the central audience for politicizing "social" problems. However, as I will show in a moment, women were actually excluded from the emerging idea of the citizen. The "war at home" had no place for women, whose job as keepers of consumption was represented not as political, but as a distraction from political matters.[25] The government's role in the domestic life of the nation had already been "feminized" during the Great Depression: safety-net social programs reached an unprecedented level and were classified as a function of central government.[26] In the post–World War II era, a more subtle refiguration was underway, concerned less with the government's role inside the borders of *nation* than with reorganizing the citizen's self-policing of social conflict: how should we balance the citizen's vigilance toward alien invaders with the need to dampen attention to differences within the body politic that seemed to cause civil strife?

The production of "the problem" through melodrama is significant not because of literal audience demographics but because it suggests that learning about the new social problems would occur less through direct experience or political debate, than through acquisition of the proper emotions and structures of identification.[27] The proposed affectivity was both a blessing and a curse, a solution and a new problem: intrinsic to the construction of "social" (as opposed to political) issues for the entertainment-consuming national public was a conviction that cross-identification would ultimately result in social progress. However, segregation was still the law, and "mixing" still held frightening connotations for whites. Expansion of mass media made it possible, even desirable, to promote an imaginary social equality—the domestic multicultural equivalent of the global village—while leaving intact the systems that make individual prejudice politically effective.[28] Indeed, what the problem works finally produce is a new definition of the citizen as one who can identify with the other members of the melting pot. What *Gentlemen's Agreement* provides is a blueprint for transforming unwitting bigots into citizens with an aptitude for empathy, who could know all about "others" without ever meeting "them."

INTO THE CLOSET

Most of the widely circulated Hobson books are organized around the idea of journalism and the journalist as the site and personification of the truth about America.[29] But this was a new kind of journalism, a journalism not of complete unbias but of affectivity, the "information" equivalent of Method acting. After searching for an angle for his series on anti-Semitism, Phil Green, the protagonist in *Gentlemen's Agreement*, realizes he'll "have to go at it from *inside*," be "Jewish for three months . . . Or six weeks or however long, till I get the feel of it" (72). Despite his worries that his attempt to pass as a Jew is fraudulent (and no wonder!—he had apparently only known one Jewish person, Army buddy Dave), he sometimes forgets that he is in character: "'Funny thing,' he said, 'the way I felt so man-to-man with Miss Wales [a passing Jew] when she pitched me [an anti-Semitic remark]. Asking her right out how she felt, as if we both were really on the inside. I keep forgetting it's just an act'" (106).

As a new kind of journalist, Phil, who has previously gone undercover as a miner and as a migrant worker, has the right combination of personal disinterestedness and neurotic, queer capacity to "understand the other fellow." This affectivity is the postmodern relative of the modern conviction, which Eve Kosofsky Sedgwick recognizes in the apt phrase: it takes one to know one. Here, the empathetic social chameleon politicizes instead of demonizes the man with the special sensitivity to temporarily lose himself to the other. In fact, such an individual might be able to capture an experience *better* than someone who has lived it their whole life. The non-Jew passing as a Jew is more objective: the actual Jew is both desensitized to, and in a sinister reintroduction of the stereotype under attack, hypersensitive to anti-Semitism. It is both his lack of defenses and his lack of group investment that makes the (Gentile) journalist the best person to report on the experience of the other: "identification" can reveal the essence of experience, which is mired in the individual pathologies (paranoia and overidentification) of those who have actually lived it.

Gentlemen's Agreement is loathe to admit that it is about the white man's burden of becoming nicer toward those whom he has exploited. Displacing the history of Christian white men's disastrous global escapades, Phil figures the person who alone has the capacity for the irrevocable transformation that marks the new citizen; the one who will turn America from a sea of bigots into a nation of empaths. Granting present readers' inescapable association of the images employed here with the now-overdetermined relation between semen, HIV, and homosexuality, Phil's account of his transformation nevertheless reads like the aftermath of an unexpected—even unwanted—but exhilarating sexual encounter. Emotions are slightly unpleasant and unformed goo. Experience enters the body through a portal other than the brain, becomes inseparably mixed with cells that are more properly one's own.

> Gluey and inescapable, the extraordinary melancholy clung to him. . . . Phil tried to locate the source of this new infection of moodiness—the inn, his mother's stroke, the hostility of Miss Wales, the continued fruitlessness of Dave's search for a place to live, the postponement of the wedding—but not any one of them, nor the sum of them all, convinced him that he had isolated the cause of the sticky sadness in him.
>
> He had accepted the fact that in a few weeks he'd undergone a swift and deep transfusion into his own blood of a million corpuscles of experience and emotion. (182)

This "identification" short of identity loss, this emotional miscegenation, was a desperate gambit for new citizenship: domestic, but political, or as Phil's mother keeps saying, "each home decides." Offering an alternate, but still complementary, solution to HUAC's hysteria, this new system of identification is the best plan against communism; it humanizes and individualizes the citizen in a way that "world orders" will not. Implicitly, it is the capacity to produce and order emotions in service of freedom that makes Americans:

> "Jobs and economic security, sure—even the Fascists and Communists promise that. No, [publisher Minify] said it had got down to a matter of equal self-respect, pride, ego, whatever. Take Communism. It's got one good thing, anyway—equality among white and black, all minorities—only the price there is so big, too. If we did it, without the price of free speech, free opposition, free everything—then we'd really be fighting the Communists where it counts. . . . beating antisemitism [sic] and antinegroism is a political must now, not just sweet decency." (184)

To some extent, the book depends on the class stereotypes of masculinity, in which prejudice is situated "in a dark crackpot place with low-class morons" (192). The implicit masculinity of these "obvious" anti-Semites helps make it easier to imagine the empathetic citizen not as feminized, but as combating a dangerous form of masculinity. In the shift from decency to national security that partially sutures social issues to the task of beating the communists, liberal pluralism joins hands with the red-baiting that, if understood as a dimension of racial or class conflict, it would have opposed. The *liberal* postwar ethic adopted the paranoid political fantasy of unseen threats to America, now thought to be an exclusive property of the right: "Millions [of people who don't think they are anti-Semitic] back up the lunatic vanguard in its war for this country—forming the rear echelons, the home front in the factories, manufacturing the silence and acquiescence" (192). This careful reinscription of the appropriate amount of masculinity quietly sets itself against the woman whose role in capitalist consumption and whose emotions, which lead to confusion rather than transformation, exclude her from the sensitivities required of the new citizen.[30] Though "subterranean," her emotions do not have the "goo" that transforms the man: "The subterranean paths that twined through human impulses and motives always eluded you if you tried to follow them. At least for her they did. There was no use to will herself to the task. She never had a road map. She always got lost" (88). The patriotic male bond encourages identification across comparatively small social difference in order to stave off the dramatic difference that can be recognized in the company of women. This gulf separates empathy from emotion, reconstructs identification as a masculine activity that connects buddy-love not to desire or sexuality, but to defense of country. Women are no longer part of the war effort, not Rosie the Riveters, but "pale plump softness" concerned more with "parties" and "summer cottages" than the serious business of national defense, the "tight" "tracks of reality":

> As he sat talking with Dave, a preference for male companionship beat through him, surly, superior. Women talked of parties, of family, of children and summer cottages and love. This with Dave was what a man needed, this bone and muscle for the mind instead of pale plump softness. This men's talk was all in the hard clean outlines of battle, impossible bridges to be built under fire, the split of the atom, the greed of looting armies. Dave had begun in Italy and gone through the whole business of D Day and the rest. He'd been wounded and mended and thrown back in. Women clawed softly at your manhood. War and work and the things you believed in gave it back to you. *This* gave it back to you, lounging in opposite chairs, taking the good short cuts men could take who'd been through the same things, fiddling through long drinks, arguing, differing or agreeing, but always tight on the tracks of reality. (129)

That men's empathy cannot be feminine or feminizing is made clear in two asides about gender identification. Early in his contemplation of difference and identification, Phil notes that: "My trouble is, he thought, the only difference that rates with me is people's sex." Hobson goes on to have Phil reflect that: "The notion amused him. I *do* care whether somebody's a man or a woman" (47–48). At the book's end, the magazine staff wonders what Phil's next assignment will be. " 'I was a woman for eight weeks?' Phil asked, and they all shouted" (268). The hilarity with which the staff greets this possibility turns a blind eye to the possibility of high heels as the next step in "walking in the other guy's shoes."[31]

The homopatriotic fusion of Phil and Dave masculinizes empathy as long as non-Zionist Jewishness is contained within America. With "oversensitiveness" attributed to the Jew (a patriot, an object of empathy, but not a citizen), with women ruled out as subjects for cross-identificatory empathy, the new citizen turns out to be a Christian, white, heterosexual male.[32] Without explicitly naming it, queerness is projected as the outer limit of mutual understanding. The admonitions against Zionism trace the edge of the alternate misalliance—to religion over nation.

Despite its surface discourse of personal attitude, anti-Semitism is approached from the perspective of nation, rather than of those subject to its devastation. Anti-Semitism is as dangerous as communism, because it produces a Jewish identification—Zionism—that is in grave danger of pursuing another kind of world order. Anti-Semitism is both an individual threat and a force that can engender a response that runs against the most basic premise of modernity and its embodiment, America. The brilliant scientist Lieberman admonishes Phil to be discriminating in "experiencing" his brief Jewishness: "Phil had defended 'the Palestine solution' for the immediate present at least, [but] Lieberman's words came back to him. "Don't let them pull the crisis over your eyes. You say you oppose all nationalism—then how can you fall for a *religious* nationalism? A rejoining of church and state after all these centuries?" (212). This logical gambit reveals how liberal pluralism can promote freedom while at the same time presuming American dominance. Hiding America within the concept of freedom invokes a national identity that simultaneously transcends nation to speak of humanity, but does so in the context of a community of nations, not world communism. The invocation of human rights is, always and simultaneously, a form of opposing particular figures of world order and allegiance beyond the nation: both the communist and the Zionist Jew.

Identity—the common referent of civil-rights and human-rights rhetoric—is the Rosemary's Baby of contemporary liberal pluralism. Born in a response to communism and installed at the heart of the identity politics it underwrites, identification has a deep sympathy with a particular kind of national identity that preaches melodramatic empathy in place of a potentially erotic comrade-love. With the empathetic citizen having absorbed much of what once marked suspect masculinities, the homosexual could figure empathy gone awry. It was not so much feminization that was the homosexual's crime, as the failure to make the turn from the strongest masculine identification of soldier into an empathy that served the nation. Queerness is the collapse of political love into something else, a subterranean place in which goo produces not transformation but fusion. Queerness is, in this instance, beyond, even, *against* identity. An antiqueer inscription of anticommunism lies at the heart of the political constellation that has produced contemporary gay politics.

ALIENATING QUEER

Recounted by victims of the event who subsequently became gay activists, repeated in virtually every history gay Americans have written about ourselves, HUAC is a touchstone in the countermemory that has provided unity for our otherwise fragmentary politics. By creating an affective attachment to the very nation that has reviled us, the hagiographic incorporation of victims (and victimizers—Roy Cohn works in *Angels in America* because he had figured the complexities of queer unity for several decades of gay and lesbian activists) of HUAC into *our history* helps secure our place as citizens. In articulating ourselves as unjustly deprived of civil rights, we participate in American citizenship, we respond to the desire for rights that will assimilate us to the whole of the nation. For many of us, that affective response has proven lifesaving. To the extent that it has succeeded, gay political efforts have convinced many—perhaps even a majority of—Americans that, as Newt Gingrich put it, most gay people are good citizens on most days. Perhaps that is as much as we can get. Perhaps it explains why we were offered a place, albeit it equivocally, in the military before we were given protection against discrimination under federal law.

Clearly, much has changed in the constellation of alien, queer, protected class, but their interconnection is only loosened, not rent. It may seem heartless to look beyond the stark evidence of blatant, vicious homophobia in the early Cold War, but revisiting this period with post-identitarian eyes has practical consequences for the queer politics that have framed themselves around disrupting or taking over the idea of nation-ness. If nothing else, it will provide a clearer understanding of how to disrupt the easy accusation, only latent in some responses to the Roy Cohn character in *Angels in America*, that neither AIDS nor HUAC counts as oppression because "we," or the loose cannons "among us," brought these disasters on ourselves. Even better if "In Your Face" politics can recognize that the term under assault (citizenship?) and the idea under erasure (nation) are themselves already multiple and labile, that queer politics are not exclusively cultural, but should go to the heart of definitions of the citizen that are woven into concrete practices of the state. I've made some guesses why communistic activity—even by the natural-born citizens—could be construed as treasonous, while the homosexual's practice, although making him suspect as a citizen, did not alienate him from the nation. Perhaps we should imagine how a Queer Nation might prepare to expatriate itself, to *become alien*, as a means to substantially challenge the very idea of nation. Without truly putting one's American citizenship at risk, without seriously entertaining the consequences of becoming a person without a nation, Queer Nation, though it refuses to specify its rules of membership, will continue to collapse into the identity politics that are, as I've suggested here, inextricably tied to American nationalism. Operating above the threshold of citizenship, trading in its privileges instead of criticizing the fantasies of nation and of rights, queerness risks being just another labeled group that liberal pluralism can easily accommodate.[33] The discourse of identity that Hobson places in the mouth of the book's most secular Jew suggests a way to more fully activate the suggestive phrase "queer nation," to fricatively align queer citizenship with citizenship in America, to *queer* the legal categories and models of nationality that still lie as fissures in the citizen-nation complex.

The stereotypical-looking but secular-thinking scientist of *Gentlemen's Agreement* suggests a politics that must have seemed nearly incoherent in its day. As a totally nonreligious and noncultural Jew, he proposes to queer the category "Jew" by claiming not to be what he "obviously" is in order to disrupt the claim that such a thing has a particular significance: "'My crusade will have a certain charm,' Lieberman continued now. 'I will go forth and state flatly, "I am not a Jew."' He looked at Phil. 'With this face that becomes not an evasion but a new principle. A scientific principle.'" But this plan has a problem, "Because this world still makes it an advantage not to be one. . . . Only if there were no anti-Semites could I do it" (212–13). He cannot, or rather, Hobson cannot, imagine a way to, succeed in this politics as long as such a refusal of an attributive identity could be misunderstood as an attempt to pass, and therefore reinforce the shackling identity by appearing to desire or evade it. For Hobson, this politics can only be successful when it is no longer necessary.

Then why even propose it? Hobson has sensed the possibilities of this strange space of attributive identity and passing, even though she can't quite work them out. In fact, it may be that it is the invisible queer, from a rather different vantage point, who can make use of the strange lever she locates. The suggestion is to doggedly avoid the reverse discourse, like that of the slogan, "Gay is good," to step away from a discourse of the relative advantages and disadvantages of particular social locations. Instead, the good doctor hints, we need to mobilize the perverse side of cross-identifications and "natural" political love—his plan has "an innocence—no, a sort of purity" (213)—that both invokes and dissembles in the face of the "grandeur from the degree to which [revolution] is felt to be something fundamentally pure."[34] What the good doctor realizes is that face is less a mask, than a hole gouged out in the social landscape.

The seduction of identity is great, and the geophagia of the nation is terrifying. To be an effective new form of politics, queer must break from the legacy of nation that social movements have inherited, must avert the collapse of community into quarantine camp that the fact of AIDS makes all too easy.[35] Queer must find a way to place its face outside nation, not, as some activists have urged, as a sinkhole in the circulation of capital, but as a refusal of political love. A truly queer nation would offer habitation, a resting place for face, that we would not have to die for.

NOTES

1 Laura Z. Hobson, *Gentlemen's Agreement* (New York: Arbor House, 1947), p. 204. Further citations to this work will be given parenthetically in the text.

2 The "suspect class" is the law's slip-of-the-tongue attempt to neutrally define a group that it has not yet anointed a group, a group the law has not previously "seen" and "named."

3　See Janet E. Halley, "The Construction of Heterosexuality" in *Fear of a Queer Planet,* ed. Michael Warner (Minneapolis: University of Minnesota Press, 1993), pp. 82–102.

4　This new structure of citizenship would undergo another change in the 1980s when empathy would be fine-tuned into a sense of compassion toward people with AIDS. This would, ostensibly, dampen the negative consequences of discrimination (that infected people would "go underground," depriving science of its research object and threatening the mainstream with misrecognized contact). But tough love was required if the citizen was to feel compassion but not vote for care and education funding measures that might have more equitably distributed health care and more rapidly halted transmission.

5　Cindy Patton, "Queer Space/God's Space: Counting Down to the Apocalypse," in *Rethinking Marxism* (forthcoming).

6　The legal issues in this period are extremely complex, and the changes occurring in legislation, the courts, the HUAC trials, and in popular culture did not work in concert. The consolidated law regarding how "aliens" might be present in America reveals two fears of invasion: first, that totalitarians will infiltrate and overthrow the government in a bloodless coup (as in, for example, the slightly later *The Manchurian Candidate* and its countless imitators), but second, that "outsiders" espousing certain social doctrines—especially those concerning race relations—would use "propaganda" to agitate Americans to destroy each other. Thus, communists will exaggerate racism in favor of world communism and totalitarians like Nazis will use racial strife to supplant the legitimacy of the American government. Both conclusions are wistful displacements of the still officially sanctioned separation of blacks and whites. Indeed, the Supreme Court was, at this very moment, hearing the *Brown v. Board of Education* case along with two cases regarding censorship of racial images/ideas—one concerning the 1949 film *Pinky* and a second concerning the 1950 film version of Richard Wright's *Native Son.* Until the mid-1940s, "political propaganda" was conceived largely as ideas directed toward issues of governmental and economic form. Unable to individually compete in a global market of ideas, Americans had to be protected from the "bias" of outsiders' opinions. What *our* government said to us was not considered biased, indeed, the government stated that it had a duty to shout down opinions (attributed to outsiders) that did not agree with its own. See Elizabeth Hull, *Taking Liberties: National Barriers to the Free Flow of Ideas* (New York: Praeger, 1990).

Assigning alienness to ideas post–World War II grew increasingly difficult, because the very idea of propaganda and the value of suppressing it were changing. The Supreme Court case *Winters v. New York,* redrew the parameters of a once comfortable linkage between suppression of propaganda (through things like alien registration) and the support of freedom of speech. Taste was newly an issue, at least covertly. *Winters v. New York* concerns the criminalization of behavior for publishing or distributing violent or graphic printed material. In its conclusions the Court held that "[t]he line between the informing and the entertaining is too elusive for the protection of that basic right [a free press]. Everyone is familiar with instances of propaganda through fiction. What is one man's amusement, teaches another's doctrine. [N.B.: "Doctrine" has a specific legal meaning in the later act, it "includes, but is not limited to, polities, practices, purposes, aims, or procedures."]"

While this gambit of legal dismantling was slowly changing what Americans could read and see, the dislocations of the war and postwar eras stirred the mix of America's urban melting pots, newly highlighting the cultural diversity of Americans. The increasing mobility of popular culture screened these differences to Americans, suggest-

To Die For　347

ing that alternate world views were, within limits, not so threatening. If laws regulating speech had attempted to distinguish between social problems and political issues, the latter uniquely affecting national security because of its contact with a world outside America, the Civil Rights movement offered a new class of political speech about the social. Because they demanded recognition of a class-based experience, the representatives of those classes, with their "authentic" speech, came to be a sign for a particular political belief. To the extent that this belief was designated political propaganda, that *person* became something like a foreign agent; speech was protected to the extent that a speaker had legitimacy. In Public Law 414, this complex play of status, speech, and advocacy constructs two asymmetrical categories—being categorized as a communist is performative: any show of support—giving money or advocating through speech—is treasonous. Public Law 414, 1952, *Act to Revise the Law Relating to Immigration, Naturalization, and Nationality.* Pervert status is cast against a grid of already-designated acts of immorality: more explicitly corporeal, evidenced through the trace of past acts (history of incarceration) or through acts or solicitations of outlawed sex.

7   Cindy Patton, "Tremble, Hetero Swine!" in *Fear of a Queer Planet*, ed. Michael Warner (Minneapolis: University of Minnesota Press, 1993), pp. 143–77, and "Refiguring Social Space," in *Social Postmodernism*, ed. Linda Nicholson and Steven Seidman (Cambridge: Cambridge University Press, 1995).

8   That homosexuals are now considered a class is not largely in dispute: what kind of class and whether they should be added to the list of potential discriminees is the issue in current debates.

9   Theorizing the relationship between political activism and the discursive effects of production and consumption of the media in the forties, fifties, and sixties is beyond the scope of this essay. I offer the following comments more as a caveat to the reader than a promise of a future analysis of these differences.

The quantity, stylistics, and content of television news was radically different during the time period under consideration than today, and the speed at which ideas and information circulated was slower. The production of the self as a resident of a global village was less articulated, or at least different: Black Power advocates relied on a pan-Africanist cultural politics, but with less rapid access to events and contacts in Africa than would be possible today. If we are all framed through our "embodiment" in different registers of face-to-face and imagined community, then activists of the forties, fifties, and sixties had different technological capabilities and a different sense of what it meant to be in a world of struggle. Perhaps most importantly, as I'll discuss briefly in a moment, film had come to occupy a new place in America's concept of the media's role in political debate.

10   One of the remarkable elements of both Public Law 414 and *Gentlemen's Agreement* is the presumption that the political subject is male. His masculinity may be at stake, but he is, apparently, fully insulated from collapsing into his morphological counterpart. The danger of queerness is not one of collapse into the feminine, but a problem of masculine affect. It would be easy to read queers as the line one crosses between masculine and feminine. But Hobson consistently describes women as having emotions, rather than something I am here calling affectivity.

11   Public Law 414, 171. This act reorganized and assembled in one place a range of "laws relating to immigration, naturalization, and nationality; and for other purposes" (p. 163). Most importantly for our purposes here, it revised and altered the use of the 1936 *Alien Registration Act*, meant to require agents ("natural" or alien) of alien govern-

ments to register their activities. The original intent of this act, an earlier stage for the ambivalence about excluding "foreign" influences while not fully allowing Americans their promised political freedoms, seems to have been to regulate the importation of Nazi propaganda. Thus, this chapter in the drama of American civility is first played out around the figure of the Jew, who is both the object of Nazi propaganda but also, because of the alienness of the Jew/Zionist, considered by the anti-Semite to be a different race. Even the less overtly anti-Semitic viewed Jews as teetering on the brink of allegiance to another nation. Because propaganda connotes foreign ideas, the original law, supposedly protecting the Jew who would become the Zionist, is already full of uncertainty about what constitutes a "foreign" idea. It appears that until the 1960s, "propaganda" applies largely to political ideas proposed by entities other than the U.S. government.

12 Gay civil-rights efforts of the 1970s and 1980s, and AIDS activism of the late 1980s and 1990s, were directed toward removing the sexuality- and health-related sections of this law.

13 This partially explains the curious difference in temporality installed between the communist and the pervert or criminal, an ontological difference expressed in the act through specification of a period of time for which the "good moral character" of applicants for permanent residence or naturalization must be demonstrated. Among the violators of the various sections that cover the morally suspect—stowaways, people who lie about their intentions to eventually apply for naturalization, drug addicts, and people with histories of incarceration—are prostitutes, procurers, and people "coming to the United States to engage in any immoral sexual act" (Public Law 414, sec. 212 [a] [13], 183). Exactly how long one must have been "moral" before entering the United States varies, as does immoralities' alienating capacity should they appear after gaining entry or naturalization. For example, criminality resulting from poverty that has occurred after one's admission is not grounds for deportation. The length of time during which one risked un-naturalization, or alienation, varied: naturalized citizens who acquired communist ideas or affiliations were immediately stripped of citizenship, as were those who in other ways lied to gain admittance. Those involved with sex-related activities had a better chance of beating the charges and retaining their naturalization despite the unnaturalness of their bodily activities.

14 Public Law 414, sec. 101, (e) (1, 2, 3), 172.

15 Public Law 414, sec. 101, (f) (1–8), 172. At this time, the issue of dual citizenship was exhausted by individuals born in a place to parents whose national allegiance was directed elsewhere. The law spells out in some detail the circumstances under which birth does not immediately determine the place of one's "natural" citizenship. Apart from the American-held territories that lacked statehood, only Canada is mentioned as a sovereign nation whose citizens are not automatically suspicious—technical aliens, but virtual Americans. Soon, natural Americans would be allowed to also hold an Israeli passport. It was not until the 1980s that Americans were widely allowed to hold dual citizenship with any other country: in the midst of renewed right-wing concern about illegal aliens, Irish immigrants filed a suit claiming discrimination, because, unlike American-Israeli dual citizens, they could not hold two passports. Subsequently, the U.S. government enumerated a list of countries with which Americans could hold dual citizenship. Of course, this listed countries viewed as permanent allies, but the policy change also made clearer against whom the xenophobia that is expressed as immigration law was to be directed. On the one hand, the idea of citizenship as a

monogamous relation was diluted. But on the other, the United States's magnanimity only acknowledged the advantages to its more mobile wealthy citizens of easy physical passage between the bloc of economically allied post-superpower powers.

16 Benedict Anderson, *Imagined Communities: Reflections on the Origin and Spread of Nationalism*, rev. ed. (London: Verso, 1991), p. 4. Briefly, Anderson argues that "nation" is a form of imagining a deep, political connection, a tie to territory, in the absence of face-to-face contact. The nation sees itself as sovereign, limited, and as a community. What differentiates nations is the *way* in which they are imagined, not some criterion of true or impostor nation-ness. For Anderson, the proliferation of print capitalism, a force used by, but also autonomous from, states, is the medium through which nations have been differentially imagined. In some cases, print capitalism helps produce an official language, while in others, it allows for the stabilization of vernaculars that together form the imagined community of nation. The educational trajectories that allow certain classes of officials to acquire and use the variety of languages and governmental systems cut across the capital interests of media, but also carve out the particular ways in which sovereignty and community are produced as nation. A second edition of the book (1991) takes a slight turn away from the English Marxist spin on Foucault that characterizes this analysis. Anderson examines the role of census, map, and museum in sustaining the sensibility of nation for a given group of people whose affectivity is circumscribed by the iconization of a particular national border.

17 Anderson, *Imagined Communities*, p. 144.

18 Ibid., p. 143.

19 The intransigence and sturdiness of biblical references—New Testament and Old (rather than "Hebrew")—in American political rhetoric belie, in a way that even head counts of the Christian Right cannot, the extent to which America, despite a technical separation of Church and State, is, perhaps all the more, a deeply Christian nation.

20 See Richard Winnington, *Film Criticism and Caricatures 1943–1953* (New York: Barnes and Noble, 1976).

21 Contemporaneous reviewers and subsequent historians compared these works to each other.

22 The larger project to which this essay is related examines some of the prefigurative "I passed for white" stories in widely circulated women's magazines. Obviously, since *Gentlemen's Agreement* was released before *Pinky*, it cannot literally "copy" its discourse of passing. But the tropes about passing were already well-established for many audiences. Hobson published extensively in these women's magazines, was influential on and influenced by their style and perceptions of audience. That her book became an international best-seller and the subject of an enormously popular film certainly, but only accidentally, helped solidify the interpretive affinity between these different media.

I cite *Pinky* as the sentinel "problem" film about racial passing: notice the sharp contrast with the more often discussed film versions of *Imitation of Life*, released before the war (Stahl, 1934) and after the problem film cycle (Sirk, 1956). Although they are melodramas about women and race relations, their passing character is an example of the racial problematic, not structured as a character of identification for the film's viewers—black and white, though no doubt with different *techne* of self-construction. In the *Imitations*, the ineluctably black and white protagonists carry the audience's principle identification. While providing alternative perspectives on the issue of racial identity, the films do not attempt to teach the viewer how to "walk in the other guy's shoes."

23 David A. Cook, *A History of Narrative Film* (New York: W. W. Norton, 1981), p. 26.

24 Or are, perhaps, central to the problematic of democracy in America. The Republicans' Contract with (on) America, and the debates surrounding health care, social welfare programs, and the federal budget, are primarily about the responsibility and geography of American domestic affairs.

25 Finance Kathy's wartime work is mentioned in order to express her frustration that the identificatory subtlety required for the new kind of war eluded women: "During the shooting war, she worked herself half sick in factories, sold bonds, accepted all the discomfort of ration books and shortages like a good soldier. But during this covert war for this country's future, this secret war in which antisemitism [*sic*] is one of the most familiar weapons, she is unable to do more than offer little clucking sounds of disapproval" (228–29).

26 But the government's original forays into social welfare had come after the Civil War, when thousands of mangled soldiers and the women and children who had lost their breadwinners were brought under government care. This was something of an embarrassment: America continues to be uncertain how to manage the peacetime presence of the broken remains of its wartime heroes. See Theda Skocpol, *Protecting Soldiers and Mothers: The Political Origins of Social Policy in the United States* (Cambridge, Mass.: The Belknap Press of Harvard University, 1992).

27 Film viewership figures for the period, along with the wide and cross-class popularity of women's magazines suggest that women were the major consumers of the product forms in which the "problem" was discussed, but this only tells us the brute demography of the most direct form of consuming these ideas. The last decade or so of research on television soap opera suggests that while women still constitute the major direct audience for these latter-day relatives of film and magazine melodrama, many men, despite their stated disdain of "women's" products actually consume them, or keep up with their plots through reviews or discussion. The compounding role of "presentation of self" through media ("I'm the sort of person who reads the *Times*, not the sort who watches daytime TV") means that demographic data do not tell the whole story of who directly or indirectly consumes and how the content and sensibilities presented in gendered or class-structured media circulate, or how discussions occurring within particular classes of media frame individuals' sense of political values.

28 The imaginary space of a multicultural America was already present in the "boy gang" films of the 1930s and the war films of the 1940s and 1950s. Each featured a-real groups with "one of each" ethnicity, marking itself by performing the stereotyped role that contributed to the whole. War films, for example, gave black or Native American soldiers a sixth sense to "know" when the enemy was near.

29 This desire for a true account of the other would not die: novels, film, and television would continually revive the plot of someone who intentionally or unintentionally ends up living out a part of their life as an other. The 1990s television series *Quantum Leap* would take this obsession to new heights with a sci-fi show organized around a brilliant, affable scientist who discovers a theory of space-time that allows him and his homo-erotic/panicked holographic friend to "leap" into the lives/bodies of others to redo history, sometimes saving individual's lives for their private benefit, sometimes altering the course of history (the white, married protagonist gets to start the Civil Rights movement, the women's movement, the gay movement, and save chimps who are being abused by his own agency—NASA).

30 Anti-Semitism is dangerously demasculinizing for the Jew as well as the country: "But

day by day the little thump of insult. Day by day the tapping on the nerves, the delicate assault on the proud stuff of a man's identity. That's how they did it. A week had
shown him how they did it" (p. 97).

31 Compare with the multiple *Quantum Leap* episodes where Sam actually does "land"
in a woman's body.

32 The book is finally incapable of figuring the citizen outside of a Christian heritage.
In sorting out why the image of a tree keeps coming into his mind, Phil unself-
consciously links Christianity with the founding of America. He finds what he is
looking for (with the aid of *Barlett's*) in the New Testament Book of Matthew:

> "Either make the tree good, and his fruit good; or else make the tree corrupt, and
> his fruit corrupt: for the tree is known by his fruit." There it was, uncompromising,
> noble—Jesus addressing the Pharisees. It was the everlasting choice for wholeness
> and soundness in a man or in a nation.
>
> They had known it, the patient stubborn men who for years had argued and writ-
> ten and rephrased and fought over the Constitution and the Bill of Rights. (p. 205)

It is also worth noting that the plot occurs in December: for his fiancée, Phil's passing
ruins Christmas.

33 Elsewhere (forthcoming) I have suggested that at least some framings of queerness
are incompatible with the liberal pluralism that underwrites lesbian and gay civil-
rights politics, because it holds a different theory of space, a fundamental category in
U.S. law and political theory. However, I also believe that the pressure to make claims
comprehensibly political—*to have an agenda*—has caused Queer Nation as an activist
force to primarily function as a civil-rights movement, albeit one that refuses to be
clear about what it wants.

34 Anderson, *Imagined Communities*, p. 144.

35 In recent human-rights discourse, the queer and the communist may have swapped
places. The assertion of human-rights discourse as essential to halting the AIDS epidemic participates in the effort to corral bodies that threaten not to conform to national
projects of sexual austerity in service of nation. For example, when the Cuban government established quarantine camps for people with HIV, many Americans touted
this not as another example of communism's inhumanness, but as a compassionate
solution for those infected and those who were cordoned off from them.

Robert F. Reid-Pharr

Tearing the Goat's Flesh: Homosexuality,

Abjection, and the Production of a

Late-Twentieth-Century Black Masculinity

Thou shalt not seethe a kid in his mother's milk. — Exodus 23:19

Chivo que rompe tambor con su pellejo paga. — Abakua proverb.

Diana Fuss has argued in a recent discussion of contemporary gay and lesbian theory that the figure of what we might call the undead homosexual, the homosexual who continually reappears, even and especially in the face of the most grisly violence and degradation, is absolutely necessary to the production of positive heterosexual identity, at least heterosexual identity produced within bourgeois-dominated economies of desire that, as Eve Kosofsky Sedgwick demonstrates, deploy homophobia to check slippage between (male) homosociality and homosexuality.[1] The inside/out binarism, then, the distinction between normalcy and chaos, is maintained precisely through the mediation of the sexually liminal character, that is to say, the homosexual. Fuss writes: "Those inhabiting, the inside . . . can only comprehend the outside through the incorporation of a negative image. This process of negative interiorization involves turning homosexuality inside out, exposing not the homosexual's abjected insides but the homosexual as the abject, as the contaminated and expurgated insides of the heterosexual subject."[2] Fuss's point is well taken. For she suggests not simply that the innate pathology of the homosexual must be revealed in order to produce the heterosexual community, but also that the homosexual works as the vehicle by which hetero-pathology itself might be negotiated; that is, the homosexual as "the contaminated and expurgated insides of the heterosexual subject."

In relating this insight to the production of African American masculinity, I would argue that the pathology that the homosexual must negotiate is precisely the specter of black boundarylessness, the idea that there is no normal blackness to which the black subject, American or otherwise, might refer. Following the work of René Girard, especially his 1986 study of the place of violence, real and imagined, in the production of communal identity, *The Scapegoat*,[3] I will suggest that homosexuality operates mimetically in the texts that I examine, standing itself as the sign of a prior violence, the violence of boundarylessness, or cultural eclipse — to borrow Girard's language — that has been continually visited upon the African American community during its long sojourn in the new world. Indeed Orlando Patterson, Henry Louis Gates, and Paul Gilroy, among others, have argued that the black has been conceptualized in modern (slave) culture as an inchoate, irrational nonsubject, as the chaos that both defines and threatens the borders of logic, individuality, and basic subjectivity.[4] In that schema, all blacks become interchangeable, creating among the population a sort of continual restlessness, a terror. Girard writes: "The terror inspired in people by the eclipse of culture and the universal confusion of popular uprisings are signs of a community that is literally undifferentiated, deprived of all that distinguishes one person from another in time and space. As a consequence all are equally disordered in the same place and at the same time."[5] Though Girard's discussion here proceeds from a consideration of societies suddenly thrown into confusion — plague ridden medieval Europe, revolutionary France — his work suggests that all terror, all confusion, works to undifferentiate the subjects of the (newly) chaotic society, such that the members of the society come to stand in for one another in their common experience of vertigo. The scapegoat, then, would be the figure who reproduces this undifferentiation, this chaos, this boundarylessness. The violence directed against the goat would mitigate against the prior violence, the erosion of borders that has beset the entire community.

I would add to this only that antihomosexual violence operates in the production of black masculinity on two levels. First, as I have argued already, the strike against the homosexual acts as a seemingly direct confrontation with the presumption of black boundarylessness, or we might say the assumption of black subhumanity and black irrationality that has its roots deep in the history of slavery and the concomitant will to produce Africans as "Other." To strike the homosexual, the scapegoat, the sign of chaos and crisis, is to return the community to normalcy, to create boundaries around blackness, rights that indeed white men are obliged to recognize.

Second, and perhaps more importantly, this violence allows for a reconnection to the very figure of boundarylessness that the assailant is presumably attempting to escape. As a consequence, black subjects are able to transcend, if only for a moment, the very strictures of normalcy and rationality that have been defined in contradistinction to a necessarily amorphous blackness. My point here is to argue for reconsideration of the process of abjection, a process referenced by Diana Fuss and developed most fruitfully by Julia Kristeva, in the *de*articulation of meaning and identity.[6] Rather, I would suggest that abjection is characterized by an excess of meaning. As a consequence, we might use the figure of the abject to access "slips" in the ideological structures of modernity, if not a complete reworking of the entire process. To put it bluntly, we must empty our consciousness of that which is contradictory and ambiguous and most especially that which disallows our differentiation. Still we seem not to be able to complete this process. We become uncomfortable with "realness" at precisely those moments when it appears to be most firmly established. Even as the profligate subject is destroyed, we retain "him" within the national consciousness, always on the brink of renewal, lest we find ourselves entrapped within a logic of subjectivity from which the black is excluded already.

I

The formal and rhetorical strategies that link Eldridge Cleaver's *Soul on Ice,* James Baldwin's *Giovanni's Room,* and Piri Thomas's *Down These Mean Streets* are not immediately apparent. Cleaver's and Thomas's texts are "autobiographical" and analytical whereas Baldwin's is fictional. Cleaver documents what has become one of the most recognizable, one might even say trite, markers of black masculinity, incarceration, while both Thomas and Baldwin attempt to push against the confines of American blackness altogether. Thomas charts the difficulty that a young, dark-skinned Puerto Rican encounters as he tries to make sense of an American racial economy that creates him as "black" while Baldwin opts to step outside of the confines of American race literature altogether, producing a novel in which there are no black characters, but, as I will argue below, in which race is one of the central signifiers.

At the same time, there is the pressing question of how we are to read Baldwin's "gay" novel in relation to the virulent homophobia of Eldridge Cleaver, a homophobia that reaches its apex at precisely those moments when it is directed specifically at Baldwin and his work, particularly *Another Country.* A similar question surrounds the work of Piri Thomas, whose antigay sentiment is just as apparent, if somewhat less virulent, than Cleaver's. One might argue, in fact, that Cleaver, Thomas, and Baldwin belong to distinct literary camps such that any attempt to read the three together can proceed only by pointing out the variety of the diametric oppositions. Still, as Paul Gilroy has suggested in a discussion of John Singleton's *Boys in the Hood* and Marlon Riggs's *Tongues Untied,* even as the black neomasculinist heterosexual attempts to distance himself from homosexuality, he draws attention to the "similarities and convergences in the way that love between men is the common factor."[7] It follows that the key to understanding the depth of Thomas's and Cleaver's homophobia lies precisely in the fact that the universe that both represent in their literature is so consistently and insistently masculine and homosocial.

Much has been made of Cleaver's vicious and repeated attacks on women and gay men. In almost every treatment of this issue, however, Cleaver's misogyny and homophobia have been chalked up to his male privilege and antiquated notions of what constitutes properly black gender and sexual relations. To date no one has examined seriously Cleaver's tragicomic struggle to construct a black heterosexuality, to finally rid the black consciousness of the dual specters of effeminacy and interracial homoeroticism. One might argue, in fact, that Cleaver's woman hating and fag bashing were, for all his bravado, failed attempts to assert himself and the black community as "straight."

Soul on Ice is in large part an explication of the difficulties of black subjectification within the highly homosocial, homosexual prison. Women, though present, operate only as the means by which social relations between men are communicated. Early in the text Cleaver confesses to having been a racially motivated rapist, perfecting his craft on the bodies of black women before he "crossed the tracks" to seek out his "white prey."[8] Clearly the abuse of the black female body acts as a means to an end, a type of cultural production in which Cleaver's manhood, his sense of self-worth, is established and articulated. I would be wrong, however, to suggest that Cleaver's ultimate goal is to possess and abuse white female bodies. Again women act only as conduits by which social relations, relations that take place exclusively between men, are represented. Cleaver may indeed be fucking black and white women, but it is white men whom he intends to hurt. "Rape was an insurrectionary act. It delighted me that I was defying and trampling upon the white man's law, upon his system of values, and that I was defiling his women—and this point, I believe, was the most satisfying to me because I was very resentful over the historical fact of how the white man has used the black woman. I felt I was getting revenge" (*SI*, 26). The peculiarity of Cleaver's twisted logic rests not so much in the fact that he saw sexual violence as an insurrectionary tool. On the contrary, the rape of women, is used regularly to terrorize and subdue one's "enemies." The difficulty in Cleaver's logic rests in the fact that he raped both white *and* black women. Was he, I must wonder, seeking revenge on the white man when he violated poor, black female residents of his quintessentially black ghettos?

This question is not simply rhetorical. Cleaver himself argues that there is a tendency within some segments of the black community to understand the black woman as having collaborated, particularly through the vehicle of sex, with the white master. Indeed, Angela Davis attempts to contextualize this sentiment in her seminal essay, "Reflections on the Black Woman's Role in the Community of Slaves."[9] Raping the black woman could be interpreted, then, as an attack on the white man's stooge. The black woman becomes the means of telegraphing a message of rage and resistance to the white male oppressor, a figure Cleaver recodifies as the Omnipotent Administrator.

It becomes clear that the ultimate target of Cleaver's sexual attacks is always the white man. Both white and black women act as pawns in an erotic conversation between Cleaver and his white male counterparts. This fact is emblematically represented in an exchange between Cleaver and a white prison guard who enters Cleaver's cell, rips a picture of a voluptuous white woman from the wall, tears it to bits, and then leaves the pieces floating in the toilet for Cleaver to find upon his return. The guard later tells Cleaver that he will allow him to keep pictures of black women, but not whites.

The clue to how deeply homoerotic the exchange between Cleaver and the guard actually is lies in Cleaver's description of his initial reaction. He writes, "I was genuinely beside myself with anger: almost every cell, excepting those of the homosexuals, had a pin-up girl on the wall and the guards didn't bother them" (*SI*, 21). Cleaver's pinup girl acts as not only a sign of interracial desire, but also a marker of his heterosexuality. This fact, which seems easy enough to understand, actually represents a deep contradiction within Cleaver's demonstration of the black male hetero-sexual self. It points directly to the disjunction between the reality of the interracial homoerotic, *homosexual* environment, the prison, in which Cleaver actually lived and wrote and the fantasy of black heterosexuality that he constructs in his narrative.

Indeed Cleaver's one rather ethereal representation of heterosexual love seems artificial and contrived, coming as it does from the pen of an admitted serial rapist and committed homophobe. He spends some time in *Soul on Ice* describing the exchange of "love" letters between his lawyer, Beverly Axelrod, and himself. Strangely enough, there is little of Cleaver, the rapist, in these works. His love seemingly transcends the corporeal. By turns he describes Axelrod as a rebel and a revolutionary, a person of great intelligence, compassion, and humanity, a valiant defender of "civil rights demonstrators, sit-iners, and the Free Speech students." And just at the moment when he has produced her as bodiless, transcendent saint he interjects, "I suppose that I should be honest, and before going any further, admit that my lawyer is a woman . . . a very excellent, unusual, and beautiful woman. I know that she believes that I do not really love her and that I am confusing a combination of lust and gratitude for love. Lust and gratitude I feel abundantly, but I also love this woman" (*SI*, 32–33). I am less concerned with pointing out the obvious homoerotic reference than with voicing how strikingly measured and cerebral his relationship with Beverly Axelrod actually was. Indeed, lust and gratitude are distinct from "love," which is presumably a type of transcendent, *trans*sexual appreciation for the intrinsic worth of the individual.

Yet Cleaver's description of his noncorporeal, non-funky love for Beverly Axelrod can only redouble upon itself. It directly challenges the claim that Cleaver's work is a product of the stark reality he has experienced. Cleaver has, much like the white man, the Omnipotent Administrator he so despises, excised his own penis, his lust, his physical self from the conversation. "The Omnipotent Administrator, having repudiated and abdicated his body, his masculine component which he has projected onto the men beneath him, cannot present his woman, the Ultrafeminine, with an image of masculinity capable of penetrating into the psychic depths where the treasure of her orgasm is buried" (*SI*, 175). Still, even as Cleaver decries the bodilessness of the Omnipotent Administrator, his love for Beverly Axelrod is no more physical than is the white man's for the ultrafeminine. Beverly Axelrod is unlike the victims of Cleaver's rapes in that she is all intellect and no body. The "sexual" passion between the two is even more rarefied than that of the Omnipotent Administrator and the Ultrafeminine, because there is never even the promise of physical contact, raw sex, but only endless *literary* representations of their desire. Beverly Axelrod should be understood, then, as a fiction, or rather as the site of yet another fictional exchange. In this manner the idea of heterosexual normalcy becomes a sort of caricature of itself. The body gives way to the intellect, lust to love.

"Love" was for Cleaver always the terrain of conceptual struggle. Indeed "love" becomes in *Soul on Ice* the very site at which normalcy is constructed in contradistinction to the sense of boundary crisis that mitigates against the production of a stable black masculinity. Perhaps the most telling moment, in this regard, is Cleaver's confrontation with his white intellectual mentor, Chris Lovdjieff, a prison teacher and a man whom Cleaver describes as "The Christ." Lovdjieff introduces Cleaver to what the great novelists and playwrights had said of love. He reads poetry on the subject and plays his students tapes of Ashley Montagu, then instructs them to write responsive essays. Cleaver writes that he cannot love whites, quoting Malcolm X as evidence: "How can I love the man who raped my mother, killed my father, enslaved my ancestors, dropped atomic bombs on Japan, killed off the Indians and keeps me cooped up in the slums? I'd rather be tied up in a sack and tossed into the Harlem River first."[10] Lovdjieff responds in a fit of tears to what he takes to be a personal attack. Cleaver remarks, "Jesus wept" then leaves. Soon thereafter the San Quentin officials begin to curtail Lovdjieff's access to the prisoners, finally barring him from entry altogether.

The ideological work that the reenactment of this Oedipal ritual accomplishes is both to detach Cleaver and his narrative from the deeply homoerotic relationship he maintains with Lovdjieff and to clear the way for a purely black masculinity. It is important to remember here that the country was in the midst of rather striking changes in the manner in which the official "reality" of both race and sexuality were articulated. In 1949, the United Nations Economic and Social Council (UNESCO) launched a study to identify means by which racism might be eradicated. The result of these efforts was a document, written by the same Ashley Montagu whose words Lovdjieff attempted to use as a bridge between his young protégé and himself.

Montagu, who began life as Israel Ehrenberg in London's East End, was trained as an anthropologist first at the University of London's University College and eventually at Columbia, where he received his graduate education under no less a light than Franz Boas.[11] By the time he wrote UNESCO's statement on race, he already had published widely in the field, developing a critical apparatus that not only called for a markedly relativistic understanding of "racial attributes," but that altogether called into question the efficacy of maintaining race as an analytical category. Montagu observed, "For all practical social purposes, 'race' is not so much a biological phenomenon as a social myth. . . . Biological differences between ethnic groups should be disregarded from the standpoint of social acceptance and social action. The unity of mankind is the main thing."[12] I would suggest again that when Cleaver severs his ties with Lovdjieff he is helping to reestablish an ontological economy that would take racial difference as primary. The resolution of the crisis represented by their relationship leads to the renormalization of received racial thinking.

At the same time it is important to point out that the post–World War II period witnessed an incredible bifurcation in the means by which sexual desire was articulated and actualized. The typical narratives of the postwar sexual ethos would have it that Americans rushed into a sort of suffocating domesticity, erecting, in the process, an image of the nuclear family that would maintain a stranglehold on the nation's consciousness for at least two decades. There was also, however, a huge increase in the visibility of homosexual communities, particularly in the nation's cities, the same locations that were opening themselves more and more to black immigrants.[13] Indeed the most prominent chroniclers of the black urban male experience, including not only Cleaver, Baldwin, and Thomas, but also Claude Brown, Malcolm X, and Amiri Baraka, all reference the increased visibility of the urban homosexual. What I would argue, then, is that the homosexual, and in particular the racially marked homosexual, the black homosexual, represented for the authors I am examining the very sign of deep crisis, a crisis of identity and community that threw into confusion, if only temporarily, the boundaries of (black) normalcy.

II

Piri Thomas's narrative, *Down These Mean Streets,* proceeds in much the same manner as Cleaver's. Like his Anglo contemporary, Thomas gains his sense of manhood from within the confines of racist urban America. Moreover, like Cleaver, and indeed like a variety of late-twentieth-century black male "autobiographers," most notably Malcolm X, his loss of freedom opens the path by which he *gains* his "freedom." Thomas uses the experience of prison to resurrect that part of himself that presumably has been squelched by the realities of racism and poverty, affecting in the process a *counter*scripting of the antebellum slave narratives. It is as if the literal loss of control over the self returns the narrators to the primal scene of black subjectification, the moment when the black, particularly the black man, enmeshed within a system defined by the policing of black bodies, turns for "escape" to the life of the mind, much as Douglass turns to literature and literacy in his struggle to construct himself as "free." The focus becomes, then, the immense effort necessary to maintain one's humanity or one's subjectivity, in the face of intense pressures to suppress or deny them. I would like to suggest, however, that unlike the antebellum slave narratives, in which the black male slave risks being brutalized viciously, or worse yet having his familial and conjugal prerogatives trampled upon by licentious white men, the twentieth-century black male narrators are in danger of being *homosexualized.* I have discussed this phenomenon in the work of Cleaver already. I would add here that Thomas's understanding of himself is altogether mediated by his relationships with men. His adoration for his father gives way to his loyalty to the gang and then finally to his respect for the prison ethos. Throughout, the homosexual acts as the emblem of the border between the inside and the out. Thomas deploys the figure of the homosexual at precisely those moments when the complex ambiguity of his "standing" within his various communities is most apparent, that is to say, those moments when he cannot avoid a declaration of his status as either the Insider or the Outsider.

The great difficulty of maintaining the distinction between the homosexual and the homosocial is made explicit from almost the beginning of Thomas's narrative. The young man begins to develop as an adult, as a subject constructed by—but nevertheless greater than—the various identities he inhabits, at precisely that moment when he proves that he has heart, *corazon*, and is accepted into an all-male Puerto Rican gang. The test of his spirit, the challenge that he must accept if he is to be integrated fully into the gang's social life, is a fist fight, a strikingly physical struggle of wills between Thomas and the gang's leader, Waneko.

> He had *corazon*. He came on me. *Let him draw first blood*, I thought, *it's his block*. Smish, my nose began to bleed. His boys cheered, his heart cheered, his turf cheered. "Waste this chump," somebody shouted.
> *Okay, baby, now it's my turn.* He swung. I grabbed innocently, and forehead smashed into his nose. His eyes crossed. His fingernails went for my eye and landed in my mouth—crunch, I bit hard. I punched him in the mouth as he pulled away from me, and he slammed his foot into my chest.[14]

By standing his own in this fight Thomas not only gains acceptance into the gang, but initiates a relationship with Waneko that lasts over many years. This fact is not, however, so terribly remarkable. The idea that violence often helps to strengthen the bonds between men is hardly new or surprising. Still, I would argue that the strikingly physical nature of the contest between Thomas and Waneko ought to alert us to the multiple levels on which this interchange resonates. Thomas allows Waneko to draw first blood out of deference to his position in the neighborhood and the gang. The abuse that the two young men mete out to one another in the course of their fight should not be understood, then, simply as a sign of masculine aggression. Thomas is not allowed into the gang solely because he is good with his fists. Instead, the emphasis is on that elusive entity, heart, that place of deep feeling and masculine determination, to which the young Puerto Ricans gain access through ritualized violence. One might argue, then, that the fight between Thomas and Waneko is at once an act of aggression *and* an act of love.

I am supported in this claim by the fact that the gang members expend so much energy denying homoerotic feeling. This is even while all of them, including Thomas, seek out and willingly engage in (homo)sex. It is telling that only a few pages after the fight scene the young men decide to stretch themselves to the limits of their masculinity by visiting the apartment of a trio of stereotypically effeminate gay men. Indeed, their interaction with the three homosexuals is itself designed to reflect their own hypermasculinity. They assure themselves, "Motherfuckers, who's a punk? Nobody, man," as they "jumped off the stoop and, grinning, shuffled towards the faggots' building" (*DMS*, 55).

The episode in the gay men's apartment is from the very outset over-determined by the intense ambiguity that suffuses the extremely homo-social world of the gangs. The faggots, the *maricones*, stand in for the constant danger that the macho young men, with their relentless empha-sis on masculinity and the male body, will stumble themselves, inadver-tently, or not so inadvertently, across the line that separates the homo-sexual from the homosocial. "I had heard that some of them fags had bigger joints than the guy that was screwing. *Oh shit, I ain't gonna screw no motherfuckin' fag. Agh—I'm not gonna get shit all over my peter, not for all the fuckin' coins in the world*" (*DMS*, 55; emphasis in original). The fag refuses, in this passage, to conform to the boys' stereotypes. His joint, his penis, the marker of his worth within the logic of patriarchy, is larger than the guy doing the screwing, the real man who stands in for Thomas and his comrades. Even more striking is the fact that Thomas's fear, the fear that he will screw a fag, (thereby, compromising his own mascu-linity), the fear against which he must assure himself constantly, turns upon the idea that he will get shit all over his penis. This aversion to feces points directly to the immense ambiguity, the boundary crisis, that the homosexual represents. Instead of Thomas's pulling blood from the gay body, much as he regularly pulls blood from the bodies of his fellow gang members and presumably also from the bodies of recently deflow-ered (female) virgins, he takes only shit from the fag, shit that acts as evidence of the nonproductive, perverse nature of the (homo)sexual act.

Let me make it perfectly clear that what I am interested in here is not the cataloging of homosexual content in the work of late-twentieth-century black male autobiographers, but instead a reading of homosexu-ality that pays attention to the way in which the homosexual stands in for the fear of crisis and chaos, or rather, the fear of slipping to the outside, that pervades the work of both nineteenth- and twentieth-century black writers. As the young "heterosexual" Puerto Rican men enter the apart-ment of the young "homosexual" Puerto Rican men, as the former fuck the latter and the latter suck the former, it becomes difficult, even in the face of the "straight" men's many protestations, to maintain a distinction between the two. Indeed it becomes nearly impossible to continue the inside/out binarism.

The rather lengthy group sex scene that Thomas describes takes on a strikingly surreal aspect. The air that they breathe is heavy with the smell of marijuana smoke, thereby pushing *all* the young men beyond their *normal* limits, creating the space of the gay men's apartment as a type of liminal terrain; we might even say a *no*-man's land. Moreover, the effect is not simply that the *normalcy* of their erotic lives is jettisoned, but also that the sexual act becomes transposed onto a variety of experiences and sites.

> I opened my eye a little. I saw a hand, and between its fingers was a stick of pot. I didn't look up at the face. I just plucked the stick from the fingers. I heard the feminine voice saying, "You gonna like thees pot. Eet's good stuff."
> I felt its size. It was a king-sized bomber. I put it to my lips and began to hiss my reserve away. It was going, going, going. I was gonna get a gone high. I inhaled. I held my nose, stopped up my mouth. I was gonna get a gone high . . . a gone high . . . a gone high . . . and then the stick was gone, burnt to a little bit of a roach. (*DMS*, 58).

Though this passage is taken from a scene that is heavily determined by the notion of profligate sex and sexuality, there is apparently no sexual activity at all. No penis, vagina, breasts, or buttocks are here to alert the reader that what we are experiencing is a type of *sexual* intercourse. There is, moreover, neither blood, nor feces to act as evidence of the all-important penetration. I would argue, however, that the very fact that this passage lacks the normal markers of sexual activity is precisely what produces it as a representation of profligacy. Here the erotic content is transferred from the sexual organs to the lips, a key site of homoerotic, homosexual pleasure. As the pot stick enters Thomas's lips, chipping away at his reserve until he is altogether gone, or we might say, spent, sexuality is severed from its association with the genitals and thus with heterosexual reproduction.

Moreover, Thomas accepts neither the passive nor active role. Though he receives the stick of pot into his mouth, he does the penetration himself, plucking the stick from between extended fingers, fingers attached to a never visible face. Still, it is once again the size of the faggot's pot stick, or rather, his joint that intrigues the youth. He is literally blown away by the innate power of this king-sized bomber, reaching, in the process, a type of homoeroticized epiphany: "Then it comes—the tight feeling, like a rubber band being squeezed around your forehead. You feel your Adam's apple doing an up-an'-down act—gulp, gulp, gulp—and you feel great—great, dammit! So fine, so smooth. You like this feeling of being air-light, with your head tight" (*DMS*, 59).

Perhaps the most telling aspect of this rather remarkable scene in Thomas's narrative, is the fact that when he returns from what I will call his drug-induced orgasmic moment, he immediately sets about tidying up the mess that he has just described. I do not mean to suggest, however, that he denies the homosexual activity. On the contrary, the descriptions of the various acts taking place between men are rather straightforwardly rendered.

> I tried to make me get up and move away from those squeezing fingers, but no good; . . . I pushed away at the fingers, but it grew independently. If I didn't like the scene, my pee-pee did. . . .
>
> I dug the lie before me. Antonia was blowin' Waneko and Indio at the same time. Alfredo was screwing La Vieja. The springs on the bed were squeaking like a million mice. . . . Indio's face was white and scared and expectant, but his body was moving in time with Antonia's outrage. I tightened my own body. It was doing the same as Indio's. It was too late. I sucked my belly and felt the hot wetness of heat. I looked down in time to see my pee-pee disappear into Concha's mouth. I felt the roughness of his tongue as it both scared and pleased me. *I like broads, I like muchachas, I like girls*, I chanted inside me. . . . Then I heard slurping sounds and it was all over. . . . I smelled the odor of shit and heard Alfredo say, "Ya dirty *maricon*, ya shitted all over me."
>
> "I'm sor-ree," said La Vieja, "I no could help eet."
>
> "ya stink'n faggot—" . . . I heard the last sounds of Alfredo's anger beating out against La Vieja—blap, blap, blap—and the faggot's wail, "Ayeeeeee, no heet me, no heet—" (*DMS*, 61)

We can see, in this passage, the reestablishment of the line separating the inside from the out at precisely the moment at which the spectacle of homosexual intercourse is realized most fully. Thomas maintains a distinction between himself and his sexual desire, producing, for a moment, the former as the victim of the latter. It is his "pee-pee" that refuses to allow him to exit this scene. Moreover, the word, *pee-pee*, with its connotations of childhood innocence, helps exonerate Thomas from any responsibility for the act in which he is engaged. Instead, by reasserting his genitalia as the privileged site of sexual pleasure, Thomas rescues himself from the never-never land of oral and anal eroticism. It is Concha, a name that can be translated as either shell or pussy, who steps to the nether side of the phallic economy, allowing his mouth to be "used" like the presumably (dis)empowered site of the vagina. Throughout, Thomas reminds himself that what he is experiencing is a lie. The satisfaction he feels is the product of a simple substitution, the mouth for the vagina, in which his pee-pee is fooled but he is not. He chants, "I like broads, I like *muchachas*, I like girls," as if to remind himself, in three different vernaculars, that the spectacle of his pee-pee within the faggot's mouth is but a representation of, or perhaps, a signification upon the truth. And if this were not enough, the scene ends with the smell of the marijuana smoke giving way to the stench of shit, the proof that the boys have stumbled beyond the limits of normalcy, sullied themselves in the confusing, if always false, pleasures of the outside. As Alfredo beats La Vieja, the old woman, a man who despite his name is described as no more than thirty, the sexual and erotic economies seemingly have come back into order, the highly stylized—and stereotypical—rendering of La Vieja's screams—"Ayeeeeee, no heet me, no heet—"—acting as irrefutable evidence of the incommensurability of *el macho* with *la maricon*.

It is striking that even as Thomas paints the faggot as the quintessential outsider, he seems incapable of dispensing with him. Homosexuals and homosexuality intervene throughout the text to help Thomas give definition to his fledgling masculinity. It is during their attempt to rob a gay nightclub, or rather a site in which there are nothing but "faggots and soft asses" that leads to Thomas's arrest and incarceration. The would-be robbers—Thomas, his friend, Louie, and their two white accomplices, Danny and Billy—are thwarted in their efforts, precisely because they underestimate the ability of the homosexual to turn their expectations and desires back in on themselves. When Billy jumps to the stage and interrupts the drag show taking place, the audience refuses to respond in a fit of hysteria as he had expected. Instead they laugh, taking him for one of the performers. It is as if the sight of a poor, undereducated white man attempting to assert his masculinity, his lack of lack, is itself a greater spectacle than the transvestite performance. It is only after he fires two shots over their heads, shattering the mirrors in the process, that they give him their full attention, or rather reflect back the image of himself that he wants to see. Of course the entire affair is bungled. Thomas is shot by an undercover police officer whose own incognito status within the gay bar implicates him as fully in the transvestite spectacle as any of the drag performers. Indeed, the whole scene turns upon the recognition that things are not always what they seem. The "women" on stage are not really women. Thomas is not really a macho gangster, but instead just a Puerto Rican teenager, who when struck by the bullet of an undercover police officer, reverts to an infantile state: "I felt like a little baby, almost like I was waiting to get my diapers changed. . . . Mommie . . . I don't . . . Mommie, *no quiero morir*" (*DMS*, 237, 238).

I have argued already that the prison acts as a primary site for the articulation of a late-twentieth-century black American masculinity. When the black narrator enters prison he returns to the primal horde, as it were, a state in which the brothers are corralled together by the capricious violence and deprivation enacted by the father. Here the Oedipal crisis has not been enacted, but only imagined. Thomas's focus remains on the unattainable female, his former girlfriend, Trina, even though the truth of his situation is that homosociality has given way altogether to homosexuality: "the real action was between men. If you weren't careful, if you didn't stand up for yourself and say, 'Hands off, motherfucker,' you became a piece of ass. And if you got by this hassle, there always was the temptation of wanting to cop some ass" (*DMS*, 262). We have reached the point in Thomas's text when the danger—and the promise—of abjection become most apparent. In prison the rational norms no longer continue to operate. In spite of all his *corazon* and macho bravado, even Thomas is tempted to "cop some ass."

We should be careful not to slip into the trap of conceptualizing abjection as simply the opposite of normalcy. The abject is not the same as the object. The relationship of abject to subject is similar to that of the inside to the outside, only in that the abject is *not* the subject and indeed that it *may* hold a contradictory or even confrontational relationship to it. As Julia Kristeva argues, abjection, "lies outside, beyond the set, and does not seem to agree to the latter's rules of the game. And yet, from its place of banishment, the abject does not cease challenging its master."[15] The danger that Thomas confronts, then, when he gives voice to his own nascent homosexual desire is not simply that he will implicate himself further as an outsider. On the contrary, the episode in the apartment of the three effeminate gay men had proven already that he could maintain his macho image even in the midst of homosexual intercourse. The danger, then, is that he will lose hold on the logic of the inside/out binarism, that he might forget that his desire for Trina is real, while his "desire" for men is only a substitution.

> One time. That's all I have to do it. Just one time and it's gone time. I'll be screwing faggots as fast as I can get them. I'm not gonna get institutionalized. I don't want to lose my hatred of this damn place. Once you lose the hatred, then the can's got you. You can do all the time in the world and it doesn't bug you. You go outside and make it; you return to prison and you make it there, too. No sweat, no pain. No. Outside is real; inside is a lie. Outside is one kind of life, inside is another. And you make them the same if you lose your hate of prison. (*DMS*, 263; emphasis in original)

Thomas clearly sees the danger of blurring the distinction between the inside and the out. He is afraid to screw faggots not because it is displeasing, but because it will allow for the articulation—and actualization—of an alternate logic of pleasure. Prison becomes, in this schema, not simply the wretched underside of normal life, but an alternative site of meaning, truth, even love and life.

This is represented emblematically by two characters whom I will treat briefly here. The first, Claude, is a black man who is extremely attracted to Thomas and who offers his reluctant paramour a host of prison treasures if he will agree to be "his daddy-o." Thomas refuses. Claude then takes up with another prisoner, Big Jules, a man sentenced to a life sentence for cutting someone up into little pieces. The couple celebrate their union in a wedding complete with preacher, best man, and attendants.

The second is Ruben, a muscular and exceptionally violent inmate, who is attracted to Thomas's "cousin," Tico. The naive youth accepts Ruben's many presents upon his arrival in prison until he receives a note from the older man, expressing his real intentions.

> Dear Tico:
>   Since the first moment I saw you, I knew you were for me. I fell in love with your young red lips and the hair to match it. I would like to keep on doing things for you and to take care of you and not let anybody mess with you. I promise not to let no one know about you being my old lady and you don't have to worry none, because I won't hurt you none at all. I know you might think it's gonna be bad, but it's not at all. I could meet you in the back part of the tier cell hall and nobody's going to know what's happening. I've been doing a lot for you and I never felt like this about no girl. If you let me cop you, I'll do it real easy to you. I'll use some hair oil and it will go in easy. You better not let me down 'cause I got it bad for you, I'd hate to mess you all up.
>
> XXX   Love and Kisses
You know who
R.
>
> P.S. Tear this up and flush it down the shit bowl. (*DMS*, 266)

The most intriguing thing about Claude's desire for Thomas and especially Ruben's desire for Tico, particularly as it is represented within his note, is the fact that in both instances the emphasis is precisely *not* on sex, but instead on the production of a new type of (homosexual) romantic relationship. Claude wants not only an intercourse partner, but a husband, a daddy-o, one willing to express his commitment within a "public" ceremony. Moreover, one might argue that instead of pining away for some unattainable outside, some reality beyond his grasp, Claude empowers himself through the structures of the prison itself, subverting, in the process, the many constraints on his freedom. He refuses to understand Big Jules as solely a sadistic murderer, but instead reconfigures him as husband, lover, mate. Ruben, for his part, never even attempts to sever his tendency for violence from his love. He assures Tico that he will just as quickly "mess him up" as love him. Yet the highly romantic nature of his note is undeniable. Strikingly, his love for Tico does not begin at the cock or anus, but indeed at the lips and hair, the redness of which excite his passion. The beauty of the young man's red mouth and lips belies the necessity of the woman's (red) vagina. Ruben assures Tico, "I never felt like this for no girl," and then closes with a series of salutations that seem jarringly feminine and trite: "Love and Kisses, XXX, You Know Who, R." He reminds Tico, in a postscript, to flush his note down the *shit* bowl, emphasizing once again the *counter*rationality of his desire.

III

I would like to turn, at this point, to the work of James Baldwin, who achieves in his *Giovanni's Room* perhaps one of the most developed explications of the possibilities inherent within abjection yet written. The progress of Baldwin's early career might be narrated, in fact, as a series of successively more explicit and stark representations of the black abject, or as I will demonstrate below, the ghost of the homosexual. The whisper of adolescent longing for distant fathers and virile young men in *Go Tell It on the Mountain* gives way in *Another Country* to the tragically inverted "straight" man, Rufus, who, on the one hand, passionately fucks his white girlfriend, a woman Cleaver refers to as a southern Jezebel, and, on the other, takes a white male Southern lover, or again to quote Cleaver, "lets a white bisexual homosexual fuck him in the ass."

To be fucked in the ass by the white man is not simply to be overcome by white culture, white intellect, white notions of superiority. Nor can it be understood solely as the undeniable evidence of the desire to be white. Instead, Cleaver's fear is that Baldwin opens up space for the reconstruction of the black imaginary, such that the most sacrosanct of black "truths" might be transgressed. The image of the white (male) Southerner fucking the (unwilling) black woman resonates with a long history of African American literature and lore in which the licentious white man acts as the absolute spoiler of black desire. The image of the white (Southerner) fucking the black *man*, however, throws all this into confusion.

On the one hand, we see a rescripting of Frederick Douglass's famous account of the whipping of his aunt Hester. The black male subject is no longer able to remain, in the closet, as it were; instead, he takes the woman's place on the joist, becoming himself the victim of the white man's scourge. On the other hand, it seems that the white man needs not force his "victim" at all. The reader cannot find comfort in the idea that the image of the white male "abuse" of the black male body is but a deeper revelation of white barbarism. The black subject willingly gives himself, becoming in the process the mirror image of the culpable female slave whom Angela Davis has described so ably. One might argue, in fact, that the spectacle of interracial homosexual desire puts such pressure on the ideological structures of the black national literary tradition that it renders the continuation of the inside/out binarism nearly impossible.

These are the issues that shape the narrative of Baldwin's second novel, *Giovanni's Room*. This work, which is widely thought of as Baldwin's anomaly, the work with no black characters, the work in which Baldwin stretches, some might say unsuccessfully, to demonstrate his grasp of the universal, has been neglected by both students of black and gay literature, many of whom assume Baldwin had first to retreat from his blackness in order to explore homosexuality and homophobia. I would argue, however, that the question of blackness, precisely because of its very apparent absence, screams out at the turn of every page. As we have seen already, the *non*existence of the black, particularly the black homosexual, is a theme that Baldwin starts to develop as early as *Go Tell It on the Mountain*. My reading of *Giovanni's Room* will proceed, then, via an exploration of the absences in the text. I will suggest that Baldwin's explication of Giovanni's ghostlike nonpresence, his nonsubjectivity, parallels the absence of the black from Western notions of rationality and humanity, while at the same time pointing to the possibility of escape from this same black-exclusive system of logic.

Baldwin initiates his discussion of race in the very first paragraph, alerting the reader that even though there are no blacks present, this is yet a race novel: "I watch my reflection in the darkening gleam of the window pane. My reflection is tall, perhaps rather like an arrow, my blond hair gleams. My face is like a face you have seen many times. My ancestors conquered a continent, pushing across death-laden plains, until they came to an ocean which faced away from Europe into a darker past."[16] There are a number of clues in this passage to alert the reader to the ideological work accomplished within Baldwin's text. His use of the autobiographical "I" both conflates his identity with that of his protagonist, David, and signals us that what he is interested in here is the subject of identity formation. David's consideration of his reflection, moreover, demonstrates Baldwin's fascination with the relationship of the Object to the Inverse, the One to the Other. David is indeed the *real-life* (American) character who considers the fate of the already, or the almost already dead Giovanni. In the process, he faces away from Europe, away from whiteness, and from received notions of masculinity and sexuality to a nebulous darker past. Moreover, as Toni Morrison has recently suggested, the production of whiteness, American and otherwise, turns largely upon a complex process in which the black is at once rendered invisible and omnipresent.[17]

Like Cleaver, then, Baldwin's task in *Giovanni's Room* is to examine the relation of the black to the white, the body to the mind. Indeed, it is the desire for the Other's body, in the person of Giovanni, that dictates the action of this text. Giovanni's nominally white, southern Italian body is bought and sold in the course of the novel. One might argue, in fact, that Giovanni becomes simply a creature of his body, a creature of sex and desire, by which other men are able to gauge their own humanity. That is to say, the paradox of the *male* homosexual is precisely that he usurps the woman's position as the site on which, or by which, fictional relationships between subjects are represented.

This explains why the central tragedy of the novel is the fact that Giovanni is never able to achieve his one true dream, the transcendence of the ideology of the corporeal: "Me, I want to escape . . . this dirty world, this dirty body. I never wish to make love again with anything more than the body" (*GR*, 35). It is not that Giovanni simply despises his flesh. On the contrary, he loves his flesh. It is the *idea* of his flesh, or rather, the fiction that his flesh represents that he so despises. He wishes to make love again, but only with his body, a body onto which others will no longer project notions of either filth and bestiality, or respectability and autonomy. Indeed, Giovanni begins his process of pushing against the strictures of Western thought not in Paris, but in Italy, where he leaves behind his wife after their failed attempt to produce a child, the marker of both husband's and wife's authenticity within the patriarchal economy. Giovanni struggles throughout not only to escape the position of the Other, but to produce a new identity, to move beyond the logic of self and other altogether. His work in Guillaume's bar, his relationship with David, and especially his squalid, overcrowded and never quite finished room are all testimony to his desire to achieve an alternative "realness," to enter the world of the living without becoming trapped there, to create a universe of his own making.

It is at this juncture that Baldwin's work so profoundly intersects with both Cleaver's and Thomas's. Like his heterosexually focused, heterosexist counterparts, Baldwin is concerned with both the body and the image of the body constructed by the white (European) mind. More importantly, all three men, even as they are divided by the yawning chasm of sexual desire and practice, give voice to the fear that the fiction of a pure heterosexuality no longer can be maintained, that the processes by which the "black" male subject is imagined as autonomous, virile, and invulnerable can no longer be rendered transparent. In each case, it is the homosexual who stands in for this concern, the homosexual who becomes the (scape)goat. It is almost as if the dissolution, in the gay body, of the strictures concerning "proper" black male sexual desire and practice parallel the dissolution of a transparent black American national consciousness. The homosexual is there when the "respectable" black male protagonist gives way to the criminal Eldridge Cleaver. He stands by as Anglo-American centered notions of race and "blackness" are thrown into disarray by the Spanish-inflected "English" of the New York–born Puerto Rican, Piri Thomas. Moreover, it is the search for the homosexual that drives the narrative of *Giovanni's Room*, a novel in which Baldwin, an author who has at times represented the apex of (black) American liberal sentiment, abandons black America, as it were, producing a text in which received racial thinking is inverted, if not *subverted*.

The character, Giovanni, might be read, in fact, as a rather odd and startling twist in Cleaver's notion of the Supermasculine Menial, the black and immensely physical opposite of his Omnipotent Administrator. That is to say, the white bourgeoisie: the French Guillaume and the Belgian (American) Jacques, are competing constantly to claim both Giovanni's labor power and his sex, a process that necessarily restricts Giovanni to the realm of the corporeal and the dirty, and that creates him at once as both the brutalized black male slave *and* the sexualized black female slave. In this sense, Giovanni has been dirtied, much as Puerto Rican boys are sullied with shit as they cross the line between the inside and the out, in their traffic with already marginal—and ambiguous—homosexuals. Indeed, as Giovanni suggests, *the* central task of modern life is the struggle to rid oneself of the dirt: "what distinguished the men was that they seemed incapable of age; they smelled of soap, which seemed indeed to be their preservative against the dangers and exigencies of any more intimate odor" (*GR*, 118). Strikingly, cleanliness acts as the very definition of manhood in this passage. The men are *cleanly* delineated from women, *cleanly* established as members of a community, *cleanly* recognized as insiders and subjects.

The struggle for cleanliness, the denial of the body that might protect one from the dangers of intimate odor, is precisely the struggle that David faces when he looks into his darker past. He attempts throughout to maintain a *clean* masculinity, to maintain his sense of respectability even as he, much like Thomas's gang, is pulled ever more deeply into the dirty muck. David's immersion into the Parisian demimonde has as much to do, then, with his desire to understand himself as *not* dirty, as *not* vulnerable and indeed as *not* homosexual, as with any real affinity for the people by whom he finds himself surrounded. "Most of the people I knew in Paris were, as Parisians sometimes put it, of *le milieu* and while this milieu was certainly anxious enough to claim me, I was intent on proving, to them and to myself, that I was not of their company. I did this by being in their company a great deal and manifesting toward all of them a tolerance which placed me, I believed, above suspicion" (*GR*, 32–33). This precisely replicates the process of denial that I demonstrated in my discussion of *Soul on Ice* and *Down These Mean Streets*. Real identity, meaning heterosexual identity, is formed through concurrent acts of repression and projection. The homosexual nonsubjects of *le milieu* not only reflect David's own subjectivity, creating him as a real man, they also stand in for the erasure of boundaries that render the entire real/not real logic unworkable.

David's abandonment of Giovanni for his female lover, Hella, a woman whom we only hear about in the second person until rather late in the novel, is, then, both a demonstration of his heterosexuality *and* his authenticity. With Giovanni, David can only exist in the shadowy and confined spaces of back alley cafes, late-night bars, and most especially, Giovanni's cramped, suffocating, and disheveled room. It is this room, much like the gay men's apartment in Thomas's narrative, that acts as the marker of Giovanni's gallant, if quixotic, effort to construct a space for himself. "But it was not the room's disorder which was frightening; it was the fact that when one began searching for the key to this disorder, one realized that it was not to be found in any of the usual places. For this was not a matter of habit or circumstance or temperament; it was a matter of punishment or grief" (*GR*, 115). I think it important here that we not get stuck in a reading of this passage that would proceed solely from the assumption that the homosexual Giovanni has been punished for his efforts to break out of normalcy by being banished to the realm of "the never quite finished," "the always in process." That is not to say that I intend to disallow this reading altogether. Instead, I would suggest also that the joy that David and Giovanni are able to achieve, however briefly, is itself a product of this same disorder. "In the beginning our life together held a joy and amazement which was newborn every day" (*GR*, 99). The attraction for both David and Giovanni is that they are obliged to recreate themselves—and the room—daily. Each has refused already to settle down. Both have left their "homelands." Both throw off the strictures of male heterosexuality. Moreover, both leave behind the mores and values of *le milieu*. Perhaps, then, the greatest tragedy—and the promise—of this work is that while David and Giovanni are cast out of the "mainstream," neither is able—or willing—to inhabit the margin. They are not the other, but the vehicles of the abject.

It becomes impossible for either to claim status in the "real" world or even its underside. Giovanni cannot simply give in to the abuse and manipulation of Guillaume. Instead, he kills him, creating himself as the marginal's marginal, the fugitive. Moreover, like both Cleaver and Thomas, he is eventually caught and incarcerated, remaining in prison until he undergoes the ultimate dissolution of the inside/out binarism—death. David has run away already from "America," which in this instance refers not simply to a geographical location, or a complex of political and social structures, but also to a patriarchal economy that produces maleness as the lack of lack, a fiction that David is never able to maintain. After the death of his mother, the family fiction is thrown into a profound crisis. His domineering aunt becomes the primary source of power and order in the household, reembodying his father, in the process, such that the notion of masculine invulnerability is exploded. Indeed, the tragedy that David brings with him from America is precisely that he both sees and knows his father. "Fathers ought to avoid utter nakedness before their sons. I did not want to know—not, anyway, from his mouth—that his flesh was as unregenerate as my own" (GR, 26).

David can never go home again, as it were, to the wide open plains of America. And yet even as David attempts to create his (American) female lover, Hella, as a surrogate for his homeland, as he mounts one last desperate attempt to save himself, to create for himself an identity that can be seen and acknowledged within respectable (American) society, he is always haunted by the dual specters of Giovanni and his own homosexuality. David becomes himself a type of ghost, growing ever distant from Hella, retreating into a world of memory and denial to which she has no access. "And I look at my body, which is under sentence of death. It is lean, hard, and cold, the incarnation of a mystery. And I do not know what moves in this body, what this body is searching. It is trapped in my mirror as it is trapped in time and it hurries toward revelation" (GR, 223). Here again we see the reference to death, the site at which the distinctions between the inside and the out, the self and the other give way, allowing only the articulation of ghostlike subjectivities. Strikingly, David's ghost-body becomes inexplicable. He can no longer fashion a narrative by which to describe it. It is distinct from the self, which remains a victim to a type of body logic that he cannot yet understand.

It is at this point, then, that we can see most clearly the process by which the figure of the homosexual is conflated with the figure of the ghost, a process that occurs throughout the production of African American literature and that is intimately tied to the production of the abject. The specter of the nonproductive, unauthentic, weak, effeminate, and antisocial homosexual had not, it seems, been exorcised with the virulently homophobic diatribes of Eldridge Cleaver, nor even with the deaths of Rufus and Giovanni. Indeed, in the process of creating the authentic black subject, a process that necessarily involves concurrent practices of negation and projection, one has always to resurrect the ghost of the black devil, as it were. That is to say, we must point to that which is unauthentic, base, and perverse in order to adequately define the borders of black "realness." At the same time, in the process of traveling through the underworld, the muck, the shit that is represented by the black homosexual, we are able to access, if only briefly, new modes of understanding and existence that seem to wait just beyond our grasp. As a consequence, the black abject never dies. On the contrary, it is only more deeply woven into the fabric of the black American (literary) imagination. As David says of Giovanni, "in fleeing from his body, I confirmed and perpetuated his body's power over me. Now, as though I had been branded his body was burned into my mind, into my dreams" (GR, 191).

I opened this essay with two epigrams: "Thou shalt not seethe a kid in his mother's milk," and "Chivo que rompe tambor con su pellejo paga," or, the goat who breaks the drum will pay with his hide. Both statements, taken from different, if not altogether dissimilar religious "texts," the Bible and the proverbs of the Cuban Abakua societies, reflect a profound concern with the question of perversity. To cook the goat in the same milk with which it has been nourished is to subvert a number of "self-evident" truths, among them the distinctions between right and wrong, inside and out, such that it becomes impossible to maintain the coherency of the society's logical order. Moreover, the very existence of the prohibition bespeaks the reality of a desire that stands outside of received logics. Indeed, it may be perverse to eat the kid prepared with its mother's milk, but this does not make it less enjoyable.

That the concern with boundary crisis, with the goat's tendency to break out of its proscribed roles within society should be repeated among Cuban Yoruba–based religious groups reflects not only the intersection of Christianity with New World religions, but also and importantly the fact that the articulation of the perverse and the grotesque is absolutely necessary to the production of a variety of national cultures. As Coco Fusco has suggested, even while the Abakua proverb points directly to the grave consequences of troublemaking,[18] it demonstrates the necessity of the untamed "outsider" to the continued creativity of the rest of the community. As James Baldwin's Giovanni is slaughtered and as Thomas's effeminate gay men are fucked and beaten, a type of music is produced, a music that points the way to new modes of existence, new ways of understanding, that allow the community to escape, however briefly, the systems of logic that have proven so enervating to the black subject. The importance of the (scape)goat, then, is not so much that with its death peace returns to the village, or that crisis ends. The point is not simply to expurgate all that is ambiguous and contradictory. On the contrary, as the kid is consumed and the drum is beaten, the community learns to gain pleasure from "the possibilities just beyond its grasp." It receives proof of its own authenticity and insider status while leaving open a space for change, perhaps even the possibility of new forms of joy. The boundaries are for a moment reestablished, but all are certain, even hopeful, that once again they will be erased.

NOTES

1 Eve Kosofsky Sedgwick, *Between Men: English Literature and Male Homosocial Desire* (New York: Columbia University Press, 1985).

2 Diana Fuss, "Inside/Out," in *Inside/Out: Lesbian Theories, Gay Theories*, ed. Diana Fuss (New York: Routledge, 1991), p. 3.

3 René Girard, *The Scapegoat* (Baltimore: Johns Hopkins University Press, 1986).

4 See Henry Louis Gates Jr., *Figures in Black: Words, Sign and the "Racial" Self* (New York: Oxford University Press, 1987), Paul Gilroy, *The Black Atlantic: Modernity and Double Consciousness* (Cambridge: Harvard University Press, 1993); and, Orlando Patterson, *Slavery and Social Death* (Cambridge: Harvard University Press, 1980).

5 Girard, *Scapegoat*, pp. 15–16.

6 Julia Kristeva, *Powers of Horror: An Essay on Abjection* (New York: Columbia University Press, 1982).

7 Paul Gilroy, "It's a Family Affair," in *Black Popular Culture*, ed. Gina Dent (Seattle: Bay Press, 1992), p. 312.

8 Eldridge Cleaver, *Soul on Ice* (New York: Laurel, 1968), p. 26. Further citations to this work will be abbreviated *SI* and given parenthetically in the text.

9 Angela Davis, "Reflections on the Black Woman's Role in the Community of Slaves," *Black Scholar* 3, no. 4 (December 1971): 2–15.

10 Malcolm X, quoted in Cleaver, *Soul on Ice*, p. 47.

11 See Pat Shipman, *The Evolution of Racism: Human Differences and the Use and Abuse of Science* (New York: Simon and Schuster, 1994).

12 Montagu, quoted in Shipman, *Evolution of Racism*, p. 163.

13 See John D'Emelio and Estelle B. Freedman, *Intimate Matters: A History of Sexuality in America* (New York: Harper and Row, 1988); and, John D'Emelio, *Sexual Politics, Sexual Communities: The Making of the Homosexual Minority in the United States, 1940–1970* (Chicago: University of Chicago Press, 1983).

14 Piri Thomas, *Down These Mean Streets* (New York: Vintage, 1967), p. 50. Further citations to this work will be abbreviated *DMS* and given parenthetically in the text.

15 Kristeva, *Powers of Horror*, p. 2.

16 James Baldwin, *Giovanni's Room* (New York: Laurel, 1956), p. 7. Further citations to this work will be abbreviated *GR* and given parenthetically in the text.

17 Toni Morrison, *Playing in the Dark: Whiteness and the Literary Imagination* (Cambridge: Harvard University Press, 1992). See also, Michael Banton, *Racial Theories* (New York: Cambridge University Press, 1987), Alexander Saxton, *The Rise and Fall of the White Republic: Class Politics and Mass Culture in Nineteenth-Century America* (New York: Verso, 1990), David R. Roediger, *The Wages of Whiteness* (New York: Verso, 1991), Eric Lott, *Love and Theft: Blackface Minstrelsy and the American Working Class* (New York: Oxford University Press, 1993), Robert C. Toll, *Blacking Up: The Minstrel Show in Nineteenth-Century America* (New York: Oxford University Press, 1974), Ruth Frankenberg, *White Women, Race Matters: The Social Construction of Whiteness* (Minneapolis: University of

Minnesota Press, 1993), Shelley Fisher Fishkin, *Was Huck Black?: Mark Twain and African American Voices* (New York: Oxford University Press, 1993); and, George M. Fredrickson, *The Black Image in the White Mind: The Debate on Afro-American Character and Destiny, 1817–1914* (New York: Harper and Row, 1971).

18 See Coco Fusco, "Pan-American Postnationalism: Another World Order," in *Black Popular Culture*, ed. Gina Dent (Seattle: Bay Press, 1992), pp. 279–284.

PART V Libidinal Intelligence:

Shocks and Recognitions

Maurice Wallace

The Autochoreography of an Ex-Snow Queen:

Dance, Desire, and the Black Masculine

in Melvin Dixon's *Vanishing Rooms*

To be liberated from the stigma of blackness of embracing it is to cease, forever, one's interior agreement and collaboration with the author of one's degradation. — James Baldwin, *No Name in the Street*

O f all the peculiarly American spectacles Charles Dickens encountered during his 1842 visit to the United States, few seem to have struck him with so much satisfied amusement as a "lively young Negro" in New York City, dancing an inimitable "Negro breakdown." Dickens described the nimble young dancer in his *American Notes*: "Single shuffle, double shuffle, cut and cross-cut: snapping his fingers, rolling his eyes, turning in his knees, presenting the backs of his legs in front, spinning about on his toes and heals like nothing but the man's fingers on the tambourine; dancing with two left legs, two right legs, two wooden legs, two wire legs, two spring legs — all sorts of legs — what is this to him?"[1] The "lively hero" of Dickens's Five Points sketches was the Master Juba himself, William Henry Lane, a Rhode Island "Negro," who was, by 1845, "the greatest dancer known"[2] in America. A member of the Ethiopian Minstrels, a troupe of four white men in blackface and him, Lane was a popular minstrel performer who regularly got top billing. But "far from fitting into [the] prefitted stereotype" of the malapropic, melon-eating buffoon typically associated with blackface minstrelsy, William "Juba" Lane succeeded in presenting minstrel audiences what only *seemed* as imitations of black life: Juba's "seeming counterfeit" performances, begrudged by white performers like P. T. Barnum's John Diamond, masked more authentic displays of black theatrical self-presentation than nineteenth-century audiences — or indeed twentieth-century ones — could imagine.[3] Where white minstrel imitations of black dance forms were "all stammers and jerks and gracelessness," Juba's were an ironic "combination of [muscular] mobility . . . flexibility of joints . . .

boundings . . . slidings . . . [and] gyrations."⁴ Such "firmness of foot, such elasticity of tendon, such mutation of movement . . . such natural grace,"⁵ one English critic wrote after Lane entertained there in 1848, never had been seen before in England.

By the time Juba's celebrity peaked in Europe, his dancing reflected such virtuoso talent that his acts routinely defied description. One observer, writing for the *Illustrated London News*, wondered how Juba could "enter into [such] wonderful complications so naturally . . . and make his feet twinkle until you lose sight of them altogether in his energy?"⁶ Another spectator wrote, "The manner in which he beats time with his feet, and the extraordinary command he possesses over them can only be believed by those who have been present at the exhibition."⁷ Undoubtedly, the allure of Juba's London "exhibition[s]" owed as much to a promised, percipient "aura of 'blackness'"⁸ in his act, as to the "extraordinary command" he demonstrated of the intricacies of black dance forms. But Lane seemed to have learned to transcend the racial gaze by the time of his London performances. The "wonderful complications" of his dancing were sufficiently spellbinding to cause audiences to "lose sight" of him *as* spectacle, but not "without losing sight of the reality of [black masculine] representation" altogether.⁹

Perhaps there is no more apt description of Juba's dancing, though, than that published by London's *Theatrical Times*. This highbrow organ of theater arts referred to Juba's performances as "an ideality . . . at once grotesque and poetical,"¹⁰ an expression that conveys an implicit and preterite apprehension, I would suggest, of ways in which *the mastery of form* and *the deformation of mastery*, as theorized by Houston Baker,¹¹ have historically coalesced to shape black masculine subjecthood in Eurocentric contexts.

When Juba died in 1852 in London, barely twenty-seven years old, he was already regarded "the most influential single performer of nineteenth-century American dance."¹² I highlight him here because I believe, like Marian Hannah Winter, that he "represents an independent Black dance tradition" of masculine self-expressivity. William Henry Lane is, by my reckoning, the primogenitor of black masculine dance history, the "initiator and determinant of the form itself,"¹³ a form that lends visible expression to the dialectics of black masculinity I shall pursue in this essay.

By close and careful consideration of Melvin Dixon's 1991 dance novel, *Vanishing Rooms*, I want to demonstrate that, if modern middle-class American manhood is finally an affair "between men," as Eve Kosofsky Segdwick has put it so famously, then black masculinity emerges as the contender identity in a bitter interracial conflict over sex and stereotype, which reveals itself performatively in a *proprioceptive improvisation on the black male body under white objectification*. Put another way, black masculinity coheres in a kinesic decolonization of the fetishized black male body, in a representational subversion, that is, whose most vivid illustration, as far as I can tell, is in the reappropriative power of dance, in "sweaty, sensual, fully efforted bodies" discovering themselves, as Marta Savigliano writes, despite burdens of otherness they bear.[14]

Admittedly, dance is one of the few remaining disciplines that we literary-cum-cultural critics have not formally explored. After film, photography, music, painting, even sport, dance is among the last frontiers of interdisciplinarity in cultural studies. Although we seem to find few occasions for thinking or writing about dance as an academic and popular discipline, it is, nevertheless, like speech and writing, a worthy sign system, a kinetic metalanguage impervious to the signifying limitations of words. Communicating paralinguistically, dance may be regarded as the visible dramatization of the invisible pursuit of "being what I am" in language, as Jacques Lacan puts it, and consequentially, in life. Because dance speaks, as it were, without words, it holds within it a potential to transcend them, to tell us something about ourselves that won't be pinned/penned down on a page. Further, if it is indeed true, as Cornel West has posited, that black masculinity reveals itself as a stylization of the body "over space and time,"[15] then it is precisely this attention to the expressive capacities of black *body language* that warrants inquiry into the theory and practice of dance in black masculine contexts. From the limbo performance of the Middle Passage (brilliantly historicized by the eminent Guyanese writer Wilson Harris) to the Calendia Dances of eighteenth-century West Indian Calienda slaves[16] to twentieth-century tap, break dancing, and voguing, the history of black male performativity in dance, popular and performance, reveals itself as a fertile field for uncovering, or perhaps *recovering*, a hermeneutics of black masculinity that owes no necessary allegiance to black macho (e.g., tap), or compulsory heterosexuality (e.g., voguing), but emerges nevertheless from a uniquely male racial experience. As dance does clearly offer black masculinity "recourse and access to another reality in the experience of masculinity," as one theorist argued was precisely what was missing from masculinity studies,[17] who can then doubt that the body-conscious careers of dancing black men like Bill "Bojangles" Robinson, Arthur Mitchell, or Alvin Ailey are as critical to comprehending twentieth-century black masculine identity as, say, Jack Johnson, Joe Louis, or Muhammad Ali? (As Ali taught us so well, boxers are not so far removed from dancers as we think. Where else, but in boxing and ballet, do men yearn for grace to "float like a butterfly," as Ali did?) In the deepest structures of boxing and dance, I submit, lie an alternate reality of black masculine subjecthood, one characterized by "new stylistic options," as West has called for in black masculine representation,[18] ones that render dance self-transforming.

In her book *Dance and the Lived Body*, Sondra Horton Fraleigh declares that to dance "is to discover [more of oneself] by uncovering, revealing and creating something not seen before . . . out of one's own bodily being."[19] To dance is to expand the repertoire of human representation, to pursue with one's body the extreme limits of self-knowledge. It is precisely this aesthetic that inheres in Melvin Dixon's 1991 novel, *Vanishing Rooms*. Like Toni Morrison's *Jazz*, *Vanishing Rooms* is a performance piece. Its alternating narration approximates a choreographic ronda variation in four (book) parts, which never fails to keep the tallest concerns of the novel corporeal. As a dancing book,[20] *Vanishing Rooms* makes literal what Henry Louis Gates Jr. intended only figuratively as "the dance of language that is writing."[21] Dance is not only in the design of *Vanishing Rooms*, however; it is both text and subtext of the novel. In its representation of the black gay dancer coming into being as a cohesive queer subject of color, *Vanishing Rooms* puts forward the symbolic power of dance as a curative for the self-abnegating devices of everyday life and language for gay black subjects under a racial and sexual hegemony.

DECONSTRUCTING DESIRE

I think that I know something about the American masculinity which most men of my generation do not know because they have not been menaced by it in the ways that I have been. It is still true, alas, that to be an American Negro male is also to be a kind of walking phallic symbol: which means that one pays, in one's own personality, for the sexual insecurity of others. The relationship, therefore, of a white boy and a black boy is a very complex thing.—James Baldwin, "The Black Boy Looks at the White Boy"

Some boys hug each other for reassurance.—Alex Hirst, introduction to Rotimi Fani-Kayode's *Black Male/White Male*

Jesse and Metro, Dixon's protagonists, meet at a small Connecticut college against the backdrop of a black student protest over the college administration's refusal to observe Malcolm X's birthday. Jesse is one of the protesters occupying the main office buildings at Wesman University. Metro, "one of those disadvantaged white boys from the South"[22] and a reporter for the *Wesman Herald*, shows up to cover the story for his paper. His "journalist's eyes" (37) find Jesse's "locked inside the building, barricaded away" (38), looking down on him from a second-story window in

Clarkson Hall. Moving "from window to window, from one empty class-room to another," Jesse sees Metro moving with him. "I watched him follow me as I moved," he recounts. "I knew we would meet somehow on the outside. . . . My hands felt empty with nothing to touch" (39). Like an exercise in body mirroring to Jesse's unchoreographed lead, their inability "to touch" across the racial divide of the scene's symbolic barricades, while politically portentous, intensifies the desire building between Jesse and Metro: "His stare made me feel weightless," Jesse revels, "light angles toward him on wings suddenly fluttering from inside me and begging for air. I wanted then to get under his skin, travel at break-neck speed through his veins and right to his heart" (38). Though the barricades around Clarkson Hall finally come down and Jesse is offered, at long last, *something* to touch in/on Metro's "pale body," race proves a more enduring barrier between them than any material obstruction.

When the demonstration ends several hours later, Jesse is among those who march proudly, militaristically out of the building. Armed with pad and pencil, Metro, ever the journalist, follows. Although his attempts to get a comment from Jesse are met each time with steely, soldierly silence—one must keep up the nationalistic pretense—Jesse's eyes betray his indifference. They coyly invite Metro back to his room. Metro's own eyes answer graciously, and it is not long before the pretense of the one's politics and the other's professionalism falls away. Sex ensues as Jesse revels in the warmth of Metro's thighs against his and "how close [their] faces held in making love" (10). That "making love" misnames their copulative act, however, is not long hidden from plain view.

Despite its billing, *Vanishing Rooms* is not a gay love story exactly, as love stories between men go. It is, more accurately, a bitter, and passionate rivalry in which sex is the weapon of choice. To call sex between Jesse and Metro "making love" is to seriously misname it, to be sure. It is rather little more than an act of spite and envy. As Dixon himself explained in a 1991 *Christopher Street* interview: "[S]exual desire can be an expression of hatred as much as it can be an expression of love. There are people who can just get off on having sex with someone *because* they hate them. The force of that hate can be as powerful as love."[23] *Vanishing Rooms*'s dual rape scenes, one involving the gang rape of Metro and in the other a similar attack on young Lonny Russo, represent the most extreme instances of sexual hatred. But *Vanishing Rooms* also discreetly reveals that sex needn't be violent or murderous to convey enmity. Though their relationship appears amorous, Jesse and Metro evince little that is loving in their reciprocal obsession for the other. While Metro's eventual murder in the novel serves as the unmistakable symbol of gay victimization and vulnerability under homophobia, it is also a sign of the potential destructiveness of sexual congress within impoverished relationships like Jesse and Metro's. Theirs is a poisoned relationship sustained by each one's political and parasitic need for the other's racial bodiliness. Their desire, in other words, is merely iconic, the false consciousness of one desire, sexual, mistaken for another: the fundamentally political wish for patriarchal privilege where the erotic stands in for unconsciously political desires, and the penis, an anatomical fact, is confused with the phallus, a political metaphor. In *Vanishing Rooms*, it is clear, "A desire to be, to become, [therefore] becomes a desire to possess or be possessed." [24]

When several gay-bashers chase Jesse to his apartment, hurling "black nigger faggot" at him like so many stones, Jesse runs directly into Metro's arms. "He held my head and hands until I calmed down," he relates, waxing sentimental. "It'll be alright," he remembered Metro saying. Metro's sexual compassion for the indignity of the racial stigmatization that Jesse has suffered represents sanctuary for Jesse, a skin-tight cover from the insult of racial caricature. Not surprisingly, then, Jesse's fear of his harassers quickly dissolves into longing for Metro. Done "slowly, deliberately" (15) sex with Metro rescues Jesse temporarily from public specularity as a "black nigger faggot." But Jesse's desire for Metro is not singularly sexual. For Jesse, to want Metro's body is not, in this instance, unlike wanting *to be* Metro, "a white boy from Louisiana, [educated at] New England prep schools and college" (15), who, despite Jesse's first impression of him outside Clarkson Hall, is not so "disadvantaged" after all.

Although Metro disputes his white-skin privilege ("Don't you think [I] have some weight to bear?"), Jesse sees differently and reproves him sharply: "You're white, Metro. At a distance you blend in with the crowd. Shit, they can see me coming, and in a riot they don't stop me to ask if I've been to college or live in the suburbs. They start beating any black head they find" (103). Jesse bears in his reproach the resentment of a black nigger faggot's double jeopardy. While Metro's queerness doesn't let him "blend in the crowd" as easily as Jesse imagines (he is murdered because of it), the burden of blackness, a condition of visual determinism, is Jesse's alone. I emphasize the deterministic nature of Jesse's condition in order to distinguish his specular condition from Metro's. This is not to deny that Metro suffers as severely as Jesse under the scopic regime. But each appears to suffer the consequences of social scopophilia differently.

In his book *Homographesis*, Lee Edelman puts forward an inestimable theorization of homophobia as "a powerful tropological imperative . . . to produce a visible emblem or metaphor" [25] for the homosexual person "whose sexuality must be represented as legible precisely because it 'threatens' to pass unremarked." [26] To permit homosexuality to "pass unremarked" is to put the so-called naturalness of heterosexuality in jeopardy. "Yet while the cultural enterprise of reading homosexuality must affirm that the homosexual is distinctively and *legibly* marked [i.e., made uninvisible], it must also recognize that those markings have been, can be or can pass as, unremarked and unremarkable"[27] in ways unavailable to racial subjects. In other words, although " '[r]acial' discrimination, . . . like . . . [homophobia] is propped up on, or as Freud might put it, occupies an anaclitic relation to, the privileging of the scopic drive in the psychic structuring of sexual difference,"[28] homophobia and racial discrimination differ in that unlike the racial Other, the subjecthood of the white queer is not optically *predetermined*. Homophobes tend to read backward onto white queer bodies, marking them—I can think of no better way to put it—*a posteriori*. (About Metro, Lonny recalls, "I thought he was one of the guys 'cause he didn't swish. . . . This guy walked like a regular fellah. . . . He [didn't] look like no faggot" [27].) Negrophobes, on the other hand, tend to read black bodies prescriptively, according to stereotypical forms and narratives that anticipate and fix the conditions of black possibility in advance.

In her essay "National Brands/National Bodies," Lauren Berlant argues that "the white male body is the relay to [social and political] legitimation." "The power to suppress that body," she writes, "to cover its tracks and its traces, is the sign of real authority."[29] However much Jesse may misjudge the "weight" borne by (white) queer subjects, he conveys to Metro in his rebuke an implicit apprehension of Berlant's point. He seems to know, like Berlant, that the male body of color, in contrast to the white male body, leaves its trace everywhere like ruins in the white imaginary. The persistent spectacle of dread and desire, of sin, sex, and stereotype that blackness commonly evokes in the white imagination effectively disqualifies black men for whatever "real authority" they might otherwise have gotten on the basis of shared gender. Because Jesse cannot ever hope to "suppress [his] body" or "blend in the crowd," he seeks a refuge from the unbearable hypervisibility of so-called black faggotry squarely in Metro.

Not until Metro's death, however, does Jesse come to face the truth of Metro's serviceability as his "underground man" (42). Symptomatically, when Jesse receives the news of his lover's fate, an unconcealable panic overtakes him: "Suddenly voices filled the outer hallway. Rushing footsteps. Laughter. Banging on doors somewhere. My hands shook again and my stomach tied itself in knots. Where could I hide?" (12). Jesse's concern is an urgent one. The commotion outside his apartment conjures images of the earlier harassment. With Metro dead, who now will protect *him*? Who, in other words, will "hide" the black nigger faggot from the physical and psychic violence of racial stigmatization? Eventually, Jesse finds in Ruella McPhee another refuge from the insufferable panopticism of the straight white gaze his tormenters personify. As a black woman, Ruella faces a similar social jeopardy. It is reasonable then for Jesse to find sympathy and safety in her. Symbolic of her availability as hiding place from the public spectacle of black faggotry, he nicknames Ruella "Rooms."

Although Jesse confesses to have "found other spaces to touch, other windows to touch" in Ruella's arms, sex with "Rooms" understandably fails. "There was one door [that remained] locked" and only "Metro had the key" (45). If Ruella offers Jesse a "safe place to go" from the taunts and torment that accompany racial and sexual difference, Metro embodies a *secret* place of specular disembodiment that Ruella, being black and female, is "locked" out of. Unlike Ruella, Metro is a "relay," as Berlant says, to the untraceable condition of white male corporeality. His touch sends consuming currents throughout Jesse's overdetermined body. "I wanted his hands on me," he says. "Five fingers and five more. I wanted the electricity of his touch, his hands on me" (11). Desiring what Whitman once called "the curious sympathy one feels when feeling with the hand the naked meat of the body,"[30] Jesse requires Metro's touch as the conducting instrument of white male (dis)embodiment and "abstract legitimation."[31] "How many times did I tell him, 'Just touch me. Dance your fingers across my chest, my thighs. Press my flesh. Take off my clothes real slow'" (11). As Metro's "wiry" hands "do their marvelous work," exciting Jesse with "the electricity of . . . [his] touch," they also become the medium of "relay," relieving Jesse of the weight of his color as well as his clothes. Jesse's desire is not only physical, then, but at the very heart of the matter, metaphysical. The "tender. . . aching" (11) in his body yearns a deeper thing for which Metro is both prosthesis and propitiation.

Metro's surrogacy for Jesse, however, is no less dire than that of Jesse for Metro. While Metro's caress appears to allay the pain of racial insult and scopic torment, it is precisely that pain that Metro requires of Jesse. When Metro beds Jesse in *Vanishing Rooms,* it is not in spite of the stamp of "black nigger faggot" on his head. He beds Jesse *because of it.* Whereas Jesse's sexual longings seem motivated by racial envy, Metro's are fueled by racial stereotype.

In less than a year of their cohabitation, Metro had already begun seeking higher pleasures than Jesse alone could provide. A regular patron of Paradise Baths, Metro hoped to seduce Jesse into his fantasies there: "Don't you see? All this is part of it, what we came to New York for. The streets, the sweat, beer and cigarettes. And here? You'd walk in, anybody would walk in, hands hooked in the belt, your jeans torn just so around the crotch. You'd lean against the wood and I'd find you, smell you waiting there. I'd kneel just so and you'd talk dirty to me" (43). Not only the pungency of "sweat, beer and cigarettes," but also the added "smell of mildew" (3) and the "stink of the warehouse" (5) suggest, in an olfactory sense, what Metro lacks, and therefore desires most profoundly in Jesse: *funk*.

In contrast to the slow, deliberate sex that gratifies Jesse, Metro requires its rougher, dirtier obscenities, which he has come to believe black men embody. The raw sensualism he seeks at the bathhouse—the funkiness of black sex—he seems to know less by sight than by scent. In Jesse, Metro desires a boorish "natural" blackness, a funk that confirms for him the half-savagery of black life he needs to cast back at him a self-affirming shadow of his privileged and powerful white male self.

As Metro's narcissistic obsession with Jesse's blackness deepens and Jesse accedes to Metro's fantasies, the truth of the racial politics of desire driving Metro's queer compulsions is articulated orgasmically. "Take it baby. Take it all" gives way to a whiny "Give me what you are" (210) not much later. Exactly what Jesse is to him, Metro seems incapable of suppressing. "Nigger" (113) bursts from his lips at the peak of pleasure, realizing simultaneously the verbal and the sexual significations of *ejaculation*. "What did you say?" Jesse asks, stunned. Brazenly, Metro answers, "I said, 'nigger.' . . . You wanted it low, didn't you? You wanted it dirty. . . . You wanted to ride the rough train, huh? Well, ride it, nigger." Not unexpectedly, Jesse strikes Metro in a rage. One body's defiance against the power of another, he expects Metro to retaliate. Much to his astonishment, though, Metro "just lay there moaning and fighting the air" maniacally: "He wasn't fighting me. He wasn't even seeing me. He was pulling at himself. I stopped and watched him pulling and punching and pulling and punching again until he moaned again and stopped as abruptly as he had begun. The bed was wet, his groin was wet. His hands slippery with his own semen" (114). Metro's autoerotic display is a revelation to Jesse. Its self-flagellative element reveals something of the pain and pleasure involved in the ritual purgings of white identity by displacement "on the backs of blacks" (to borrow that stunning phrase from Toni Morrison). "I was his nigger," Jesse later bemoans. "He called me nigger [because] . . . I was something he couldn't stand in me or himself anymore" (128). Inasmuch as fetishism is their mutual and coincident debility, then, it is a sharper logic that judges each one's surrogacy as a function of double parasitism, wherein sex belies the primacy of race as the animating feature of Jesse and Metro's relationship. Only through the difference accorded by race, after all, will either ever achieve the mundane out-of-his-own-body experience he is desperately seeking.

Of course, Metro and Jesse are not extraordinary types. Neither is *Vanishing Rooms* far removed from the psychic reality of black and white men's contemporary lives. By realizing the homosocial/homosexual enactments of dread and desire that more broadly structure historic masculine identity, *Vanishing Rooms* proffers an imaginative "critique of [the] relations of power and desire"[32] produced by what Baldwin calls "the obscenity of color" within the broad span of male-to-male relations, from combat to caring. On the other hand, what *is* extraordinary about Dixon's novel is its emphasis on the recuperative potential of dance for the fetish-framed body. In Dixon's novel, the black masculine reclaims itself, unfettered, in the dance, in a particular stylization of the gay black male body over ritualized time and space, which, following an important trope in Pierre Bourdieu's *Outline of a Theory of Practice,* I wish to call, in a word, *improvisation.*

It should be understood that the formal distinction between choreographed performance (rehearsed dance) and improvisation (unrehearsed dance) in modern dance practice does not hold in this essay. By "improvisation" I do not mean to invoke the unrehearsed performance specifically, but any motile expression "play[ing] on the equivocations, innuendos, and unspoken implications of verbal or gestural symbolism,"[33] which may be formalized in a choreography (rehearsed dance) or not. More important than improvisation's physical exercise, however, are the interior deliberations over what Daniel Nagrin calls "the specific image"[34] that, in the dancer's mind, thematizes a performance and against which his improvisation asserts itself, oscillating, as Bourdieu writes, "between playfulness and seriousness, abandon and reserve, eagerness and indifference."[35] Problematically, black masculinity has for its "specific image" the picture of itself *as it is (mis)recognized by racialists,* an image that is virtual but not real. It is this virtual image, then, that alienates the black man from himself and for which improvisation, substituting "*strategy* for the *rule,*"[36] seems an effectual antidote.

The beginning of Jesse's self-transformation is his "first solo," performed to Billie Holliday's "Strange Fruit" in the spring concert at Wesman. His dance is his personal statement, he says, an enactment "of where I might go from this limited space of light and shivering movement" (102) as a (gay) black male under the public gaze. Sweeping the stage "in a series of small, contracted movements in a circle," his body sweating "in the light that held [him] . . . tight . . . against the thick suggestion of night," Jesse is the fictional realization of what Ramsay Burt, in his book *The Male Dancer: Bodies Spectacles Sexualities,* refers to as dance's "restive and oppositional [resistance] to 'the body's placement within a

system of power relations'" inimical to it.[37] Jesse's circumambulation resists the boxlike quadrangularity of the stage, while his glistening body
opposes the "thick suggestion of night." Little wonder his performance
bewildered the (white) audience ("The next day someone asked me what
the dance meant"). Far from being a mere divertissement, here was, in
the best traditions of black dance, "an inner drama occurring on stage, . . .
an activity of self-definition"[38] in spite of its public exhibition.

Notwithstanding his "journalist eyes," Metro fails with the rest of the
audience to see through the sweaty spectacle gleaming under the spot-
light to the deeper "complex of tensions" (Baldwin's phrase) being dramatized in Jesse's dance. "Why did you choose that dance, Jesse? . . . [W]hy
do you act like black people are the only ones oppressed?" (103). Though
obviously vexed, Jesse evades Metro's provocation: "Look Metro, I don't
want to discuss it. It's my favorite Billie Holliday song and I wanted to
dance" (103). This evasion and the subsequent struggle to convincingly articulate his black difference is not to be taken to mean that between Jesse
and Metro, both gay, their racial difference is negligible. Rather, Jesse's
inability to get Metro *to really see,* and therefore comprehend, his black
particularity underscores his need to dance in the first place; for, quite
apart from most other calisthenic arts, "dance functions as a luminous
symbol of unspeakable human truths." It is, as one dance theorist put it,
"an ephemeral event whose immediate appeal can never be captured in
words."[39] When Jesse ultimately relents in the argument that follows, his
exasperation is also a capitulation to the logocentric prejudice that exalts
verbal expression (the word as signifier) above body language (the gesture
as signifier). Consequently, Metro has little difficulty convincing Jesse
that there are no significant differences between them: "[W]e're faggots.
Two faggots. That's what we are," (103) he argues. Of course, Jesse cannot
dispute Metro. As a journalist, naturally Metro has the word on his side.

For the moment Jesse gives up on his self-clarifying blues solo as he
and Metro now "danced together" (41). Their shared routine is closer to
slapstick, however, than serious dance. In the giddy excitement of gradua-
tion day "We tussled and danced in our gowns" Jesse remembers, "holler-
ing ourselves silly. I bowed to him. He pulled wide the edges of his sleeves
and curtsied." Later in the novel, they would make their egress from Paradise Baths wobbling "like two dancing drunks, vying for balance" (3). But
so frivolous and involuntary a production as this is far from gratifying
for Jesse and, leaving Metro there in front of the bathhouse to "dance"
alone, he hurries off to the studio for—what else?—"improvisations" (4).

Significantly, in his improvisations class, Jesse pairs up with Ruella. If
their duet resembles the one aptly titled "A Duet" outlined by Nagrin in
Dance and the Specific Image: Improvisations, then the specific image be-

fore Jesse is no longer black and male but black and female. In Nagrin's sketch of "A Duet," the dancers "dance looking at [their] partners and dancing about [their] partners, *about* his.her hair [*sic*], clothing, personality traits, eyes—anything that gets your attention."[40] As Jesse dances "about" Ruella, it is the specific image of black womanhood with which he identifies and around which he improvises. As it is constructed in *Vanishing Rooms*, the black masculine is not so much opposed to the black feminine as it is symbiotically joined to it. The relation would seem to confirm Hortense Spillers, when she writes that "the black American male embodies the *only* American which has had the specific occasion to learn *who* the female is within itself."[41] This much, Jesse perceives clearly. He sees Ruella anew at improvisations. "She was pretty," he told himself. "And I knew right away through the dance of our black skins that if I didn't feel her full beauty, I'd never know my own" (197). Ruella satisfies in Jesse's self-image exactly what Metro grieves.

Left alone on the pier near Paradise Baths, Metro is easy prey for the young gay bashers who ultimately murder him. Although Jesse grieves bitterly for Metro, his grief is most certainly for himself as well. In an sudden reversal of circumstances, Metro's death leaves Jesse alone, as decidedly as Jesse had abandoned him by the river, to face the intolerable fact of blackness by himself. It is exactly this aloneness, though, that Jesse demands for the critical second dance, "the *pas de deux*," which liberates him at last from his fetish condition. Through Dixon's exercise of what Susan Leigh Foster calls "writing dancing," Jesse is transformed from the body-object of Metro's "rough love" (209) into a self-satisfied body-subject. Jesse reclaims control over his body in a choreography that reimagines and redeems his relationship with Metro, discovering in the dance the possibility for a more authentic partnership with Metro than the racially inflected machinations of their former union allowed. In the process, Jesse overcomes the self-alienation of the surveilled body-object who "is [inevitably] made other to [himself] when [he] takes account of its appearance to others."[42] In the critical "dance for two men," Jesse's "Strange Fruit" solo is vindicated.

Like Dixon's *Vanishing Rooms*, Langston Hughes's poem "Dream Variations" recognizes the resuscitative powers of the body-in-ritual-motion. The second stanza of that work follows:

> To fling my arms wide
> In the face of the sun,
> Dance! Whirl! Whirl!
> Till the quick day is done.
> Rest at pale evening . . .

A tall, slim tree . . .
Night coming tenderly
Black like me.[43]

Here, dance and desire conjoin as the romantic will to "fling my arms wide / In the face of the sun / Dance! Whirl! Whirl! / Till the quick day is done" is also, the will to a subject-position that is, in the final analysis, as irrevocable as that "tall, slim tree," and as singular, of course, as "Black . . . me." One might imagine that the oneiric confession at the center of "Dream Variations" is a pronouncement of Hughes's hopefulness for "new stylistic options," repeating West, "for black men caught in the deadly endeavor of rejecting black machismo identity"[44] that the dancing figure, like "Night coming tenderly," presumes to embody.

Literary critic and Hughes's biographer, Arnold Rampersad, has written that "Dream Variations," unlike the other poems Hughes composed shortly after dropping out of Columbia University, is "more contrived, though with a typically childlike, perhaps androgynous persona."[45] While the poem's "childlike" quality is to be wondered at, it is no surprise that Rampersad finds Hughes's dreamer "androgynous," since the whole choreographic repertoire, the flinging and the whirling, expands the otherwise narrow range of body stylizations currently available to black men. That a poet rather than a dancer could conceive of the greater possibilities for black masculine self-knowledge that lay in the dance is not unremarkable. Before his death in 1989, choreographer Alvin Ailey wrote in his autobiography, *Revelations,* that he and Hughes had become "good friends and often used to meet and talk, usually about music and dance — he was very fond of and knowledgeable about both."[46] Hughes had even composed a few poems that he hoped Ailey would put to choreography. In addition to the poetry, Hughes wrote at least one sexually "adventurous"[47] short story he called "Seven People Dancing." Its protagonist, Marcel Smith, was a gay epicurean Harlemite whose dancing was "too fanciful to be masculine and too grotesque to be feminine." Although it is doubtful that "Seven People Dancing" or "Dream Variations" was included in the collection of poems offered to Ailey by Hughes,[48] both works represent the promise of new discursive improvisations — perhaps, following Rampersad, "androgynous" ones — on an otherwise tedious masculinist theme.

THE AUTOCHOREOGRAPHY OF AN EX-SNOW QUEEN

You think I'm going to please you, but I'm going to show you something we both have trouble looking at. It's in my legs and hips, my face filled with clouds passing to reveal the sun, and now clouds again, its in my voice. Perhaps I am pretending, but this is my habitat, this place of illusion.—Bill T. Jones, *Last Night on Earth*

While Dixon's *Vanishing Rooms* and Hughes's dance writings reveal textually something vital about the symbolic effectuality of the kinetic body, there are few articulations of the black man performatively "coming into being" more lucid than the recent choreographies of Bill T. Jones. The parallels between *Vanishing Rooms*, particularly, and Jones's memoirs, *Last Night on Earth*, are especially striking. Reading *Last Night on Earth*, one must consciously resist the suspicion that it must be Jones's life on which *Vanishing Rooms* is based. The interracial romance, the bathhouse, and the dance in *Vanishing Rooms* reappear in *Last Night on Earth* with uncanny resemblance. However fortuitous these parallels may be, though, they are, in themselves, beside the greater point of this essay. Whether or not Dixon owes anything to Jones's story (or Jones, Dixon's), the similarities between the texts permits the self-expressive limits of fiction to be transcended by the formal virtues of autochoreography. With its combination of personal narrative, poetic meditations, and choreographic outlines, *Last Night on Earth*, "a performance in text,"[49] elucidates *Vanishing Rooms*'s dance elements where literary terms alone won't do. In other words, Jones's compositional preoccupations following the 1988 death of his late partner, Arnie Zane, illuminate dance's survivalist function in *Vanishing Rooms*.

Probably no devotee to modern dance failed to recognize Jones and Zane during their shared career as the most visual pair in modern dance. Few critics could resist discussing the stark physical contrast between Jones, "tall and black with an animal quality of movement," and Zane, "short and white with a nervous, pugnacious demeanor" (150). While there is little evidence in *Last Night* to suggest that these men were attracted, like Jesse and Metro, because of racial difference (who can rightly tag these two as "false lovers"?), it would be naive to think that their partnership was not also vexed at times by racial difference, stereotype, and fetishism. At its deepest levels, Jones confesses, their relationship was vexed by certain demons of race and class.

In chapter 7 of *Last Night*, "Amsterdam," Jones admits that in the early stages of his relationship with Zane, "[their] lovemaking and [their] fights took on a relentless dependency" (93):

> *"Why does Arnie want so much?"*
> *"Why is he so business-minded? He's such a white man. He's such a Jew."*

"He's that way because you need him to be that way. . . ."

"Why do I feel used all the time?"

"Because you *are* used. And why shouldn't you be used, since you refuse to use youself?"

With his therapist's help, Jones recognized for the first time his own complicity in Zane's latent prejudice. Perhaps just as importantly, with Zane dying a slow AIDS-related death, Jones's therapist helped him recognize in his own complaints a more genuine fear of his losing Zane's bodily sanctuary/surrogacy as an incorrigible "white man" whom, Jones learns, he "need[s] . . . to be that way." Without Zane as collaborator and lover, Jones worried, as Jesse had, that he would lose emotional and artistic "balance" all at once: "Tell me what to do, baby, I'm coming apart. You've always been the one telling me what to do" (174). Zane's rattled reply, "You'll figure it out," simple if unappeasing, was to prove prophetic. Like Jesse, Jones "figure[s] it out" in a dance.

With Zane's death, Jones discovered his discrete black masculine difference, his identity apart from the mutual dependency reflected in "*BillandArnie* or *ArnieandBill*," (93) as they had come to be inextricably referred to. In a 1992 *Transitions* interview, Jones explained, "I felt very much how my world had changed when Arnie was no longer there: the work began to speak more as that of a black man. And of a gay man, too, because there was reason to."[50] As someone "who never really had to be a black artist until that other member was dead,"[51] Jones looked more purposefully to black dance. What he discovered there was a solacing "tension"[52] that not only kept him from "coming apart," but challenged the smug aesthetics of white avant-gardism he and Zane had for so long opposed. Taking full choreographic advantage of the dialectical themes of black cultural production, Jones came to realize that beyond the binary emphasis on black and white, slave and master, Africa and America common to black aesthetic practices, attention to "the mysterious intimacy between audience and performer" (164) was also vital to the processes of decolonizing the black arts. Just as crucially for Jones's career since then has been his understanding of the importance of decolonizing the black body.

Consistently, from his earliest performances, Jones's critics have been overwhelmed by his dark, elegant musculature. One (white) female critic, "*deeply* regretting the fact that he [was] gay," spoke wistfully of Jones's "long limbs, the trim but defined muscles, [and] the rich mocha sheen of his skin."[53] Even today, Jones is not unaware of his public image. As Henry Louis Gates Jr. writes, "Jones. . . has an acute sense of [his] physicality." Describing himself as having the face of "a young prizefighter, with intelligent eyes, sensitive mouth, lips not too thick, nose not too flared. . . an ass that is too high but firm like a racehorse,"[54] Jones's picture of himself suggests the dual character of his performance style and compositional intent "to challenge the implicit ritualism of performance, acknowledge its boundaries and subvert them" (164). "[Y]oung," "intelligent," and "sensitive," on the one hand, Jones's solos immediately following Zane's death, were consistently "coupled with [a kind of] wild anger and belligerence."[55] His strategy is designed to estrange, not ingratiate itself with, the spectator's gaze, to participate in his fetishization in order, finally, to subvert and transcend it. As Gates has pointed out, he "does not disavow the gaze of white fascination: he works within it, plays with it," and, recalling his therapist's advice, "*uses* it."[56] And as Jones explains in *Last Night*, he has often "opted for improvisation to accomplish this" (164). In this way, "I [have been] able to deconstruct [my own] identity," Jones writes. "Deconstruction [has] yielded solos that [are] confessional, often painful, taking unpleasant emotions and exposing them spontaneously in a fashion that [is] brutal on both the audience and me" (165).

From Jones's "largely improvised solo" (165) at the American Dance Festival in 1981, the first of his self-consciously antagonizing performances, to his 1992 choreography "Last Night on Earth," and beyond, Jones has taken for his philosophy of performance what cultural theorist Michael Taussig calls "the magic of mimesis"—namely, the notion that "in some way or another one can protect oneself from evil spirits by portraying them."[57] That is, by portraying the fetish image in his dances, Jones gains "power over that which is portrayed,"[58] demystifying it and "out-fetishizing the fetish."[59] "Last Night on Earth," a solo composition that casts Jones as "the possibility of Eros" (238), typifies his deconstructive strategy.

Scantily clad in "a short white skirt—a tunic really" (239), obscuring gender and history with a single garment, Jones's leaps and jumps expose "a glistening sequined codpiece and [his] naked ass" (239), which flash the audience indiscreetly. Unembarrassed, Jones playfully "cast[s] a coy glance at the audience, as if I were Marilyn Monroe," he explains, "in her lace bustier, teasing a bit of cleavage" (239). More duplicitous than playful, however, Jones's "glance" defies his audience with *a resistant look*[60] that is not only an ocular challenge to the collective look (*le regard*) of a white racialist audience, but a proprioceptive self-display as well. In classic vogue fashion, Jones strikes a cross-gendered, cross-racial pose imitative of the pictorial "look" (*l'image*) of Marilyn Monroe, whose voluptuous image is precisely that which black men, it is alleged, desire most to ravish. Whether the defiance in *Jones's* look lies principally in the coquetry of the eyes or, alternately, in the simulation of Monroe "teasing a bit of cleavage," it is clear that the dance undertakes to seduce the audience into the erotic fantasy Jones is (de)constructing on stage:

> I roll from standing to all fours, grip an imaginary partner, and thrust two time aggressively with my pelvis. I roll, repeat the rutting action, stop, stare at the audience, caught in the act, then continue with vehemence.
> I am dancing about fucking. Unfettered fucking. Obscene, joyous, wildly defiant, desperate fucking. (239)

While "Last Night on Earth" is a solo, the "fucking" fantasy he enacts in this choreography involves more than one persona. Jones realizes in his dance a colonial fantasy always already present in the white spectatorial gaze, which his stare is intended to disrupt. As Jones lures his spectators into imaginary erotic play, they too are "caught in the act," publicly confronted by the very fetish image of black male sexuality they have privately held in their racialist minds. Jones projects their guilt before them, entrapping them within the racial fictions of their own scopic imaginations by seizing a sex partner on stage they cannot see but must nevertheless visualize. Just whom each spectator imagines Jones to be humping so feverishly—another man or a woman, a black persona or a white one—will inevitably vary, but his or her participation in the fantasy produced by "Last Night on Earth" remains invariable. Whomever it is the spectator imagines in the sex act with Jones, Jones's look suggests that *he* imagines he is "fucking" the spectator "with no consequence," as the colonial fantasy gets revisited on its authors with "unfettered . . . obscene . . . wildly defiant" abandon.

Perhaps, only through "a language that is parsed by the configuration and movement of bodies,"[61] then, can a black man, by an aggressive improvisation on the very stereotypes that objectify and restrict his subjective possibilities (Eros in this case), ever hope to escape the unbearable psychic and social stigmas attached to him. Such language, of course, needn't be that of dance only; however, as Jesse discovers in *Vanishing Rooms*, the expressive language of the black male body is "everywhere":

> I watched black men everywhere for movement: in barbershops, on street corners, some reading the *New York Times*, some going in and out of expensive hotels by the front door and some by the service entrance. And I watched myself: my bend of waist while making the bed, washing dishes, stretching on the parquet floor. And I watched [my new lover] Rodney without him knowing it. . . . I saw his grace, his sureness and poise of movement. . . . I watched black Wall Street

executives leaping from taxis and the man selling subway tokens near our block. I watched the kids playing handball against the supermarket wall and under the sign reading "No Ball Playing." I watched black boys dribbling imaginary basketballs while waiting to take the subway to the next playground. And some balancing real basketballs while riding in the car. (198)

Jesse's study of black men moving within and across gender, class, sexual, and physical boundaries, underscores the deep structures of dance in black men's everyday lives, their particular stylizations of bodiliness, their improvisations on white American themes of subalternity. In this context, it is not difficult to see why dancing is so crucial to Jesse's representational self-recovery. Only through the deconstructive power of dance, as exemplified by Jones, can Jesse extricate himself from self-abnegating "porno-house of language"⁶² into which "blackniggerfaggot" has immolated him. His dance for two men, one black, the other white, recasts his poisoned relationship with Metro, his "underground man," in the redeeming light of a new choreography fittingly performed to Duke Ellington's *A Train*. Having recognized his own difference in the lived collage of black men around him, Jesse understands, by the novel's end, that he, as Jones concludes, "can't even quite begin to position [himself] in the world matrix without taking into account the issue of [his] humanity as a black man."⁶³ Like Jones, too, Jesse comes to subjective self-knowledge, too much aware of his body's sensual and serpentine powers to be merely an object among other objects anymore.

Vanishing Rooms concludes with Jesse's *pas de deux* in performance. Representing the culmination of his quest for black masculine subjecthood, Jesse's choreography, "the opportunity for improvisation in the rhythm, the solo, and personal statement" (199), takes him "someplace else" (200) other than the "filthy abandoned [bathhouse] where the single word 'nigger' had already sealed [Metro's] fate" (197) and stood to seal Jesse's. When the performance ends, the hush of the theater breaks "into a gathering wave of hands clapping. Pools of sweat dotted the stage. The applause showered over me. . . . Then quickly, the [hall] burst into light, and the room holding us there vanished" (211). The baptismal resonance of metaphors like "wave," "pools," "showered," and "light" underscores the psychic transformation the dance has inspired in Jesse.

While Dixon's portrayal of Jesse's *A Train* choreography is vibrant and spirited ("Wheels of legs spinning, leaping. Tiny runs ending in arabesque. Turn-two-three, plié-two-three. Relevé" [209]), it is brief, only a few lines long, and those who lack an appreciation for dance movement may still fail to visualize it. I suspect that Bill T. Jones's "Last Night on

Earth" as well as his works "Absence," "Forsythia," "Achilles Loved Patro-clus" (for Arthur Avilles), "Fever Swamp" (for the Alvin Ailey Repertory Company), and his own "Pas de Deux for Two," however, may help us have a clearer vision of Dixon's novel and what it really means to be a (gay) black man under the public gaze in America.

But Jones is only one touchstone among many for reading dance in *Vanishing Rooms*. The recent works of Ronald K. Brown ("Life Lesson"), Dwight Rhoden ("Black or White"), and David Rousseve ("The Whisper-ing of Angels"), may yet have lessons to teach us cultural and literary critics about the theory and practice of black masculinist production. These men may know better than any of us the urgency behind the words of theorist/choreocritic Erick Hawkins, who writes, "A man danc-ing will have to go far beyond entertainment. A man dancing will have to stand for what a man can become."[64] This, of course, is the hope the late Melvin Dixon has bequeathed us, the promise that Bill T. Jones and so many other dancing black men presently realize.

NOTES

1 Charles Dickens, *American Notes*. (1842; reprint, Gloucester, Mass.: Peter Smith, 1968), pp. 110, 112.

2 Ibid., p. 110.

3 Eric Lott, *Love and Theft: Blackface Minstrelsy and the American Working Class* (New York: Oxford University Press, 1993), p. 113.

4 Ibid., p. 115.

5 Quoted in Marian Hannah Winter, "Juba and American Minstrelsy," in *Chronicles of the American Dance*, ed. Paul Magriel (New York: Henry Holt, 1948), p. 50.

6 Ibid.

7 Ibid.

8 Lott, *Love and Theft*, p. 113.

9 Winter, "Juba and American Minstrelsy," p. 50.

10 Ibid.

11 See Houston Baker, *Modernism and the Harlem Renaissance* (Chicago: University of Chicago Press, 1987).

12 Winter, "Juba and American Minstrelsy," p. 39.

13 Ibid.

14 Marta Savigliano, *Tango and the Political Economy of Passion* (Boulder, Colo.: Westview Press, 1995), p. 4.

15 Cornel West, *Race Matters* (New York: Vintage, 1994), p. 129.

16 According to black dance historian Edward Thorpe, in his *Black Dance* (London: Chatto and Windus, 1989), "one of the favorite dances which reappeared among slaves in the West Indies was the Calenda," from which the Calienda, a vigorous eighteenth-century jig "performed by males only, stripped to the waist and twirling heavy sticks in a mock fight" (15) evolved. By contrast, the Calenda was a line dance in which "the men and women faced each other in two lines and danced to an impromptu song"

intoned by the onlookers. In Calenda dancing, "the dancers made contact, slapping their thighs together, kissing and making 'lascivious' gestures" (14). Thorpe distinguishes the Calenda from its male counterversion, the Calienda, by the supposition that, owing to its inherent homosociality, the Calienda "must have been rather different from the 'indecent' versions performed by mixed couples" (15). Given the partial nakedness of the Calienda dancers and the phallicism of "the heavy sticks" wielded in the performance, however, the Calienda, if performatively different from the Calenda, might actually have been just as "indecent."

17 Arthur Flannigan Saint Aubin, "Testeria: The Dis-ease of Black Men in White Supremacist, Patriarchal Culture," *Callaloo: A Journal of African American and American Arts and Letters* 17, no. 4 (1994): 1068.

18 West, *Race Matters*, p. 129.

19 Sondra Horton Fraleigh, *Dance and the Lived Body: A Descriptive Aesthetics* (Pittsburgh: University of Pittsburgh Press, 1987), p. xxxii.

20 The idea of the "dancing book" extends from Henry Louis Gates Jr.'s archaeology of the talking book, the "ur-trope of the Anglo-African [literary] tradition." Just as the talking book "seems to concern itself with the possibilities of representation of the speaking black voice in writing," the "dancing book" as I have called it, aims to represent, in style and subject, orchestrated and improvised dance movement. We might go further, as I suggest in the text of this essay, to think of Toni Morrison's 1992 novel, *Jazz*, similarly. In a sense, *Jazz*, a novelistic approximation of the jazz sound, is the "music book" to Dixon's "dancing book." Both would seem to be postmodern derivatives of the talking book theorized by Gates. See Gates's *The Signifying Monkey: A Theory of African-American Literary Criticism* (New York: Oxford University Press, 1988), pp. xxv, 127–69.

21 Henry Louis Gates Jr., review of *Jazz*, by Toni Morrison, in *Toni Morrison: Critical Perspectives Past and Present*, ed. Henry Louis Gates Jr. and K. A. Appiah (New York: Amistad, 1993), p. 54.

22 Melvin Dixon, *Vanishing Rooms* (New York: Plume, 1991), p. 97. Further citations to this work are given parenthetically in the text.

23 Clarence Bard Cole, "Other Voices, Other Rooms: An Interview with Melvin Dixon," *Christopher Street*, May 1991, 27. Emphasis added.

24 Saint Aubin, "Testeria," p. 1067.

25 Lee Edelman, *Homographesis: Essays in Gay Literary and Cultural Theory* (New York: Routledge, 1995), p. 8.

26 Ibid., p. 43.

27 Ibid., p. 7.

28 Ibid., p. 46.

29 Lauren Berlant, "National Brands/National Body: *Imitation of Life*," in *Comparative American Identities: Race, Sex, and Nationality in the Modern Text*, ed. Hortense Spillers (New York: Routledge, 1991), p. 113.

30 Walt Whitman, "I Sing the Body Electric," in *The Whitman Reader*, ed. Maxwell Geismar (New York: Pocket, 1955), pp. 63–72.

31 Berlant, "National Brands/National Body," p. 112.

32 Michael Moon, introduction to Guy Hocquenghem, *Homosexual Desire*, trans. Daniella Dangoor (Durham: Duke University Press, 1993), p. 17.

33 Pierre Bourdieu, *Outline of a Theory of Practice*, trans. Richard Nice (Cambridge, England: University of Cambridge Press, 1977), p. 10.

34 See Daniel Nagrin, *Dance and the Specific Image: Improvisations* (Pittsburgh: University of Pittsburgh Press, 1994).

35 Bourdieu, *Outline*, p. 10.

36 Ibid., p. 9. Emphasis Bourdieu's.

37 Ramsay Burt, *The Male Dancer: Bodies, Spectacle, Sexualities* (New York: Routledge, 1995), p. 46.

38 Gerald Myers, "African Americans and the Modern Dance Aesthetic," in *African American Genius in Modern Dance*, ed. Gerald Myers (Durham, N.C.: American Dance Festival, n.d.), p. 31.

39 Susan Leigh Foster, *Reading Dancing: Bodies and Subjects in Contemporary American Dance* (Berkeley: University of California Press, 1986), p. xvi.

40 Nagrin, *Dance and the Specific Image*, p. 28.

41 Hortense Spillers, "Mama's Baby, Papa's Maybe: An American Grammar Book," *Diacritics* 17 (1987): 80. For reminding me of the importance of this relationship, I wish to thank those graduate students in English who participated in the Americanist Colloquium at Yale University where, in the spring of 1996, I delivered an early version of this paper.

42 Fraleigh, *Dance and the Lived Body*, p. 17.

43 Langston Hughes, "Dream Variations," in *The Collected Poems of Langston Hughes*, ed. Arnold Rampersad and David Roessel (New York: Vintage, 1995), p. 40.

44 West, *Race Matters*, p. 129.

45 Arnold Rampersad, *The Life of Langston Hughes, Volume I: 1902–1941, I, Too, Sing America* (New York: Oxford University Press, 1986), p. 78.

46 Alvin Ailey and Peter Bailey, *Revelations: The Autobiography of Alvin Ailey* (New York: Routledge, 1993), p. 88.

47 Arnold Rampersad, *The Life of Langston Hughes, Volume II: 1941–1967, I Dream a World* (New York: Oxford University Press, 1988), p. 333.

48 According to Rampersad, Hughes offered Ailey his ballet libretto, "St. Louis Blues" and his long poem *Ask Your Mama* for choreographic consideration in 1955 and 1961 respectively. Whether or not the specific poems Ailey referred to in *Revelations* were related to these, it is not known. Ailey was also retained to provide choreographic direction to two gospel musicals by Hughes, *Black Nativity* and *Jericho Jim-Crow* (Ailey did not stay with the former production). See Rampersad, *Life of Langston Hughes* 2:248, 343, 346–47, 371.

49 Bill T. Jones and Peggy Gillespie, *Last Night on Earth* (New York: Pantheon, 1995), p. ix. Further citations to this work are given parenthetically in the text.

50 Eric K. Washington, "Sculpture in Flight: A Conversation with Bill T. Jones," *Transitions* 62 (1992): 194.

51 Ibid., p. 191.

52 Ibid.

53 Henry Louis Gates Jr., "The Body Politic," *New Yorker*, 28 November 1994, p. 84. Emphasis Gates's.

54 Ibid.

55 Ibid., p. 121.

56 Ibid. Emphasis Gates's.

57 Michael Taussig, *Mimesis and Alterity: A Particular History of the Senses* (New York: Routledge, 1993), p. 13.

58 Ibid.

59 Ibid., p. 3. Taussig derives his theory of "the magic of mimesis" from the ritual magic practices of the Cuna Indian in and around Panama, Central America.

60 See Kaja Silverman, *Threshold of the Visible World* (New York: Routledge, 1996), pp. 154–61.

61 Gates, "Body Politic," p. 121.

62 See Calvin Thomas, *Male Matters* (Urbana: University of Illinois Press, 1996), pp. 19–26, 190–94.

63 Gates, "Body Politic," p. 124.

64 Erick Hawkins, *The Body Is a Clear Place: And Other Statements on Dance* (Princeton, N.J.: Princeton Book Company, 1987), p. 56.

Stephen Barber

Lip-Reading: Woolf's Secret Encounters

Queer, . . . a book coming out, why one writes them? How much part does 'coming out' play in the pleasure of writing them? Each one accumulates a little of the fictitious V. W. whom I carry like a mask about the world.—Virginia Woolf[1]

There was Dodge, the lip reader, her semblable, her conspirator, a seeker like her after hidden faces.—Virginia Woolf[2]

The only way to get outside the dualisms is to be-between, to pass between, the intermezzo—that is what Virginia Woolf lived with all her energies, in all of her work, never ceasing to become.—Gilles Deleuze[3]

Virginia Woolf's declaration in 1940 to her diary that her books constitute fictitious selves, that they are masks that are simultaneously acts of "coming out," adumbrates the presence of a queer force within both her impulsion *to* write and that passion's progeny. "Coming out" signifies for her not as the revelation of a putative lesbian self; neither are her "masks" to be glossed as merely so many dissimulations by a closeted lesbian.[4] Woolf's accumulated "Woolfs," her stylized selves, these masks, her fictions, inscribe, rather, just as they are inscriptions of, a critically queer technology of self. Thus, while at work on *The Pargiters* (arguably the first of her queer works) in 1933, she characteristically records the transformation of her character, Elvira Pargiter, into a (counter)discursive position that the author comes to inhabit:[5] "It is an utterly corrupt society I have just remarked, speaking in the person of Elvira Pargiter, and I will take nothing that it can give me. . . . [N]ow, as Virginia Woolf, I have to write . . . to the Vice Chancelor of Manchester University and say that I refuse to be made a Doctor of Letters. . . . Lord knows how I'm to put Elvira's language into polite journalese. What an odd coincidence! that real life should provide precisely the situation I was writing about. I hardly know which I am, or where: Virginia or Elvira:

in the Pargiters or outside" (D, 4:147–48). Upon completing her work, Woolf again expresses uncertainty as to whether it is within or outside her textual practice that she dwells; this undecidability, in turn, admits the most decisively joyful of discoveries: that writing not only is, but does. About this performativity—for her, distinctly queer—she claims the accomplishment of an ability to "pass from outer to inner, & inhabit eternity. A queer, very happy free feeling, such as I've not had at the finish of any other book" (D, 4:355). From now on, a "moment" whose timing is queer,[6] Woolf accounts for her *rapport à soi* in terms of writing as performativity; "then I am so composed," she realizes in 1937, for example, "that nothing is real unless I write it."[7]

Eve Kosofsky Sedgwick's far-reaching explication of "queer" as "hing-[ing] . . . radically and explicitly on a person's undertaking particular, performative acts of experimental self-perception and filiation" unequivocally bestows upon its practitioner an agency less obviously attributable to the "homosexual," that "modern invention [that] embodies less a set of subjective desires than a particular, historically contingent process of labeling applied in the first place from without."[8] While evincing the mutually supportive and indeed inextricable aspects of performativity identified by Sedgwick, Woolf's "queer" is also vigorously indebted to a preoccupation with social codifications or regulatory labeling. The task of problematizing the concept of "gay self" is crucial to Woolf's queer aesthetic, since sexual identification and assignment (through processes of normalization) are at once consequences and functions of the government of individualization that continues to "trap us in our own history."[9] As Sedgwick has argued, "'gay' and 'lesbian' still present themselves (however delusively) as objective, empirical categories governed by empirical rules of evidence (however contested)."[10] In order to devise a means for deindividualization whereby new forms of ethics may emerge, the practices of which are queer, Woolf's gay figures make use of countermemories incurred by their subjectification to homophobic processes of identification. The diacritical mark of queerness *is* its deindividualized agency, a peculiar self-performativity: "there are important senses in which 'queer' can signify only *when attached to the first person*. One possible corollary: that what it takes—all it takes—to make the description 'queer' a true one is the impulsion *to* use it in the first person."[11] The particularity and peculiarity of this *rapport à soi* owes to a queerly critical awareness that motivates and determines the "ensuing" course of action (the time is out of joint here: who, for instance, *precedes* the other— Woolf, or Elvira? the writing "I," or the "reality" written?), which in turn renders this first person obstinately unavailable, indeed nonpresentable, to empirical rules of evidence, let alone to "itself," for it is always irreducibly, ineluctably, and *strangely, relational* to *others.*[12]

Nicholas Pomjalovsky of *The Years* as well as William Dodge and Miss La Trobe of *Between the Acts* succeed in countering paleonymic constraints of "homosexuality"—being named from without through legal, medical, and religious discourses—by queering themselves, that is, by critically using the *naming* of their homosexuality to advance a manner of living counter to, and discontinuous with, the violating yet perversely enabling epistemic configuration within which they find themselves. In her last novel, *Between the Acts*, Woolf stages a deliberate resistance to regulatory procedures of labeling homosexuality by giving the name "Dodge" not only to a gay character, but to this text's queer performativity. The *effect* of Woolf's queer nominalism ("I . . . like buggers; I can't think of a word to fit them—that's all")[13] on her writing—Mallarmé: "On a touché au vers"—is, in a word, this: the *dis*continuous and lacunary narrative of the text's continous and "initial" narrative comes to be ethically privileged (hence the title, *Between the Acts*). Woolf's outlaws produce these discontinuous ruptures that, although never finally achieved, are ever enacted as queer performativity.

"Where people mistake," Woolf submits, "is in perpetually narrowing and naming these immensely composite and wide flung passions—driving stakes through them, herding them between screens. But," she sincerely (and not in the least antithetically) demands, "how do you define 'Perversity'? What is the line between friendship and perversion?" (*L*, 6:200). Like Woolf's avowed passing from "outer" to "inner" and back again, the woven line between friendship and perversion is, in its Woolfian sense, precisely a fiction, *her fiction.* Impossible to separate from this privileged version of *friendship* distinguishing her final two fictional experiments, Woolf's textual investment in *perversion* entails a self-intimate relationship that is always also a "*conspiracy.*" For instrumental to the inauguration of women's accession to positions of self-agenting in these works are the gay figures whose collective presence underpins Woolf's counterdiscourse. The textual cathexis of these queer *relations* is all the more pronounced since their nominalist inscription is *by* a queer-filiated woman (it is, after all, Woolf who is activating these forces). Beginning with *The Pargiters*, Woolf invariably represents queer novelistic subjectivities in the defamiliarizing light of conspiratorial relationships between women and gay men. "I am writing about sodomy at the moment and wish I could discuss the matter with you," she reveals about this work in 1934 to her nephew, Quentin Bell; significantly, immediately following this remark, Woolf emphasizes the relation between her writing "I" and queer. "How far," she wonders, "can one say *openly* what is the *relation* of a woman and a sod?" (*L*, 5:273; emphasis added). Woolf's queer textual practice, as figured by and in this "openness," that relationality, sets off "the immemorial current that *queer* represents, [which is as] antiseparatist as it is antiassimilationist. Keenly, it is relational, and strange." [14]

In both *The Pargiters* and *The Years*, Elvira (who becomes Sara in the latter) and Eleanor Pargiter are quite literally reflected upon by the text in the numinous light of their relationship with that gay "bounder," Nicholas. [15] Woolf's inscription of gay men as forces of intervention in normalizing procedures of subjectification transforms—both thematically and technically—her preceding conceptualization of sexual difference, a point left mostly unacknowledged or, when taken up, misunderstood if not misrepresented by critical work on Woolf. [16] It has not been acknowledged, for example, that the very philosophy of *Three Guineas*, which is so frequently mobilized as a source text for separatist feminist thought, is initially elaborated by *Nicholas* in the "1917" section of *The Pargiters*. [17] Neither has it been noted that the persistent, if formally unarticulated, textual desire of *The Years* and *Between the Acts* to make (in Walter Benjamin's memorable phrase) "the continuum of history explode" develops in the figures of Nicholas and, in the latter novel, William Dodge, and all the more radically in the counterdiscursive positions these characters (including La Trobe) generate as queer novelistic subjectivities (just as Elvira is at once character and counterdiscursive position in the passage I cite above).

Although *The Pargiters* was finally transformed into two works, her penultimate novel, *The Years*, and the critical essays comprising *Three Guineas*, Woolf's inscription of queer relationality, explicit in the former and implicit in the latter, remains central to the ethical positions of both works. The ethic of *Three Guineas* signifies in the rationalist sense of "doing the right thing"; in *The Years* and *Between the Acts*, ethics is *thematized* thus, but at the level of *techne*, the mechanics of "telling," yet another manifestation occurs: the effort, that is, of ethical singularity or, what Gayatri Chakravorty Spivak names in another context, the "secret encounter." [18] Communication fails to transpire between subjects in these novels *except* during secret encounters between those who are moved by queer *rapport à soi* and/or those who inhabit the queer *relation* of a woman and "a sod," in which, diacritically, each refuses mastery, to master the other, to treat it as a mere extension of the ego. The writing subject, "Woolf," too, takes the lead from the other in a textual economy that harbors a lesson: that the most difficult accomplishment, but also the most necessary, is to arrive at the most extreme proximity while guarding against the trap of projection, identification. The other must remain strange within the greatest possible proximity.

What might it mean to give form to the following sentence from the "1917" section of *The Years* if we attend seriously to it at the level of content: "[Nicholas] was *saying* what Eleanor *felt* herself" (*Y*, 272; emphasis added)? The political analysis immanent within these aesthetic works is generated by Woolf's critical philosophy of "being-displaced," of being queer in a homophobic, misogynistic sociocultural order. Owing to a political regime vigilantly scrutinized by Woolf,[19] being queer in modern Britain meant, in her shorthand, "being at risk," "being despised" (a critical position attributed initially to Nicholas),[20] this last phrase the one that resonated most to her thinking and that, for a brief while at least, she intended as the title for *Three Guineas*.[21] On being despised: Woolf critically and vitally identified with this position, as is indicated not only in the political philosophy advanced by *Three Guineas*, but in the narrative drive of the *The Years* and *Between the Acts*, as well. In these latter works, Woolf "finds" or cathects in her gay characters a mode of joyful experimentation with being. From *The Pargiters* onward, then, textual investment in queer performativity intensifies, and the gestural codes of gay bodies—their corporeal morphology—are read by other characters with several possible consequences: self-transformation, for example, or reactions that compel readers of these texts to become cartographers of subjectifying force-fields.

Communion with Dodge in *Between the Acts* is, we shall see, the condition of possibility for the emergence in the suicidal Isa Oliver of critical consciousness, which, nonetheless, since her knowledge fails to be acted upon, remains incapable of fundamentally countering the ventriloquism that constitutes her life. Such Woolfian encounters between women and gay men invariably allow for a transition from ventriloquism to (possibilities for) a critical awareness or a political ontology by means of which "being despised" becomes a position to be affirmed in efforts both to trace the prudent administration and policing of bodies and desires, as well as to ignite novel ethical possibilities. This is not to invoke an imaginary and, to be sure, impossible line from "false consciousness" to "conscientization"; rather it is to insist with Gilles Deleuze and Félix Guattari on Woolf's line of "transition" as an experience of "the middle":

It is in the middle where one finds the becoming, the movement, the velocity, the vortex. The middle is not the mean, but on the contrary, an excess. It is by the middle that things push. That was Virginia Woolf's idea. Now the middle does not at all imply to be in one's time, to be historical—on the contrary. It is that by which the most diverse times communicate. It is neither the historical nor the eternal, but the untimely. A minor author is just that: without future or past, she has only a becoming, a middle, by which she communicates with others, other times, other spaces.[22]

I. PATH-CLEARING: NUMINOUS NIGHTS IN *THE YEARS*

There was something queer about Nicholas, Eleanor thought.—Virginia Woolf (*Y*, 277)

Anyhow my Elizabeth [Bowen] comes to see me, alone, tomorrow. I rather think, as I told you, that her emotions sway in a certain way. . . . I'm reading her novel to find out. What's so interesting is when one uncovers an emotion that the person themselves, I should say herself, doesn't suspect. And it's a sort of duty don't you think—revealing people's true selves to themselves?—Virginia Woolf (*L*, 5:111)

[E]thics is the experience of the impossible.—Gayatri Chakravorty Spivak[23]

In *The Years*, Eleanor perceives Nicholas as a purveyor of a new form of "*pouvoir/savoir*," of (in Spivak's demonumentalizing account of Michel Foucault's term) critical practices based upon "being able to do something only as you are able to make sense of it."[24] Since "*pouvoir/savoir*" has translated conceptually into Anglo-American thought as a necessarily imperfect identification of a dominant constellation of power-knowledge-subjectivity relations, to understand it as an indispensible name for self-agenting may appear, at least initially, as counterintuitive. The productive discomfort this term summons in critical thought is conveyed by Spivak's insightful formulation that "*pouvoir/savoir* is the ontophenomenological truth of ethics, to the very extent that it is its contradiction in subjecting."[25] This richly suggestive account of "power/knowledge" requires remembrance of two senses given by Foucault to "subject": being subject, on the one hand, *to* prevalent discursive formations, *and*, on the other, *rapport à soi*, or self-agenting. Ethics "happen" when the subject subjects him- or herself by means, necessarily, of a critical manipulation of the very subjectifying processes that "initially" obstruct ethics.

An instance of the inauguration of a queer *rapport à soi* finds Eleanor musing for the first time in *The Years* about "freedom," the lack of which she suffers as "daily life" until her encounter with Nicholas. "Eleanor wished that he would go on talking—the man she called Nicholas," we read. "*When*, she wanted to ask him, when shall this new world come? When shall we be free? When shall we live adventurously, wholly, not like cripples in a cave? He seemed to have released something in her; she felt*

not only a new space of time, but new powers, something unknown within her"
(Y, 282–83; emphasis added). Immediately preceding Eleanor's passage,
she anxiously concludes that "had she told them [what she was think-
ing] nobody would know what she meant" (Y, 280); at Nicholas's urging
("What are you thinking, Eleanor?" [Y, 281]), however, she imparts her
thoughts, an action that initiates the movement toward a sense of release
from the text's proffered record of a gendered inability to act. Her subsequent indication (in the "Present Day" section) of an achieved gaiety and
of an ongoing practice of freedom, as well as her desire to explicate them,
signify a radical discontinuity, a rupture that, like Nicholas's ceaselessly
interrupted and eternally deferred speech (about which more soon), the
rest of the text dramatizes as historically lost, although never entirely
or successfully irreclaimable, since something of it always remains. In
order for the remainder *to* remain as radical discontinuity, though, effortful readings are called for. "Nothing that has happened should be
lost for history," claims Benjamin in his attempt to open temporality to
ethics.[26] Woolf enables a reading practice *for* such a timing, as exemplified in Nicholas's gift to Eleanor of being, here and now, and, we shall
see, as further evinced in Eleanor's responsible reading and accounting
of (as well as responsiveness and accountability *to*) Nicholas.

Nicholas, who as Sara informs Eleanor "ought to be in prison . . .
because he loves . . . the other sex, the other sex, you see" (Y, 283), develops a philosophy based upon the bestowal of ontological gravity to a
historically contingent identity that provides the discursive position with
which he is able to counter paleonymic constraints. Upon first encounter,
Sara's sentence surprises for at least two reasons: first, since it would
seem Nicholas is subject to discipline and punishment *simply because he
loves* and, second, because gay men are implicitly, *queerly,* identified with
women: the "other" sex. This "identification," which makes operative a
displacement of identification, is ultimately less asserted or described than
forcefully put into play by Woolf's textual practice, which gives "writing"
over to "queer-becoming," and "gay men" and "women" over to the other,
as the site of admission "qu'il y ait de l'autre." This is a *coup de force*
against near insuperable odds, against the resistant logic of opposing
names, for Woolf here renames "gay men" *and* "women" with the name
of the other even while retaining the same name. The text thus advances
through contra-diction, countering logical diction with a queer force.

Among the few politicized women in the novel is Rose Pargiter, who
has been in prison (as it is observed Nicholas ought to be), and to whom
Kitty Malone raises a glass of wine in honor of her feminist insurgency:
"Rose had the courage of her convictions. Rose went to prison. And I
drink to her!" (Y, 399). Outside of prison Nicholas is no less subject to the

law that condemns him to the sentence "ought to be in prison." Let us pause to heed that sentence and its subject's name, as well as Nicholas's own sentences. When Eleanor is introduced to him she cannot catch his surname, in part, she reflects, because "it was so long," and in part because his *language*, ostensibly "the same" as hers, differs so from her own. "A foreign name, she thought. A foreigner. He was clearly not English." *And then we read:* "He shook hands with a bow like a foreigner, and he went on talking, as if he were in the middle of a sentence that he wished to finish" (*Y*, 267). Both within Britain specifically and the community generally, Nicholas (like La Trobe in *Between the Acts*) is a foreigner in several senses: "one who is from a place other than the one being considered"; "one who is [deemed] alien; not natural" (*OED*). A relation emerges between Nicholas's outsider status, his homosexuality, and (his) aesthetics (of existence, as well as in its common sense). We find him in the *middle* of a sentence he wishes to finish, a predicament we can better grasp with recourse to Foucault's distinction between ethics and the code that stresses as fundamental the difference that obtains between a moral problematization and an interdiction. (The code refers to behaviors that are permitted or forbidden or excluded; it determines "the positive or negative value of the different possible behaviors.")[27] Nicholas uses critical consciousness about his position in order to transform the code into ethics. If he is to elaborate a relation to self in which desire and reality are connected (an association both Woolf and Foucault conceive as "a revolutionary force"),[28] he must keep in mind the sentences "ought to be in prison" and the unknown, unknowable, unfinished sentence he wishes to complete.

In *Three Guineas*, Woolf explicitly discriminates between the sociopolitical code and ethics—or, in its own words, between "two kinds of laws: the written and the unwritten" (*TG*, 184). For Woolf, establishing ways of existing is not exclusively an aesthetic matter, for it also requires what Foucault opposes to morality: ethics. In this relationship of ethics and aesthetics, devised so as to create "ways of living with what would otherwise be unendurable," "we're no longer in the domain of codified rules of knowledge (relations between forms), and constraining rules of power (the relation of force to other forces), but in one of rules that are in some sense *optional* (self-relation): the best thing is to exert power over yourself."[29] Although Woolf argues in this "guide" to the "good life"[30] that written law must and will be interpreted differently by the sexes ("since 'reason' and imagination are to some extent the product of our bodies" [*TG*, 185]), her inscription of queer relationships in *The Years* and *Between the Acts* troubles the codified rules of knowledge and the oppositional logic of a certain familiar conceptualization of sexual difference by making gay men figures of displacement who engender critical and ethical thinking in their gendered interlocutors. The name Woolf lends to these friendships is "conspiracy," which denotes "a combination of persons for an unlawful purpose" (*OED*). Through Woolf's lens homosexuality and queerness appear in the forms of a transvalued impropriety and unlawfulness, for queer displacement writes "unwritten law" into being and, breaking with convention, opens a time-space where being may manifest otherwise. Woolf's commitment to pursue "endeavors of an experimental kind to discover what are the unwritten laws" is revealed in her creation of queer combinations. These endeavours lead, she avers, to the "fact that it may sometimes be necessary to improve the written law by *breaking* it" (*TG*, 185).

Since the counterdiscursive position of homosexuality in *The Years* is fabricated tropologically and subjectively in the face of an ever-portending possibility of confinement, its *pouvoir/savoir* proves a telling position from which to theorize oppression. "Before we can fully achieve and use our intuitive grasp of the leverage that sexual relations seem to offer on the relations of oppression," Sedgwick suggests, "we need more—more different, more complicated, more diachronically apt, more off-centered—more daring and prehensile applications of our present understanding of what it may mean for one thing to signify another."[31] In a letter to a writer all too familiar with confinement, Jean Genet, Jacques Derrida locates in the prison the possibility for analysis of just this kind: "In a prison—this one and others—where it thought it had put its outside in chains, the system of (Western-white-capitalist-racist) society has made possible, *by this act*, an analysis that is at once the most implacable, the most desperate, but also the most *affirmative*." The temporality of this disruptive analytic force is invoked in Derrida's observation of George Jackson's letters from prison that "[t]hey are not only cries, although they *also* remain that, nor writings of political history. The time of their history is worked out *between* the precipitation of absolute impatience, of immediate bliss and the endless work of preliminary mediations."[32] So too *The Years* works (toward) a temporality that (perhaps) breaks with the continuum of history: "[Eleanor] had seemed to be looking into the future. . . . We shall be free, we shall be free, she thought" (*Y*, 282–83).

In both *The Years* and *Between the Acts* secret encounters occur in and call forth this radically indeterminate time, a time that is also a figural space, nameable only with the periphrasis "*between* the acts," a time, moreover, that gathers around the names of queer men when recollected by women. Nicholas's name eludes the memory of almost every character in *The Years*, a point to which the text draws much attention.[33] But names *are* important to Eleanor, who *does* recollect his (lost) name; when, for example, during their initial meeting she is asked by him to disclose her thoughts, she considers, "He calls me Eleanor . . . that's right" (Y, 281). Only following their talk of "the true and good life," of self-elaboration—during which Eleanor "seemed to be looking into the future"—does she learn from Sara of Nicholas's homosexuality:

> '. . . And Nicholas,'—[Sara] patted him on the knee—'who ought to be in prison, says, "Oh, my dear friends, let us improve the soul!"'
> 'Ought to be in prison?' said Eleanor, looking at him.
> 'Because he loves,' Sara explained. She paused. '—the other sex, the other sex, you see,' she said lightly, waving her hand in a way that was so like her mother's.
> For a second a sharp shiver of repugnance passed over Eleanor's skin as if a knife had sliced it. Then she realized that it touched nothing of importance. The sharp shiver had passed. Underneath was—what? She looked at Nicholas. He was watching her. (Y, 283)

Although the revelation to Eleanor of Nicholas's sexuality is met with an instant (and it would seem instinctive) shiver of repugnance, this news ultimately enables her to conceive of their earlier secret communion or conspiracy ("they had been overheard" [Y, 282]) as a mode of exchange based on the re-cognition of an experience of the impossible, which is to say, of the other. ("They are aware of each other," Eleanor will realize of Nicholas and the queer Sara. "They live in each other; what else is love?" [Y, 352].) The following passage thus channels repugnance and then indifference ("it touched nothing of importance") into a form of passionate acknowledgment of difference:

> 'Does that,' he said, hesitating a little, 'make you dislike me, Eleanor?'
> 'Not in the least! Not in the least!' she exclaimed spontaneously. All the evening, off and on, she had been feeling about him; this, that, and the other; but now all the feelings came together and made one feeling, one whole liking. 'Not in the least,' she said again. He gave her a little bow. But the clock on the mantelpiece was striking. . . . She went to the window and parted the curtains and looked out. All the houses were still curtained. The cold winter's night was almost black. It was like looking into the hollow of a dark-blue stone. Here and there a star pierced the blue. She had a sense of immensity and peace—as if something had been consumed. (Y, 283–84)

All is transformed for Eleanor following this introduction to Nicholas. Before their meeting she feels "numb all over—not only her hands, but her brain" (Y, 268). "She spoke without any meaning," we are given to understand slightly earlier, and then that "[Renny's] silence oppressed her" (Y, 271). Approaching Nicholas, "She looked at the man whose surname she had not heard. He was very dark; he had a rounded head and dark eyes. . . . [He] must be Russian, she thought. Russian, Polish, Jewish?—she had no idea what he was, who he was. . . . Did she like him or not? She did not know. I've interrupted them, she felt, and I've nothing whatever to say. She felt dazed and cold" (Y, 269). As their communion transpires, we notice, if we attend, strange things happening to perception and/or bodies. "[T]hey all seemed to have lost their skins; to be freed from some surface hardness," Eleanor muses of her group of friends (Y, 276). This atmosphere intensifies when, in order to wait out an air raid, she accompanies the group to the cellar—"With its crypt-like ceiling and stone walls it had," we note, "a damp ecclesiastical look" (Y, 276). And again a numinous reflection: "They looked at each other," we read as the raid ends; "[d]raped in their quilts and dressing gowns, against the grey-green walls, they all looked whitish, greenish" (Y, 278). Maggie acknowledges, " 'It's partly the light. . . . Eleanor,' she said, looking at her, 'looks like an abbess' " (Y, 278).

The atmosphere is thus highly charged, but not all are participants in its creation; that conjugal pair, Renny and Maggie, for example, do not contribute to talk of "good life," the talk that saturates the air. "I was saying," Nicholas proffers, "we do not know ourselves. . . . and if we do not know ourselves, how then can we make religions, laws, that—." Eleanor comes to his help: "That fit—that fit" (Y, 268). Nicholas then "take[s] the word and repeats it as if he were grateful for her help" (Y, 268). Guarding a space for the other's thought, Nicholas typically makes questions of his statements: "The soul—the whole being. . . . It wishes to expand; to adventure; to form—new combinations?" And Eleanor, combining with him, answers, " 'Yes, yes,' . . . as if to assure him that his words were right" (Y, 269).

By the time Eleanor watches Nicholas with Sara—their combination—in the "Present Day" (1936) section, she is able to disinter subjective possibilities that hitherto she found unimaginable.[34] In "1917," for instance, she remarks of Sara as the latter "gave her hand to Nicholas and he kissed it" that "she wore no engagement ring" (Y, 270). Such normalizing "observations" are refused by Eleanor in "Present Day." "What an odd-looking couple!" North exclaims to his Aunt Eleanor as he watches the dance of Nicholas and Sara. To North's ensuing query, "Why don't they marry?", Eleanor responds:

'Why should they?'
'Oh, everybody *ought* to marry,' he said. 'And I like him, though

he's a bit of a—shall we say "bounder"?' he suggested, as he watched them circling rather awkwardly in and out.

'"Bounder"?' Eleanor echoed him. . . . 'No, not a bounder,' she said aloud. 'He's—' (Y, 353)

Instead of announcing what Nicholas "is," however, Eleanor turns to a *refusal* of what is: "Marriage isn't for everyone," she tells North again (Y, 354).

Toward the novel's conclusion, Eleanor, now "a fine old prophetess, a queer old bird" (Y, 311), descries as the party draws to its close "a curious pallor on all the faces. . . . North's head—he was sitting on the floor—was rimmed with whiteness" (Y, 405). She "sink[s] back into her chair, exasperated." For what *she* glimpses—this numinous glow—is not present as such; it remains what *Eleanor* is able to perceive *because* of her reading practice. So, she thinks,

> There must be another life. . . . Not in dreams; but here and now, in this room, with living people. She felt as if she were standing on the edge of a precipice with her hair blown back; she was about to grasp something that just evaded her. There must be another life, here and now, she repeated. This is too short, too broken. We know nothing, even about ourselves. We're only just beginning, she thought, to understand, here and there. She hollowed her hands in her lap. . . . She held her hands hollowed; she felt that she wanted to enclose the present moment; to make it stay; to fill it fuller and fuller, with the past, the present and the future, until it shone, whole, bright, deep with understanding. (Y, 406)

Hollowing her hands, Eleanor repeats a queer gesture ("[Nicholas] hollowed his hands as if to enclose a circle" [Y, 281]) which summons "another life." The queer life she intuits both is and is not *this* life; when requested by Sara to narrate her life, therefore, Eleanor feels "she must put her thoughts into order; then she must find words. But no, she thought, I can't find words; I can't tell anybody" (Y, 348).

Now why can Eleanor find no words? She thinks, "My life's been other people's lives," a statement rife with antagonistic senses. For example, "My life's been other people's lives. . . . my father's; [my brother] Morris's" (Y, 349): patriarchal society is founded upon "her" suppression (Eleanor's niece asks her, "Was it that you were suppressed when you were young?" [Y, 318]); she is confined to family relations; she does not, like her father and brothers, act in the universal. She does not accede to the public sphere to which the man in his masculinist inscription has access *because* his particular needs are looked after in the family.[35] Before "1917," then,

Eleanor is not acting for-herself; on this plane, she is portrayed as re-actively fulfilling a function of the State: "A Victorian spinster," her niece dismissively summarizes (Y, 312). Yet another (and this time livelier) possibility presents itself: "My life's been other people's lives. . . . [M]y friends' lives; Nicholas's" (Y, 349): this is a self-intimate, secret "know-ing," a conspiratorial position produced through and present-ed as queer relationality. On this plane, Eleanor, rejecting marriage, forms combina-tions that, the text dramatizes, interrupt the order of things.

Unable to tell Sara about her life, Eleanor discovers Nicholas mani-festing before her. "Just as I was thinking of you!" she cries with relief. *"Indeed it was like a part of her, a sunk part, coming to the surface"* (Y, 349; emphasis added). "And what were you thinking about me?" Nicholas in-quires as he takes the proffered seat (Y, 350). Eleanor's response is re-markable in that while Nicholas's availability for identification and love is predicated on his being homosexual, Eleanor is able to resist her cul-ture's discursive practice of privileging sexuality for its telling relation to individual identity, truth, and knowledge, by demonstrating a respon-sible unwillingness to bind Nicholas *to* identity. This passage unfolds as her contemplation of him: "If I can't describe my own life, [she] thought, how can I describe him? *For what he was [Eleanor] did not know;* only that it gave her pleasure when he came in; . . . and gave her mind a little jog. . . . She knew exactly what he was going to say. . . . As she thought it, he said it. Does everything then come over again a little differently? she thought. . . . The thought gave her extreme pleasure. . . . But . . . [h]er mind slipped. She could not finish her thought" (Y, 350–51; empha-sis added). Again Eleanor turns to Nicholas for assistance:

> 'Nicholas . . .' she said. She wanted him to finish it; to take her thought and carry it out into the open unbroken; to make it whole, beautiful, entire.
> 'Tell me, Nicholas . . .' she began; but she had no notion how she was going to finish her sentence, or what it was she wanted to ask him. (Y, 351)

No wonder Eleanor "fails" to narrate her life and desires that Nicholas, who remains in the middle, complete her sentence: the discontinuity with her previous subjectification is experienced by her as an *ongoing* miracle set off by him. A "feeling of happiness" possesses her, an "unrea-sonable exaltation," for "[i]t seemed to her that they were all young, with the future before them. Nothing was fixed; nothing was known; life was open and free before them" (Y, 363–64). "Isn't *that* queer?" asks Eleanor. "Isn't that why life's a perpetual—what shall I call it?—miracle? . . . [I]t's been a perpetual discovery, my life. A miracle" (Y, 364).

Nicholas is cathected by *The Years* as figuring forth this unnarrativizable miracle. Toward the novel's end, Kitty presses him to describe what his interrupted speech was to have been about. Woolf may have excised Nicholas's speech from *The Years* (one may find it whole in the original holograph draft of *The Pargiters* or versions of it in Grace Radin's important study of *The Years*) in order to dramatize its conspicuous absence as the persistent becoming of an inarticulable radical discontinuity (such as Eleanor knows through encounters with him). "'My speech?' he laughed. 'It was to have been a miracle!' he said. . . . 'But how can one speak when one is always interrupted!'" (*Y*, 405). *Stretching his hand out, touching each finger separately*, Nicholas concludes of his speech that it was to close with a "'drink to the human race. The human race,' he continued, raising his glass to his lips, 'which is now in its infancy, may it grow to maturity!'" (*Y*, 405).[36] Eleanor, too, knows that her experience of discontinuity can only remain, like Nicholas's speech, (if) unsaid, a miracle about to have happened. She manages to handle it, to point to it, though, when she reminds Renny of her first meeting with Nicholas. "'I feel . . .' she stopped. She put her hand to her head: 'as if I'd been in another world! So happy!' she exclaimed." As always, Renny, impatient with Eleanor's ecstasy, cuts her off. "'Always talking of the other world,' he said. 'Why not this one?'" (*Y*, 367). Eleanor counters: "'But I *meant* this world! I meant, happy in this world—happy with living people.' She waved her hand as if to embrace the miscellaneous company, the young, the old, the dancers, the talkers. . . . 'What I mean is, we've changed in ourselves. We're happier—we're freer'" (*Y*, 368).

II. QUEER FILIATIONS

I daresay I get an infinity of pleasure from the intensity of my own emotions. But I can't write without thinking of Lytton.—Virginia Woolf (*L*, 5:11)

I find I can't write without suddenly thinking, Oh but Lytton wont read this, and it takes all the point out of it. I always put things in my mind to say to Lytton. —Virginia Woolf (*L*, 5:11)

I am aghast at the futility of life—Lytton gone, and nobody minding. —Virginia Woolf (*L*, 5:16)

He was so good to me
Who's going to make me gay, now?—Nina Simone

Woolf traces the origin of her own critical transformation—her achievement of "happiness" and "freedom"[37]—to queer filiation, and especially to her friendship with Lytton Strachey. "Suddenly the door opened," she recalls in her 1921/22 memoir, "Old Bloomsbury," "and the long and sinister figure of Mr Lytton Strachey stood on the threshold."

> He pointed his finger at a stain on [Woolf's sister] Vanessa's white dress.
>
> 'Semen?' he said.
>
> Can one really say it? I thought and we burst out laughing. With that one word all barriers of reticence and reserve went down. A flood of the sacred fluid seemed to overwhelm us. Sex permeated our conversation. The word bugger was never far from our lips. We discussed copulation with the same excitement that we had discussed the nature of good. (*MB*, 200)

"Everything was going to be new," Woolf prophesied as the Bloomsbury group formed through its declared commitment to the practice of freedom; "everything was going to be different. Everything was on trial" (*MB*, 188). Certainly everyone of the group was on trial owing to its queer ethos; "Henry James," for example, "on seeing Lytton . . . at Rye, exclaimed . . . 'Deplorable! Deplorable! How could Vanessa and Virginia have picked up such friends? How could Leslie [Stephen]'s daughters have taken up with young men like *that?*'" (*MB*, 195–96).

"With his idiosyncratic posture and dress," Strachey embodied, as David Eberly notes, "a visibly effeminate man whose mannerisms came to encode homosexual recognition in a hostile society for the next two generations."[38] "The drooping Lytton," Woolf's erstwhile lover Vita Sackville-West complained when describing the Bloomsbury group, "must have done its cause a great deal of harm. I hated him."[39] A contiguous metonymic chain in which "Strachey" stands in for "Bloomsbury," which in turn functions as a code word for a vilified effeminate homosexuality emerges at the outset in personal memoirs about the group (by people outside it) and in public criticism of its works. "Consistently behind—or metaphorized within—the varieties of intellectual charges made against Bloomsbury," Christopher Reed astutely discerns, "is the Group's transgression of patriarchy's ultimate prohibition: the feminized man."[40] If cultural critics, along with Sackville-West, despised Strachey for his queerness, Woolf cherished him; moreover, as the *primum mobile* of *Between the Acts*, this passion vigorously confronts the homophobic impulse of modern British culture to extinguish queer existence.

Although Woolf describes herself in "Old Bloomsbury" as surrounded by, and surrounding herself with, the company of queer men since at least her twenty-eighth year, it was not until the last decade of her life (at the beginning of which, notably, Strachey died) that she self-avowedly sought relationships with "out" gay men.[41] Shortly before Strachey's death she informs Ethel Smyth, "After all, I don't suppose I care for anyone more than for Lytton. . . . He's in all my past—my youth" (L, 4:415). And to Ottoline Morrell she observes, after his death, "*I get a queer feeling I'm hearing him talk in the next room—the talk I always want to go on with. I wonder how many talks I've had with him*—sometimes I think I never talked so much to anyone" (L, 5:129; emphasis added). During the same year (1932), Woolf's queer affect takes the form of inestimable admiration for Strachey's decision to "write violently, proclaiming his sodomy, and cutting adrift from society" (L, 5:46). In the midst of revising *The Years* four years later, Woolf confides to Smyth that she is contemplating a book on him (L, 6:44).

Let us briefly turn to one of the relationships I have described as developing out of Woolf's queer yearning: the Hugh Walpole–Virginia Woolf assemblage. Although her relationship with the popular novelist compares neither in biographical significance nor in affective intensity with the Woolf-Strachey friendship, Walpole's gossip and accounts of gay life worked to seal their bond. Finding him otherwise to be of little appeal,[42] Woolf attributes her cathexis to his fear of "monstrosity," *his* self-avowed monstrosity, which is his "sodomy": "Then he told us the true story of Frank Vosper & Mr Willes—sodomy—a sudden impulse—how his face grew; he was afraid of being a monstrosity. This is what I milk Hugh for" (D, 5:78). At a later date she decides of another visit that "it was a good idea having Hugh alone. He gave me a full account of his sexual life, of which I retain these facts. He only loves men who don't love men. Tried to jump into a river; stuck in mud; seized a carving knife; saw himself in the glass; all became absurd. reconciliation" [sic] (D, 5:211). After recounting Walpole's description of the London baths and the prestigious men who frequent them, Woolf enthusiastically focuses on his "married life with a policeman," and concludes: "All this piles up a rich life of wh[ich] I have no knowledge: & he can't use it in his novels. They are therefore about lives he hasn't lived which explains their badness. Hasn't the courage to write about his real life. Would shock people he likes. Told me how he had a father & son simultaneously. Copulation removes barriers. Class barriers fade" (D, 5:211).

Michèle Barrett glosses this last passage as "extraordinarily unsympathetic," "extremely harsh," and "the response of a securely married woman." Woolf's remarks are misconstrued by Barrett to be symptomatic of her "vexatious attitudes" toward gay men; after all, Barrett advances as evidence, "[homosexual] experiences were at the time deemed criminal, and even in modern times publishers have felt it necessary to omit names from Woolf's account."[43] The reactionary accusation against

Woolf that she makes no "effort to empathize with the experiences of those inhabiting the margins of sexual/social life"[44] owes to Barrett's mistaken identification of the actual object of Woolf's criticism, which is *not* (as Barrett assumes) Walpole's style of life, but his literary aesthetic. Although Woolf's demand for "courage," for a counterdiscursive truthtelling that would confront homophobia and generate queer possibilities, is not satisfied by Walpole's literature,[45] it is accomplished in his talk; *thus* her preference for the latter: "All this is a great deal better than his literary talk," Woolf judges of Walpole's "sodomitic confession[s] of affection," which she later laments as an *"intimacy"* ceaselessly *"interrupted"* (*D*, 5:282), reminding one not only of her longing for Strachey's company and "the talk I always want to go on with," but also of Eleanor's interrupted dialogue with Nicholas, as exemplified in the following scene:

'But how . . . , how can we improve ourselves, live more naturally, better . . . ? How can we? [Eleanor asks.]
They seemed to be talking, privately, together. . . .
'It is only a question,' he said—he stopped.
He drew himself closer to her—'of learning. The soul. . . .' Again he stopped.
'Yes—the soul?' she prompted him.
'The soul—the whole being,' he explained. He hollowed his hands as if to enclose a circle. 'It wishes to expand; to adventure; to form— new combinations?'
'Yes, yes,' she said, as if to assure him that his words were right.
'Whereas now,'—he drew himself together; put his feet together; . . . 'this is how we live, screwed up into one hard little, tight little— knot?'
'Knot, knot—yes, that's right,' she nodded.
'Each is his own little cubicle; each with his own cross or holy book; each with his fire, his wife . . .'
'Darning socks,' Maggie [Renny's wife] interrupted.
Eleanor started. She had seemed to be looking into the future. But they had been overheard. Their privacy was ended. (*Y*, 281–82)

Let us return now to the particular privacy Woolf knew with Strachey or, more accurately, to the reasons she deliberately and "courageously" ended (by publicly enacting) their secrecy. In a retaliative effort to prevent the cultural compulsion she witnessed to erase Strachey's gay imprint (so evidently had he influenced a generation of aspiring artists and intellectuals),[46] Woolf abandoned the privacy that had been consigned to their friendship decades earlier. The public treatment of his queer life as expendable, indeed as the target of a cultural will to amnesia, is referred to by Woolf in what Nigel Nicolson correctly calls "one of her angriest letters,"[47] written to the biographer and bookseller Francis Birrell, a gay friend who was himself, as he read Woolf's words, facing death in a hospital (cf. *L*, 5:278). Significantly, Birrell, a friend to both Strachey and Woolf, was the first of the Bloomsbury group to be slandered by D. H. Lawrence in a series of letters that became part of the subject of John Maynard Keynes's Memoir Club essay, "My Early Beliefs," which the latter read aloud to Bloomsbury in the summer of 1938. Keynes's explication of Lawrence's hostility toward Bloomsbury was clearly unacceptable to Woolf: the manifestation in fictional form of the content of these letters in *Between the Acts* demonstrates that she associated Lawrence's criticism not with mere "intellectual differences," as did Keynes, but with a murderous homophobia of genocidal scope.

Among the relevant letters is a 1915 tirade to Ottoline Morrell, in which Lawrence, referring to Birrell, complains of "men lovers of men [who] give me a sense of corruption, almost of putrescence that I dream of beetles. It is abominable. . . . I like sensual lust—but insectwise, no—it is obscene. I like men to be beasts—but insects—one insect mounted on another—oh God! They are teeming insects. What massive creeping hell is let loose nowadays."[48] To David Garnett, Duncan Grant's former lover, Lawrence prescribes in another of the letters, "Never bring Birrell to see me any more. There is something nasty about him like black beetles. He is horrible and unclean. I feel I should go mad when I think of your [Bloomsbury] set, Duncan Grant and Keynes, Strachey and Birrell. It makes me dream of beetles. . . . [Y]ou must leave these friends, these beetles. Birrell and Duncan Grant are gone forever. . . . It sen[ds] me mad with misery and hostility and rage."[49] In *Between the Acts* Woolf translates Lawrence's depicted rage into Giles Oliver's homophobia (which is directed at the effeminate Dodge), and portrays it thus:

> It was a bit of luck—that [Giles] could despise [Dodge], not himself. (*BA*, 83)

> [Dodge's] expression gave Giles another peg on which to hang his rage as one hangs a coat on a peg, conveniently. A toady; a lick-spittle; not a downright plain man of his senses; but a teaser and a twitcher; a fingerer of sensations; picking and choosing; dillying and dallying; not a man to have straight-forward love for a woman— [Dodge's] head was close to [Giles's wife] Isa's head—but simply a ———— At this word, which he could not speak in public, he pursed his lips; and the signet ring on his little finger looked redder, for the flesh next it whitened as he gripped the arm of his chair. (*BA*, 48)

Lawrence's vituperation ends by claiming of the "Bloomsbuggers" that "[t]hey made me dream in the night of a beetle that bites like a scorpion. But I killed it—a very large beetle. I scotched it and it ran off—but I came upon it again, and I killed it."[50] Woolf has Giles conduct an action as homophobically invested and symbolically suggestive as Lawrence's dream, the latter of which the former is surely a disturbing echo:

> There, couched in the grass, curled in an olive green ring, was a snake. [Woolf's terms of endearment for her beloved 'Strache' were 'the old Serpent,' 'the bearded serpent.'][51] Dead? No, choked with a toad in its mouth. The snake was unable to swallow; the toad was unable to die. A spasm made the ribs contract; blood oozed. It was *birth* the wrong way round—*a monstrous inversion*. So, raising his foot, he stamped on them. The mass crushed and slithered. The white canvas on his tennis shoes was bloodstained and sticky. (*BA*, 75; emphasis added)

That this brutality against the toad-engorged snake operates as a metaphor for the siting of homosexuality in an instant of murderous homophobia is "recognized" by Dodge; in perhaps the most numinous scene of the novel, after all, as he responds to Lucy Swithin's call to follow her into the recesses of a private chamber, where he wishes to kneel before her and offer for witness his history of persecution and shame, Dodge thinks, "I'm a half-man, Mrs Swithin; a flickering, mind-divided little snake in the grass, Mrs Swithin; as Giles saw; but you've healed me" (*BA*, 90). In this never-quite-performed self-outing to Mrs. Swithin (which is nonetheless an outing and opening of another kind by the novel), Dodge's initial recourse is to a logic and rhetoric of among the most authoritative of technologies for self-fashioning and self-knowledge: the psychoanalytic narrative of psychosexual development. "I'm a *half*-man," he wishes to "confess" to her, "*as Giles saw.*" Giles's "seeing" enacts the homophobia that Dodge, as a gay effeminate man figured by the epistemology of the closet in this English militaristic world of 1939, always already has directed against himself. Dodge cites Giles's "seeing," which is itself a sociocultural citation, an iteration that *Between the Acts* writes against in and indeed as *its* recitation.[52] While the Freudian narrative arguably construes homosexuality as a *failure* of teleology,[53] Woolf's novel *raises* this "half-man," this "half-breed," to the noble height of a gaiety that *cuts* (with) teleology and *figures* Dodge the misfit as an emancipatory instance of catachrestical homosexuality.[54]

Against Alex Zwerdling's assertion that "there is no character in [*Between the Acts*] whose vision emerges as authoritative,"[55] then, I wish to cast light on this novel's transvaluation of "failure" and "authoritative vision" by demonstrating its minimal idealization of "misfits," which is to say queer figures. Contrary to Kathy Phillips's assertion that "[w]asting their lives, the characters in *Between the Acts* are indicted as the walking dead,"[56] Dodge, as well as La Trobe (the pageant's writer and director), Mrs. Swithin (Giles's paternal aunt), and to some extent, Isa, are textually invested as vital, active forces in this otherwise moribund, reactive culture. The transvaluation of authoritative vision is by no means obvious; in order for it to appear, a queer reading is required, lessons for which are offered, even rehearsed, in and by the text. La Trobe's pageant dramatically provokes such a reading, and the event as well as consequences of that reading, in turn, are staged as Isa's encounters with Dodge between its acts.

The "initial" narrative line of *Between the Acts* is relatively simple to rehearse. The Olivers, who own the property upon which La Trobe is to present her pageant, are unexpectedly called upon by Mrs. Manresa, whose sexual rapaciousness is to be satiated temporarily by Isa's husband, Giles Oliver. The latter, along with "the Manresa," are portrayed as at once typically British and of the "type" associated by Woolf with fascism.[57] In tow with Mrs. Manresa is Dodge, her rather unwilling companion. The novel, which Woolf was completing in early 1941 (and which reflects the impact of contemporaneous, catastrophic international events), takes place in a village in "the heart of England" on a 1939 June day (*BA*, 14).

La Trobe's pageant and Woolf's novel offer immanent critiques of capitalism, imperialism, misogyny, and homophobia, and it *matters* that in both cases the authors are queer. Sophisticated commentaries on some of these critiques exist,[58] but none addresses the text's queer aesthetic or its handling of homophobia, despite the centrality of these concerns to Woolf's thinking. "I am writing about sodomy at the moment," she announces in a letter from which I have already partially quoted. "[H]ow far can one say openly what is the relation of a woman and a sod? *In French, yes; but in Mr Galsworthy's English, no*" (*L*, 5:273; emphasis added).[59] This allusion to queer relationality in terms of language intimates the inseparability for Woolf of "queer" from literary concern. *Between the Acts* unravels, indeed, as a queer passion for those ever-elusive " 'perverse' " *figures* (within and beyond characterology): the "dillying and dallying" Dodge and the "swarthy, sturdy, and thick set" La Trobe (*BA*, 75, 48, 46).

[S]ometimes the very term that would annihilate us becomes the site of resistance, the possibility of an enabling social and political signification: I think we have seen that quite clearly in the astounding transvaluation undergone by "queer." This is for me the enactment of a prohibition and a degradation against itself, the spawning of a different order of values, of a political affirmation from and through the very term which in a prior usage had as its final aim the eradication of precisely such an affirmation. — Judith Butler[60]

Words . . . ceased to lie flat in the sentence. They rose, became menacing and shook their fists at you. — Virginia Woolf (*BA*, 47)

Inextricable from these queer figures are the bodies that present them. Hands, specifically hands belonging to queer bodies, are (once again) sites of investment in the libidinal economy of *Between the Acts* capable of issuing a time-space given over to the ethical. Since boots also signify in this novel—but as the *antithesis* to queer being; indeed, as its annihilator—Nietzsche's self-observation rises to mind and pleases inasmuch as it strikes one, perversely, as words issued by Woolf: "To me," he reports, "it seems one of the rarest distinctions that a man can accord himself if he takes one of my books into his *hands*—I even suppose that he first takes off his shoes, not to speak of boots."[61] Giles Oliver, the model of masculinist authority in *Between the Acts*, is nothing if he is not his boots.[62] So, "No, I don't admire you," his wife, Isa, decides as she looks not at Giles's face, nor at his hands, but at his feet. "Silly little boy, with blood on his boots" (*BA*, 84).

Without replicating the same trajectory, *Between the Acts* establishes Giles, the white, Christian, straight man of property, as the ethical universal of a history in which all feel imprisoned. *On the one hand*, that figure is shown to be the organizer of meaning—"'Our representative, our spokesman,' [Isa] sneered" (*BA*, 156)—who scripts the plot *against* which Isa and La Trobe ("or" Dodge, "or" the narrator) write: Isa in a hidden book ("the book bound like an account book in case Giles suspected" [*BA*, 16]) and the counterdiscursive positions named Dodge, La Trobe, and/or the narrator, between the acts of *Between the Acts*. Thus, *on the other hand*, a disseminating force of a differing repetition is at work, the writing of which is queer. "'Yes,' Isa answered. 'No,' she added. It was Yes, No. Yes, yes, yes, the tide rushed out embracing. No, no, no, it contracted. The old boot appeared on the shingle" (*BA*, 156). The final chord of negativity occurs simultaneously with the exposure of an otherwise inexplicable boot (by this moment in the text its association with Giles is incontrovertible), which becomes covered with the blood of the snake/Dodge/Strachey assemblage, the "fluid" of the text that is "pre-vent[ed] from overflowing" (*BA*, 132). On the one hand, then, there is repetition that recites the continuum of history; on the other, a repeti-tion that gathers, recuperates, and disseminates difference.

On the former hand is a signet ring, an engraving of straight com-panionate "love": this is Giles's hand, on which "the flesh next [the ring] whitened as he gripped the arm of the chair" in reaction to Dodge's " 'perversion' " (*BA*, 48). Giles may fathom "homosexuality," but it re-mains publicly "private," ostensibly unnamed, just as Dodge's name re-mains "unknown" to most of the novel's characters. The latter hand, the disseminating hand, the hand that effects queer difference (as affirmation and action), is Dodge's. "But what did he do with his hands, the white, the fine, the shapely?" (*BA*, 42), the text poses with suggestive anxiety *and* considerable mirth.

Hands make way for other incorporations. *Between the Acts* stages a history of the present that entails an embodiment of the supplement in the form of history's outsiders. The presence of " 'the idiot' " in La Trobe's pageant vexes Mrs. Parker, one of the audience members, whose husband is equally disturbed by the exclusion of the army from representation. ("Why leave out the British Army? What's history without the army, eh?" [*BA*, 115].) When Dodge contends (speaking *for* and, as it is to turn out, *with* Isa) that difference is always already inscribed *within* tradition, that it has only to be traced, he is rebuked by Giles.

> Mrs Parker was deploring to Isa in a low voice the village idiot.
>
> 'Oh that idiot!' she was saying. But Isa was immobile, watching her husband. She could feel the Manresa in his wake. She could hear in the dusk in their bedroom the usual explanation. It made no dif-ference; his infidelity—but hers did.
>
> 'The idiot?' William [Dodge] answered Mrs Parker for [Isa]. 'He's in the tradition.'
>
> 'But surely,' said Mrs Parker, and told Giles how creepy the idiot— 'We have one in our village'—had made her feel. 'Surely, Mr Oliver, we're more civilized?'
>
> '*We?*' said Giles. '*We?*' He looked, once, at William. He knew not his name; but what his left hand was doing. It was a bit of luck— that he could despise him, not himself. (*BA*, 83)

Giles's despisal of what he will not publicly name—"queer"—is coun-tered by the text that welcomes this very name both for its economy of writing and for the trace by means of which social desolation and indi-vidual alienation are recathected in terms of hope, in terms of the certainty that one's careful interpretations of those traces will ensure repetition of and as difference.

Each character who comes across Dodge attempts either to fix him or to figure him out, in order, respectively, "to know" so as to drive him into oblivion or to encounter him secretly so as to admit ethical singularity. We are presented "first" with the interpretive work of Giles, who sees him as "not a man to have straight-forward love for a woman — [Dodge's] head was close to Isa's head — but simply a ———" (*BA*, 48). Yet another practice of reading gracefully emerges: Mrs. Swithin, for example, "guesse[s] his trouble" (*BA*, 55), and "Isabella opened her mouth, hoping that Dodge would open his, and so enable her to place him" (*BA*, 37). As Isa "guesse[s] the word Giles had not spoken," she wonders, "Well, was it wrong if he were that word? Do we know each other? Not here, not now" (*BA*, 49). (Now Nicholas's voice reaches across to this text. "If we do not know ourselves, how then can we make . . . laws . . . that fit?")

Ultimately, it is impossible to decide who or what Dodge is, since his nature is to be what he is not. As his name insists, Dodge the misfit is an undecidable whose "deviance" discloses itself in terms of the "not itself," in terms of distancing: metaphor. Dodge is felt to be a "thief" of identities who mobilizes *différance* and occupies the text's privileged metaphoricity. Such mimetic disturbance is a writing of illicit borrowings, of illegal masks intimately associated with the so-called sexual deviation of homosexuality itself. To be queer in Woolf's hands is not simply to be an outlaw, a thief of prohibited identities, one who succeeds in saying "no" to the name, but to exist metaphorically. Such a conception of metaphor as a transgressive activity based upon illicit modes of exchange (the taking on of identities that do not "properly" belong) not only confuses but threatens distinctions ostensibly required by the operation of "justice," which Nietzsche diagnoses as man's alibi for the desire to punish, a desire that is written *into* masculinist being. In other words, "in the interest of a survival game, man produces an alibi which is called justice. And in the interest of that alibi, man has to define and articulate, over and over again, the name of 'man.'"[63] Against the writing of *that* name is an *other* writing, an inscription that is knowable, if unrepresentable as such, through and as responsibility to the trace of the other. "There was Dodge, the lip-reader," Isa reflects, "*her* semblable, *her* conspirator, a seeker *like her* after hidden faces" (*BA*, 50; emphasis added).

Between the Acts is written through the kind of proximate distancing enacted around encounters with Dodge: one never seizes his name or identity; one never arrives at it. His name, like Nicholas's in *The Years*, remains ungraspable: first you have it, then you don't. As the beyond of the closure of this text, "queer" is neither to be awaited nor to be refound. It simply "is" there like the shadow of Dodge the text, the third party between the hands holding the book, the deferral within the now of writing, the distance between the book and that other hand. Dodge's shadow casts his figure as dissemination, as a living interruption that, even as the handful of grains is never "actually" scattered, remains as dissemination: "The fish had come to the surface. [Mrs. Swithin] had nothing to give them—not a crumb of bread. 'Wait, my darlings,' she addressed them. She would trot into the house and ask Mrs Sands for a biscuit. Then a shadow fell. How vexatious! Who was it? Dear me, the young man whose name she had forgotten, not Jones; nor Hodge" (BA, 149). Lucy Swithin may temporarily forget Dodge's name, but she is responsible to the trace of the other: "She had leant [Dodge] a hand to help him up a steep place. 'We have other lives, I think, I hope,' she murmured. 'We live in others, Mr . . .'" (BA, 55; emphasis added). Even as she too temporarily "fails" to gather his name, her encounter with Dodge signals the way the trace in the text is the pre-condition of hope, the starting place of hope. It must be, after all, in that undecidable "time"—between the concealment of queerness and its revelation—that the expectation emerges of an encounter with queerness grounded on the experience of being where queerness is not. Hope is dramatized during Dodge's encounter with Mrs. Swithin thus:

> 'I took you,' she apologized, 'away from your friends, William, because I felt wound tight here . . .' She touched her bony forehead upon which a blue vein wriggled like a blue worm. But her eyes were still lambent. He saw her eyes only. And he wished to kneel before her, to kiss her hand, and to say: 'At school they held me under a bucket of water, Mrs Swithin; so I married; but my child's not my child, Mrs Swithin. I'm a half-man, Mrs Swithin; a flickering, mind-divided little snake in the grass, Mrs Swithin; as Giles saw; but you've healed me . . .' So he wished to say; but said nothing. (BA, 57; emphasis added)

Dodge may "say" nothing during his encounter with Mrs. Swithin, but his presence marks everything in this text.

Dodge's description of himself as a "half-man" echoes Giles's condemnation of him as a "half-breed" (BA, 40). As a character in this fictive world, Dodge cannot have known that Giles brutally kills the toad-engorged snake in the grass (BA, 75) with which, by way of abjection, Dodge temporarily identifies. But that identification remains finally unachieved since the text critiques Giles's response to Dodge (the paleonymic "queer") and, indeed, reads as a writing against Giles's interpretation (signaling the emergence of "queer" as catachrestical).[64] This reading/writing practice is thematized as a queer performativity that operates paradoxically as the weaving of *unweaving*; a *text-ing*, in other words, of unweaving.

Mrs. Swithin tells Dodge that she feels "wound tight" (*BA*, 88) — a telling phrase since it is a "knot" that La Trobe's pageant, as well as *Between the Acts* as a whole, *cuts*. In the scene of the secret encounter between Dodge and Mrs. Swithin, Dodge feels "healed," discovering himself in a situation that both allows for his alterity (it is, after all, precisely this that brings the two together) and opens to a witnessing that makes allowable an account of his painful history of abjection and subjectification. The knot that makes Mrs. Swithin "feel wound tight here" and that Isa also discerns in Dodge the moment she guesses his " 'perversion' " — "she had her finger on the knot which had tied itself so tightly, almost to the extent of squinting, certainly of twitching, in his face" (*BA*, 54) — is itself the text against which the counterdiscursive writing positions itself. "Perhaps Miss La Trobe meant that when she cut this knot in the centre?" Isa "or" the narrator ventures (*BA*, 69). This *coupure* is the *POTENCE du texte*, the strategy that ensures the double scene of writing (one hand *and* its other) as well as the affirmative appropriation of what, in *Glas*, Derrida names "more or less a loss."[65] *Between the Acts* rides the margin of the *POTENCE du texte*, that threshold between the presence of queer and its absence, a threshold where the difference between the two is never quite thematically established yet always textually maintained. For the writing of the *coupure* is decisively marked as queer productivity and passion. Mrs. Swithin will approach La Trobe with reverence to thank her for initiating hitherto unknown pleasures, for arousing queer potential, for "stirring my unacted part" (*BA*, 112).

La Trobe's lesbianism, which makes her an outcast in the village, is exactly that which guarantees her productivity and the text's will to power. The narrator portrays her as "always all agog to get things up. But where did she spring from? With that name she wasn't presumably pure English. . . . Outwardly she was swarthy, sturdy, and thick set; she strode about the fields in a smock frock; sometimes with a cigarette in her mouth; often with a whip in her hand; and used rather strong language — perhaps, then, she wasn't altogether a lady? At any rate, she had a passion for getting things up" (*BA*, 46). The text intimates a connection between queer productivity and the fact that La Trobe is not "altogether a lady": "she had a passion for getting things up." This eagerness or passion or impropriety is a property of her difference in relation to law. "She was an outcast," according to the narrator, an outlaw: "Nature had somehow set her apart from her kind. Since the row with the actress who had shared her bed and her purse the need of drink had grown on her. And the horror and the terror of being alone. One of these days she would *break* —

which of the village laws? Sobriety? Chastity? *Or take something that did not properly belong to her?*" (*BA*, 153; emphasis added). The certainty that La Trobe is to break with law is inscribed in her will to power: against all propriety, her text is a counterfactual account in which *queerness* reworks reproduction ("it was birth the wrong way round") as *agent* of production (the pageant), thus enabling a position against the masculinist manipulation of women's agency.[66] Hence what *Between the Acts* suspends is that which La Trobe raises (recall her passion for getting things up): the siting/citing of queer difference as ethical/textual productivity.

Between the Acts is located within this space of the producer's "uncouthness," an uncouthness characterized not only by rudeness (La Trobe's rather strong language—remember, too, that Nicholas is said to be a "bounder" and, like La Trobe, a "foreigner") but also by alienation and estrangement (she is "cut off," "distanced"). That which does not "properly" belong is this uncouth space within which it is guaranteed she will have "broken" with law. She is further distinguished by the narrator from other characters (excluding, notably, Dodge) in terms of portraiture. While histories are given for each of the other "central" characters, La Trobe's biography can only be surmised, "guessed at," just as Dodge's (sexual) identity is conjectured by those around him: "Rumour said that she had kept a tea shop at Winchester; that had failed. She had been an actress; that had failed. She had bought a four-roomed cottage and shared it with an actress. They had quarrelled. Very little was actually known about her" (*BA*, 46). Very little, to be sure; moreover, when comments about La Trobe begin to circulate we are no more "in the know" than before. Or are we? Does not apparent undecidability about La Trobe become legibly queer as we heed the text's affirmative appropriation of social castigation? The earlier question, for example, that "perhaps, then, she wasn't altogether a lady?" includes the possibility that La Trobe incurs not only the villagers' but *also* the narrator's disapproval; the inverted moral schemes of both the novel's and the pageant's satire, however, undermine any inclination to construe the narrator's representation of La Trobe as condemnatory. Descriptions of La Trobe's life as well as the prediction of her future thus leave rumor and castigation behind precisely as the content of conjecture is confirmed and affirmed.

Another and more intriguing possibility of reading offered by the novel allows that the narrator of *Between the Acts* "is" the producer of the pageant; in other words, La Tro(p)e "her" "self." Or is it that La Trobe is somehow the "author" of *Between the Acts*, just as Elvira of *The Pargiters* is, in a sense, the author of Woolf's letter to Manchester University, in which she declines its invitation to make of her a Doctor of Letters? The final words in the novel about La Trobe signify, after all, that she hears the first words of what is to become her subsequent work. That to which she extends her ear "is" *Between the Acts,* for the first words she hears echo those with which Woolf's final novel concludes. These words, "authored" by La Trobe but part of the narrative we take to be Woolf's, correspond to those which comprise the text's conclusion while simultaneously threatening, or promising, its incapacity to end: "'I should group them,' she murmured, 'here.' It would be midnight; there would be *two figures half concealed by a rock. The curtain would rise. What would the first words be?* The words escaped her" (*BA,* 152; emphasis added). But words do come, for a scene gathers in her mind of "high ground at midnight; *there the rock;* and *two scarcely perceptible figures.* Suddenly the tree was pelted with starlings. She set down her glass. She heard the first words" (*BA,* 154; emphasis added). The final words of *Between the Acts* recall—which is to say, figure forth—La Trobe's vision: "It was the night that *dwellers in caves* had watched from some high place among *rocks. Then the curtain rose. They spoke*" (*BA,* 155; emphasis added). The novel *begins,* moreover, on a summer's night with people speaking. The words La Trobe finally hears are those delivered by Isa and Giles as the curtain rises. Those words are what we know to be *Between the Acts.*

To grasp the novel as La Trobe's, or *as* La Trobe, is to reject various interpretive constraints that standardly lead to glossing its conclusion as nothing less—and nothing more—than an affirmation of straight companionate "love." Elizabeth Abel's otherwise dazzling and groundbreaking readings of Woolf with and against both Freud and Klein miss the mark in their dealings with the queer works, finding in *Between the Acts,* for example, not only that "heterosexuality is repeatedly insinuated as our covert truth," but that "Woolf . . . generates a new insistence on female heterosexuality."[67] *Between the Acts* vigilantly prepares against such handlings by training its readers to perceive, map, and counter the homophobic and misogynistic force-fields within and by which characters' souls, their emotions, gestures and postures, are formed. Isa's desolation, for instance, is ascribed to her subject position within a straight regime: she "loathed the domestic, the possessive, the maternal" (*BA,* 18). And when her father-in-law mocks Isa's son for "insufficient" masculinity, she feels "pegged down on a chair arm, like a captive balloon, by a myriad of hair-thin ties into domesticity" (*BA,* 18). We may intially believe, moreover, that it is the narrator who concludes, "'Abortive' was the word that expressed her" (*BA,* 16), but since this word is placed under citation we may infer that Isa is accused of this by other characters (Bart, for one, who suspects and resents her hatred of the domestic [*BA,* 18]).

If the novel's final scene appears to present Isa and Giles as instinctively preparing for sex in response to teleological inevitability, then, readers should keep in mind the text's critique of how such alliances are fabricated and fabulated. We would hear in that case a discordant tone (and, with Zwerdling, the "sinister implications"[68]) emanating from this scene: "Giles crumpled the newspaper and turned out the light. Left alone together for the first time that day, they were silent. Alone, enmity was bared; also love. Before they slept, they must fight; after they had fought, they would embrace. From that embrace another life might be born. But first they must fight, as the dog fox fights the vixen, in the heart of darkness, in the fields of night" (BA, 158). In this passage, which is preceded and followed by, as well as indebted to, the monumentality of history,[69] the newspaper crumpled by Giles should not go unnoticed; rather than casting it aside we might acknowledge its presence as a simultaneous reproduction and interruption of that history. For Woolf, certainly, journalism functions more complexly than commentaries on the novel generally allow. Zwerdling denounces "journalism (and its implied obsession with the present moment) [as] the enemy of cultural continuity,"[70] a position similarly elaborated by Benjamin during Woolf's lifetime. Modern Western culture is, of course, characterized by information isolated from experience, but Woolf's novel manipulates another relation between information, culture, and experience. Like Zwerdling, Benjamin holds that "information does not enter 'tradition,'" but, in one sense at least, "tradition" in Between the Acts perniciously posits as the ethical universal that which the text (attempts to) displace(s) precisely by means of the insertion of journalistic "information." The final passage writes "tradition" in the monumentality of history as Giles lives it (and, to be sure, as it "plays" Giles), but the newspaper he crumples contains another story, an account the content of which vies for representative status—like the idiot about whom Dodge argues is (always already) included in (if occluded by) history and its official representation.

In a manner that resonates with Woolf's treatment of modern experience in Between the Acts, Benjamin maintains that "experience has fallen in value": "And it looks as if it is continuing to fall into bottomlessness. Every glance at a newspaper demonstrates that it has reached a new low, that our picture, not only of the external world but of the moral world as well, overnight has undergone changes which were never thought possible."[71] The atrophy of experience for Isa (she is desperate for "something to happen" [BA, 144]) structures her reality ("O that our human pain could here have ending!" [BA, 131]), which, it is emphasized, represents present-day experience (Isa is "the age of the century—thirty-nine" [BA, 18]). Early in the novel Isa takes up the Times and reads an account of a gang rape that will continue to haunt her even as it functions as a catalyst for discursive change. As she begins, her reading moves from fantasy to romance, but "then, building word upon word" she arrives at a "real" meaning, an apprehension of sense that permits for an intervention in her worlding:

'The troopers told [the girl] the horse had a green tail; but she found it was just an ordinary horse. And they dragged her up to the barrack room where she was thrown upon a bed. Then one of the troopers removed part of her clothing, and she screamed and hit him about the face . . .'

That was real; so real that on the mahogany door panels [Isa] saw the Arch in Whitehall; through the Arch the barrack room; in the barrack room the bed, and on the bed the girl was screaming and hitting him about the face, when the door (for in fact it was a door) opened and in came Mrs Swithin carrying a hammer. (*BA*, 19)

The "real" is worked by Isa's manipulation of this information in such a way as to form her critical awareness. "Tradition" does not help her thus; her poetry is often mired, ventriloquially, in poetic conventions that, Woolf's novel holds, enforce the narrative of romance within and by which Isa as gendered individual is herself written. Of course, the irreducibility of art to ideology means that while *Between the Acts* is itself incorporated into literary tradition, it is able to produce a conscientized position *against* the political regime of bodies that incites, regulates, and dissimulates violence against history's scorned and derided: "foreigners," "perverts," "women," and "idiots."

Isa's struggle against subjective obliteration unfolds as an attempt to reach a non-ventriloquial position. The account of the rape, she fathoms, is an "unheard rhythm" of her own subjectification, as it is, indeed, of the text (*BA*, 51). And just as Isa must build "word upon word" for that story to release its potential for critical interpretation and transformation, so too must readers glean narrative allusions to swallows in order to grasp how they attribute sense to her world. For the swallow and the absent nightingale (*BA*, 7) recall the myth of Procne and Philomela,[72] itself representing an instance of *coupure* since it entails a weaving fabricated by a woman, a victim of rape, whose tongue is *cut out* in order to prevent her from telling the story of that rape. The mythical story enables yet another telling in which *re*-cognition comes into being through another *coupure*, rupture or tearing; for that which breaks the unbearable repetitive strain of what Isa experiences as monumental history ("O that our human pain could here have ending!") is discursive (power/knowledge) change: "The same chime followed the same chime [as it did year after year], *only this year beneath the chime she heard: 'The girl screamed and hit him about the face with a hammer'*" (*BA*, 20; emphasis added). What Isa hears beneath the chime constitutes the text's subtext, but such a distinction cannot obtain here since text and subtext constantly bleed into one another. Isa condenses her vision of Mrs. Swithin carrying a hammer, for example, with the image of the reported rape: "What an angel she was—the old woman!—... to beat up against those immensities and the old man's irreverences her skinny hands, her laughing eyes! How courageous to defy Bart" (*BA*, 21–22).

The story of the rape, then, crucially inaugurates Isa's attempt to establish critical awareness. Slightly before she reads the article, Isa, we are informed, is in need of "relief": "What remedy was there for her age . . . in books?" (*BA*, 18). What remedy, indeed, when books script the family romance within which Isa is held captive or feels confined? Yet the pageant demonstrates that literature can function as both poison and remedy. "The play keeps running in my head," she complains, significantly, to Dodge (*BA*, 79). "'I wish the play didn't run in my head,' she said" (*BA*, 85). Dodge, in turn, notes that Isa's relation to Giles is "as people say in novels 'strained'" (*BA*, 80). Isa's resigned despair (*BA*, 131) weaves the very continuum of history, which in turn so bitterly and desolately figures or knots her: "'In love,' was in her eyes. But outside, on the washstand, on the dressing table, among silver boxes and toothpaste, was the other love; love for her husband, the stock-broker—'The father of my children,' she added, slipping into the cliché conveniently provided by fiction" (*BA*, 14). Having fallen into longing for dissolution ("'Dispersed are we,' she murmured. . . . 'That the waters should cover me,' she added, 'of the wishing well'" [*BA*, 78]), Isa nonetheless manages to make use of the story of the rape in order to rouse herself into critical "knowing" during the interval (the break: between the acts) of La Trobe's pageant: "She roused herself. She encouraged herself. 'On little donkey, patiently stumble. *Hear not* the frantic cries of the leaders who in that they seek to lead desert us. Nor the chatter of china faces glazed and hard. *Hear rather* . . . the brawl in the barrack room when they stripped her naked'" (*BA*, 114–15; emphasis added). Isa attributes her alienation and atrophy of experience to her inability to activate critical thought; so, closing her ears to "the frantic cries of the leaders," she "held her cup out to be filled. She took it. 'Let me turn away,' she murmured, turning, 'from the array'—she looked desolately round her—'of china faces, glazed and hard . . .'" (*BA*, 78). Three times her turning away signals a decision made: "'No,' said Isa, as plainly as words could say it. 'I don't admire you,' and looked, not at [Giles's face], but at his feet. 'Silly little boy, with blood on his boots'" (*BA*, 84). Isa's criticism of Giles is directed at his murderous aggression, which she temporarily allows makes for the historical continuum whose coercive recitation she is. Giles's intolerance of queer difference as evinced in the slaughter of the snake and toad (*BA*, 75)—that figure for Dodge and La Trobe ("'a monstrous inversion'";

"birth the wrong way round": queer production)—is held in scorn by his wife, who later refuses his emblematically proffered sexuality: "Here . . . exposing a white cone, Giles offered his wife a banana. She refused it. He stubbed his match on the plate. Out it went with a little fizz" (BA, 155).

The novel reads Isa's rejections as merely reactionary since such differences ultimately appear ineffective as they are reabsorbed into a dominant worlding sequence. After all, although Isa will once again sneer, "Our representative, our spokesman" (BA, 156) as she stares with disdain at Giles's feet, she finds herself—immediately following this denunciation—finally reproducing the very conditions that necessitate such an utterance: this, of course, is the conclusion of the novel cited above. The temporary accomplishment of this critical position does nevertheless prevent the *text* from finally falling into those convenient clichés that promote, script, and (attempt to) sustain the illusion of a heterosexual *telos*. Moreover, La Trobe's pageant makes possible not only an erotics for Lucy Swithin ("You've stirred in me my unacted part"), it also *produces* the counterpositions Isa and Dodge come to occupy as they take up the pageant's parody of Elizabethan drama. This act spawns in Isa a critical recognition of ventriloquism and overturns, if only momentarily, her initial aversion to the play (cf. BA, 79):

'Look where she comes!' [the young Prince] cried. . . . Who came? Isa looked. The nightingale's song? Love embodied.

All arms were raised; all faces stared. 'Hail, sweet Carintha!' said the Prince, sweeping his hat off. And she to him, raising her eyes: 'My love! My lord!'

It was enough. Enough. Enough, Isa repeated.

All else was verbiage, repetition. (BA, 70)

. . . she started. William Dodge was by her side.

He smiled. She smiled. They were conspirators; each murmuring some song my uncle taught me.

'It's the play," she said. 'The play keeps running in my head."

'Hail, sweet Carintha. My love. My life,' he quoted.

My lord, my liege," she bowed, ironically. (BA, 79)

No longer is that verbiage (the repetition associated with straight companionate "love": "love embodied") accepted uncritically by Isa. "The father of my children," she repeats to herself earlier in the novel. "It worked, that old cliché; she felt pride; and affection; then pride in herself, whom he had chosen" (BA, 39). Such unions are now linked by her with the myth of Procne and Philomela ("Who came? Isa looked. The nightingale's song? . . . Love embodied"). This "knowing" interrupts her capacity simply to watch or attend passively, for "It was enough" signifies not satisfaction but the critical position against which "[a]ll else was verbiage, repetition."

Mrs. Manresa impels and embodies the verbiage briefly condemned by Isa. "Mrs Manresa applauded loudly. Somehow she was the Queen; and he (Giles) was the surely hero" (BA, 71). "I am the Queen, he my hero, my sulky hero," she reiterates shortly afterward (BA, 81). Giles "was the very type that Mrs Manresa adored"; "[t]here was something fierce [after all], untamed, in the expression which incited her, even at forty-five, to furbish up her ancient batteries" (BA, 38–39). In the world of the novel, Mrs. Manresa stands in for the very characters of the pageant parodied by Isa, Dodge, and, of course, La Trobe, who mobilizes as her pageant's critical force what Benjamin describes as allegory's destructive impulse with regard to such apparently immutable appearances and their social order.[73] La Trobe accomplishes this by means of her genealogical enactment of a history in which the alienation and atrophy of experience characteristic of this summer day unfold.

The variety of intense engagements with and violent reactions to the pageant betray the extent to which Between the Acts perceives and represents responses as investments. Some characters find to their horror that "the words rose and pointed a finger"; others will wonder, "Well, was it wrong if [Dodge] were that word?" ("What else is love?"); still others will experience subjective, even erotic, change: "You've stirred in me my unacted part." Giles at least derives no pleasure from La Trobe's text if only because he suspects a "lesson" therein: "A moral. What? Giles supposed it was: where there's a Will there's a Way. The words rose and pointed a finger of scorn at him" (BA, 109). The exegetical force of La Trobe's pageant is suspected by Giles to be its queer aesthetic: where there's a Will(iam) there's a way.

Woolf's text thus inscribes its ethic—a way there is if Will there be —through the presence of queer misfits, which subverts logocentrism at times by a peculiarly wrenched subordination. William Dodge's encounter with Lucy Swithin, for example, is framed by mirror-image sentences that are modified by framing participial phrases. The proper subject of the first sentence ("Sitting on the bed . . ."), however, is modified by the participial phrases of the second. The subject of the first is Lucy Swithin. Her guest, William, is the subject of the other. The occasion of double vision is a visit to Mrs. Swithin's childhood bedchamber, where she perches on the bed (dangling her feet) and where the dangling participles deposit Dodge in her lap. Actually he is standing so that their eyes meet in a mirror opposite the bed. This is a seesaw of vision, a layering of the mind's objects and the narrative's objects in a band of illusion, until all the story is told, even and especially the "unacted parts":

'Here,' she said, 'yes, here,' she tapped the counter-pane, 'I was born. In this bed.'

Her voice died away. She sank down on the edge of the bed. She was tired, no doubt, by the stairs, by heat.

'But we have other lives, I think, I hope,' she murmured. 'We live in others, Mr . . . We live in things.'

She spoke simply. She spoke with an effort. She spoke as if she must overcome tiredness out of charity towards a stranger, a guest. She has forgotten his name. Twice she had said 'Mr' and stopped.

The furniture was mid-Victorian, bought at Maples, perhaps, in the forties. The carpet was covered with small purple dots. And a white circle marked the place where the slop pail had stood by the washstand.

Could he say 'I'm William'? He wished to. Old and frail she had climbed the stairs. She had spoken her thoughts. . . . She had lent him a hand to help him up a steep place. She had guessed his trouble. [And then the relevant two sentences:] Sitting on the bed he heard her sing, swinging her little legs, 'Come and see my sea weeds, come and see my sea shells, come and see my dicky bird hop upon its perch'—an old child's nursery rhyme to help a child. Standing by the cupboard in the corner he saw her reflected in the glass. Cut off from their bodies, their eyes smiled, their bodiless eyes, at their eyes in the glass.

Then she slipped off the bed. (*BA*, 55–56)

The way the narrator slips into the other dramatizes an ethically motivated distancing instantly recuperated into closeness. Suspended from time to time, the narrator is the "I" who leads ("leads" not in the sense of "the leaders who in that they seek to lead desert us" [*BA*, 114]), the "I" who receives the impulse to write from the other and who receives the other in the text itself. One character in particular recognizes this giving-face to unacted parts and active traces; enough, indeed, to approach La Trobe so as to acknowledge that which her pageant miraculously figures forth. When Mrs. Swithin attempts to express gratitude for the gift of La Trobe's production ("*with a little wave of her hand*, as if asking Miss La Trobe to help her" [*BA*, 122; emphasis added]), "[t]heir eyes met in a common effort to bring a common meaning *to birth*" (*BA*, 122; emphasis added). Just as Mrs. Swithin's eyes have met with Dodge's, so too are they to meet La Trobe's, and to a similar end. "You've stirred in me my unacted part" is one articulation of that meaning. At least this is the sense La Trobe wrests from Lucy's declaration of "What a small part I've played! But you've made me feel I could have played . . . Cleopatra!" (*BA*, 112).

The lesson that Giles construes as condemnatory is welcomed by Isa as much as by Mrs. Swithin. For Isa that lesson is acted out in and by means of her encounters with Dodge. "There was Dodge, the lip reader, her semblable, her conspirator, a seeker like her after hidden faces" (*BA*, 150). The hidden face, the trace of the other, begins to manifest as queer force fissures the text. "The tune began; the first note meant a second; the second a third. Then down beneath a force was born in opposition; then another. On different levels they diverged" (*BA*, 137). "Now Miss La Trobe stepped from her hiding" to present herself as a producer of queer presence, performativity, and temporality (*BA*, 74). "She wanted to expose them, as it were, to douche them, with present-time reality" (*BA*, 130). This revelation, a gift, offers the lesson of displaced being, of being displaced, where difference is identical ("her semblable, her conspirator") and the identical is precious. Unrestrained dialogue, self-elaboration, and disclosure become possible in this book only for "seekers after hidden faces": "[Dodge and Isa] talked as if they had known each other all their lives" (*BA*, 85). Isa "could say—as she did—whatever came into her head. And *hand* him, as she *handed* him, a flower" (*BA*, 85; emphasis added). Before taking leave of the village, Dodge searches for Mrs. Swithin, whom he reveres, in order to fare her well. *They take hold of one another's hands:* "'I thank you,' he said. He took her hand and pressed it. Putting one thing with another, it was unlikely they would ever meet again" (*BA*, 150). So the wait begins, again.

IV. WE'RE HERE, WE'RE QUEER . . . SAME AS ALWAYS

[T]hey talked as if they had know each other all their lives; which was odd, [Isa] said, as [women] always did, considering she'd known [Dodge] perhaps one hour. Weren't they, though, conspirators, seekers after hidden faces? That confessed, she paused and wondered, as they always did, why they could speak so plainly to each other. And added: 'Perhaps because we've never met before, and never shall again.'—Virginia Woolf (*BA*, 85–86)

> The wait's begun again,
> The long wait for the angel,
> For that rare, random descent.[74]
> —Sylvia Plath

> We were never being boring,
> We had too much time to find for ourselves,
> We were never looking back, thinking that
> Time would come to an end. . . .
> —Pet Shop Boys, "Being Boring"

If, as is often claimed, *The Years* and *Between the Acts* generally engender a sense of claustrophobia, perhaps this is because they are written from within, but queerly beyond, too, a form of prison. Certainly, "Isabella felt prisoned. Through the bars of the prison, through the sleep haze that deflected them, blunt arrows bruised her; of love, then of hate" (*BA*, 52). Bodies, emotions, and patterns of thought in these works are realities constantly produced, effects of techniques promoting and criticizing specific gestures and postures, sensations and feelings. "Love and hate—how they tore [Isa] asunder! Surely it was time someone invented a new plot, or that the author came out from the bushes" (*BA*, 156). Between the Acts hands over to consideration this question: "Did the plot matter?" (*BA*, 69). And it answers in its unfolding: If one wishes to *live* in these works, abilities to queer are crucial. For the plot *matters* in that it *works*, and "[t]he plot was only there to beget emotion. There were only two emotions: love; and hate. Perhaps Miss La Trobe meant that when she *cut* this knot in the centre?" (*BA* 69). As evinced in the novel subject-positions and assemblages generated by and producing Woolf's textual practice of *coupure*, queer combinations radically disturb enframing and unfolding, and fissure the plot to provide vital lines of flight.

"'What's this knot in the middle of my forehead,'" North frantically demands in *The Years*. "'Untie it.' For he had enough of thinking alone. Thinking alone tied knots in the middle of the forehead" (*Y*, 394). Eleanor and Nicholas, tired as well of living like "cripples in a cave," wish "to expand; to adventure; to form—new combinations." For, as Nicholas indicates,

'. . . this is how we live, screwed up into one hard little, tight little—knot?'
'Knot, knot—yes, that's right,' she nodded.
'Each is his own little cubicle; each with his own cross or holy book; each with his fire, his wife . . .' (*Y*, 281–82)

So bound are the effects of individualization and normalization to procedures of sexual identification that *Between the Acts* posits Giles's homophobia as complicit with and integral to his war-bound society's version of "civilization." Yet another version of civilization is held by both works (if only as a portent): this is what drives North's ultimate criticism of the possessiveness and murderous appropriation that underpin conformist intra- as well as intersubjective relations. "This is the conspiracy," he comes to think: "[T]his is the steam-roller that smooths, obliterates; rounds into identity; rolls into balls. . . . *My* boy—*my* girl . . . they were saying. But they're not interested in other people's children, he observed. Only in their own; their own property; their own flesh and blood, which they would protect with the unsheathed claws of the primeval swamp, he thought. . . . How then *can* we be civilized?" (*Y*, 359). To ask *that* question, Woolf's novel offers, is to broach its answer.

Life in *Between the Acts* feels "maddening" to all "caught and caged; prisoners; watching a spectacle. Nothing happened" (*BA*, 128), but *we* have only to trace events unraveling between and in its acts to disinter and discern, in fact, *everything* happening: *life opening out*. Dodge may indeed "say" nothing about himself, for instance, but his queer presence touches upon everything in the text. And if La Trobe's production, as well as events between its acts, interrupt a continuum only to find these discontinuities returned to, for, and as history's recitation, a stutter, we remark, nevertheless remains. A tear in the fabric appears; an interval opens. "They were suspended, without being, in limbo. Tick, tick, tick went the machine." "The cheap clock ticked." "The second hand jerked on." "The clock ticked." " 'This year, last year, next year, never . . .' Isa murmured." Then: "*There was an interval*" (*BA*, 129, 153, 156, 157, 155, 126; emphasis added). Radical discontinuity cannot appear as such, but inasmuch as it remains, it discloses a temporality born of an effortfulness that makes the peculiar present-tense that occupies and performs Nicholas, La Trobe, as well as Eleanor. "We shall be free. . . . We shall be free," Eleanor rehearses, and so saying, "*is*" freed from her "knottedness."

Nicholas's speech may be ever-interrupted or forever-deferred but, as a discontinuity, a *coupure*, it does remain the text's privileged discourse. " 'To the New World!' they cried and drank," we read after Eleanor's first meeting with Nicholas.

> The yellow liquid swayed up and down in their glasses.
> 'Now, Nicholas,' said Sara, setting her glass down with a tap on the box, 'a speech! A speech!'
> 'We don't want any speeches,' Renny interrupted him. (*Y*, 278–79)

Renny's "we" does not participate in the formation of other subjective possibilities (such as those *present*-ed by Nicholas and Eleanor). Are *we* not finally left wondering, though, we of that present, the recipients of this gift, we who gratefully pursue and trace the specters of Nicholas's speech, of Dodge's textual presence, and of La Trobe's pageant, as to whether these *are* enough to ensure the persistence of queer in so homophobically inscribed a socius? We are not alone in advancing the question, for William too wonders, " 'Isn't that enough?' . . . Beauty—isn't that enough?' But here Isa fidgetted. Her bare brown arms went nervously to her head. She half-turned in her seat. 'No, not for us, who've the future,' she seemed to say. The future disturbing our present" (*BA*, 62).

"We have no future," Woolf thought in the early months of 1941. "I'm fished out of my element and lie gasping on the ground" (L, 6:321). "As for us," T. S. Eliot mournfully recorded two months after Woolf's death by drowning in March of that year, "l'on sait ce que l'on perd. On ne sait jamais ce que l'on rattrapera."[75] Speaking for the literary and cultural elite as he penned these words, Eliot most certainly was not speaking to real or imagined queers, even as, for many of us, his remarks seem to belong to that uncanny realm of words in which we feel, perhaps, they should have been spoken by us if their subject, Woolf, is to be responsibly— which is not to say properly—rememorated.[76] We may content ourselves, however, with lip-reading those words. Despite her conviction in 1937 that her "little reputation lies like an old cigarette end" (D, 5:68), Woolf remains alive in rememoration since her writing is not content to offer by means of the ennobling of art a mere alternative to history and its discontents; its production of queer life, that is to say, its queer presentation, disseminates a readership ("Dispersed are we" [BA, 144]) that in turn presents other ethical histories and futures. In The Years and Between the Acts, communion and communication may finally fail to transpire between subjects generally ("We cannot help each other," North concludes in The Years, "we are all deformed" [Y, 361]), but "during" the secret encounters of those figures handled between these pages, to "whom" we have turned an ear, a numinous intra- and intersubjective responsiveness transpires and remains as the diacritical mark of Woolf's queer work. This handling, that turning, is preceded by a call, which has only to be heard, and whose time is now, and queer.

NOTES

I am especially grateful to Adriana Benzaquèn and David Clark for their encouragement of and vigorous responses to the various incarnations of this essay. Their interest, engagement, and intelligent criticisms provided the qualities of encounters with the kinds of readers I most wanted to reach. I wish also to extend warm thanks to Ian Balfour, Lesley Higgins, Marie-Christine Leps, and Karin de Weille for more local, but equally insightful, comments. This article was prepared under a fellowship from the Social Sciences and Humanities Research Council of Canada. It is dedicated to Matias Milet, and to the memory of Christel Barber and Alice Titta.

1   Virginia Woolf, The Diary of Virginia Woolf, ed. Anne Olivier Bell and Andrew McNeillie, 5 vols. (London: Hogarth Press, 1977–84), 5:307. Further quotations from this work will be abbreviated in the text as D, followed by volume and page number.
2   Virginia Woolf, Between the Acts (1941; London: Grafton, 1978), p. 150. Further cited in the text as BA.
3   Gilles Deleuze, The Deleuze Reader, ed. Constantin V. Boundas (New York: Columbia University Press, 1993), p. 126.
4   For examples that fit the first clause—that is, commentaries that find in Woolf various textual strategies of lesbian disclosure—see Blanche Wiesen Cook, "Women Alone

Stir My Imagination: Lesbianism and the Cultural Tradition," *Signs* 4, no. 4 (summer 1979): 718–39, and Sherron E. Knopp, "'If I Saw You Would You Kiss Me?' Sapphism and the Subversiveness of Virginia Woolf's *Orlando*," *PMLA* 103, no. 1 (January 1988): 24–34. Examples of the second clause, which tend to conceive sexuality as seamless, monolithic, and unfractured, manifest in Madeline Moore (for whom Woolf is a "closet lesbian who hid her lesbianism in marriage" [p. 25]), *The Short Season Between Two Silences: The Mystical and the Political in the Novels of Virginia Woolf* (Boston: Allen and Unwin, 1984), and in Catharine Stimpson, "Woolf's Room, Our Project: The Building of Feminist Criticism," in *The Future of Literary Theory*, ed. Ralph Cohen (New York: Routledge, 1989), pp. 129–43.

5 Woolfian counterdiscursive truth signifies neither as scientific certainty nor as metaphysical correspondence between concept and object; it is, rather, a coterminous aesthetic practice *and* technology of self (engendering new affective and epistemological possibilities) that link belief and risk.

6 "Queer" is doing duty here for a temporal dimension emerging in Woolf's effortful responsibility and accountability: it is a "nondimensional verbal mode—not a future present but a persistent effortfulness that makes a 'present'" (Gayatri Chakravorty Spivak, *Outside in the Teaching Machine* [New York: Routledge, 1993], p. 156).

7 Virginia Woolf, "Appendix C: Virginia Woolf and Julian Bell," p. 255, in Quentin Bell, *Virginia Woolf: A Biography*. Vol. 2 (London: Triad/Paladin, 1987), pp. 255–59.

8 Eve Kosofsky Sedgwick, *Tendencies* (Durham: Duke University Press, 1993), pp. 9, 79.

9 Michel Foucault, "Afterword: The Subject and Power," in *Michel Foucault: Beyond Structuralism and Hermeneutics*, ed. H. L. Dreyfus and P. Rabinow, 2d ed. (Chicago: University of Chicago Press, 1983), p. 210.

10 Sedgwick, *Tendencies*, p. 9.

11 Ibid.

12 Woolf's care for self as a deliberate practice of freedom is ethical in itself but, as Foucault rightly points out, such an ethic "implies complex relations with others, in the measure where this *ethos* of freedom is also a way of caring for others" ("The Ethic of Care for the Self as a Practice of Freedom: An Interview with Michel Foucault," in *The Final Foucault*, ed. James Bernauer and D. Rasmussen [Cambridge, Mass.: MIT Press, 1988], p. 7).

13 Virginia Woolf, *The Letters of Virginia Woolf*, ed. Nigel Nicholson and Joanne Trautmann, 6 vols. (London: Hogarth Press, 1975–84), 5:10. Further quotations from this work will be abbreviated in the text as *L*, followed by volume and page number.

14 Sedgwick, *Tendencies*, p. xii.

15 Virginia Woolf, *The Years* (1937; London: Oxford University Press, 1992), p. 353. Further cited in the text as *Y*.

16 To my knowledge, Christopher Reed's essay ("Bloomsbury Bashing: Homophobia and the Politics of Criticism in the Eighties," *Genders* [fall 1991]: 58–80) is unique in its concern with homophobic biographical accounts of Woolf's relationships with gay men. David Eberly ("Taking It All Out: Homosexual Disclosure in Woolf," in *Virginia Woolf: Themes and Variations. Selected Papers from the Second Annual Conference on Virginia Woolf*, ed. Vara Neverow-Turk and Mark Hussey [New York: Pace University Press, 1993], pp. 128–34) provides among the first of distinctly queer readings of Woolf, and Barbara Fassler's history of Bloomsbury's responses to and representations of "available homosexual positions" remains indispensable ("Theories of Homosexuality as Sources of Bloomsbury's Androgyny," *Signs*, 5, no. 2 [winter 1979]: 237–51).

One significant tradition of Woolf scholarship and criticism has consigned Woolf to an orbit that unwittingly associates her with gays in a dominant cultural logic that construes as death-wish both gay sexual pleasure and Woolf's narrative drive. (The association of Woolf with a desire for death is pervasive; see for example Hélène Cixous, "Rethinking Differences: An Interview," in *Homosexualities and French Literature: Cultural Contexts/Critical Texts*, ed. George Stambolian and Elaine Marks [Ithaca: Cornell University Press, 1979], p. 83.) Another influential critical tradition (inasmuch as Woolf functions as exemplary figure in Anglo-American feminisms [cf. Rachel Bowlby, "Who's Framing Virginia Woolf?" *diacritics* (summer–fall 1991): 3–10, and Catharine Stimpson, "Woolf's Room, Our Project: The Building of Feminist Criticism"]) almost unanimously represents Woolf and gay men as necessary antagonists. For a vivid example see Jane Marcus, *Virginia Woolf and the Languages of Patriarchy* (Bloomington: Indiana University Press, 1987), esp. pp. 79–80, 137, 159, 165. Marcus construes Woolf's position on gay men as logically hostile (given opposing interests) and "understandably" antagonistic, thus providing in her commentaries an especially powerful and pernicious instance of homophobic feminism, disavowals notwithstanding (p. 76).

17 In *Three Guineas* Woolf, refusing what "is," transmits a series of duties and conditions for women entering the public sphere. If taken up, she claims, this ethic would allow daughters of educated men to accede to a "true life" that would not fall prey to masculinist, liberalist individualism. These duties include poverty, chastity, derision, and freedom from unreal loyalties, all of which Woolf redefines (*Three Guineas* [1938; New York: Harcourt Brace Jovanovich, 1966], pp. 92–93. Further cited in the text as *TG*). The similarity of that list with a statement by Nicholas (addressed to and about Eleanor) in *The Pargiters* is noteworthy and only one example: "Not to earn money; not to have power, not to be famous—obscurity, inferiority, to be despised—not to possess; that's the finest education in the world" (qtd. in Grace Radin, *Virginia Woolf's The Years: The Evolution of a Novel* [Knoxville: University of Tennessee Press, 1981], p. 73).

18 Gayatri Chakravorty Spivak, *The Spivak Reader*, ed. Donna Landry and Gerald MacClean (New York: Routledge, 1996), p. 270. Spivak's exquisite description of ethical singularity (pp. 269–70) characteristically and movingly does what it says.

19 Brenda Silver documents how, in the 1930s, Woolf became "a systemic reader of her culture" ("Introduction," in *Virginia Woolf's Reading Notebooks*, ed. Brenda Silver [Princeton, N.J.: Princeton University Press, 1983], p. 22).

20 James King concedes this point in his critical biography of Woolf (*Virginia Woolf* [London: Hamish Hamilton, 1994]). "In *The Pargiters*," he remarks, "much attention is devoted to Nicholas's criticisms of the social order; his remarks on such subjects are sketchily hinted at in *The Years* (this material was now being diverted to 'On Being Despised'" [p. 535]). Immediately following this, however, King minimizes the importance of Nicholas's homosexuality to the novel: "Although Nicholas's homosexuality is still *mentioned* . . ." (p. 535; emphasis added).

21 See Woolf, *D*, 4:6.

22 Deleuze, *The Deleuze Reader*, p. 208.

23 Spivak, *The Spivak Reader*, p. 270.

24 Spivak, *Outside in the Teaching Machine*, p. 34.

25 Ibid., p. 38.

26 Walter Benjamin, *Illuminations*, ed. Hannah Arendt, trans. Harry Zohn (New York: Schocken, 1969), p. 254.

27 Michel Foucault, *The Use of Pleasure*. Vol.2 of *The History of Sexuality*, trans. Robert Hurley (New York: Vintage Books, 1990), p. 29.

28 Michel Foucault, "Preface," *Anti-Oedipus: Capitalism and Schizophrenia*, by Gilles De-

leuze and Félix Guattari, trans. Robert Hurley et al. (Minneapolis: University of Minnesota Press, 1983), p. xii.

29 Gilles Deleuze, *Negotiations: 1972–1990*, trans. Martin Joughin (New York: Columbia University Press, 1995).

30 Woolf frequently describes *Three Guineas* as a conduct book; in June 1937, for example, she tells her diary, "No I will [no longer] write for the larger paying magazines: in fact, couldn't. In this way I put 3 Guineas daily into practice" (*D*, 5:96).

31 Eve Kosofsky Sedgwick, *Between Men: English Literature and Male Homosocial Desire* (New York: Columbia University Press, 1985), p. 11.

32 Jacques Derrida, "Letter to Jean Genet" (unpublished, 1971), p. 5. Ian Balfour kindly showed me this letter.

33 See, for examples, pp. 293, 296, 299, 373.

34 Eleanor's niece, Peggy, finds such positions not unimaginable but deplorable. She wonders if she dislikes Sara because of "the croak of some ancestral prudery—did she disapprove of these friendships with men who did not love women?" (*Y*, p. 310). The irony, of course, is that in *The Years* "men who [do] not love women"—that is, gay men—are precisely those who *do* love women.

35 Woolf famously advances this thesis in both *A Room of One's Own* (1929; London: Grafton, 1977) and *Three Guineas*.

36 For Foucault, the catachrestical figure of "mature adulthood," perhaps never to be arrived at and therefore structurally ethical as a pursuit, relates radically to Kant's project of Enlightenment. A most Nicholas-like explication of enlightenment as a "critical ontology of ourselves . . . a philosophical life in which the critique of what we are is at one and the same time the historical analysis of the limits that are imposed on us and an experiment with the possibility of going beyond them," is to be found in Foucault's well-known essay on Kant's article, "What is Enlightenment?" (in *The Foucault Reader*, ed. Paul Rabinow [New York: Pantheon Books, 1984], pp. 32–50, esp. pp. 49–50).

37 Just as Eleanor's talk with Nicholas is to be interrupted (more than once) by the subject (in two senses) of marriage, so too Woolf's exhilaration about *her* newfound freedom comes to be threatened. " 'Of course, I can see that we shall all marry. It's bound to happen'—and as [Woolf's sister, Vanessa] said it I could feel a horrible necessity impending over us; a fate would descend and snatch us apart just as we had achieved freedom and happiness" (Virginia Woolf, *Moments of Being: Unpublished Autobiographical Writings*, ed. Jeanne Schulkind [London: Triad Grafton, 1978], p. 196. Further cited in the text as *MB*. For her account of the supersession of straight "love" by queer possibilities, see Woolf, *MB*, pp. 195–96).

38 Eberly, "Taking It All Out," p. 129.

39 Vita Sackville-West, "The Vitality of Bloomsbury," in *The Bloomsbury Group: A Collection of Memoirs, Commentary, and Criticism*, ed. S. P. Rosenbaum (Toronto: University of Toronto Press, 1975), p. 249.

40 Reed, "Bloomsbury Bashing," p. 59.

41 More often than not, Woolf's "search" appears strikingly as its opposite: a magnetic force propelling gay men to seek her out. Consider, for example, Stephen Tennant's remark upon encountering her: "Stephen later recalled how much he enjoyed arriving at Kiln Cottage in Piddinghoe. Virginia turned to Leonard and said, 'What can they think, when this bird-of-paradise arrives?' Stephen was very pleased: 'After that, I decided I must cultivate her acquaintance!' " (Philip Hoare, *Serious Pleasures: The Life of Stephen Tennant* [New York: Penguin Books, 1990], p. 198).

42 "Not much real interest in human nature in Hugh" is just one of her condemnations (*D*, 5:78).

43 Michèle Barrett, "*A Room of One's Own* and *Three Guineas*," in *Virginia Woolf: Introductions to the Major Works*, ed. Julia Briggs (London: Virago Press, 1994), p. 214.

44 Ibid.

45 "Isn't the great artist," Woolf queries while composing *The Pargiters*, "the only person to tell the truth?" (*L*, 6:453). "I prefer," she avows in that text, "where truth is important, to write fiction" (Woolf, *The Pargiters: The Novel-Essay Portion of* The Years, ed. Mitchell A. Leaska [New York: The New York Public Library and Readex Books, 1977], p. 9). Woolf considers "the novel" to be "truly" itself only as it counters established and conformist power-knowledge-subjectivity relations, a task she sees as especially well-suited to art. "The form of the novel, so rich, elastic, and alive," she contends, has been evolved "not to preach doctrines . . . or celebrate the glories of the British Empire" (*Collected Essays*, ed. Leonard Woolf, 4 vols. [New York: Harcourt, Brace & World, 1953], 1:324), but to "tell the truth" (*L*, 6:453).

46 For accounts of Strachey's queer self-stylization and its effect on succeeding generations of the cultural elite, see Michael Holroyd, "Lytton Strachey," in *The Bloomsbury Group*, ed. S. P. Rosenbaum, pp. 184–86; Osbert Sitwell, "Armistice in Bloomsbury," in *The Bloomsbury Group*, ed. S. P. Rosenbaum, pp. 250, 254; and Leonard Woolf, "Lytton Strachey," in *The Bloomsbury Group*, ed. S. P. Rosenbaum, pp. 178–79.

47 Nigel Nicolson, "Introduction" to *The Sickleside of the Moon. The Letters of Virginia Woolf* ed. Nigel Nicolson and Joanne Trautmann (London: Hogarth Press, 1979), 5:xi.

48 Quoted in Quentin Bell, *Bloomsbury*, new ed. (London: Weidenfeld & Nicolson, 1986), p. 76.

49 Quoted in Bell, *Bloomsbury*, p. 78.

50 Quoted in Bell, *Bloomsbury*, p. 72.

51 See Virginia Woolf and Lytton Strachey, *Virginia Woolf and Lytton Strachey: Letters*, ed. Leonard Woolf and James Strachey (London: Hogarth Press, 1956), pp. 115, 128.

52 Judith Butler's formulation of this operation of power is helpful: "[T]here is no power, construed as a subject, that acts, but only a reiterated acting that *is* power in its persistence and instability. This is less an 'act,' singular and deliberate, than a nexus of power and discourse that repeats or mimes the discursive gestures of power" ("Critically Queer," *GLQ: A Journal of Lesbian and Gay Studies* 1 [1993/4]: 17). Woolf rehearses this understanding in her dramatization of Giles's slaughter of the toad-engorged snake and Dodge's identification with it.

53 Homosexuality, which various psychoanalysts have promised to convert into heterosexuality, is often construed as sexual impulses that have yet to find resolution and stabilization in "proper" object-choices. (There is a whole critical literature on this topic. A particularly interesting example is Paul Morrison, "End Pleasure," *GLQ* 1, no. 1 [1993]: 53–78.) In her book *Virginia Woolf and the "Lust of Creation": A Psychoanalytic Exploration* (Albany: State University of New York Press, 1987), Shirley Panken betrays this "tendency": "Following the mother's death, Woolf's inability to mourn, to resolve her submerged anger regarding her mother, *interfered* with the *evolution* of her feminine and *heterosexual* identification" (p. 16; emphasis added).

54 As early as 1922 Woolf declares that "Beauty is only got by the *failure* to get it" (*L*, 2:366; emphasis added). Following her completion of *The Years*, she returns to her notion of a transvalued failure and decides of her writing that "its failure is deliberate. I . . . know that I have reached my point of view, as writer, as being" (*D*, 5:65).

On catachrestical master-words as necessary misfits, see Spivak, *Outside in the Teaching Machine*, p. 297 n. 22.

55 Alex Zwerdling, *Virginia Woolf and the Real World* (Berkeley: University of California Press, 1986), p. 322.

56 Kathy J. Phillips, *Virginia Woolf Against Empire* (Knoxville: University of Tennessee Press, 1994), p. 200.

57 Woolf's descriptions of fascisms abound, but see in particular *Collected Essays*, 4:174, and *TG*, p. 142, where a common rhetoric respectively and decisively implicates Mrs. Manresa and Giles. See also Foucault, "Afterword: The Subject and and Power," p. 209, and "Preface," in *Anti-Oedipus*, by Deleuze and Guattari, p. xiii, for similar accounts.

58 See especially Patricia Kleindienst Joplin, "The Authority of Illusion: Feminism and Fascism in Virginia Woolf's *Between the Acts*," *South Central Review* 2 (summer 1989): 88–104; Phillips, *Virginia Woolf Against Empire*; Sallie Sears, "Theater of War: Virginia Woolf's *Between the Acts*," in *Virginia Woolf: A Feminist Slant*, ed. Jane Marcus (Lincoln: University of Nebraska Press, 1983), pp. 212–35; and Zwerdling, *Virginia Woolf and the Real World*.

59 "In French, yes" refers not only to Proust, but also to Colette's *The Pure and the Impure* (New York: Farrar, Straus & Giroux, 1966), which contains an "essay" on relationships between women and gay men, and which Woolf was just then reading.

60 Butler, "Critically Queer," p. 22.

61 Friedrich Nietzsche, *On the Genealogy of Morals and Ecce Homo*, ed. Walter Kaufmann, trans. Walter Kaufmann and R. J. Hollingdale (New York: Vintage, 1969), p. 259.

62 Giles's tennis shoes, with which he stamps to death the snake, are inexplicably transformed several pages later into boots.

63 Spivak, *Outside in the Teaching Machine*, p. 136.

64 Failing to acknowledge the critical leverage Dodge offers Isa, Madeline Moore contends that "[s]o apparently ingrained are the stories of straight, masculine culture to the English middle classes that even the homosexual outcast, William Dodge, has internalized them." Dodge, she concludes, has "acquiesced to his oppressors' view of the homosexual as a 'mind-divided little snake in the grass'" (Moore, *The Short Season*, pp. 165–66).

65 Jacques Derrida, *Glas*, trans. John P. Leavey, Jr. and Richard Rand (Lincoln and London: University of Nebraska Press, 1986), p. 216.

66 According to Engels, and implicit in Woolf, class exploitation originates in the sexual division of labor, which is required for "the structure of support around the reproduction of society." In Spivak's fabulation, women's labor-power is socially "fetishized as a relationship of dependence and subordination" (*Outside in the Teaching Machine*, p. 71).

67 Elizabeth Abel, *Virginia Woolf and the Fictions of Psychoanalysis* (Chicago: University of Chicago Press, 1989), p. 108.

68 Zwerdling, *Virginia Woolf and the Real World*, p. 306.

69 "He looked leafless, spectral, and his chair monumental"; " 'Prehistoric man,' [Mrs. Swithin] read, 'half-human, half-ape, roused himself from his semi-crouching position and raised great stones'"; "It was the night before roads were made, or houses. It was the night that dwellers in caves had watched from some high place among rocks" (*BA*, pp. 158–59).

70 Zwerdling, *Virginia Woolf and the Real World*, pp. 303–4.

71 Benjamin, *Illuminations*, pp. 83–84.

72 Several characters in *Between the Acts* are thinking about this myth; Bart, for example, twice recites passages from Swinburne's version of it (*BA*, pp. 56, 62).

73 See Walter Benjamin, *The Origin of German Tragic Drama*, trans. John Osborne (London: Verso, 1977).

74 Sylvia Plath, *Collected Poems*, ed. Ted Hughes (London: Faber and Faber, 1981), p. 57.

75 T. S. Eliot, "Virginia Woolf," in *The Bloomsbury Group*, ed. S. P. Rosenbaum, p. 202.

76 Spivak formalizes responsibility thus: "It is that all action is undertaken in response to a call (or something that seems to us to resemble a call) that cannot be grasped as such. Response here involves not only 'to respond to,' as in 'give an answer to,' but also the related situations of 'answering to,' as in being responsible for a name (this brings up the question of the relationship between being responsible for/to ourselves and for/to others); of being answerable for. . . . It is also, when it is possible for the other to be face-to-face, the task and lesson of attending to her response so that it can draw forth one's own" ("Responsibility," *boundary 2* 21, no. 3 [1994]: 22).

Melissa Solomon

The Female World of Exorcism and Displacement

(Or, Relations between Women in Henry James's

Nineteenth-Century *The Portrait of a Lady*)

W hen Henry James introduces the sophisticated and mesmer-izingly intense Madame Merle to a likewise beautiful but younger female counterpart, Isabel Archer, many governing but displaced lesbian interests in *The Portrait of a Lady* radiate from the nucleus of their relationship. Even before Isabel, with her practiced taste for appreciating other women, sets eyes on Madame Merle alone in the drawing room at Gardencourt, the various introductions of Isabel to other, lesser characters in the novel make figurally clear, by degree and by contrast, how much Madame Merle will mean to a girl in whose "soul . . . lay a belief that if a certain light should dawn she could give her-self completely."[1] The centrality of their evolving attachment undergirds the wealth of interconnection between James's other characters and the fascinating, almost illusory holds they (don't quite) have over each other: so much does the novel direct light away from the relation of Madame Merle and Isabel and onto other relations, only to reestablish later with centripetal force how *those* relations have been little but refractions and shadows of that original light. Although nothing more erotic than a walk in the rain happens between Isabel and Madame Merle, their relationship is the central combustive experiment without which Isabel's marriage to Gilbert Osmond, maneuvered as one woman's deliciously proprietary, ample, and salacious trade in the mocked charm, wealth, and submis-siveness of "the young female," could not have occurred.

Erotic displacement, more than romance, accounts for the sinking im-pression that terribly much of what happens between Isabel and Osmond has to do with what happens between Isabel and Madame Merle. So much, that "romance" of *any kind*, endlessly mocked by James through-out, is possibly the least interesting facet of *The Portrait of a Lady*. The stakes of the novel are somewhere far left of that center, and nowhere does complication, interest, or even a sense of vitality come into micro-focus from anybody being "in love." The expendability of romance in this Victorian novel about a young, beautiful, wealthy, eligible, desirable girl is, itself, one signal that whatever you think matters about the plot of Isabel's courtship, marriage, and married life literally complicates itself out of existence as one subject and reemerges as another.

Why might it be important to note such an odd, or at least uncustomary, flattening of romance and love, in a novel where hauntingly the two people most attuned to each other and indeed most inextricably bound to each other are two women? This is not a rhetorical question, nor is it a question meant to imply that this novel is in any simple or predetermined way about lesbians prevented from being lesbians. Between Isabel and Madame Merle, there exists nothing like that familiar "Victorian" moment (so figured in boarding-school stories, medical literature, or fables for the young distributed by the Catholic church, parole board, or dean's office), when one female repudiates the advance of another. Which is to say, there is no acknowledged terrain of female-female desire exiled at the level of plot; as such no critical exercise of lesbian redemption, allowance, or repatriation does justice. The female world of exorcism and displacement operates, I think, by more complicated and covert means.

Concurrently, however, undressing the operations of exorcism and displacement between the two female protagonists, Isabel Archer and Madame Merle, does depend on lifting the prohibition against reading anything but platonic complication in the presentation of a same-sex female dyad in nineteenth-century American literature.[2] One is bound to reckon with the historian's hush of caution against "conclusive" lesbianism[3] in at least two ways: first, with the speculation that Victorian female same-sex association would not, most probably, have been "genital"[4] and second, with the imperative that same-sex female passion is by nature platonic anyway. To the extent that *The Portrait of a Lady* might be read as a queer text, the interpretation of Isabel Archer—an obsessive preoccupation for every character inside the novel—is insistently programmed by and routed through a series of imbricated identity-making substitutions, whereby if Isabel is at all a subject, her passion for and ultimately blind submission to Madame Merle is the dialectical ground by and against which she achieves her (necessarily queer) subjecthood.

I. ARCHITECTURE

a. The Blueprint
Depending on how one credits James in his preface to the New York edition, Isabel is "the image of the young feminine nature."[5] Most of her "satellites"[6] think of her as a composite. The Countess Gemini remarks:

"You're very brilliant—you know that's the way you're always spoken of; you're an heiress and very good-looking and original, not *banal;* so it's a good thing to have you in the family" (300). The narrator assures that Isabel "was, however, at all times a keenly-glancing, quickly-moving, completely animated young woman" (254). Of her visit to Rome, no less than a paradigm: "It is enough to say that her impression was such as might have been expected of a person of her freshness and eagerness" (245).

To explore the implications of the charming young woman, registering what aspects might make up her composition and what desires lie within her constellation, is a fundamental portion of the scaffolding here; why is it or how is it that Isabel falls in love with Madame Merle as she does? Is lesbianism the hidden but coeval space comprising this charming young thing, not asexual, accustomed at first to her own company (when masturbating on the "old haircloth sofa" [33] in the room beyond the library in Albany) or maybe to the company of Henrietta Stackpole, and later to the machinations, or perhaps literally to the "large white hand" (302), of Madame Merle? No one would seriously argue that lesbianism is simply the default setting for absent heterosexuality; but might lesbianism (in a heterosexist universe) have a stolen viability in a text about a young woman who becomes totally obsessed with an older woman? Never stable and never allowed, but never preventable, lesbianism becomes tricky to locate insofar as the middle space—into which it is relegated by heterosexism—must be teased out with the especially sharpened pincers of subliminal insight. Where is Isabel's desire? It is nowhere and everywhere, present both without male satellites (on which James admits he presses the "least hard" [P, 51]) and because of them. Within this ontology, perception itself (as a tool for detecting the range of one's own queer desire and a marker of the facility to locate it in other people, texts, spaces— even *negative* spaces) is frightfully at stake, and one scrambles to employ the finely calibrated senses of taste, touch, and smell.

b. The Blueprint's Reception

If it happens, then, that this American girl, an unburnished, unfinished young embodiment of pure (shall we say) capital, is introduced to Europe[7] under the tutelage of an already industrialized and clarified expatriate such as Madame Merle,[8] this tutelage initially seems to exist for the remaking of Isabel. Such a pygmalion project is an insistent, although ultimately ineffectual and perhaps definitionally impossible, subtext of *Portrait*. It may also be a uniquely queer one, in that the filling out of her definitional space has (they think) not yet taken place, has not yet succumbed to compulsory heterosexuality (or compulsory anything), and yet that emptiness is simultaneously part of what rivets the erotic energy of her satellites. Except for Madame Merle (who knows better and registers, for instance, that Isabel is not empty but *suffused* with desire for her), all who encounter Isabel read her as an archetype and undertake manipulation of her seemingly plastic circumstance. These drives deserve suspicion and inspection.

One pauses, then, to separate two individual but affectively related tributaries:

First, the pressures of "queer" others (especially Ralph, Lord Warburton, and even Mr. Touchett)—whose queerness lies in the inexactness and peculiarity with which each one is not at all settled within the motions of a straight marriage, estate, or even body (the queer complexities of which beg their own queer space—unfortunately not this one) and whose incumbent queer anxieties, energies, projects, repressed hopes, repressed desires (the list continues indefinitely) become rerouted through and projected onto the perceived empty space of "the charming young thing" (wherein one sees how immediately and totally the energies of this text turn toward Isabel the minute she enters, stage right);

And second, Isabel's own queer desire, which no one but Madame Merle can read and which may in part be the necessity of resisting "all that" coming from Ralph, Warburton, Touchett, and others as "not me," and which resistance certainly fuels the passion with which Isabel discovers and submits to Madame Merle, as one who is starving and invisible in a queer desert reacts to another who spots her and brings food.

c. "What do you mean by rich?"

When Ralph Touchett asserts that he "should like to make [Isabel] rich," Mr. Touchett queries: "What do you mean by rich?" Ralph's answer moves shakily between Isabel as the subject of address and the vague category of "people": "I call people rich when they're able to meet the requirements of their imagination. Isabel has a great deal of imagination." Mr. Touchett, who listens "attentively but a little confusedly," registers this answer as a displacement of Ralph's own subject status, doubly removed, first onto Isabel and then onto even more general terrain. Hearing Ralph in just the right key, his loving retort ("So have you, my son" [160]) insists that the person having "imagination" is actually Ralph himself; for, in fact, Ralph's desire to make Isabel rich is a collation of material good intention and the hidden pressure of his own bound-up imagination. He labors under the formulation that Isabel needs the same kind of freedom he needs and that freeing her will, by proxy, free himself. When his father asks what good he will get out of sharing his money with Isabel, he answers, "that of having met the requirements of my imagination" (163). This kind of identification (or, displacement) dies hard. Even much later, when Isabel is unhappily married to Gilbert Osmond and it is clear that Ralph's most basic impression and hope (one, that "she wishes to be free," and two, this "bequest will make her free" [160]) were not true and did not come to pass, his very revisitation of her in Rome seems a denial or a categorically willed and scrupulously maintained ignorance of facts that would make his vision of Isabel—and of himself—dead: "What kept Ralph alive was simply the fact that he had not yet seen enough of the person in the world in whom he was most interested; he was not yet satisfied" (332).

It is not inconsequential that Warburton returns to Rome with Ralph on this same occasion. His fascination with Isabel can be refracted through a similar lens: namely, that he projects onto Isabel a vitality he lacks. She becomes, in his fantasy, a split-off part of himself, whereby she is invested with interest, life, even the power to decide the fate of their relationship and he with no alternative but to appeal—in his "poverty"—to her. From the beginning, he ascertains, "If I marry an interesting woman, I shall be interested" (23). Isabel's willingness to be "the world" to him is limited, although extricating herself from her (necessarily fixed) role in his universe proves difficult. Even the act of dismissal, which falls to her, bears the weight of his pitiful lack of facility and the requirement that Isabel take charge and scold him (whereupon "he coloured like a boy of fifteen" [257]) just to escape from his repeated scenarios. In effect, Lord Warburton and Ralph are blind to the subject position Isabel Archer wants to and will occupy in her most intimate and structuring relationship with another human being.

II. "ELLE CHERCHE TOUJOURS LE MERLE BLANC,"[9] OR, TRANSFERENCE

More than marriage proposals, a footing in aristocratic society, or a hefty bequest, what Isabel's European tutelage brings is Madame Merle. Occurring on the solemn occasion of bearing witness to and giving solace at the death of Mr. Touchett, the initial months Isabel is to spend in the company of Madame Merle become months of courtship and of falling in love. If Mrs. Touchett's and Ralph's efforts of acculturating Isabel have not hit the mark of enlightening and satisfying her (and if her refusal of Warburton is any measure, they have not), but have served more to enlighten and satisfy *them*,[10] then the effects of Madame Merle's presence are a spellbinding contrast. It is not incidental that Madame Merle appears around the time Ralph is arranging what he thinks will be Isabel's ticket to adulthood (the bequest) or later that it is Madame Merle who relays to Isabel Ralph's role in the bequest. The feebleness with which the bequest does not fulfill Ralph's fantasy injunction (that Isabel become x, y, or z, which is more about what Ralph desires than what Isabel does) contrasts starkly with how instantly and forcefully Madame Merle does fulfill Isabel's desires and does become the agent of Isabel's privileged access to (or prohibition from) knowledge or power.

What are the filaments of love in this fabric, and how does someone looking for the world come to find it residing in Madame Merle? For a young woman accustomed to others making declarations of love to her (that is, finding the world in *her*), Isabel's first sensory impression of Madame Merle, that of hearing "the sound of [her] low music proceeding apparently from the saloon" (150), reverses this cathexis; Isabel's immediate exertion is to find out who is at the piano. The skill with which the Schubert piece is executed (need one suggest, the deftness of a woman's fingers on ivory?) and the beauty of the sound delight her and draw her into engagement, an experience of Isabel discovering pleasure and life in something or someone else. She seems surprised that such an embodiment is possible:

> The drawing-room at Gardencourt was an apartment of great distances, and, as the piano was placed at the end of it furthest removed from the door at which she entered, her arrival was not noticed by the person seated before the instrument. This person was neither Ralph nor his mother; it was a lady whom Isabel immediately saw to be a stranger to herself, though her back was presented to the door. This back—an ample and well-dressed one—Isabel viewed for some moments with surprise. (150–51)

The geography of the scene is of places at their "furthest removed," distance that Isabel must actively cover to reach a stranger whose identity interests her; Isabel's thoughts follow a repetitive trope to deduce who "the person," "this person," "a lady" might be. The acquaintance stretches her, but only with the hope that it "would exert some momentous influence on her life" (151). "Skill," "feeling," "strong desire," "rapture," "pleasure," "radiance," beauty, interest, and delight are all alive in this meeting. In addition, when Isabel presents herself as the proverbial "charming young thing," Madame Merle brilliantly resists engagement with this persona and responds to the content of Isabel's speech, rather than to the style in which it is spoken:

> "That's very beautiful, and your playing makes it more beautiful still," said Isabel with all the young radiance with which she usually uttered a truthful rapture.
> "You don't think I disturbed Mr. Touchett then?" the musician answered as sweetly as this compliment deserved. (151)

The adjustment in how Isabel is heard is slight but critical; with this tone, Madame Merle establishes a structuring voice, rather than one that flutters and cloys and pines to serve "young radiance." Nothing pleases Isabel more. The more she sees of Madame Merle, the more she loves: "'Ah then she's not French,' Isabel murmured; and as the opposite supposition had made her romantic it might have seemed that this revelation would have marked a drop. But such was not the fact; rarer even than to be French seemed it to be American on such interesting terms" (152).

Isabel's transfixion includes an acute focus on Madame Merle's physical body, as well as her notice of when that body allusively reveals/revels in its practice of lesbian sex. After the sound of her playing has enticed Isabel toward her, Isabel's first sight is her "ample and well-dressed" back. Later, on a rainy walk together, Isabel watches as Madame Merle enjoys the sensuality of the rain: "There's always a little of it and never too much at once . . . and it never wets you and it always smells good," Madame Merle says, adding, "that in England the pleasures of smell [are] great" (165) as she buries her nose in the fine English wool of her overcoat. Isabel knows that Madame Merle is not boastful or bashful and that her statements "dropped from her like cold confessions" (164). (And so, presumably, she knows the "confession" in this instance. Madame Merle's physical delight in the texture and smell of "fine wool," her poetic and epicurean preference for the kind of fragrant, succulent wetness that "never wets you," and her inclination to elucidate and also demonstrate, with her nose and her overcoat, these kinds of pleasures to Isabel affectively, metaphorically, and dramatically recreates the degree of olfactory and sexual pleasure that performing cunnilingus provides her.) Therefore, it is uniquely *not* the level of literalness in Madame Merle's enjoyments, but rather how consistently she and Isabel enjoy each other, how their conversations traverse the usual boundaries of decorum, how there are no limits to what they will say to each other, do with each other, or to the unending respect and reverence Isabel feels for Madame Merle—all this in a text where such relations are totally absent, the torsion in a girl who looks away from all who look at her, the torsion in a text that is all about who applies to Isabel and what happens to them.

Isabel understands how different, in scale and magnitude, her relation to Madame Merle is. She records the level of sensuality between them accurately, and she is conscious of how much power Madame Merle wields over her. She reflects that "she [herself] wandered, as by the wrong side of the wall of a private garden, round the enclosed talents, accomplishments, aptitudes of Madame Merle" (165). So appreciable, palpable, and even obdurate, despite the formidable literal and figural displacements of sex they might or would have, their erotic relation is still mysteriously accountable to the fact that between would-be lovers, there is sometimes an evolution, insensible to any timetable, agenda, or applied pressure, from sexual fantasy to probable erotic channeling, sometimes coincident with loving and caring, or at least to being in the real orbit of another person's life. When Madame Merle expresses her reciprocal interest in Isabel (and Isabel's body), the fixity of their gazes on each other is exponentially amplified with sexual possibility. Different from fantasy in which one imagines the fullness of another's attention, each now acknowledges a growing telepathy of sensual reading, occurrences of knowing that one's own erotic images are fed by and perhaps exist because of erotic responsiveness in another. "You dress very well," Madame Merle tells her. And when Isabel protests, in the perfect countervoice of erotic playfulness, that clothes mean very little, her partner takes the cue: " 'Should you prefer to go without them?' Madame Merle enquired in a tone which virtually terminated the discussion" (175). Ultimately, Isabel submits that, "she said things to this amiable auditress that she had not yet said to anyone. Sometimes she took alarm at her candour; it was as if she had given to a comparative stranger the key to her cabinet of jewels" (163). It will take the entire space of the novel to witness and understand the degree and effect of this relinquishment.

a. Castles and Visitations and Longings
One of Madame Merle's most cherished, European pleasures is visiting some of the "best" homes and castles, to which she has the honor of a standing invitation. Another of her chief pleasures is letting Isabel know the meaning and magnitude of such privileges: "[Madame Merle] was on the point of leaving Florence, her next station being an ancient castle in the mountains of Tuscany, the residence of a noble family of that country, whose acquaintance (she had known them, as she said, "forever") seemed to Isabel, in the light of certain photographs of their immense crenellated dwelling which her friend was able to show her, a precious privilege" (266). What Madame Merle implies by showing Isabel her portfolio of castles is that a visit, a relation, or a place has value that is regulated, determined, and acquired by who offers it and who else has been there. In part, the excitement of a castle lies in its barring stature and in the determination of the question, "Who shall be allowed in?": a question of historically and materially scaled propriety for the vagina, as well.[11] If the novel is preoccupied with ratifying who shall be allowed Isabel's society, what are the pressures surrounding Isabel's nearly inexhaustible capacity to refuse and Madame Merle's savvy reapplications to

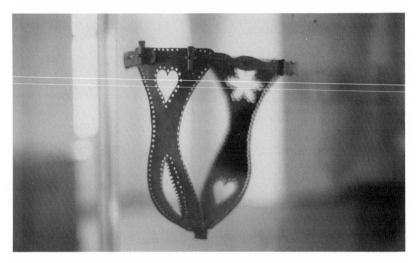

Photo courtesy of Gregory Tomso.

Isabel, who has never prevented, in fact has welcomed, her visitations (and only *her* visitations)? Endlessly proving and cross-proving such a terrain might mean some or all of the following:

(a) this terrain is unstable, even in the face of unquestioned government;

(b) this terrain can never be proven, despite every positive indication that it has been or is; and/or

(c) the desire for this terrain is so excessive and so complete it cannot be attenuated by the illustration that, in this (heterosexist) sign system, one woman's highly charged concentration (need, grievance, demand) on/for/of another woman is made impossible by (among other things) sheer lack of signification.

Madame Merle's insistent self-positionings before Isabel might be paraphrased in the following way: "This is where I have been. This is what you must long for. Only through me will you have the translation of this experience. Everything you could want is in me. I am what you want."[12]

b. Dialectical Reversal

Moving from the novel to Jacques Lacan's essay, "Intervention on Transference," in which Lacan searches through the components of Ida Bauer's (Freud's "Dora") case history for what he calls the "truths" and "dialectical reversals," provides this assertion about Dora's "inverted" lesbian desire for Frau K.:

Here takes place *the second dialectical reversal,* which Freud brings about by commenting that, far from the alleged object of jealousy providing its true motive, it conceals an interest in the person of the subject-rival, an interest whose nature, being much less easily assimilated to common discourse, can only be expressed within it in this inverted form.[13]

What Lacan names "the second dialectical reversal" is a reversal, whereby Dora's seeming love for her father and jealousy over Frau K.'s demands on him are actually masks for her true interest in the "subject-rival," Frau K. herself: a reversal enabling expression of a lesbian desire that is "much less easily assimilated to common discourse" than, for instance, jealousy over a father.

The linchpin of this antihomophobic inquiry is my hypothesis that Madame Merle is predetermined to underwrite a kind of dialectical reversal or substitution or displacement of Isabel's desire for her onto Gilbert Osmond. With such a displacement, Isabel still belongs to her, but at a more easily assimilable distance. Certain (theoretical) preconditions ensure this substitution:

(a) the instability of the (dis)allowed, truncated, monitored, censored paramenters of lesbian affiliation in a heterosexist (and misogynistic) framework;

(b) the sheer "unsignifiability" of two women who desire each other but whose desire surfaces via the very homophobically governed medium, world, text that cannot name or depict the ramifications of that desire; and

(c) therefore, the seeming impossibility—to the degree that language, signification, and/or art signal life—of lesbian representation.

If it is true that "displacement involves the transference of affect from a highly charged idea to an apparently unimportant idea,"[14] there seems no other space in this novel, short of mutual suicide, where Isabel's desire could still be maintained as Isabel's desire and Madame Merle's still that of her structuring counterpart. Marrying Isabel to Osmond is one way to discharge "the highly charged idea" of Isabel's and Madame Merle's relationship, while still allowing it to exist with at least its essence, if not original form, nearly intact.

III. THE MARRIAGE

The fixed betrothal of Isabel to Osmond might, thus, be read as a shift in Madame Merle's subvocal utterance from "I am what you want" to

"I have what you want" (fill in the blank: vagina, Pansy, Osmond). Lest there is any doubt Gilbert Osmond may be read as her functionary or transitional object, Osmond himself is cast in the following ways. First, as negative space:

> Mrs. Touchett had from far back found a place on her scant list for this gentleman, though wondering dimly by what art and what process—so negative and so wise as they were—he had everywhere effectively imposed himself. As he had never been an importunate visitor he had had no chance to be offensive, and he was recommended to her by his appearance of being as well able to do without her as she was to do without him—a quality that always, oddly enough, affected her as providing ground for a relation with her. (234)

As negative space, his desire, if it can be said to exist, is determined by Madame Merle; that is, his desire is Madame Merle's desire. Madame Merle gives him Isabel (who is her desire) and, with the weight and sway of bestowal, determines Isabel will suit him perfectly. In this conversation, Madame Merle first tells Osmond about Isabel:

> "[Isabel's] young—twenty-three years old. She's a great friend of mine. I met her for the first time in England, several months ago, and we struck up a grand alliance. I like her immensely, and I do what I don't do every day—I admire her. You'll do the same."
> "Not if I can help it."
> "Precisely. But you won't be able to help it." (206)

Later, Osmond admits he cannot help but fall into rank and file: " 'The girl's not disagreeable,' Osmond quietly conceded" (244).

Madame Merle's recognition of her governing centrality in the lives of both Osmond and Isabel, echoed at various times in the novel by both Ralph and Mrs. Touchett in the degree to which each routes Isabel's path to Osmond through Madame Merle, is present in her declaration, "I don't pretend to know what people are meant for. . . . I only know what I can do with them" (207). In order for this substitution of Gilbert Osmond for herself to function as a dialectical reversal, not only must Osmond accept Isabel via Madame Merle, but Isabel must accept Osmond, without question or even further need of proof from Osmond himself, on the recommendation of Madame Merle. This almost instantly accepted shift, from Madame Merle to Osmond, has already happened by the time Isabel reveals her plan to visit Pansy in Florence, and Madame Merle decides not to accompany her, exclaiming, "*Ah, comme cela se trouve!*" (Ah, so that's how it is!) (266). From the moment Madame Merle introduces Osmond's name to Isabel, the process of Isabel's becoming affixed to him commences at a gallop. There is little weighing in the manner she weighs Warburton and Goodwood, and her initial interactions with Osmond happen in the presence of Madame Merle and are interpreted for her by Madame Merle. Once the shift is successful,[15] Isabel's engagement and marriage happen "offscreen," as if the events themselves are of comparatively minute importance.

Isabel is not subconsciously unaware that Madame Merle's initial interpretations of Gilbert Osmond carry the terms of his eventual substitution for her, and like many psychic operations, this one is unpleasant when it is exposed to the light of day. Nevertheless she cannot resist either the process of the substitution or her need—which will continue during her marriage[16]—for Merle's translation of it. In a conversation about Osmond's impression of Isabel, Madame Merle and Isabel subliminally transact and enact what will be the new parameters of their relationship, centered around and displaced onto discussion of Gilbert Osmond and what loaded meanings those discussions will have:

> "You were charming, my dear; you were just as one would have wished you. You're never disappointing."
>
> A rebuke might possibly have been irritating, though it is much more probable that Isabel would have taken it in good part; but strange to say, the words that Madame Merle actually used caused her the first feeling of displeasure she had known this ally to excite.
>
> "That's more than I intended," she answered coldly. "I'm under no obligation that I know of to charm Mr. Osmond."
>
> Madame Merle perceptibly flushed, but we know it was not her habit to retract. "My dear child, I didn't speak for him, poor man; I spoke for yourself. It's not of course a question as to his liking you; it matters little whether he likes you or not! I thought you liked *him*."
>
> "I did," said Isabel honestly. "But I don't see what that matters either."
>
> "Everything that concerns you matters to me," Madame Merle returned with her weary nobleness; "especially when at the same time another old friend's concerned." (213–14)

What Isabel and Madame Merle mean to each other, how those meanings exceed what the text can express outright, how these covertures operate, can all be found in this passage. Insofar as Osmond is negative space taken up by Madame Merle, Isabel will submit to Osmond, so long as Madame Merle sets up the formula of this submission, interprets the formula, reassures her the formula is of paramount concern between herself and Isabel, and institutes the law that such a formula will not be death (to the subjecthood Isabel gains through submission to Madame Merle), but life: "Everything that concerns you matters to me."

There are fewer neighborhood vicinities closer and more important to love and yet trickier to delineate than absence . . . of a mother's love, of a lover's application, of the very instance of the hottest and most bothersome, haunting, preoccupying flirtation and subsequent sexual desire, as well as the consequent attentions, silences, perceptual breaks, and resuming double-strength hopes. Absence links passion experientially to numbness and death. What keeps the banality of this assertion equally weighted by a sense of riveting horror is the surprising scope of its reaches and also its nightmarish funereal dimension, which necessitates discerning whether the proverbial person in the casket being lowered into the ground might very well be alive (never mind that it might very well be oneself).

What are the special repercussions of absence, the effects of yearning but never getting? Goodwood articulates that "there are disappointments that last as long as life" (423), and surely the most compelling and complicated "disappointment" of the novel is (not Goodwood's), but Isabel's. I pause here to wonder, literally, what it means for Isabel never to have the one woman who could satisfy her. This is not precisely to highlight how little tangible sensual relief, or even desire, Isabel finds or gets to express during the course of her marriage to Osmond. Nor is it to discount how, even in the end, Madame Merle reads Isabel's slightest mood, feeling, and/or response in every conversation with the telling depth, precision, and spine-tingling sensitivity of a lover who can read the body like no one else . . . especially if there is orgasm or if orgasm is missing. Insofar as Isabel has to or does make do with them, Madame Merle's reading abilities are a *kind* of relief in an impoverished existence in which most people in Isabel's circle can't understand her at all or are suspicious of her or try to force her to be someone she is not or admit something she will not. But whether or not Madame Merle's "reading abilities" are a positive relief or actually the opposite remains an important question. She is the one person in this novel whose provisions to Isabel really most signify absence, substitution, and displacement in the vicinity of passion, so that her facility in reading Isabel becomes in some ways an aching and painful marker of limit and boundary. The implications and consequences of this kind of absence, denial, emptiness, and ache on a "lady" hover closely around death. Someone who mobilizes the hope of satisfaction in so many others and whose very signification is supposed to be the *service* of desire, but never the satisfaction of her own desire, is not fully a person, if personhood means entitlement and place.

Isabel Archer's misery peculiarly exceeds that which others believe is the cause: her marriage to Osmond, his treachery, Madame Merle's supposed duplicity, and that trump card of he-done-me-wrong matrimonial defilement, the idea of being married for one's money. All the components of every woman's fantasy (marriage) and every woman's nightmare (betrayal) should make this novel a well-worn close-up of the most familiar kinds of scenarios. Narrating the plot out loud—depending on how deeply one succumbs to the directional pull of heterosexism on the surface of events (woman gets money, woman marries, woman is betrayed, and above all, woman is conventional) and how discouraging it seems, on a given day, to conduct an antihomophobic inquiry without the literal support beams of plot—feels like the worst kind of public media trial in which the fate of the prosecuted is predetermined before the evidence is weighed. And if there is evidence, it either doesn't matter (because it fails to signify) or it is ready-to-serve (like a TV dinner) exactly what the audience recognizes and was expecting, without labor, anyway. Neither are these discouragements separate, identifiable, and discrete, but rather pervasive, sometimes working in consort and with the battalion of universal conviction. Therefore, must it, by definition, be with the gravest hesitation that one doubts that Isabel's marriage and betrayal, her misery and seeming conventionality, are really at the eye of this tornado? In truth, their lack of cumulative impact on her in good times and bad make the plight of her marriage seem like a dead end that does not lead to deciphering meaning in the novel. Isabel does not seem to fit, indeed she exceeds, the room the plot has made for her.[17]

And so, what can be made of the novel's finale, of Isabel's discovery of Madame Merle's betrayal, of Madame Merle's response to her discovery, and of Isabel's decision to return to Italy after Ralph's death at the end of the novel?

Whenever others have attempted to enlighten Isabel about something or someone, she has either steadfastly refused to be enlightened or the "enlightenment" fails to have the effect on her that the enlightener hoped it would. The crowning example: Isabel first resists Mrs. Touchett's belief that Madame Merle is opportunistic, but later admits this is perfectly correct. Both responses, of either repudiation or bored agreement, deny Mrs. Touchett the power of knowing something Isabel does not and disrupt the subsequent command such a position usually entails. They also guard Isabel's custom of interpreting people and situations in her own, often queer manner. "Rightness" (Mrs. Touchett's) effects no impact or excitement and amounts to no degree of insight . . . in this case as to why Isabel persists in her association with one who others find (as it were) dishonorable.

The Countess Gemini encounters a similar frustration. In telling Isabel that Pansy is the daughter of Osmond and Madame Merle, the Countess imagines this knowledge will break apart the "flimsy" ignorances she believes have kept Isabel tied to Osmond and to Madame Merle. She says to Isabel, "*Ça me dépasse* [it's beyond me] if you don't mind my saying so, the things, all round you, that you've appeared to succeed in not knowing" (451). Later, Isabel responds:

> "It's very strange. I suppose I ought to know, but I'm sorry," Isabel said. "I'm much obliged to you."
> "Yes, you seem to be!" cried the Countess with a mocking laugh. "Perhaps you are—perhaps you're not. You don't take it as I should have thought."
> "How should I take it?" Isabel asked.
> "Well, I should say as a woman who has been made use of." Isabel made no answer to this; she only listened, and the Countess went on. (455)

In order to register an important implication of Isabel's silence in the face of being "used" by Madame Merle, this scene may be read against an earlier moment between Isabel and Madame Merle, in which Isabel demands to know why Madame Merle is so concerned with the fate of Pansy, Osmond, and herself: " 'What have you to do with me?' Isabel went on. Madame Merle slowly got up, stroking her muff, but not removing her eyes from Isabel's face. 'Everything!' she answered" (430). "What have you to do with me?" is Isabel's plaintive, nearly desperate cry, elicited by no one but Madame Merle. It asks, in one breath, 'Who am I?' yet demands, in the next, that Madame Merle's answer be 'I am You.' As both questioning demand and demanding question, it neatly encapsulates the positively unshakable primacy of her interest in, need of, grievance with, and identification with Madame Merle. It is also asked and answered as a sexualized question. The physical world is, in the space of their gazes, a place full of heat and electricity, where eyes transfix and hands cannot keep themselves from stroking.

And so, more than the actual treacherousness of the idea that Madame Merle has "used" Isabel, the meaning of her "use" bears the intensity of a sexual command and Isabel's utility a sexual utility. So it is that Isabel's new "knowledge" of her use does not result in her abandonment of Madame Merle and satellites—it fails to effect any such preconceived result, anger, or break between them (more on this later)—but rather in Isabel's taking another step toward the woman who compels her. What the knowledge succeeds in doing is closing the universe of the novel ever tighter around Madame Merle and Isabel, reestablishing that it has been about their interwoven interests all along, so much have the others been the mask of that, the pawns of that, and the blind substitution of that all at once.

What events indicate Isabel turns toward Madame Merle? Answering this question fully requires understanding the forces dictating Madame Merle's life, her arrangements under the weight of these forces, and what these arrangements will mean to her and to Isabel. What, in effect, are the options, desires, and preoccupations—to say nothing of "assets"—of a widow with a child, of a woman whose occupation is to have no occupation but making social calls; indeed, according to the Countess Gemini, "No one knows, no one has ever known, what she lives on, or how she got all those beautiful things. . . . I don't call Madame Merle a success, you know. I don't know what she may accomplish yet, but at present she has very little to show. The only tangible result she has ever achieved— except of course, getting to know every one and staying with them free of expense—has been bringing you and Osmond together" (453). In short, what has Madame Merle to give Isabel but what she has given? If one believes the Countess, Madame Merle is nothing but a pathetic collection of ladylike attributes such as playing, painting, and conversation, all of which have failed in their supposedly predetermined efforts to win her an important husband. One of the insistent questions constantly resurfacing in *The Portrait of a Lady* is, What is to be done with a marriageable woman? There is no end to the stream of unmarried females (Pansy, Henrietta Stackpole, Lord Warburton's sisters), and one of the trompe l'oeil thrills of this novel is realizing that either no marriage works out as planned and/or that we don't really care if it does anyway. (What is only minimally interesting in Stackpole's engagement to Bantling is that others are surprised she really is a woman and that somehow her engagement is/must/should be proof of that . . . except it really isn't.) From the minute Isabel first passes up those chances for happy-ever-after marriage with Warburton and Goodwood (chances that annoyingly persist in being offered, first as grand prizes, then as consolation prizes, but just refuse to disappear from the novel), one knows that marriage will be an unstable element on this periodic table. Isabel's marriage to Gilbert Osmond does not mean what others think it should mean or change what others hope it will change. In a novel where characters have so much trouble interpreting each other and where the surface of relationships sometimes offers little to no hint at the depth beneath, can one accept the image of Madame Merle as a used-up collection of charm-school achievements? Others' impressions and even insights about her are likely to prove a dead end.

At least two elements that reify Isabel's and Madame Merle's desire for each other take shape once Isabel has "found out" her use-value and as much confronted Madame Merle:[18] one regards gift exchange or dowry (hence the nature of betrothal, marriage, and property exchange), and the second regards the sanctity of eternity (the part in which both parties say "as long as we both shall live") whose agent and proof is obedience. I have earlier asserted that Isabel's marriage to Osmond is Madame Merle's vehicle for displacing her own lesbian attachment to Isabel. It seems logical to suggest that, as an additional part of this displacement and substitution, Isabel's money and devotion has been dispatched to care for Madame Merle's child. The net result is that there is no part of Isabel's life, resources, or passion that is not conscripted into service by Madame Merle. To the extent that Madame Merle has secured anyone with her charms in her years of visiting grand houses (and remember, Gardencourt is her favorite), it has not been an affluent husband, but an affluent wife. It would be harder to find a more faithful wife than Isabel or a turn of events more uniquely tailored to the kinds of surrogacy that saying "I do" to Madame Merle would require. Love me, love my child. Their very last meeting at the convent proves the unshakable fidelity of this arrangement. Madame Merle's departure to America actually ensures that Isabel will return to Italy for Pansy: each one bowing in obedience to the wishes of the other. If Madame Merle goes to America in order to fulfill Isabel's wish never to see her again (and, please note, to whom other than Isabel has Madame Merle ever given this kind of promise or immediate obedience?), then Isabel's return to Italy merely obeys the attachments (to Madame Merle) she undertook in the first place.

The idea that Madame Merle makes "a convenience of" (475) Isabel does not really strike at the heart of her relationship with Isabel. Ultimately, there is nobody whom Madame Merle makes "a convenience of" more than Gilbert Osmond: nobody who serves as more of a go-between, nobody more emasculated (his threats to Isabel so flagrantly disregarded), and nobody less the focal point of anyone's desires. Even Goodwood's blind, self-driven single-mindedness keeps himself better company.

IV. ISABEL'S "PRIMITIVE NEED"
(OTHERWISE KNOWN AS "SHAME")

What had become of all her ardours, her aspirations, her theories, her high estimate of her independence and her incipient conviction that she should never marry? These things had been absorbed in a more primitive need—a need the answer to which brushed away numberless questions, yet gratified infinite desires. It simplified the situation at a stroke, it came down from above like the light of the stars, and it needed no explanation. There was explanation enough in the fact that he was her lover, her own, and that she should be able to be of use to him. She could surrender to him with a kind of humility, she could marry him with a kind of pride; she was not only taking, she was giving. (297)

The unknowing that defines Isabel's unnameable "primitive need" is exponentially intensified by the phrase "There was explanation *enough*" (emphasis added); the word "enough" admits that what follows will be not an explanation, but compensation for *lack* of explanation. That caesura, the immediate shift from wondering what the "primitive need" is to the shrunken topic of marriage which does not fit the space made by the "light of the stars," indicates that there are at least two oppositional spaces at work in Isabel: one space that loosely binds freedom and desire and another default space associating marriage with truth. The latter space is marked by the words "enough," "fact," "should," "use," "humility," "pride," "taking," and "giving." She "surrenders" as one who surrenders from high ground to low ground, from the ground of "primitive need" to ground that must or should be right. Part of that rightness lies in the hope of concrete service rendered: "Pansy already so represented part of the service she could render, part of the responsibility she could face" (298). And this concrete nature is implicitly different from where Isabel has been: allusive, unmassed needs and pleasures either exorcised or displaced onto marriage.

The drive to root out the satiation of "primitive need," to institute this division—between Isabel's past and her fantasy about a necessarily different future in which "none of that" will take place—is where shame lives. Eve Kosofsky Sedgwick names this "the conceivable shame of a past self."[19] Poor Isabel will later consciously realize that shame lives as well in her marriage to Osmond, insofar as it is an integral part of Madame Merle's performative (or periperformative?) substitution:

> The fact of Madame Merle's having had a hand in Gilbert Osmond's marriage ceased to be one of the titles to consideration; it might have been written, after all, that there was not so much to thank her for. As time went on there was less and less, and Isabel once said to herself that perhaps without her these things would not have been. That reflection indeed was instantly stifled; she knew an immediate horror at having made it. "Whatever happens to me let me not be unjust," she said; "Let me bear my burdens myself and not shift them upon others!" (339–40)

"Let me bear my burdens myself and not shift them upon others!": this is the inevitable, but heartbreaking philosophy and goal of a lady whose aches have never been satisfied, the mantra of one who has had to go without. This is Isabel's frustration with her own subjecthood defined as submission to Madame Merle (and of lesbianism that can no longer be contained peacefully within these mechanisms). That the mechanisms standing for lesbianism and being substituted for lesbianism fail is perhaps built into the need for their very existence. One central question bears on its functioning. How does the novel in some ways illustrate "the moment when the proscenium arch of the [performative of] marriage is . . . displaced"[20] and the periperformative of lesbian attachment threatens to become the most structuring (albeit warping, occluded, and shame-ridden) voice of the narrative? Estimating the circumscription of that voice is an act of divination, the importance of which is equal in stature to locating whatever heretofore monstrous and unseen, but identity-making undercurrents exist and to providing the space these pressures demand above ground in the light of day.

NOTES

This essay is *also* dedicated to Nayra Atiya and Gregory Tomso, for whom and without whom . . .

1 Henry James, *The Portrait of a Lady* (New York: W. W. Norton, 1975), p. 56. Further citations will be given parenthetically in the text.

2 To exclude the words "love" and "ritual" in a reappropriation of Carroll Smith-Rosenberg's 1975 title is to deroutinize an assumption about the goodness and kindness, the near utopic empathy, fixed as definitional to female same-sex affiliation by a dominant narrative unable to fathom why else or what else—since women are simply configured as sisters—would be appealing about or, in addition, complicated by an equation without the phallus: mythmaking in this instance actually serving to make mythic what is, in fact, the status quo.

    See "The Female World of Love and Ritual: Relations Between Women in Nineteenth-Century America," by Carroll Smith-Rosenberg, which originally appeared in *Signs: A Journal of Women in Culture and Society* 1 (Autumn 1975): 1–29. Reprinted in *A Heritage of Her Own*, ed. Nancy F. Cott and Elizabeth H. Pleck (New York: Simon and Schuster, 1979); all citations from this edition.

3 I do not signal "lesbianism" as a medicalized identity, per se, (the birth of which Foucault dates at 1870), but as a site of same-sex female erotic complication.

4 Did Victorian women even have vaginas or know what to do with them? This is one possible question to ask of the alienating and pseudo-clinical use of the term "genital," as if Victorian genitals were automatically estranged from the Victorian subjects being studied. What, in fact, is "genitality"? Can there be no sex without "genitality"? Rosenberg asserts that, "The essential question is not whether these women had genital contact." And any consideration of such "genitality" (a term her article mandates using, even amidst repudiation of it as a subject) is something that "distorts the nature of these women's emotional interaction" (p. 316). This "emotional interaction" is cast so broadly it shames any mention of "genitality" by making it seem a reductive and misdirected twentieth-century absorption. More interesting to Rosenberg is her cloying and necessarily truncated vision of how, "female friendships served a num-

ber of emotional functions. Within this secure and empathic world [of nineteenth-century America?] women could share sorrows, anxieties, and joys, confident that other women had experienced similar emotions. . . . This was a world in which hostility and criticism of other women were discouraged, and thus a milieu in which women could develop a sense of inner security and self-esteem" (p. 321).

For a more finely calibrated series of questions on historical dismissals or side-steppings of the question of homosexuality, see Eve Kosofsky Sedgwick, *Epistemology of the Closet* (Berkeley: University of California Press, 1990), p. 52.

5   Henry James, "Preface to 'The Portrait of a Lady'," collected in *The Art of the Novel* (New York: Charles Scribner's Sons, 1934), p. 48. Further citations will be abbreviated P and given parenthetically in the text.

6   "Satellites" is another term from James's preface to the New York edition.

7   And by introduced one does not signal her introduction at Gardencourt, a contained and domesticated Europe-unto-itself, where Isabel can do little but walk up and down a certain hall with each new visitor looking at the same collection of paintings (and here it is, of course, Isabel on exhibit as well for the delight of, say, Warburton), but more Florence and Rome themselves, as cities exhibiting themselves before Isabel.

8   Madame Merle is convincing in her imitation of an original "European" and also illustrates that the original can be imitated.

9   I thank Nayra Atiya for her reference to this ornithological French idiom. *Le merle* is a black thrush. Atiya's translation of this idiom is: "She's still looking for her dream love" or "To search for the impossible."

10 Touchett family self-interest in Isabel is palpable; Isabel's consolidation of her own charm, even in exercising her power of "no," has from the first delighted them.

11 Figure 1 depicts a chastity belt (date unknown) on display at Hohensalzburg Castle in Salzburg, Austria. The vaginal opening (unlike the anal opening) is sharply crenulated, barring entrance. Photo courtesy of Gregory Tomso.

12 It is *nearly* as if Madame Merle says to Isabel, "My pussy would be your privilege, and yours mine."

13 Jacques Lacan, "Intervention on Transference" in *In Dora's Case: Freud—Hysteria—Feminism*, ed. Charles Bernheimer and Claire Kahane, 2d ed. (New York: Columbia University Press, 1990), p. 97. Heather Findlay, in her essay, "Queer Dora: Hysteria, Sexual Politics, and Lacan's 'Intervention on Transference'" *GLQ* 1, no. 3 (1994): 323–47, alerted me to the existence of this piece.

14 Jonathan Scott Lee, *Jacques Lacan* (Amherst: University of Massachusetts Press, 1991), p. 210.

15 The success of this shift is signaled by Isabel's desire to visit Pansy without Madame Merle (insofar as the agent must recede momentarily into the background in order for the "other" to stand in successfully for her) and, later, by their rather platonic trip to Greece (the most exotic and potentially homoerotic testing site available for judging the totality of Madame Merle's reduplication.)

16 See pp. 343–44 for an example of this.

17 The flatness of Isabel's marriage to Osmond does not imply that his treachery and sadistic impulses toward her are dull, but that ultimately they drive the novel nowhere. Isabel perceives them, bears them, and unsuccessfully tries to hide them from public view. His treatment of her is the secret that isn't a secret, the secret that isn't powerful enough to stay hidden or, conversely, isn't powerful enough for its disclosure to mean much in terms of impact. Isabel's friends talk a lot about Isabel's miserable marriage (in fact, they discuss little *but* this) as if to position themselves inside her intimate

space. Yet, her friends (Goodwood, Ralph, Warburton, Stackpole) are no closer to her now than they ever were. Osmond's treachery is the conduit for precisely nothing. It fails to signify her life in any meaningful way. Osmond may be a sadist, but Isabel is not (at least in response to *him*) a masochist. Their marriage is like bad theater in which one partner fails to take the scripted cues of another's involved scenario.

18 Inside the walls of Pansy's convent . . .

19 Eve Kosofsky Sedgwick, "Queer Performativity: Henry James's *The Art of the Novel*," *GLQ* 1, no. 1 (1993): 10.

20 Eve Kosofsky Sedgwick, "Around the Performative: Periperformative Vicinities in Dickens, Eliot, and James," unpublished manuscript.

Jonathan Goldberg

Strange Brothers

first read Willa Cather when I was in high school. I can no longer remember which novel we were assigned—it must have been *O Pioneers!* or *My Ántonia*—but I can still recall what it felt like to be reading Cather then. Once I had read the assigned novel I went on to others— among them, I am certain, *The Professor's House*, to which I will be turning in the pages below. I didn't know Cather's well-known pronouncement in "The Novel Démeublé" on "the thing not named," but it was just that quality of Cather's writing that spoke to me.[1] I found the writing intense, atmospheric, heavy with something that was not said, which I nonetheless recognized. I couldn't tell what it was, aslant the calm surface of narration, that I heard. But whatever it was spoke to me precisely along the wavelengths of a silence that I found irrestible. As if, somehow, the novels were written in a language that I could not myself articulate and yet in which I found myself articulated. Not, I should add, that I knew what they said, or what part of me they found; or, rather, I knew, but couldn't tell how the novels I was reading spoke so uncannily, couldn't see what it was in the novels that made the connection. My reading was rapt; indeed, I can still recall a kind of fevered sense that overcame me when I read "Tom Outland's Story"; at the time I knew nothing about the Anasazi ruins at Mesa Verde, and read the story as if it were some kind of science fiction. The place was unimaginable, I could not imagine it as being real. It was the place of reading. It was where I was.

Now, in hindsight, I know several names for that place. And thanks to the criticism on Cather that I value most—Eve Kosofsky Sedgwick's "Across Gender, Across Sexuality: Willa Cather and Others"; Judith Butler's "'Dangerous Crossing': Willa Cather's Masculine Names"—I know better where I was reading.[2] The essay that follows suggests, I trust, my indebtedness to those I have just cited; perhaps it finds some words for the experience I have described and still have reading Cather. The translation of her texts into the language of sexual knowledge remains an elusive task. In titling this essay as I have done, I call up the strange kinship of these texts through an allusion to a 1931 novel by Blair Niles, *Strange Brother*, often identified as one of the few homosexual novels of the early twentieth century, and I will have a word or two to say about the inexplicitly gay project of *The Professor's House* (1925) and Niles' programmatic work.[3] But the title aims mainly at the resonances of Cather's work, and not, I hope, only those that vibrate with this reader.

In an essay detailing the relationship of Cather's fictionalized version of the "discovery" of the Mesa Verde cliff dwellings by Tom Outland in *The Professor's House* to the December 1888 sighting of the ruins of the Cliff Palace by Richard Wetherill and his brother-in-law Charlie Mason, David Harrell is guided by the thesis that "the creative route from Richard Wetherill to Tom Outland was not all that straight."[4] Harrell's "not . . . straight" says more than he means. The aim of his essay is simply to measure passages in *The Professor's House* against other tellings offered by Cather (both in a 1916 piece of journalism and in the letter she published on *The Professor's House* in 1938)[5] and to detail factual slips: such things as Cather's description of the thirty-year-old Wetherill as a "young boy"; or of her 1916 informant, in all likelihood Clayton Wetherill, as "a very old man," when he was only forty-seven when she spoke to him; or the misspelling and misnaming to be found in Cather's claim simply to have built upon the facts: "The Blue Mesa (the Mesa Verde) actually was discovered by a young cowpuncher in just this way. . . . I myself had the good fortune to hear the story of it from a very old man, brother of Dick Wetherell. Dick Wetherell as a young boy forded Mancos River into the Mesa after lost cattle. I followed the real story very closely in Tom Outland's narrative."[6] Harrell chalks up the divergencies (in this telling, for instance, Wetherill is as unaccompanied as Cather's Tom is) to some "private myth of discovery."[7] In a footnote he records the fact that while Cather is not alone in misspelling Wetherill's surname, "he was never known to anyone as Dick,"[8] an error neither he nor an expert he has consulted can understand as anything but "curious."

Harrell seems accurate in his claim that Richard Wetherill was always Richard to those who knew him, but it is not quite true that he was only Cather's Dick.[9] Edith Lewis, in *Willa Cather Living: A Personal Record,* tells the story of how Cather heard from "a brother of Dick Wetherill . . . the whole story of how Dick Wetherill swam the Mancos river on his horse and rode into the Mesa after lost cattle."[10] Lewis follows Cather here, not only in making Wetherill the sole "discoverer" (Lewis uses the scare quotes) of the Cliff Palace, but also in naming him Dick. Yet to say that she follows Cather is too easily to grant her the secondary, behind-the-scenes status she often has. Her narrative, in fact, moves in and out of a position in which "we" (she and Cather) go to Mesa Verde and spend a week there, passing an entire day alone in the Cliff Palace; telling how, on the way out, they got lost and passed four or five hours waiting to be rescued, sitting on a rock as the moon rose on the canyon before them. Lewis describes events participated in by a couple, but registers their effect in her secondhand understanding of Cather's response to them. "The four or five hours that we spent waiting there were, I think, for Willa Cather the most rewarding of our whole trip to the Mesa Verde." [11] The syntactic complications of that sentence perhaps can be read along-side the *folie à deux* of their shared Dick, an overdetermined instance, to be sure, of the masculine name. As Lewis joins and separates with the person she always calls Willa Cather (never either one or the other name, always both), she presents as her thought her hypothesis about what Cather felt. Not explicit in this passage is the very "personal record" that Lewis claims to present and yet for whose absence she is often blamed. [12] There is no narrative of how this "we" operated. There is, rather, the movement of identification and distance, of displacement and overlapping. Dick is one of the sites where Cather and Lewis meet, the shared misnaming that makes Cather's Dick also Edith Lewis's or perhaps the other way around. Dick is a (mis)naming of their relationship.

If the route from Richard Wetherill to Tom Outland was not "straight," it is, in part, because it passed through this couple, and through the misnaming instanced here. It is, moreover, I would argue, the relationship with Lewis that needs to be read as a sustaining condition not only of Cather's life but also of her writing. Lewis writes that "*The Professor's House* is, I think, the most personal of Willa Cather's novels," [13] interpolating and ventriloquizing Cather in just the way in which she described their Mesa Verde experience. A compelling case has been made by Leon Edel for thinking that the elegiac, despairing tone of *The Professor's House* is rooted in Cather's loss of Isabelle McClung, newly married to Jan Hambourg (the likely prototype for Louie Marsellus). [14] The professor's rejection of the backyard study at Outland that Rosamond and Louie are building finds a parallel in Cather's similar refusal in 1923 of Isabelle's offer of a study in Ville-D'Avray. But one must also recall that Cather, unlike the professor, had unthreatened places to write; in the Bank St. apartment or the cabin on Grand Manan that she and Lewis shared, the locales where *The Professor's House* was written; indeed, the summer after the novel was completed, Lewis reports, "we decided to build a small cottage on Grand Manan." [15] Critics like Doris Grumbach, who assume that Cather's loss of Isabelle signaled the kind of terminus that she finds in the professor's condition—"The tragedy of St. Peter's love for Tom is that it is private, unconfessed, sublimated," and that Cather is similarly letting go of something she never had—too easily conflate Cather and her professor, and in treating Isabelle as Tom, ignore the existence of Edith Lewis, the houses they shared and built together.[16]

What makes *The Professor's House* so personal? Lewis, characteristically, fails to say, indeed stresses the symbolic nature of the novel as a sign of its personal import. Harrell thinks the novel conforms to a "private myth of discovery" found as early as in the 1909 story, "The Enchanted Bluff," which he describes as concerning "a group of boys" who "dream of conquering a legendary mesa where ancient Indians once lived,"[17] ignoring in this summary the crucial fact that the narrator of the story is an unnamed boy who forms part of the group. Grumbach finds a precedent for *The Professor's House* in an even earlier story, the 1902 "The Professor's Commencement," in which a delicately feminine bachelor professor who lives with his masculine sister humiliates himself at his farewell party as he had when he had graduated; in this professor's bleak life of retreat and overrefinement, the one moment of life had been a stunning student, dead in his early twenties. These stories suggest that whatever was "personal" in *The Professor's House* went back further than the loss of Isabelle to Jan Hambourg. But however much they express Cather's early anxieties, they do not lead "straightforwardly" to *The Professor's House*. Tom Outland lives on the mesa; Cather wrote his story on Grand Manan. The awful fear of having missed the chance to love—the overwhelming sadness of the professor in his recognition of and resignation to what has been lost—is, arguably, not Cather's position. This is not to deny what many critics have argued, that Cather's identifications in the text extend both to the professor and to Tom; they are versions of the old man and the boy that also structure her account of the route from "Dick" Wetherill to Outland. The two coalesce, condensing the double trajectory of identification, in Godfrey St. Peter's belated discovery of his earlier self, the boy with whom "he had meant . . . to live some sort of life together."[18]

That boy might well have been Tom. It is one of the crucial points about the novel that "Tom Outland's Story" is not the interpolated and autonomous central episode it appears to be, but woven throughout *The Professor's House*. Dead Tom exerts his influence on the living, as the figure between the professor and Dr. Crane, his one valued colleague, for instance, but also, and more centrally, between every member of the professor's family. Indeed, it is impossible to describe the tensions and difficulties of the family—and of the initial section of the novel, which bears that name—without seeing how Tom is at the core of all of them. He is there most obviously as the source of the money that is such a sore spot between the professor's daughters, but was there before Tom's legacy was ever a question. Rosamond's announcement of her engagement to Tom triggered Kathleen's acceptance of Scott McGregor (53), and it is difficult not to believe that her precipitous marriage to someone her father finds unworthy of her, however decent Scott is in himself (something of a question), registers her disappointment at losing Tom to Rosie.[19] Indeed, when the professor and Kathleen bond together in the novel against Rosamond it is through their shared possession of that earlier Tom: "Our Tom is much nicer than theirs" (113). Moreover, it is arguably this position of identification that inflects the professor's wife's misunderstanding of St. Peter's position. "You didn't get the son-in-law you wanted" (38), she opines; but the professor's critical attitude toward Rosamond seems more straightforwardly jealous. Tom only saw her as others do—as a ravishing beauty (47); had he seen better, he would not have chosen her. If, within a heterosexual logic of choice, this means that the professor wanted Tom for Kitty, their bonding over Tom could as easily suggest how the professor wanted Tom for himself, how the animus against Rosamond is motivated not only by her having forgotten Tom, but by her having gotten him in the first place.

One sign of this can be seen in the relationship Tom had to the two when they were girls. They were his confidants, and to them he told the story that only belatedly he relates to the professor (as "Tom Outland's Story"). Their response to his narrative was to identify with its protagonists, "to play at being Tom and Roddy" (105). This means that in desiring Tom they took up the place of the male partner. It implies, too, that in shaping themselves through Tom's stories their desires were formed through same-sex ones, and that their gender identities are similarly inflected. If one reason the professor bonds so tightly with Kathleen has to do with their shared relation to Tom, it is expressed in the limits of Kitty's drawing abilities: she can only render the professor, a mark of her identification with him. So, to the professor, Rosamond is his wife's daughter, especially after she marries Louie Marsellus. However, these questions of identification are more complex; in looks, at least, Rosie resembles her father. Perhaps in erotic choice as well.

Mrs. St. Peter's mistake about the professor's desired son-in-law brings up the vexed relationship to Tom's successor, Louie Marsellus, the man who turned Tom's scientific discovery into cash and who married Rosamond. Lillian's relationship to Louie is, of course, a close one, and in part registers her former aversion to Tom. He is a kind of substitute lover for her. Louie obviously lives in the shadow of Tom, and his decision to name his new house Outland is one gesture toward this. Much in Louie is clearly repellant: his need to dominate social situations, his miscalculated attempts at intimacy and generosity. While the professor expresses aversion and resentment over Louie's appropriation of Tom ("I can't bear it when he talks about Outland as his affair" [36]), he also allows himself to acknowledge him as "magnanimous and magnificent" (149), as he exclaims when Louie is even willing to forgive Scott if he has blackballed him. For Louie is clearly trying to live up to an impossible ideal. Found to be in possession of Tom's fortune without, unlike the others, having had any direct knowledge of Tom, he is the illegitimate inheritor that is scorned for having what is not rightly his. (Even McGregor can score a point of resentment against Louie precisely on the basis of the fact that he at least knew Tom at school.) Louie's position as an interloper is constituted by his being outside the ways in which all the others are related through the figure of Tom. His outsider status is registered too in the Jewishness that emblematizes it, but which also accounts for the desperation of his attempts to please and to ingratiate himself. He overdoes it, and one recognizes in his flamboyance something that raises Cather's hackles as well. His is the sin for which she had so much earlier lambasted Oscar Wilde, in a gesture at once self-protective and self-hating.[20]

That sins of the Oscar Wilde sort attach to Louie must be remarked. He loves to shop; he sits over a jewel case with Lillian, whom he always calls "dearest." He embodies the "florid style" (36). Louie is marked, as a Jew, as an outsider, as distinctly effeminate and effusive. But these are also signs of identifications with Tom even as they also register as attempts to deflect that identification. Tom, too, was an outsider, an orphan who comes from nowhere. "He departs leaving princely gifts" (103), and Louie is similarly generous, also "princely" (141). And, as Lillian points out, invidiously, jealously, Tom also was "highly coloured" (138). Moreover, Louie knows against whom he is being measured, and that he can never quite measure up. Still, Cather allows him to speak the book's epigraph, a recognition of value in a locus of indistinction: "A turquoise set in silver, wasn't it? . . . Yes, a turquoise set in dull silver" (90). Ostensibly a description of a gift from Tom to Rosamond that she wore when Louie first met her, it also evokes the shimmering value found in the dull setting, the thing not said glimmering in Cather's deliberately understated prose. These are qualities she attributes to Tom's diary: "To St. Peter this plain account was almost beautiful, because of the stupidities it avoided and things it did not say. . . . Yet through this austerity one felt the kindling imagination, the ardour and excitement of the boy, like the vibration in a voice when the speaker strives to conceal his emotion by using only conventional phrases" (238). Louie is the flaming version of Tom, easy enough to be scorned; he is the protective flare that draws off from Tom the signs of a flamboyance that otherwise might be all too legible. If

Rosie and the money are the most visible signs of Louie's inheritance, the recognition of the bracelet points to the secret path of their identification.

St. Peter himself posts the warning that is meant to safeguard his relationship with Tom and to ward off the making legible of such secrets: "My friendship with Outland is the one thing I will not have translated into the vulgar tongue" (50). (By the vulgar tongue, the professor means cash; hence the figure of Louie and his translations of Tom are implicated.) Thus, one can understand how readers sympathetic to Cather's work balk at finding sexual meanings in texts that so protect against that "vulgar" translation. Hermione Lee, for one, points out that the professor's recovery of the boy that he meant to make his lifelong companion is couched in explicitly asexual terms, the recognition of a primitive, original self replaced with maturity:[21] "The Professor knew, of course, that adolesence grafted a new creature into the original one, and that the complexion of a man's life was largely determined by how well or ill his original self and his nature as modified by sex rubbed on together" (242). "Sex" in this formulation is almost unnatural, a social grafting; but sex is also explicitly heterosex; "[a]fter he met Lillian Ornsley, St. Peter forgot that boy had ever lived" (240), and his life has been shaped by the demands of marriage and family, the demands of the "secondary social man" (240). So, earlier, he insists to Rosamond that while her bond to Tom was social (and therefore monetary, a matter of property and possession), his was not (50).

If the professor's ultimate state of resignation involves a refusal to live in these social terms and a regrasping of an elemental self, the question remains of where and how Tom fits into this reordering, whether he can really be cordoned off to a nonsocial, nonsexual state of the self, or whether the social-sexual state, by being heterosexual, leaves open other sexual possibilities for the asocial state of the primitive boy. The "secondary social man" would seem to be related to the "accidental" chance elements of life, which the professor regards as having shaped his existence ever since he lost touch with the original boy. Even in these terms, Tom cannot be so easily allied to the primitive condition, since he represents "a stroke of chance he couldn't possibly have imagined" (233), and one that changed everything—gave shape to the professor's work, imbricating itself in every domain of his family; but also—and far more importantly—Tom came close to filling the role of the imagined boyhood companion. As the professor reflects back upon his past, his happiest moments are vacations away from his family shared with Tom, trips to the mesa, to Mexico, and the projected trip to Paris never accomplished (which undoubtedly explains why the professor has refused to go there with his family). Remaining instead in the study of the old house, he returns to the place where, when the family had been on vacation, he had been a bachelor again, the "back garden" (5) where he and Tom had spent summer evenings together, the very place where Tom finally narrates his story:

> Over a dish of steaming asparagus, swathed in a napkin to keep it hot, and a bottle of sparkling Asti, they talked and watched night fall in the garden. If the evening happened to be rainy or chilly, they sat inside and read Lucretius.
>
> It was on one of those rainy nights, before the fire in the dining-room, that Tom at last told the story he had always kept back. (155)

Tom ends his story back in the garden—"I landed here and walked into your garden" (229)—just as it was by its "green door" (95) that he first entered, "the hottest boy" the professor had ever seen (100). The professor's French garden is a seemingly sterile place where "trees . . . don't bear not'ing," as his landlord puts it (40), a site of barren shrubs, devoid of grass. "It was there he and Tom Outland used to sit and talk half through the warm, soft nights" (7). The back garden is Tom's site, outward reflection of his inner nature: "The boy's mind had the super-abundance of heat which is always present where there is rich germination" (234). What he makes grow are the professor's "sons," his books (144). While the professor acknowledges this as a romance of the mind, this abstracted translation conflicts with the heat and generativity of this backdoor site of unnatural graftings. "Nature's full of such substitutions, but they always seem to me sad, even in botany" (165); this sentence, pronounced by Tom on Roddy's failure to have children, Hermione Lee takes as Cather's most explicit acknowledgment of her own sexuality. The sad substitutions are nonetheless within nature. Just as Outland's story runs throughout the narrative, so too his relation to the professor cannot be stabilized on one or the other side of the divide (natural/unnatural, natural/social, sterile/germinative, asexual/sexual). Tom's position is continually belied by the doubling most explicit through the figure of Louie. He is both inside and out; the homosexual lining of the heterosexual as well as the homosexual irritant to the heterosexual; the Lucretian rub of chance that might be nature or might be nature as written and grafted: "It struck him that the seasons sometimes gain by being brought into the house, just as they gain by being brought into painting, and into poetry. The hand, fastidious and bold, which selected and placed—it was that which made the difference. In Nature there is no selection" (61).

If the professor's legacy from Tom is memory, it materializes in a diary written in his hand, even more in the hand itself as the focus of the professor's interest and revery. At first, turquoises in it, St. Peter looks instead at "the muscular, many-lined palm, the long, strong fingers with soft ends, the straight little finger, the flexible, beautifully shaped thumb that curved back from the rest of the hand as if it were its own master. What a hand!" (103). Contemplating what would have become of Tom had he survived the war and profited from his invention, it is the desecration of "his fine long hand with the backspringing thumb, which had never handled things that were not symbols of ideas" that the professor regards as what Tom has avoided by dying (236). If this is the choosing hand— the hand that refuses to be natural, the artistic hand—it is also evidently a sexual hand. The translation out of the vulgar and into the ideal and the symbolic is a sign of that, as Lewis teaches us by remarking how Cather registered the most personal through the most symbolic.[22] "Nice hands" (36), the professor comments to Lillian: the hand in Cather is not necessarily attached to a body of either gender; the professor's responsiveness to Tom and to Lillian focuses on an organ they both share.

Tom's hand or his manuscript (read only by St. Peter) in its anything but "florid style" are not the only sites for the transmission of the unspoken. There is also the blanket Tom gave the professor, Rodney Blake's blanket in which Tom had been wrapped when Roddy nursed him through pneumonia. Kathleen reads it as a symbol, like the cups passed between "*Amis* and *Amile*" (111), a token of identity that is also a sign of identification. The blanket functions as this legacy, and not simply in these immaterial terms. Louie characteristically seizes upon the purple blanket as a costume (144), but the professor wraps himself in it when he is chilly. "Nothing could part me from that blanket. . . . It was like his skin" (111). Like the token that passes between friends, the blanket doubles as Tom's body. This is how the professor sleeps with Tom, beneath his blanket/skin, or inside his book, divining the lode between the plain words on the page, fantasmatically grasping or being penetrated by the hand, the flexible thumb, springing in the back garden. Tom embodies these forms of transmissions. Tom-the-boy, the Tomboy of Cather's enchanted mesa. The blanket takes us from Tom and the professor to Tom and Roddy and to the scene of discovery.

As in "The Enchanted Bluff," with its "big red rock" that "no white man" has ever been atop, and which is the site of "a village way up there in the air,"[23] so, too, the "tantalizing" (170) sight of the Blue Mesa draws Tom and Roddy; they similarly plan to "be the first men up there," and "climbing the mesa" is their "staple topic of conversation" (166). The dream proves realizable after Tom has his unforgettable first sight of the cliff dwellings, a moment literally breathtaking: "In stopping to take breath, I happened to glance up at the canyon wall. I wish I could tell you what I saw there, just *as* I saw it, on that first morning, through a veil of lightly falling snow. Far up above me, a thousand feet or so, I saw a little city of stone, asleep" (179). Tom's first impulse is to keep secret what he has seen, and part of the powerful effect of the mesa and its city in the sky has to do with its being the locus of the kind of numinous secret to which Cather's art is devoted. The city is a site of perfect geometry, modernist harmony organized around a red tower. The symbolic architecture is, thus, one place toward which Cather's Dick drives. The rupture with Roddy is likewise to be explained by what the city in the cliffs keeps secret: "I never told him just how I felt about those things we'd dug out together, it was the kind of thing one doesn't talk about directly. But he must have known; he couldn't have lived with me all summer and fall without knowing" (216). The "things" are meant to be like the cups by which Amis and Amile recognized each other as ideal friends.[24]

As the symbolic site of the unspoken relationship between Tom and Roddy, it is the Blue Mesa that makes "gorgeous" their homo romance (to recall Sedgwick's description).[25] This is not to say that in itself that traces of romance cannot be read in Tom and Roddy's relationship. It can be seen in the way in which Tom reports himself entranced by this surly stranger in their midst ("I'd been interested in this fellow ever since he came on our division; he was close-mouthed and unfriendly" [161]), drawn back in fascination to rescue him from a poker game threatening to turn nasty; or in the scene in which he follows him from behind to his room where he strips him of the gold pouring out of his pockets and lying around his hips (162), finally seeing to the money being safely deposited in a bank. That this friendship is reciprocated is evident in the reversal that follows, as Roddy now tends the ailing Tom who had watched over him. Roddy quits his job for Tom, does his work for him, finally selling the "curios" and setting up an account in Tom's name so that he will be able to afford to go to college. If they are at first in a quasi-filial relationship (Blake calls Tom "kid" [163] and "son" [163], and Tom himself is the sad substitute he remarks [165]), they become a pair of "boys" (175), age difference erased by fraternity and friendship in an all-male family in which Henry Atkins does their cooking, cleaning, and interior decoration. From the start, Tom is drawn to Roddy by his strong silence, and they bond together over the unspoken mystery of the mesa. When Roddy turns it into cash, making that vulgar translation, the rift is opened. Cash makes the mesa a social site and one couched in terms of property and possession. Yet, once Roddy disappears down the hole, Tom comes into "possession" of the mesa (226), living in the cliff dwellings, doing his Latin. The contradiction here between the avowals of disinterest and the luxuriance of Tom's summer and fall "feeling that I had found everything, instead of having lost everything" (227) is perhaps built into the mesa's symbolic function as the site of unspeakable desire. Tom comes into himself there, without Roddy, much as the professor will come into himself alone in the closing pages of the book; but the mesa is also the locus of a series of sad substitutions and sublimations, not least in its lure of self-possession after betrayal and loss.

For it must be remarked how transitory that exultant moment of possession is; Tom remains haunted by the need to make restitution to Roddy; indeed, this sense of guilt has been passed on to the professor and to the family who keep up the search for Roddy. When Rosie and Kathleen play Tom and Roddy, they play a version of the relationship in which Roddy was "noble. He was always noble, noble Roddy!" (106). It is, of course, the Roddy that Tom has depicted for them. His betrayal of Roddy is perhaps a deeper betrayal than Roddy's—for Roddy had treated the "relics" as things to be sold for the sake of his friend; and his friend had insisted on a panoply of symbolic meanings—many of them, as he admits, invented on the spot (219)—to place the mesa and the ruins above their relationship.

This excruciating moment in the story—anything but adequately described as "nothing very incriminating, nothing very remarkable; a story of youthful defeat, the sort of thing a boy is sensitive about—until he grows older" (155)—suggests, I think the "double life" of this text, divided between the gorgeous mesa romance and the relations between characters. The cue to this doubleness is explicit in the "two lives" (19) of the professor, the division between his teaching and his writing that only begins to name the divides: between his upstairs and his downstairs life, between Tom and his family, between past and present with its strong homo and hetero cleavages. But even more to the point is the function of the "double life" as a recognizable term for gay life in the opening decades of the twentieth century, as George Chauncey has shown.[26] If the professor lives a double life, Cather's text could be said to be written in the kind of double language that Chauncey describes, one in which "common words" are given "a second meaning that would be readily recognized only by other gay men."[27] Cather's double language is perhaps a bit more private (the "personal myth" that Harrell invokes), but not entirely so. If the mesa and the lost civilization resonate so deeply for her, it does in part because of a classical echo (Anasazi pots are said to be identical to Greek ones). The organizing red tower almost requires no comment; nor, perhaps, the "back court-yard" with its wall "like the sloping roof of an attic" (186). That rear space connects the Cliff City to the professor's study, his "shadowy crypt at the top of the house" (94), with its window and its view of Lake Michigan always inviting like an open door; it connects thus to his back garden—and to Tom: "one seemed to catch glimpses of an unusual background behind his shoulders" (112). Guarding against the drift of this reading is the remarkably pure water deep in the cave. Or, perhaps, that purifies these dark desires. The cave is on the divide, a "twilit space"; "there was perpetual twilight back there" (186), Cather repeats. In the end, the professor comes into the "twilight stage" (239) he had not had before.

"Twilight" is a key term in describing the allure of the mesa, seen over and again in the purple and gold of the fading sun, and it is also the term that leaps out as a recognizable piece of the double language that Chauncey details. Andre Tellier's *Twilight Men* (1931), for instance, makes explicit the code, just as the title of Lillian Faderman's *Odd Girls and Twilight Lovers* draws on it as well.[28] Indeed, it is a small stretch from her "odd girls" to Blair Niles's *Strange Brother* (1931).[29] That novel locates its twilight man, the "half-man" Mark Thornton (153), in a "shadow world" (the phrase recurs) in which he lives half of his double life. The "tribe" that makes him sick (50) is populated with rouged and marcelled boys with names like Pansy and Nelly; he draws solace from knowing that Native Americans had their half-men (307), from defenses of gay love by Carpenter and Ellis that go back to the Greeks, and from the possibility of being more natural and open among the "citizens" of Harlem where a number of scenes of the novel are set. Mark identifies with the suffering of Blacks (the connection is thematized in the novel by the scientist Irwin Hesse, who links black, Latin, and European cultures together in their acceptance of so-called abnormals [184]), but especially with June West-brook, the white journalist who sympathetically responds to him and his plight (she is also able to slip under the skin of various black women in the course of the novel, one explicitly lesbian). If the novel attempts to understand a "brotherhood" that transcends homo/heterosexual division, it does so largely through its movements across racial and gendered difference. June and Mark bond over their love problems, although June never tells Mark that Palmer Fleming, her first husband (a kind of Gilbert Osmond figure), was gay, something she discovers in the course of the novel when she sees him at a Harlem drag ball clothed in Venetian garb with a companion "in the dress of a woman of the Turkish harem" (217). Nor does she tell Mark about her frustrations with her current lover, Seth Vaughan, who dies in an airplane crash never having consummated their relationship. From Beulah, her Caribbean maid, she comes to understand that Seth was the kind of man who could go through with a consummated heterosexual relationship only once in his life; she has come to him too late. If Seth, in these ways, seems a bit like St. Peter, the explanation for him lies in the novel's depiction of a homo/hetero continuum that ranges from the confirmed queer cases like Mark along a sliding scale that includes Palmer Fleming and Seth. While Mark repudiates feminine identification, the novel also depends upon cross-gender identification. But, as in *The Professor's House*, it can scarcely imagine for its hero the possibility of a sustained male-male relationship. Mark pines for a real man and learns from a boyhood mentor that he must pursue his art (Mark draws) as a way of overcoming and sublimating his desire. Mark's Midwest mentor is named Tom Burden, Cather's Tom and her Jim Burden (the narrator of *My Ántonia*) conflated. Not that this is the only possible Cather allusion; did she choose to name Marsellus after the hairstyle of pansies? Or to dress him à la Turque in the professor's little pageant for much the same reason that Palmer Fleming's date is so attired? Or to think of Louie as black (as Othello, the "extravagant and wheeling stranger of here and everywhere") when the professor, in the position of Brabantio, imagines he has lost his daughter (or, more likely, his Tom) to him?[30]

In asking these questions, I mean merely to indicate some of the ways in which Niles's "knowing" novel could be read as kind of vulgar translation of Cather's. But also for the ways in which it perhaps points one back to certain almost explicit translations in Cather. These crystallize around the figure who bears another form of the overdetermined masculine name, Rodney Blake—Roddy, for short. If the professor sees in Tom the embodiment of "the dream of self-sacrificing friendship and disinterested love down among the day-labourers" (151), those are qualities he derives from Roddy, as Tom insists in his descriptions of him as a typical workingman (161, 164). Blake's radical politics—his support of the Chicago anarchists massacred in the 1886 Haymarket Riots and his Dreyfusard position—are not Tom's, however, but may well have been Cather's (an early piece of journalism was pro-Dreyfus).[31] As Chauncey argues in *Gay New York*, the most vibrant instances of gay culture (or, more accurately, of the acceptance of same-sex desire) flourished in working-class culture in the early twentieth century. It is what makes for the same-sex family on the mesa, with its hobo figure of Henry and the railroad workers Tom and Roddy. When Roddy puts his friend above his country, he enunciates a workingman's ethos, or speaks from a position of disenfranchisement that might also attach to unjustly condemned Jews like Dreyfus (or Louie?), or to excoriated "abnormals" (anarchists were, of course, associated with free love if not usually with same-sex couplings).[32] So, when Tom attempts to link the artefacts of Anasazi civilization to his ancestry (he is, pointedly, an orphan without familial ties) or to his country (his surname suggests he has none), he seeks various forms of legitimization for and sublimations of the meaning of those objects in his relation with Roddy; but more—as his sacrifice to the Great War conveys—Tom embraces these values *to his death* as a denial of the bond of friendship and love with Roddy.

This is not the first time that Roddy has been "unlucky in personal relations" (164); it is, rather, his life's story, "skinned" by his friends, "double-
crossed" by the girl he was to have married (164). The latter double-cross
is writ large across the mesa, with its presumptively adulterous mummy
dubbed Mother Eve, and across Cather's novel with its misogynist hostility so often on the lips and in the thoughts of the professor. It is that
which has made The Professor's House difficult for many of its readers, and
which might give pause to the kinds of translations this essay has been
suggesting, the routes of painful identification across gender and sexuality to the nomination of Cather in the masculine. I don't know whether
it helps to recall that the professor has a moment of almost inarticulate
bonding with Lillian in the novel—"You, you too?" (78)—that suggests
that she was as unsuited to the heterosexual life as he was (and which
would make just a bit less malignant his fantasy of being shipwrecked
in all-male company [79]); or to note that the professor thinks of his life-
work as a piece of weaving not unlike that of Queen Mathilde (85); or to
recall that when Tom meets him for the first time and recites his Virgil,
he speaks the words of Aeneas to this demanding Dido; or to note that
at the bottom of his box-couch the seamstress Augusta's patterns and
his manuscripts "interpenetrated" (13). I do think it worth pausing over
Augusta, too often treated as a figure of maternal rescue and reconciliation in the novel, since she is there at the novel's end to save St. Peter
from his Ophelia-like suicide. Augusta, when she first appears, is called
a spinster (8). So would Cather have been called. About the only thing
St. Peter wants to know from her is about the Magnificat, a piece of
female writing celebrating pregnancy without having sex with a man. It
might be the fantasy form that solves the question of natural and unnatural graftings in the novel; it attaches them in this instance to the rough,
unsentimental hand of Augusta, and to the virgin's pen. At any rate, it
suggests that the animus against women in the novel is more pointedly
against married, procreative, heterosexual women, against the "cruel biological necessities" (13) they embody even when abstracted to the dummy
forms of the professor's attic space shared with Augusta. The professor's
female-identified moments, or his bonding with Augusta, arguably hint
at a potential movement across gender and sexuality, and in the direction
of Cather and Edith Lewis.

For if one had to name the scene that lies behind or that translates the
romance of the mesa, its "bluish rock" as seen "under the unusual purple-
grey of the sky," as the valley turns "lavender and pale gold" (178), that perpetual backlit twilight scene, the "sunset colour" dousing the valley while
"the mesa was one great ink-black rock against a sky on fire" (171), perhaps
it is here, in Edith Lewis's understated yet gorgeous prose: "The four or

five hours we spent waiting there were, I think, for Willa Cather the most rewarding of our whole trip to the Mesa Verde. There was a large flat rock at the mouth of Cliff Canyon, and we settled ourselves on this rock. . . . We did not talk, but watched the long summer twilight come on, and the full moon rise up over the rim of the canyon. The place was very beautiful."³³

NOTES

1 Willa Cather, "The Novel Démeublé," in *Not Under Forty* (1992; Lincoln: University of Nebraska Press, 1988), p. 50. The paragraph reads: "Whatever is felt upon the page without being specifically named there—that, one might say, is created. It is the inexplicable presence of the thing not named, of the overtone divined by the ear but not heard by it, the verbal mood, the emotional aura of the fact or thing or the deed, that gives high quality to the novel or the drama, as well as to poetry itself." This citation serves as the epigraph for Sharon O'Brien's "'The Thing Not Named': Willa Cather as a Lesbian Writer," *Signs* 9 (1984): 576–99.

2 Eve Kosofsky Sedgwick, "Across Gender, Across Sexuality: Willa Cather and Others," *South Atlantic Quarterly* 88, no. 1 (1989): 53–72 (reprinted as "Willa Cather and Others," in Sedgwick, *Tendencies* [Durham, N.C.: Duke University Press, 1993], pp. 167–76); and Judith Butler, "'Dangerous Crossing': Willa Cather's Masculine Names," in *Bodies That Matter: On the Discursive Limits of "Sex."* (New York: Routledge, 1993), pp. 143–66.

3 On Niles and other novels of the 1930s, see Roger Austen, *Playing the Game: The Homosexual Novel in America* (Indianapolis: Bobbs-Merrill, 1977), pp. 57–92. As Austen notes, in the twenties Niles wrote such books as *Casual Wanderings in Ecuador* and *Condemned to Devil's Island*. These suggest the degree to which her interest in the question of homosexuality was anthropological and journalistic; however, it should be mentioned that *Condemned to Devil's Island* (New York: Harcourt, Brace, 1928), which, like *Strange Brother*, is motivated by a liberal argument (in this case, a recognition of the humanity of those sent to Devil's Island, and a condemnation of their inhumane treatment), describes the system of male-male sex in the prison. While the attitude taken can be rather heterosexualizing (e.g., "In the womanless world of the Guiana prisons the men who satisfy Adam's desire for Eve are called *momes*" [53 n]; "that strange love-making which is the prison substitute for nature" [130]), Niles can be quite sympathetic in her portrayal of the tattooed tough guys with their "brats." Her protagonist Michel has forsworn such relations, however, and they are not central to the novel's story of the crushing of his spirit.

4 David Harrell, "Willa Cather's Mesa Verde Myth," *Cather Studies* 1 (1990): 130–43; citing p. 130. Harrell extends his arguments in *From Mesa Verde to The Professor's House* (Albuquerque: University of New Mexico Press, 1992). Richard Wetherill's first sighting has been disputed by his brother Al; see Maurine S. Fletcher, ed., *The Wetherills of the Mesa Verde* (Lincoln: University of Nebraska Press, 1977), esp. part 2. (The book is a version of Al Wetherill's autobiographical papers.)

5 The essay is reprinted in Susan J. Rosowski and Bernice Slote, "Willa Cather's 1916 Mesa Verde Essay: The Genesis of *The Professor's House*," *Prairie Schooner* 58, no. 4 (1984): 81–92; "On *The Professor's House*" is included in *Willa Cather on Writing* (Lincoln: University of Nebraska Press, 1988), pp. 30–33.

6 Willa Cather, "On *The Professor's House*," p. 32.

7 Harrell, "Willa Cather's Mesa Verde Myth," p. 140.

8 Ibid., p. 141 n. 6.

9 He seems always to be Richard in the biographical account offered by Frank McNitt, *Richard Wetherill: Anasazi* (Albuquerque: University of New Mexico Press, 1957); in the reminiscences of his wife compiled by Kathryn Gabriel, *Marietta Wetherill* (Boulder, Colo.: Johnson Books, 1992); in his brother Al's autobiographical writings.

   As I note in an unpublished essay, "Photographic Relations: Willa Cather, Laura Gilpin," the same "mistake" about the name can be found in Laura Gilpin, *The Pueblos: A Camera Chronicle* (New York: Hastings House, 1941), p. 34, and, as I argue there, the mistake resonates with Gilpin's sexuality and with her desire to see an edition of *The Professor's House* illustrated with her Mesa Verde photographs.

10 Edith Lewis, *Willa Cather Living: A Personal Record* (1953; Athens: Ohio University Press, 1989), pp. 94–95.

11 Ibid., p. 97.

12 Sharon O'Brien, *Willa Cather: The Emerging Voice* (New York: Fawcett Columbine, 1987), for instance, while certainly aware of the importance of Lewis's role in Cather's life, nonetheless complains that "one doesn't learn much about this relationship from Lewis' cautious memoir" (p. 354). In her "Foreword" to *Willa Cather Living*, Marilyn Arnold is rather circumspect about the personal relationship of the two women, but acute in noting how the book shows "the merging of one mind and life into that of another" (p. xxiii).

13 Lewis, *Willa Cather Living*, p. 137.

14 See Leon Edel, "A Cave of One's Own," in *Stuff of Sleep and Dreams* (New York: Harper and Row, 1982), p. 238. Edel's broader psychological reading of the novel I find quite unconvincing in its recourse to themes of regression and maternal domination.

15 Lewis, *Willa Cather Living*, p. 130.

16 Doris Grumbach, "A Study of the Small Room in *The Professor's House*," *Women's Studies* 11 (1984): 327–45; citing p. 339. Grumbach's recognition of the homoerotics of the relationship is welcome, of course, and not something most critics notice, nor would I deny Cather's identification with St. Peter, the most telling sign of which, in this context, is the fact that the study that Isabelle McClung earlier provided for Cather in her Pittsburgh house was a room, like the professor's, shared with a seamstress.

   While one might assume that O'Brien's groundbreaking work on Cather would have initiated a developing literature on the significance of Cather's sexuality, such has not been the case, save for a few exceptions. While things are perhaps not as dire as when Joanna Russ published an essay on Cather's lesbianism in 1986 ("To Write 'Like a Woman': Transformations of Identity in the Work of Willa Cather," reprinted and revised in Russ, *To Write Like a Woman* [Bloomington: Indiana University Press 1995], where Russ details her difficulty in placing the essay), it is certainly a sign of the times when Joan Acocella, writing in *The New Yorker* (27 November 1995), excoriates most feminist and gay affirmative criticism of Cather, but endorses Russ, precisely because she can take, from its account of a closeted writing practice, the opportunity to practice what Eve Kosofsky Sedgwick has summarized as the strategy of (un)knowingness that reduces to "Don't ask. Or, less laconically: You shouldn't know" (*Epistemology of the Closet* [Berkeley: University of California, 1990], p. 52). Acocella affirms that Cather was a lesbian, but that she never had lesbian sex, and that her sexuality therefore has nothing to do with her success as a writer. Acocella's essay, while claiming to be doing nothing more than rescuing Cather from the ideological extremes and flattening aims of her critics, is an exercise in a familiar "populist" anti-intellectualism.

17 Harrell, "Willa Cather's Mesa Verde Myth," p. 138.

18 Willa Cather, *The Professor's House* (1925; New York: Vintage, 1990), p. 239. Further citations to this work will be given parenthetically in the text.

19 It also explains Kathleen's otherwise unmotivated assurance to Scott that he is "the real one" (93) after they witness a scene in which Rosie seems to betray some feeling for Outland; the assurance concludes an elliptical conversation that may suggest that Scott knew that there was Tom before he came along, and before Kathleen lost him to her sister.

20 On that episode, see Sedgwick, "Across Gender, Across Sexuality," pp. 62–63. Similar energies are deployed in *The Professor's House* against St. Peter's rival colleague Horace Langtry, derisively named "Lily" (41) and "Madame" (43). Langtry seems akin to the professor of "The Professor's Commencement," and his doubled relationship to St. Peter is a sign of an attempted splitting of the professor, just as Louie and Tom serve as alter egos. On the possibilities of mobilizing anti-Semitism for antigay purposes, see Daniel Boyarin, "Freud's Baby, Fliess's Maybe: Homophobia, Anti-Semitism, and the Invention of Oedipus," *GLQ* 2 (1995): 115–47. For a reading of Louie in terms consonant with the ones that I provide, see Julie Abraham, *Are Girls Necessary?* (New York: Routledge, 1996), p. 51; Abraham's chapter on Cather, which appeared after I wrote this essay, attempts important connections between her representations of homosexuality and heterosexuality, of male-male and lesbian identifications facilitated by the figure of the "boy," and attends, in its pages on *The Professor's House*, to the relationships between Tom and Roddy as well as between Tom and St. Peter.

21 Hermione Lee, *Willa Cather: Double Lives* (New York: Vintage, 1989), p. 241.

22 One of the most extraordinary descriptions of the hand can be found in "Neighbour Rosicky" (Willa Cather, *Stories, Poems, and Other Writings* [New York: Library of America, 1992], p. 616); I owe to Judith Butler, and her "The Lesbian Phallus and the Morphological Imaginary" (in *Bodies That Matter*), the warrant for thinking about hands in this sexual fashion. I have also been implying that in this confluence of hand and back garden, Cather may share with her mentor Henry James a rich anal erotics. On this in James, see Eve Kosofsky Sedgwick, "Is the Rectum Straight?: Identification and Identity in *The Wings of The Dove*," in *Tendencies* (Durham: Duke University Press, 1993). On Cather's anal erotics, see the forthcoming essay by Michèle Aina Barale in her *Below the Belt*.

23 "The Enchanted Bluff," in Willa Cather, *Twenty-Four Stories*, ed. Sharon O'Brien (New York: Penguin/Meridian, 1987), p. 255.

24 This suggests that Native American civilization may have served something of the same function for Cather as it provided a site for homosexual projection in Hart Crane; on this, see Jared Gardner, "'Our Native Clay': Racial and Sexual Identity and the Making of Americans in *The Bridge*," *American Quarterly* 44, no. 1 (1992): 24–50.

25 Sedgwick, "Across Gender, Across Sexuality," p. 68.

26 George Chauncey, *Gay New York: Gender, Urban Culture, and the Making of the Gay Male World, 1890–1940* (New York: Basic Books, 1994), pp. 6–7, 273–80, 375 n. 8. It is, of course, ironic that Hermione Lee subtitles her book "Double Lives" without registering the salience of that term in this context.

27 Chauncey, *Gay New York*, p. 286.

28 Lillian Faderman, *Odd Girls and Twilight Lovers* (New York: Penguin, 1991). While Faderman alludes to the title of a 1950s lesbian novel, the term "twilight" has both gay male and lesbian currency in the 1920s and 1930s.

29 Blair Niles, *Strange Brother* (1931; London: Gay Men's Press, 1991). Further citations to this work will be given parenthetically in the text.

30 See Cather, *The Professor's House*, pp. 59–60, for the pageant of the sons-in-law, Louie in "a green dressing gown and turban," Scott attired like Richard Plantagenet (giving a crusading excuse for Scott's anti-Semitism, as well as pointing to the kind of possible homo resonance Sedgwick notes in the *Berengaria* ["Across Gender, Across Sexuality," p. 71]; p. 233 for the allusion to *Othello* 1.1.135, which suggests the further parallel between Tom's storytelling and the Moor's.

31 See Lee, *Willa Cather: Double Lives*, p. 251, who also reads Roddy sympathetically; as she notes, he is "an unusual figure in Cather's work, a radical working man," although I think much of what his "workingman" status conveys is often the work of immigrant culture in other Cather novels and stories—those Bohemians who may encode another form of *la vie boheme* as well (Cather herself was a Greenwich Village denizen, of course). As Lee puts it, Roddy's "personal tenderness has led him, in Forster's phrase, to betray his country rather than his friend; Tom's idealism makes him betray his friend in the interests of his country." What I think requires more thought here— and why I am not convinced by arguments like those of Walter Benn Michaels in "The Souls of White Folks" (in *Literature and the Body*, ed. Elaine Scarry [Baltimore: Johns Hopkins University Press, 1988]), and in "Race into Culture: A Critical Genealogy of Cultural Identity," *Critical Inquiry* 18, no. 4 (1992): 655–85, or in "The Vanishing American," *American Literary History* 2, no. 2 (1990): 220–41, Michaels's application of the race-into-culture argument to *The Professor's House*—is the degree to which the evocation of national culture is to be taken straight or simply as Cather's political position. It is certainly the case that Cather opposed melting-pot models for the assimilation of immigrants, but she did so from an aversion to "turning them into stupid replicas of smug American citizens" (*Willa Cather in Person* [Lincoln: University of Nebraska Press, 1966], p. 71, from a 1924 *New York Times* interview), which suggests that American citizenship may have not been as central to Cather as Michaels seems to believe. In "Affect-Genealogy: Feeling and Affiliation in Willa Cather" (*American Literature* 69, no. 1 [1997]: 5–37), Christopher Nealon shows how "Cather assembled a lesbian strategy for imagining an America in which feeling, not family, would be the basis of affiliation" (p. 11). Such an argument wrests "culture" from "ideology" and makes valuable and valued space for sexuality and affect.

32 Whether Cather made the connection always implicit in Proust, of anti-Dreyfus sentiment and homophobia, is possible. On this point, see Abraham, *Are Girls Necessary?*, pp. 50–51, 187 n. 14.

33 Lewis, *Willa Cather Living*, p. 97.

BIBLIOGRAPHY

Abel, Elizabeth. *Virginia Woolf and the Fictions of Psychoanalysis*. Chicago: University of Chicago Press, 1989.

Abraham, Julie. *Are Girls Necessary?* New York: Routledge, 1996.

Acton, William. *The Functions and Disorders of the Reproductive Organs in Childhood, Youth, Adult Age, and Advanced Life Considered in Their Physiological, Social, and Moral Relations*. Philadelphia: Lindsay and Blakiston, 1875.

Adams, James Eli. *Dandies and Desert Saints: Styles of Victorian Manhood*. Ithaca, N.Y.: Cornell University Press, 1995.

Adorno, Theodor W. *Minima Moralia: Reflections from Damaged Life*. Translated by E. F. N. Jephcott. London: Verso, 1974.

———. "On Proust." In *Notes to Literature*, translated by Shierry Weber Nicholsen. Vol. 2. New York: Columbia University Press, 1992.

———. "Short Commentaries on Proust." In *Notes to Literature*, translated by Shierry Weber Nicholsen. Vol. 1. New York: Columbia University Press, 1991.

"AIDS and the Arts: A Lost Generation." *Newsweek*, 18 January 1993, pp. 16–20.

Ailey, Alvin, and Peter Bailey. *Revelations: The Autobiography of Alvin Ailey*. New York: Routledge, 1993.

Anderson, Benedict. *Imagined Communities: Reflections on the Origin and Spread of Nationalism*. Rev. ed. London: Verso, 1991.

Apter, Emily, and William Pietz, eds. *Fetishism as Cultural Discourse*. Ithaca, N.Y.: Cornell University Press, 1993.

Armstrong, Nancy. *Desire and Domestic Fiction: A Political History of the Novel*. New York: Oxford University Press, 1987.

Arnaud, André-Jean. *Essai d'analyse structurale du code civil français. La Règle du jeu dans la paix bourgeoise*. Paris: R. Pichon et R. Durand-Auzias, 1973.

Arnold, Marilyn. Foreword to *Willa Cather Living*, by Edith Lewis. New York: Knopf, 1953.

Auden, W. H. "An Improbable Life." In *Forewords and Afterwords*, edited by Edward Mendelson. New York: Vintage, 1973.

Austen, Roger. *Playing the Game: The Homosexual Novel in America*. Indianapolis: Bobbs-Merrill, 1977.

Baker, Houston. *Modernism and the Harlem Renaissance*. Chicago: University of Chicago Press, 1987.

Baldwin, James. *Giovanni's Room*. New York: Laurel, 1956.

Balzac, Honoré de. *La Comédie humaine*. Edited by Pierre-Georges Castex. Vol. 7. Paris: Gallimard (Pléiade), 1977.

———. *Cousin Bette*. Translated by Marion Ayton Crawford. Harmondsworth, England: Penguin, 1965.

———. *Cousin Pons*. Translated by Herbert J. Hunt. Harmondsworth, England: Penguin, 1968.

Banton, Michael. *Racial Theories*. New York: Cambridge University Press, 1987.

Barale, Michèle Aina. *Below the Belt*. Forthcoming.

Bardèche, Maurice. *Marcel Proust romancier*. 2 vols. Paris: Les Sept couleurs, 1971.

Barrett, Michèle. "*A Room of One's Own* and *Three Guineas*." In *Virginia Woolf: Introductions to the Major Works*, edited by Julia Briggs, pp. 349–394. London: Virago Press, 1994.

Barthes, Roland. *Mythologies*. Translated by Annette Lavers. New York: Hill and Wang, 1957; New York: Noonday Press, 1972.

———. "The Reality Effect." In *French Literary Theory Today: A Reader*, edited by Tzvetan Todorov, translated by R. Carter, pp. 11–17. Cambridge: Cambridge University Press, 1982.

Baudrillard, Jean. *For a Critique of the Political Economy of the Sign*. Translated by Charles Levin. St. Louis: Telos Press, 1981.

———. *Simulations*. New York: Semiotext(e), 1983.

Bell, Quentin. *Bloomsbury*. New edition. London: Weidenfeld and Nicolson, 1986.

———. *Virginia Woolf: A Biography*. 2 vols. New York: Harcourt, Brace, Jovanovich, 1972.

Beller, Steven. *Herzl*. New York: Grove Weidenfeld, 1991.

Benjamin, Walter. *Illuminations*. Edited by Hannah Arendt. Translated by Harry Zohn. New York: Schocken, 1969.

———. *The Origin of German Tragic Drama*. Translated by John Osborne. London: Verso, 1977.

Berlant, Lauren. "National Brands/National Body: *Imitation of Life*." In *Comparative American Identities: Race, Sex, and Nationality in the Modern Text*, edited by Hortense Spillers (New York: Routledge, 1995).

Berman, Marshall. *All That Is Solid Melts into Air*. New York: Simon and Schuster, 1982.

Bersani, Leo. *The Culture of Redemption*. Cambridge, Mass.: Harvard University Press, 1990.

———. *Marcel Proust: The Fictions of Life and Art*. New York: Oxford University Press, 1965.

Bieri, Peter. "Thinking Machines: Some Reflections on the Turing Test." *Poetics Today* 9, no. 1 (1988): 163–86.

Bon, Michel, and Antoine d'Arc. *Rapport sur l'homosexualité de l'homme*. Paris: Editions Universitaires, 1974.

Bourdieu, Pierre. *Outline of a Theory of Practice*. Translated by Richard Nice. Cambridge, England: University of Cambridge Press, 1977.

Bowlby, Rachel. *Shopping with Freud*. London: Routledge, 1993.

———. "Who's Framing Virginia Woolf?" *diacritics*. (summer–fall 1991): 3–10.

Boyarin, Daniel. "Freud's Baby, Fliess's Maybe: Homophobia, Anti-Semitism, and the Invention of Oedipus." *GLQ* 2 (1995): 115–47.

Breines, Paul. *Tough Jews: Political Fantasies and the Moral Dilemma of American Jewry*. New York: Basic Books, 1990.

Brett, Philip, Elizabeth Wood, and Gary C. Thomas, eds. *Queering the Pitch: The New Gay and Lesbian Musicology*. New York and London: Routledge, 1994.

Brewer, Elisabeth. *T. H. White's The Once and Future King*. Cambridge, England: D. S. Brewer, 1993.

Brooks, Richard. *The Brick Foxhole*. New York: Harper, 1945.

Bruckman, Amy. "Identity Workshop: Emergent Social and Psychological Phenomena in Text-Based Virtual Reality." Internet ftp location: parcftp.xerox.com /pub/MOO/papers/ identity-workshop.* (1992):35.

Burt, Ramsay. *The Male Dancer: Bodies, Spectacle, Sexualities*. New York: Routledge, 1995.

Butler, Judith. "Against Proper Objects." *differences* 6, nos. 2–3 (1994): 1–26.

———. *Bodies That Matter: On The Discursive Limits of "Sex."* New York: Routledge, 1993.

———. "Critically Queer." *GLQ* 1 (1993): 17–32.

———. *Gender Trouble: Feminism and the Subversion of Identity*. New York: Routledge, 1990.

Butler, Marilyn. *Maria Edgeworth: A Literary Biography*. Oxford: Clarendon Press, 1972.

Caldwell, Gail. Review of *Beloved*, by Toni Morrison. *Boston Globe*, 6 October 1987, pp. 67–68.

Carpenter, Edward. *The Intermediate Sex: A Study of Some Transitional Types of Men and Women*. New York and London: Mitchell Kennerly, 1912.

———. *Intermediate Types among Primitive Folk: A Study in Social Evolution*. London: George Allen and Unwin, 1919. Reprint, New York: Arno Press, 1975.

———. *Love's Coming-of-Age*. New York: The Modern Library, 1918.

Carpenter, Humphrey. *Benjamin Britten*. New York: Charles Scribner's Sons, 1992.

Carpenter, Mary Wilson. "'Bit of Her Flesh': Circumcision and 'The Signification of the Phallus' in *Daniel Deronda*." *Genders* 1 (1988): 1–23.

Cather, Willa. "The Enchanted Bluff." In *Twenty-Four Stories*, edited by Sharon O'Brien. New York: Penguin/Meridian, 1987.

———. "Neighbour Rosicky." In *Stories, Poems, and Other Writings*. New York: Library of America, 1992.

———. "The Novel Demeuble." In *Not Under Forty*. 1922. Reprint, Lincoln: University of Nebraska Press, 1988.

———. "On *The Professor's House*." In *Willa Cather on Writing*, pp. 30–33. Lincoln: University of Nebraska Press, 1988.

———. *The Professor's House*. 1925. Reprint, New York: Vintage, 1990.

———. *Willa Cather in Person*. Lincoln: University of Nebraska Press, 1966.

Chase, Cynthia. "The Decomposition of the Elephants: Double-Reading *Daniel Deronda*." *PMLA* 93 (1978): 215–27.

Chauncey, George. *Gay New York: Gender, Urban Culture, and the Making of the Gay Male World, 1890–1940*. New York: Basic Books, 1994.

Cherny, Lynn. "Gender Differences in Text-Based Virtual Reality." Internet ftp location: parcftp.xerox.com /pub/MOO/papers/GenderMOO.* (1994).

Cixous, Hélène. "Rethinking Differences: An Interview." In *Homosexualities and French Literature: Cultural Contexts/Critical Texts*, edited by George Stambolian and Elaine Marks, pp. 7–86. Ithaca, N.Y.: Cornell University Press, 1979.

Clark, Timothy. "The Turing Test as a Novel Form of Hermeneutics." *International Studies in Philosophy* 24, no. 1 (1989): 17–31.

Cleaver, Eldridge. *Soul on Ice*. New York: Laurel, 1968.

"Cloning: Where Do We Draw the Line?" *Time*, 8 November 1993, pp. 65–69.

Cobb, William S., ed. *Plato's Erotic Dialogues*. Albany: State University of New York Press, 1993.

Cole, Clarence Bard. "Other Voices, Other Rooms: An Interview with Melvin Dixon." *Christopher Street* (May 1991): 27.

Colette. *The Pure and the Impure*. Translated by Herma Briffault. New York: Farrar, Straus and Giroux, 1966.

Concise Columbia Dictionary of Quotations. Microsoft Bookshelf, 1992.

Constant, Benjamin. *Adolphe*. In *Adolphe and the Red Note-Book*. Translated by Carl Wildman. 1948. Reprint, London: Hamish Hamilton, 1959.

———. *Adolphe*. In *Oeuvres de Benjamin Constant*. Vol. 6. Paris: Editions de la Pléiade, Gallimard, 1957.

———. *Oeuvres de Benjamin Constant*. Paris: Editions de la Pléiade, Gallimard, 1957.

Cook, Blanche Wiesen. "Women Alone Stir My Imagination: Lesbianism and the Cultural Tradition." *Signs* 4, no. 4 (summer 1979): 718–39.

Cook, David A. *A History of Narrative Film*. New York: W. W. Norton, 1981.

Courouve, Claude. *Vocabulaire de l'homosexualité masculine*. Paris: Payot, 1985.

Creech, James. *Closet Writing/Gay Reading*. Chicago: University of Chicago Press, 1993.

Crosby, Christina. "George Eliot's Apocalypse of History." In *The Ends of History: Victorians and 'The Woman Question'*, pp. 12–43. New York: Routledge, 1991.

Crossfire. Directed by Edward Dmytryk. RKO Radio Pictures.

Crouzet, Michel. *Nature et société chez Stendhal: la révolte romantique*. Villeneuve d'Ascq: Presses universitaires de Lille, 1985.

Culler, Jonathan. *Structuralist Poetics: Structuralism, Linguistics and the Study of Literature*. Ithaca, N.Y.: Cornell University Press, 1975.

Curtis, Pavel. "Mudding: Social Phenomena in Text-Based Virtual Realities." Internet ftp location: parcftp.xerox.com /pub/MOO/papers/DIAC92.* (1992):6.

"Cyberspace: The Software That Will Take You There." *Business Week*, 27 February 1995, pp. 78–86.

Davenport, John. *Curiositates Eroticae Physiologiae, or Tabooed Subjects Freely Treated*. London, 1875. Reprinted in *Aphrodisiacs and Love Stimulants*, edited by Alan Hull Walton. New York: Lyle Stuart, 1966.

Davis, Angela. "Reflections on the Black Woman's Role in the Community of Slaves." *Black Scholar* 3, no. 4 (December 1971): 2–15.

Dawkins, Richard. *The Selfish Gene*. New York: Oxford University Press, 1989.

Day, Thomas. *The History of Sanford and Merton*. New York: The World Publishing House, 1875.

de Crébillon, Claude-Prosper. *Oeuvres complètes*. 2 vols. Geneva: Slatkine, 1968.

de Saussure, Ferdinand. *Course in General Linguistics*. Edited by Charles Bally and Albert Sechehaye. Translated by Wade Baskin. New York: McGraw-Hill, 1966.

DeBord, Guy. *Society of the Spectacle*. Detroit: Black and Red Press, 1973.

Deleuze, Gilles. *The Deleuze Reader*. Edited by Constantin V. Boundas. New York: Columbia University Press, 1993.

———. *The Fold*. Translated by Tom Conley. Minneapolis: University of Minnesota Press, 1993.

———. *Masochism*. Translated by Jean McNeil. New York: Zone Books, 1988, 1989, 1991.

———. *Proust et les signes*. Paris: Presses Universitaires de France, 1976.

Deleuze, Gilles, and Félix Guattari. *Anti-Oedipus: Capitalism and Schizophrenia*. Translated by Robert Hurley et al. Preface by Michel Foucault. Minneapolis: University of Minnesota Press, 1983.

———. *A Thousand Plateaus*. Trans. Brian Massumi. Minneapolis: University of Minnesota Press, 1987.

D'Emelio, John. *Sexual Politics, Sexual Communities: The Making of the Homosexual Minority in the United States, 1940–1970*. Chicago: University of Chicago Press, 1983.

D'Emelio, John, and Estelle B. Freedman. *Intimate Matters: A History of Sexuality in America*. New York: Harper and Row, 1988.

Dennett, Daniel C. "Can Machines Think." In *How We Know*, edited by Michael Shafto, pp. 121–45. San Francisco: Harper and Row, 1985.

——. *Consciousness Explained*. Boston: Little, Brown, 1991.

Derrida, Jacques. *Dissemination*. Translated by Barbara Johnson. Chicago: University of Chicago Press, 1981.

——. *Glas*. Translated by John P. Leavey, Jr. and Richard Rand. Lincoln. London: University of Nebraska Press, 1986.

——. *Of Grammatology*. Translated by Gayatri Spivak. Baltimore: Johns Hopkins University Press, 1976.

——. "Letter to Jean Genet." Unpublished. 1971.

——. *Margins of Philosophy*. Translated by Alan Bass. Chicago: University of Chicago Press, 1982.

——. *Spurs*. Translated by Barbara Harlow. Chicago: University of Chicago Press, 1979.

——. *Writing and Difference*. Translated by Alan Bass. Chicago: University of Chicago Press, 1978.

Deleuze, Gilles. *Negotiations: 1972–1990*. Translated by Martin Joughin. New York: Columbia University Press, 1995.

Descombes, Vincent. *Proust: Philosophy of the Novel*. Translated by Catherine Chance Macksey. Stanford, Calif.: Stanford University Press, 1992.

Dickens, Charles. *American Notes*. 1842. Reprint, Gloucester, Mass.: Peter Smith, 1968.

Dixon, Melvin. *Vanishing Rooms*. New York: Plume, 1991.

Dollimore, Jonathan. *Sexual Dissidence: Augustine to Wilde, Freud to Foucault*. Oxford: Oxford University Press, 1991.

Doubrovsky, Serge. *Writing and Fantasy in Proust: La Place de la Madeleine*. Translated by Carol Mastrangelo Bové and Paul A. Bové. Lincoln: University of Nebraska Press, 1986.

Dover, Kenneth. *Greek Homosexuality*. Cambridge: Cambridge University Press, 1978.

Dyer, Richard. *The Matter of Images*. New York: Routledge, 1993.

Eberly, David. "Taking It All Out: Homosexual Disclosure in Woolf." In *Virginia Woolf: Themes and Variations. Selected Papers from the Second Annual Conference on Virginia Woolf*, edited by Vara Neverow-Turk and Mark Hussey, pp. 128–34. New York: Pace University Press, 1993.

Edel, Leon. "A Cave of One's Own." In *Stuff of Sleep and Dreams*. New York: Harper and Row, 1982.

Edelman, Lee. *Homographesis: Essays in Gay Literary and Cultural Theory*. New York: Routledge, 1994.

——. "Piss Elegant: Freud, Hitchcock, and the Micturating Penis," *GLQ* 2 (1995): 149–77.

——. "Plasticity, Paternity, Perversity: Freud's *Falcon*, Huston's *Freud*." *American Imago* 51 (spring 1994): 69–104.

Edgeworth, Richard Lovell, and Maria Edgeworth. *Memoirs of Richard Lovell Edgeworth*. 2 vols. London, 1820. Reprint, Shannon: Irish University Press, 1969.

Eliot, George. *Daniel Deronda*. New York: Penguin, 1986.

Eliot, T. S. "Virginia Woolf." In *The Bloomsbury Group: A Collection of Memoirs, Commentary and Criticism*, edited by S. P. Rosenbaum, pp. 202–3. Toronto: University of Toronto Press, 1975.

Ellman, Richard. *Oscar Wilde*. New York: Vintage Books, 1988.

Engels, Friedrich. *The Origin of the Family, Private Property, and the State*, ed. Eleanor Leacock. New York: International Publishers, 1972.

Eribon, Didier. *Michel Foucault et ses contemporains*. Paris: Fayard, 1994.

Faderman, Lillian. *Odd Girls and Twilight Lovers*. New York: Penguin, 1991.

———. *Surpassing the Love of Men: Romantic Friendship and Love Between Women from the Renaissance to the Present*. New York: Morrow, 1981.

Faillie, Marie-Henriette. *La Femme et le Code civil dans La Comédie humaine d'Honoré de Balzac*. Paris: Didier, 1968.

Falk, Avner. *Herzl, King of the Jews: A Psychoanalytic Biography of Theodor Herzl*. New York: University Press of America, 1993.

Fassler, Barbara. "Theories of Homosexuality as Sources of Bloomsbury's Androgyny." *Signs* 5, no. 2 (winter 1979): 237–51.

Findlay, Heather. "Queer Dora: Hysteria, Sexual Politics, and Lacan's 'Intervention on Transference.' *GLQ* 1, no. 3 (1994): 323–47.

Fischler, Martin A., and Oscar Firschein. *Intelligence: The Eye, the Brain, and the Computer*. Reading, Mass.: Addison-Wesley Publishing Company, 1987.

Fishkin, Shelley Fisher. *Was Huck Black?: Mark Twain and African American Voices*. New York: Oxford University Press, 1993.

Fletcher, Maurine S., ed. *The Wetherills of the Mesa Verde*. Lincoln: University of Nebraska Press, 1977.

Foster, Susan Leigh. *Reading Dancing: Bodies and Subjects in Contemporary American Dance*. Berkeley: University of California Press, 1986.

Foucault, Michel. "Afterword: The Subject and Power." In H. L. Dreyfus and P. Rabinow, *Michel Foucault: Beyond Structuralism and Hermeneutics*, edited by H. L. Dreyfus and P. Rabinow, pp. 208–26. 2d ed. Chicago: University of Chicago Press, 1983[a].

———. *The Care of the Self*. Vol. 3 of *The History of Sexuality*. Translated by Robert Hurley. New York: Random House, 1986.

———. *Dits et écrits 1954–1988*. Edited by Daniel Defert and François Ewald. 4 vols. Paris: Gallimard, 1994.

———. "Entretien avec M. Foucault." In *Dits et écrits*. 4:286–95.

———. "The Ethic of Care for the Self as a Practice of Freedom: An Interview with Michel Foucault on January 20, 1984." In *The Final Foucault*, edited by J. Bernauer and D. Rasmussen, pp. 1–20. Cambridge, Mass.: MIT Press, 1988.

———. "Folie, littérature, société." Interview with T. Shimizu and M. Watanabe. In *Dits et écrits*. 2:104–28.

———. "Friendship as a Way of Life." In *Foucault Live (Interviews, 1966–84)*, edited by Sylvère Lotringer, translated by John Johnston, pp. 203–9. New York: Semiotext(e), 1989. Translation of: "De l'amitié comme mode de vie." In *Dits et écrits*. 4:163–67.

———, ed. *Herculine Barbin. Being the Recently Discovered Memoirs of a Nineteenth-Century French Hermaphrodite*. Translated by Richard McDougall. New York: Pantheon, 1980.

———. *The History of Sexuality: An Introduction*. Vol. 1. Translated by Robert Hurley. New York: Random House, 1978.

———. "Preface." In *Anti-Oedipus*, Deleuze and Guattari.

———, ed. *I, Pierre Rivière, having slaughtered my mother, my sister and my brother . . . : A Case of Parricide in the 19th Century*. Harmondsworth, England: Penguin, 1978. Translation of: *Moi, Pierre Rivière, ayant égorgé ma mère, ma soeur et mon frère . . . : Un cas de parricide au XIXe siècle*. Paris: Gallimard, 1973.

———. "The Life of Infamous Men." In *Michel Foucault: Power, Truth, Strategy*, edited by Meaghan Morris and Paul Patton, translated by Paul Foss and Meaghan Morris, pp. 76–91. Sydney: Feral, 1979. Translation of: "La vie des hommes infâmes." In *Dits et écrits*. 3:237–53.

———. "Michel Foucault: An Interview: Sex, Power and the Politics of Identity." *The Advocate*, 7 August 1984, pp. 26+.

———. *The Use of Pleasure*. Vol. 2 of *The History of Sexuality*. Translated by Robert Hurley. New York: Vintage Books, 1990.

———. "Le vrai sexe." In *Dits et écrits*. 4:115–23.

———. "What Is Enlightenment?" In *The Foucault Reader*, edited by Paul Rabinow, pp. 32–50. New York: Pantheon Books, 1984.

Fraleigh, Sondra Horton. *Dance and the Lived Body: A Descriptive Aesthetics*. Pittsburgh: University of Pittsburgh Press, 1987.

Frankenberg, Ruth. *White Women, Race Matters: The Social Construction of Whiteness*. Minneapolis: University of Minnesota Press, 1993.

Fredrickson, George M. *The Black Image in the White Mind: The Debate on Afro-American Character and Destiny, 1817–1914*. New York: Harper and Row, 1971.

French, Robert M. "Subcognition and the Limits of the Turing Test." *Mind* 99, no. 393 (January 1990): 53–65.

Freud, Sigmund. *The Standard Edition of the Complete Psychological Works of Sigmund Freud*. Edited by James Strachey. Translated by James Strachey et al. 24 vols. London: Hogarth Press, 1953–.

———. *Beyond the Pleasure Principle*. Vol. 18 of *The Standard Edition of the Complete Psychological Works of Sigmund Freud*, pp. 3–64.

Fuller, Jean Overton. *Swinburne: A Biography*. New York: Schocken Books, 1968.

Fusco, Coco. "Pan-American Postnationalism: Another World Order." In *Black Popular Culture*, edited by Gina Dent, pp. 279–84. Seattle: Bay Press, 1992.

Fuss, Diana. "Inside/Out." In *Inside/Out: Lesbian Theories, Gay Theories*, edited by Diana Fuss, pp. 1–10. New York: Routledge, 1991.

Gabriel, Kathryn. *Marietta Wetherill*. Boulder: Johnson Books, 1992.

Gallagher, Catherine. "George Eliot and *Daniel Deronda*: The Prostitute and the Jewish Question." In *The New Historicism Reader*, edited by H. Aram Veeser, pp. 124–40. New York: Routledge, 1994.

Gardner, Jared. "'Our Native Clay': Racial and Sexual Identity and the Making of Americans in *The Bridge*." *American Quarterly* 44 (March 1992): 24–50.

Garnett, David, ed. *The White/Garnett Letters*. New York: The Viking Press, 1968.

Gates, Henry Louis. "The Body Politic." *New Yorker*, 28 November 1994, p. 112.

———. *Figures in Black: Words, Sign and the "Racial" Self*. New York: Oxford University Press, 1987.

———. Review of *Jazz*, by Toni Morrison. In *Toni Morrison: Critical Perspectives Past and Present*, edited by Henry Louis Gates Jr. and K. A. Appiah. New York: Amistad, 1993.

———. *The Signifying Monkey: A Theory of African-American Literary Criticism*. New York: Oxford University Press, 1988.

Gautier, Théophile. *Mlle de Maupin*. Paris: Editions Garnier, 1966.

Genette, Gérard. *Narrative Discourse*. Translated by Jane Lewin. Ithaca, N.Y.: Cornell University Press, 1980.

Gentleman's Agreement. Directed by Elia Kazan. 20th Century Fox, 1947.

Gibson, Ian. *The English Vice: Beating, Sex and Shame in Victorian England and After*. London: Duckworth, 1978.

Gibson, William. "The Gernsback Continuum." In *Mirrorshades*, pp. 1–11. New York: Ace Books, 1986.

———. *Neuromancer*. New York: Ace Books, 1984.

Gignilliat, George Warren Jr. *The Author of Sandford and Merton: A Life of Thomas Day, Esq.* New York: Columbia University Press, 1932.

Gilman, Sander. *The Jew's Body.* New York: Routledge, 1991.

Gilpin, Laura. *The Pueblos: A Camera Chronicle.* New York: Hastings House, 1941.

Gilroy, Paul. *The Black Atlantic: Modernity and Double Consciousness.* Cambridge: Harvard University Press, 1993.

———. "It's a Family Affair." In *Black Popular Culture,* edited by Gina Dent. Seattle: Bay Press, 1992.

Girard, René. *The Scapegoat.* Baltimore: Johns Hopkins University Press, 1986.

Gleick, James. *Chaos: Making a New Science.* New York: Viking, 1987.

Goldberg, Johnathan, "Photographic Relations: Willa Cather, Laura Gilpin." Unpublished.

Greenberg, David F. *The Construction of Homosexuality.* Chicago: University of Chicago Press, 1988.

Grumbach, Doris. "A Study of the Small Room in *The Professor's House.*" *Women's Studies* 11 (1984): 327–45.

Hafner, Katie, and John Markoff. *Cyberpunk: Outlaws and Hackers on the Computer Frontier.* New York: Touchstone, 1991.

Halley, Janet. "The Construction of Heterosexuality." In *Fear of a Queer Planet,* edited by Michael Warner, pp. 82–102. Minneapolis: University of Minnesota Press, 1993.

Halperin, David M. "Is There a History of Sexuality?". In *The Gay and Lesbian Studies Reader,* edited by Henry Abelove, Michèle Aina Barale, and David M. Halperin, pp. 416–31. New York: Routledge, 1993.

———. "Why is Diotima a Woman?: Platonic *Eros* and the Figuration of Gender." In *Before Sexuality: The Construction of Erotic Experience in the Ancient Greek World,* edited by David Halperin, John J. Winkler, and Froma I. Zeitlin, pp. 257–98. Princeton: Princeton University Press, 1990.

———. *Saint Foucault: Towards a Gay Hagiography.* New York: Oxford University Press, 1995.

Haraway, Donna. "The Biopolitics of Postmodern Bodies: Determinations of Self in Immune System Discourse." *differences* 1 (1989): 3–43.

Harrell, David. *From Mesa Verde to The Professor's House.* Albuquerque: University of New Mexico Press, 1992.

———. "Willa Cather's Mesa Verde Myth." *Cather Studies* 1 (1990): 130–43.

Harris, Daniel. "Making Kitsch from AIDS." *Harper's,* July 1994.

Hawkins, Erick. *The Body Is a Clear Place: And Other Statements on Dance.* Princeton, N.J.: Princeton Book Company, 1987.

Hawkins, Peter S. "Naming Names: The Art of Memory and the NAMES Project AIDS Quilt." *Critical Inquiry* 19 (summer 1993): 752–79.

Hein, Robert. *Studentischer Antisemitismus in Osterreich.* Vienna: Osterreichischer Verein fur Studentengeschichte, 1984.

Henderson, Philip. *Swinburne: Portrait of a Poet.* New York: Macmillan, 1974.

Herbert, Christopher. *Culture and Anomie: Ethnographic Imagination in the Nineteenth Century.* Chicago: University of Chicago Press, 1991.

Herdt, Gilbert. *Guardians of the Flutes: Idioms of Masculinity.* New York: McGraw-Hill, 1981.

Herzl, Theodor. *Altneuland.* Translated by Paula Arnold. Haifa, Israel: Haifa Publishing Company, 1964.

———. *Briefe und Tagebucher.* Edited by Alex Bein et al. Vol. 1 of *Briefe und Autobiographische Notizen, 1866–1895,* edited by Johannes Wachten. Berlin: Verlag Ullstein, Propylaen, 1983.

————. *The Complete Diaries of Theodor Herzl, 1895–1904*. Translated by H. Zohn. Edited by R. Patai. 5 vols. New York: Herzl Press and Thomas Yoseloff, 1960.

————. *The Diaries of Theodor Herzl*. Edited and translated by Marvin Lowenthal. New York: The Dial Press, 1956.

————. "Foreword." In *The Jewish State; An Attempt at a Modern Solution of the Jewish Question*. Translated by Sylvia d'Avigdor. New York: American Zionist Emergency Council, 1946.

Hinshelwood, R. D. *A Dictionary of Kleinian Thought*. 2d ed. Northvale, N.J.: Aronson, 1991.

Hoare, Philip. *Serious Pleasures: The Life of Stephen Tennant*. New York: Penguin Books, 1990.

Hobson, Laura Z. *Gentleman's Agreement*. New York: Arbor House, 1947.

Hocquenghem, Guy. *Homosexual Desire*. Translated by Daniella Dangoor. Preface by Jeffrey Weeks. Introduction by Michael Moon. Durham, N.C.: Duke University Press, 1993.

Hofstadter, Richard. *The Paranoid Style in American Politics and Other Essays*. New York: Alfred A. Knopf, 1965.

Holmes, Glyn. *The Adolphe Type in French Fiction of the First Half of the Nineteenth Century*. Sherbrooke, Quebec: Editions Naaman, 1977.

Holroyd, Michael. "Lytton Strachey." In *The Bloomsbury Group: A Collection of Memoirs, Commentary, and Criticism*, edited by S. P. Rosenbaum, pp. 181–87. Toronto: University of Toronto Press, 1975.

Home of the Brave. Directed by Mark Robson. United Artists, 1949.

Hull, Elizabeth. *Taking Liberties: National Barriers to the Free Flow of Ideas*. New York: Praeger, 1990.

Illingworth, Montieth M. "Looking for Mr. Goodbyte." *Mirabella*, December 1994, pp. 108–17.

Imitation of Life. Directed by John Stahl, Universal Pictures, 1934.

————. Directed by Douglas Sirk, 1959.

Irigaray, Luce. *This Sex Which Is Not One*. Translated by Catherine Porter. Ithaca, N.Y.: Cornell University Press, 1985.

————. *Speculum of the Other Woman*. Translated by Gillian C. Gill. Ithaca, N.Y.: Cornell University Press, 1985.

"Is There a Case for Viruses?" *Newsweek*, 27 February 1995, p. 65.

James, Henry. *The Ambassadors*. New York: W. W. Norton, 1994.

————. *The Portrait of a Lady*. New York: W. W. Norton, 1975.

————. "Preface to 'The Portrait of a Lady'." In *The Art of the Novel* pp. 40–58. New York: Charles Scribner's Sons, 1934.

————. *The Wings of the Dove*. New York: Penguin, 1988.

Jameson, Fredric. "Actually Existing Marxism." *Polygraph* 6/7 (1993): 170–95.

————. *Postmodernism, or, The Cultural Logic of Late Capitalism*. Durham, N.C.: Duke University Press, 1991.

Johnson, Thomas H., ed. *The Complete Poems of Emily Dickinson*. Boston: Little, Brown, 1960.

Jones, Bill T., and Peggy Gillespie. *Last Night on Earth*. New York: Pantheon, 1995.

Joplin, Patricia Kleindienst. "The Authority of Illusion: Feminism and Fascism in Virginia Woolf's *Between the Acts*." *South Central Review* 2 (summer 1989): 88–104.

Kaiser, Jon D. *Immune Power: A Comprehensive Treatment Program for HIV*. New York: St. Martin's Press, 1993.

Keir, James. *An Account of the Life and Writings of Thomas Day, Esq.* 1791. Reprint, New York: Garland, 1970.

Kellner, Leon. *Theodor Herzls Lehrjahre 1860–1895*. Vienna: R. Lowit Verlag, 1920.

"The Killing Quilt." *People Magazine*, 15 November 1993, pp. 93–98.

Kincaid, James. *Child-Loving: The Erotic Child and Victorian Culture*. New York: Routledge, 1992.

King, James. *Virginia Woolf*. London: Hamish Hamilton, 1994.

Klein, Melanie. *Envy and Gratitude*. London: Tavistock, 1957.

Knopp, Sherron E. " 'If I Saw You Would You Kiss Me?': Sapphism and the Subversiveness of Virginia Woolf's *Orlando*." *PMLA* 103, no. 1 (January 1988): 24–34.

Kornberg, Jacques. *Theodor Herzl: From Assimilation to Zionism*. Bloomington: Indiana University Press, 1993.

Krauss, Rosalind. *The Optical Unconscious*. Cambridge, Mass.: MIT Press, 1993.

Kristeva, Julia. *Powers of Horror: An Essay on Abjection*. New York: Columbia University Press, 1982.

Lacan, Jacques. *The Four Fundamental Concepts of Psycho-Analysis*. Edited by Jacques-Alain Miller. Translated by Alan Sheridan. New York: W. W. Norton, 1981.

—————. "Intervention on Transference." In *In Dora's Case: Freud—Hysteria—Feminism*, edited by Charles Bernheimer and Claire Kahane. 2d ed. New York: Columbia University Press, 1990.

Laplanche, Jean, and J-B. Pontalis. *The Language of Psycho-Analysis*. Translated by Donald Nicholson-Smith. New York: Norton, 1973.

Leary, Timothy. *Chaos & Cyber Culture*. Berkeley, Calif.: Ronin Publishing, 1994.

Lee, Hermione. *Willa Cather: Double Lives*. New York: Vintage, 1989.

Lee, Jonathan Scott. *Jacques Lacan*. Amherst, Mass.: University of Massachusetts Press, 1991.

Lévi-Strauss, Claude. "The Family." In *Man, Culture, and Society*, edited by H. Shapiro. London: Oxford University Press, 1971.

Lewontin, Richard, Steven Rose, and Leon Kamin. *Not in Our Genes*. London: Penguin, 1984.

Lewis, Edith. *Willa Cather Living*. 1953. Reprint, Athens: Ohio University Press, 1989.

Litvak, Joseph. *Caught in the Act: Theatricality in the Nineteenth-Century English Novel*. Berkeley: University of California Press, 1992.

Lloyd, Mary. *Borzoi Book of Modern Dance*. New York: Knopf, 1949.

Locke, John. *Some Thoughts Concerning Education*. Edited by John W. and Jean S. Yolton. Oxford: Clarendon Press, 1989.

Loewenberg, Peter. "Theodor Herzl: A Psychoanalytic Study in Charismatic Political Leadership." In *The Psychoanalytic Interpretation of History*, edited by Benjamin B. Wolman. New York: Basic Books, 1971.

London, Bette. "Guerrilla in Petticoats Or Sans-Culotte? Virginia Woolf and the Future of Feminist Criticism." *diacritics* 21 (summer–fall 1991): 11–29.

"The Long Shot." *Discover*, August 1993, pp. 66–67.

Lott, Eric. *Love and Theft: Blackface Minstrelsy and the American Working Class*. New York: Oxford University Press, 1993.

Malory, Sir Thomas. *Works*. Edited by Eugene Vinaver. Oxford and New York: Oxford University Press, 1971.

The Manchurian Candidate. Directed by John Frankheimer, 1962.

Marcus, Jane, ed. *Virginia Woolf: A Feminist Slant*. Lincoln: University of Nebraska Press, 1983.

—————. *Virginia Woolf and the Languages of Patriarchy*. Bloomington: Indiana University Press, 1987.

Marcus, Sharon. "Restless Houses: Domesticity and Urban Culture in Paris and London, 1820–1880." Ph.D. diss. Johns Hopkins University, 1995.

Marcus, Steven. "Human Nature, Social Orders, and 19th Century Systems of Explanation: Starting in with George Eliot." *Salmagundi* 28 (winter 1975): 20–42.

Marx, Karl. *Capital*. Vol. 1. Translated by Ben Fowkes. New York: Vintage, 1977.

Maya Deren: Experimental Films. Dustjacket. Laserdisk. Mystic Fire Video, 1986.

McClintock, Anne. *Imperial Leather: Race, Gender, and Sexuality in the Colonial Context*. New York: Routledge, 1995.

McGann, Jerome J. *Swinburne: An Experiment in Criticism*. Chicago: University of Chicago Press, 1972.

McGrath, William J. *Freud's Discovery of Psychoanalysis: The Politics of Hysteria*. Ithaca, N.Y.: Cornell University Press, 1986.

McNitt, Frank. *Richard Wetherill: Anasazi*. Albuquerque: University of New Mexico Press, 1957, 1966.

Mehlman, Jeffrey. *A Structural Study of Autobiography*. New Haven: Yale University Press, 1974.

Mercer, Kobena. *Welcome to the Jungle*. London: Routledge, 1994.

Meyer, Susan. "'Safely to their own borders': Proto-Zionism, Feminism, and Nationalism in *Daniel Deronda*." *ELH* 60 (1993): 733–58.

Michaels, Walter Benn. "Race into Culture: A Critical Genealogy of Cultural Identity." *Critical Inquiry* 18, no. 4 (1992): 655–85.

———. "The Souls of White Folks." In *Literature and the Body*, edited by Elaine Scarry. Baltimore: Johns Hopkins University Press, 1988.

———. "The Vanishing American." *American Literary History* 2, no. 2 (1990): 220–41.

Miller, D. A. *The Novel and the Police*. Berkeley: University of California Press, 1988.

Moon, Michael. "A Small Boy and Others: Sexual Disorientation in Henry James, Kenneth Anger, and David Lynch." In *Comparative American Identities*, edited by Hortense Spillers, pp. 141–56. New York: Routledge, 1991.

———. "Introduction to Guy Hocquenghem." In *Homosexual Desire*, by Guy Hocquenghem. Translated by Daniella Dangoor. Durham, N.C.: Duke University Press, 1993.

Moore, Madeline. *The Short Season Between Two Silences: The Mystical and the Political in the Novels of Virginia Woolf*. Boston: Allen and Unwin, 1984.

Morrison, Paul. "End Pleasure." *GLQ* 1 (1993): 53–78.

Morrison, Toni. *Beloved*. New York: Plume, 1987.

———. "In the Realm of Responsibility: A Conversation with Toni Morrison." Interview by Marsha Darling. *Women's Review of Books*, 5 March 1978, pp. 5–6.

———. *Playing in the Dark: Whiteness and the Literary Imagination*. Cambridge: Harvard University Press, 1992.

Mosse, George L. *Nationalism and Sexuality: Respectability and Abnormal Sexuality in Modern Europe*. New York: Howard Fertig, 1985.

Myers, Gerald. "African Americans and the Modern Dance Aesthetic." In *African American Genius in Modern Dance*, edited by Gerald Myers, p. 31. Durham, N.C.: American Dance Festival, n.d.

Nagrin, Daniel. *Dance and the Specific Image: Improvisations*. Pittsburgh: University of Pittsburgh Press, 1994.

Napheys, George H. *The Transmission of Life. Counsels on the Nature and Hygiene of the Masculine Function*. 2nd ed. Philadelphia: J. O. Fergus, 1871.

Native Son. Directed by Pierre Chenal, 1950.

Naudin, Jean-Bernard, Anne Borel, and Alain Senderens. *Dining with Proust.* New York: Random House, 1992.

Nealon, Christopher. "Affect-Genealogy: Feeling and Affiliation in Willa Cather." Forthcoming, *American Literature.*

Newton, K. M. "*Daniel Deronda* and Circumcision." *Essays in Cultures* 31 (1985): 313–27.

Nicolson, Harold. *Benjamin Constant.* London: Constable, 1949.

Nicolson, Nigel. Introduction to *The Sickleside of the Moon. The Letters of Virginia Woolf,* edited by Nigel Nicolson and Joanne Trautmann. 5 vols. London: Hogarth Press, 1979.

Nietzsche, Friedrich. *On the Genealogy of Morals and Ecce Homo.* Edited by Walter Kaufmann. Translated by Walter Kaufmann and R. J. Hollingdale. New York: Vintage, 1969.

Niles, Blair. *Condemned to Devil's Island.* New York: Harcourt, Brace, 1928.

———. *Strange Brother.* 1931. Reprint, London: Gay Mens Press, 1991.

Nordau, Max. *Degeneration.* New York: D. Appleton and Company, 1895.

Nye, Robert A. *Masculinity and Male Codes of Honor in Modern France.* Oxford: Oxford University Press, 1993.

O'Brien, Sharon. "'The Thing Not Named': Willa Cather as a Lesbian Writer." *Signs* 9 (1984): 576–99.

———. *Willa Cather: The Emerging Voice.* New York: Fawcett Columbine, 1987.

Ozick, Cynthia. *The Shawl.* New York: Vintage International, 1990.

Painter, George D. *Marcel Proust: A Biography.* 2 vols. in one. New York: Random House, 1987.

Panken, Shirley. *Virginia Woolf and the "Lust of Creation": A Psychoanalytic Exploration.* Albany: State University of New York Press, 1987.

Paterson, Orlando. *Slavery and Social Death.* Cambridge: Harvard University Press, 1980.

Patton, Cindy. "Queer Space/God's Space: Counting Down to the Apocalypse." Forthcoming in *Rethinking Marxism.*

———. "Refiguring Social Space." In *Social Postmodernism,* edited by Linda Nicholson and Steven Siedman. Cambridge: Cambridge University Press, 1995.

———. "Tremble Heteroswine." *Fear of a Queer Planet,* edited by Michael Warner, pp. 143–77. Minneapolis: University of Minnesota Press, 1993.

Pawel, Ernst. *The Labyrinth of Exile: A Life of Theodor Herzl.* New York: Farrar, Straus and Giroux, 1989.

Phillips, Adam. *On Kissing, Tickling and Being Bored: Psychoanalytic Essays on the Unexamined Life.* Cambridge: Harvard University Press, 1993.

Phillips, Kathy J. *Virginia Woolf Against Empire.* Knoxville: University of Tennessee Press, 1994.

Pickering, Samuel F. *John Locke and Children's Books in Eighteenth-Century England.* Knoxville: University of Tennessee Press, 1981.

Pinky. Directed by Elia Kazan. 20th Century Fox, 1949.

Plath, Sylvia. *Collected Poems.* Edited by Ted Hughes. London: Faber and Faber, 1981.

Poppel, Stephen. *Zionism in Germany, 1897–1933: The Shaping of a Jewish Identity.* Philadelphia: The Jewish Publication Society of America, 1977.

Preston, Richard. *The Hot Zone.* New York: Random House, 1994.

Proust, Marcel. *A la recherche du temps perdu.* Edited by Jean-Yves Tadié et al. 4 vols. Paris: Gallimard, 1987–89.

———. *Correspondence. Texte établi, présenté et annoté par Philip Kolb, tome XX. 1921.* Paris: Plon, 1992.

———. *The Guermantes Way.* Vol. 4 of *In Search of Lost Time.* Translated by C. K. Scott

Moncrieff and Terence Kilmartin. Revised by D. J. Enright. 6 vols. New York: Modern Library, 1992–93.

———. *In Search of Lost Time*. Translated by Andreas Mayor and Terence Kilmartin. Revised by D. J. Enright. New York: Modern Library, 1993.

———. "Sentiments filiaux d'un parricide." In *"Contre Sainte-Beuve," précédé de "Pastiches et mélanges," et suivi de "Essais et articles,"* edited by Pierre Clarac with Yves Sandres, pp. 150–59. Paris: Gallimard, 1971.

———. *Time Regained*. Vol. 6 of *In Search of Lost Time*. Translated by C. K. Scott Moncrieff and Terence Kilmartin. Revised by D. J. Enright. 6 vols. New York: Modern Library, 1992–93.

Radin, Grace. *Virginia Woolf's The Years: The Evolution of a Novel*. Knoxville: University of Tennessee Press, 1981.

Rampersad, Arnold. *The Life of Langston Hughes, Volume I: 1902–1941, I, Too, Sing America*. New York: Oxford University Press, 1986.

———. *The Life of Langston Hughes, Volume II: 1941–1967, I Dream a World*. New York: Oxford University Press, 1988.

Reed, Christopher. "Bloomsbury Bashing: Homophobia and the Politics of Criticism in the Eighties." *Genders* 11 (fall 1991): 58–80.

Reid, Roddey. *Families in Jeopardy: Regulating the Social Body in France, 1750–1910*. Stanford, Calif.: Stanford University Press, 1993.

Reingold, Howard. *The Virtual Community: Homesteading on the Electronic Frontier*. New York: HarperPerennial, 1993.

Richard, Jean-Pierre. *Proust et le monde sensible*. Paris: Seuil, 1974.

Ricoeur, Paul. *Freud and Philosophy: An Essay on Interpretation*. Translated by Denis Savage. New Haven and London: Yale University Press, 1970.

Roediger, David R. *The Wages of Whiteness*. New York: Verso, 1991.

Rosenbaum, S. P., ed. *The Bloomsbury Group: A Collection of Memoirs, Commentary, and Criticism*. Toronto: University of Toronto Press, 1975.

Rosowski, Susan J., and Bernice Slote. "Willa Cather's 1916 Mesa Verde Essay: The Genesis of *The Professor's House.*" *Prairie Schooner* 58, no. 4 (1984): 81–92.

Rousseau, Jean-Jacques. *Emile, or On Education*. Translated by Allan Bloom. 1762. Reprint, New York: Basic Books, 1979.

Rubin, Gayle. "Sexual Traffic." Interview with Judith Butler. *differences* 6, nos. 2–3 (1994): 62–99.

———. "The Traffic in Women: Notes Toward a Political Economy of Sex." In *Toward an Anthropology of Women*, edited by Rayna Reiter, pp. 157–210. New York: Monthly Review Press, 1975.

Rudler, Gustave. *Jeunesse de Benjamin Constant 1767–1794*. Paris: Armand Colin, 1909.

Rushkoff, Douglas. *Media Virus!* New York: Ballantine Books, 1994.

Russ, Joanna. "To Write 'Like a Woman': Transformations of Identity in the Work of Willa Cather." 1986. Revised in *To Write Like a Woman*. Bloomington: Indiana University Press, 1995.

Sackville-West, Vita. "The Vitality of Bloomsbury." In *The Bloomsbury Group: A Collection of Memoirs, Commentary, and Criticism*, edited by S. P. Rosenbaum, pp. 248–49. Toronto: University of Toronto Press, 1975.

Saint Aubin, Arthur Flannigan. "Testeria: The Dis-ease of Black Men in White Supremacist, Patriarchal Culture." *American and American Arts and Letters*. 17, no. 4 (1994): 1068.

Saffo, Paul. "Have Your Agent Call My Agent." *Newsweek*, 6 February 1995, p. 76.

Sartre, Jean-Paul. *Being And Nothingness*. Translated by Hazel Barnes. New York: Pocket Books, 1956.

Savigliano, Marta. *Tango and the Political Economy of Passion*. Boulder, Colo.: Westview Press, 1995.

Saxton, Alexander. *The Rise and Fall of the White Republic: Class Politics and Mass Culture in Nineteenth-Century America*. New York: Verso, 1990.

Scheuermann, Mona. *Social Protest in the Eighteenth-Century English Novel*. Columbus: Ohio State University Press, 1985.

Schor, Naomi. *Reading in Detail*. New York: Routledge, 1987.

Scott, Sir S. H. *The Exemplary Mr. Day*. London: Faber and Faber, 1935.

Sears, Sallie. "Theater of War: Virginia Woolf's *Between the Acts*." In *Virginia Woolf: A Feminist Slant*, edited by Jane Marcus, pp. 212–35. Lincoln: University of Nebraska Press, 1983.

Sedgwick, Eve Kosofsky. "Across Gender, Across Sexuality: Willa Cather and Others" *SAQ* 88, no. 1 (1989): 53–72.

———. "Around the Performative: Periperformative Vicinities in Dickens, Eliot, and James." Unpublished.

———. *Between Men: English Literature and Male Homosocial Desire*. New York: Columbia University Press, 1985.

———. *The Coherence of Gothic Conventions*. New York: Methuen, 1986.

———. "Inside Henry James: Toward A Lexicon for *The Art of the Novel*." In *Negotiating Lesbian and Gay Subjects* edited by Monika Dorenkamp and Richard Henke. New York: Routledge, 1995.

———. *Epistemology of the Closet*. Berkeley: University of California Press, 1990.

———. *Tendencies*. Durham, N.C.: Duke University Press, 1993.

———. "Queer Performativity: Henry James's *The Art of the Novel*." *GLQ*, vol. 1, 1 (1993): 1–16.

Sedgwick, Eve Kosofsky, and Adam Frank. "Shame in the Cybernetic Fold." *Critical Inquiry* 21 (winter 1995): 496–522.

Shipman, Pat. *The Evolution of Racism: Human Differences and the Use and Abuse of Science*. New York: Simon and Schuster, 1994.

Skocpol, Theda. *Protecting Soldiers and Mothers: The Political Origins of Social Policy in the United States*. Cambridge, Mass.: The Belknap Press of Harvard University.

Silver, Brenda. Introduction to *Virginia Woolf's Reading Notebooks*, edited by Brenda Silver. Princeton, N.J.: Princeton University Press, 1983.

Silverman, Kaja. *Male Subjectivity at the Margins*. New York: Routledge, 1992.

———. *Threshold of the Visible World*. New York: Routledge, 1996.

Simmel, Georg. "The Metropolis and Mental Life." In *The Sociology of Georg Simmel*, translated and edited by Kurt H. Wolff. New York: The Free Press, 1950.

Sitwell, Osbert. "Armistice in Bloomsbury." In *The Bloomsbury Group: A Collection of Memoirs, Commentary, and Criticism*, edited by S. P. Rosenbaum, pp. 249–59. Toronto: University of Toronto Press, 1975.

60 Minutes. 26 February 1995.

Sloterdijk, Peter. *Critique of Cynical Reason*. Translated by Michael Eldred. Foreword by Andreas Huyssen. Minneapolis: University of Minnesota Press, 1987.

Smith-Rosenberg, Carroll. "The Female World of Love and Ritual: Relations Between Women in Nineteenth-Century America." In *A Heritage of Her Own*, edited by Nancy F. Cott and Elizabeth H. Pleck, pp. 311–42. New York: Simon and Schuster, 1979.

Spillers, Hortense. "Mama's Baby, Papa's Maybe: An American Grammar Book." *diacritics* 17 (1987): 65–81.

Spivak, Gayatri Chakravorty. *Outside in the Teaching Machine.* New York: Routledge, 1993.

———. "Responsibility." *boundary 2* 21, no. 3 (1994): 19–64.

———. *The Spivak Reader.* Edited by Donna Landry and Gerald MacClean. New York: Routledge, 1996.

Stimpson, Catharine. "Woolf's Room, Our Project: The Building of Feminist Criticism." In *The Future of Literary Theory,* edited by Ralph Cohen, pp. 129–43. New York: Routledge, 1989.

Stockton, Kathryn Bond. "Heaven's Bottom: Anal Economics and the Critical Debasement of Freud in Toni Morrison's Sula." *Cultural Critique* (spring 1993): 81–118.

"Stop! Cyberthief!" *Newsweek,* 6 February 1995, p. 37.

Straayer, Chris. *Deviant Eyes, Deviant Bodies: Sexual Re-Orientation in Film and Video.* New York: Columbia University Press, 1996.

Strachey, Lytton, and Virginia Woolf. *Virginia Woolf and Lytton Strachey: Letters.* Edited by Leonard Woolf and James Strachey. London: Hogarth Press, 1956.

Sullivan, Robert. "The Search for the Cure for AIDS: A Special Report from the Frontiers of Science." *Rolling Stone,* 7 April 1994, p. 61.

"A Superhacker Meets His Match." *Newsweek,* 27 February 1995, p. 43.

Swinburne, A. C. *Lesbia Brandon.* Edited by Randolph Hughes. London: Falcon Press, 1952.

———. *The Novels of A. C. Swinburne.* Edited by Edmund Wilson. New York: Noonday: Farrar, Straus and Cudahy, 1962.

———. *The Swinburne Letters.* Edited by Cecil Y. Lang. 6 vols. New Haven: Yale University Press, 1962.

Taussig, Michael. *Mimesis and Alterity: A Particular History of the Senses.* New York: Routledge, 1993.

Taylor, Mark C., and Esa Saarinen. *Imagologies: Media Philosophy.* London: Routledge, 1994.

"TechnoMania: The Future Isn't What You Think." *Newsweek,* 27 February 1995.

Thomas, Calvin. *Male Matters.* Urbana: University of Illinois Press, 1996.

Thomas, Piri. *Down These Mean Streets.* New York: Vintage, 1967.

Thomson, Patrice. *La Religion de Benjamin Constant. Les Pouvoirs de l'image.* Pisa: La Goliardica, 1978.

Thorpe, Edward. *Black Dance.* London: Chatto and Windus, 1989.

Toll, Robert C. *Blacking Up: The Minstrel Show in Nineteenth-Century America.* New York: Oxford University Press, 1974.

Tomkins, Silvan. *Affect Imagery Consciousness.* Vol. 2. New York: Springer, 1963.

———. *Shame and Its Sisters: A Silvan Tomkins Reader.* Edited with an introduction by Eve Kosofsky Sedgwick and Adam Frank. Durham, N.C.: Duke University Press, 1995.

Trilling, Lionel. Introduction to *Emma,* by Jane Austen. Boston: Houghton Mifflin, 1957.

Turing, A. M. "Computing Machinery and Intelligence." *Mind,* October 1950, pp. 433–60.

United States Congress. *Public Law 414: An Act to Revise the Law Relating to Immigration, Naturalization, and Nationality,* 1952.

Verhoeff, Han. *'Adolphe' et Constant: une étude psychocritique.* Paris: Klincksieck, 1976.

Waller, Margaret. *The Male Malady: Fictions of Impotence in the French Romantic Novel.* New Brunswick, N.J.: Rutgers University Press, 1993.

Warner, Sylvia Townsend. *T. H. White: A Biography.* New York: Viking Press, 1967.

Washington, Eric K. "Sculpture in Flight: A Conversation with Bill T. Jones." *Transitions* 62 (1992).

Weininger, Otto. *Sex and Character.* 6th German ed. London: W. Heinemann, 1906. Reprint, New York: AMS Press, 1975.

West, Cornel. *Race Matters.* New York: Vintage, 1994.

White, Terence Hanbury. *The Book of Merlyn.* Austin and London: University of Texas Press, 1977.

————. *The Ill-Made Knight.* New York: G. P. Putnam's Sons, 1940.

————. *Letters to a Friend: The Correspondence between T. H. White and L. J. Potts.* Edited with introductions by François Gallix. Gloucester: Alan Sutton, 1984.

————. *The Once and Future King.* London: Collins, 1958; New York: G. P. Putnam's Sons, 1958.

————. *The Sword in the Stone.* London: Collins, 1938.

————. *The Sword in the Stone.* New York: G. P. Putnam's Sons, 1939.

————. *The Witch in the Wood.* New York: G. P. Putnam's Sons, 1939.

Whitman, Walt. "I Sing the Body Electric." In *The Whitman Reader,* edited by Maxwell Geismar, pp. 63–72. New York: Pocket, 1955.

Wilde, Oscar. *Lady Windermere's Fan.* In *The Complete Plays.* London: Methuen, 1989.

————. "The Portrait of Mr. W.H.." In *The Artist as Critic: Critical Writings of Oscar Wilde,* edited by Richard Ellmann, pp. 212–13. Chicago: University of Chicago, 1982.

————. *The Picture of Dorian Gray.* Edited by Donald Lawler. 1891. Reprint, New York: Norton, 1988.

Williams, Linda. *Hard Core: Power, Pleasure, and the 'Frenzy of the Visible.'* Berkeley: University of California Press, 1989.

Winnington, Richard. *Film Criticism and Caricatures 1943–1953.* New York: Barnes and Noble, 1976.

Winter, Marian Hannah. "Juba and American Minstrelsy." In *Chronicles of the American Dance,* edited by Paul Magriel. New York: Henry Holt, 1948.

Wittig, Monique. *The Straight Mind.* Boston: Beacon Press, 1992.

Wood, Dennis. *Benjamin Constant: A Biography.* London and New York: Routledge, 1993.

Wood, Mary McGee. "Signification and Simulation: Barthes's response to Turing." *Paragraph* 11 (1988): 211–26.

Woods, Gregory. "High Culture and High Camp: The Case of Marcel Proust." In *Camp Grounds: Style and Homosexuality,* edited by David Bergman, pp. 121–22. Amherst: University of Massachusetts Press, 1993.

Woolf, Leonard. "Lytton Strachey." In *The Bloomsbury Group: A Collection of Memoirs, Commentary, and Criticism,* edited by S. P. Rosenbaum. Toronto: University of Toronto Press, 1975.

Woolf, Virginia. "Appendix C: Virginia Woolf and Julian Bell." In vol. 2 of *Virginia Woolf: A Biography,* edited by Quentin Bell, pp. 255–59. New York: Harcourt, Brace, Jovanovich, 1972.

————. *Between the Acts.* 1941. Reprint, London: Grafton, 1978.

————. *Collected Essays.* Edited by Leonard Woolf. 4 vols. New York: Harcourt, Brace and World, 1953.

————. *The Diary of Virginia Woolf.* 1941. Edited by Anne Olivier Bell and Andrew McNeillie. 5 vols. London: Hogarth Press, 1977–84. London: Grafton, 1978.

————. *The Letters of Virginia Woolf.* Edited by Nigel Nicholson and Joanne Trautmann. 6 vols. London: Hogarth Press, 1975–84.

————. *Moments of Being: Unpublished Autobiographical Writings.* Edited by Jeanne Schulkind. Sussex: Sussex University Press, 1976.

————. *The Pargiters: The Novel-Essay Portion of The Years.* Edited by Mitchell A. Leaska. New York: The New York Public Library and Readex Books, 1977.

————. *A Room of One's Own.* 1929. Reprint, London: Grafton, 1977.

————. *Three Guineas.* 1938. Reprint, New York: Harcourt Brace Jovanovich, 1966.

————. *The Years.* 1937. Reprint, London: Oxford University Press, 1992.

Woolf, Virginia, and Lytton Strachey. *Virginia Woolf and Lytton Strachey Letters.* Edited by Leonard Woolf and James Strachey. London: Hogarth Press, 1956.

Wright, Robert. "Hyper Democracy." *Time,* 23 January 1995, pp. 15–21.

Žižek, Slavoj. *Looking Awry: An Introduction to Jacques Lacan through Popular Culture.* Cambridge: MIT Press, 1991.

————. *The Sublime Object of Ideology.* London: Verso, 1989.

Zwerdling, Alex. *Virginia Woolf and the Real World.* Berkeley: University of California Press, 1986.

INDEX

Abjection, 353, 355, 366, 368; identity and, 355; race and, 368, 374. *See also* homosexuality; scapegoat; waste

Activism: internet and, 44

Adler, Hermann, 300

Adolescence, 76–78, 85, 88; and humiliation, 88

Adorno, Theodor, 74–76, 86, 90–91; homophobia of, 90–91; on Proust, 74–76, 86

Aesthetics: of advertisement, 30, 160; and Proust, 87; Woolf and, 402, 408, 417, 432

Affect, 9, 12–16, 23–24, 36n, 335, 340–341, 345; in *The Ambassadors*, 95, 106, 109–114, 116, 121, 123; and Benedict Anderson, 337; of boredom, 153; gay politics and, 345; positive and negative, 9, 15–16, 23–24; and nation, 335; and sexuality in Balzac, 175, 185–187; Silvan Tomkins and, 12; transfer of, 95, 106, 109, 111, 112–115, 123 (*see also* James, Henry: *The Ambassadors*). *See also* affectivity; boredom; humiliation; paranoia

Affectivity, 335, 340–341, 345, 348n; and identification, 340–341. *See also* affect

African-American literature: abjection in, 373–374; ghosts in, 373. *See also* Baldwin, James, works of; black masculinity; black subjectivity; Cleaver, Eldridge, works of; Dixon, Melvin, works of; Morrison, Toni, works of

Age: and innocence in *The Ambassadors*, 96, 108–109, 116, 125n; and friendship, 26–27; in *The Picture of Dorian Gray*, 163–164. *See also* body

AIDS, 3–4, 42, 44, 46, 54, 57, 61–62, 72n–

73n; and citizenship, 347n; memes as, 57; and paranoia, 3–4. *See also* HIV; viruses

Ailey, Alvin: Hughes and, 391, 399n

Albia, 314–316. *See also* anti-Semitism; Herzl, Theodor

Allegory, 432. *See also* figures of speech

Alliance, in Balzac, 186–187, 192, 193; and sexuality, 186–187, 190, 193–194

Anachronism, 31. *See also* prolepsis

Anal eroticism, 76–77, 87–88, 97; in *The Ambassadors*, 95–97, 106–108, 117–118; in *Down These Mean Streets*, 364; and face/butt metonymy, 274–277, 281, 285, 288; in Proust, 76–77, 87–88; in T. H. White's work, 240–241; in Swinburne's work, 270, 288–290. *See also* body; flogging; hands; orality; waste

Anderson, Benedict, 32, 335–336, 350n; on affect, 335; on political love, 336

Animals, in Day, 205–210, 213–214

Anti-Semitism, 214, 314–316; of Albia, 314–316; anti-, 332; in *Gentlemen's Agreement*, 337, 343–344; of German fraternity movement, 314–315; and homophobia, 84, 315, 338; and misogyny, 315; in Proust's works, 84; and racism, 337–338; in Vienna, 314; of Weininger, 315. *See also* racism

Artificial Intelligence (AI), 128–147; absence of motive and, 130–131; gender and, 132–134; in "The Gernsback Continuum," 135; in *Neuromancer*, 129–134. *See also* intelligence; Turing test

Assimilation, 310–312, 314–315, 323–325, 346. *See also* Jew, non-national; *Daniel Deronda*; Herzl, Theodor

Arthurian narrative: versions of, 227–244, 245n. *See also* White, T. H., works of

Avuncular figures, 232, 238–239. *See also* White, T. H., works of

Baker, Houston, 380

Baldwin, James, works of: *Another Country*, 355, 368: Cleaver on, 368; interracial (homo)sex and, 368; *Giovanni's Room*, 355, 368–374: abjection in, 368; absence/invisibility of blackness in, 369; the body in, 370–371, 373–374; denial in, 371–372; ghost of homosexuality in, 369, 373; Giovanni's labor power, 371; Giovanni's non-subjectivity, 369–370; Giovanni as Cleaver's Supermasculine Menial, 371; Giovanni as slave, 371; homosexuality in, 369–373; identity formation in, 369–370, 372; inside/out binarism in, 373; masculinity in, 371–373; narrator of, 369; the Other in, 369–370; as prison narrative, 372–373; race in, 368–371; and representation of the body, 370; refusal of heterosexuality in, 372; whiteness in, 369–370; *Go Tell It on the Mountain*, 368

Balzac, Honoré de, 30, 167–194, 197n; Foucaultian readings and, 168–169, 186; and French history, 193–194; novels of as disciplinary, 168; psychoanalytic readings of, 170–171; same-sex sexual relations in novels of, 180–181; sexuality in novels of, 170–171, 181, 191. *See also* Balzac, Honoré de, works of

Balzac, Honoré de, works of: *Cousin Bette*, 167, 180–194: affect in, 184–187; and alliance, 186–187, 190; Bette and Valerie, 180–194; Bette's lesbianism, 180–181; capital in, 189; classism in, 190; family in, 185–190; friendship in, 190; gossip in, 180–183; inheritance in, 186–189; kinship in, 186–187, 190; lesbianism in, 181; marriage in, 182–183, 188–189; narrator of, 180, 183, 190–191; same-sex sex in, 180–181; sentiment in, 185; and sexuality, 186–187; *Cousin Pons*, 167–180, 171–172: art and economics in, 174–175; family in, 170–180; and heterosexuality, 172–173, 175–177; inheritance in, 173–180; kinship in, 174–175; marriage in, 172–175; Pons's collection, 171, 173–180; Pons's gastronomy, 171; Pons's homosexuality, 171–172, 181; Pons and

Schmuke, 171–180, 192 (*see also* friendships); and queerness as redistribution of wealth, 176–177, 179; scholarship on, 168; sexuality in, 171–173, 175–177, 179–180; the state in, 179–180; and traffic in women, 173; wills in, 177–179; *Cousin Pons* and *Cousin Bette*, 169–171, 181, 191–194: and alliance, 192, 194; endings of, 192; and friendships, 191–192; and gender, 191; as parallels, 169–170, 181, 194

Barbin, Herculine, 169

Bardéche, Maurice, 78

Barthes, Roland, 25, 62–63, 65–66, 98, 104–105

Baudrillard, Jean, 96–97

Bauer, Ida, 452–453

Bell, Quentin, 403

Bergson, Henri, 100

Berlant, Lauren, 385

Berman, Marshall, 98

Benjamin, Walter, 104

Bersani, Leo, 6, 36n, 92n–93n

Bestiality. *See* White, T. H., works of

Bildungsroman, 229, 256. *See also* Development, narratives of

Binarisms, 1, 353, 366, 369, 373, 472; of texture, 95–96, 99, 107, 117, 122. *See also* queerness

Birrell, Francis, 418. *See also* Bloomsbury group; homophobia: of Lawrence

Black literary tradition, 360, 368–369: and autobiographies, 355; freedom in, 360; interracial homosexual desire and, 368–369. *See also* prison narratives; slave narrative

Black masculinity, 353–374, 379–397, 397n–398n; anti-homosexual violence and, 354–355; black homosexuality and, 360; boundaries of, 360; and the body, 381; dance and, 379–397, 397n–398n; effeminacy and, 356; heterosexuality and, 356; homosexuality and, 356, 360, 370; homosexuality as scapegoat to, 370–371; imprisonment and, 355–357, 360, 365–368; in Jones's dance, 392–397; performativity of, 381; queerness and, 382; the scapegoat and, 354–355, 370; and self-expression, 380; and slavery, 368–369; in *Soul on Ice*, 358–359; specularity and, 388; in *Vanishing Rooms*, 380, 382–384, 386–388, 390, 397; and white spectatorship, 381. *See also* Baldwin, James, works of; Cleaver, Eldridge, works

Cleaver (continued)
black masculinity, 358–359; the body in, 358; gender in, 356–357; heterosexuality in, 356–358; homosexuality in, 356–357; homosociality and, 356–357; interracial homoeroticism in, 357–359; love in, 357–358; the Omnipotent Administrator, 357–358; prison and, 355–358; process of denial in, 357; racial difference in, 359; rape in, 356–357; and sexual violence, 356–357; and sexuality, 359; slave narrative and 360; women in, 356–358. See also black masculinity

Cloning, 42–43. See also reproduction

Closet, the: in Adolf, 259, 261; and flogging, 285; Jewish, 84; in Proust, 76–77, 83–84; in T. H. White

Cold War, 20–21, 32–33, 330–346, 347n–352n

Coming out: and Woolf, 401. See also homosexuality; queerness

Commodity culture. See commodity fetish; consumerism

Commodity fetish, 97–98, 125n. See also consumerism

Computers. See artificial Intelligence; cyberspace; internet

Conduct books, 201; Three Guineas as, 440n

Constant, Benjamin, 249–264, 265n–268n; homosexuality and, 263; masculinity and, 263; relationship with father, 250, 254, 263

Constant, Benjamin, works of: Adolf, 249–264, 265n–268n: absence of mother in, 257; blackmailability in, 259; as canonical, 249; closeted homosexuality in, 258–259, 261; empathy in, 253–254; the father in, 250, 254–261; the feminine in, 254–25, 258, 261; gender in, 249–253, 261–262; gender dissonance in, 249–251, 256; heterosexuality in, 256, 258–260, 262; homoeroticism in, 249, 261; and homosexuality, 249; and the homosocial, 253, 261; irony in, 251–252, 255; masculinity in, 249–262; mimetic desire in, 260; and misogyny, 261; and the Oedipus complex, 256–257, 261; pain in, 250, 255–256, 261–262; and plot, 249; prefaces to, 250–254; and psychoanalytic criticism, 254; and prolepsis, 252; as queer, 250, 262; and romanticism, 249; seduction in, 250–251; sentiment in, 250–252, 255–262; and sentimental

novel, 256; and sexuality, 251; shame in, 253–254; women in, 250–252, 257, 259–262

Constant, Jute de, 254, 263, 265n–266n

Consumer culture, 30; anti-, 331, 333–335, 341–342, 349n; and boredom, 160–161, 165; and homosexuality, 330–331, 333; women and, 339, 342–343. See also commodity fetish; fetishism

Contract with America, 20

Crebillon, Claude-Prosper de, 264n–265n

Crossfire (1947), 337; Anti-Semitism and homophobia in, 338

Cultural eclipse, 354. See also black subjectivity: and boundarylessness; scapegoat

Curtis, Pavel, 142–143

Cynicism, 19; in The Ambassadors, 113. See also paranoia; snobbery; sophistication

Cyperspace, 135–137; and culture, 136–137; as ideological, 137. See also internet; virtual: reality

CYRUS, 140–141. See also artificial intelligence; intelligence: and gender; Turing test

Dance, 33–34, 379–397, 397n–398n; and black masculinity, 380–382; and the body, 382; and body language, 381; and boxing, 381–382; Calienda, 381; improvisational, 388–390; Langston Hughes on, 390–391. See also black masculinity; Dixon, Melvin, works of: Vanishing Rooms; Jones, Bill T.

Dandy, 152, 155–157; and desire, 153–165. See also boredom; Wilde, Oscar, works of

Daniel Deronda. See Eliot, George, works of

Davis, Angela, 357, 369

Dawkins, Richard, 56–58, 67n, 70n–71n

Day, Thomas, 201–221, 222n–226n; and Edgeworth (Richard), 203; on education, 223n; and heterosexuality, 203; and marriage, 202–203; misogyny of, 203, 205, 221n–222n; relationships with men, 203; and Rousseau's Emile, 202–203; and training of pupils, 202–203

Day, Thomas, works of: Sanford and Merton, 201–221, 222n–226n: animals in, 205–210, 213–214; as anti-developmental, 203, 206; as children's literature, 202, 223n; and development, 201–221, 222n–226n; education in, 201, 206–207; effeminacy in, 203–210, 215–216, 225n; Harry's

Homoeroticism (*continued*)
  Portrait of a Lady, 444–453, 458–459,
    462n; in *Sanford and Merton*, 212–221;
    and violence, 204, 212, 217–220, 227, 361
Homographesis, 74
Homophobia, 384–385, 415; and Adorno,
    90n; anti-, 146; and anti-Semitism, 84,
    315, 338 (*see also* anti-Semitism); and
    cuckoldry in White, 235; and the internet,
    145; Lawrence, D. H. and, 418–419; and
    metaphor, 384; negrophobia and, 385
    (*see also* racism); Nordau's, 328n–329n;
    and paranoia, 6–7; in *Vanishing Rooms*,
    384–385, 390; of Woolf scholarship,
    438n–439n, 441n; Woolf's representa-
    tion of, 418–419, 421–422, 424, 427,
    430–431, 435 (*see also* Woolf, Virginia;
    Woolf, Virginia, works of)
Homosexual/homosocial distinction: in
    Down These Mean Streets, 360–361
Homosexuality, 32–33, 84, 257, 353, 402;
    the abject and, 353; in *Adolf*, 249; black,
    360; and black boundarylessness, 353;
    and boredom, 85; and citizenship, 331–
    332, 334–335, 344–346; closeted in *Adolf*,
    258–259; and communism, 330–331,
    333, 352n; in *Down These Mean Streets*,
    360–364, 367–368; and feminization,
    257; ghost of, 353, 368 (*see also* Baldwin,
    James, works of, *Giovanni's Room*); in
    Giovanni's Room, 369–373; in *The Guer-
    mantes Way*, 83–84; and homosociality,
    360–368 (*see also Down These Mean
    Streets*); HUAC and, 330–331, 333, 344–
    345; interracial, 368–369; as liminal,
    360, 362–363, 366; pathologization of,
    353; and *The Picture of Dorian Gray*, 161–
    162, 164–165; psychoanalysis, 5–6, 441;
    race and, 384–385; scapegoat and, 354; as
    sophistication, 74; in *Soul on Ice*, 356–
    357; and taste, 83; in *Vanishing Rooms*,
    383–385; visibility of, 359–360, 384–385;
    and White, 230–231, 233–234, 238–239,
    242–243, 246n; in Woolf, 403–405, 407–
    410, 413, 418–419, 422–426. *See also*
    Cather, Willa; Cather Willa, works of;
    desire; homoeroticism; James, Henry,
    works of; lesbianism; queerness; sexu-
    ality; White, T. H.; White, T. H., works
    of; Wilde, Oscar; Wilde, Oscar, works of;
    Woolf, Virginia; Woolf, Virginia, works of
Homosexual panic: internet and, 144–145.
    See also homophobia
Homosociality, 265, 253, 261, 265n; in

Adolfe, 253, 261; in *Daniel Deronda*, 310–
    311; and homosexuality, 360–368 (see
    also *Down These Mean Streets*); and Zion-
    ism, 319. *See also* alliance; friendship;
    kinship; women: traffic in
House Committee on Un-American Activi-
    ties (HUAC), 330–331, 333, 341, 345, 347n;
    and gay political history, 330–331; and
    homosexuality, 330–331, 344–345
Hughes, Langston, 390–391; Alvin Ailey
    and, 391, 399n
Hughes, Randolf, 272
Humiliation, 12–15, 24, 87–88; adolescence
    and, 88; and narratives of development,
    229. *See also* mortification; shame
Hyperlink, 43; Beloved as, 43, 45, 71n;
    in *Beloved*, 45, 49. *See also* internet;
    Morrison, Toni, works of: *Beloved*
Hypolink, 46–47

Identification: affect and, 340–341; and
    citizenship, 332, 339; empathy and, 332,
    341–343; and flogging, 272 (*see also* Swin-
    burne, August); gender, 8, 10, 17, 27,
    196, 257, 266n, 343; and love of country,
    342; melodrama and, 340, 344; method
    acting and, 332, 339–340; with minority
    experience, 332; and nation, 346. *See
    also* melodrama; nationalism; sentiment;
    sexuality; subjectivity
Illingworth, Montieth, 143–144
Illness, 46; in *Beloved*, 54, 58. *See also* AIDS;
    HIV; Morrison, Toni, works of
Impressionability, 204–207, 217–218. *See
    also* empathy; melodrama
Incest: prohibition of, 193, 254, 257, 266n;
    prohibition of homoerotic, 254, 257. *See
    also* desire
Inheritance. *See* alliance; Balzac, Honoré
    de, works of; family; kinship; sexuality
Ingestion. *See* Orality
Innuendo: in *The Ambassadors*, 94, 96,
    108–112, 115–116, 118. *See also* James,
    Henry, works of: *The Ambassadors*;
    vulgarity
Intelligence: 29, 128–129, 138–139,
    140–141; gender and 138–142; world
    knowledge as, 140–141. *See also* artificial
    intelligence
Internet, 29, 42–45, 68n, 128; activism
    and, 44; gender and, 142–147, 148n. *See
    also* hyperlink
Irigaray, Luce, 253
Irony, 251–252, 255; in *Adolf*, 251–252, 255;

Power (continued)
on, 167–169; Miller on, 168, 194n. See
also pouvoir/savoir; sexuality
Preston, Richard, 67n
Prison, 409; and Woolf, 435–436. See also
prison narrative
Prison narrative: black masculinity
and, 355–357, 360, 365–368; as
counterscripting of slave narrative, 360.
See also Cleaver, Eldridge, Soul on Ice;
Thomas, Piri, Down These Mean Streets
"Problem" genre, 32: Home of the Brave
(1949) as, 337–338; and melodrama, 337;
Pinky (1949) as, 338–339, 347n, 350n. See
also citizenship; cold war; empathy
Prolepsis, 252. See also figures of speech
Prophylactics, 71n; and Beloved, 46, 48–
49, 51–53, 62; internet as, 44; and "The
Shawl," 47. See also brain, the; memory;
viruses
Proust, Marcel, 26, 29, 33, 37n, 74–90,
91n–93n; adolescence and, 76–78, 85,
88; Adorno on, 74–75; and aesthetics,
87; and le beau monde, 76; anal eroticism
and, 76–77, 87–88; and "behindsight,"
88; the closet and, 76–77; and desire,
78–79, 85; and demystification, 79; and
gay alchemy, 86; as gay writer, 74; and
hom(e)opathy, 86; and humiliation, 88;
identification with the Duchess (in The
Guermantes Way), 83; immediacy and, 75,
77; and literature, 87–88; and naïveté,
77; and narration, 78, 83, 86, 88–89;
Sedgwick on, 76; and snobbery, 79, 88;
and sophistication, 74–77, 81, 83, 86–
90, 93n; gayness of, 75; wealth of, 76;
and wit, 87; and worldliness, 75, 80–81
Proust, Marcel, works of: The Guermantes
Way, 77–90, 91n–93n: adolescence in,
85; anal eroticism and, 87; bad objects
in, 85 (see also object-relations theory);
boredom in, 85, 88, 90; closet-effects in,
83–84; family in, 84–85; the fecal in, 80–
81, 86–87; gender in, 83; homosexuality
in, 83–84: and Jewishness in, 84; homosexualized heterosexuality in, 84; love in,
82–85, 87; melancholia in, 89; mondanité
of, 77, 86; naïveté, 85; narrator of, 78, 83,
86, 88; and orality, 82, 89; as reprise of
Jean Santeuil, 78; snobbery in, 79, 83–
84, 88; and sophistication, 74–77, 81, 83,
86–90, 93n; taste in, 77, 80–83, 85–86,
88–89; and the vulgar, 81; waste in, 76–
77, 79–81, 87–88, 90; worldliness in,
80–81; Jean Santeuil, 78: and snobbery,
78; Swann's Way, 80
Psychoanalysis, 11–12, 170–171, 187, 254,
265n; on boredom, 153; and feminism,
12; and homophobia, 6; and literary
criticism, 196n; on paranoia, 5–6. See
also Freud, Sigmund; Klein, Melanie;
Tomkins, Silvan
Punishment, 18–19. See also disciplinary
power; flogging; humiliation; mortification; pedagogy

Queerness, 1–3, 26–28, 31; and The Ambassadors, 95, 109–111, 115, 123; citizenship
and, 331, 344–346; communism and,
330–331, 333, 352n; definition of, 402;
performativity of, 402–403; politics,
344–346; and reading, 2–3, 95, 249–250,
262–264, 420, 424, 457, 465; reading
for, 172; as redistribution of wealth, 177;
relationality of, 402–404; and Woolf,
401–437. See also gender; homosexuality; queer readings; queer recognition;
sexuality
Queer performativity: and Woolf, 402–403,
405, 424, 434
Queer reading, 2–3, 25, 95, 249–250, 262–
264; and Cather, 457, 465; and evidence
for, 263, 457; and Woolf, 420, 424. See
also literary criticism; queerness; queer
recognition
Queer recognition, 3, 31, 33, 250, 262–264,
465, 475; and Woolf, 410–412, 415, 434.
See also homosexuality; queer readings
Queer theory, 1–2, 249

Race, 355; in Giovanni's Room, 368–371;
UNESCO statement on, 359; in Vanishing
Rooms, 382–389. See also black mascu-
linity; black subjectivity; masculinity;
anti-Semitism; Jewishness
Racism, 314, 316, 385; and anti-Semitism,
337–338; negrophobia, 385. See also
anti-Semitism
Radzik, Jody, 54–55. See also hackers
Rampersad, Arnold, 391
Realism, 98, 302
Reality principle, 16
Reed, Christopher, 415, 438n
Reid, Roddey, 167
Renault, Mary, 245n
Reparative position, 27–28; in criticism,
8, 22, 24, 27–28, 35. See also Kleinian
positions; paranoia

Repressive hypothesis, 110, 167–168. *See also* disciplinary power; Foucault, Michel

Reproduction: family and, 171. *See also* Morrison, Toni: *Beloved*: birth in; Viruses: reproduction of

Resistance, 169; and pedagogy, 210. *See also* disciplinary power

Responsibility: Morrison on, 73n; Spivak on, 443n. *See also* ethics

Ricoeur, Paul, 4–5, 17. *See also* hermeneutic of suspicion

Rousseau, Jean-Jacques, 201–202, 204, 210–213, 265n

Rousseau, Jean-Jacques, works of: *Emile*, 211–212, 225n; and erotics of pedagogy, 211–212; heterosexuality in, 212; subjection of Emile in, 211–212. *See also* development, narratives of

Rubin, Gayle, 186, 196n, 253. *See also* sex-gender system

Rushkoff, Douglas, 44, 54–56

Sackville-West, Vita, 415

Sade, Marquis de, 273; *Justine*, 273

Sado-masochism (S/M): and *The Ambassadors*, 112–114. *See also* masochism

Saffo, Paul, 67n–68n

Sartre, Jean Paul, 99–100

de Saussure, Ferdinand, 58

Scapegoat, the, 354, 370–371, 374–375; and black masculinity, 354–355, 370; and black subjectivity, 354, 374–375; and boundarylessness, 354; homosexuality and, 354, 370–371; violence and, 354. *See also* Baldwin, James, works of; black masculinity; black subjectivity; Cleaver, Eldridge, works of; Thomas, Piri, works of

Schizophrenia, 9. *See also* paranoia

Schor, Naomi, 98

Schreber, Dr., 5, 9. *See also* anal eroticism

Sedgwick, Eve Kosofsky, 72n, 76, 259, 253, 353, 402, 409, 465, 474, 480n; on Proust, 76; on Silvan Tomkins, 72n

Sentiment, 250–253, 255–262; in *Adolf*, 250–252, 255–262; and family structure, 185 (*see also* Balzac, Honoré de: works of); gender and, 250–253, 255–262; prohibition against, 255–256. *See also* melodrama

Sex/gender system, 142, 173, 186, 256, 265n. *See also* sexuality

Sexual difference, 11–12, 14, 25. *See also* gender; masculinity; sexuality

Sexuality, 2, 167–169, 172, 186–187, 194, 359, 402; in *The Ambassadors*, 94, 96, 106, 110–111; and alliance, 186–187, 190, 193–194; in Balzac, 170–173, 175–177, 179–181, 186–187, 191; and Cather, 474, 480n (*see also* Cather, Willa); and class, 442; and disciplinary power, 167–169, 194; in *Down These Mean Streets*, 363–364; and ethnology, 193; and the family, 186–187, 193; Foucault's history of, 110, 167–169, 224n–225n, 333; and French history, 167, 193–194, 257; and friendship, 190–191; and Herzl, 312; and incest taboo, 193; impulse to produce, 172, 181 (*see also* Balzac, Honoré de; disciplinary power); inheritance and, 186–187 (*see also* Balzac, Honoré de: works of); and kinship, 186–187, 196–197n; and narratives of development, 212, 229; and the novel, 167–169; and queer reading, 2–3 (*see also* queer reading); and race, 357, 359; and texture, 95–96; in *Soul on Ice*, 356–359; and Weininger, 315; in White, 229, 232–235; and Woolf, 401, 404. *See also* black masculinity; desire; gender; homosexuality; homosexual panic; masculinity; queerness

Shame, 461: in *Daniel Deronda*, 303, 305; and flogging, 273; in *Lesbia Brandon*, 286; in *The Portrait of a Lady*, 460–461. *See also* affect; humiliation; mortification

Shit: gift of, 76; in *Down These Mean Streets*, 362; in Proust, 76, 79–80, 87; wit as, 87. *See also* anal eroticism; waste: fecal

Signification: in *Beloved*, 51–52, 65–66. *See also* figures of speech

Simmel, George, 165n

Skin, 29, 48–51; in *Beloved*, 48–52, 62; as origin of the brain, 50; and projection, 51; as prophylactic, 49–51. *See also* Morrison, Toni: *Beloved*: texture; touch

Slavery, 354, 360, 368–369: and *Beloved*, 42, 45, 56, 73n; *Beloved* as compression of, 45; and the Holocaust, 46, 66; infant mortality and, 61; myths of in *Beloved*, 62–66; narrative of, 360; as virtual remains, 45. *See also* black masculinity; black subjectivity; Morrison, Toni: works of

Sloterdijk, Peter, 19, 21

Smith-Rosenberg, Carol, 462n–463n

Snobbery: in Proust, 79–80, 83–84, 88, 92n. *See also* boredom, sophistication, taste

Sodomy: and Woolf, 403, 416–417, 420. *See also* anal eroticism; flogging; homosexuality

Sophistication: and boredom, 88; gayness as, 74; in *The Guermantes Way*, 74–77, 81, 83, 86–90, 93n; in *The Picture of Dorian Gray*, 152 (*see also* boredom); and snobbery, 83; and wit, 74, 87; and worldliness, 75, 80. *See also* naïveté; Proust, Marcel, works of; snobbery; taste

Sociobiology, 58, 71n

Spillers, Hortense, 390

Spivak, Gayatri, 34, 406, 443n. *See also* ethics

Strachey, Lytton: and effeminacy, 415; James on, 415; and Woolf, 414–416. *See also* Woolf, Virginia: and gay men

Strong theory, 9, 12–15; as tautological, 15

Subject: liberal, 18–19

Subjectivity: civil rights and, 332; human, 29, 129–131; and flogging, 284, 286, 293–294; and the internet, 128–129, 142–147; and the novel, 168. *See also* Baldwin, James, works of: *Giovanni's Room*; black subjectivity; disciplinary power

Supplement, 107–108, 122

Swinburne, A. C., 32, 269–294, 294n; and face/butt metonymy, 274–277, 281–283, 285, 288; and flogging, 269–294; and spectacle of flogging, 269

Swinburne, A. C., works of: *The Flogging Book*, 269–271; *Lesbia Brandon*, 269–294: anal eroticism in, 288–290; drag in, 292; flogging in, 274–294; gender in, 286; lesbianism in, 291–292; the sea in, 276–277; writing in, 286; and masochism, 270–272; pleasure and pain in, 272, 275, 283; *Love's Cross Currents*, 269; *The Whippingham Papers*, 269. *See also* anal eroticism; flogging

Taste: in Proust, 77, 80–83, 85–86, 88–89. *See also* snobbery; sophistication; orality

Texture, 29, 94–126; and *The Ambassadors*, 94, 106–108, 111–123; binarisms of, 95–96, 99, 107, 117, 122; definitions of, 98–102, 123–125; etymology of, 123–125; and fetishism, 102–106, 126n; and innuendo, 29; and James, 101–102; and postmodernism, 103; and sexuality, 95–96; and TEXXTURE, 99–103, 107, 118–119; and threshold, 123–124; types of, 95–96, 99, 101–107, 117, 122; and vision, 29, 99, 101, 106, 117–188. *See also*

fetishism; James, Henry: works of: *The Ambassadors*; skin; touch

Theory, 5, 12–15, 22–24; everyday, 22; and paranoia, 5–6, 12–15; strong and weak, 12–15, 23, 35n–36n; and tautologies, 14, 16; Tomkins on, 12–15. *See also* literary criticism; paranoia; queer theory

Thomas, Piri, works of: *Down These Mean Streets*, 355, 360–368, 371, 372: abjection in, 366; anal eroticism in, 364; denial in, 361–365; and desire, 364, 366, 368; effeminate gay men in, 361–364; and slave narrative, 360; homoeroticism in, 361–364; homosexuality in, 360–364, 367–368; homosexuality as liminal in, 362–363, 366; and homosociality, 356; homosexual/homosocial distinction in, 360–368; homosexual romance in, 367–368; insider/outsider status in, 360, 366; love in, 367; masculinity in, 362, 365; object relations, 29 (*see also* Klein, Melanie; Kleinian positions); oral eroticism in, 363–364, 368; prison in, 360, 365–368; racism and, 360; sexuality in, 363–364; shit as marker of gay sex in, 362, 365, 368; violence in, 361–362, 367

Tomkins, Silvan, 7, 12–15, 24–25, 36, 72n

Touch, 99–100, 106, 117–120; and *The Ambassadors*, 106, 117–120. *See also* skin; texture

Transference, 450, 452–454, 460. *See also* affect: transfer of; displacement; James, Henry, works of: *The Portrait of a Lady*

Truth, 1, 9

Turing test, 29, 137–147; and gender, 138–142, 145–146. *See also* intelligence

United Nations Economic and Social Council (UNESCO), 359

Violence: in *Down These Mean Streets*, 361–362, 367; Foucault on, 18; and the scapegoat, 354–355; visibility of, 18–19. *See also* flogging; mortification; punishment

Virtual, 41: reality; remains and slavery in *Beloved*, 45–46; text based, 142–147, 148n. *See also* Gibson, William, works of; internet

Viruses, 41, 44–45, 55–57, 61; computer, 44–45, 54–56; as forms of cultural transmission, 56; HIV, 41, 44, 46, 57, 61; memes as, 56–57; personification of,

61–62; reproduction/transmission of, 41, 44–45, 61

Vision, 1; and texture, 99, 101, 106, 117–188. *See also* texture, touch

Von Portheim, Paul, 314–315

Vulgarity: and Cather, 471, 473, 477; in Proust, 81. *See also* anal eroticism; waste

Warner, Sylvia Townsend, 231–232, 242, 245n–246n

Waste: in *Beloved*, 46, 53–54; in Ozick, 46, 48, 53; and Proust, 76–77, 80–81, 86–88, 90. *See also* anal eroticism; orality; shit

Weininger, Otto: anti-Semitism of, 315; and homophobia, 315; misogyny of, 315; and sexuality, 315

West, Cornel, 381, 382

White, Constance Aston, 236, 247. *See also* White, T. H.

White, T. H., 31, 227–244, 245n–246n; anal eroticism, 240–241; and animals, 227–228, 230–232, 242–244; as anti-heterosexual, 232–233; closet, 233; and homoeroticism, 229; and homosexuality, 230–231, 233–234, 242–243; identification with Lancelot, 233; and love, 231–232; Malory and, 244n; and mother, 236–237; and the open secret, 234–235; and orality, 236–237; and pederasty, 230–231; poems of, 230; and sexuality, 227–229; at Stowe, 230–231; women in writings of, 236–237, 242, 246n

White, T. H., works of: *Book of Beasts*, 231; *Book of Merlyn*, 228, 230, 243–244: animals in, 243–244; Arthur's vitality in, 242; *Candle in the Wind*, 228, 230; *England Have My Bones*, 231; *The Godstone and the Blackymore*, 231; *Ill Made Knight*, 228–229, 23–234, 248n: discipline in, 229; humiliation in, 229; *Of Whom the World*, 242; *Once and Future King*, 227–244, 245n–248n: animals in, 230; Arthur's drained vitality in, 232; avuncular figures in, 232, 238–239; cannibalism in, 236–237; the closet in, 233; homosexuality in, 238–239, 242, 246n; Lancelot's sexuality, 232–235; motherhood in, 232, 235–237; open secret in, 234–235; pedagogy in, 229–230; the Questing Beast in, 232; sexuality in, 229; *Sword in the Stone*, 227–230, 232, 236–238, 247n–248n: and homoeroticism, 227; and orality, 236–237; *Witch in the Wood*, 227, 229, 236–237, 239–242, 248n: anal eroticism

in, 240–241; the Questing Beast in, 240–241; and sadism, 227–228

Whiteness, 385; audiences and, 389, 394–395; in *Vanishing Rooms*, 384–385, 387

Wilde, Oscar, 29–30, 152; trial of, 151–152

Wilde, Oscar, works of: "The Decay of Lying," 157; *The Picture of Dorian Gray*, 152–165: and boredom, 151, 153–165; consumerism in, 160–161; the dandy in, 152, 155–157; desire and the body in, 153–157; desire for the end of desire in, 153–167; and homosexuality, 161–162, 164–165; on the "Love that dare not speak its name," 157–158; passion in, 158–159, 165n; reader of, 151

Wit, 74, 87; as shit, 87. *See also* sophistication

Women: in *Adolf*, 250–252, 257, 259–262; and citizenship, 339; and consumer culture, 339, 342–343; friendships between, 191, 462n–463n; and gay men, 403–405, 407–418, 420, 438n, 440n (*see also* Woolf, Virginia; Woolf, Virginia, works of); in *The Professor's House*, 478; and the public sphere, 439n; traffic in, 173, 186 (*see also* Girardian triangles; homosociality; sex/gender system); and White, 236–237, 242, 246n (*see also* White, T. H., works of). *See also* gender; genitality; homoeroticism; lesbianism; misogyny; sexuality

Wood, Denis, 263, 265n–267n

Woods, Gregory, 90n

Woolf, Virginia, 34, 401–437, 438n–445n; and aesthetics, 402, 408, 417, 432; and the Bloomsbury group, 415–419, 438n–439n; death of, 436–437; and ethics, 402, 404–406, 408, 421; and gay men, 405, 409, 415–418, 438n–440n; and lesbianism, 401, 437n–438n; and marriage, 440n; and metaphor, 423; and naming, 402–403; on the novel, 441; and outlaws, 403, 407–409; on perversion, 403; and plot, 435; and prison, 435–436 (*see also* Woolf, Virginia, works of: *The Years*); queer legacy of, 437; and queerness, 401–437; and queer performativity, 402–403, 405; and queer recognition, 410–412, 415, 434; scholarship on, 404, 415–420, 427, 438n–439n, 441n (*see also* homophobia); and sexuality, 401, 404; on sodomy, 403, 416–417, 420; and Strachey, Lytton, 414–418; and Walpole, Hugh, 416–417; on women and gay men,

CONTRIBUTORS

Stephen Barber is Assistant Professor of English at the University of Rhode Island. His essay in this collection derives from his dissertation on the parrhesiastic ethics and aesthetics of Michel Foucault and Virginia Woolf. He is completing a book, provisionally entitled *On Being Ill with Proust and Woolf*, on counterdiscursive inscriptions of illness in Proust, Woolf, and Jarman.

Renu Bora is a graduate student in the Department of English at Duke University. He is currently writing his dissertation on texture.

Anne Chandler teaches English literature at Southern Illinois University at Carbondale. Her research on Thomas Day and the Edgeworths continues, alongside current work with Mary Wollstonecraft's educationism and fiction.

James Creech is Professor of French at Miami University. His latest book is *Closet Writing/Gay Reading*. The present article is excerpted from his current project entitled "The French Closet."

Tyler Curtain is a graduate of the Department of Computer Science, School of Engineering, University of Colorado at Boulder. He has worked with the Nation Center for Atmospheric Research's Scientific Computing Division and AT&T's Advanced Technology Group in Denver, Colorado. He is currently a graduate student in English at the Johns Hopkins University, writing about problems of moral philosophy and sexuality in eighteenth- and nineteenth-century literature.

Jonathan Goldberg is Professor of English at Duke University. He is the author of *Sodometries: Renaissance Texts, Modern Sexualities* and has edited both *Queering the Renaissance* and *Reclaiming Sodom*.

Joseph Litvak is Associate Professor of English at Bowdoin College. He is the author of *Caught in the Act: Theatricality in the Nineteenth-Century English Novel* and, most recently, "Pedagogy and Sexuality" and "Discipline, Spectacle, and Melancholia in and around the Gay Studies Classroom." His essay in this issue is a part of a book he is currently completing on the politics of sophistication from Jane Austen to cultural studies.

Michael Lucey teaches in the departments of French and Comparative Literature, and in the Lesbian, Gay, Bisexual, and Transgender Studies Program at the University of California, Berkeley. He is the author of *Gide's Bent: Sexuality, Politics, Writing* and of articles on Virginia Woolf, Hervé Guibert, Jean Genet, and others. He is currently writing a book on Honoré de Balzac, tentatively titled *The Misfit of the Family: Sexuality in the Social World of Balzac's Novels.*

Jeff Nunokawa teaches English at Princeton University. He is currently working on a book on economics, erotica, and Victorian literature.

Cindy Patton teaches lesbian and gay studies in the Graduate Institute of the Liberal Arts at Emory University. The most recent of her several books on the social dimensions of the HIV epidemic is *Fatal Advice: How Safe Sex Education Went Wrong.* She is currently working on a book concerning the production of ideas of identity in post–World War II mass media.

Jacob Press is a graduate student in the department of English at Duke University. He received a B.A. in History and Literature from Harvard University and then traveled to Israel as a Dorot Fellow. He is coeditor with Amir Sumakaái Fink of *Independence Park: The Lives of Gay Men in Israel* (forthcoming).

Robert F. Reid-Pharr is Assistant Professor of English at the Johns Hopkins University. He is the author of *Conjugal Union: Gender, Sexuality and the Development of an African American National Literature* (forthcoming).

Eve Kosofsky Sedgwick is the Newman Ivey White Professor of English at Duke University. She is the author of *Between Men, Epistemology of the Closet, Tendencies,* and *Fat Art/Thin Art.*

Melissa Solomon is currently a graduate student in the Ph.D. program in English at Duke University.

Kathryn Bond Stockton is Assistant Professor at the University of Utah and is the author of *God Between Their Lips: Desire Between Women in Irigaray, Brontë, and Eliot.* Her articles have appeared in, among other places, *boundary 2, Novel,* and *Cultural Critique.* She is currently writing a book on debasement engaging switchpoints between black and other queer connections to anal economics, miscegenation, stone butch wounds, and the brain's prophylactic relations with the dead.

John Vincent received his M.F.A. from Warren Wilson College and is a Ph.D. candidate in the English program at Duke University. His poems have appeared in *The Cream City Review, The Beloit Poetry Journal, The Plum Review,* and elsewhere.

Maurice Wallace is Assistant Professor of English and African and African American Studies at Yale University. His teaching and research include studies in African American literature, nineteenth-century American literature and cultural criticism. He is the author of *Constructing the Black Masculine: Identity and Ideality in African American Men's Literature and Culture* (forthcoming).

Barry Weller is Professor of English at the University of Utah and editor of *The Western Humanities Review.* He is also coeditor (with Jerome McGann) of *Byron's Dramas* for *The Oxford University Press Complete Poetical Works of Byron* and (with Margaret Ferguson) *The Tragedy of Marian, 1617.* He has published articles in, among others, *ELH, MLN, The Kenyon Review,* and *Modern Philology.*

Library of Congress Cataloging-in-Publication Data
Novel gazing : queer readings in fiction / edited by
Eve Kosofsky Sedgwick.
p.   cm. — (Series Q)
Includes bibliographical references and index.
ISBN 0-8223-2028-2 (cloth : alk. paper). — ISBN 0-8223-2040-1 (pbk. : alk. paper)
1. American fiction—History and criticism.   2. Homosexuality and literature—United
States.   3. English fiction—History and criticism.   4. French fiction—History and
criticism.   5. Gays' writings—History and criticism.   6. Homosexuality and literature.
7. Gays in literature.   I. Sedgwick, Eve Kosofsky.   II. Series.
PS374.H63N68   1997
813.009'353—dc21   97-7608 CIP